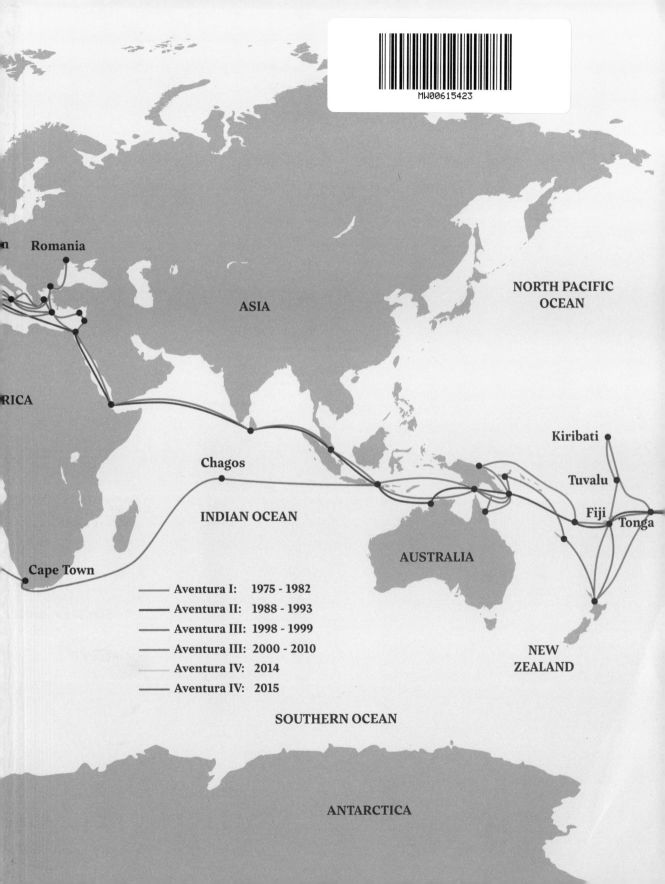

Jimmy Cornell

200,000 MILES

A LIFE OF ADVENTURE

CORNELL SAILING

Published by Cornell Sailing Ltd
50 Great Russell Street
London WC1B 3BA
www.cornellsailing.com

First edition published 2017

Paperback ISBN: 978-0-9572626-8-3

This book is produced using paper that is made from wood grown in managed, sustainable
forests. It is natural, renewable and recyclable. The logging and manufacturing processes conform
to the environmental regulations of the country of origin.

Typeset in 9pt on 13pt Inka
Designer: Jörg Baginski
Editor: Gwenda Cornell
Subeditor: Vicky McGinley
Maps: Mark Silver

Printed by
Loire Offset Titoulet
82, rue de la Talaudière
42964 Saint-Etienne
France

Distributed in USA and Canada by
Paradise Cay Publications
120 Monda Way
Blue Lake
CA 95525
USA
www.paracay.com

Note: while all reasonable care has been taken in the publication of this book, the publisher
takes no responsibility for the use of the methods or products described in the book.

To Stéphan Constance

Without whose vision and support Aventura IV would not have been created and there would have been no reason to write this book.

Reviews from the international sailing press

As both a fascinating memoir and a first-person guide to long-range, offshore sailing, Jimmy Cornell's 200,000 miles is a terrific account of a sailor's life well-lived. From the tales of a contemptuous childhood in communist Romania, to a fresh start in Great Britain with his English bride, to a lifetime spent exploring the world's oceans from Antarctica to the Northwest Passage, Cornell's story reads like something out of the movies. Richly illustrated and tightly written, 200,000 Miles just might be Cornell's best book of them all.

Herb McCormick, senior editor, Cruising World magazine, USA

Jimmy Cornell is one of the most famous blue ocean sailors navigating the oceans today. 200,000 miles is a fascinating tale, not only about sailing but also about the adventurous spirit that brought a young man from the forests of Romania to become a master of the seas.

Ole Henrik Nissen-Lie, editor-in-chief, SEILmagasinet and Seilas, Norway

Jimmy Cornell's journey through life has been as fascinating and varied as his seagoing feats. 200,000 Miles blends anecdote, philosophy and hard-won experience into one enjoyable narrative spanning a lifetime of voyaging under sail. Essential reading for aspiring cruisers.

Peter Nielsen, editor, SAIL magazine, USA

In one book, Cornell not only shares all he knows about sailing, he also lets loose with his well-formed opinions on long-distance cruising. A cruising life requires skills, talents, virtues, luck, doggedness and a certain will of personality. Thankfully, not only does Cornell have these in spades, plus many more, he has also always been willing to share. This book epitomises his lifelong philosophy.

Phil Ross, editor, Cruising Helmsman, Australia

Jimmy Cornell has gained experience from three world circumnavigations, a couple of trips to Antarctica and a transit of the Northwest Passage. He also has a unique ability to share his knowledge through books that have inspired and guided sailors across the seas for many years. This book is an inspiring guide filled with facts and hands-on advice for anyone heading out on a long-distance voyage, but it is also a plain good read thanks to Cornell's personal stories and a great many anecdotes from all over the world.

Camilla Herrmann, editor of Cruising magazine for the Cruising Association

Jimmy has devoted his professional life to discovering and sharing knowledge on world cruising. This book provides a more personal perspective on a lifetime's voyaging, but is still far from being a straightforward autobiography because it maintains the same focus on providing useful information. Starting with his 2015-16 voyage through the Northwest Passage, Jimmy looks back on his early days and then his world trips in four yachts, all called Aventura. His thoughts on equipment, sailing strategies, navigation and living aboard, all interspersed with very honest stories of his own mistakes and successes, make this a book worth reading for any cruiser who has ever planned or dreamed of heading for blue waters.

Johan Boström, editor of På Kryss magazine for the Swedish Cruising Association

Other Cornell titles

World Cruising Routes

Long established as the bible for long-distance cruisers and a bestseller since its first publication in 1987, World Cruising Routes is a comprehensive guide to over 1,000 routes covering all the oceans of the world from the tropical South Seas to the high-latitudes of the Arctic and Antarctic. Geared specifically to the needs of cruising sailors the latest edition assesses the effects of climate change on cruising routes and provides over 6,000 waypoints to assist navigators in planning individual routes. It is the perfect one-stop reference for planning a voyage anywhere in the world.

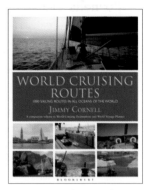

'The serious cruiser's bible… don't leave report without it.'
Cruising Magazine, UK

'The venerable World Cruising Routes is the must-have guide to world cruising.'
Latitudes & Attitudes

'A must for every circumnavigator and fascinating armchair reader for the rest of us.'
Yachting Monthly

World Voyage Planner

This comprehensive guide deals with all the elements that ensure a successful voyage by providing practical advice for would-be voyagers. Essential aspects of preparations for an offshore voyage are based on Jimmy Cornell's personal experience gained both from his own voyages and the transatlantic and round-the-world sailing rallies he has organised over the years. While the main focus is on the most popular cruising routes, there are also suggested voyages to some less-frequented destinations.

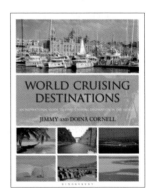

Jimmy Cornell's remarkable depth of knowledge shines through.
Yachting World, UK

This book provides more than just knowhow: it entertains, it makes you dream, it paints a picture of a beautiful world – it is pure enjoyment.
Die Yacht, Germany

World Voyage Planner is a book to pick up for five minutes and put it down, reluctantly, two hours later.
Ocean Cruising Club

World Cruising Destinations

A substantial handbook that profiles every cruising destination in the world is a companion volume to *World Cruising Routes* and *World Voyage Planner*. It contains information on all maritime nations of the world with details of local attractions, formalities, facilities, charter opportunities, websites and cruising guides. Lavishly illustrated throughout, this book is not only a must-have onboard reference manual for long-distance sailors, but will undoubtedly inspire the adventurous to explore new and challenging destinations.

An indispensable addition to the cruising sailor's library.
Yachting World

'The most complete and practical handbook… full of what every cruiser needs to know and an inspiration to those who dream of sailing away.'
Seven Seas Cruising Association

'Essential for cruisers worldwide, whether planning a circumnavigation or a two-week cruise.'
noonsite.com

Cornells' Ocean Atlas

Jimmy and Ivan Cornell have produced this global atlas of pilot charts aimed at sailors planning offshore voyages. Monthly charts of all oceans of the world show wind speed and direction, current speed and direction, the extent of the Intertropical Convergence Zone, the common tracks of tropical storms, and the mean location of high-pressure cells for each hemisphere. Now in its second edition (October 2017), the pilot charts have been updated with the most recent weather data gathered by meteorological satellites. An indispensable tool for anyone planning an offshore passage and companion to *World Cruising Routes* and *World Voyage Planner*.

Jimmy Cornell belongs on the very short list of modern sailing's most trusted authorities on long-distance cruising.
Cruising World, USA

Jimmy Cornell is the leading star for sailors planning ocean voyages anywhere on the globe. For this publication he has researched and collected facts about weather, winds and currents from all over the world.
Seilas, Norway

A very impressive and valuable publication that will be of great assistance to sailors worldwide.
Herb Hilgenberg, Southbound II

Child of the Sea

Doina Cornell's memoir of sailing around the world with her family from the age of seven to fourteen gives a glimpse into a life that most children couldn't imagine, of visiting some of the most beautiful islands in the world and falling in love with the sea in all its ever-changing moods. The book also tells the story of a girl's coming of age, of family life on a small boat, and the challenges of settling back on land when the voyage is over.

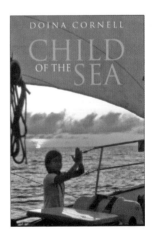

A rare memoir of tenderness and exquisite detail.
Boat US

A unique and poignant autobiographical saga. A must-read for kids ages ten and up, parents, or others who dream either of adventure or exploring the world under sail.
Cruising World, USA

This book should be read by all who are going to sell up and sail away into the Blue Yonder with their kids.
Yachting Monthly , UK

A vivid and personal account perfect for any nautical or adventure travel collection.
The Midwest Book Review , USA

A poignant story – told with appealing freshness – of a very different, fascinating childhood and coming-of-age. It is a must read for any young would-be sailor or traveller.
Sailing, USA

We are with you from the tropics to the Arctic   You can depend on us 24/7

THE CHOICE OF CRUISING SAILORS

Topsail
INSURANCE

HIGHFIELD
aluminium boats

Table of Contents

Foreword

Looking back on a long, happy and fulfilled life, I realise just how lucky I have been to achieve everything that I could have hoped for: a successful professional career, my childhood dream of sailing around the world and, above all, a wonderful family life, without doubt due to the six years spent cruising together during Doina and Ivan's formative years.

Having been so fortunate, I feel that I have a duty to pass on my experience to other sailors planning to set off on their own voyage. Rather than write a typical autobiography, I decided that a memoir would be more helpful to anyone who, like me, has a passion for the sea and sailing. I have tried as much as possible to keep away from theory and concentrate instead on practical examples from my own or other's experience that are relevant to the subject under discussion.

In the 10 years since the publication of my book Passion for the Sea, a lot has happened both in my personal life and in sailing generally. Having sold Aventura III in 2010, I resumed my previous activity as an event organiser and launched a new series of cruising rallies. The Blue Planet Odyssey and the 10 transatlantic rallies that followed have brought me once again into close contact with sailors. Soon I realised that the new generation of sailors setting off on long voyages were, in many aspects, very different to those I had come across on my previous voyages, or while running the ARC and round-the-world rallies. What struck me most was how many of those who had little offshore sailing experience tried to make up for this by buying all the latest gear, thus becoming totally dependent on equipment, much of which they could not repair if it failed. It has been said that sailing is not rocket science, although it seems to be getting very close to it when one looks at the array of equipment on some yachts, including my own Aventura IV, not to speak of those latest America's Cup racing machines. But as far as cruising is concerned, I believe that one should resist becoming a slave to technology. After all, offshore sailing is one of the activities that is closest to nature, and much of the pleasure and satisfaction it gives derives from being on your own boat in the middle of a vast ocean, facing the same challenges as navigators of yesteryear, helped by technology but not dominated by it.

As a journalist trained by the BBC, both in this book and at my lectures and seminars, I have followed its dictum to inform, educate and entertain. The BBC also instilled in me the importance of objectivity in everything that I say or write. This is what led me to conduct the first of many surveys in which I attempted to find out how other sailors dealt with various aspects of cruising. Many of their comments as well as the results of those surveys have been a valuable source of material for this book.

From my earliest days of sailing, I have learned much from my own mistakes as well as those of others, often participants in the rallies I organised. The observations, incidents and anecdotes on the various aspects of ocean cruising mentioned in this book seem to have resulted not in a how-to manual, but rather in a how-not-to guide to long-distance cruising. I hope you enjoy it.

A new Aventura is born

One of the first lessons I learned early in my cruising life was the importance of having a well-thought-out voyage plan. A second lesson was to be prepared to abandon that plan should a more attractive alternative present itself. Indeed, some of the most memorable experiences in my four decades of roaming the oceans of the world were detours to places that had not featured in the original plan.

My life generally has followed the same tortuous route, and these last years have been no exception. In 1998, after 12 years of organising transatlantic and round-the-world rallies, I decided to stop all that and focus on doing what I like best: sailing. In the next dozen years, on Aventura III, I sailed 70,000 miles, that included voyages to Antarctica and Alaska, followed by a circumnavigation of the globe, my third. That should have been enough, so in 2010, at the age of 70, I decided to sell my boat and renounce any plans for more distant voyaging... or so I thought.

During my third circumnavigation I revisited some of the places I had been to previously and was often shocked by the changes that had occurred in the intervening years. The worst was pollution, on land, underwater and on the surface of the ocean. Once-pristine beaches were now covered in garbage, all kinds of plastic debris was carried by wind and waves, and in many places where I had dived in the past, the coral reefs were dead. Most of this damage was obviously man-made, but there were other signs that pointed to a change in the global climate, which many scientists have been predicting.

My personal concern for the state of the oceans was not new. In 1997-1998 I organised a round-the-world rally sponsored by the Expo 98 world exhibition, which was held in Lisbon to commemorate the 500th anniversary of Vasco da Gama's historic voyage. The 32 boats taking part carried the message of Expo 98: 'The Ocean, our heritage for the future.'

Sixteen years after Expo 98, that message had become even more relevant and urgent, and I felt that there ought to be a global sailing event to raise awareness of the threat to the oceans. The Blue Planet Odyssey was thus launched in late 2012 with the aim of carrying around the world a clear message: 'The oceans – our future.' The itinerary of the rally included a southern route that called at some of the most endangered island nations, and also a more challenging northern route through the Northwest Passage, the once-impenetrable waterway, which had been open to navigation in recent years as a result of climate change. The Arctic has been described as the canary in the mine for global weather and what has been happening in the Northwest Passage highlights a trend that eventually may have grave repercussions for the entire planet. Bearing in mind the Blue Planet Odyssey's stated mission, I simply had to go. Although I knew that the chances of a successful transit of the Northwest Passage were still limited, I decided that it was my responsibility to lead by example and attempt to sail the Arctic route myself.

With little over one year left until the start of the event, I had to find a suitable boat quickly and, having looked around at all that was available, I realised that I had an unmissable opportunity to come up with my own concept of a cruising boat suitable for both tropical and high-latitude voyages. For much of my sailing life I had been trying to find out if there was such a thing as an ideal cruising boat. Over the years I had conducted several surveys among cruising sailors, spoken to designers and boat builders, but the more I tried, the farther my target seemed to recede. And here was this unexpected opportunity to give it another try, especially as I knew exactly what I wanted: a strong, fast, comfortable, functional and easily handled boat, perfectly suited for all seas and all seasons.

I was very fortunate in being able to infect with my enthusiasm Stephan Constance, the CEO of Garcia and Allures Yachting, the best aluminium yacht builders in France, and Olivier Racoupeau, one of France's top naval architects. I made it clear that I wanted to keep the best features of my previous Aventura, such as an unpainted aluminium hull, integral centreboard, shallow draft and cutter rig. What was new was my idea of transplanting to a monohull the almost all-round visibility that I found so attractive on catamarans. A deck saloon was something that had never been attempted before on a yacht with an integral centreboard, primarily because the added height might affect its stability. By settling for a low profile the designer produced what I believe to be the perfect solution: a comfortable deck saloon with 270-degree visibility, as well as an inside navigation-cum-watchkeeper's station, without compromising either the stability or the looks of the new Exploration 45.

From right to left: Stéphan Constance, Olivier Racoupeau, Jimmy Cornell and Benoit Lebizay, MD of Garcia Yachting

Much thought went into the safety aspects, the hull being of very strong construction and provided with watertight collision bulkheads, fore and aft. The two aluminium rudders are supported by skegs, and as an added protection the upper section of each rudder blade incorporates a crumple area. Should the rudder be pushed upwards in a collision, this sacrificial area made of light composite material would crumple and compress without causing any damage to the hull itself.

Furthermore, each wheel and rudder is provided with an independent steering mechanism. In an emergency the connecting bar between the two steering mechanisms can be disconnected and the rudders can be used independently of each other. This system also allows for either wheel to steer with either rudder. Aventura is equipped with two entirely autonomous autopilots, either of which can steer the boat with either rudder or

both. Also with safety in mind, as I regard a traditional propeller shaft to be more suited to this type of boat, I decided against a saildrive.

As I believe that comfort is such an important element of overall safety, I told the designer that I wanted to have as many comfortable sea berths as he could possibly squeeze into a 45-foot boat. As a result, besides the two double cabins, Aventura IV has four single sea berths, two in the starboard aft cabin and two on the portside of the salon.

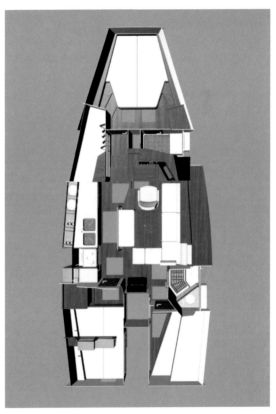

Just as much thought went into ensuring a high level of self-sufficiency, so the boat could be easily handled by a small crew, and sailed single-handed if necessary. All essential lines lead back to the cockpit, to two electric and two primary winches. As an extra safety

Wow! This certainly looks like a boat to take on the Northwest Passage

have been developed for marine use were considered unsuitable for the kind of voyage that I had in mind. As none of my previous boats had a diesel generator nor would the new Aventura. I made up for it by covering as much of the energy needs as possible from renewable sources. The combination of a D400 wind generator, Sail-Gen hydro-generator, and a 140W solar panel should be able to supply most energy needs from renewable sources whether on passage or at anchor.

There are many other features that make Aventura both comfortable and enjoyable to sail, such as the spacious well-protected cockpit, with the coachroof extending over its forward part to provide a sheltered corner for the on-watch crew with immediate access to instruments and aids to navigation.

Work on my new Aventura started in summer 2013, and by May 2014 I was on my way to the Northwest Passage.

precaution, each of the two electric winches is provided with an easily accessible emergency cut-off switch.

One of my top priorities was to have as low a carbon footprint as possible. To my great disappointment, I was unable to implement the original plan of having a hybrid engine, for the simple reason that the few that

The Northwest Passage

Sailing above the Arctic Circle was everything we'd hoped it would be: challenging, frightening, beautiful, fulfilling. We'd been hypnotised and dazzled by the stark landscapes, the whales and polar bears, the never-ending daylight. The Passage remains one of the most remote and difficult voyages on the planet, yet it is also a place that seems forever changed.

Herb McCormick

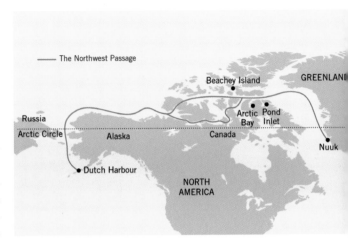

All my previous boats started their maiden voyage in London, and the new Aventura was no exception. A short delivery trip across the English Channel from the boatyard in Cherbourg took us up the River Thames into the heart of London. At the appointed time on 31 May 2014, we locked out of Limehouse Basin and passed into the Pool of London through the iconic Tower Bridge that was raised especially for us.

Sailing along the Thames is akin to leafing through a book of English history. Close to us on the north shore, the remains of the Roman defence walls of ancient Londinium were overlooked by the Tower of London. It was built in the 11th century by William the Conqueror, who invaded England from Normandy in 1066. Nearly one millennium later, my own Norman-built Aventura was hoisting her sails for a second passage through Tower Bridge. The last

time I had made that request was at the start of the previous Aventura's voyage to Antarctica as part of the Millennium Odyssey. This time I was heading in the opposite direction, bound for the Northwest Passage.

As the favourable tide took us fast downstream, we passed Greenwich, the attractive London suburb bisected by the Zero Meridian, which gave its name to Greenwich Mean Time, on which all time zones are based. It was from here that the explorer Martin Frobisher had set off in 1576 on the first unsuccessful voyage to find a high-latitude shortcut from the Atlantic to the Pacific through the mythical Northwest Passage. In the history of maritime exploration no other part of the world has proved to be more difficult and has taken longer to conquer than the Northwest Passage. Since Roald Amundsen's successful transit in 1903-1906, a total of only 86 sailing boats (as of 2015) have been able to follow his example and transit this challenging waterway unassisted. To put it in perspective: for every sailor who has successfully completed a transit of the Northwest Passage, 15 climbers have scaled the highest mountain summit in the world.

The reason is quite simple: in spite of all the advances in boat design, technology and means of navigation, the challenges faced by those sailing in the High Arctic have remained basically the same. Climate change, whose effects are more obvious in the Arctic than anywhere else in the world, has certainly played a role in making conditions for a successful transit somewhat easier but, as I found out myself on my first attempt in 2014, however well prepared you are, Mother Nature always has the last word.

Compared with other high-latitude destinations where I have sailed in the past, namely Antarctica and Spitsbergen, the challenge posed by the Northwest Passage is entirely different. Whereas in the former places, the success of a voyage depends primarily on the experience of the skipper and crew, as well as the suitability of the vessel, in other words, on objective criteria, in the case of the Northwest Passage there is one major factor that is entirely out of your control: ice.

Sunrise in the North Sea

Centuries of failed expeditions have resulted in a well-defined strategy for a transit of the Northwest Passage, but its successful completion is still entirely at the mercy of ice conditions. During the short summer season, the sea ice, which has formed over the long winter, as well as the old ice left from previous winters, melts to a greater or lesser extent. The ice usually retreats from west to east (Pacific to Atlantic), which means that in most years the eastern sector of the

Northwest Passage is the last to become free of ice. If planning an east to west passage, the way to deal with this phenomenon is to plan on arriving in the eastern approaches in the second half of July, and be prepared to wait until the ice has retreated to such an extent that a transit of the central section of the Northwest Passage may be safely attempted.

A transit starting from the Pacific is somewhat easier to plan, as in most years the western approaches to the Northwest Passage become free of ice by late July or early August, making it possible to follow the retreating ice eastwards. In recent years, the main hurdle to overcome has been Peel Sound, the symbolic exit gate for those coming from the west, and the gateway to the Northwest Passage for boats coming from the east. This potential choke-point had been entirely blocked by ice during the summers of 2012 and 2013, although a few boats managed to bypass it by using the shortcut provided by Bellot Strait. I was hoping that luck would be on my side again, as on so many occasions in the past, and conditions in summer 2014 would be more favourable.

Downstream from Greenwich we passed London City Airport, built on the site where once stood the old Royal Albert Docks. It was there that I had fitted out the first Aventura and had set off, almost exactly 40 years previously, on my first world voyage. And here I was again, setting off on board her namesake on the most ambitious of all my sailing projects.

After a fast passage up the North Sea, and following the tradition of previous expeditions to the Northwest Passage, we stopped for fresh provisions at Stromness in the Orkney Islands. Lying on almost the same latitude as Cape Farewell at the southern extremity of Greenland, Stromness has been used as a port of departure for westbound expeditions since the time of the Vikings, who were able to establish their latitude by measuring the altitude of the North Star. Probably for the same reason, later explorers had also left from there, such as Henry Hudson, James

Cook, Edward Parry and John Franklin as well as John Rae, a native of Orkney, who was born there in 1813. The statue of the most famous Orcadian overlooks the perfectly sheltered harbour. A true adventurer, Rae despised the Royal Navy's elaborate and mostly misguided preparations for Arctic expeditions, and decided to learn from the Inuit how to survive the harsh Arctic climate. He wore their clothing, covered long distances on snowshoes, built icehouses for shelter, and didn't use dogs but pulled with his team sledges loaded with provisions. This admirable explorer was the first European to survive an Arctic winter in 1846 without outside help and was the first to confirm that the Northwest Passage was indeed an open waterway, albeit choked by ice for most of the year.

Choosing the right time for our departure from Stromness was crucial in order to avoid the fierce tidal streams that swirl around these islands. As we were swept out into the Atlantic Ocean through Hoy Sound, we passed the Man of Hoy, a rocky outcrop akin to a smaller Easter Island statue, and the last land we were likely to see before our distant destination.

On the third day of Aventura's passage to Greenland, it suddenly felt as if we had been miraculously transposed to the Mediterranean. The sun was shining out of a deep-blue sky, the sea was sparkling in the late afternoon, the air temperature rose to 20°C, and off our port bow a school of dolphins were busy having a late lunch. After dinner, with the skies still clear and a good wind, we hoisted the Parasailor spinnaker, agreed on the order of night watches, and were all set up for a quiet night. At 2230, while a full moon was showing its pale face veiled by a thin cloud, the sun finally started its long descent towards the northern horizon, and we were rewarded by a spectacular sunset worthy of a Turner painting.

Alternating between our Code Zero when reaching and the Parasailor spinnaker when the wind was abaft the beam, we romped along in what can only be described as Arctic trade wind conditions. As we got close to Cape Farewell, we launched the first of the two weather buoys that we had been given by Météo-France on behalf of the World Meteorological Organisation. We had been asked to deploy it in the area of the

Ivan steering past the first iceberg we encountered

East Greenland Current, a cold current that sweeps through the Denmark Strait separating Greenland from Iceland. Along the way it picks up icebergs calved by the glaciers along Greenland's west coast and carries them southwards. It is believed that it was one of these that collided with the Titanic.

As the ice charts issued by the Danish Meteorological Office showed a heavy concentration of ice all along Greenland's coast, we started keeping a lookout for icebergs, usually by radar when the visibility was poor. Sailing in thick fog, the air temperature dropped suddenly to zero and that of the sea to one degree. The cause was soon clear as the radar showed a large area of ice concentration right ahead of us. Soon we were dodging small bits of ice, then larger ones, and finally mini-icebergs the size of Aventura. Slowly the visibility improved, and we found it easier to slalom between them. We passed close to a small iceberg with a bearded seal looking quizzically at my son Ivan, and his much less impressive beard. As the sun came up, it started burning off the fog, and visibility gradually became better.

With less ice to worry about, we prepared the second oceanographic buoy to be launched, as requested, close to 61°N and at some distance off the west Greenland coast. Ivan decided to dedicate his

silent cabinmate to his niece Nera and nephew Dan, and wrote their names on the buoy.

Although we had planned to stop in southern Greenland, with all harbours and bays along the coast still blocked by ice, we decided to continue nonstop to the capital Nuuk. On the last night before landfall, the sun set at quarter to midnight local time and throughout the short period of relative darkness it stayed barely hidden just below the northern horizon, fringing it with a palette of reddish hues. Just after 0300 the colours intensified and slowly the upper limb of an enormous blood orange made its appearance over Greenland's high mountain range. My last night watch on this Viking passage came to an end and although we were still some distance from the coast, I hoisted the Greenland courtesy flag, whose symbolic blood-red rising sun perfectly mirrored the spectacle I had just witnessed.

Fortis fortuna adiuvat

"Fortune favours the bold" is a Roman saying and throughout my eventful life I have been convinced that Fortuna, the goddess of luck, has been by my side. Aventura's 1700-mile passage from Scotland to Greenland was the latest example, as for ten days we enjoyed favourable sailing conditions gifted by a prolonged spell of southeasterly winds across an area of the North Atlantic where prevailing westerly winds are the rule. Such a spell of favourable winds in late spring/early summer explains how 1,000 years ago Viking navigators managed to sail this very same stretch of the North Atlantic and discover in the process Iceland, Greenland and even Newfoundland, which they called Vinland. They had thus landed in what we now call North America.

Slowed down by a spell of strong contrary winds, we only arrived at Nuuk at midnight. I had called the harbour master on my satphone earlier to report our arrival and warned him that we might not get in before

midnight. He replied that it was no problem, and that he would wait for us. When we entered the outer harbour and called him on the VHF radio, he replied immediately, told us where to tie up and met us on the dock to take our lines. He introduced himself as Johannes Lindenhann, gave me his card with a phone number to call if we needed any help, and told us to

enjoy the weekend, as it was not only midsummer day, but also Greenland's national holiday.

In the morning we walked into the town, which is home to one quarter of Greenland's population of 57,000. Every one of them seemed to be out on this brilliant sunny and warm day to celebrate their national holiday. The great majority were Kalaallit (related to the Canadian Inuit), and some women were wearing the attractive national dress with short deerskin trousers and moccasins, and a wide colourful cape made of beads, while the men wore plain white. The name of Greenland is Kalaallit Nunat, and while the official language is Kalaallisut, Danish continues to be widely spoken.

Greenland was settled by indigenous people from North America around 2500 BC, and was followed by Viking settlers about 1,000 years ago. During that later period, the climate was much milder than today, and could support several Norse settlements. Some of their remains are scattered around Nuuk and the 100-mile-long Nuup Kangerlua fjord. After being briefed by a local friend on the highlights not to be missed, we turned Aventura's bows inland.

As we sailed into the steep fjord a magnificent rainbow bridged the waters ahead of us. Moving deeper into the fjord, we encountered increasingly more ice, bergy bits giving way to small icebergs. The nearby Narsap Sermia glacier must have been very active calving its offspring, as a seemingly solid ice barrier appeared to be blocking the way to our chosen anchorage at the head of a secondary fjord. As we got closer, a narrow lead opened in the ice, allowing us to make slow progress, although it was near midnight by the time we finally dropped anchor in the perfectly landlocked Kangiussaq Bay. As we stepped ashore in the morning, the scenery surrounding us was as green as the island's name, the soft grassy meadow sprinkled with clumps of flowers. We had to ford a swift torrent

to the site of the Norse settlement, where only the remains of an old stone and turf wall bore witness to the former human presence.

Our exit from this idyllic spot was even more difficult than our access, and dodging the ice proved to be even more challenging than the previous day. In spite of some close shaves, Aventura made it safely through and, after one night anchored off the picturesque village of Kapisillit, we closed the loop in Nuuk.

On the leg from London to Nuuk I had been accompanied by my son Ivan and Nick Carter, a consultant in rheumatology and sports medicine, who had taken a career break to sail in the Arctic. Ivan left in Nuuk, where I was joined by three other family members: daughter Doina, granddaughter Nera and niece Marianne. Doina and Nera had been instrumental in persuading me to conceive and build the latest Aventura, and sailing the Northwest Passage reflected

Front row: Doina and Nera, middle row: Nikki, Emily, Marianne, Jimmy. Back row: Nick and Jean-Luc

for both of them, passionate environmentalists, their concern for the state of the planet. I have always been very close to Marianne and, having once sailed with me from Tahiti to Hawaii on Aventura III, she begged me to take her along. We achieved the full complement with the arrival of Jean-Luc, a French journalist, Nick's

partner Nikki, and Emily, who had been commissioned to conduct a series of tests to research the presence of plastic in Arctic waters.

Throughout our stay in Nuuk, Aventura had been tied up alongside Kisaq, a 20-metre workboat, strongly built and perfectly suited for these waters. The owner, Anders Pedersen, a former Danish Coast Guard officer, has been based in Greenland for the last 30 years. As it is compulsory to have a gun in Arctic Canada to protect against possible attacks by polar bears, I asked Anders's advice where to buy one.

'Jimmy, before you leave you can buy a gun at the fuel station here in the harbour.'

'At the fuel station?' I asked incredulously.

'Yes, of course.'

We took Aventura across the harbour to the fuel station, tied up to its dock and filled up our two tanks as well as an extra 200 litres in plastic jerry cans. The first thing I saw as I entered the shop to pay for the fuel was an entire wall displaying every conceivable type of gun. I explained to the young assistant what kind of gun I needed, and he showed me half a dozen rifles suitable for the job. As I couldn't make up my mind, he said:

'If I were you I'd buy this one, a military rifle, former Soviet Army issue. It's very reliable, and the steel-tipped bullets are the best if you ever come to use it.

Also, it comes with the original bayonet.'

I produced a credit card and also my passport as an ID for the gun.

'No need for that,' the man said, pointing at the passport.

'Do I need to go to the police to register the gun?'

'No, here in Greenland anyone can have a gun, and, in fact, everyone does.'

I walked back to the boat with the gun on my shoulder, the bayonet affixed, and a box of ammunition in my hand, half waiting to be called back. But it didn't happen. When I went to say goodbye to Anders, I expressed my astonishment at how simple it had all been. I also asked if there is much crime given the ease of obtaining a gun.

'None really. I think Greenland must be one of the safest places in the world.'

Across the Arctic Circle

There is a certain fascination about crossing specific lines on a chart by boat, be it the equator, international dateline, Tropic of Cancer or Capricorn, Antarctic or Arctic Circle. In my many years of wandering I have passed them all while on passage to some distant destination. But sailing across the Arctic Circle as we made our way along Greenland's west coast had a unique feeling as my voyage had a specific objective: a transit of the Northwest Passage. Those who had braved the challenges of the Northwest Passage in recent years have determined that a successful transit

only counts if their track had crossed that magic line in Davis Strait, in the east, and Bering Strait, in the west. From that point of view, we were now truly on our way. Using an orange as a convenient sphere, I explained to Nera the meaning of the Arctic Circle. Spanning the

earth at 66°33'27" N, its location is determined by the angle of inclination of our planet as it revolves around the sun. That same angle also dictates the seasons, and the fact that as we were now well above 70°N, we had continuous daylight during the brief Arctic summer.

We spent the next day cruising through the spectacular Disko Bay, where several glaciers calve icebergs into the sea, the mightiest of them all being the Sermeq Kujalleq glacier. As we got closer, the mass of icebergs that had been calved recently formed an impenetrable barrier. We sailed slowly alongside it, savouring the splendour of nature's artistry. As we slalomed through the crowded waters we gasped

the Northwest Passage, much of which was still choked by ice in late July. While waiting for an improvement in the ice situation, and in readiness to go as soon as conditions were favourable, we headed for Dundas Harbour, a perfectly protected anchorage on the south coast of Devon Island.

As we made our way slowly through the poorly surveyed area, we passed a noisy colony of walrus, then noticed ahead of us a whitish shape moving swiftly through the water towards the nearby shore. A polar bear! As it reached shallow water, it stood up, looked

in turns at the amazing shapes of the sculptured behemoths, while catching brief glimpses of humpback whales surfacing with a blast of steam after a deep dive feeding in these rich waters.

After exactly one month to the day, we bade farewell to Greenland and set a course across Baffin Bay to the Canadian side. Those icebergs continued to keep us company, and on our toes, during our 500-mile passage to Lancaster Sound. This is the start of the intricate maze of straits and narrows that make up

in our direction, then started climbing a steep hill behind the beach. Every now and then it turned with a quizzical look towards Aventura. I suddenly felt rather embarrassed by the purchase of that rifle, to be used in self-defence against such a beautiful animal, and hoped that it would never come to it.

By late July we were joined in that sheltered anchorage by several other boats just like us waiting for the ice situation to improve. As we needed to get fuel for the continuation of the voyage and with no prospect of an imminent improvement in the ice situation, we

Lancaster Sound

decided to cross Lancaster Sound to Arctic Bay. Set in a little bay inside Admiralty Inlet, at about 100 miles from where we were, the small Inuit settlement was the closest option for fuel. I called the Royal Canadian Mounted Police station in Arctic Bay and spoke to the duty officer. He confirmed that the bay was entirely free of ice, so I checked once again the latest ice chart issued by the Canadian Ice Service. The approaches through Admiralty Inlet looked clear enough to allow us to reach Arctic Bay, so we left Dundas Bay and headed south. Friends on Suilvan, an Oyster 47 yacht, decided to join us.

With a favourable easterly wind we had a fast sail across the 50-mile wide Lancaster Sound. Before we had reached the mouth of Admiralty Inlet, we encountered the first ice, but the floes were well spread out and we could easily find a way through them. We continued confidently on our way south, but as we got deeper into the inlet, the ice concentration gradually became higher. Ice concentration on the charts is graded on a scale from 1 to 10. A concentration of 1, shown as 1/10, represents approximately 10% ice and 90% open water. Any concentration between 1/10 and 3/10 is acceptable; passing through an area between 3/10 and 5/10 is difficult but may still be possible, preferably with a metal hull, but only if there is no other alternative. Any concentration higher than 6/10

is considered dangerous, and not suitable to be tackled by a small boat.

Having advanced about 10 miles into the inlet, our progress became increasingly more difficult, and we barely managed to keep heading in the desired direction. As the ice situation had turned out to be far worse than expected, and the chances of reaching Arctic Bay looked quite improbable, going any further seemed too risky, so I decided to turn around. We turned north and tried to follow our outbound track. Whereas earlier we had encountered scattered ice floes and small bergs that were relatively easy to avoid, we now found that in the meantime the ice had been concentrated by the tide or wind, and we had serious difficulties finding a way through. The crew of Suilvan, whom we had warned not to continue as we were turning around, stopped to wait for us to catch up. We

did, and continued together, but the ice got worse and worse. With Suilvan following closely behind, as we felt more comfortable to open up leads with a metal hull, we zigzagged and slalomed, but to no avail. Whereas before we could still follow short leads to proceed roughly in the direction of the open sea, by now the ice floes were setting tighter and tighter. Looking back, I saw that Suilvan was no longer following us, and they confirmed by radio that they were beset by ice and could no longer move. We continued looking for a way

Nera looking concerned

out, but the ice was so thick that we had to give up. Held firmly in its grip, with no obvious alternative but to wait, our only hope was that the tide or wind would loosen the ice and help us escape. Earlier, we had seen close to the edge of a floe we were passing, some clear polar bear footprints. As there were seals about, and bears are known to use such floes to attack seals, we had the rifle at the ready in the cockpit all the time.

Although we appeared to be stationary, the chart plotter showed that we were drifting with the ice pack at a rate of 0.6 knots, not in the direction of the open sea, but towards the coastline, some five miles distant. I realised the situation was becoming critical, but

reassured the crew that sooner or later the ice would start breaking up and loosen its grip. Doina took my word, tethered herself to the boat, and stepped down on the nearest floe to take some photos of Aventura moored alongside a large floe, while Marianne filmed both that telling scene and our subsequent predicament.

Suddenly, the crew of Suilvan called to say that they had been freed, and were attempting to reach the nearest lead. They kept updating us on their progress, saying that they had to push their way through some floes to reach open water, and soon their AIS signal was showing them heading north at a rate of 7.2 knots.

Still stuck and with our situation seeming to get worse rather than better, I decided to attempt to force our way out. Firmly trapped by the surrounding floes, I rammed Aventura's bows into a narrow gap, and revved up. Slowly the floes drifted apart, and we were on the move. We continued forcing our way through with the engine while also pushing the floes out of the way with two long ice poles, Aventura brutally ramming those that refused to yield. The worst were the older, blue-coloured bergy bits, broken off larger icebergs and thus

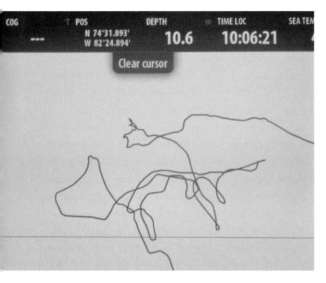

COG — T POS N 74°31.893' W 82°24.894' DEPTH 10.6 m TIME LOC 10:06:21 SEA TEM — Clear cursor

made of denser ice. They extended underwater both sideways and downwards, and several times we could not avoid being stranded with one rudder stuck on a protruding underwater ledge. Now I was thankful I had insisted on the rudders being supported by massive steel stocks protected by skegs.

Although we attempted to make our way towards the open sea, more often than not the leads would point away from the direction in which we wanted to go. Several times we passed floes marked by our green antifouling paint, showing that we had been there before. I was totally confused as to our actual location until it occurred to me to look on the chart plotter at our previous southbound track, and attempt to follow the openings that pointed closest to it. Eventually we reached an area with less ice concentration, finding open leads became easier and soon we were in clear water.

The tortuous route recorded on the chart plotter shows clearly our 14-hour ordeal and the challenge it had been to get out of the grip of the ice. It was a relief and certainly satisfying to be free, but I must admit that I could have done without the experience. However, it was a very valuable lesson and showed how

well Aventura could cope in such a situation. After all, this is what she had been conceived and built for.

Back in Dundas Harbour we joined the other boats in the frustrating waiting game. A forecast of an easterly gale turned into a proper storm with gusts of over 60 knots. As the wind increased, my main concern were two boats that had arrived recently and had anchored quite close to us. Gaia, a small steel boat from Hungary, started dragging and the crew only managed with great difficulty to raise their anchor. As they passed perilously close to us, I had to swerve hard with the help of the engine to avoid a collision. In the middle of a violent gust, the foresail on the neighbouring Gjoa started unfurling. With the crew fighting to tame the billowing sail, while the boat was dangerously yawing closer and closer to us, I somehow managed to power Aventura out of their way.

With half of August gone and still no realistic signs of an impending improvement in the ice situation, I was forced to admit that the long-term ice forecasts had been wrong, and we were faced with a repeat of the previous year's scenario, when the ice situation had been just as unpredictable. Although in

2013 the Passage did open briefly in late August/early September, few of those who attempted an east to west transit, managed to continue their voyage into the Pacific, so some had to overwinter in the Arctic. Faced with a similar prospect I knew that a decision had to be taken soon, and as with reefing, you should reef as soon as you think of it, or leave a doubtful anchorage before it may be too late - I knew that within days I would have to make up my mind whether it was time to give up.

Beechey Island

Located at the western end of Lancaster Sound, Beechey Island is the site where the ill-fated expedition led by Sir John Franklin spent their first Arctic winter in 1845-46.

Terror and Erebus

Two well-equipped ships, Terror and Erebus, had left London in May 1845 with the task of completing the charting of the Northwest Passage, and thus establishing beyond any doubt the existence of this waterway linking the Atlantic and Pacific oceans. Neither the ships nor any of the 129 men were ever seen again*. In the following years, several search expeditions were mounted and eventually their tragic fate became known. With their ships beset by ice, the crews were forced to abandon them and try to save themselves by walking overland. Only a few managed to make it to the mainland, where they all perished. Over the years there has been much speculation as to the real reason why such a well-prepared expedition could have come to such an unexpected end. It was only in the early 1980s that it was finally proven that the high content of lead in the human remains that had been analysed would have caused severe lead poisoning owing to badly soldered cans among the ships' food stores. Combined with scurvy, the effects had eventually led to their deaths.

On the shore of Beechey Island are the graves of four men who had died during that first winter, as well as several memorials dedicated to this tragic expedition. For sailors attempting a transit of the Northwest Passage, the site is a place of pilgrimage, and, having anchored Aventura in Terror and Erebus Bay, we made our way ashore to pay our respects.

Our stop at Beechey Island was tinged with sadness, not only because of the tragic events all those years ago, but more so by my decision to abandon the attempt to transit the Northwest Passage that summer. With the ice situation showing little improvement, even if a late transit became possible, we would quite likely not be able to reach the Pacific before the seas started to ice up again. In such an eventuality the only solution would be to overwinter somewhere in Arctic Canada or Alaska, something that I was not prepared to do. I therefore decided to turn around, while the weather conditions in the Northern Atlantic were still favourable for the passage south.

It was a painful but not very difficult decision, as I had known all along that such an eventuality could not be discounted. I never had any doubt that the Northwest Passage presented a considerable challenge, but what I had learned from the example of Roald Amundsen, and the many Arctic explorers who had preceded him, was that challenges are there to be overcome, and that the success of any expedition depends not only on good preparation but above all on perseverance.

* The wreck of Erebus was discovered in 2014 and that of Terror in 2016 about 200 miles south of Beechey Island.

The first reaction to my decision came from my son Ivan, who had accompanied me on all my previous high-latitude adventures. I quote his words, as they reflected exactly my own feelings:

Marianne and Jean-Luc were going to continue to Nuuk, with only Doina sailing with me all the way home.

On our last night in the High Arctic, as we made our way south across Davis Strait, we were treated to a spectacular show of northern lights.

Southbound

After the others had left us in Nuuk, Doina and I provisioned and fuelled the boat for the 2,500-mile passage to Europe. As we were about to leave, I received an urgent message from Stephan Constance, the CEO of Garcia Yachting, the boatyard that had built Aventura. He urged me to reconsider my plan and sail instead to the USA so Aventura could be exhibited at two of the major US boat shows. As he had done so much to turn my dream into reality, I found it hard to refuse, and, with Doina's agreement, we turned the bows south, now bound for St John's in Newfoundland.

'Seeing that there seems to be a 50/50 chance that the Northwest Passage won't open this year, it may be for the best to turn back. This is something my cycling has taught me about being audacious: it's better to have tried and possibly failed than not to try at all.'

After the decision was taken to abandon our attempt and sail south, Nick, Nikki and Emily moved to other boats that were still hoping to make it through. Nera,

A large sperm whale swims slowly past us on the morning after the celestial show

Doina steering past an iceberg on the way out of Nuuk

The night after a fast start from Nuuk, the predicted 30-knot northwesterly winds were soon gusting over 40 knots. We had large seas as our track crossed an area of banks with depths of only 10 to 20 metres. We were broad reaching with three reefs in the mainsail, no foresail, and the centreboard fully up, a combination I had used in similar situations in the past. Aventura was taking the strong wind in her stride, surfing occasionally at 10 to 12 knots, and when a large following wave caught us on its cusp, she swept ahead at an exhilarating speed of 14.8 knots.

We continued riding the swell comfortably with everything under control until a large steep wave approaching from abeam broke violently over us, pushing us around into a gybe. The gybe was not too violent as the boom brake controlled it, but when I got Aventura back on course, Doina noticed that the boom was at a strange angle. The fitting holding the boom to the mast had broken. As the mainsail and taut reefing lines were still holding up the boom, we could continue sailing. I checked the boom, and saw no damage apart from the broken casting. I secured the boom in place with two lines hauled in tightly to the mast winches, and was confident that we could continue, albeit with three reefs in the mainsail.

Since the gybe, we had been hand-steering as the violent shock had also put the autopilot out of action, and there was no response from the rudder sensor. As Aventura was equipped with two entirely autonomous autopilot systems, I disconnected the faulty autopilot and connected the other unit. With one faulty pilot and a broken boom, I suggested to Doina that we ought to consider diverting to the nearest port in Greenland to effect repairs.

'Why make a detour of some 150 miles when the boom seems to work, and if this pilot also goes, we can steer by hand,' was her immediate reaction.

'We still have 1,100 miles to St John's and with just the two of us that won't be easy,' I said.

'If you promise to take me to a really good fish restaurant when we get there, I'd be quite happy to carry on,' she responded.

And carry on we did. We completed the 1,200-mile passage from Nuuk in 7 days 21 hours, with a broken boom, sailing with three reefs in the mainsail, keeping permanent radar watch during the hours of darkness, as there were still icebergs about, and covered it all at an average speed of well over 6 knots.

We had hardly tied up at the customs dock in St John's when a man came over and started asking us about our trip, what kind of boat Aventura was and why the boom was lashed to the mast. I told him about the broken fitting, and he said: 'The man who will be able to make you a replacement will be here in one hour. His name is Terry Crane. I just called him to come and look at your boat as he has a metal workshop and wants to build his own aluminum yacht.'

Terry arrived soon after, had a look at the broken part, described it as unsuitable for the size of the boom, and offered to machine a better, stronger one from solid aluminium.

'I'll be back with the new part this afternoon.'

And indeed he was... and five minutes later the boom was fixed. I could not believe it. We had just arrived in this remote place, and the first person I met was possibly the only one able to help me. The goddess Fortuna was obviously looking after me.

Seeing Doina step off the boat to return home after having been together for two months was a sad moment, just as I felt when Ivan left after having helped me sail Aventura from London to Greenland. Our long voyage in the first Aventura 40 years ago has forged a strong and lasting bond between us, and nothing makes me happier than sailing with my children.

3

One more time

The most certain way to succeed is always to try just one more time.

Thomas Edison

The decision to abandon my attempt at transiting the Northwest Passage brought on a period of uncertainty, as I could not make up my mind what to do next. But what I knew was that I would certainly have another go, so the suggestion to sail south and have Aventura exhibited at some US boat shows seemed like a good stop-gap solution. After Doina's departure, I was joined in St John's by Lou Morgan, the owner of Aventura's sister ship Arctic Monkey, and Ryan Helling of Swiftsure Yachts, the US distributors of the Exploration 45. The plan was to sail to Annapolis where Aventura would be exhibited at the biggest boat show in the United States. To my great satisfaction, Aventura – and the Exploration 45 design – won the two most important design awards: Best Boat 2015, presented by SAIL magazine, and US Boat of the Year, awarded by Cruising World magazine.

South to Panama

After a winter spent in Florida, by spring 2015 Aventura was ready to head for the Panama Canal and the Pacific to join the Blue Planet Odyssey southern route in Tahiti. My new crew was Dunbar Lewis, a 38-year-old South African sailor, who had taken part in one of our events on his own boat, but was keen to expand his horizons. When I told him that I was looking for crew for my Pacific voyage, he sold his boat and joined me in Fort Lauderdale. For the passage to Panama we were also joined by Charlie Doane, whom I had first met in 1992, when he had taken part in America 500. The fourth crew was Dave, an American sailor fresh from a passage to Hawaii.

With the strong Gulf Stream sweeping north through the Florida Strait, and the bulk of Cuba blocking the direct route to Panama, I chose to make a detour via the Outer Bahamas and reach the Caribbean Sea via the Windward Passage. This was my third passage along this route, and the prolonged spell of

light winds for most of the 1,300 miles was a great surprise. Fortunately our light-weather sails, a Code Zero complemented by a Parasailor spinnaker, allowed us to make good progress even when the winds were hovering around 10 knots. Once again, the Parasailor proved its worth as its versatile design allowed us to fly it both for reaching, when it behaved just like an asymmetric spinnaker, and as a tri-radial when broadreaching or running. My crew, who were not familiar with the Parasailor, were quite impressed, so much so that one of them climbed to the top of the mast for a bird's eye view of the billowing canvas.

As we approached Panama, ships coming from or heading for the canal were constantly crossing our track, the AIS making it so much easier to guess their intentions, especially at night. We made landfall off the port of Cristobal at dawn, and having passed through the massive breakwaters, made our way to Shelter Bay Marina. As its name suggests, located in a perfectly sheltered basin, this is the most convenient place on the Caribbean side to prepare for the transit of the Panama Canal.

I transited the canal for the first time on my first Aventura in 1977, with the second in 1991 and the third in 2002, while six of my round-the-world events also reached the Pacific this way, with the Blue Planet Odyssey passing through in early 2015. Having missed transiting the canal with the rally, we were in a hurry to catch up with them in Tahiti and were therefore hoping to transit the canal in the shortest time possible. Over the years I have established an excellent relationship with the canal authorities, and we were scheduled to transit two days after our arrival, much sooner than normal.

This major feat of engineering never fails to fill me with awe regardless of how many times I have passed through it. Indeed, when the Panama Canal was opened in 1914 it was described as the eighth wonder of the world. In 1977, the United States handed over its operation to Panama, and in spite of some initial doubts about its ability to handle this complex operation efficiently, the new Panama Canal Authority has been doing an outstanding job in ensuring that this major international waterway functions like clockwork. Between 42 and 46 ships transit the canal every day, and yachts are usually locked through with smaller vessels.

Every yacht must have a minimum crew of five: one at the helm, and four to handle the mooring lines. Two days after our arrival, our course advisor boarded Aventura in the early evening, and we proceeded towards the Gatun Locks, where a set of three chambers lifts ships into Gatun Lake, 27 metres above sea level. Shortly before midnight we reached Lake Gatun, the course advisor left us, and we spent the night tied to a mooring buoy. A new advisor joined us in the morning

and we set off across the lake to the Pedro Miguel Lock, some 27 miles distant. Using every possible shortcut to gain time, we were urged by our advisor to move at our best speed to meet a tight deadline at the next set of locks. As the gates of the Miraflores Lock swung inwards, the waters of the Pacific rushed through welcoming us to the South Seas.

As soon as we had completed the transit, disembarked the pilot and extra crew, Dunbar and I set course for distant Tahiti where I intended to catch up and sail with the Blue Planet Odyssey boats as far as Fiji. From there Aventura would strike out north on her own, spend the winter in Japan and in spring 2016 sail east and make a new attempt at the Northwest Passage, this time from the west.

With 4,800 miles ahead of us, and only five weeks to get to Tahiti, there was no time to waste, so I was planning to sail there nonstop. As the prospects of a faster passage with consistent winds looked better if we stayed just north of the equator for the first part of the voyage, I decided against the traditional route that passes close to the Galapagos Islands. The tactic seemed to work as we picked up steady northeasterly winds while crossing the Bay of Panama and were making good progress reeling off the miles under the poled out Parasailor while the autopilot was doing all the work. Settling into an easy routine with Dunbar, I was looking forward to an enjoyable passage, the longest I had ever attempted.

When I woke up at dawn on the third morning, ready to relieve Dunbar, I was suddenly struck by the thought that what I was doing was not right, that the entire plan was wrong. Was sailing the projected route really important, while ignoring a more attractive and also logical alternative? Why wait another year to achieve my goal, when I could easily have another go at the Northwest Passage this season? I mulled over this dilemma throughout my watch, prepared breakfast, and then woke up Dunbar.

'Let's slow down and have a chat,' I told him.

'What? Slow down for breakfast? We've never done that,' he exclaimed, puzzled.

'No, it's not that. Something much more serious. I need to talk to you about a change of plan. How about going for the Northwest Passage this summer, not next.'

'But how feasible is it? Isn't it too late? Also, I am really keen to sail to Tahiti and continue to Japan.' He sounded disappointed.

'OK, let's have breakfast. I only thought of it now. But let's slow down while we consider our options.'

The tempting opportunity was certainly my main motivation, but I was also wondering whether this sudden decision may not have been influenced by my previous experience of sailing in my own events, the first round-the-world rally on Aventura II, and the Millennium Odyssey on Aventura III. Managing an event while also being in charge of my own boat had not been an ideal combination then; why should it be now?

The more I thought about it, the more justified I felt in embarking on this drastic change of plan. Having outlined to Dunbar both sides of my dilemma, he generously agreed to such a drastic change and sail north instead. However, once I started looking realistically at this new scenario, I realised that time was too short to sail to Alaska and catch the best time for a west to east transit. The logical solution was to ship Aventura north on the next transport to Victoria, British Columbia. I contacted Sevenstar Yacht

sail the odyssey

THE OCEAN · OUR FUTURE

Transport, and was told that a ship was due in the next two to three weeks, departing from Golfito in Costa Rica.

For many years the perfectly sheltered harbour of Golfito has been a popular destination for US and Canadian boats sailing to or from Panama and the Caribbean, or just cruising the Central American coast. As we sailed into the landlocked harbour, I was surprised to see only about half a dozen sailing boats, and a few more motor yachts anchored or docked at the two marinas, Banana Bay and Fish Hook. We were warmly welcomed at the latter and tied up to one of its floating docks.

Golfito's main attraction is its proximity to large tracts of virgin rainforest, home to a variety of wildlife, sloths, various species of monkey, and all kinds of birds, from minuscule hummingbirds to majestic toucans. Keen to stretch our legs, we set off along a steep forest road, marching steadily upwards in the sweltering heat. Having been erroneously advised about the distance to walk to the nearest wildlife spot, it took us twice as long to finally reach the summit of the ridge, where huge trees reached for the sky, their rich canopies brushing the clouds. The sun was almost setting as we crossed a small meadow with a bird's-eye view of Golfo Dulce. We were rewarded for our efforts by a spectacular sunset, as the flaming orb broke through the clouds to bathe the waves of densely clad ridges in a misty purple light.

Bound for Alaska

After four weeks of patiently waiting in Golfito, on 29 April Aventura was loaded onto M.V. Tamper, a Sevenstar yacht transporter that delivered her to Victoria 17 days later. While being prepared for a renewed attempt at the Northwest Passage, Aventura was based for one month in nearby Seattle in the care of Swiftsure Yachts. On the day of our departure, we left at dawn to go through three opening bridges before the morning rush hour. As we left the Seattle sealock and entered Puget Sound, I looked back and there was the magnificent sight of Mount Rainier bathed in soft pastel colours by the rising sun.

As we pulled into our slip in Victoria marina, I noticed right next to us an older Garcia yacht of about the same size as Aventura. I was almost blown off my feet when the captain called across and greeted me in Hungarian! Although born in the US, Peter Molnar's parents were originally from Hungary, from where they escaped during the Hungarian Revolution of 1956. Besides sailing, Peter's other passion is wine, and he is the owner of a winery in Napa Valley. We toasted to our common Magyar genes with a glass of his excellent Pinot Noir.

As we set off on the long passage to Dutch Harbor, the Canadian Ice Service published the 30-day ice outlook for the western and central Arctic. Compared to the previous year, the forecast looked much better, and there was little doubt that attempting to transit the Northwest Passage from the Pacific end might ensure a better chance of success. But, as I knew too well, long-term forecasts were not be relied upon, so all I could do was hope for the best.

We had a frustratingly slow start for the long passage from Victoria to Dutch Harbor as we had to contend with both contrary winds and current. Halfway across the Gulf of Alaska we entered an area of high pressure and thus very light winds. I decided to motor as even if the light winds persisted, which was quite unlikely, we had enough fuel to take us all the way to Dutch Harbor, by that stage under 1,000 miles distant.

After a few days, favourable winds set in and we sailed 191 miles in 24 hours, my best mileage in that time span on Aventura IV and just one mile short of an average of 8 knots. As we made landfall at Sedanka Island on day 11 of the 1,700-mile passage, to the north of us the snowy peaks of Unimak Island were

bathed in the rosy tints of the setting sun. To reach our destination, we still had to negotiate the Unalga Strait, known for its fierce tides, so I decided not to attempt it in the fading light but wait for the following morning. Having spent a peaceful night at anchor, at first light we caught the favourable tide through the narrow strait, and 15 miles farther on, entered the land-locked port of Dutch Harbor on Unalaska Island, one of the Aleutian Islands whose chain stretches southwest from Alaska in the direction of Japan. When Russia sold Alaska to the United States in 1867, the Aleutian Islands were part of the deal. Renowned as the busiest fishing port in the United States, the 300 vessels based in Dutch Harbor harvest the rich waters of the shallow Bering Sea for halibut, pollock, all kinds of salmon, as well as snow, red and brown king crabs.

As we made our way through the narrow channel leading into Ililiut Harbor, I was astonished to see perched on top of a channel marker a large bald eagle. I would never have expected to see this magnificent bird, the symbol of the United States, nesting in this busy harbour, but soon we could see bald eagles everywhere. As we passed, it took off with a rustling whoosh of its mighty wings. We were told later that this skilled predator had turned into a scavenger, attracted by the detritus from the fish processing plants.

Shortly after our arrival, Dunbar and I were joined by our new crew: Chris Eakin, a friend from London, and Martin Frey, from Salt Lake City, both experienced sailors. Dutch Harbor was the perfect place to provision for what I reckoned to be a 60-day passage to Greenland, but to be on the safe side, I decided to have enough food for 80 days. We managed to get everything we needed, even, if to my taste, our supplies were inferior to the previous year's excellent provisions bought in Cherbourg - the quality I was searching for often being replaced by quantity.

Sailing friends had put me in touch with Daneen and Andy who lived in Dutch Harbor. Andy was away,

but soon after our arrival, Daneen came by to say hello, and for the rest of our stay proved to be an invaluable help, ferrying us everywhere in her capacious truck, allowing us to go online and do our laundry at her home, and earning the title of our Aleutian guardian angel.

To the end of the world

Fully provisioned, we left Dutch Harbor on schedule and set course for the Bering Strait and the Arctic Circle. For as long as I can remember I have regarded the Bering Strait as the most remote place in the world. As we hurried north on a miserably cold and misty

day, it was just as I had imagined, a forlorn and forbidding place separating America from Asia, Alaska from Siberia. That dreaded name of frozen wastes and murderous labour camps flooded me with distant memories of a child growing up under a communist regime in Romania; the son of a political prisoner, with no prospect of ever escaping except by dreaming. And here I was, sailing on my own boat through what I once considered to be the very end of the world. As we were swept on our way by a strong current, I realised that what I love above all about sailing is the absolute freedom that it gives me to go to places I never ever dreamed possible.

Soon we crossed another milestone, the Arctic Circle, gateway to the Northwest Passage. We were now in the Chukchi Sea, which is part of the Arctic Ocean and, as the latest ice chart showed the area south of Point Barrow to be clear, we continued sailing blissfully unaware of what lay ahead of us. As I came on watch at midnight and started filling the log, I saw that the air temperature had suddenly plummeted to 0°C and that of the sea to 4°C. Ice! I rushed into the cockpit and through the swirling mist could make out the menacing shapes of large grey blocks of ice barely a few boat lengths away. I called the crew, we dropped the sails and started the engine while looking for a way out.

We attempted to steer a course towards the Alaskan coast hoping that this was just an isolated patch of ice that could be easily bypassed. It was to no avail, as, on the contrary, the ice concentration was getting higher. Turning around was no longer an option, as the situation behind us looked just as bad. Within minutes we were trapped.

My main concern was that the ice surrounding us appeared to be old ice, as the floes were larger and thicker than those I had come across in the eastern Arctic. I could only presume that they had broken off the polar ice pack and had been pushed our way by the northeasterly winds. Floes of new ice are relatively thin and usually easier to push out of the way with our 4-metre-long ice poles, but the ice surrounding us was solid and dense, hard as concrete. It soon became clear that it would only yield to the more ruthless treatment of finding a gap in the pack, and brutally ramming Aventura through that narrow space, just as I had done in a similar situation the previous year. It was an adrenaline-spiked exercise, which seemed to work and we managed to make some modest progress, only to be trapped again and repeat the procedure. On several occasions we reached a dead end and had to

backtrack. Turning in a tight space proved even more difficult than simply pushing ahead, but with the help of the bow-thruster and careful manoeuvering, we got out of some really tight corners, although I shuddered to think what those repeated collisions with solid ice might be doing to our hull.

The most worrying aspect were the underwater ledges that extended sideways from some of the larger floes and could not be easily seen or avoided. I knew that if one were to hit one of the rudders, or worse still, the propeller, we would be in serious trouble. As I attempted to make a hard turn in one narrow space, we hit such a submerged ledge sideways, the violent shock knocking me off my feet. But our luck held, and although it took us over eight hours to escape that icy maze, we eventually reached open water 27 miles from the point where the pack had taken us captive.

Late that same evening we reached Point Barrow at the northwestern extremity of Alaska and could finally turn east and into the Northwest Passage proper. At 71°23'N, this is the farthest north anyone may wish to sail, as there was nothing between here and the North Pole, just solid ice. Although we could see the dense ice pack close to the north of our course, there seemed to be a narrow gap along the Alaskan coast where the ice concentration was lower, due both to the relatively warmer water in the vicinity of land and the fact that the larger ice blocks were grounded in deeper water. By staying in shallow water and sailing a parallel course to the coast, we were able to make headway at a reasonable pace, although now and again we had to fight our way through a larger concentration of ice.

The drama of the previous day was soon forgotten as we motored and occasionally sailed through fields of ice, the floes being spaced out enough so that we could slalom between them. Being so far north we had 24 hours of daylight and we passed our time photographing the phantasmagoric shapes sculpted by the sun and wind: a crowned Neptune on his throne, a pouncing crocodile, a brooding Mayan deity. It felt like walking through the gallery of a surrealist sculptor.

We continued making unexpectedly fast progress but I knew that this wasn't going to last as the latest ice chart showed a solid choke-point barring our course where a wide tongue of drift ice appeared to merge with the coastline. Before long, the ice concentration became higher, the free leads more difficult to find, and our course more erratic. After a few dead ends had forced us to turn back, I realised that we had reached that point shown on the ice charts, and would not be able to pass it. The only alternative was to divert south and attempt to bypass it by gaining the lee of the Maguire Islands, and stay in shallow water close to the shoreline, in water that was sometimes less than two metres deep.

This group of three low sandy cays fronts a shallow lagoon, which we found to be entirely free of ice. We soon found the explanation for that, as the depths depicted on both the paper and electronic charts were entirely wrong. Several times we touched the ground with our draft of 2.8 metres with the centreboard down, where the chart showed twice that depth. As the forward-looking sonar, which would have shown us the depth ahead, was out of action, I reverted to the old and tested method of 'sounding with the board'. We would edge slowly forward until the board touched the bottom, raise it enough to pass that shallow spot into slightly deeper water, and carry on. It was slow, but it worked, and showed the advantage of having a boat with variable draft as, at a touch of a button, the electric winch would lift the board thus reducing Aventura's draft instantaneously to just over one metre.

By now we were all exhausted by the constant concentration, so I suggested we drop the anchor where we were and catch up on some sleep, so as to be rested when we came to the critical area that was still blocked by ice. We reached the latter the following morning, and by staying close to the shoreline in as shallow water as I dared, we managed to avoid the worst of it. At long last we found open water ahead and were soon sailing fast with a following westerly wind. We were also helped by an east-setting current, the circumpolar current that sets through the Northwest Passage at a rate of up to one knot.

With the ice starting to thin out, we could relax, and enjoy the beauty of the Arctic scenery. As we crossed the demarcation line between the USA and Canada,

Making progress in shallow waters south of the Maguire Islands

have conveyed better the beauty of the Arctic than that dream-like image of the distant coastline. On a more mundane level, it was also a source of satisfaction as in the four weeks since Aventura had left Seattle we had sailed over 3,000 miles, while also stopping for three days in Victoria, BC, and four days in Dutch Harbor.

Herschel Island

We made our Canadian landfall at Herschel Island and we could not have picked a better place of arrival in the High Arctic. The island has a rich and fascinating history and is rarely visited by sailing boats.

Once a busy whaling station, it has a cluster of old buildings preserved as a capsule of times gone by, and is now part of the Qikiqtaruk Territorial Park. When the whalers arrived there in the late 19th century, Thetis Bay was crowded with bowhead and beluga whales. They were 'thick as sardines' in the words of Peyton Lenny, one of the two native Inuvialuit rangers stationed on the island. Among the historic buildings,

Alaska and Yukon, the undulating snow-clad mountains were bathed in pastel colours by the midnight sun. It was a magic moment that lifted our spirits as we knew that we had achieved almost the impossible by having come so far long before the end of July. It was also a moment of quiet celebration, and nothing could

the Arctic and the possible effects of climate change on the endemic flora and fauna to measuring the depletion of the permafrost and the resulting massive leaks of carbon dioxide into the atmosphere. A German scientist, who had been monitoring the local conditions for several years, explained that on a much larger scale this could be the fate awaiting the vast Siberian tundra, where the accelerating instability of its permafrost could result in catastrophic consequences for the entire planet.

The consequences of climate change were brought to our attention on the day of our arrival when a warden shot a large grizzly bear that had swum across from the mainland and posed a serious threat to the researchers roaming the island. He explained that grizzly bears were migrating into polar-bear territory, and red foxes were displacing their Arctic cousins.

Inuit interlude

Having passed through the western Arctic and its ice fields much earlier in the season than we had expected, and with the ice situation still unfavourable in the eastern Arctic, we could slow down and turn the next stage of our voyage into a more leisurely cruise. My crew were keen to see some Arctic wildlife, but apart from some birds fishing among the ice, a few seals and a couple of beluga whales far in the distance, the most exciting so far had been a falcon dive-bombing us as we walked on Herschel Island. Nor were my crew impressed with a cute ground squirrel, which stood up and looked puzzled at seeing these large animals walking on their hind legs just like him.

the original Pacific Steam Whaling Company house built in 1893 has been converted into a museum, while the Anglican Church is now a protected nesting place for black guillemots.

Among the buildings was also an old-fashioned wood-burning sauna, and I traded a large packet of biscuits with Peyton to fire it up for us. Several scientists working on various research projects soon joined us in the overheated chamber and a young Finn challenged me to walk into the ice-cold sea with him for a proper Arctic baptism. I did, and my crew followed.

Just as the Arctic has been described as the canary in the mine for global weather, so Herschel Island is regarded as a symbol of the Arctic, because what happens in this microcosm of Arctic flora and fauna may point to the eventual consequences of climate changes in other similar environments. The research projects being undertaken range from the greening of

From Herschel Island we sailed due east across the shallow Beluga Bay, on the lookout for the whales that had given it its name, but all we spotted were some puffins diving quickly as they saw us approach. On arrival at Tuktoyaktuk (or Tuk as everyone referred to it) we tied up to a floating pontoon and walked to the Royal Canadian Mounted Police station to complete entry formalities into Canada.

The sprawling settlement of about 900 inhabitants is an important supply centre for Arctic Canada. It also marks the very end of the Trans-Canadian Highway, a route that starts in faraway Newfoundland and crosses the entire continent to reach this remotest of places. Most houses that we passed were pre-fabricated one-family units typical of the permanent settlements, which had been set up by the Canadian government to provide the native population with medical facilities, schools, supermarkets and airports.

Sailing boats are quite a rarity in the Arctic and we had not seen a single one since we had left Dutch Harbor. We were warmly welcomed wherever we stopped, as the people wanted to know what had brought us to these remote places. While at Tuktoyaktuk, the mayor, Darrel Nasogaluake, came to greet us and, seeing the Blue Planet Odyssey banner and UNESCO logo on our boom, asked us about the meaning of this event. He then spoke at length about changes in their traditional way of life, now greatly influenced by the changing climate.

In spite of the warm welcome at Tuktoyaktuk, it was not what we had expected from a native Inuvialuit settlement, so we took the mayor's advice and made a 200-mile detour to Ulukhaktok, on Victoria Island, having been assured that it was more traditional.

We dropped anchor close to the settlement in late afternoon and walked ashore, but found everything to be closed, as it was Sunday. A local man stopped his quad bike to greet us and introduced himself as Little Jack. He explained that Ulukhaktok had a supermarket, a small hotel, a kindergarten for the 12 younger children and a school with one class of 20 pupils aged between 7 and 12. There were also three churches for the 480 inhabitants: Catholic, Pentecostal and Anglican, but only the last had a resident priest. We stopped at the church in the hope of meeting him but the door was locked.

Little Jack gives Martin and Chris the lowdown on the local scene

'He's away hunting, like everyone else,' a passing man called over. There were obviously more pressing priorities on a summer Arctic Sunday and religious services could very well wait until winter.

We had been told that Ulukhaktok was a settlement where the people lived a more traditional way of life. Nowadays they all had to travel much farther than ever before and the place was so quiet because many families were at summer camps, hunting and fishing for winter supplies. Passing by were three young men who were setting off on their quad bikes to go hunting musk ox. Little Jack commented that climate change was a matter of serious concern and that in recent years they were seeing fish, birds and even bats that they had never seen before. He could have added Aventura to that list, too, as he told us that a sailing boat like ours had not been seen there for more years than the fingers of his hand.

The Arctic hub

We set sail the following morning because the ice charts showed that the route to Cambridge Bay was no longer barred so we rushed to get there. Due to its strategic location Cambridge Bay has been described as the make or break point for anyone attempting a transit of the Northwest Passage. For those coming like us from the west and chasing the retreating ice, this is often the place to pass a nail-biting time while waiting and hoping that the ice will break up in the eastern Arctic to open the way to Greenland and the Atlantic Ocean.

For those heading west, getting to Cambridge Bay is a great relief, but it is still only a relatively short step towards completing a transit during the quickly shrinking favourable season. Often the only alternative is to spend the winter there and continue the voyage the following summer. When we arrived, there were three yachts that had spent the winter in Cambridge Bay: the Australian Philos, which was heading east like

us, while the Canadian Gjoa and Wave were waiting impatiently to set off westwards. Both had been hauled out by a shore crane the previous September and could not get back in the water as there was no crane driver available nor anyone who knew how to operate a crane. After waiting for three weeks, they had no choice but to fly a professional crane driver from south Canada at great expense to end their ordeal.

With Cambridge Bay possibly the last place to get fuel in the Northwest Passage, we made arrangements to have a tanker deliver the fuel to a dock were we could tie up.

'The expected fuel barge has not arrived as it is too early in the season,' said the man at the fuel depot. 'All we have is Jet A fuel used by the prop planes. Most diesel engines manage to run on it,' he added, helpfully.

Alarm bells started ringing in my head, as this was one risk I was not going to take. Instead, I went to the school library, got online, typed in a query on Google, and had several responses reassuring me that indeed Jet A fuel can be used for marine diesel engines, but needed to be properly lubricated. This we did with a generous ratio of outboard motor oil, and our Volvo seemed to like it, as it purred contentedly when we ran it for a test.

Refuelled and with fresh provisions from the surprisingly well-stocked supermarket, we were keen

that Roald Amundsen spent the first two winters of his voyage. Amundsen and his crew put those two years to good use by learning from their hosts the art of survival in that harsh climate. Amundsen also conducted important scientific observations on earth magnetism and the North Magnetic Pole, being the first to establish that its location was not fixed but constantly moving.

The relationship between the Kabluna (foreigners) and Nattilik was very amicable, and locals still spoke about Amundsen's stay as if it happened ten, not 110 years ago. Among them was the artist Danny Aaluk, from whom I purchased a beautiful pen and ink drawing inspired by an Inuit saga. When the subject of Amundsen came up during our conversation, he shyly murmured. 'I am, in fact, related to him... on my mother's side.'

Taken aback, I looked at him and agreed that he did indeed have a certain resemblance to the great explorer. A faded photo on the Amundsen memorial overlooking the anchorage shows the explorer holding a baby on his knee in the company of a Nattilik couple.

to push on. While ice is the main hurdle in the western part of the Northwest Passage, from the navigation point of view the most difficult stretch lay ahead of us between Cambridge Bay and Gjoa Haven. This is a poorly surveyed area of shallows and submerged rocks with many blank areas on the Canadian paper charts.

Gjoa Haven is the one place that no Arctic sailor wants to miss as it was in this Nattilik settlement

Sunrise over the ice on the way to Bellot Strait

Our enjoyable stopover in Gjoa Haven had to be cut short when the ice charts indicated an imminent improvement in the conditions ahead of us. With more than 300 miles to the point that would give us access to the Atlantic, we set off immediately.

This last section of the Northwest Passage proved to be the most difficult of the entire voyage, as we had to

contend with both strong contrary winds and having our route blocked by several areas of high ice concentration. With the prospect of achieving our aim of completing a transit of the Northwest Passage almost within reach, we spared no effort to make progress and carried on valiantly towards Bellot Strait and Peel Sound, the last obstacles still separating us from our goal.

We timed our arrival at Bellot Strait perfectly as the 17-mile long strait is renowned for its fierce tidal currents and can only be negotiated on a favourable tide. Halfway through the strait we passed Zenith Point, which marks the northern extremity of continental America. Having sailed my previous Aventura past Cape Horn, at the continent's southern extremity, I now had reached its northernmost point. As we approached the eastern entrance to the strait, the current peaked at over eight knots, and we completed the transit of the entire strait in only 90 minutes... and exactly one month to the day since we had left Dutch Harbor.

After the excitement of having reached the eastern Arctic, we were rewarded by a quiet night at anchor in Depot Bay, the site of Fort Ross, a former trading station of the Hudson's Bay Company. Two of the original cabins have survived and are still in good

order. One had been converted into an emergency shelter for visiting scientists or Canadian officials, but is accessible to any visitor. We duly signed the souvenir book that records the names of those who passed through on their way to or from the Northwest Passage.

The euphoria of our achievement was soon dampened by the prospect of the remaining 1,200-mile long passage to Nuuk. As I knew from the previous year, we could expect both strong winds and flat calms in the area ahead of us. In due course we had both. We had to fight our way out of Prince Regent Inlet against headwinds and sufficient ice about to keep us alert, but as we reached Lancaster Sound, the wind dropped, the sky cleared and the sun came out. The chilly dampness was gone and we enjoyed a sweltering Arctic day of 8°C, while passing an ever-changing panorama of tall cliffs scoured by ancient glaciers, and distant mountains covered by permanent icecaps.

To reach Davis Strait and the open sea we had to negotiate a narrow strait overlooked by breathtaking scenery. The enjoyment of the beauty surrounding us was marred by a strong wind being funneled through the strait, and as we finally reached the open water, the wind dropped and on came the engine. We caught the south-setting West Greenland current that gave us a boost of one knot, but also brought with it a procession of icebergs that it had picked up from calving glaciers along the way. And then the fog descended, visibility dropped to a boat's length, and we had to be on high alert to avoid running into one of those glistening behemoths, floating silently by.

By late morning the sun had burnt the mist and my attention was caught by the attractive blue colour of a large iceberg. Knowing that soon we would be out of such a unique photo opportunity, I decided not to miss it. I had promised the manufacturer of the Parasailor spinnaker to take some photos of this colourful sail in the Arctic, and this was definitely the last chance.

We took shelter in the lee of the iceberg, hoisted the sail but kept it in its douser, and launched the tender. Dunbar and Chris agreed to sail Aventura past the iceberg, while Martin and I boarded the dinghy to lay in wait.

As we bounced up and down in the swell, waiting for Aventura to pass between the iceberg and us, Martin exclaimed:

'I bet this is the first dinghy ever to brave the Davis Strait!'

Later that day we crossed the Arctic Circle and, in the view of those who only consider a successful transit of the Northwest Passage as having crossed this symbolic gateway both on the way north and south, we had achieved our aim. Since we had passed the former point 34 days earlier, we had sailed 3,728 miles. What was remarkable is that we had completed the transit with no breakages or any serious technical problems and arrived in Nuuk with all systems in perfect working order. If the successful transit of the Northwest Passage counted as Aventura's maiden voyage, this had been a very long honeymoon indeed.

Closing the circle

The Parasailor photo shoot was the last act before declaring the Northwest Passage mission accomplished. We turned Aventura's bows for Nuuk and, although it was late August, we encountered many more icebergs than expected while crossing the Davis Strait to Greenland. Chris and Martin left us in Nuuk and our successful Arctic expedition was rapidly becoming just a memory. After almost two months in the High Arctic, arriving in Nuuk felt like coming home. As on Aventura's two previous visits, we were welcomed warmly by the

Nuuk harbour master Johannes Lindeman. This time I had come prepared and presented Johannes with a dedicated copy of my Ocean Atlas.

As there was no free space anywhere in the small boat harbour, we had to tie up alongside a boat flying the Russian flag. The crew came out to take our lines, and the captain called across: 'So nice to see you again, Jimmy. Last time we met was at the lecture you gave last spring at the Russian Geographical Society in St Petersburg.'

Daniel Gavrilov came on board and explained that his current voyage around the Arctic had been inspired by what I had said on that memorable evening. Seeing many young people in the audience, among them several Navy cadets in their uniforms, I referred to my own growing up under a communist dictatorship and urged them to make the best of the freedom their parents could not even dream about, but try to do something meaningful with their lives.

Although Aventura had just completed a long and occasionally arduous 5,000-mile passage from Dutch Harbor, we arrived in Nuuk with no list of jobs to be done. We did have a few matters to deal with along the way, but in every case I had the necessary spares and could deal with each job as it happened. Self-sufficiency is of utmost importance in the Arctic, and in that respect Aventura had passed the test in exemplary fashion.

After having loaded up with fuel for the long passage to the Canaries, I took a taxi into town to buy fresh provisions for the forthcoming voyage. When we arrived at the supermarket, I tried to pay the taxi with my credit card, as I had had no chance to get any cash.

'Sorry,' the driver said. 'Card not work, machine kaput. Only money.'

'But I have no money,' I replied.

'No problem,' he said, and zeroed the counter. This gesture most definitely did not feel like home as I remembered the annoying arguments I have had with London cabbies trying to cheat me because of my 'foreign' accent.

Less than 48 hours after our arrival, Dunbar and I were sailing again. Down to the basic crew of two, we were looking forward to what we hoped to be an uneventful 2,800-mile passage to the Canaries, where Aventura was going to spend the coming winter. To finish our sojourn in Greenland on a high, we decided to make a detour to visit the spectacular Prince Christian Sound at the southeastern tip of Greenland. As we sailed a course parallel to the coast, we started passing through large fields of broken ice discharged by the icebergs that had broken free during the summer from the many glaciers that are a feature of this coast. As the nights were getting longer, we now had to cope not just with this hazard that I had not counted on, but also with the longer nights and dense fog.

It was an eerie feeling to motor ahead in zero visibility while keeping watch from the inside nav station, monitoring the radar and steering with the help of the autopilot. After two seasons in the Arctic I had total confidence in Aventura's strongly built hull to take the occasional collision with bergy bits on the chin. I had found that the best way to deal with such obstructions was to keep up a speed of around four knots so that the ice would be deflected sideways by the bow wave and pass harmlessly by. The substantial aluminum tang welded at the base of the forefoot was a great help and was originally meant as a point of attachment to drag the boat ashore with a tractor if we were to spend the winter in the Arctic. In our case it acted just like the rostrum fitted to Roman galleys for ramming enemy ships, sweeping the ice out of our way, and allowing us to proceed unimpeded.

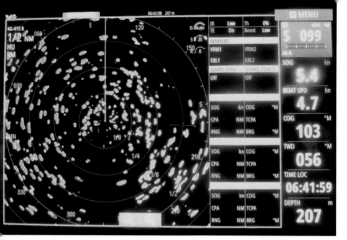

Our hope to end this Arctic trip on a high ended up instead with a low, a real low. A deep stationary depression located south of Iceland started generating strong southeasterly winds that made it impossible to reach Prince Christian Sound. Reluctantly, we tacked and ended up pointing in the general direction of Newfoundland, well off our desired course. As the wind got lighter we decided to motorsail on a more southerly course. The tactic seemed to work but after a while the engine overheated and I stopped it. I found that the impeller in the seawater circuit had been damaged and replaced it. The engine ran well but after about 20 minutes I noticed that the exhaust was no longer discharging water. On inspection, the impeller looked undamaged, so we checked with the GoPro underwater camera to see if we had picked up some obstruction on the seawater inlet, such as seaweed or a plastic bag, but it all looked clear. I tested the engine but after a few minutes it overheated again, so I stopped it to avoid damaging the impeller. I was now convinced that there was an airlock somewhere in the cooling system, and although I checked every possibility, I could not locate it. Having taken us safely through the Northwest Passage, our Volvo diesel engine must have felt like having a well-deserved rest and it showed its displeasure by refusing to work.

Concerned about setting off on such a long passage without a working engine, I had a chat with Dunbar about whether we should detour to the nearest port in Greenland, about 150 miles away, or continue without an engine. I was now in a similar situation as

the previous year, when passing through almost the same area with Doina. Dunbar's reaction was the same as Doina's: if I decided to carry on, he had no objection. So carry on we did. From that point we gave the engine the rest it obviously wanted, and just sailed. Fortunately our solar, wind and hydro-generator produced more than enough energy to keep us going.

I had always wondered why the southernmost point of Greenland had been given the attractive name of Cape Farewell. After several days of struggling to tack out of its grip, I knew I never wanted to see it again. It took us nine days to reach a point about 500 miles to the southeast of it, a distance we normally cover in three.

The culprit was a stationary and very powerful high west from the British Isles, extending halfway across the North Atlantic. It was blocking all weather systems and preventing any lows from moving from west to east and thus generate more favourable wind directions. I now gratefully appreciated the conditions we had encountered in the Northwest Passage, but once that voyage had been successfully completed, I seemed to have run out of luck. All we could sail was a southerly course parallel to Newfoundland and pointing in the general direction of Bermuda. With the latest forecasts predicting the situation would continue, I realised that Mother Nature had been trying to tell me something for the last few days. Suddenly I got the message: 'Don't fight me, you will not win. Be what you always claim to be: flexible.'

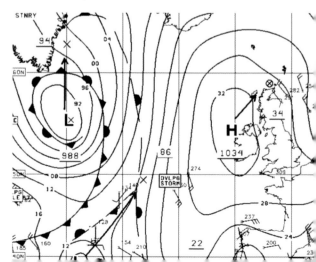

The decision was therefore taken to abandon our plan to sail to the Azores and on to the Canaries, and to turn east for Ireland instead. Once we got closer, we would let the wind decide whether we would make landfall in southern England, and sail to London from that direction, or make for Scotland and reach London via the North Sea.

With that obstinate high still blocking the weather systems in our area, in the course of four days we had two storms with sustained winds of 45 knots, and gusts of over 50 with seas to match. Being well reefed down, Aventura was holding her course and, bearing in mind the conditions outside, was quite comfortable. I made myself a hot chocolate and settled down at the navigation station for my night watch. Looking out of the windows from my comfortable armchair, it suddenly struck me that even in this kind of filthy weather, life at sea can still be enjoyable... if you have the right boat, and the mindset to go with it. But I wondered if William Shakespeare, who described the Atlantic as 'the wild and wasteful ocean', would have agreed with my assessment?

Well reefed down, we continued sailing, relishing the bursts of speed as Aventura caught the right wave and surged ahead, surfing at over 12 knots. After a while I decided not to overdo it, and hove-to. As on similar occasions in the past, I simply could not believe how almost at a stroke, everything calmed down, Aventura taking the large swell in her stride, having instantly morphed from a wildly rearing bronco to a docile flat-footed nag.

Slowly the weather improved, the wind direction promised a southern landfall, and with the temperature going steadily up we were shedding, like onions, one layer of clothing every day.

We made landfall at Falmouth, in southwest England, after a long and occasionally frustrating, but also challenging and memorable passage. We arrived off Falmouth in the middle of the night and hove-to for a few hours, as I didn't want to risk arriving in the dark with a dodgy engine. As we were drifting slowly with the tide, the VHF radio spluttered into action:
'Aventura, this is Falmouth Coastguard, calling on channel 16.'
'Falmouth Coastguard, this is sailing vessel Aventura...'
'Is that Jimmy Cornell's Aventura and is Jimmy on board?'

'Yes, I am.'

'Welcome to Falmouth. I sailed in your ARC in 1993. Where are you coming from?'

'Nuuk, Greenland, and before that the Northwest Passage.'

'The Northwest Passage? Congratulations.'

Could anyone have wished for a warmer welcome at four o'clock in the morning?

The reason for the stop at Falmouth was to have the engine checked and repaired before we tackled the busy English Channel. Fortunately I managed to get the engine to work long enough to get us into Pendennis Marina and tie up to a pontoon. I had already made arrangements via satellite phone with the local Volvo agent, and an engineer was waiting on the dockside. He gave the engine a service and, after a patient step-by-step search, located the source of the airlock at the anti-siphon valve. By early afternoon he declared the patient fully recovered, and left us with the engine in perfect running order.

Dunbar would have liked to spend at least one night away from the sea, but he was also just as keen as I to get to London. To make up for it, I took him out for a local treat: afternoon tea with oven-warm scones, covered in strawberry jam and dollops of clotted Cornish cream.

At 1800, we slipped our lines, had a quick look behind at the attractive port we were regretfully leaving, and started on the 360-mile leg to London. As we sailed into Falmouth Bay we were rewarded by the sight of a large fleet of yachts racing along the shore. The magnificent mixture of modern and traditional yachts was a perfect reflection of the picturesque Cornish town we were leaving behind.

We made a fast passage to the Thames Estuary where we caught the favourable tide for the remaining 40 miles to London. Shortly after we had passed the Thames tidal barrier, we reached the former Royal Albert Docks. It was from there that I had left in 1975 with Gwenda, Doina and Ivan on the first Aventura on our six-year-long round-the-world voyage. As we turned a wide river bend, the sight of Greenwich and the splendid buildings of the Royal Naval College came into view. In 1576 Martin Frobisher was seen off from here by Queen Elizabeth I, as he set off on the first voyage of exploration to the Northwest Passage. And here was Aventura proudly sailing past this historic site four and a half centuries later, having succeeded where

so many others had failed, and being only the 87th sailing vessel to have made it through that challenging waterway.

As we approached Tower Bridge we were called on the radio by the operator to inform us that he was stopping the traffic to open the bridge and let us pass into the Pool of London. As we passed through the open bridge, I saw Ivan and Gwenda waving from the south bank, where they had positioned themselves to photograph our arrival. Could I have ever dreamed way back in 1969, when I had just arrived in England and saw for the first time this iconic symbol of London, that one day I would arrive here on my own yacht to a hero's welcome?

4

A passion for the sea

Growing up in Romania

A young boy is sitting in the corner of a train compartment with his nose pressed to the window. With a loud screech the train slows down and starts negotiating a long bend. Suddenly a voice shouts excitedly: 'The sea, the sea! Look.... the sea!'
And there in front of us was a vast expanse of blue-grey water stretching to the far horizon. This first glimpse was the start of an abiding fascination with the sea that has lived with me to this day.

I am the little boy, the year is 1949, I am nine years old and on my way to a state-run vacation colony. A holiday by the sea seemed a dream after the traumatic events I had been through. I could not believe my luck.

Just a few weeks earlier I had been staying with my father in a small village in southern Transylvania where he was working on a roadbuilding site. One day, against his express orders, I had swum across the Olt, one of Romania's swiftest rivers, probably to impress my friends. When my father came to fetch me and saw my little head bobbing in the middle of that brown water, he could barely control his anger. Without a word, he yanked me home and gave me a good hiding, the first and last I ever got from him.

That same night, shortly after midnight, we were woken up by loud bangs on the door and, when my father opened it, a group of policemen burst into the room and, in front of me and my equally terrified sister Doina, took him away. Over 100,000 political undesirables, so-called unreliable members of the ancient regime, were seized that night. Each was sentenced to 15 years hard labour at the Danube-Black Sea Canal, one of Stalin's death camps, which was abandoned immediately after that tyrant's death in 1953. That night raid was the first nationwide dragnet carried out by the communists after they had taken over power in Romania, expelled King Michael and imposed a ruthless dictatorship that was to last half a century.

The River Olt

My father and other survivors were freed shortly after Stalin's death. With his health ruined and weighing only 40 kg, my father was unable to climb the stairs to our first floor flat and had to be carried by a neighbour. Although he recovered some of the lost weight, his mind and body remained scarred by those experiences to his dying day.

My father's fate has been a constant inspiration for me, but in a strangely negative way, as all my life I have done my best not to follow his example. One of the first lessons along this steep learning curve happened when my uncle came to take us home the day after my father's arrest. As we stood on the platform waiting for the train, he suddenly turned and said: 'Never pee against the wind.' I may not have understood the real meaning then, but now, a lifetime later, I realised that I have followed that simple advice all my life, trying to navigate the best course through life and, later, across the oceans.

My uncle followed his own advice to the letter: as a social democrat he did what many others in his situation decided to do and joined the communist party. He never went to prison, always had a well-paid job, lived happily into retirement and died in his sleep aged 88.

My father was the exact opposite: never able to compromise he put his principles above everything else including his family. His tragic fate was a relentless downward spiral, which started when he was barely 16 and his entire class were drafted into the Austro-Hungarian army, as Transylvania belonged to Hungary in those days. Sent to the Italian front, they suffered heavy losses when his company tried to cross the Piave River and were repelled. As my father was trying to reach their side of the river, a drowning man grabbed hold of him and started dragging him down. Realising that he did not have the strength to save his dying comrade, my father reached down and, grabbing hold of the man's open mouth, pushed him away, sending him to a certain death. This incident left him with a deep sense of guilt and made him deeply religious. He would pray every morning and evening in front of a crucifix, and often stopped to pray in churches he walked past.

Demobbed at 19, he finished his schooling in his tattered uniform, then managed to get a grant and study law in Budapest. Shortly after completing his studies, he decided to seek his fortune in South America. With interesting travel experiences but no fortune, he returned home and got a job as a village notary in eastern Transylvania. There he met my mother, they married in 1929, my sister Doina was born in 1935, and

I in 1940. In 1942, the quiet notary life was swapped for a glamorous and well-paid job as administrator of a private royal estate in the village of Savarsin in western Transylvania.

My father's fate was sealed days after the communists took over in late 1947 and forced King Michael into exile. The new regime had decided to expel the entire royal entourage and was allowing anyone connected with the King to join the special royal train leaving for Switzerland. My mother was so convinced we were going that she had packed four suitcases and was waiting hopefully for its arrival, but when the train finally arrived in Savarsin my father just went to pay his respects to the King and was the only person left behind on the platform. As he later explained to my distraught mother, he simply could not give up the great honour of staying behind and taking care of the King's estate in his absence.

For my poor mother this was the last straw. In the dying days of the war she had lost her parents, younger sister and two nephews when their refugee train was bombed. She had put all her hopes on starting a new life. Days after the departure of the royal train, my father was visited by the local communist party chief, who told him that the new regime needed people of his reputation and would do anything for him if he agreed to cooperate.

'I'd rather be dead,' my father replied.

'I hope you realise what you are saying. You must know Lenin's words that "who is not with us is against us". Take my honest advice: do it, otherwise you will be in a very dangerous situation.'

'So be it.'

My father had the mandate papers empowering him to administer the estate on the King's behalf torn up in his face and was given 24 hours to leave the village. My uncle managed to get him a job as a cashier on a remote roadbuilding site. My mother, Doina and I joined her sister in Brasov, where we arrived early in 1949.

My father in Rio de Janeiro

The medieval centre of Brasov with the Gothic Black Church

Set in a picturesque valley in the bend of the Carpathians, Brasov has a long and eventful history, having been founded in the 12th century by German settlers from Franconia, sent by a Hungarian king to defend this outpost of the empire. Mistakenly referred to as Saxons, they developed a thriving city whose wealth was founded on trade with the Orient. The Honterus Gymnasium, which I later attended, was the oldest school in Eastern Europe. It stood next to the equally famous Gothic Black Church, the first Lutheran church in Eastern Europe. Determined to give my sister Doina and me the best possible education, my mother mysteriously managed to enrol us into this prestigious school.

Our dingy flat was in a 400-year-old dilapidated building, its only advantage the central location right by the Black Church and its attendant school. With help from a family friend, my mother had found a job at a small enterprise dealing with hygiene and pest control. Everything under communism depended on your contacts, and friendship was the foundation of everything, which probably explains why for me having friends and being loyal to them is among the most important thing in life.

My mother's meagre salary was 400 lei, which covered exactly the cost of the monthly 5 kg parcel sent to my father in the labour camp. It contained honey, nuts and cigarettes, the universal prison currency. Without such life-saving parcels my father would not have survived. To supplement her earnings, pay for the flat and feed us, my mother played gin rummy. She was very good at it and although the stakes were low, she somehow always managed to win. Her sister and husband also helped, and having a comfortable house it was there that we all went for the weekly bath.

Every summer from the age of 12 I got some kind of work. Being well developed and strong, one job I got was as a porter with a vegetable wholesaler, owned like everything else in Romania by the state. After having been there for a while I started taking vegetables home, first for our own use, then to sell to neighbours. To earn more money I was doing two full shifts, working from six in the morning to ten in the evening. Before finishing my late shift I'd load in the last delivery truck a carefully selected sack of vegetables. Out of the gate the truck had to slow down to negotiate a crossroads and it was there that I jumped off with the sack and headed for home. Each dawn before leaving for work I would have an auction among our neighbours and take orders for the next day. It worked well for a while until one day I was hauled in to see the boss.

'You'll end up in prison like your father,' he shouted at me.

'My father is a political prisoner and I'm proud of it,' I replied.

'Yes and so you should, but the way you've started, you'll end up a common criminal and should be ashamed of it. You're fired!'

It was once again my advice-giving uncle who put my mind to rest.

'The state is the biggest thief. There is nothing wrong in stealing from it.'

With my rugby team, I am in the middle looking to my left

In a drive to get young people to start work as soon as possible, the communist regime had reduced the time at school from twelve to ten years, so the end of school, in summer 1956, had come early for me. I was only 16 and had no idea what I really wanted to do in life. I had started playing rugby for the local Brasov team while still at school, which suited me as I was tough, strong and recklessly fearless. It certainly used up some of my excessive energy, especially once my team advanced to Romania's first division, in which I became the youngest player. That same year I was selected for Romania's national under-18 team and played in Bucharest against France's under-18s. I also worked as a photographer, taking photos in parks, restaurants and a nearby mountain resort, earning good money.

After leaving school, on my parents' insistence I reluctantly agreed to study forestry at the local faculty in Brasov. Having grown up on an estate in the middle of a forest, this was my father's idea of heaven, and being a forestry manager was probably the fulfilment of his own dream. Once again, as so many times in my life, fate intervened and solved the forestry career dilemma. By the time I had reached the second year of studies I was expelled because of my social background. This was a period when universities were

being cleansed of 'bourgeois' elements among both students and professors. My situation was not helped by the fact that my father had been arrested again and was now in prison at Jilava, a notorious prison for political detainees near Bucharest, where he died one year later aged 59. My life as the son of a political prisoner was now severely restricted and I knew that the future held little promise for me.

The news of my father's death came out of the blue when one of my father's sisters had written to my mother to express her condolences. Under communist bureaucracy, the prison had sent the death certificate to my father's village of birth where his death was entered on the official register next to his birth and marriage entries. This is how his sisters, who still lived there, had found out and how, by this cruel roundabout way, the news had reached my mother. She asked me to accompany her to the prison near Bucharest to try and find out more and get him re-buried.

Jilava prison was a death machine for political prisoners from which few escaped with their lives. During 1959 there had been a temporary thaw and we somehow managed to be received by the prison governor. He listened to my mother quite sympathetically, but explained that the body could not be released, as according to the law, it had to remain in the prison cemetery until the expiry of my father's 15-year sentence. Hearing this, my mother collapsed, and I exploded:

'Having murdered this innocent man, the least you could do is let his family give him a decent burial!' I screamed at the governor.

Terrified that she might now lose her son as well, my mother begged me to stop, but I would have none of it and continued shouting at the governor. For reasons I never understood, the governor gave in, told us where the cemetery was located and gave us the necessary release papers, asking us insistently to keep all this to ourselves. That was the first breach in the communist regime that I had witnessed and showed that there were a few officials with a sliver of humanity.

In the corner of a rundown village cemetery, my father's grave was identified by a small wooden plaque: 1006/58. When the gravedigger reached his remains it fell to me to identify him, an image that I can never forget and that fills my heart with unbearable pain on the occasions when it flashes through my mind. We took his remains to Brasov where they now rest in a quiet cemetery that overlooks the city from a lofty hill, next to my sister, who died in 1973, and my mother who passed away in 1988.

It was not long after the death of my father that I came across by chance in our flat some Red Cross papers issued by the missing person's office in Geneva, which stated that the named persons had not been able to be tracked down. That evening, when I confronted my mother, she broke down and, sobbing uncontrollably, exploded the family myth and finally cleared up the painful lie that had haunted her all her life. As the only Jewish family living in a remote Hungarian village, my two grandparents, David and Regina Neuwirth, who were already in their seventies and were looking after my twin four-year-old cousins Peter and Ivan, had been rounded up by the Hungarian Police and sent to a German death camp. Taken separately, the twins' mother, my mother's sister, Agnes, had died in Auschwitz, while the only survivor, her husband, Joseph, had died of hunger or typhus on his long walk home after the liberation of his camp. Suddenly all the question marks and suspicions that had plagued me even as a child came into focus. Not only had I Romanian, Austrian, Serb and possibly Hungarian blood, but now a proportion of Jewish blood as well. Strangely enough, rather than being shocked I was quite pleased and proud of my heritage, I suppose a normal reaction in an air-brained teenager like I was then.

In the summer of 1997 I drove to Romania with Gwenda and Doina and visited my grandparents' small village in eastern Transylvania. Strolling down the muddy main street, we met an older looking man walking towards us. As this was an area entirely populated by Hungarian Szeklers, I addressed him in Hungarian.

'Good day, uncle, you look old enough to maybe remember David and Regina Neuwirth.'

'Of course I do, God bless them. I was their driver. And who are you?'

'I am their grandson, Anna's son. This is my wife and our daughter.'

'God, oh God, what a tragedy. The entire village witnessed it, and it was me whom the gendarmes asked to drive your grandparents and their poor grandchildren to the first camp at Sighisoara. Let's go and see Uncle Lajos. He is now in his nineties but lived across the street from them and he used to play cards with Mr David.'

He knocked loudly on a wooden gate and a sprightly old man came out and greeted us.

'Isten hozta! God brought you!'

'Uncle Lajos this is Dragos, Anna Neuwirth's son.'

He shook my hand warmly. 'So good to see you. Your mother has visited a few times but hasn't come for many years now.'

'No, she passed away in 1988.'

'Sorry to hear that. We all pass on. Even I expect to go soon. I am 96 and I am tired of this life.'

'Oh don't say that Uncle Lajos,' the other man exclaimed. 'You'll outlive us all.'

'The entire village witnessed their arrest. It was incomprehensible,' said the old man. 'The war was at its end, the Russians 100 km to the east and those filthy gendarmes had nothing better to do than round up these kind people who many of us didn't know, or even care, that they were Jews. As far as I know they were the only Jews in this whole area.'

'Yes, and I remember to this moment hitching up their beautiful horses, the bay on the left, the chestnut roan on the right,' the other man said.

'Oh no, you didn't,' interjected the old man. 'The bay was always hitched on the right, the roan on the left.'

'Well, sorry Uncle, but I should know. I was, after all, the driver.'

'You might have been, young man, but you are dead wrong, so stop arguing.'

In spite of being churned up inside, I burst out laughing. Here we were, 53 years later, and these two villagers were arguing heatedly about something that they seemed to remember as vividly as if it had happened the previous summer.

'Unfortunately Mr David's house was demolished soon after the war but let's walk over to speak to the man who bought the land from your mother and her sister,' said Uncle Lajos.

A man my age who was working in front of a barn came out and greeted us warmly.

When he was told who we were, he exclaimed. 'This is such a coincidence, I can hardly believe it. Last week I was rummaging in that barn and came across a few things that must have belonged to your grandparents. Among them I found two small snow sleds that can only have belonged to...'

'Poor Ivan and Peter,' the old man interjected.

'I'll go and fetch them.'

He came back with two small black sleds and I could not control myself any longer. Gwenda burst in tears too, and so did Doina and the three men. The utter cruelty of that day, the grotesque senselessness of the entire operation hit me as never before. This was the Holocaust as I had never really understood it: taking two innocent old people in their seventies and those four-year-olds to their death simply because, by a quirk of nature, they had been born with the wrong genes. Wishing to bring the painful scene to an end, the man handed me the two sleds.

'Take them, I have no use for them, but for you they must have a lot of meaning.'

They do and are mounted now on a wall at our house in Provence, a permanent and painful reminder of my family's tiny part in the bloody history of the 20th century.

The lure of freedom

In the summer of 1959, exactly ten years after the first of my many vacations by the Black Sea, I was back there again: this time with a precise mission. My best school friend, Günter Oberth, and I had come to see if we could find a way to escape to the west. Two of our early attempts to gain entrance into the commercial harbour of Constantza had failed at the first hurdle when we found that the boarding steps of every foreign ship were guarded by a soldier accompanied by a large guard dog. We agreed to have one last try. Having explored the vicinity of that busy port for several days, watching the movements and routines of arriving and departing ships, we had found out that those that had no immediate place in the harbour would spend some time anchored about three miles offshore. Early one evening we found a suitable hideaway amongst the large boulders of the breakwater that protected the old casino. We got undressed, hid our clothes and dove in. The most difficult part was right at the start as the bright lights from the promenade above lit up the water along a wide band. We managed to swim underwater until we hit darker water. Earlier we had located three ships at anchor and headed for the nearest one. The night was pleasant, the water warm and we were making good progress. About halfway to the ship we saw the lights of a small coaster crossing in front of us but didn't give it a second thought. Finally we reached the ship and saw on its stern in huge letters: Anita B, Oslo.

'Perfect choice,' I said to Günter and started screaming: 'Man overboard, man overboard!'

A small head appeared high above us, then more heads and finally a boarding ladder was lowered over the side. After we clambered up the swaying rope ladder we found the whole crew waiting for us. In my limited English I managed to explain what we had in mind, so they took us to the mess, gave us dry towels, and fed us like kings. The captain was called and I told him who we were, that my father was a political prisoner, and described our plan. I begged him to hide us somewhere safe, leave us in hiding while unloading and loading the ship in Constantza, then drop us off anywhere he wanted, ideally Istanbul as it was the closest non-communist port.

The captain left, and we were happily chatting with the sailors when the radio officer was called away. When he came back, his face was grim and he told us that the captain had ordered us to leave the ship immediately. A ship leaving the port had seen a man in the water and had alerted the authorities, which were now patrolling the area looking for him. The radio officer had received a call already, asking if they had seen anything suspicious. The game was up.

Reluctantly we had to say goodbye, climb down the swinging ladder and head for the shore. For a while we stayed together but I could tell from the way we were being taken sideways that there was a current setting us towards the harbour entrance and we had to fight hard to keep our course. Suddenly I lost sight of Günter and, as I was the better swimmer, I was very concerned that he might have been swept into the harbour.

The lights of the casino were shining like a beacon and eventually the current eased and I managed to make for them. As there was no sign of a patrol and I suspected that perhaps the Norwegians had lied just to get rid of us, I made for the corner nearest to our hideaway. As I was clambering over the slippery rocks I suddenly saw a soldier on the promenade above, and as I dove

back into the sea he loosened a spray of bullets from his automatic rifle. As I was sinking, I felt a sharp blow under my right knee but, stayed underwater and swam as far as I could parallel to the building, then climbed out quickly and made my way carefully up to the promenade. I looked around the corner but the wide promenade was clear, and I supposed that the patrol must have gone down to the water expecting to find me shot. I ran across the promenade into a small park and safely reached our hideaway. Only then did I dare look at the wound, which, by now, was bleeding profusely. Fortunately it did not appear to be too serious. I used

A mariner at last

my shirt to staunch the blood, then stood shivering, wondering what had happened to my friend. Much later, when it started to get light, I heard the slap-slap of bare feet. Shaking uncontrollably and totally exhausted, Günter told me how he had also managed to beat the current but had landed much further away. He had walked along the promenade all the way back unaware of the risk he was taking.

'What happened to you?' he asked, pointing at my bloody shirt.

I was just about to tell him, then thought otherwise. For some reason, I felt that I'd better keep that incident to myself and, although I trusted my friend, I didn't trust him enough to divulge the true source of my injury. This was one essential lesson that one learned living under a dictatorship: never to say more than absolutely necessary and always refrain from asking questions if you didn't want to know the answer.

'As I came out by the side of the casino, I slipped and hit something underwater. It felt like a piece of reinforcement sticking out of a concrete block. It looks worse than it is; it just needs to be disinfected.'

'OK, what now?' asked Günter.

'Three times unlucky is enough for me,' I replied. My gut feeling told me that it was time to stop, but he disagreed. While waiting for Günter, I kept thinking of my mother and how devastated she would be if I had been caught and sent to prison just like my father. Günter thought otherwise. He soon teamed up with another friend and headed for the Yugoslav border, trying to cross it by land. They were caught at the railway station when they arrived without the required permit and could not explain what they were doing there. They were sentenced to three years hard labour and were taken to the Danube Delta, where they spent all day in leech-infested water up to their chests cutting reeds for a paper factory. Ironically, around the same time I got a job at that same paper factory, working as an interpreter for the East German team who were building a large extension.

My very first outing as a budding sailor happened the following year, when a departing German gave me an inflatable kayak and paddle. At the end of the summer I headed straight for the Danube, got off the train at a large bridge spanning the mighty river and descended with my heavy load to the embankment below. The inflated two-man kayak nearly sank under the combined weight of tent, provisions and myself. I pushed off and paddled towards the middle of the river, where I was caught by the swift current. As I passed under the enormous bridge, I looked up in wonder as a train trundled over my head. The day was beautiful, sunny and warm, dragonflies were flitting over the brown waters and I was in heaven. Here I was, on my own little ship, heading into the unknown without a care in the world. The throbbing noise of an engine made me turn as a grey patrol boat came fast alongside. A uniformed officer shouted from the foredeck. 'What flag?'

'Sorry?'

'What is the national flag of your vessel?'

'Well, I don't understand.'

'Where the hell are you from?' He shouted impatiently.

'Oh, I am Romanian all right.'

'Not all right at all! This is an international waterway and every vessel must fly its national ensign.'

'But how can I get a Romanian flag here in the middle of nowhere?'

'Well, you should have thought about it before.'

The man at the wheel leant out of the window and beckoned for me to get closer. He came out, handed me a tatty tricolour and said, 'Hang it at the stern and bon voyage, but keep out of the way and stay closer to the sides.'

Proudly flying the red, yellow and blue from a tent pole, I was now legal, having been instantly promoted from ordinary seaman to a fully-fledged captain commanding his own vessel on an international waterway.

The Danube Delta

Drifting in Bucharest

The onward journey was sheer joy. Much of that area of the Danube was deserted, with few villages and, as I approached the delta, two large ports. The final days passing through the wilderness of the delta were like a dream. There were countless water birds, thick avenues of tall reeds and friendly fishermen who shared their tasty meals with me. The inhabitants of the delta are of Ukrainian origin and are called Lipoveni – burly, hefty men with penetrating blue eyes and large bushy beards. They spoke Romanian with a heavy accent that I could barely understand. They were dedicated watermen to their fingertips and handled their narrow pitch-covered craft with such ease, as if they were part of their own bodies. Around that time someone had had the brilliant idea to train some younger Lipoveni and send them to the Olympic Games, where they grabbed several gold medals in rowing.

Having reached Tulcea and the Black Sea, I packed my gear, took the train home… and was hooked for life. I knew that this was what I wanted to do more than anything else: to roam the world on my own boat. That dream had to wait a few years to come true, but true it came and how!

Not wanting to return to Brasov after the loss of my father, I moved to Bucharest, where I felt there were more opportunities for an ambitious young man like me. As my identity card was issued in Brasov, I was not able to work in Bucharest, and in fact was not supposed to be there at all. In those days people were not allowed to live anywhere except where they were registered.

Living illegally in Bucharest, I had to keep as low a profile as possible. I found a small attic room in the centre where no questions were asked, but without any source of income life was tough. I did the occasional portering job in the market, then one day I met a girl who introduced me to her friends, and life suddenly took a turn for the better. She was part of a group of kids belonging to the communist elite. All her friends' parents were high officials in the party, government, or heads of some large company. One day, at a party at a sumptuous villa in an exclusive quarter of Bucharest, attended by various boss kids, a guy my age made a dramatic entrance, looked around and asked: 'Where is that provincial yokel from the country who has been making waves here of late?'
'Here, you creep, and what do you want?'

'First of all I want to give you a good hiding for encroaching on my territory, and then bugger off to where you came from!'

'Suits me, let's go outside and sort it out now!'

As I advanced towards him meaning every word I had said, the local bully must have realised that finally he had met his match.

'OK, you seem to be as impatient as a virgin on her wedding night. But I like you, so let's have a drink first.' We eventually became friends and I never had any more trouble from him or anyone else in his gang.

As the party was breaking up a boy of about 14 sidled up to me and said:

'Jimmy, I like what you did, standing up for yourself. Would you like to be my friend?'

Tudor was the son of a high party official, and his mother a well-known actress. Being Jewish, and in spite of the status of his parents, he was constantly pestered by bullies at his school, antisemitism always having been a shameful trait among many of my countrymen. Every afternoon, I waited outside Tudor's school gates to accompany him home. Occasionally I had to put on the heavy act, but the message quickly spread and he was never taunted again. Although much younger than me, we got on well together, and I spent many afternoons at their luxurious home, being fed regally and being waited on by their servants. This was communism in great style. Every evening, just before his father came home and his mother left for the theatre, Tudor would hand me a 100 lei note, which he had liberated from his mother's handbag. This was a large amount in those days and allowed me to live well and even occasionally send some money to my own mother.

It was almost too good to be true, but gradually I got bored with this inactive hedonistic life, especially as some of my new friends started going to university and had less time to hang out with me. I decided to try and do the same and join the newly formed faculty of foreign trade that had just opened at the Institute of Economics. I was told that due to my background I would only succeed if I could pass the tough entrance examination with the highest marks, so I studied hard and managed to be among the top three of the 500 candidates competing for the 100 places.

Studying economics and languages interested me greatly and my life seemed to have settled down. Then in 1963, while on a trip to the western town of Oradea, I met some young people from England on a tour of Eastern Europe. Among them was Gwenda. After one winter of writing letters, she came back to Bucharest and we decided to get married... and that's when more problems began. As a Romanian citizen I was not allowed to marry a foreigner, so I had to make a special application to the State Council. While we were waiting to get married, a family friend had lent us her small flat, which looked straight out of the 1920s and made a cosy home for us. Meanwhile, Gwenda commuted by car between England and Romania, always arriving loaded with things that we could sell on the black market to survive. The years went by and our marriage application was still not approved.

As soon as I had put in the application to get married, I was expelled from the university, but I wasn't too bothered as I saw it as just a first step towards freedom. So as to continue being together, Gwenda managed to get a job with a British tour operator that was sending tourists to Romania. To be close to her I got a job as a barman in a small fishing village next to the Black Sea resort where she was working. Later, my languages helped me secure the much better job of chief of reception at the old Hotel Rex, a beautiful art deco building from the 1920s. It was there that one morning I received a cable from Gwenda's mother saying that our daughter Doina had been born, and that both Gwenda and the baby were well. It was the happiest day of my life.

While working at the Rex Hotel I met the head of foreign coproductions at the Romanian Film Studio. Romania had just started attracting large foreign productions, due mainly to the low costs and cheap rates paid to easily available extras. These were drawn primarily from the Army and were paid the equivalent of one US dollar per day. A new production was about to start and they needed someone with languages because both the main production team and all the main actors were either German- or English-speaking. Thus I managed to land the best job of all. The Last

Roman was an old style epic describing the dying days of the Roman Empire. The main actors were Laurence Harvey, who played Cethegus, a Roman senator, Orson Welles, who was the Byzantine Emperor Justinian, and Sylva Koscina who was Empress Theodora.

My own work on the film was as assistant production manager. I had to look after the foreign stars but also to find immediate solutions to the many problems that crop up in film making all the time. The job fitted me like a glove: I had always been good at improvisation, got on well with people and always managed to get them to do things for me. This problem-solving talent soon earned me the nickname Mr Fix It, which I was very proud of. Now I realise just how much those talents that I developed in my work in films helped me in my life at sea, where a capacity to improvise and find solutions is even more vital that on land.

Apart from production jobs, the stars asked me to do them various personal favours: from finding ancient Romanian icons or traditional embroidered blouses to sourcing caviar on the black market. The latter job took off when trouble erupted on the streets of Paris. This was May 1968 and all flights to Paris were cancelled, amongst them the cargo plane supplying the top Parisian restaurants and nightclubs with Romanian caviar. In those days Romania was a leading exporter of caviar from the Danube Delta. Suddenly Bucharest was flooded with caviar and I snapped it up by the kilo for the stars. Gwenda took an instant liking to caviar and learned to eat it with a large spoon.

During this time, Gwenda had made the acquaintance of the actress wife of a government minister, who was also high in the communist party hierarchy. She was charmed by Doina and promised Gwenda to talk to her husband to see if he could move our marriage application along. Gwenda had also lobbied her Member of Parliament in England, who promised to speak to the Foreign Secretary, who was due to make an official visit to Bucharest. We will never know which was the more important contact, but

In the role of a bishop in the First Crusade

The long awaited moment of our civil marriage in Bucharest

that autumn, after three years of waiting, our marriage application was approved. I sneaked a day off from the film studios, not telling anyone where I was going, and we hotfooted it to the City Hall. Once married, I applied to leave Romania and join my family in England, stipulating that I wanted to renounce my citizenship and leave the country as a stateless person. I made it to England just in time to be present at the birth of our son Ivan.

A new start in London

Ten-year intervals have marked my life like milestones; in 1949 my father's arrest and my first encounter with the sea, in 1959 my father's death and the failed escape attempts at the Black Sea, and my arrival in London in June 1969. That very evening I told Gwenda that I needed to tell her something important that I hadn't wanted to tell her in Romania. I could tell from her shocked expression that she obviously expected something bad, so I blurted out: 'I want to go to sea. I want to be a seaman. I want to see the world.'

Gwenda burst out laughing.

'What's so funny?'

'I thought you were going to tell me that you had only used me to get out, or that you have another woman, maybe even another family back in Romania.'

'Oh no, none of that. You are and will forever be the only one... It's only that I have this urge, this life-long passion to go to sea.'

'Yes, but how are you going to do it? First you need a job, you have a family to support, one young child and another due soon. Can't the sea wait?'

She was right of course, but I did have a mistress, and eventually, albeit reluctantly, Gwenda wisely accepted this 'ménage a trois', realizing that in spite of my undoubted love for her, the sea would always compete with her for my affection.

Having passed that first hurdle, my next priority was to change my name, as I realised that with a name like Dragoș Corneliu Cismașiu life in England would be difficult or, at the very least, a constant bore. Before Doina had been born, Gwenda had already changed her name to Cismașiu so the baby would have our name. As Mrs Cismașiu she hated always having to spell her surname and was tired of being asked by her English tourists, 'Where did you learn to speak such good English?'

One morning I went to a lawyer, signed a few papers, paid a modest ten shillings fee and instantly became James Cornell. Gwenda and I had already agreed on Cornell as an Anglicisation of my middle name and, we felt, a good surname that worked in several languages. Everyone in Bucharest already knew me as Jimmy so that was an easy choice. My nickname of Jimmy had been bestowed on me shortly after the

Gwenda with Doina and baby Ivan at home in London

53

war when an English pilot came to visit the King in Savarsin. He landed his plane at the airstrip nearby, where my father was waiting to receive him with me in tow. In typical British fashion he ignored my name Dragoș, and said he'd prefer to call me Jimmy as I reminded him of his son... and Jimmy I have remained to this day.

Our choice of name seems to have been so inspired that when she got married Doina decided to keep the name Cornell, and even registered her children, Nera and Dan, as Cornell as well. I suppose this is how dynasties are born.

My next real challenge was to find a job in London. I wrote and visited countless companies, most of them in the City, quite sure that with my background and languages I could find some job in exports. As a stopgap solution, I took a job as a night porter in a large hotel, the tips for one night being as much as I was paid by the hotel for a week of 12-hour night shifts. About one month after Ivan's birth I received in the same mail two offers: one from a large British paper manufacturer to

work as their sales representative in Western Europe, and one from the BBC World Service to be a radio announcer in the Romanian section. Having always believed that my field would be in business, and having studied economics, I instantly preferred the former, but Gwenda had other ideas. After so many years of hardship and separation, she wanted me to be closer to home. Head won over the wallet and I became a journalist, a choice I have never regretted.

With help from Gwenda's mother, supplemented by 2,000 dollars I had managed to smuggle out of Romania, we bought a small early-Victorian house in a London suburb, the absolute cheapest we could find and afford. We immediately set about making it habitable as it had no bathroom and even the toilet was out in the garden. My shift work at the BBC was very convenient, and I could spend every free moment fitting out and painting our cosy nest.

The sea, however, never went away, and was only put on the backburner temporarily. The BBC had both a sailing and a yacht club, so I immediately joined the former, learning to sail 14-foot Wayfarer dinghies on the Upper Thames. I soon graduated to the yacht club, which had an elderly 40-foot sloop called Ariel based on the Hamble, on England's south coast. I signed up for a sailing weekend, and Charlie McLaren, a friend from BBC television news, came to collect me in his bright yellow Lotus sports car. Out of London we joined the motorway towards the south coast, cruising happily in a light drizzle at around 100 miles per hour. While overtaking another car the Lotus suddenly took off, having probably hit an oily patch. The light car was airborne, with the crash barrier to one side and the other car close and slightly below me.

'Oh my God!' Charlie exclaimed, doing his best to keep the car under control. We somehow managed to land squarely, slow down and complete our journey without any further excitement. We found the rest of the crew already waiting, so the captain told us to quickly hop on, stow our gear and help get underway. As our

Our first home in London

docking lines were being taken off by the others, I did my best to look busy, as there seemed nothing for me to do. As the captain pushed the tiller to clear the dock I noticed a large hawser that was running across our cockpit from the stern of a big steamer docked ahead of us. I tried to point it out to the captain but he brushed me aside. With an almighty crack the hawser swept our flagstaff off the stern, the proud BBC yacht club ensign now floating out of reach on the murky surface.

'Get a boat hook... quick!' the captain ordered, and Charlie, as mate, managed to retrieve our flag.

The captain turned with a glowering look to me. 'That was quite stupid, wasn't it?'

I was about to reply that I had tried to warn him, but remembered just in time that the captain was always right.

'I am very sorry.'

'And so you should be.'

Although I had done a bit of dinghy sailing on the Thames, I knew that I was so green that I had better lie low and observe. So I offered to do the washing up and that instantly ensured my popularity.

We stopped for lunch at a pub in a small port and then the captain suggested we sail across to the Isle of Wight and spend the night at Yarmouth. We zigzagged around a bewildering forest of buoys of different colours, shapes and sizes, dodged fast ferries and other yachts, and eventually pointed the bows towards what looked like a fairly large harbour. Just as the captain was telling Charlie to get the crew to lower the sails, there was a crunch and Ariel came to an abrupt halt. Even I could tell that we had run aground. The captain revved the engine hard astern, then tried to go sideways but to no avail. We were well and truly stuck.

The boat heeling over at a slight angle and rocking in the swell, Charlie organised us crew to lower the sails, but before we could do so, the wildly swinging boom hit one of the crew hard on the head, the violent blow splitting his scalp open. With blood gushing all over the place, we took him below and put a towel around his head. Although bleeding profusely he didn't seem in much danger so, in proper English fashion, Charlie offered to make him a cup of tea. As he was pouring the water into a mug the boat gave a sudden lurch and all the boiling water ended up in his sea boots. Screaming like mad, Charlie ripped them off, and when he pulled off his woollen socks both legs

Editing my weekly programme in a BBC studio

were already covered in blisters. With the situation now bordering on the desperate, and no prospect of coming off on our own, the captain hailed a passing motoryacht, shouted across what had happened and asked them to pull us off, which they did. He then contacted the Coast Guard by VHF who told him to head immediately across the Solent to Portsmouth, where the hospital had an accident and emergency department. We motored as fast as we could across the busy waterway, while trying to make our patients as comfortable as possible. An ambulance with its blue lights flashing was waiting at the nearest dock, and the two casualties were taken off and driven to hospital.

With Charlie out of action, I bade goodbye to the captain and remaining crew and took the train back to London.

'How was your weekend?' asked Gwenda.

'Very interesting. I think I've learnt a lot. Not much about sailing, but a lot about what NOT to do on a boat.'

Building Aventura

My urge to see the world never left me, but I realised that trying to become a seaman at my age was not practical, whereas leaving on a sailing boat might be a more feasible solution. I discussed this with Gwenda over many evenings after the children had gone to bed, and slowly a plan began to coalesce. While setting off on a small boat with two young children was not Gwenda's preferred way of seeing the world, she agreed that, from the purely practical and financial point of view, it made sense. Once that decision was taken, we both started making serious preparations. The children's education was our main concern, so Gwenda, a trained pharmacologist, decided to go back to college, and over two years of evening courses, she qualified as a teacher. During the long winter months I joined an evening course in seamanship and navigation, and also sailed a few more times on Ariel. In 1974, with a loan secured on our house, we managed to raise enough

funds to order a 36-foot GRP hull. All we could afford was the bare hull, but I was convinced that I could somehow manage to fit the boat out myself.

One day in spring 1974, a gleaming white hull was wheeled into a large shed in the Royal Albert Docks on the Thames. It was only then that I was struck by the enormity of my undertaking. I didn't even know where to begin, but begin I did. In the huge shed there were many other dreamers, most of them building ferrocement boats. We were always helping each other and it was a pleasant, friendly atmosphere. With a little help from my friends, Charlie McLaren, Dominic Coll, a carpenter I had met on my navigation course, and a Swedish rigger living on his boat in the docks, Aventura started taking shape.

It was my great fortune to make friends with Harold Valman, a typical Cockney from East London: wise, funny and extremely kind. He was the greatest expert on diesel engines that I have ever met. He had owned a variety of launches and small vessels, mostly ex-Navy auxiliary craft, which he bought for a song at auctions, cleaned up, fitted out and sold for a tidy profit. My greenness in all matters mechanical moved Harold to tears and he became a permanent presence by my side. He took charge of the engine installation, decided on fitting a hydraulic steering, as this was the cheapest and easiest option, and lent me tools from his vast collection, which he kept on a beautiful Admiral's launch outside the shed.

It was chance friendships like this that helped me finish Aventura in such record time and it only reinforced my firm belief, I could almost say my life philosophy, that it is always easier to achieve something if you have good friends around you. I value my friends more than anything else and keep in regular touch regardless of time or distance. For our joint 60th birthday in 2000, Gwenda and I invited all our closest friends for a long weekend of celebrations at a hotel in the mountains near Brasov. All they had to do was get there. And they all came, some 72 of them, from

Australia, the USA, from all over Europe and from Romania itself. It was one of the happiest occasions of my life being surrounded by my oldest and best friends.

Quite miraculously, by July 1974, although the interior was only partially finished, Aventura was launched, and we set sail on our maiden voyage across the English Channel to France. Motoring down the Thames at the helm of my own boat was exhilarating. My crew, however, were not so enchanted. I looked into the aft cabin as we left the Thames and saw not only the protruding bolts from the unlined ceiling and lockers without doors, but also four children, Doina, Ivan, Marianne and Klausi, rolling about like bags of potatoes in the rough swell. My sister had died the previous year in Romania and her husband Klaus and two teenage children had emigrated to Germany. Marianne and Klausi had joined us in London for a vacation, and I decided to take them back to the continent on Aventura's maiden voyage.

As we hit the English Channel, the weather deteriorated and soon a southwest gale was upon us. We ran for shelter into Ramsgate harbour, which was already crowded with all types of craft seeking shelter. A fisherman beckoned me to come alongside his trawler, lying four deep alongside the high quay.

While I was still tying the lines, a uniformed port official popped up above me: 'That will be £2.50. Thank you!' Welcome to my first English landfall!

The following morning the weather was calmer so we crossed over to Boulogne, being amazed and frightened in equal measure by the stream of car ferries plying between Dover and France, and the even denser pack of ships of all shapes and sizes moving equally fast at right angles, literally squeezing through the narrowest part of the English Channel. I was totally mesmerised by the hubbub and it took all my non-existent skills to find a suitable hole and quickly cross behind the nearest threatening monster. I had little idea that we were in the busiest shipping lanes in the world, so I thought that the sea was always going to be like this and it worried me.

When we arrived at Boulogne we found the small boat harbour and made our way in. Gwenda was at the helm and I was preparing fenders and ropes. We spotted my brother-in-law Klaus waving frantically from the end of a pontoon so Gwenda headed that way. She saw an empty slip and pointed for its middle, still seeming to advance at the same speed. I realised what was going to happen and shouted at her to slow down, but she didn't and so hit the pontoon with a might blow, while Klaus valiantly tried to stop the boat. Aventura's bows had ridden right up onto the pontoon where she stopped, then gracefully slid back in. The crash must have been heard in the entire marina, but apart from Klaus no one had witnessed our dramatic arrival.

'Why did you do that?' I asked Gwenda. 'Why didn't you slow down?'

'I tried.'

'Tried how?'

'I put the gear in neutral...'

'And?'

'It didn't slow down much.'

'Why didn't you go astern?'

'Why?'

I then explained exactly how to stop the boat.

'You never told me that before.'

As I had already learned from my days as a BBC yacht club crew, the responsibility rests squarely with the captain, so there was no point in arguing. We handed over Klausi and Marianne to their father and continued our summer cruise to the Channel Islands. On our return to London, the mast was taken down and Aventura moved back into her place in the huge shed. That maiden voyage had shown up all the mistakes I had made in her construction but, as she was mostly unfinished, I could easily put things right. There followed a most gruelling work schedule as I was determined to get Aventura ready to sail by the following May. I would get up at five every morning, drive to the boat and work until ten, then drive to the BBC for the afternoon shift, which finished around seven. Then it was back to the boat for more work and I'd finally get home around midnight. By the following spring we were ready.

I resigned from the BBC, but had secured a freelance contract to continue my weekly programme Aventura (adventure in Romanian), a music and adventure programme for young listeners, which attracted a large audience in Romania, once estimated by a British newspaper as being in the millions. That this estimate may not have been exaggerated was proven shortly before Christmas 1974, when a large sack of mail arrived from Romania all addressed to me. In the past we had received only the odd letter posted by someone who had gone abroad. The arrival in one single day of over 1,500 listeners' letters from Romania got everyone at the BBC excited. It was quite clear that the sack had either slipped past the censors by mistake, or, as I prefer to believe, a friendly guy at the Romanian post office, probably one of my listeners, had put the bag into the wrong, or rather, right pile. As I had launched and presented the most successful weekly programme of the Romanian Service, my boss wanted me to continue it by sending reports throughout our forthcoming voyage. I had also been asked by a couple of English language programmes to look out for interesting material from the countries we were going to visit.

Camping in our hippy days

When I handed in my resignation to the head of the personnel department she warned me not to withdraw my pension contributions. 'Better leave them here, as you will only get whatever you had paid in yourself and that amounts to only about £500. But if you leave the money here the BBC's own contributions will more than double your fund.'

'I understand, but I badly need that money as otherwise I can't pay for my sails.'

Withdrawing that money was probably the worst financial decision of my life as in those days the BBC pension fund was extremely generous. Had I kept that fund untouched, as I did with the one I started on my return, I would probably have received now almost the same amount as a monthly payment. And yet I do not regret for one moment that decision. How could Aventura leave on such a voyage without sails?

With all the hard work done, Aventura was finished and the world was waiting. The dreaded Bay of Biscay received us with a benign smile, and although there was a large swell, the winds were favourable and we arrived safely in Lisbon after a few days. Soon we headed for the Mediterranean, where we planned to spend one year getting acquainted with the boat and life aboard before continuing on an open-ended world voyage. My dream had come true.

5.

The voyage of Aventura

In the early 1970s, when I started looking for a suitable boat for our planned voyage, I knew next to nothing about boats, offshore sailing and what such a voyage would actually entail. So I read voraciously every book I could lay my hands on, from Joshua Slocum to Eric Hiscock, Francis Chichester to Bernard Moitessier, and countless others. Those famous sailing pioneers' well-written tales were not only fascinating but also full of excellent advice. As I ploughed through those books, I made notes and listed essential features to look out for. Later I rearranged the list in order of priorities. I also compiled a separate list of things to avoid.

In those days the choice of a suitable boat for a long voyage was quite limited. On top of that I had my own serious limitation: I did not have enough money for a completed boat, not even for a used one. So very soon I realised that the only solution was to buy the best hull I could afford and do the fitting out myself. By that stage I had not even been able to decide between a monohull and a catamaran. I was attracted by the spaciousness of a catamaran and I approached a couple of British manufacturers building fibreglass

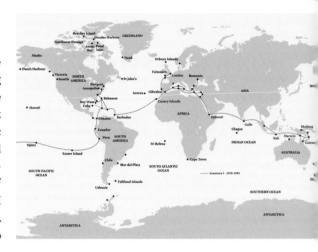

The voyage of Aventura 1975–1981

catamarans, but both refused to sell me a bare hull. I also considered a Wharram catamaran, whose plans were available as a home-build kit, but I didn't have the confidence to build a complete boat.

With catamarans out, the choice became somewhat easier and eventually I decided on a Van de Stadt design, the 36-foot Trintella IIIA. The builders, Tylers, were based close to London, and when I visited the yard I was impressed by the high standard of their work and also the friendly and helpful attitude of their staff. Tylers built only hulls, leaving the fitting out to outside contractors, so I immediately placed an order.

Over the years Aventura proved to have been the best choice I could have made at that time. She was rigged as a ketch, a decision heavily influenced by the desire for manageable sails in the absence, in those days, of furling gears. She was easy to sail, especially for a beginner, and in spite of her modest size, she had an aft cabin, which made it comfortable for a family of four. Her main quality was that her hull was very strongly built. I found this out when we ran aground on a reef in the Turks and Caicos Islands and spent several hours pounding hard on a coral head. When we eventually came off and I had a look with a mask at the keel and hull I was amazed that there was no serious damage except for a few superficial scratches. Amazed maybe, but not surprised, because while fitting

out I had to cut a hole through the hull for one of the seacocks and found that the thickness in that area was 40 mm, the layers of fibreglass clearly marked in different colours. In those days some builders did not know how to build flimsy hulls. That came later.

Robert Louis Stevenson, who was an inveterate traveller and whose sailing adventures took him right across the Pacific Ocean, wrote: 'I travel not to go anywhere, but to go; I travel for travel's sake.' If 'travel' is replaced by 'sailing' it should become immediately clear why the title of the predecessor of this book was A Passion for the Sea. Besides the sheer joy of sailing, my voyages were also rich in new experiences, most of them well off the beaten track. Few of the many detours were due to chance, but mainly to my insatiable journalistic curiosity, which led us into some lengthy and ambitious detours. This willingness to put up with some inconvenience was the price both Gwenda and I were ready to accept as the unavoidable sacrifice that committed travellers have to pay.

In spring 1975, with all essential jobs on Aventura finished, we left England with the intention of spending one year in the Mediterranean before deciding whether we should continue across the Atlantic and beyond. From Gibraltar we headed east and spent most of the summer in the Aegean. We were planning to cross the Atlantic during the following winter, but a major fault with the engine forced us to stop for repairs in Corsica. We resumed our voyage with an overhauled engine in the spring of 1976 and headed once again east, continuing into the Black Sea as by that stage I had received my British passport and could return for the first time to visit my family and friends in Romania. Later that summer we sailed all the way to Gibraltar as we had by then decided that we were ready and keen to see more of the world. My freelance work was proceeding well, we were managing with the children's education and we were very happy living on board Aventura.

Caribbean to USA

After stops in Madeira and several of the Canary Islands, on 15 November we set sail from the island of La Palma bound for Barbados. We made a very slow but highly enjoyable passage of 28 days, as I had failed to have Aventura antifouled before leaving the Canaries, which meant that we hardly ever sailed faster than five knots.

The Caribbean more than lived up to our expectations, especially as I managed to do quite a lot of work for the BBC, which meant we met many interesting local people. Soon after our landfall in Barbados, I started looking for a suitable subject to use in my reports for the BBC. At the local radio station I happened to arrive just as the studio was recording an interesting-sounding song, which I was told was of African origin and had been preserved from the early days of slavery. I got my portable tape recorder and taped the song then asked the leading singer to explain, on tape, the story behind it. He got into quite a stride and was soon digressing into the heartrending story of his ancestors, how they had been cruelly snatched away from their roots and transported in the most inhumane conditions across the Atlantic.

Carlisle Bay in Barbados

Back on board, I made a rough edit with the help of my second tape recorder and sent the tape to a friend with whom I had been on a BBC training course and who was now editing a programme called Good Morning Africa. When my report was broadcast to the African audience it was an instant success as they knew about the history of African slaves in the USA but knew little about those in the Caribbean. That was the beginning of one of my biggest journalistic successes, my regular reports becoming part of a long-running series called The African Connection.

The African Connection turned out to be a never-before-explored treasure trove of original material: folk tales and legends, bush medicine, tribal dances, working songs, lullabies, wedding songs and much else besides. My reports recorded in various Caribbean islands became a great hit with the audience of the daily Good Morning Africa programme as very few of the listeners knew that Caribbean islands had been settled by African slaves. The series continued to Panama, Peru and all the way to Fiji, where my African Connection finally fizzled out. By then I was even more involved in a different kind of BBC programme called Hello Tomorrow, which dealt with practical subjects in developing countries. The programme was produced in London and was then sent by the BBC to various national radio stations around the world, from Sri Lanka to Zimbabwe, Samoa to Jamaica. Often an interview that I had recorded at some previous stop preceded me and had already been broadcast in the country where we had just arrived. It happened in Fiji, where people had already heard my reports and recognised my name and voice. This made my life much easier and I had no problem finding new material everywhere: visiting an experimental farming station in the jungle of Panama; the Potato Institute high in the Peruvian Andes; a pig farm in Tonga producing methane gas from manure, which was then used by the villagers as cooking fuel; a fish farm in Fiji and later a tea plantation in the highlands of Sri Lanka.

By this time we were sailing in company with a French yacht Calao owned by a couple of a similar age to us and who had children slightly younger than Ivan and Doina. We had met Erick and Muriel, Sidonie and Fabien just before leaving La Palma and agreed to meet again in the Caribbean. While sailing from Puerto Rico to the Bahamas in their company we stopped at Grand Turk and decided to explore the nearby Ambergris Cays on the edge of the Caicos Bank. As we moved from the deep channel into the shallow waters of the bank, I could see a clear-unobstructed way ahead, leading to an area of darker blue water where

Calao was already anchored. Suddenly a passing cloud obscured the sun and the transparent water all around us turned to quicksilver. I slowed down and continued on what I believed was the same course, but came to a crunching halt on top of a massive coral head. Even with the engine on full power ahead, and then astern, we didn't budge. We were stuck. I donned my mask, leapt overboard and saw that Aventura's long keel was jammed in a deep coral cleft. What I still remember, however, was that instead of being concerned by our predicament, I was absolutely fascinated by the beauty of the underwater scenery. I had dived before in many attractive places, but the scenery that confronted me was beautiful beyond imagination. Fishes of all colours, shapes and sizes darted among large swaying coral fans, spiny lobsters were sweeping their antennae from their hidey-holes, while a large Napoleon wrasse with thick lips glanced with a bored look at this intruder into its territory. I had to firmly grip the edge of the coral head to avoid being swept away by the strong current that I realised had swiftly pushed Aventura off course when I could no longer see the way ahead.

Back on board, I got a spare anchor, tied it to a halyard and swam it some distance away in the hope of heeling Aventura over, and thus reduce its draft to get out of its trap. But it was to no avail. The keel was firmly gripped in the coral vice.

Erick sculled over in his Optimist but all he could do was lend moral support in what I now considered to be a desperate situation... unless your name was Lucky Jim and you managed to run aground on a rising tide! So the saintly Moon came to our help by lifting the water level by enough inches for Aventura to float free. We dropped the anchor close to Calao and I dived to inspect the damage. We were very fortunate to have such a strong hull and got away with only a few scratches. Now anchored on clear sand, there were no fishes about... but I knew where to get some tasty lobsters for a celebratory dinner with our good French friends.

With Erick, Muriel, Sidonie and Fabien on a visit to Washington

A chance encounter in Gibraltar with an older American couple, who invited us to visit them at their home in the USA, led us to change our plans and not continue to the Pacific immediately, but make a long detour to the US east coast. After stops in the Turks and Caicos Islands and the Bahamas, we arrived in Florida where I discovered to my dismay that our friends lived in the state of Maine, which is as far north on the US east coast as one could possibly go. But go we did. Erick and Muriel on Calao were just as adventuresome and curious as us, so they decided not to miss such an opportunity and joined us on our voyage along the US east coast.

Sailing in the Intracoastal Waterway virtually along its entire length from south to north was a wonderful experience, especially the stops along the way in Washington, New York, Mystic Seaport Museum, Newport, Boston and countless other interesting places. In those early days of cruising, the sight of a British and a French boat with children on board was something rare and we were received everywhere with great interest and open arms. Our hosts, Wolly and Louise Weiss, were surprised and pleased in equal measure seeing us drop our anchors virtually on their doorstep in Casco Bay.

By late August we turned around and retraced our steps through New York and the Intracoastal Waterway all the way to Beaufort, North Carolina, from where we sailed to the Bahamas and south to Panama.

South America

According to our original plan, after transiting the Panama Canal we intended to sail the traditional route to the Marquesas, possibly stopping in the Galapagos Islands to shorten the long passage. As by now we had become addicted to detours, rather than sail to the Marquesas, from Panama we decided to turn left for Ecuador and Peru.

After a slow passage along the South America coast, one day before Christmas we made landfall in Callao, the port of the Peruvian capital Lima. The detour was inspired by Doina and Ivan's wish to visit the country of birth of Paddington, a Peruvian bear from the High Andes. For those who may not be familiar with him, I must explain that this delightful little bear, one of the most popular fictional characters for

Neptune's baptism on our first equator crossing

English children, was found wandering on Paddington railway station in London and was adopted by a kind English family. Paddington's adventures left such an impression on Doina and Ivan that they managed to persuade us to divert from our planned itinerary.

At the Callao Yacht Club we met Alan Sitt, a young American, whose father had a small factory in Peru. Alan agreed to look after Aventura while we toured the interior of the country. After Christmas we took a bus into the High Andes, a bone-rattling two-day ordeal on a rickety bus that took us to Cuzco, the ancient capital of the Inca empire. From there we took a train to Machu

At Cuzco in the High Andes

Picchu in the hope of meeting some of Paddington's relatives. While visiting the ancient remains at Machu Picchu, Ivan was wearing a Paddington bear T-shirt. We met an elderly gentleman, who, noticing Ivan's shirt, asked him, 'Are you looking for Paddington? Just carry on along this path as I think I caught a glimpse of him.'

Having got so far inland into Darkest Peru, we decided that we might as well make the best of it and see more of South America. From Lake Titicaca we crossed the border on foot to Bolivia, and continued by train to Rio de Janeiro, where my BBC credentials allowed us to attend the world-famous carnival. One more detour took us to the Iguazu Falls in Argentina, and finally to Asuncion in Paraguay, before we flew back to Callao to resume our voyage.

South Pacific

There are few places in the world that can inspire the awe one feels from the moment you land on this enigmatic island with its scores of mysterious giant statues. I cannot think of any other detour, before or after, that had been more justified or satisfying.

A chance encounter on Easter Island led to an even longer detour and extended our South Pacific sojourn by at least one year. While walking ashore in Hanga Roa, the main settlement of the island, we were stopped by an Englishman who asked whether we had come from the boat anchored offshore. Hearing that I was a journalist and working for the BBC, he asked whether we were planning to sail to the Ellice Islands for the forthcoming independence celebrations in October. I told him that we had absolutely no intention of going that far out of our way, as our plan was to continue west to Australia. He then painted a very attractive and tempting picture of the planned festivities, but even so we would not commit ourselves.

'Well, if you change your mind and come, let me know and I'll do my best to welcome you.'

'And how are we going to find you?' I replied.

'It's a very small place. Just ask for me. I am Tom Layng, the British Commissioner of the Ellice Islands, or Tuvalu as they will soon be called.'

It was a very tempting offer, especially as it could provide some interesting material for the BBC programme Hello Tomorrow.

From Easter Island we sailed west to Pitcairn Island and on to Mangareva. At long last we had reached the first of the widespread islands of French Polynesia, scattered over an area larger than that of Europe. Unfortunately on our arrival at Mangareva in the Gambier Islands, I was told at the gendarmerie that

Bounty's original anchor

we could not stay as the islands were off limits because of the ongoing nuclear tests being carried out at nearby Mururoa Atoll.

'We are a family with two young children,' I pleaded. 'We have sailed all the way from Peru to get here. I cannot believe that we are asked to leave,' I told the burly Polynesian sergeant. 'Surely you could make an exception.'

'Yes, but only in exceptional circumstances... and if I understood well, your wife is not well. Is that correct?' I got the hint.

'Yes, and I'd be really grateful if we could have a rest here and a chance for her to get better as we haven't been in a secure anchorage for three months.'

'OK, I will telex Papeete straightaway and ask permission. In the meantime please be our guests and enjoy your stay here.'

Iotua was true to his word, he did obtain the needed permission, and we spent an unforgettable month in Mangareva. Doina and Ivan enrolled in the local school; I took Iotua, his French colleague, Manou, and Doina's teacher, Lucas Paeamara, fishing on Aventura off the reef, while Gwenda was entertained by their wives.

After a restful month spent among those wonderful people, we asked Iotua to obtain the permission to sail to Tahiti. When it came, I was shocked to see that it proscribed a northabout route that had to clear by 50 miles the prohibited area around the nuclear testing sites at Mururoa and Fangataufa. Sailing that route would have put us on a direct course for several hazards in the southern Tuamotus, so aptly called

by Captain James Cook the Dangerous Archipelago. No other passage in my entire sailing life was more nerve-racking than having to sail over 1,000 miles to Tahiti through a poorly charted area, swept by strong currents, and relying entirely on astronavigation.

From Tahiti we continued west stopping at each of the Society Islands. After the bustle of Tahiti's capital Papeete, they all felt like sleepy places, except Bora Bora where something unusual seemed to be afoot. A film crew led by the Italian producer Dino de Laurentiis was on the island filming a new version of Hurricane with a cast of stars led by Mia Farrow, Leslie Howard, Jason Robards, Max von Sydow and Timothy Bottoms. Set in Samoa shortly before the Second World War, there is one scene in which a group of American sailors on shore leave are seen dancing with a group of pretty Polynesian girls. Finding pretty Polynesian girls as extras had been easy on Bora Bora, but young men looking like American sailors was much more difficult. One day a production assistant asked me bluntly, 'How would you like to earn 50 dollars a day as an extra?' In those days we were living on 50 dollars a week! As we were cruising on a very tight budget made up entirely from my taped radio reports sent to the BBC World Service, such an unexpected offer was almost too good to be true, even if it meant having to shave off my bushy beard and curtailing my long hair to the regulation crew cut. This is how for a week I was one of a number of US Navy sailors recruited from among the yachts, spending our days being filmed dancing with some beautiful Polynesian girls.

The film was shot on a small islet inside Bora Bora's lagoon, with the imposing profile of Mount Otamanu making up the picturesque background. We were fed regally, treated almost like film stars and were actually paid for all this. Never before or since has the term 'work' meant the same thing to me!

My film career over, but several hundred dollars richer, we continued on our leisurely amble through the South Pacific. From Bora Bora we sailed west, with

Mangareva farewell

'Yes sir.'

We took our turns to stand in the shower cubicle while Semisi was busy pumping on the outside. I somehow felt that I was back in Ancient Egypt.

The 9,000-strong population had pulled out all the stops to celebrate their impending statehood, and various celebrities, foremost among them Princess Margaret, Queen Elizabeth's sister, started flying in. There were plenty of naval ships too, from a US destroyer to ships from New Zealand, Australia, France and Fiji. One ensign that was glaringly and surprisingly missing was the one of the departing colonial power. One of the celebrations took place at the Philatelic Bureau, as Tuvalu stamps were a prime collection item for enthusiasts. I was reporting on the event for a British newspaper and when, after all the dignitaries as well as the ship captains had received their special souvenir collection, I piped up from the back: 'How about an album for the captain of the only British ship to attend these celebrations?'

There was a moment of embarrassed silence followed by loud laughter. I was called forward and was duly presented with an album containing a collection of Tuvalu stamps. The biggest laugh however came the following day when the correspondent of the prestigious The Age newspaper of Melbourne told me that my story headed the front page.

'Ex-Romanian yachtie represents British Navy at Tuvalu independence celebrations.'

many intermediate stops in the Cooks and Tonga until we reached Fiji. By now we had decided that a 1,000-mile detour to the Ellice Islands was a relatively short hop by Pacific standards, so we left Suva and headed north.

The first impression as we arrived in Funafuti, the capital of Tuvalu, was utter amazement at how small a place it was. Fangataufa, the island it was built on, was maybe one kilometre long and about 200 metres wide. A landing strip had been carved somehow out of the available terrain but it was normally used as a village green. On the rare occasions when an aeroplane was expected to land, the one and only policeman had to cycle all over the strip to chase children, dogs and chickens away.

Finding Tom Layng was indeed easy. He welcomed us warmly at his residence and asked us if we wanted to take a shower. Oh yes, we all exclaimed enthusiastically, so Tom turned to his secretary and told her, 'Get a prisoner, will you?'

I thought I misunderstood, but a while later there was a knock on the door and a man in what looked like prison garb stood there expectantly.

'Semisi, you go pump water for these people who want take shower. OK?'

Doina and Ivan with Tuvalu's Prime Minister and Governor General awaiting the arrival of Princess Margaret

It was just the kind of story Aussies relish – any chance of putting down the mother country. I was later sent that front page, which now occupies place of pride in my collection of souvenirs, as does that special stamp album.

Later that day, I was stopped by a young man asking me whether having made the effort to attend Tuvalu's independence celebrations, would I do the same for the independence of the Gilbert Islands, planned for the following year?

'I haven't thought of it,' I replied.

'I assure you that as a journalist you should. We are planning something much more spectacular than you have seen here.'

'And who are you?' I asked.

'I am Ieremia Tabai, now chief minister, and future president of Kiribati as our independent country will be called.'

'Sounds tempting, I'll think about it.'

'You'll be warmly welcomed. I assure you of that,' he said, shaking my hand with a firm grip.

By now we were so seduced by the South Pacific and its people that we decided to spend as long as possible there instead of rushing west to complete the second half of our circumnavigation. The education of Doina and Ivan was proceeding well, my freelance work was going from strength to strength, and we had no pressing reason to bring such a wonderful life

to a premature end. After a highly enjoyable time at the festivities in Tuvalu, we sailed south to Fiji and continued to New Zealand, where we made our base in a small marina in the centre of Whangarei. Doina and Ivan enrolled in the local school, and we embarked on an overdue maintenance blitz.

While on a visit to Auckland, I went to the Maori and Pacific Island Section of Radio Aotearoa. I was received by its Maori director, Haare Williams, a former international rugby player, who sounded more interested in my rugby past than my journalism. At the end of a friendly conversation, he asked me to be their roving correspondent and to send him recorded interviews with any island people who would be of interest to his audience. Once again, just as in the Caribbean, I gave free rein to my imagination and sent back taped reports, interviews and music recordings from every island. We had wonderful encounters at every stop, with the most memorable occurring on the island of Uvea (Wallis), where Georges Pilioko, a local art historian, helped me record the most beautiful traditional music, performed alternately by the royal choir of old men and a group of young men. We spent the entire night sitting on the ground, with the flickering coconut-oil torches projecting phantasmagorical shadows on the hanging mats, listening mesmerised to the soft, mellifluous voices.

The port of Whangarei

From Wallis we turned due north, crossed the equator and, shortly before the appointed day for the independence celebrations, made landfall at the capital Tarawa. No one was more surprised to see us show up than Ieremia Tabai, soon to become the president of independent Kiribati. Every single island of this widely scattered nation had sent a delegation of dancers and singers to the capital, but for us, the highlight of the festivities were the hotly disputed races of the over-canvassed double-hulled canoes.

Back in Fiji, we rejoined the main Pacific trunk route, and, after several stops in Vanuatu and the Solomon Islands, arrived in Papua New Guinea, where we had decided to spend the impending cyclone season. Among all the countries that we visited during Aventura's circumnavigation, no other country stood out more for the variety and originality of its folklore,

music and dress than Papua New Guinea. Over the coming months, as we explored some of the most remote areas of New Guinea, we came to understand the reason for that, as we came across several isolated communities that had moved in one generation from stone age to the modern world.

Our first contact with this incredible country and its fascinating people was the Amphlett Islands. We had been told that traditional beliefs and lifestyles had been remarkably resilient in those islands, so we decided

to sail there first. We had hardly dropped the anchor off a small village, when Aventura was surrounded by an armada of small canoes, most occupied by a single child. Their curiosity in us was matched by ours in them. They seemed fascinated by Ivan and Doina, and it was only later that we found out that not only was Aventura the first yacht to be seen there, but that the islanders had seen only a few male Australians never a European woman or children.

We landed later in the village and walked among the simple dwellings, but people seemed extremely shy and we felt like intruders, so we left. In the shadow of a huge tree we were fascinated to see a woman fashioning a large clay pot without the use of a potter's wheel.

From Papua New Guinea we sailed to Australia and made our temporary base at Cairns in Queensland. We left Aventura in the care of a boatyard, hired a car and set off on a long road trip that took in all of Australia's east coast and some of the south coast as far as Melbourne. While there I visited the headquarters of Radio Australia, met the director of the overseas service, and landed a major job to report on the 1980

South Pacific Festival of Arts. The fourth edition of this pan-Pacific event was to be hosted that year in Port Moresby, the capital of Papua New Guinea.

A large fleet of sailing canoes was going to gather off the southeast coast of Papua New Guinea, and sail in company to Port Moresby to signal the start of the festival. We set off from Australia to join them and, as we made our way along the Papuan coast, the fleet of traditional canoes got larger and larger as more and more boats arrived from the outlying islands. Aventura was the only non-traditional sailing craft to accompany the ever-growing fleet, which by the time it reached Port Moresby had become an armada of over 200 canoes of all types, shapes and sizes.

The festival brought together hundreds of artists, singers, dancers and craftsmen from all over Polynesia, Melanesia and Micronesia for a fortnight of music, dance and stupendous displays of traditional dress. Passing through the Torres Strait shortly after the end of the festival was a painfully sad moment. Like countless sailors before us, we had fallen irredeemably in love with the Pacific and its people, and didn't want to leave. By way of compensation, we decided to ease the pain by spending longer in Indonesia, in those days a country as yet undiscovered by cruising boats.

Indian Ocean

Over a period of two months, we sailed along the entire chain of islands, from the Tanimbars in the east all the

Opening ceremony of the South Pacific Festival of Arts

Ferried ashore at our first Indonesian landfall

way to the Riau Islands in the northwest. Discovering the astonishing beauty of this vast unexplored area was a wonderful experience, especially as it was mostly unexpected.

The sixth year of our voyage dawned at Lumut, in Western Malaysia. Doina was by now 13 and starting to display a typical teenager's behaviour. Also the demands of satisfying her enquiring mind were getting more difficult and she was keen to go to school. We realised that we may be heading for a crisis point, so decided to pre-empt it by having a serious discussion with Doina. We admitted that the situation had reached a stage where we could see that she was no longer happy so suggested she return to England and live with Gwenda's mother while we would make haste to bring the voyage to an end and rejoin her.

'No, that would be unfair! 'Doina exclaimed. 'I started this voyage like you, and I want to complete it just like you. If you promise to do your best to get back to England as quickly as possible, I promise to put up with it and stay.'

It was a very reasonable suggestion that we all liked and accepted.

Romania

We crossed the Indian Ocean to Aden, transited the Suez Canal and completed our circumnavigation on reaching the Mediterranean. We continued via Greece and Turkey to the Black Sea, and made landfall at the port of Constantza in May 1981, exactly five years since our previous visit. In spite of the restrictions imposed by the Ceausescu regime, many friends came to welcome us, among them a few courageous listeners who had followed our entire voyage on my weekly radio reports broadcast on the BBC short-wave transmissions. Some daring journalists even took the considerable risk of reporting our arrival, mentioning my achievement of being the first Romanian to have sailed around the world.

But the nicest surprise awaited us at a party put on by our friends in Bucharest, where I was pleased to finally meet Maxim Berghianu, our benefactor who had made it possible for us to get the permission to marry, and eventually for me to leave and join Gwenda in England. Although he was by then No 2 in the communist hierarchy, he accepted the invitation to this

welcoming party arranged by our closest friends. Even in his position, he had taken a great risk to come and meet us, but he did, and I will never forget his words when he shook my hand: 'I am proud of you.'

Back to London

From Romania we sailed back to Greece, laid up Aventura in a boatyard near Athens, bought a used car, filled it with all the souvenirs gathered over the last six years, and drove to England. Our main priority was to enrol Doina and Ivan into a good school where they could resume their studies, reintegrate into the British educational system and, most important, ease their way into life ashore after their long absence.

My colleagues at the BBC gave me a hero's welcome on my return, and a few days later I was called to a meeting with the new head of the department where I had worked before my resignation. My former boss had been replaced by a younger man, who was determined to adapt the service to the expectations of a new, better-informed and more discriminating audience.

Peter Udell received me warmly, congratulated me on my successful voyage and then got straight to the point.

'I understand that you are not planning to settle down, and I guess this is the reason why you have not applied to rejoin us?'

'Yes, on both counts. I simply cannot see myself resuming a life pattern as if the last six years had not happened.'

'I do understand, but surely you have some alternative in mind?'

Suddenly I realised that telling him about my plan to sail all the way to Australia to take up the offer of a job with Radio Australia would sound crazier than even I had started to see it.

'To be honest, no, I don't.'

'As you know we have a high opinion of you as a journalist, and the excellent work you have done for this and other BBC departments during your voyage. We have already decided that in view of all this, we would offer you all the benefits you had before you left, as well as the seniority and salary you would have reached had you not resigned.'

I was flabbergasted. All I could say was, 'Thank you. May I think about it?'

As always at key moments in my life, Gwenda's reason and common sense prevailed, and I accepted. By that stage I was forced to realise that even the most beautiful dream has to end, and for better or worse one has to face reality.

Aventura's voyage has been in every respect a dream come true, and whenever I think back to those wonderful years I cannot believe how fortunate we were to have seen the world during a relatively peaceful time, and to visit places and encounter people as yet unaffected by the outside world. I regret not having written an account of that voyage, but I have tried to make up for it by including some of its highlights at various relevant points of this book.

6

Evolution: Aventura II, III, IV

There are no shortcuts in evolution.

Louis D. Brandeis

Aventura II

After that early near-disaster on Caicos Bank, Aventura looked after us well for the remainder of our six-year-long voyage totalling 68,000 miles. When the time came to choose a successor, in which I also planned to set off around the world, the choice was much wider. This time, however, I had many ideas of my own based on my previous voyage and, as there seemed to be nothing on the market that came close to what I

wanted, I decided to have my new boat designed and built for me. I made a list of all the desirable features and went to see Bill Dixon, a young naval architect, who had already made his name as an original thinker. Bill liked my ideas and managed to produce plans for a boat that included all my essential points. Having witnessed a number of total losses due to navigational errors as well as collisions with mysterious objects, Aventura II had to be as strong as possible, which in those days meant steel. An overall length of 40 feet, which I regarded then as ideal, had been easily decided upon.

As I regarded shallow draft to be an invaluable advantage when cruising, we came up with a design for a retractable keel, operated hydraulically. Fully retracted, the keel passed through a box, which ended at deck level. Inspired by the Australian victory in the America's Cup, I asked Bill to provide the keel with two large wings. They gave additional stability and when retracted rested snugly against the bottom of the hull. With the keel fully down the draft was an acceptable 1.8 metres. To maintain the shallow draft of just under one metre with the keel retracted, she had twin rudders. Manoeuvrability was further aided by twin Perkins 28 HP engines. Each engine could power the boat on its own, which I usually did to conserve fuel, but the main advantage of this arrangement was that one engine also acted as a generating unit, having been fitted with an oversized alternator. Both engines drove MaxProp folding propellers. The rig was a standard cutter with a Hood in-mast furling mainsail, which was then very much in vogue.

Aventura II's underwater configuration

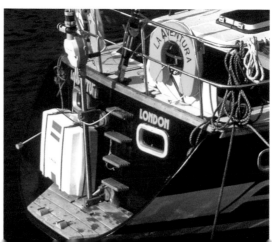

The decks were clear and, unusual at that time, the boat had a stern platform. This functional feature neatly incorporated the Hydrovane self-steering gear, and also allowed locating the liferaft in a place from where it could be easily launched in an emergency.

An eye-catching feature was a fixed dodger (calling it a pilot house would be an exaggeration), which not only gave good cockpit protection but also was highly attractive and gave the entire boat a beautiful overall look.

The interior was also unusual, but suited us perfectly. The main accommodation was in the stern, where a large table and U-shaped comfortable settee gave the crew a good view of the outside. The two cabins occupied the centre of the boat and were separated by the keel box. The entire width of the starboard cabin was taken up by a double bunk. The port cabin was provided with two superimposed bunks with high sides that made them very comfortable at sea. A passageway through that cabin led forward to a massive steel door provided with submarine-type clamps, which turned the forepeak into a sacrificial collision or crumple zone. With so much accommodation available elsewhere, this forward cabin was not used for sleeping. Instead, to port there was a full-size workbench, while the starboard side was left for storage and held a diving compressor, my diving gear, two inflatable dinghies, spare anchors, ropes and fenders.

Although Aventura II sailed well in anything over 15 knots, when the winds were light she could be frustratingly slow. Designed to be of a reasonable displacement of 12.5 tons, which in hindsight may have been rather optimistic for a steel boat, when she was launched she weighed in at a mighty 17 tons. The builder had promised to build me a solid boat and ended up building a tank. Slowly I learned to get the best out of her and she proved to be everything I had expected.

Aventura II incorporated several original features for a long-distance cruising boat, and I still believe that her basic concept was right. Her versatility proved to be a great advantage in the first round-the-world rally. By the time she was sold in 1995 she had sailed some 40,000 miles. The only major job that I had to do up to that point was to completely repaint the hull. If a steel hull is not extremely well prepared for the first coat application, there will be unending problems later on, as I found out to my cost. Her new owners, an Australian couple, still have her and emailed me recently that they are still extremely happy with her.

The voyage of Aventura II 1987-1992

Aventura I was sold in 1982 and for several years I was boatless. Like any sailor, I must have been thinking about my next boat, but however hard I try I cannot remember the reason why I decided to design and build a new boat at that point in my life. What I remember distinctly is that with Doina and Ivan settled down and at or about to enter university, and Gwenda quite happy with our shorebound life, a new voyage was not on my books. Or not yet.

In 1986 I had launched the ARC transatlantic rally, whose instant success kept me fully occupied, so much so that, reluctantly, I decided to resign from the BBC as I felt that I might have chanced upon a more rewarding occupation. Although my plans for another long voyage were undefined, being in close contact with so many sailors and their boats, I felt that the design of long-distance cruising boats had hardly advanced in the years since I had left on my previous voyage.

The new Aventura saw the light of day in the middle of England, about as far from the sea as one could be on an island. The small boatyard was located close to Stratford-upon-Avon of Shakespeare fame. After her launch in 1987, Aventura II spent the first two years on a relaxed European shakedown cruise from England

Start of ARC 1989

Aventura II at Fatu Hiva in the Marquesas where she joined the first round-the-world rally

to the Azores, Madeira and Gibraltar. For much of this highly enjoyable cruise I was accompanied by Doina. In 1989 I crossed the Atlantic in the ARC, continuing via the Bahamas to the USA and on to Panama.

Although I was not planning a new voyage for myself, that didn't stop me from devising one for others... and this is how the idea came of a round-the-world rally that would circumnavigate the planet by way of the Panama and Suez canals. Like the ARC five years previously, it was an instant success and 35 yachts took the start from Gibraltar in early January 1991. Aventura was not among the starters as by then I was already on my way to Panama. Eventually Aventura II joined the rally in Tahiti and from there on served as a very useful and convenient floating base for rally control, mobile office, communications hub, committee

vessel and storage space for rally material. From Tahiti she continued with the rally all the way to the finish in Gibraltar in May 1992.

It is only now, as I am writing these lines exactly a quarter of a century later, that I realise that some of the most memorable highlights that I experienced on Aventura II happened along the route of that round-the-world rally. As the first global sailing event for cruising boats, we were warmly welcomed at every stop, and our hosts did everything in their power to ensure that we left with the best impression of their country. It was that kind of experience that inspired me to organise other special events culminating in the Millennium Odyssey in 1998-2000, a global event that carried a message of goodwill for the coming millennium to all corners of the planet. But that story belongs to the next Aventura.

Aventura III

By the time I started to think seriously of a third Aventura I was rapidly approaching the age of 60 and, as I had already decided that I did not want to continue working after that age, I was determined to do from then on what I like best: sailing. A participant in one of my round-the-world rallies, once paid me a great compliment, when he said, referring to the event which he had just successfully completed: 'Jimmy Cornell forces people to realise their dreams.' I felt that the moment had now arrived for Jimmy Cornell to force himself to realise his own dreams.

In the late 1990s I was still deeply involved with the annual ARC transatlantic rally, which I had launched in 1986, had sailed in ARC 1989 and later in the first round-the-world rally. Having seen so many wrong choices among participants in my various rallies, I knew exactly what mistakes to avoid. One major lesson I had learned from the process of designing Aventura II, was to force myself not to be too influenced by my previous boat. A common mistake people make when it comes to choosing their next boat is to look back at the boating scene that they knew and were familiar with, rather than

be bold and find out what new developments had been made in yacht design since they last bought a boat.

Fortunately the choice of the third Aventura was relatively easy as I knew what I wanted, a light but robust boat that was fast and easy to sail shorthanded, and that could take me anywhere in the world, from icy polar regions to shallow tropical lagoons. Because I do listen to my friends, especially those who know more than I, the determining factor in my final decision was the advice of my friend Erick Bouteleux. On completing his circumnavigation, some of which we had done in company, he became the agent for OVNI yachts for the French Riviera. In the 1980s OVNIs were still a novel concept, very original and very French. The name OVNI suited them very well, as Objet Volant Non Identifié in French means UFO i.e. unidentified flying object.

Anchored in a shallow cove that could only be reached with the centreboard up

Dried out on a beach in Patagonia for a quick coat of antifouling paint

All lines were led back to the cockpit as were those of the boom brake.

Another useful feature was a generous stern platform that gave easy access to the selfsteering gear and kept the messy business of gutting a fish away from the cockpit.

The cockpit also featured a strong rollbar to hold onto...

... or for the younger crew members to show off their acrobatics.

The functional stern arch provided a convenient place to install various pieces of gear and also doubled up as a davit for the tender.

Regardless of length, all OVNIs shared a number of basic elements: hardchined, flat bottomed, with an integral centreboard and folding rudder. That meant that with both rudder and centreboard up they drew very little. For a 43-footer, Aventura drew one metre with the board up, and 2.40 metres with the board down. With a displacement of 9.5 tons, the sailing performance of the OVNI 43 was very good.

The voyage of Aventura III 1998-2010

Aventura II would have been the perfect boat for our first round-the-world voyage: strong, safe, comfortable, spacious, easy to handle, capable of having its draft reduced to one metre, and equipped with a diving compressor. In other words, everything I could have wished for in 1974, but a dozen years later, when I

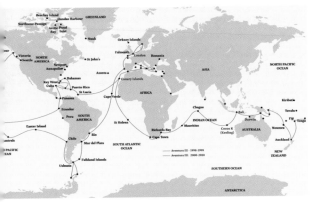

conceived Aventura II, I should have looked into the future, not the past, and this was a mistake I was determined to avoid when I came to decide on the main features of Aventura III. In contrast to Aventura II, for which I did not have a specific voyage in mind, by 1996 I knew exactly what I wanted: a boat that would take me on a new world voyage, starting with a foray to Antarctica.

Aventura III was launched in western France in April 1997 and the initial plan for its maiden voyage was

a summer cruise to the Norwegian Arctic outpost of Svalbard (Spitsbergen). The usual delays and teething problems put paid to that ambitious plan, although we did make it to Norway, albeit its very southern part. That shortened Scandinavian cruise proved that the new Aventura was indeed the boat that I wanted, and allowed me to confidently draw up an even more ambitious schedule.

In summer 1998 Aventura left London as part of the Millennium Odyssey, a global event that would carry around the world a symbolic flame as a message of goodwill for the new millennium. In Lisbon she joined up with the slowly growing fleet, which eventually would reach a total of 40 boats. From Lisbon we sailed to Madeira and the Canaries, where the fleet split in two, as in order to cover as much of the world as possible I had devised two very different routes: a warm

water route that went through the Panama Canal and the tropics, which attracted the bulk of the fleet, and a cold-water high-latitude alternative via Antarctica, Chile and the Cape of Good Hope.

While the warm-water fleet headed west from the Canaries to the Caribbean and the Panama Canal, Aventura was among the seven daring yachts that sailed south to Brazil, Argentina, the Falklands and Patagonia. At Puerto Williams on the Beagle Channel the small

Anchored in Puerto Angosto possibly in the same spot as Joshua Slocum's Spray

fleet split into two with three yachts remaining on the mainland, and four yachts, including Aventura, crossing the Drake Passage to Antarctica.

Three years after my trip to Antarctica with Doina and Ivan on Skip Novak's Pelagic, I was back on my own boat. It was a happy occasion that would have been even happier if Gwenda and Doina could have been with us. Ivan had taken a one-year sabbatical break from work to join me on this voyage, and our old friends Erick and Muriel made up the rest of the crew.

After Antarctica we continued north via the Chilean fjordland as far as Valdivia where Erick and Muriel left and I continued with Ivan on our own. The small Millennium southern fleet was reunited in Valdivia and we proceeded westwards via Easter, Pitcairn and the Gambier Islands to Tahiti. By the time we had reached that point, I had decided that continuing around the world at a rhythm imposed by the rally was not to my taste, and also that the conflict of interest of being both participant and organiser was not an ideal situation. In Bora Bora Ivan and I left the Millennium fleet and sailed north to the Line Islands, Hawaii and finally Alaska, as described in chapter 13. Although I had a good team to run the Millennium Odyssey on a day-to-day basis, for me to manage that complex event by remote control proved more and more difficult. As a result, in Vancouver, Aventura was loaded onto a ship specialising in yacht transport, and six weeks later she arrived in the Mediterranean port of Toulon. I could now dedicate myself fully to the Millennium Odyssey, and by the time the Millennium boats reached Rome for the grand finale of this unique event, Aventura was also among them.

The Millennium Odyssey brought to an end my activities as rally organiser and I could now focus all my time on preparing Aventura III to resume her interrupted world voyage. I left the Mediterranean in 2001 and after a lengthy stop in the Canaries, crossed the Atlantic to St Lucia and spent the winter cruising the Caribbean. Stops in Puerto Rico, Turks and Caicos, the Bahamas and Florida were followed by a long delayed visit to Cuba. The San Blas Islands made an interesting stop en route to the Panama Canal, from where I sailed the traditional route via Galapagos to the Marquesas, Tuamotus, Tahiti, Cook Islands, Niue, Tonga and Fiji. The cyclone season was spent in New Zealand before I continued to New Caledonia, Vanuatu, Papua New Guinea and the Torres Strait. A leisurely cruise across the South Indian Ocean included stops at Cocos Keeling, Chagos, Mauritius and La Reunion. From South Africa I decided to sail the rarely travelled route to Gibraltar via St Helena, Ascension, the Cape Verde and Canary Islands. After five years Aventura was back in the Mediterranean where she spent the following four years visiting places that we had missed in the past and reacquainting ourselves with some of our favourite places. The many highlights of my voyage on Aventura III are interspersed with the practical chapters in the following pages, starting with the foremost of those highlights: Antarctica.

In 2010, at the ripe young age of 70, I decided that with no further long voyages in mind, this kind of Mediterranean sailing was really not my style, and the time had come to call it a day. Aventura III was sold and, at Gwenda's insistence, I agreed to finally give retirement a try. But it didn't work and the outcome was... a new Aventura.

Aventura IV

As to be expected, the latest Aventura incorporates the best features of her predecessors. However, in my quest to conceive a cruising boat which would come closest to my ideal, the final product was based not only on my own experience, but also influenced by the many useful things that I had learned from several surveys I had conducted over the years on the subject of the 'ideal cruising boat' as well as from my interaction with hundreds of participants in the various rallies.

Material

The first Aventura was a strong and well-built GRP boat that survived running aground on a reef on the Caicos Bank with only superficial scratches. For my next boat I decided to go for steel mainly because I was planning to explore some remote places and believed that a metal boat was better suited for such a purpose. Eventually I realised that while metal had indeed been the right choice, the careful maintenance required by a steel hull was too much of a burden, and for the third Aventura I chose aluminium. I became totally converted to this wonderful material. The greatest advantage of aluminium over any other boat building material is that it naturally forms a durable oxide layer on the exposed surface that prevents further oxidation. Aluminium oxide is impermeable and it adheres strongly to the parent metal. As my main priority was not only to have a strong boat but also a functional one, I decided to go, as on the previous Aventura, for an unpainted hull. The advantage of an unpainted aluminium hull is that it can deal with the rough treatment of unfendered docks, unfriendly pilings, not to speak of encounters with ice.

Centreboard

One of the first questions everyone asks me is how safe it is to sail on a boat without a keel. Having sailed twice across the Drake Passage to Antarctica and back, both times on a centreboard boat, and having experienced on two occasions winds between 50 and 60 knots, this was a perfect opportunity to test the boat's stability under such conditions. On both occasions the boats performed perfectly well and took the high cross-swell in their stride. Both Aventura III and IV have an integral centreboard, which means that when the board is raised, it is fully retracted into the hull. The ballast is also internal. The ballast to displacement ratio of both was 32, which is similar to that of most modern cruising yachts.

One of the main reasons for choosing a centreboarder is to increase my cruising options, and having a boat whose draft can be reduced instantly is an important advantage. But shallow draft is not only ideal for exploring places that other boats cannot reach, but also a safety factor, because it allows you to access a protected shallow spot if needing shelter in an emergency. Also, as most integral centreboard boats have a flat bottom, it means that with the board fully up, the boat can dry out on any beach, tidal bay or estuary. When the tide runs out, the boat settles down comfortably. We dried out Aventura III on many occasions, whether to put on a quick coat of antifouling between tides while cruising in Southern Chile, or to access a shallow bay in Alaska so we could watch grizzly bears fishing for salmon. One other advantage of a centreboard is that it can be used as a sounding board when entering an unfamiliar shallow anchorage. It is a technique I learned from Erick Bouteleux and taught me a new meaning for the term 'sounding board'. To my shame, I did not put that unique feature to good use when we entered an anchorage in the Northwest Passage and hit an uncharted rock in an area that showed a minimum depth of four metres. Although we hit the rock quite hard, the centreboard did its job and swung up, it scraped along the top of the rock, then dropped back into its lowered position. The only damage was to my ego, but any other boat would have been in serious trouble.

Shallow draft is a major attraction of centreboard yachts, but there are also some considerable performance advantages. The main role of the board is to provide lift when sailing closehauled, and to reduce leeway when reaching. With the board fully down Aventura III drew 2.4 metres and, when sailed properly, it could point as high, or almost as high, as most keeled cruising boats. Sailed properly means that when sailing on the wind sail trim is critical and the sails must be perfectly set to achieve the desired performance. It also means that a good speed must be kept up, and heeling too much must be avoided, or you end up making too

Aventura IV in slings

much leeway. With a draft of 2.8 metres with the board down, Aventura IV performs even better than her predecessor.

There is a certain technique in sailing a centreboarder efficiently, not just on the wind but off the wind as well. This is when the centreboard becomes a true asset as it allows you to reduce the wetted surface. Also, the ability to lift the board gradually as the apparent wind goes past 135°, and then continue lifting it up to the point where the board is fully retracted, is a great advantage as the risk of broaching is virtually eliminated. The absence of a keel to act as a pivot in a potential broaching situation means that the boat does not tend to round up when, in a similar situation, a keeled boat would do just that. It is a feature that I have blessed on many occasions, and that has allowed me to continue keeping the spinnaker up longer than I would have done otherwise. The board is normally retracted when motoring in calm waters and the reduction in wetted surface provides an extra 0.3 to 0.5 knots of speed.

I must admit that before acquiring Aventura III I also had doubts about having a boat with a centreboard, being primarily concerned about stability. My doubts were put to rest after sailing to Antarctica on Skip Novak's Pelagic, a 50-foot centreboarder, and seeing how well she coped with the mountainous seas we encountered. I therefore went ahead with my plan to sail to Antarctica on the new Aventura III. Before leaving London, I decided to have a photo-shoot on the River Thames, where I hoped to get some spectacular photos with the iconic Tower Bridge as background for the benefit of the sponsors of the Millennium Odyssey. Gwenda was at the wheel, the crew were some friends and I was strategically located on a floating pontoon with my camera. Aventura III made a couple of passes in front of Tower Bridge sporting a large spinnaker adorned with the Canary Islands logo.

The framing was absolutely perfect for the third pass, when a violent gust rolled down from one of the tall buildings nearby, hit Aventura with all its might, and tipped her over until the spreaders touched the water. To her credit, Gwenda kept her cool, gripped the wheel firmly, the boat righted herself, and shot past my pontoon at breakneck speed. Having watched this unfolding disaster through my viewfinder, I froze when I saw Aventura tipping over, thus missing the most dramatic shot. That loss was more than compensated by my having witnessed such a convincing demonstration of Aventura's unquestionable stability.

Rig

The first Aventura was rigged as a ketch, a decision greatly influenced by the desire for manageable sails in the days before jib furling gears. Most early world voyages had been done in two-masted boats, so the wisdom of such a rig was not even questioned. It didn't take me long to realise that, except when reaching, Aventura's mizzen rig was of little use. Doina and Ivan adopted the mizzenmast and its sail as their own and had a lot of fun putting up the small mizzen sail.

I have no doubt that a single taller mast would have greatly improved Aventura's performance and

so, when I decided on a rig for Aventura II, I chose a straightforward sloop with a relatively high-aspect mainsail. The advent of reliable furling gears had made sail handling much easier, so having larger sails was no longer regarded as a problem on a short-handed boat. Under most conditions, having a large genoa on a roller furling gear, seemed to be a good solution and Aventura II ended up with this setup and an in-mast furling mainsail. Purely from the performance point of view, the result was quite disappointing as the battenless in-mast furling mainsail performed poorly when close-hauled. Based on that experience, I decided that Aventura III should have a cutter rig. The versatility and ease of handling the combination of a high-cut yankee and staysail, both on furling gears, proved to be an excellent choice. As a 130% genoa had been included in the original sail wardrobe, I kept it as a spare, but when I once swapped the yankee for it, it only took me a couple of days to realise just how much more efficient the yankee/staysail combination performed than the large overlapping genoa. So the genoa was taken down, packed up and sent into permanent retirement.

Aventura IV's windward-sailing capability was put to a good test in the Arctic when we had to beat our way through a narrow strait in 25-knot winds to reach the open sea

Sailing close-hauled is the weakest point of a centreboard boat, and this is where a well-cut jib is essential. Aventura IV had a fractional rig (7/8) with a Solent jib, which is a low-cut, relatively flat sail, plus a staysail for stronger winds. They were not meant to be used together, as on a cutter, although occasionally I experimented with using both sails, usually with the Solent partially rolled up.

Windward performance is certainly a potential weakness of a centreboard boat with a relatively flat bottom, but with the sails well trimmed and the board down, we managed to sail as close as 35 degrees to the

Aventura IV like a knife through water

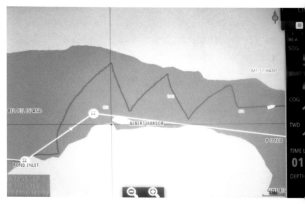

This diagram shows clearly how we managed to tack our way out

wind. On a test sail in Cherbourg harbour, in 25 to 28 knots of wind, with a full staysail and two reefs in the mainsail, we once hit 9.5 knots. I must stress that she was not yet fully laden, although the fuel and water tanks were full. This meant that we could try out one of Aventura's special features by using the two transfer pumps to quickly move close to one tonne of weight into the windward tanks.

Although Aventura IV has a jib and staysail, technically it is not a cutter rig. Initially I was determined to have a similar cutter rig as on her predecessor, but I was eventually persuaded by both the builder and

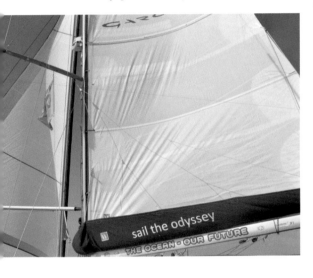

architect that, in their experience, a fractional rig, as extensively tested on the Allures range, had proved to be more efficient on a centreboard boat than a standard cutter rig. In the event, the Solent jib performed indeed better when close-hauled than Aventura III's yankee-staysail combination. Aventura IV's mast was also much better stayed than on my previous boat and due to the swept-back spreaders the lower shroud was not obstructing the side deck. The running backstays only had to be set up when using the staysail in strong winds.

One clear disadvantage of swept-back spreaders is that they prevent the mainsail being fully let out

when sailing off the wind. Having the mainsail coming to rest against the spreaders threatened to be a serious source of chafe. I managed to overcome this by buying two lengths of foam pipe lagging from a builders merchant in the Orkney Islands. This improvised protection worked well, but, to be on the safe side, later I had anti-chafe patches sewn onto the mainsail in all critical areas.

Mainsail

My own experience with different types of mainsail has been quite enlightening. The first Aventura had a standard mainsail, which was adequate when we started the voyage but ended up baggy and out of shape halfway through the voyage, having been affected by UV light. In the early 1970s synthetic sail materials were still being developed and Dacron hadn't been around for long. Reefing in those days was usually done in the old-fashioned way, but I also had a backup as Aventura's mainsail could be furled around the boom with a winch handle. The system was simple to use even if it made the boom sag and the sail ended up in rather poor shape when it was partly rolled up.

The second Aventura had a Hood in-mast furling mainsail, in those days seeming the perfect solution on a short-handed cruising boat. In some ways it was, even if the sail was not that efficient when sailing close-hauled. There was one early incident that happened on her maiden voyage across the Bay of Biscay and made me regret that I had chosen this type of mainsail. We had left England for the Mediterranean early, and in March the weather in the Bay of Biscay was, as to be expected, rough. Right in the middle of that dreaded bay, with the wind increasing, I tried to roll in some of the mainsail but it refused to budge and I realised that it was jammed. With the wind getting stronger, the only solution seemed to be to put a knife to it, something I was not prepared to do to my expensive new sail. The other alternative was to carry on with the full mainsail and no foresail, and hope for the best. Sailing like this in over 30 knots was certainly fast and exciting, and Aventura took it surprisingly well. On my dawn watch, at the end of a nail-biting night, I looked back and in the half-light saw right behind us, at no more than 20 metres, the bow of a large yacht advancing fast towards us riding high on a wave. The yacht veered slightly and passed within a few metres, the lone man at the wheel shouting a greeting. We made it safely into Lisbon, where we docked the boat with some difficulty with the full mainsail still up. Close to us I saw the Swan 65 that had passed us and went over to speak to the crew. That same guy was sitting in the cockpit having a coffee.

'You certainly looked a sight,' he exclaimed when he saw me, 'and I was quite impressed how well you were sailing with that full mainsail up! But I only understood now, seeing you coming in with one of those stupid in-mast furling jobs, that you weren't doing it deliberately.'

'You guessed right...it's stuck. So where are you going?'

'Delivering this tub to Mallorca.'

'I suppose it takes some crew to sail such a large boat.'

'It certainly does...that's why I decided to do it on my own?'

My mouth fell open. 'On your own?'

'Yeah. Some friends let me down at the last minute and as I couldn't wait, I simply left. OK, I'd better explain that I have done a lot of singlehanding, a couple of transat and round-the-world races.'

He then kindly offered to help me with my mainsail, asked me to hoist him to the top of the mast where he found the problem.

'It's the halyard that got jammed around the swivel. I'll get some tools and fix it for you. It's an easy job, but I admit that I wouldn't have gone aloft in that weather, so you were very wise to do what you did.'

When he had finished he explained exactly how to fix the problem if it ever happened again, and also what to do to prevent it. Needless to say, it never occurred again. As a result, a fully battened mainsail was the logical solution for both Aventura III and Aventura

IV, as I realised that only such an efficient sail would ensure a satisfactory performance from a boat with a flat bottom and centreboard.

Rudders

The first Aventura had a massive rudder supported by a skeg. Aventura II sported twin rudders, which was quite a novelty in those days. Aventura III had a folding rudder that was standard on all but the larger OVNIs.

Aventura IV had two rudders of strong aluminium construction, supported by short skegs. An ingenious solution to protect the rudders was put to the test when we collided with the underwater ledge of an iceberg while sailing in the Northwest Passage. The shock was so hard that it knocked me off my feet in the cockpit. It was only about two weeks later that I noticed the damage from the dinghy. The crumple zone had done its job and the damage was purely superficial. Aventura continued sailing like that for several months until we returned to the boatyard in Cherbourg where the rudder blade was extracted and the crumple zone could be rebuilt.

Aventura IV's clean decks as all lines are led back to the cockpit through concealed tunnels

All this shows that the Exploration 45 is not a standard production boat, but a specially-designed long-distance cruising boat conceived as a safer boat than any other currently on the market. The steering arrangement was an intrinsic part of this safety aspect and there was even provision for an emergency rudder that could be hung from a universal bracket on the stern platform.

The same bracket was used for the Sail-Gen hydro-generator and could also be used to mount an outboard motor in an emergency.

Deck layout

As I wanted to be able to sail Aventura IV on my own, or at least be able to handle her without calling the crew, all lines were led back to the cockpit to two primary and two electric winches. Therefore I could easily reef the mainsail on my own, set up the spinnaker pole to run downwind, or hoist the Parasailor spinnaker.

At all seminars I stress the importance of being able to handle your boat on your own if necessary. It is an essential aspect of self-sufficiency and I am often surprised how badly thought-out some production boats are. I am profoundly impressed by those heroes of our times, the single-handed sailors in the Vendée Globe round-the-world race, and cannot see why any able-bodied sailor should not be able do the same on a boat sailing at one third of the speed of an Open 60.

Electronics

Aventura IV's state-of-the-art electronics system was taken in hand by Ivan, who managed to tailor it to my own requirements, making it as user-friendly as possible.

There were three networks running on Aventura IV. The Iridium Pilot provided our satellite communications with two phones (captain and crew had their own lines), and a permanent 128 kb/s data link. Due to bandwidth charges of $7 per MB, Ivan decided to play safe and limit this to only allow connections to our email service provider, and a web service for when we needed to download ice charts, weather maps, and other large files.

The fully integrated Brookes & Gatehouse instruments displayed all the navigational data, including charts, radar and autopilot, and were

configured to share the network over wifi to allow iPads to connect via a custom app. This had been bridged via a firewall into another wireless router to create a single wifi network for all onboard laptops to connect to. This allowed us to download email weather forecasts, such as GRIB data, and upload the data directly to the chart plotters for display. The firewall was also configured to continuously capture data from the Brookes & Gatehouse network, which allowed us to transmit on a regular basis automated reports via email of wind conditions, sea temperature and barometric pressure to the World Meteorological Organisation.

Ivan also set up a network to keep a regularly updated log including detailed information pertaining to our voyage, although I also kept a proper ship's log with entries updated at regular intervals. While in the Northwest Passage, an edited version of the electronic log was emailed every 4 or 6 hours, as required, to the Canadian or Greenland Coast Guard.

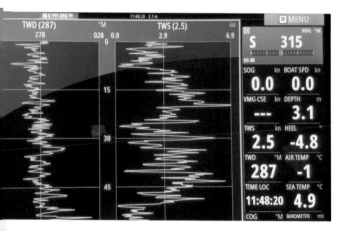

Day tank

Every Aventura has been fitted with a day tank and I am still surprised why so few boats have them. Many engine failures on cruising boats seem to be caused by dirty fuel and on many production boats the fuel supply and filtering systems are often woefully inadequate.

As on all my previous boats, Aventura IV has a 40-litre tank mounted higher than the engine so that the fuel is gravity-fed to the engine. The tank is topped up every four or five hours by manually activating a fuel transfer pump. I have deliberately avoided having an automatic filling system so that the person who fills the tank needs to actually look at what is happening. The manual switch is placed in such a position that you can see the filter and its glass water-separator while filling the tank, thus making sure that the fuel that enters the tank is always clean. Apart from this pre-filter, there are two more filters before the fuel reaches the injection pump. A crossover valve allows the day tank to be bypassed if necessary, so that fuel is then drawn directly from the main tank. Besides feeding the engine clean fuel effortlessly by gravity, a further advantage of a day tank is that it can act as a final reserve tank by showing exactly how much fuel is left before the main tank is empty. In my view, the day tank should be regarded as a safety feature, and I regard it as essential on any long-distance sailing boat.

Concern for the environment

Some of the most important features on Aventura IV were dictated by my determination for my new boat to be as eco-friendly as possible. None of my previous boats had a dedicated diesel generator nor does Aventura IV. Electricity consumption on the first Aventura was so low, and the equipment so basic,

that we could easily manage with what our Perkins 4108 engine produced. On Aventura II one of the twin Perkins 28 HP engines doubled up as a virtual generator and amply covered our modest needs. By the time Aventura III came about, a solar panel, wind and towing generators allowed us to cover most of our needs from renewable sources.

On Aventura IV, a similar but more efficient combination of a D400 wind generator, Sail-Gen hydro-generator, and a 140W solar panel, supplied our energy needs on all offshore passages. This was demonstrated on the passage from Greenland to England when we had a problem with our engine and had to rely on the above equipment to provide all our energy needs, which it did perfectly. Finally, also with the environment in mind, the contents of both grey and black waters were treated by an Electroscan purifying system before being discharged.

7

Voyage planning

Voyage planning is common sense.
  International Convention for the Safety of Life at Sea

My interest in voyage planning goes back even further than my interest in sailing. As a young boy I often leafed through an old atlas, imagining all those places where one day I would land from my own boat. Dreamily, I would trace with my finger a route across an ocean that would take me to a tiny dot of an island: Abemama or Nuku Hiva or some other such beautifully enticing name. I could not have been much older than eight when I started writing an adventure book in which I set off with my closest friends on a world voyage in a boat with the English name of Friend Ship.

My practical interest in ocean routing was born during our first round-the-world voyage when I realised, mainly from the books of previous travellers, just how important it was for the overall safety of a voyage to plan the best route possible. Immediately after our return in 1981, I started working on what was to become World Cruising Routes. My research work took me from the British Library to the Maritime Museum in Greenwich, right on the zero meridian, where I was given permission to study the original logs of many ships that roamed the oceans in the early 19th century. I was even allowed to look at Captain Cook's original logs, and I can still feel the thrill of seeing the neat writing of the man whom I regard as the greatest navigator of all time.

My own voyaging, and the lessons learned from all those captains, as well as the writings of some of my near contemporaries such as Erick Hiscock, have formed the basis of my attitude to routing. Put simply, it is to always do your best to be in the right place at the right time and, conversely, to avoid at all cost being in the wrong place at the wrong time. I have no doubt that this is the reason why in all these years of ocean sailing I have never been in really serious trouble. There may be a contradiction here between my willingness to take risks in my earlier shorebound life and this cautious attitude when sailing. As I have become more experienced, I have occasionally taken some calculated risks. Some recent examples are the decision to leave Fiji for New Zealand early in the season on Aventura III, or setting off the following year for New Caledonia when the safe season had barely started. On the other hand, the marathon that my son Ivan and I sailed from Antarctica to Alaska had been carefully planned to coincide with the safest seasons, and was consequently accomplished without any mishap.

World Cruising Routes

When I started planning my first voyage in the early 1970s there was only one book dealing specifically with ocean routing, the British Admiralty Ocean

Plotting the noon position

Passages for the World. Aimed primarily at commercial shipping, it had very little relevant information for sailing yachts. The only sailing information, which had been retained from earlier editions, described weather conditions along some of the well-established trade routes, such as the tea-clipper route from Hong Kong to England, or the wool and grain route from Australia to Europe. While those details still made interesting reading, the routes described were very different from those sailed by modern cruising yachts, and thus the information was irrelevant.

All through the first Aventura's voyage I gathered material on ocean routing, and soon after our return to London I started writing the kind of book that I would have liked to have had myself when I was planning our own round-the-world voyage. World Cruising Routes was first published in 1987 and is now in its eighth edition. It has been translated into German, French, Italian and Spanish. It contains essential routing and weather information on all popular cruising routes throughout the world, with details of tropical-storm seasons and areas affected by them, prevailing winds and currents, suggested landfalls, relevant waypoints, recommended cruising guides and suggestions on the best time and tactics for each particular route. Over the years, the book has gradually grown in scope so that its latest edition lists over 1,000 different routes, with a much wider selection of destinations.

One of the greatest compliments I ever received for my book came from the most unexpected direction. One day, while in Las Palmas before the start of the ARC, a participant who I knew to have been an officer in the Royal Navy barged into my office and exclaimed breathlessly, 'Jimmy, you will never believe this. I have just visited a British nuclear submarine that is here on a goodwill mission and guess what? On the shelf above the nav table I saw a copy of your Routes! So I asked the captain why on earth he would carry that doorstopper of a book with him.'

'So I know where those silly yachts go and can be extra careful not to smash into one when we surface,' he replied.

I had a similarly backhanded compliment from the captain of an Indonesian sail training yacht that was taking part in the Hong Kong Challenge, a round-the-world race that I organised to mark the handover of Hong Kong to China. At the stopover in Japan, he came to my office and told me proudly, 'Mr Jimmy, I have a copy of your book. Would you sign it for me, please.'

'Really? Is it World Cruising Routes?'

'Yes. Look at it.'

I had already noticed the battered copy he was holding but it certainly didn't look like any of my books. He handed it over and I saw it was a poor photocopied job.

'Very nice,' I said.

'Yes, the Ministry of Maritime Affairs has made enough copies to distribute to the entire Indonesian Navy,' he told me proudly.

'How very interesting,' was all I could say, trying to sound as impressed as I obviously was not, as no author would be when faced with a pirated copy.

The biggest compliment, however, came from a British single-hander whom I met in New Zealand. One day he came over to look at my boat and, before leaving, said rather sheepishly, 'I want to tell you something that may amuse you.'

'Go ahead.'

'After transiting the Panama Canal, a group of us were headed for the Galapagos Islands. We soon separated and I continued on my own. I had great difficulty getting out of the Bay of Panama and, whichever way I turned, the wind and current always seemed to be against me. Rather than the hoped for eight- or nine-day passage, it took me 16 days to get there. When I finally arrived, everyone told me how concerned they had been for my safety.

'What had actually happened?' one of them asked me.

'Not much.' And I told them of my ordeal.

'But didn't you have Jimmy Cornell's book on board?'

'Yeah, I do have it but never looked at the thing.'

'Well, you fool, you'd better look now as it tells you exactly where to go. We did that and got here in under eight days.'

'So, Jimmy, I do owe you an apology. I did read what you wrote and the information is very clear on the tactics on leaving Panama, where to find favourable winds and currents, the lot.'

'Well, at least I hope you're using the book now.'

'Of course, all the time. Otherwise I would never have told you, as I find it so stupid and embarrassing.'

Weather routing

To know the laws that govern the winds, and to know that you know them, will give you an easy mind on your voyage... Otherwise you may tremble at the appearance of every cloud.

Joshua Slocum

Having done all my early sailing at a time when there were no weather forecasts available on ocean passages, my offshore strategy had to be based on the actual conditions being experienced, which wasn't of much help in forward planning. In those days one of my favourite aids were the monthly pilot charts that showed average conditions for every month of the year: wind strength and direction, percentage of gale force winds, tropical storms and their tracks, currents, etc. The charts had been compiled over a number of years and were based on observations made by ships' captains, so they presented a fairly accurate picture of what could be expected at certain times in any given area of an ocean. Plotting a hypothetical route with this kind of information at one's fingertips was not only easy but also highly enjoyable and satisfying.

This is how I learned my trade and there is nothing new in this because ever since man ventured onto the seas, he always tried to make the most of existing conditions. In historic times, it is well known that the Phoenicians had an almost instinctive way of choosing the right time to sail west across the Mediterranean during spells of easterly winds, and got their timing right to sail home with favourable westerlies. In Roman times there were regular trading voyages between the Red Sea, Persian Gulf and India, sailing east during the favourable SW monsoon of summer, and west with the NW monsoon of winter. The Vikings made repeated westbound voyages from Scandinavia by taking advantage of the prevailing easterly winds of high latitudes and returning home with the westerlies that blow further south. In the process they discovered the Shetland, Orkney and

Faroe Islands, Iceland and Greenland. They were also the first Europeans to land in what they called Vinland (Newfoundland) in present-day North America. Since ancient times Arab navigators embarked on regular trading voyages between the Persian Gulf and East Africa, sailing southwest during the favourable NE monsoon and returning home with the equally favourable SW monsoon. Some of the greatest navigators in history were the Polynesians who, during a relatively short time, managed to discover virtually all the Pacific islands, simply by observing and using the prevailing conditions to best advantage.

Christopher Columbus was probably the greatest opportunist among navigators, having instinctively picked the best route to sail from the Canaries to what was to become the New World with the prevailing NE winds and returning home the following spring by presciently (or miraculously) sailing NE from the newly discovered lands to the area dominated by prevailing westerly winds. He was the first to realise that there was a logic to this clockwise Atlantic merry-go-round and there is still keen debate as to whether he discovered this simply by chance.

The sailing ships of the 18th and early 19th centuries are the best example of how commercial considerations were responsible for the development of some of the most effective sailing machines ever built. However well they sailed, their masters always made sure that weather conditions were in their favour. After all, what is more telling than the fact that those favourable winds are called 'trade' winds? In all other languages they have a generic name to do with their regularity or seasonality such as Passat (German), alisée (French) but only a mercantile nation such as the British could think of naming winds as 'commercial'.

As sailing vessels evolved and were no longer dependent on being able to sail only with following winds, navigators became more daring and started going against the established weather systems, but the principle of planning long voyages to coincide with the best season was never abandoned. In this respect contemporary cruising sailors have remained highly traditional in their approach, even if today many prefer to play safe and obtain as much weather-routing information as possible. The main cruising routes of the world have remained virtually unchanged and still follow the old trade wind routes from east to west across the oceans.

I have always used pilot charts for my voyage planning or when adding new routes and updating the information on existing ones in World Cruising Routes. I try to give my readers the best information and advice on how to safely plan a voyage or a passage virtually anywhere in the world. On a few occasions I have gone against my own advice, such as when I decided to take the shortest route from Cape Town to the Mediterranean via the Canaries, rather than the traditional but much longer route via the Caribbean, or the Azores. My gamble paid off and has shown that this rarely sailed route is quite feasible. On the other hand, maybe I was, as often in the past, just plain lucky.

While I never deny that I have had luck on my side, I must add that often I help my luck by being pragmatic. After my first attempt to transit the Northwest Passage from east to west in summer 2014, I realised that because of the ice conditions, attempting a transit from west to east might have a better chance of success. So in early 2015 I sailed through the Panama Canal into the Pacific and managed a successful transit, this time from the Pacific to the Atlantic.

Boats leaving on an Atlantic crossing to the Caribbean during the favourable winter season

Passage making

The tactics outlined in *World Cruising Routes* for specific routes all follow the principle of being in the right place at the right time, and also take advantage of prevailing weather conditions. The book describes the best tactics for the successful completion of such classic passages as crossing the Atlantic from the Canaries to the Caribbean, sailing around the Cape of Good Hope into the South Atlantic, or returning from the Caribbean to the USA or Europe at the end of the winter season. In more recent editions I have also tried to help those who wish to divert from the beaten track, for instance, sailing from New Zealand to Tahiti via the Austral Islands, or getting from Micronesia to Hawaii against winds and current, or, as I did myself, taking the shortest route from South Africa to the Mediterranean. As increasing numbers of sailors are interested in high-latitude cruising, I have added routes and information on Antarctica, Greenland and the Northwest Passage.

This is a suitable point at which to consider some of the reasons why people attempt to sail, as it were, against the grain, not just by going against the prevailing conditions but often setting off in the wrong season or along an illogical route. Most do it simply out of ignorance, but they soon learn that there is more to ocean routing than drawing a line along a desired track. Countless such cases, some with unhappy consequences, have come to my knowledge over the years but I will mention only one.

While in Chagos, in the Indian Ocean, I was approached by the American owner of a 50-foot boat who told me that he was planning to sail to Perth, in Western Australia, as he had arranged to meet his family and grandchildren there.

'Not easy at the best of times,' I warned him. 'You will be sailing hard against the prevailing winds and, if you do not leave soon, you risk running into the next cyclone season.'

'I can deal with both. I still have 200 gallons of fuel and avoiding cyclones is not all that difficult if you know what you are doing.'

A few months later I got an email from another sailor, whom I had met there, who told me that the American yacht did leave soon after my own departure, and got back to Chagos three months later, battered, exhausted, with all its sails torn, only having been able to make less than 1,000 miles towards its intended destination.

Route planning

If one does not know to which port one is sailing, no wind is favourable.

Lucius Annaeus Seneca

At lectures and seminars I am always asked about sailing a certain route or planning a certain passage. Often the intended passage is either plainly wrong, planned to be sailed during the dangerous season, or both. My usual reaction is to say that I would not attempt to sail such a passage myself and suggest a safer alternative. Occasionally, a few months later, I get a contrite email admitting to having been proven wrong, and wishing they had listened to my advice.

Eventually I realised that, while World Cruising Routes was doing an adequate job in helping sailors plan a passage, there seemed to be a need for a book specifically dedicated to voyage planning. In my initial research on the subject, I came across this statement by the International Convention for the Safety of Life at Sea: 'Voyage planning is common sense.'

I tend to agree, but how can one define common sense? Obviously I wasn't the first to ask this question as even the philosopher Voltaire seems to have had doubts about its meaning, when he wrote: 'There is nothing so common about common sense... so it should really be called "uncommon" sense.'

More researching led me to this old saying from the Ivory Coast, which I am sure Voltaire would have greatly enjoyed: 'What is the one thing that you'd never be able to sell in the market? Common sense! Those

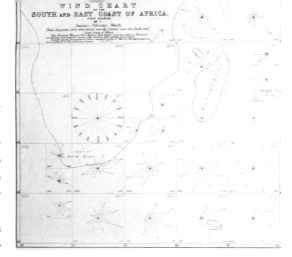

who have it wouldn't need to buy it. Those who don't have it wouldn't know what to do with it.'

What led to my decision to write a book on voyage planning was the realisation that many of those who had asked my advice about setting off, or planning to set off, on a certain voyage or offshore passage actually lacked that essential common sense themselves.

To illustrate weather conditions in certain parts of the world, I intended to use in World Voyage Planner the existing pilot charts. The first person to chart winds and ocean currents was the American meteorologist and oceanographer Matthew Fontaine Maury.

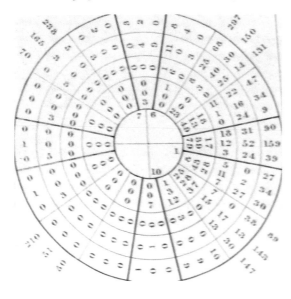

Those early wind charts were difficult to interpret and in 1856 a British chart was published showing the direction of winds in the South Indian Ocean. These were the original windroses, which are still used on the current pilot charts.

Over the years monthly pilot charts depicting winds and currents in every ocean have become the main tool in voyage planning. For a long time they were based on observations made by ship's captains or navigators. I realised that some of them had not been updated for decades and the information depicted on them had probably been affected by changes in global climate, thus rendering them inaccurate. Ivan came to my help by pointing out that NOAA (National Oceanic and Atmospheric Administration) satellites have been gathering global data on winds and currents for the past 20 years, although for some reason none of that information had been used to produce new and up-to-date pilot charts. As this vast amount of data was in the public domain, and thus freely accessible, Ivan wrote a program to process it. The result is Cornells' Ocean Atlas, which gives monthly details of winds, currents, tropical storms and the seasonal location of atmospheric highs for all the oceans of the world. The Atlas and World Voyage Planner have established themselves as essential companions to World Cruising Routes.

An interesting phenomenon highlighted by the new pilot charts is the change in the prevailing wind direction in the area north of the Galapagos Islands. In the circled areas, there appears to have been a drastic change, from southeast to northeast winds.

This change can be a major factor for anyone planning to sail nonstop from Panama to the Marquesas, as more favourable conditions may be encountered by initially sailing north of the equator until the point is reached to cross the Line and set course for one's destination.

To help those planning a particular passage we have used the atlas data to produce for the latest edition

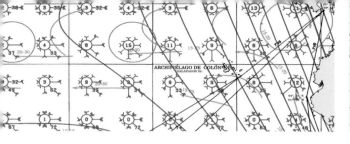

Old pilot chart

Latest pilot chart

of World Cruising Routes so-called windgrams which depict a summary of wind conditions for the months when passages are undertaken along some of the most commonly sailed routes. Each windgram is a synthesis of wind direction and strength along a specific route. The average wind strength is on the Beaufort scale. Here are some examples:

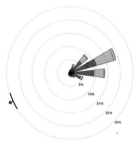

Gran Canaria to Saint Lucia
November

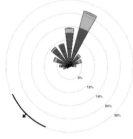

Gibraltar to Canaries
September

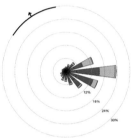

Antigua to Bermuda
May

Cape Town to Saint Helena
January

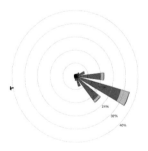

Galapagos to Marquesas
March

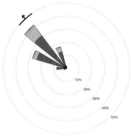

Cabo San Lucas to San Diego
May

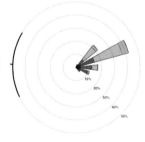

Saint Helena to Eastern Caribbean
January

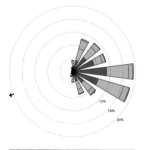

Mauritius to Richards Bay
October

Passage planning

The latest pilot charts should be the first source of information to be consulted whether planning a longer voyage or just an ocean passage. I was once asked by the owner of a 80-foot sailing yacht to advise him on the best route to sail from Singapore to Western Australia. Just as in the earlier example, he was going to do it close to the start of the South Indian Ocean cyclone season, so I warned him about this, and also told him that even at the best of times the voyage would be difficult or even impossible to accomplish along his proposed route across Indonesia to the Sunda Strait and on to Fremantle in Western Australia.

'I am sure it can be done,' he replied confidently. 'I have a good crew and a good boat. Anyway, the alternative route that you described is far too long, so I'd rather take a chance on the shortest available option.'

My advice was to sail the longer, but ultimately safer route, by heading east from Singapore towards Micronesia, make easting by staying just north of the equator to take advantage of the east-setting North Equatorial Counter Current, cross the Line far enough east to get a good angle across the SE trade winds of the South Pacific, then take a long sweep so as to sail south of Australia during the narrow window at the height of the southern summer (December to February). At that time there was a good chance of having a spell of easterly winds to sail across the Great Australian Bight to reach Western Australia. The main problem with such a route was that, in order to take advantage of the safest seasons on both sides of the equator (January to April in the North Pacific, May to October in the South Pacific), the voyage could take as long as one year.

About a month later, my worst expectations were confirmed when I received an email from the boat owner saying that I had been absolutely right. Having made it past the Sunda Strait without too much difficulty, once they hit the South Indian Ocean proper, the strong southeast winds made it impossible for them to make any headway towards their goal. They took long tacks to no avail; they tried shorter tacks with

the same result. Gear started to break, the crew were close to mutiny, so eventually they turned around and sailed back to Singapore.

'You were absolutely right and now I wish I had listened to you and taken the longer route as you so wisely suggested. I realise that not only is it a much safer option but it would give us also an opportunity to do some cruising and visit some places en route, both in the North and South Pacific. I assure you that once I manage to get the boat back into shape, that's exactly what I am going to do,' wrote the contrite owner.

'Best of luck,' I replied. 'It's always better to be safe than sorry.'

So what are the reasons for such illogical decisions? As I mentioned earlier, ignorance or wishful thinking are usually a factor. Other causes include time pressure from crew or family, or simply the need to deliver a boat on time.

As Joseph Conrad pointed out: 'More accidents have happened at sea because the captain believed that he needed to be in a certain place by a specific date than any other reason.' Indeed, one of the worst things to do is to take on certain commitments without considering the possible consequences, something that happened repeatedly among participants in the ARC and more recently the Atlantic Odyssey. I was often amazed to hear how boats got into trouble sailing from Europe to the Canaries late in the season because the owner had other priorities. Every year boats heading south from Northern Europe bound for the Canaries get into trouble crossing the Bay of Biscay, and however much skippers are warned to do this early in the summer, when conditions are the best, almost every time a boat gets into serious difficulty it is because the voyage had started too late in the season.

Many of the sailors joining a transatlantic rally have little offshore experience, and although they have sailed to the start in the Canaries, and have successfully completed a passage that can be more difficult than a transatlantic crossing, they are nevertheless much more concerned about the actual Atlantic crossing. At the pre-start briefings I always tried to make them understand the importance of a well-prepared boat, backed by good planning and timing. The impending crossing of an ocean can be a frightening prospect for inexperienced sailors so I try to reason that offshore experience can only be acquired by practice, and the only way is to bite the bullet and do it. Often, the main source of anxiety was the size of the Atlantic. One way to deal with this is to reduce it in your mind into a number of shorter, perhaps daily, segments, thus making the task look more manageable. As the captain of a charter boat explained to his guests, even an elephant can be eaten one bite at a time.

Forward planning

In 2016 I had to take some important decisions for the timing of two events that I organised: the Blue Planet Odyssey and the Pacific Odyssey. I mention them here as they are a telling example of good voyage planning being not just a matter of common sense, but also show that when planning ahead and faced with the uncertainty of seasonal weather conditions it is always better to err on the side of caution.

Blue Planet Odyssey, Southeast Asia
January-May 2016
Because of safety concerns caused by the deteriorating political situation in the Red Sea and Middle East, it was decided not to take the Blue Planet Odyssey along the planned route from Southeast Asia across the North Indian Ocean to the Mediterranean, but sail instead the Cape of Good Hope route.

The main difficulty in planning a voyage from Southeast Asia to the South Indian Ocean is to schedule a departure during the favourable NE Monsoon but avoid arriving in the South Indian Ocean before 30 April, the end of the cyclone season. As we were in the midst of an El Niño episode, I was seriously concerned

about the possibility of a late cyclone occurring in the South Indian Ocean.

Taking these factors into account, the solution that I suggested was to leave Southeast Asia before the end of the NE Monsoon (March) to avoid contrary southwest winds along the route, and spend the intermediate period until the start of the safe season in the South Indian Ocean in western Sumatra, an area that is not affected by tropical storms. Fortunately this schedule was adhered to, as in late April Cyclone Fantala northeast of Madagascar was upgraded to a grade 5 cyclone, the strongest ever cyclone recorded in the South Indian Ocean. Its effects were felt not only in Madagascar, Mauritius and Chagos but also as far as the equator. Fantala was one of several tropical storms associated with El Niño and the unusually high water temperatures in some tropical areas. According to the initial schedule, the BPO boats would have been at that time in Chagos, but instead enjoyed benign conditions in western Sumatra. They left Sumatra in mid-May bound for Cocos Keeling, before continuing to Rodrigues and Mauritius.

Pacific Odyssey, South Pacific
April-May 2016
Similar safety considerations came into play in the case of the Pacific Odyssey between Panama and the Marquesas. Initially, the rally was planned to follow the timing used in the previous years, by leaving from Martinique in January, transiting the Panama Canal in February, and setting sail from Galapagos to the Marquesas in March. Once again, my concerns were caused by the possible effects of El Niño on weather conditions in the South Pacific Ocean, when during an El Niño episode there is a higher probability of a late cyclone in the eastern South Pacific. All participants agreed that an early arrival in French Polynesia was not advisable and the schedule was delayed, with a transit of the Panama Canal in April and a start from Galapagos in early May. As a result, they had excellent

winds on the 3,000-mile passage to the Marquesas, which the first boat, an Outremer 51 catamaran, covered in 15 days, and even the last, a Najad 36, in a remarkable 22 days.

Atlantic Odyssey, North Atlantic Ocean
November 2016-January 2017

Ever since I launched the first ARC in 1986, my rallies, whether transatlantic or around the world, have been a valuable source of information on offshore weather conditions. In the new series of transatlantic rallies that I initiated in 2013, some started from Lanzarote, Tenerife or La Palma in the Canaries, others from São Vicente in the Cape Verde Islands. Some finished in Martinique, others in Grenada or Barbados. Some started in November, while others set off in January. As a result, they provided a good overview of weather conditions for passages to the Caribbean in early- or mid-winter. Every rally seems to have encountered different weather conditions, from consistent trade winds to light winds and long periods of calms. The obvious conclusion was that the effects of climate change on ocean passages were become increasingly visible, and the days when you could confidently expect consistent trade winds on a winter crossing from the Canaries to the Caribbean may be a thing of the past.

Climate change

Much has been written about this phenomenon and few sailors would disagree that global weather conditions appear to be undergoing a radical change. This is also the irrefutable conclusion of the recently published report of the Intergovernmental Panel on Climate Change. Its main conclusion is that the warming of the climate system is unequivocal. The atmosphere and oceans have warmed, the amounts of snow and ice have diminished, sea levels are rising, and the concentrations of greenhouse gases have increased.

There are still many, including some scientists, who refuse to accept that climate change is a direct result of human activity, insisting that it is a cyclic phenomenon that has occurred repeatedly in the history of the planet. This was an argument raised at some of the presentations that I held while promoting the Blue Planet Odyssey round-the-world rally. My answer was always the same: as far as we sailors are concerned, climate change is happening, and whether it is the result of human activity or a natural phenomenon is an irrelevant argument. What really matters is that global weather conditions are changing.

Some of the changes are becoming increasingly evident: the Arctic icecap is melting at an unprecedented rate, the Northwest Passage has been free of ice for several summers, extra-seasonal tropical storms are more common, and the tropical-storm seasons themselves are less clearly defined and becoming more active.

Tropical storms have affected areas where they had never occurred before. In the South Pacific the cyclone seasons now last longer than in the past, and in the Coral Sea extra-seasonal cyclones have been recorded as late as June and even July. In the Northwest Pacific both the frequency and force of the typhoons is on the increase, with some super-typhoons having gusts of close to 200 knots. In recent years, typhoons have been recorded in every month of the year, with a well-defined safe season now sadly a thing of the past.

My personal concern for the state of the oceans is supported by my own observations during four decades of roaming the world, as I noticed the disastrous effects of climate change in places like Tuvalu, which faces the threat of disappearing before the end of this century, and witnessed the death of coral reefs in the tropics, visible changes in Antarctica between my two visits there, and the absence of steady trade winds even on previously reliable routes. My one-season transit of the Northwest Passage was only possible due to climate change.

Looking at all this from the point of view of a sailor, I believe it is no longer acceptable to deny that there has been a significant change in weather patterns during the last decades. Although some people still refuse to take notice of what scientists and meteorologists have been saying for many years, weather patterns are changing and there is no longer any excuse for not taking these warnings seriously. This affects sailors perhaps more than anyone else, so we need to take heed and be even more cautious when planning a voyage.

Aventura IV's Northwest Passage route and the extent of the shrinking of the polar icecap

Carpe diem

The lovely thing about cruising is that planning usually turns out to be of little use.

Dom Degnon

I started this book by stating: 'One of the first lessons I learned early in my cruising life was the importance of having a well-thought-out voyage plan. A second lesson was the willingness to abandon that plan should a more attractive alternative present itself.' And this is how I want to end this chapter on voyage planning. I have come across too many examples of people who were stuck with a predefined plan and were unwilling or perhaps unable to see the wisdom or attraction of a possibly better alternative. For me the greatest pleasure in sailing is being on passage, sailing for days on end; enjoying the solitude, the wildlife and the ocean at its best and, occasionally, at its worst. In such moments, the destination is of no importance and the only thing that matters is the here and now.

Never forget that you are an intruder on the oceans of the world. Respect all life forms for whom the sea is their home.

Bill Butler

Tips

» Use small-scale paper charts for passage planning to have a proper overview of the ocean area to be crossed, of dangers to avoid, of island groups close to the chosen route, and of possible alternative routes.

» Consult seasonal data along the proposed route: tropical-storm seasons, storm tracks and frequency, probability of extra-seasonal storms.

» Consult up-to-date pilot charts that synthesise meteorological observations over long periods of time.

» There is a certain value in researching archival material when planning a voyage.

8

Navigation in the age of electronic charts

The wind and the waves are always on the side of the ablest navigator.

Edward Gibbon

One essential aid to navigation that has made cruising not only safer but also much more enjoyable is electronic charts. For a time I resisted their temptation because over the years I had acquired a vast collection of paper charts that cover the entire world. Although most of my old charts are out of date, and allowances have to be made to match them with GPS data, they can still be used, especially on offshore passages. The best way to describe my attitude to this important subject is to call it old-fashioned. Having completed a first circumnavigation with a sextant and paper charts, I still find such charts useful for route planning and offshore navigation. The main reason, however, for my reluctance to move with the times was that I felt that in offshore navigation paper charts were more user-friendly as they provided a general picture of a passage, and both myself and my crew enjoyed watching the daily positions creep slowly towards our destination. At a recent seminar, I had great pleasure in showing my chart of the eastern South Pacific, crisscrossed with the lines of positions of my four previous passages through that area.

But even if sometimes reluctantly, I do attempt to move with the times, and am extremely happy to take advantage of the amazing progress made in what I am pleased to see are aptly described as 'aids' to navigation. On offshore passages I still mark the latest noon position on a small-scale chart, a leftover from my early cruising days when the daily noon sight was always something to look forward to.

That routine was followed religiously every day, with one sight just before the sun crossed the local meridian followed by another sight soon after the sun started its slow descent. Those two sights were the most important of the day, as a simple calculation allowed me to work out both latitude and longitude. I have followed this noon routine throughout my sailing life, although nowadays I simply plot the latest noon position from the GPS. The distance run from noon to noon is announced to the crew, and then it's time for lunch. Those early noon sights had played such an important role in our life that, at Ivan's suggestion, we named the website we created noonsite.com.

However, there is an obvious drawback to using old paper charts, and this is their possible inaccuracy. Whereas in more frequented areas, both paper and electronic charts have been brought up to date to accord with GPS, in some remote areas charts are rarely corrected, nor do they tally with GPS positions. This should not be a serious handicap: not expecting charts to be entirely accurate forces me to keep alert all the time. As I stress in the chapter discussing safety, the conviction that you know exactly where you are can be quite dangerous, and I know of several boat losses caused by such overreliance on GPS.

Having been struck by lightning four times, of which three times were in a span of only 17 days, I am a real advocate of using paper charts... Or at the least to carry the essential charts as a backup.

Michelle LaMontagne

On the day we left Vava'u for Fiji on Aventura III, I heard on the radio of an incident that highlighted the limitations of modern navigation systems. A boat sailing the same route as us had been struck by lightning and had lost its computer and everything that was stored on it. The situation was exacerbated by the fact that the boat used only electronic charts for navigation and wasn't carrying any paper charts. The crew were unable to plot a course through the reef-infested waters they needed to cross to reach a port in Fiji. Fortunately they managed to get their radio to work so other sailors came to their assistance by giving them a series of waypoints. They were thus able to follow them on a handheld GPS that luckily had not been obliterated by the lightning strike, which had destroyed the rest of their electronic equipment. Electronic charts are undoubtedly a great improvement, but incidents such as this make me continue in my old-fashioned habit of always carrying some essential paper charts as a backup.

To follow up on a survey I had done on overreliance on GPS, I decided to find out from some of my cruising friends who were using electronic charts if they were aware of other drawbacks. The first to reply was a former radio-net controller for the western Caribbean who confirmed that many cruisers sailed without any paper charts. He gave the example of a boat that broke into his radio net, stating that they were in heavy seas and needed a GPS position to find an anchorage along the coast of Nicaragua. They were in gale-force winds and had been knocked down. Their computer had hit the floor and been put out of action. They had no paper charts and were desperate. The net controller provided the GPS coordinates, and they managed to find shelter in an anchorage off Media Luna Reef.

Anchored behind the reef in Chagos

Moving with the times

The same reef played a role in another incident, which also highlighted the limitations of electronic charts. It involved a boat that went aground on Media Luna Reef while sailing from the island of San Andres towards Honduras. The crew were convinced that they had hit an uncharted reef. Their statement made over the radio net that they had hit an uncharted reef caused great anxiety among other sailors cruising in that area. Some of them spent hours poring over their charts while comparing paper and electronic charts. Eventually they established that inaccuracies could occur when zooming in from a higher to a lower level of some electronic charts. The mystery of the stranded boat was cleared up when it became apparent that, according to its GPS position, the boat appeared to be indeed safely offshore, while the same coordinates showed that on the zoomed-in chart it was right in the middle of the reef. This seemed to be caused by an error that can occur when charts are scanned and the chart is not perfectly aligned. Fortunately the tale had a happy ending, as after spending 24 hours on the reef, the stranded boat was rescued by the US Coast Guard and the boat was not seriously damaged.

One sailor responded to my survey by giving as an example the stranding of a boat that arrived in Chagos in the dark and drove onto a reef about 0.3 miles from the pass. The crew realised later that the electronic chart they were using needed a correction for the specific chart of Chagos. Fortunately it was a steel boat and it managed to come off with only superficial damage.

A practice that I became aware of while conducting this survey was the fact that a number of sailors appeared to use unauthorised copies of some electronic charts. Apart from the fact that such pirated copies are illegal, their use can also have grave consequences as they are never corrected, whereas electronic charts bought through the normal channels are regularly updated by their manufacturers or distributors.

Over the last four decades, offshore navigation has taken bigger strides than in the previous four centuries. The first Aventura's navigation system was quite rudimentary as I only had a sextant, a radio direction finder (RDF) and a depth sounder. Aventura II's system was a great improvement as by the late 1980s Transit, the first satellite navigation system, had come into use and profoundly revolutionised the art of navigation. I also had a radar and integrated instrumentation so life indeed became much easier. Aventura III was even better equipped, having the full range of Brookes & Gatehouse instrumentation and autopilot, GPS, radar, forward-looking sonar, SSB radio, Iridium satellite phone and Inmarsat C. Not surprisingly, Aventura IV was even better equipped, with a full range of Brookes & Gatehouse instrumentation, two autopilots, radar, AIS, forward-looking sonar, Iridium Pilot and SSB radio.

Throughout Aventura IV's voyage I used C-map electronic charts produced by Jeppesen. I found their accuracy to be quite remarkable wherever we sailed, not just in such well-charted areas as the waters of the UK or USA, but even in the remote Arctic areas of Greenland and Canada.

While we relied on electronic charts for navigation, I still carried small-scale paper charts for the entire route, as well as the entire set of detailed charts for the Northwest Passage. Old habits die hard.

Bahamas, December 2014
Having spent Christmas with Gwenda and my crew Dunbar on Aventura IV at Marsh Harbour on Great Abaco Island, on 26 December we resumed our voyage bound for Key West. We reached the open ocean via the Man O'War Pass and set a course for the Northwest Channel and the Great Bahama Bank, which I planned to cross the following day. Suddenly the entire B&G system crashed, the autopilot froze and all screens went blank. I tried to restart the system, but nothing happened. As we were well offshore and in no immediate

danger, I gave Dunbar an approximate compass course to steer, and went below to find the paper chart for the area. Unfortunately it wasn't detailed enough to navigate those intricate waters, so I decided to take the safe deep-water route via the Northeast Providence Channel and reach Florida that way. Just as suddenly as the system had gone off, it came on again and started working as if nothing had happened. Indeed it continued working without a hitch, so we reverted to the original plan, crossed the Great Bahama Bank and reached our destination safely.

I was not able to find the reason for that total blackout, nor could B&G when I contacted them later. But it certainly shook my confidence in relying entirely on electronic navigation, and made me worry about what would have happened if it had occurred not in the open sea but in a more difficult area, possibly at night.

Accuracy of electronic charts

Northwest Passage, August 2015

In some remote areas even the latest electronic charts may be based on older inaccurate paper charts that may not have been updated for years. I came across such a discrepancy in summer 2015 when the latest Canadian paper charts for the Northwest Passage were grossly inaccurate on at least a couple of occasions. From a navigational point of view, the most difficult stretch of the Northwest Passage is between Cambridge Bay and Gjoa Haven. This is a poorly surveyed area of shallows and submerged rocks, with many blank areas on the Canadian paper charts, where I was amused to read: 'The magnetic compass is useless in this area.' Being very close to the magnetic north, the compass did indeed behave in an erratic manner and was entirely unreliable, so we used a GPS-based compass instead. The warning 'Positions on the chart may be in error by as much as 5 miles' was no exaggeration either, because at one point we found ourselves in very shallow waters, and suspected that we were about 6 miles off our

presumed position. Having learned my navigation long before the days of GPS, I managed to plot our position on the paper chart by taking bearings with the hand-held compass of three conspicuous land features. The intersecting lines gave us a fix which showed clearly that we had indeed strayed dangerously off the safe course. In this case the paper and electronic charts were both wrong.

South Indian Ocean, November 2014

During the night of 29 November 2014, the yacht Vestas Wind, taking part in the Volvo round-the-world race and bound for Abu Dhabi, ran aground on the Cargados Carajos Shoal, 240 miles northeast of Mauritius. The subsequent investigation established that both the captain and the navigator had wrongly presumed that the minimum depth in that area was 40 metres and had not zoomed in further on the electronic chart to actually see the shoal. The nine-man crew stepped off the stranded yacht onto the reef and were later rescued. Eventually, so was the damaged yacht.

These were the comments of Elaine Bunting, editor of Yachting World magazine: 'My guess is almost certain that this happened for the same age-old reason: the crew were sure they were where they were not... The biggest danger is certainty.'

When I heard about the Vestas Wind grounding, I remembered my own passage through that area on Aventura III. Having spent an enjoyable sojourn in Chagos, I realised that a tropical depression forming to the southeast of the area might result in a favourable angle to the southeast trade winds. Rather than miss

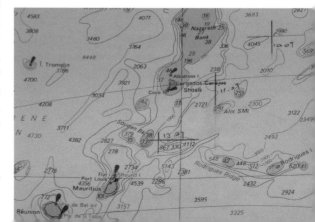

Paper chart of Aventura III's route

this fortunate opportunity to have good winds on the notoriously closehauled passage to Mauritius, I decided to leave immediately, to the visible disappointment of the friend sailing with me. Being very much aware of the infamous shoals lying almost astride of our course, I set a cautious course to pass well to the east of them. After the news of the Vestas incident, I found my own chart for that passage and noticed the careful course I had plotted to pass well clear of that notorious area.

For this to happen to a fully-crewed yacht brimming with state-of-the-art navigation equipment is unforgivable. A very similar incident to that of Vestas Wind occurred in 2010 in another round-the-world race, when the Clipper Ventures yacht Cork was lost at night on the Gosong Mampango Reef in the Java Sea. The reef is close to a mile off its charted position, and while this warning was printed on paper charts it did not appear on their electronic equivalent.

While sailing in the Tuamotus on Aventura III, not called the Dangerous Archipelago for nothing, I also found the latest paper charts, which I had bought for that trip, to be often inaccurate. In one instance, the chart of Makemo Atoll was not only totally inaccurate but the western pass into the lagoon did not agree with its charted location by over three miles. This was no exception, as in many parts of the world the charted position of some reefs and even islands is still inaccurate. Satellite observations have allowed hydrographers to accurately plot the actual position of such dangers. As a result, most charts have been corrected to the WGS (World Geodetic System) 84 datum, which is the reference coordinate system used by the Global Positioning System. It was introduced in 1984 and last updated in 2004, and older charts may still need to be checked and updated manually. Paper charts normally show all relevant dangers that may not appear on electronic charts. The problem with electronic charts is that they show different amounts of detail at different zoom levels, as in the case of the Vestas incident.

On our way south from the Tuamotus, we made landfall on Tahiti's north coast and Gwenda noticed that the beautiful engraved chart I was using to navigate in coastal waters had been printed in 1862. In spite of its age it was still reasonably accurate. It is quite likely that it was based on Lieutenant James Cook's original drawings, when he visited this same area to observe the transit of Venus in 1769. The three-year expedition on the Endeavour, his first voyage into the Pacific, rates as one of the most significant journeys of European exploration. The rare transit of the planet Venus was used to calculate the distance from the earth to the Sun.

Hard landings

Even Captain Cook's navigation skills, or perhaps just his luck, failed him on a few occasions, so it shouldn't be surprising that in all the miles that I have sailed over the years I ended up in some difficult situations myself.

Caicos Bank, February 1978
As mentioned on page 62, my first Aventura was nearly lost when she ran aground on a coral head on the edge of the Caicos Bank. We had sailed across from Grand Turk and, as we moved from a deep channel into the shallow waters of the bank, a passing cloud obscured the sun completely reducing the visibility ahead of us. We eventually came off on the rising tide, but it had been a narrow escape.

Chesapeake, USA, October 1978
On our way south from New York bound for Annapolis, we passed through the Chesapeake & Delaware Canal.

On a pilgrimage with Aventura III anchored close to the spot where we had run aground 25 years earlier

Having been slowed down by the tide, by the time it got dark we couldn't find any shelter for the night, so had no choice but to continue. As the breeze started getting stronger around midnight, I realised that we needed to stop somewhere. I had a chart of the area, the lights were clearly marked on it, so we prepared to enter the long channel that led into Annapolis Harbour. I identified the red light flashing every 2 seconds that marked the outer approaches and, believing it to be the right place, I told Gwenda to head for it. As we passed close to the buoy, we touched the bottom and then ran firmly aground right next to the light. Aventura started shaking and banging in the swell, the rigging making a horrible noise that sounded much worse than the situation probably was. I tried to back down at full revs but we were stuck in the soft mud. My hope was that we were not in serious danger, as, after the hard grounding in Caicos, I knew that Aventura's strong hull should be able to survive this less threatening ordeal.

To my surprise, we were so far inshore that a busy road was running only some 200 metres away. I checked the chart and realised that we must have run aground somewhere different from where I thought we were, and certainly nowhere near Annapolis. A driver appeared to realise our predicament, as he flashed his lights repeatedly, which I understood as meaning he was going to call for help. This is what he must have done, because a quarter of an hour later, a small US Coastguard launch headed for us, but when the officer realised that we were in very shallow waters, he stopped short and called us on his loudhailer. As we did not have a VHF radio, communication had to be carried out in this way. He first went through a lengthy procedure of identifying our boat, home port, number of people on board and a host of other – to me – irrelevant questions. Finally, he said that he would try to tow us out, but as he did not have a tender and there was no way he could get any closer, I shouted across that I would swim across with a long line, an offer which he vehemently opposed. I ignored him, tied the end of a line around my waist and dove overboard. I reached the launch, handed one end of the rope to the crew and swam back to Aventura. While still a few metres short of Aventura's stern, my rope came to an end and, as Aventura only drew five feet and I could stand in the soft mud, I asked Gwenda to hand me another rope to make up the difference. With a violent jerk, the line tied round my waist tightened and I felt myself being yanked away. Obviously the officer had presumed that I had secured the line and that we were ready to be towed off. While I was bodysurfing at great speed through the warm water, the skipper must have realised that the rope could not have been attached to Aventura so he stopped the launch and the crew looked flabbergasted when I surfaced spluttering at their side. I told them what had happened and asked them to repeat the operation, ensuring they give me enough time to secure my own end of the rope to Aventura. I made my way back and attached the line to a cleat.

Meanwhile, a second USCG launch had arrived on the scene and was standing by. I shouted across to our helpful friends to start pulling. However hard they tried nothing seemed to happen, until I saw the line go slack and… someone shouted across that they had got my line around their propeller! So now we had two stranded boats with the wind steadily increasing, and a Coastguard officer whose very red face I almost believed I could see shining through the dark. The incoming tide eventually came to our aid, allowing me to slowly back off the bank. I motored over to the stranded launch to thank the officer.

'Nothing to worry about, we'll come off soon as well. You just proceed into Annapolis. The entrance is about half a mile over there. Make sure you come to our office in the morning to sign a report and retrieve your line.'

I found the proper entrance this time and was puzzled to see that it was also marked by a red light flashing every 2 seconds. I realised that the strong tide had carried us south and I had picked up the wrong set of lights. We anchored in the inner harbour, and as soon as it got light I donned my mask and had a quick look at the hull. There didn't seem to be any damage, although later I found that the repeated pounding on the grounded rudder had caused the hydraulic steering ram to be bent, so it had to be replaced.

In the morning I made my way to the USCG office overlooking the attractive Annapolis Bay. A different officer received me because our saviours had finished their shift. He told me that they had managed to come off soon after we had left, and handed me the neatly coiled rope.

'Tell me officer, why do you have lights with the same characteristics so close to each other?'

'Good question,' he replied, 'but I don't really know the answer. Maybe the bosses had bought a whole identical batch. All I know is that it seems to cause a lot of confusion, as you are not the first boat to have made this mistake.'

At least I had a reasonable excuse for my navigational error, but I was still puzzled by such an example of incomprehensible bureaucracy.

Bali, July 2004

We had benign weather conditions for the 1,000-mile passage on Aventura III from Darwin to Bali across the Arafura and Timor Seas, which gave us one week of glorious sailing, all of it under spinnaker. The only hiccup occurred right at the end when a strong contrary current slowed us down, so that it was already dark by the time we arrived off the entrance channel into Benoa Harbour.

Having been in and out of the small port on several occasions, I decided to attempt to enter immediately rather than spend the night outside. I lined up the boat with the leading lights and moved slowly forward, but something didn't seem right... and suddenly the forward-looking sonar showed shallow water right in front of us. I quickly swung the wheel to port, but it was too late and we touched the bottom lightly with the centreboard, the slight impact pushing the board up. One quick look around showed that the current had pushed us out of the approach channel and we had barely avoided running seriously aground. I now knew

Traditional canoes lined up on the bank overlooking Benoa's entrance channel

exactly where we were and realised what had got me into trouble: the fact that I thought I knew where I was. It is something that has got many other navigators into serious trouble and could have had grave consequences also for me, as will become clear from the following examples.

Sardinia, April 2006

A more serious mistake happened on a night passage on Aventura III between Sardinia and Tunisia. Having left from the island's west coast, we followed the coast closely to its southwest corner, which we had to clear before being able to set a course for Tunisia. I had checked the route on both my paper and electronic charts, and there were no dangers close to our course. It was a clear night, Aventura was sailing beautifully and I was ticking off the navigation lights as we passed them. Before turning the corner we had to pass between an islet and the main island, and as there seemed to be clear water between, I readjusted the autopilot to steer for the middle of the narrow gap. As the rocky islet loomed out of the dark to starboard I suddenly glimpsed a dark shape right ahead of me. I dashed to the wheel, disengaged the autopilot and turned the wheel sharply to port. From the corner of my eye I saw a rocky pinnacle surrounded by frothing water that we passed by only a few metres. It all happened so quickly that I hadn't even had time to worry – or breathe. With the boat sailing at 6 knots, if I had not taken that avoiding action we would have hit the rock square on and I doubt that even Aventura III's strong hull would have escaped unscathed. And all this close to the end of my third round-the-world voyage! How could I have been so careless?

Later, I had a closer look at the paper chart. I hasten to add that it was not an old chart but the most recent one, which I had bought for this very occasion. As I examined the area we had just passed, I saw that in the narrow gap between the main island and the off-lying islet there was indeed a tiny blob but, as it was almost entirely obscured by some writing, I had not noticed the rock itself. This was also confirmed by the electronic chart when I zoomed in. Worse still, before going off watch, Gwenda had told me that I should look out for a dangerous rock that lay close to our course and I had reassured her that I certainly would be careful, imagining that she had meant the off-lying islet, not some other rock. I had committed a gross error, but being on watch and also quite vigilant had saved us. It was an unforgivable mistake and, in fact, my worst-ever navigational error.

GPS: a false sense of security?

The danger I see is that more and more cruisers rely blindly on GPS navigation.

Luc Callebaut

Two months after leaving Ecuador, Aventura III was tethered to a pontoon at the Tahiti Yacht Club. This

Ancient site on the stretch of coast we passed during the night

was the fourth time I had come to Tahiti on my own boat, but this time the satisfaction of just being there was accompanied by a sense of relief after the anxious moments we had experienced in the Tuamotus. Although we were never in any danger, there had been times when things could have gone worse and I agreed with Gwenda that cruising the Dangerous Archipelago demanded a high price and was definitely not for the faint-hearted. We had avoided the Tuamotus on our previous trips, initially by force, as in the 1970s much of the area was out of bounds because of the French nuclear tests, or by choice, preferring to spend longer in the Marquesas or Gambiers.

We were certainly not alone, as many of the boats that we encountered in the Society Islands had stopped at the Tuamotus en route to Tahiti. Over the radio, and from people we met, we were hearing stories of boats getting into trouble, and it made me wonder if perhaps GPS was to blame for giving navigators a false sense of security. My friend Antti Louhija, who earlier had sailed with me from Ecuador to the Marquesas, had answered the question already. While in the Red Sea, 600 miles short of completing his circumnavigation, Antti lost his 36-foot Pegasos on a reef off the coast of Sudan. In his own words:
'During the darkness of a moonless night we hit a coral reef 40 miles offshore. We had been heading for a GPS waypoint and the course had been laid so as to bypass by two miles the islet of Barra Musa Kebir and its off-lying reef. We struck the reef where it should not have been, and the boat was a total loss. Luckily nobody on board was hurt. GPS is a wonderful tool but do not trust the charts.'

You've got to be very careful if you don't know where you are going, because you might not get there.

Yogi Berra

In my own experience as a rally organiser I had witnessed several instances when boats were damaged or lost due to a navigational error caused by being overreliant on GPS. The worst case was that of a delivery crew who ran their boat onto the east coast of Barbados, having set their landfall waypoint in the approaches to Bridgetown Harbour, which happens to be on the opposite side of the island.

The more I thought about such incidents, the more came to mind, so I decided to widen the scope of my enquiry and contact friends sailing in other oceans. My ad-hoc poll by email brought forth a host of incidents, with entering an unfamiliar port or anchorage at night being one of the principal causes. In some cases the problem was compounded when GPS was used in conjunction with the autopilot, and the navigator relied slavishly on both. I remember sailing on a friend's boat from Crosshaven to Kinsale in Southern Ireland. It was a bright clear day with no wind, and we were motoring under autopilot. We seemed to take a long way round a headland and I asked my friend why he didn't cut the corner, as there were no dangers closer inshore. He told me that he had already pre-programmed a route to the next port and didn't want to interfere with the autopilot as it was doing such an excellent job.

Sailing to a waypoint, often on autopilot, and not keeping a proper watch appears to be the most common cause of groundings, and one of my correspondents mentioned the case of a French yacht that had run aground and was lost at Cayo Holandes in the San Blas Islands. Apparently the captain had tried to find his way at night into an anchorage solely by GPS, relying on his electronic charts and the waypoints someone else had given him. This incident reconfirmed the fact that even the latest electronic charts for some parts of the world, the San Blas included, may be inaccurate, especially if they have not been updated, and thus do

Lovely anchorage in San Blas but only to be entered in daylight and with good visibility

not entirely agree with current GPS positions. This is the reason why the landfall waypoints listed in World Cruising Routes are set at a safe distance offshore because I don't want anyone to take that term 'landfall' too literally. Unfortunately some navigators do, and one of the first to reply to my survey was Nick Wardle of the Bahamas Search and Rescue Association (BASRA), who described the case of a large motor yacht whose captain went for a nap and asked the mate to set a waypoint for the Northwest Providence Channel light. The mate did such a good job of making for that waypoint that he actually crashed into the light, the large tower landing on their foredeck.

In the late 1970s I conducted a survey on the causes of boat losses in the South Pacific, of which there seemed to be quite a high number in those days. Just by talking to sailors whom I had met while cruising I compiled a list of 50 total losses, most of which had been caused by navigational errors. A similar survey conducted nearly 30 years later did not produce even a quarter of that number, so there is no doubt that cruising has become much safer thanks to GPS. Nevertheless, there are still many situations in which

this magnificent tool has its limitations, and the safety of ship and crew depend ultimately on a high degree of vigilance at all times.

Tips

» In remote areas regard all charts, whether paper or electronic, with caution.

» Never sail to a waypoint without keeping a good lookout.

» Never set a landfall waypoint that is not at a safe offshore distance from the intended destination.

» Avoid entering an unknown port or anchorage at night.

» Resist overreliance on GPS.

» If in any doubt when approaching landfall, slow down, double-check your position, and only proceed to your waypoint if absolutely certain that you know where you are.

» In remote areas where charts are suspected of being inaccurate, it may be advisable to refer to Google Earth images and use them in conjunction with electronic charts.

9

Destination Antarctica

Antarctica is more than an addiction; it's almost a curse. You'll be back!

Skip Novak

Skip was right because three years after my Antarctic cruise on Pelagic I was back, but this time on my own boat. The prospect of several weeks of sailing in the ice had persuaded Gwenda to stay at home. But when Ivan heard of my plans, not only to sail to Antarctica, but also to continue from there all the way to Alaska, he quit his job as systems manager at a film postproduction company in London to accompany me. We were also joined by Erick and Muriel Bouteleux. This voyage to Antarctica had been on the books even before Aventura III had been launched, so the trip to the frozen continent was planned as her proper baptism, albeit by ice rather than fire.

Aventura's voyage south from the Canaries to the Cape Verdes, Brazil, Argentina, Falklands and finally Patagonia, along with several Millennium Odyssey boats, had gone according to plan and, like the dozen or so boats that sail to Antarctica at the start of the southern summer, we made the last preparations for the 600-mile passage to Antarctica in Puerto Williams. The main role of this small port set on the southern shore of the Beagle Channel continues to be that of a military base, with little interest in tourism or foreign visitors. As Chile continues to claim a large wedge of ocean to the south, which includes both Horn and the surrounding islands as well as much of the Antarctic Peninsula, yachts planning to visit the latter have to clear in and out of Puerto Williams. This is a base for the Chilean Navy, but as the bitter dispute with Argentina over the Beagle Channel has been settled, its military role is mostly symbolic. Apart from priding itself on being the southernmost settlement in the world, its only other claim to fame is a strange monument consisting of the cut-off bows of the M.V. Yelcho, commemorating the rescue of Ernest Shackleton's crew by the Chilean Navy in 1916. A recent wreck, that of the auxiliary ship Micalvi, has been put to more practical use as a yacht club of sorts. The walls of its bar are adorned with mementoes from the Antarctic yachts whose crews never fail to stop here for a Pisco sour on the way to or from the frozen continent.

Less than 60 miles from Cape Horn, Puerto Williams is an excellent place to wait for a favourable forecast to cross the Drake Passage, and the best time to head south is on the back of a depression, as usually the winds veer gradually from west to northeast. With Aventura fully provisioned for a voyage of four weeks, we didn't have long to wait before I deemed the time to be right to head south. One valuable lesson I had learned from my previous trip was that in this part of the world if conditions look reasonably good, you go. I set a course straight across the Drake Passage and as we sailed south past Cape Horn under spinnaker, my only concern was to get south of latitude 60°S as quickly as possible. A large and vicious-looking low was building west of Cape Horn, and, as I followed closely the twice-daily weatherfax transmissions from the Chilean meteorological office in Valparaiso, it became obvious that, as usually happens, the low would track right through the middle of Drake Passage. By hurrying south at the right moment, we had the benefit of good winds all the way and made a satisfyingly fast passage to Deception Island, off the tip of the Antarctic Peninsula.

On the fourth morning after our departure, we had covered over 400 miles and were sailing fast on a beam reach. Aventura was surrounded by lots of birds: storm petrels, Mother Carey's chickens, Cape pigeons (also known as painted petrels), the back of their wings akin to a checkerboard, and the first wandering albatross. It was such an overwhelming feeling to be sailing in glorious weather several hundred miles south of Cape Horn.

Fifty miles from land we met the first icebergs, but the visibility was so good we could easily avoid them. By mid-morning we were closing with the land and were met by three humpback whales sounding together for krill. The Antarctic Peninsula was by now clearly visible, as were its surrounding mountain ranges. The view all around us was truly spectacular. Several blue icebergs stood out against the blinding-white background of the snow-clad mountains. Lots of gentoo penguins were diving in close formation ahead of us. We passed seals and more penguins sunning themselves on smaller icebergs floating by, then glided silently past a large glacier calving a string of small bergs. A stunningly beautiful introduction to an amazing world!

The crossing of the 600-mile-wide Drake Passage had shown Aventura III at her best, as we rarely sailed below seven knots and managed to keep pace with our nearest rival, the American Risqué, a new Swan 57 sailed with a crack crew of eight compared to our modest crew of four. Our secret weapon was Erick, who had sailed in his native port of Le Havre virtually before he could walk and, having been involved with OVNI yachts for many years, knew these boats better than anyone else. Not only did he manage to get the best out of Aventura but whenever something broke, as it does more often when he is around and pushes the boat harder than me, I just smile slyly and let Erick fix it.

Deception Island 62°57'S, 60°38'W

Discovered in 1802 by the explorer Bransfield, who must have been very disappointed by what he found when he named it, Deception Island is a fascinating place. This horseshoe-shaped island is the partly submerged caldera of an active volcano, which last erupted in 1991, and its unique landscape of barren volcanic slopes, steaming beaches and timeworn glaciers is covered in a thick layer of black lava dust. A narrow channel, called Neptune's Bellow, leads into the circular harbour. It is one of the few places in the world where a ship can sail into the flooded crater of a restless volcano. As we made our way in, the wind funnelled through the narrow entrance channel, justifying its inspired name, and we were rocked and pushed sideways by violent

gusts as if Neptune were having fun at our expense, pumping his bellows. Expecting to be caught by that threatening depression we moved into the innermost anchorage at Telefon Bay. By the time the strong winds from the passing depression had arrived, we were safely tucked in the northwest corner of the submerged crater.

The strong winds lasted only one night, and in the morning we went looking for a famous warm-water volcanic spring that gushes up near the shore. Watching closely the cockpit display showing the temperature of the sea water, I saw it steadily climbing from 5°C to 12°C, settling finally at an amazing 18°C. With a mighty glacier nearby on the shore, it was almost impossible to believe that my instruments were telling the truth, but they were, and we had the proof when we dipped our feet in the water.

Further along, we came across the derelict site of an abandoned Norwegian whale-processing factory. The huge machinery was strewn all over the black land while in front of a building stood the remnants of a small spotter airplane with all its windows broken. We had the entire place to ourselves and spent all morning walking around the ruins that reminded us of those grim whaling days.

Deception Island is a good starting point for a cruise along the Antarctic Peninsula. We started our trip along its western shore and the many off-lying islands, an area with good protection and plenty of sheltered anchorages. As on my previous visit, I was overwhelmed by the sublime scenery and the richness of the wildlife. But these were only secondary reasons for my addiction, as beyond all that natural beauty, for me Antarctica's main attraction is the overpowering feeling of being a witness to a pristine world hardly touched by man, of being part of something that has remained virtually unchanged for tens of thousands of years.

Love at first sight

The scenery of Antarctica takes centre stage, and rightly so, but the wildlife is equally attractive. Because the animals have no fear of man, it is possible to observe them at close quarters without interfering with their daily life. We stopped at penguin colonies almost every day, but to see other animals we sometimes had to go out of our way. From my previous visit I remembered a large elephant seal colony and, very close to it, a large number of giant petrels' nests. I retraced our route from three years previously, anchored in the same spot and went ashore. I had expected the petrels to be still there, but was quite surprised to see instead the beach heaving with massive blubbery shapes.

There were at least 20 elephant seals stretched out lazily in total abandonment, and the first impression that sprung to mind was that even pigs couldn't have looked happier lolling about in their own smelly mess. They were all young males, quite clearly bonding as single blokes do and enjoying a carefree summer vacation before family responsibilities put an end to their hedonistic existence. The master of the congregation, a huge bull probably weighing in excess of a ton, was lying on his own, right by the water's edge, and growled at me unconvincingly when I stopped to take his photograph. Only later, when I had a close look at the result, did I realise that my own image was perfectly reflected in his large eyes.

Leaving the elephant seals to revert to their rudely interrupted siesta, we climbed up a glacier and reached the bare summit of a hill, where scores of giant petrels had their abode. Most had a young chick in the nest, but what was surprising was that at almost every nest there was also a young adult, which was last year's offspring. Apparently young petrels are not keen to face the problems of the outside world and prefer to prolong their adolescence by staying with mummy and daddy. Their indulging parents seem happy with this arrangement and continue to provide them with food and lodging even when the youngsters have reached the size of adults, as in the case of some urban two-legged late starters. Like many city teenagers, they were also badly behaved and rude to strangers, receiving us with shrieks and aggressive gestures, true bullies in the making. We didn't dare go too close, as I had been warned that these petrels tend to spit at intruders, their saliva being slightly venomous. It sounded quite improbable, but we kept our distance nevertheless, just as most of us wise oldies do when faced with a similar situation back home.

Danco Island 64°44'S, 62°37'W

We arrived at Danco Island in brilliant sunshine with a blue sky. The island was named after Emile Danco, a geophysicist who died here during the Belgian expedition led by the explorer Adrien de Gerlache in the closing days of the 19th century. With our large inflatable dinghy we started exploring the immediate area, and close by, on a tiny islet, we found the remains of several small whaling boats. Before all whaling and fishing activities were banned south of the Antarctic Circle, this area had been frequently visited by whalers during the Antarctic summer. Also on Danco Island is an old cabin belonging to the British Antarctic Survey. The unoccupied wooden hut is still maintained as an emergency shelter for scientists and has a reserve of tinned food. Later we came across several such food depots, set in prominent places and marked by a perch, which would provide survival rations to anyone lost in this wilderness.

Ivan and I climbed to the top of the 200-metre-high island to visit an amazing penguin colony. There were thousands of gentoo penguins all the way to the summit. Penguins need bare soil or rock for their colonies, and as such places are difficult to find on the ice-covered islands, they were prepared to climb quite high to find a suitable nesting place. The adults were in continuous motion, waddling up and down the mountain. To reach the sea they would slide down on their backs through the snow, and there were several parallel shiny grooves from the top of the island to the shoreline. By late afternoon there was a procession of penguins coming home to feed their chicks – a proper commuter traffic at the end of the working day. It was intriguing to see how the parents recognised their own offspring from among a mass of identical-looking balls of fluff. The parent gave a cry, which attracted a response from several chicks, but the adult penguin ignored them and went straight to his or her own, pushing the pretenders out of the way. The lucky chick stretched its head straight up and opened its beak wide, while the parent pushed its own beak in as far as it would go and disgorged a half-digested lump of krill. Watching the daily life in a penguin colony is one of the most fascinating activities in Antarctica and I could never get enough of it.

proved to be the best answer to local conditions: rocky ground interspersed with patches of mud. Across the sound, snowy peaks of the Antarctic Peninsula reared up giddily either side of a mighty glacier. Countless icebergs that it had calved were littered about, grounded in shallow water. Two icebergs, slightly larger than Aventura, had parked themselves close by during the night, their powder blue mass almost transparent in the brilliant sunshine. It was one of those Antarctic mornings, crisp and clear, that filled you with awe at nature's beauty. We had now reached nearly 65°S, but the intention was to carry on south as far as the ice would allow, although we doubted whether we could get further than 67°S, where the sea was reported to still be completely blocked by last winter's ice.

The following morning, we took the dinghy to the opposite shore and started climbing up a glacier. Because of the warm weather, the slopes were covered in small pools of melted water and the going was quite exhausting in the slushy heavy snow. Suddenly I fell into a crevasse up to my armpits, and had it not been for my quick reaction I would have dropped to the bottom, some 10 metres below. That put an end to this kind of mountaineering activity, as at that time of year the risks were too high. On the way down, I was attacked by two irate skuas protecting their nests. I braved their fury and took several photographs as they dive-bombed me. In one of the photographs a skua is right in front of me, its wings outstretched, its eyes boring menacingly into mine. Who would blink first? It was certainly not I, but my Nikon's shutter.

Cuverville Island 64°41'S, 62°38'W

We woke up to find the boat covered in a thick coating of snow. During the short night, a blizzard had moved in from the south, obliterating all visibility. Securely anchored with two anchors in tandem and lines tied by stainless-steel strops to large boulders ashore, we had nothing to fear. This anchoring technique

Antarctic glaciers calve continuously and release huge icebergs, some several miles long. Caught by winds and currents, they drift aimlessly across the oceans, melting slowly and thus making up for the seawater lost by evaporation or other reasons. Under normal climatic conditions nature keeps the balance by replacing the missing mass with the snow of the following winter. On this visit I was shocked to see the obvious changes that had occurred during my relatively short absence of only three years. Most glaciers that I still remembered well had retreated significantly, and in many places their sides were covered in green lichen, apparently the first surface plant to survive in that environment. I had no doubt that climatic change was underway.

The smaller glaciers along the Antarctic Peninsula, or on the islands facing it, were also busy calving, but their offspring rarely got far and they grounded in the shallow waters. With less than one quarter of an iceberg's mass visible above the water, most of it being hidden under the surface, the largest icebergs were grounded in depths of several hundred feet, while the smaller bergs came to rest in the shallow waters close to the shores. Pushed by an onshore wind, they usually ended up in one of the bays, and it was imperative to be aware of this when choosing an anchorage. We always attempted to anchor in the shallowest depth possible, where only the smallest bergs could follow us in. With Aventura's shallow draft this was not a problem, and if the weather looked at all threatening I pumped up the centreboard; with a draft of only one metre, the risk posed by visiting bergs was greatly reduced. Even so, we were often woken up by the noise of an amorous intruder the size of Aventura, which, after hopefully parking itself alongside us, would rub us up, expectantly waiting for a response. Pushing off such unwanted visitors was a waste of time, as each weighed at least twice as much as their chosen victim, so I did what I normally do in foreign lands when faced with pushy locals: I shrugged and put up with it. After all, it was their territory we were invading.

Although these waters have been relatively well charted, landmarks often do not tally with the GPS coordinates and some small rocks may have been overlooked entirely, so we had to keep a constant lookout and rely more on our eyes than on the instruments. Although we touched the ground on a few occasions, Aventura's forgiving centreboard let us get away without any damage, but other yachts found the experience quite unnerving and ended up moving very little.

Pléneau Island, 65°06'S, 64°04'W

The weatherfax from Chile at 0815 didn't show anything threatening, so we decided to move on. Having retrieved the shorelines and anchors, we hoisted the inflatable with its outboard onto the foredeck and started moving slowly out of the bay. Before we had time to react to the depth sounder moving speedily upwards, there was a crunch and we were aground. 'No problem,' exclaimed Erick, who was at the wheel, 'we'll lift the centreboard and come off.' And that's what we did. As a committed centreboarder he never enters shallow waters with the board up, but waits until the board makes contact first. 'It is better to touch with the 40-mm-thick aluminium plate at slow speed, as it will swing upwards into its casing without any damage, than run aground with the hull. Then you do have a problem!'

Sounding with the board we reached places that other boats could not even consider. This attitude, coupled with our willingness to scout ahead of the other Millennium Odyssey yachts and, where necessary, push our way through ice, turning Aventura into a mini-icebreaker, had earned us the nickname Risky, as opposed to our rival Risqué. But then, we had a metal hull and they didn't!

Pitt Islands 65°25'S, 65°29'W

There was a certain symmetry in our position, with latitude and longitude almost the same. I was tempted to go a little more to the east where both would be equal, but that would have meant anchoring in open water. We had reached the furthest point south we could go, as from here on mostly unbroken ice stretched to the southern horizon, more suitable for a real icebreaker.

Determined to be the yacht that reached furthest south that season, we left Pléneau Island and headed southwest. As soon as we left the protection of the islands and encountered open water, the ice started thickening, and by the time we closed with the small island group, we were ploughing through a lot of brash ice. The dull grey day made this bleak place even bleaker. There were hardly any animals about, except a couple of large leopard seals that gave us a most hateful look for invading their territory.

After we had anchored and taken our lines to some rocks, we went ashore. As we got closer, with me following in the smaller dinghy and taking photographs, the leopard seals growled, then turned around and ignored us. These aggressive animals have no enemy and obviously these two did not regard us as such. We explored the small area and found a more promising anchorage. But as we were not going to stay long it wasn't worth moving. I realised that this was going to be our turning point, and the thought filled me with a deep sense of regret, as none of us were ready to leave this wonderful and unique world. Skip's words kept surfacing in my mind and made me understand just how addicts must feel.

Port Circumcision 65°10'S, 64°10'W

We anchored in this most delightfully protected spot on the east side of Petermann Island. The French explorer Jean-Baptise Charcot named it after the traditional Feast of the Circumcision of Christ on which it was first sighted, 1 January 1909. The French expedition spent a long winter here and Aventura was anchored close to the spot where their ship Pourqoui Pas? (Why Not?) had been anchored. A plaque commemorating their stay had been placed near an Argentinian refuge hut.

With threatening weather approaching from the east, we had made for this sheltered bay as it promised to give us protection from all directions. After going through the routine of anchoring and taking lines ashore, this time even more carefully than usual as I knew that we were in for a blow, we landed on the nearby rocky beach right in the middle of a large penguin colony. As we stepped ashore, a penguin followed us closely, covered in blood and badly wounded. It had obviously been mauled by a leopard seal, but had miraculously managed to escape and was now determinedly making its way to feed its chick. I hoped it would survive but I doubted it, as even if it didn't die of its wounds the skuas would probably finish the job. These aggressive

predators are always to be seen on the edges of penguin colonies, watching their potential prey with a beady eye. They rarely attack a healthy penguin but pounce at the first sign of weakness, their usual victim being a famished chick whose parent has failed to return from a feeding expedition.

Back on board we were having a late dinner when we heard Vegewind, one of the Millennium Odyssey yachts, calling us on VHF. I looked out and saw them steaming past and heading for Lemaire Channel.
'Where are you going?' I asked the captain.
'We plan to anchor for the night just the other side of this strait.'
'But there is no protected anchorage there and the weather doesn't look good.'
'Oh, we'll be all right,' he replied confidently.
'I wouldn't be so sure. Look, there is space in this bay and even with your draft you could make it just by the entrance.'
'No thanks, my crew want to go through the strait.'
Thick low black clouds precipitated nightfall and the gradually increasing wind started pushing more and more ice into the anchorage. Having lifted the centreboard and anchored in the shallowest spot possible, we were soon surrounded by a wall of ice, with only a slither of open water around Aventura. We looked quite safe and went to bed.

Vernadsky, formerly Faraday, Arctic station

When we woke up, the scenery looked even worse than the night before, but our snug location couldn't have been safer. Later in the day the wind dropped, the sun came out and the ice started retreating, so we upped anchor and headed for Lemaire Channel. As we came out at its end we saw Vegewind anchored close inshore, but there was no sign of life on board, so, presuming they were still asleep, we carried on towards the Ukrainian base on Argentine Islands.

Argentine Islands 65°15''S, 64°16'W

This large base prides itself on running the southernmost bar in the world, boldly stated on a piece of driftwood displayed on the shore. Located more than 500 miles south of Cape Horn, its claim is beyond dispute. Also it is probably the most welcoming bar anywhere in the world. The base commander, Viktor Systov, recognised me from my previous visit on Pelagic, when we arrived only a few days after the Ukrainian Academy of Sciences had taken over the British Antarctic station Faraday, renamed Vernadsky after Ukraine's most famous physicist. Britain handed over the fully equipped station for the token payment of £1 on condition that the Ukrainians continued a number of projects started by the British, most important among them being a study of the ozone

layer above Antarctica. Indeed, the Ukrainian scientists were carrying out their tasks fastidiously and sending daily reports to their colleagues in Cambridge. The specialist in charge, Mykola Leonov, gave us a detailed demonstration of his work as an ozonometrist, but insisted that on present data he would not commit himself to say whether the ozone hole was getting larger or smaller. All he could say was that 40 years of observations covered too short a span to be able to draw any meaningful conclusions. He did stress that the size and intensity of the ozone layer showed a remarkable seasonal variation, having a lower intensity in the Antarctic spring than at other times, which could also point to a cyclic variation that could only be measured over a number of decades, if not centuries.

For the Ukrainian scientists, playing host to the four Millennium Odyssey yachts was a highlight of their 14-month-long Antarctic sojourn, which was going to end the following month, when the 11-man team would be relieved by a new group from the Ukraine. So the party that they put on for us was also an early farewell party for their own imminent departure. True to the East European tradition of hospitality, the 34 Millennium guests were regally entertained, and the bar was kept open from eight in the evening until three the following morning. At some point, when I could still speak clearly, I made a toast to our hosts and said how happy we all were that the message of the Millennium Odyssey had reached as far as Antarctica, then handed them some Millennium souvenirs. To my shame, I had not thought of setting aside a Millennium Lamp for Antarctica, as I never imagined that we would have a chance of a flame ceremony. It didn't really matter as the message of peace and friendship was what our hosts appreciated.

The crew of Vegewind had been the first to arrive, making a beeline for the bar and hogging it for the rest of the night, putting away the Ukrainian vodka and chain-smoking the base cigarettes as if there were no tomorrow. As one younger crew member passed by, I asked him what they were celebrating.

'To put it briefly: our miraculous survival!'

'What happened?'

'After we had passed you and came out of the Lemaire Channel, we anchored quickly as it was getting dark, but we had hardly gone to bed when the wind came up and we started dragging and were being driven fast towards the beach. Even with the engine at full blast we could hardly control our drift, so we tried to set a second anchor. As we drifted into shallow water we managed to take lines ashore and just about stop the worst. The wind and ice pushed us further in, we touched the ground, but somehow that terrible night passed.'

'Sorry to hear that and even more sorry that I didn't insist more strongly that you joined us at Circumcision.'

'Yes, I overheard your chat with our captain and couldn't understand why on earth we continued. Anyway, let's drink to our amazing luck.'

Vodka was being poured out generously in ever-larger glasses, accompanied by freshly baked bread covered in a thick layer of juicy red caviar. The cook, Vassily, having learned that I was originally from Romania, told me that his native village was only 20-km from the Romanian border, and, in a display of regional bonding, that same night baked six large loaves of bread for the crew of Aventura. Indeed, our hosts' generosity was almost embarrassing and as they firmly refused any payment for the large hole left behind in their bar (probably larger than the ozone hole above), we tried to make up for it by buying some of the souvenirs they had made during the long Antarctic winter.

Viktor the boss came over to me and wished me the best for the continuation of the voyage. Then he added: 'Jimmy, these Germans sure know how to drink!'

Coming from a Ukrainian, I could only interpret this as a compliment.

'It's probably because they are sailing on a dry ship and had a most horrible night almost losing their boat.'

'Well, that makes it easier to understand, but I am still impressed!'

As several of our Ukrainian friends came from Odessa and were keen sailors at heart, they asked us to put up our sails as we left the anchorage the following morning so they could take photos and videos to show their families back home. Aventura duly obliged by running up our most colourful spinnaker, the Canaries logo of the Millennium Odyssey sponsors looking rather incongruous against a background of snow and icebergs, but it must have made an impressive picture nonetheless.

With improved visibility, by mid-morning we could see Cape Renard clearly at the entrance to Lemaire Channel, our day's objective at a distance of some 15 miles. Not to be confused with Le Maire Strait off Staten Island, this is a 5-mile-long narrows between Booth Island and the Antarctic Peninsula. The stunning scenery has made it the most visited site in this part of the world. In a relatively small area are concentrated all the elements that make up the grandeur of Antarctic scenery: soaring snow-covered peaks, majestic glaciers and countless icebergs, large and small. As if on cue, a large cruise ship steamed into view, the passengers crowded on the upper deck taking pictures of my small sailing boat weaving her way amongst the icebergs piled up in the approaches to the narrows. With all sails up, we must have been a sight. I tuned the VHF radio to channel 16 expecting to be called in appreciation for having provided the 400 passengers with such a rare photo opportunity. We even joked among ourselves that if asked if we needed anything, we would say, 'Yes, please could we have our garbage collected?' This is indeed a major problem as, under the terms of the Antarctic Treaty, nothing must be left behind, nor anything taken out. So all our solid waste, degradable or not, had been collecting in large plastic bags tied to the aft rail. But the ship sailed silently past, not answering our call, not even saying hello.

Photo session over, we furled the sails because slaloming amongst icebergs and growlers was markedly easier under power than sail. We followed the ship into the narrows but as the ice was getting thicker and progress slower, I climbed to the first set of spreaders to eyeball a way through.

Dead ahead of us two grey-brown shapes were undulating in the slight swell. Every once in a while one would raise itself and blow: two humpback whales resting on the surface, right in the middle of Lemaire Channel. We edged closer with the engine barely ticking over. Only when we were about one boat length away did they react to our presence: they rolled over in perfect synchronisation and swam towards us. The larger of the two, probably the male, raised its head out of the water, gave us a reproachful look, then both dove under our stern. The whites of their huge flukes shimmered greenly for a long while through the clear water as they gradually disappeared from sight. From the spreaders I had had an even better view than the rest of the crew in the cockpit, and we all agreed that this could very well be the highlight of our Antarctic trip.

Back to reality, we found a passage through the ice and motored slowly through the narrows. More ice had piled up at their southern end, but by now our ice-dodging technique was tried and tested, and we headed for the nearest anchorage behind Pléneau Island. In order to reach it, we had to pass a relatively shallow area littered with grounded icebergs, and aptly described by Doina on our previous trip as the 'iceberg cemetery'.

Wind and sun work relentlessly on the stranded icebergs, moulding them into shapes undreamed of even by the most inspired sculptor. We took a dinghy trip through this ice gallery, competing with each other in naming the surrounding shapes: a sphinx, a jumbo jet, a cathedral spire, a stranded whale, even a diminutive creature looking just like the Loch Ness monster.

Having sounded our way as per the well-tried routine into the shallow corner of the anchorage, we quickly ran through the mooring technique: put the two anchors down in tandem, lower the dinghy, run two or four lines ashore, collect some ice for a well deserved happy hour. Nothing, believe me, tastes better than a Pisco sour with 20,000-year-old ice!

Port Lockroy 64°49'S, 63°29'W

What turned out to be our last day in Antarctica was also the most exquisite. Perfect is, in fact, the only word to describe it. My second trip to Antarctica reinforced my conviction that it is the most interesting cruising destination in the world, and our cruise along the Antarctic Peninsula and its off-lying islands had

allowed me to experience some of the most exciting and satisfying moments of my entire sailing life.

After a rendezvous with the other Millennium Odyssey yachts at Port Lockroy, each captain had the option to pick his own time to start the leg back to Cape Horn. We spent a highly enjoyable time at Port Lockroy, the site of the first British base in Antarctica, now a museum run by the Antarctic Heritage Trust. Two of its members had spent the entire summer there, welcoming visitors both from cruise ships and yachts. The logbook kept at Port Lockroy recorded the arrival of 17 yachts that season, about half of which were regular visitors to the Antarctic Peninsula, being engaged in charter work. Because of its strategic location and excellent shelter, every yacht stops at Port Lockroy, so the number gives a fair indication of yachts visiting the Antarctic Peninsula. If the four Millennium Odyssey boats were not included, the number of cruising boats was only about eight, which was close to the average recorded in recent years. Among recent arrivals was an Australian singlehander who had sailed nonstop from New Zealand, and was planning to spend the coming winter in Antarctica, having laid in stores for a stay of well over one year. Singlehanders appeared to be attracted to the frozen continent – as on the day we were leaving we heard that a Brazilian singlehander had just completed a circumnavigation of Antarctica, the first to do so, and was resting in the bay next to Port Lockroy.

Dave Burkitt and Nigel Millius were the ideal hosts at Port Lockroy and were a font of information on Antarctica. By profession a shipwright, Dave was an old Antarctic hand and had been working for the British Antarctic Survey since the early 1970s, when he was in charge of a dog team. The departure of the last huskies from the Antarctic in 1994, under pressure from environmentalists, was deeply regretted as it wiped out at one stroke the true spirit of adventure of overland explorations by sledges pulled by teams of huskies.

'They were replaced by noisy, smelly skidoos - a poor replacement for the hard-working huskies, and an odd way to protect Antarctica from pollution,' commented Dave with a bitter smile.

Nigel, an ornithologist, was spending his third season in Antarctica observing the life of penguin colonies and the impact of human visitors. In spite of the steady increase in the number of tourists, this did not seem to have affected local wildlife significantly, although Nigel stressed the fact that keeping a check on the size of groups that were landed by the cruise ships, and such groups being always accompanied by a qualified guide, had helped minimise the potential risks.

From Port Lockroy we followed the Gerlache Strait towards the Melchior Islands, our chosen point of departure. In brilliant sunshine and with a light breeze on the quarter, we hoisted the spinnaker, gliding silently past icebergs and surprising several pairs of humpback whales feeding or resting in the calm waters of the mountain-ringed fjord. By early evening we had reached our destination, but as the weather looked settled, I decided not to wait, like the others, for a weather window, but to carry on without stopping. The crossing of the Drake Passage is the price one has to pay for the privilege of visiting Antarctica, so with no depression showing close to the west on the daily weatherfax, we agreed that we'd rather swallow the bitter pill sooner than later. Indeed, with depressions passing through at an average of one every three days, it is almost impossible to do the 600-mile passage to Cape Horn without getting a pasting, a risk we had to be ready to take.

The tactic for the northbound voyage from Antarctica across the Drake Passage is to leave from as far west as possible, and also to keep some westing in hand for the intended landfall at Cape Horn, where the prevailing winds are from the northwest and there is also an east-setting current. The Melchior Islands, off the Antarctic Peninsula, are the best departure point, and there were a few other boats there waiting to cross to Cape Horn. The radio was abuzz with advice, comments and speculations, as captains defended their pet theories. I knew that Risqué had commissioned a well-known offshore-weather expert to give them daily routing advice, and I was taken by surprise when the captain told everyone listening to the radio that, in view of possible deteriorating weather, he had been strongly advised to wait a few more days for an improvement. I butted in and explained that, according to the way I read the latest weatherfax, I begged to differ, but neither Risqué nor any of the other captains took any notice.

We left immediately and had a reasonably good passage to Cape Horn, where we made landfall almost exactly four days after leaving Antarctica. Whether we now deserved to wear an earring or not didn't bother me, as I never wear any jewellery, not even a wedding band. However, having passed Cape Horn from west to east, to make sure our claim was beyond dispute, we anchored in the lee of Horn Island and started preparations to actually step ashore at this famous landmark. But that story belongs elsewhere.

(at least 5 metres in circumference) to be slung across rocks ashore. To ease the handling of the mooring lines, they should be stored on drums installed on the fore and aft decks and provided with handles so the lines can be wound on the drums when not in use. For us, these same mooring lines came in handy later when we were cruising the Chilean fjordland and had to moor the boat four-ways in some restricted anchorages.

Practical tips for Antarctica

The boat

Safety and comfort are the two most important criteria. For the passage across Drake, where one can expect to encounter icebergs, a collision bulkhead forward will give peace of mind, although collisions even with the smaller growlers can be avoided by keeping a good lookout. This is not too difficult as the summer nights are short and get even shorter moving south. Radar is essential in detecting and tracking icebergs at night. The boat should be easily steered from a sheltered position, although the cold is not normally a major problem provided one is well dressed. Some type of heating is essential as the daytime temperatures rarely rise above freezing. Condensation can be a major problem if the boat is not well insulated. The worst areas are hatches and portholes, and these should be either provided with a second, transparent framed cover, or be covered in a plastic film sheet, which will cut down condensation considerably. We used what I believe was quite an ingenious solution by filling the space between the retractable mosquito screen and the actual hatch with bubblewrap packing material.

As many anchorages have limited swinging space, being moored safely is greatly facilitated by having four lines (floating propylene is best) at least 50 metres long to moor the boat securely while at anchor. The lines should be provided with stainless-steel cable strops

Clothing

Adequate clothing is an essential item in cold-water sailing. Personal comfort is of utmost importance when sailing in extreme conditions, and I must stress that in two Antarctic voyages I was never cold, either inside or outside the boat. This makes it possible not only to enjoy the unique scenery to the full, but is also a major safety factor. There is now a wide range of good-quality clothing suitable for cold climates and it is recommended to buy those that are of the breathable type. The so-called middle layer is excellent to wear under the outside wet-weather gear, and some middle layers have the advantage of being able to be worn on their own when off-watch. The third, innermost, layer should be some sort of thermal underwear. I found that cotton suited me best as my skin is sensitive to synthetic fibres, but some people prefer silk.

For walking ashore, a good windproof jacket or anorak is needed. I found ski salopettes worn with such a jacket to be perfect for shore expeditions. Also needed are good hiking boots with a non-slip sole, such as Vibram, and, if the trousers do not fit well over the boots, also gaiters. Both on board and ashore, it is recommended to use dark glasses as well as sun-block cream. As the nose is the most exposed part of the body, a nose cover made of leather or plastic and fitted to the sunglasses works best.

Sea boots should have a thick non-slip sole and should be at least two sizes larger to accommodate two or even three additional pairs of socks. You should have between four and six pairs of fibre-pile or wool socks. Gloves are just as important and should be worn in two layers, the inner fingered glove to be of wool and the outer of a waterproof material (Gore-Tex), ideally also with fingers. One should take sufficient woollen gloves, as they do get wet. A place on board is needed to dry them as well as the rest of the wet-weather gear. As I could not find any good-quality waterproof gloves I solved this by buying a pair of dry diving gloves, which

were perfect for steering or handling wet ropes. Good head cover is also required, such as a Polartec balaclava. Rather than a standard survival suit, it may be more useful to acquire a dry diving suit that can be used on watch under extreme conditions and also for wet dinghy landings. To play safe, I had both.

Walking ashore

Much time will be spent ashore, in penguin colonies, watching other animals or just exploring the shoreline and enjoying the peaceful scenery. There are two aggressive animals to be aware of: fur seals, who should not be approached too closely, and skuas.

Skuas are in the seagull family, and are very territorial and aggressive, especially if they have chicks and you get too close to their nest. They will take off and dive-bomb an intruder, giving a sharp and painful peck on the scalp. The best protection is a walking or ski stick that can be held upright above your head if attacked. A stick is also very useful when walking on glaciers, where it is easy to slip or even fall into a crevasse, as happened to me. Suspicious-looking cracks filled with fresh snow should be explored with the stick first and, generally, when the weather starts getting warmer it is wiser not to walk on glaciers at all.

A good camera with a telephoto lens is highly recommended. Spending time ashore, it is good to carry some energy bars, as one gets hungry in the cold, and also water as although there is ice everywhere, melted ice water from the ground is not drinkable because it is soiled from penguin droppings. A portable VHF radio to communicate with the boat is essential.

Crew changes

There are no commercial flights to anywhere on the Antarctic Peninsula, although the Chilean base on King George Island may help in a real emergency. Puerto Williams is connected by a small plane to Punta Arenas and on to Santiago de Chile. A better solution for crew changes is Ushuaia, in neighbouring Argentina, which has frequent flights to Buenos Aires for onward international connections. Flights between Buenos Aires and Ushuaia are often fully booked by cruise-ship passengers so bookings should be made well in advance.

Tips

» Good-quality high-latitude foul-weather gear
» Survival suit
» Windproof trousers and jacket (lightweight Gore-Tex) or anorak
» Middle-layer clothing
» Sea boots with non-slip sole (two sizes larger)
» Hiking boots with Vibram soles and gaiters
» Thermal underwear
» Fibre-pile jacket and trousers
» Two balaclavas or wool hats with ear protection
» Several pairs of wool or fibre-pile gloves/mittens
» Rubber or Gore-Tex overmitts
» Several pairs of wool socks
» Dark glasses
» Strong sun block
» Small rucksack for shore trips
» Walking stick
» Dry diving suit and, ideally, diving gear and two tanks in case of being forced to dive in an emergency
» Satellite phone. Iridium has the best polar coverage

10

Weather and weather routing

The pessimist complains about the wind; the optimist expects it to change; the realist adjusts the sails.

William A. Ward

I might as well start with a confession. In spite of all the years I have spent at sea, for a long time my knowledge of weather forecasting was quite rudimentary. It all changed when I started sailing to high-latitude destinations such as Antarctica, Patagonia or Alaska, where being able to assess impending conditions was much more important than when sailing in the tropics during the safe season.

I still look at the sky and clouds, see that some are white and others grey, some large, some small, some fluffy, some ragged at the edges, trying to guess what they may be telling me.

Could this be an extraterrestrial craft about to land?

The distinctive trade-wind clouds are obvious and so are the tropical squalls, which announce themselves so clearly that even a child could recognise their arrival. Furthermore, having spent so much time observing the sea and sky at close quarters, I seem to have developed a sixth sense and cannot explain why most of the time I surmise what is going to happen. Usually I can guess how much power an approaching squall will pack, if we are going to be in for a real blow, or even smell if rain is coming. This sense-based approach to weather

is backed by an overcautious attitude, which means that I always prefer to reef early, reduce sail if a squall is approaching, make all necessary preparations at the first sign of impending bad weather or leave an anchorage at short notice if I deem it unsafe. Put simply, over the years I have learned never to take anything for granted and not to allow wishful thinking to override common sense. So my approach to weather is pragmatic: in other words, I take it as it comes. In fact, fatalistic is a better definition. I may not leave a marina or safe harbour if there is a gale blowing outside, but if a strong wind is likely to continue and is blowing from the right direction, I prefer to go.

Weather tactics vary in different parts of the world. Basically, in temperate zones what really matters is the direction of the wind, so if winds are predicted from an unfavourable direction one has little choice but to wait. This is why I stressed that if the direction is right, I prefer to go even if the actual strength may not be entirely to my liking.

The situation is very different when sailing in the tropics, where what really matters is the strength of the wind because the direction, especially in trade-wind areas, is normally more constant and predictable. So I know that a spell of reinforced trade winds blowing at around 30 knots will eventually diminish their strength to the more pleasant 15-20 knots. If I am not in a hurry, I prefer to wait.

Strangely enough, on passage I find it much more interesting if I do not know what to expect. As I mentioned in the chapter dealing with routing, I have always followed the dictum of attempting not to be in the wrong place at the wrong time. This usually means planning a voyage that avoids known bad-weather areas or seasons, particularly tropical cyclone seasons. With a few exceptions, I have managed to avoid really bad weather, and have coped with what came my way. I must add that I had complete confidence in all my boats, and knew that I could trust them to take me safely out of trouble, as they have done on many occasions.

It is important to point out that there were very limited sources of information on offshore weather when I started cruising, so anyone setting off on an ocean voyage in those days had little choice but to take things as they came. Eventually, this became a habit. As I enjoy so much being at sea, taking the weather as it comes is an intrinsic part of the mystery of the sea and one of the reasons why I love being out there.

Tropical squalls

Recognising an approaching tropical squall is quite easy as they are always preceded by an impossible-to-miss black cloud that often has a straight bottom, usually parallel to the horizon, hence their definition as line squalls. Outside the tropics, squalls are more difficult to detect and can occasionally come out of a clear sky without any warning, so they are called white squalls. Tropical squalls always travel with the wind, so if you look regularly to windward their approach can hardly be missed. They also show up well on radar and are quite visible to the naked eye even at night. If a squall is detected in good time and if the advancing front is small, it may be possible to avoid being in its path by altering course. Sail should be shortened promptly, as

by the time the squall hits it is usually too late to do much except pray that whatever sail has been left up will cope with the increased wind and that the person at the helm or the autopilot will manage to keep things under control. I avoid using a wind vane in squally conditions as a strong gust may overpower it, and disconnecting the gear to take over steering by hand will take longer than pushing the autopilot button.

A massive squall at sunrise

Most tropical squalls generate winds of about twice the force of the current wind. As they strike the boat, the wind often changes direction, so the autopilot must always be set to steer to wind. If I am hand-steering, my usual tactic is to try and keep the wind on the quarter, enough to keep the apparent wind speed down but not too close astern to risk gybing. This is easily avoided in such situations, as I would have the centreboard fully up.

Squalls do not always bring stronger wind but are usually accompanied by rain. There is a useful German ditty for this: 'Kommt der Regen mit dem Wind, nimm die Segel in geschwind; kommt der Wind und dann der Regen, kann der Segler sich schlafen legen.' Translated roughly, it says that if the rain comes before the wind,

A typical line squall

you must reef quickly, but if the rain comes after the wind, the sailor can go to sleep. What it actually means is that the rain is propelled by a strong wind that soon will reach the boat itself. Conversely, a squall that is not preceded by rain is a sign that the accompanying wind cannot be that strong.

Apart from keeping a keen lookout at all times, there is nothing else that can be done to predict an approaching squall, as the barometer gives no indication, although they do show up clearly on radar. In some areas squalls occur with boring regularity, although occasionally on some passages days can go by without a squall, while at other times they can hit every hour. With time being usually too short to reef the mainsail, when sailing through a squally area it is best to use a sail combination that can be quickly reduced to about half its total surface; rolling up a foresail or dousing the spinnaker being the preferred option. The mainsail is best left alone, especially because putting in a reef just as the squall approaches may not be easy, as most likely you will be broad-reaching or running. Also, once the squall is gone, you have saved yourself the job of taking the reef out of the mainsail. Usually I aim to have the right amount of mainsail up to cope with a squall of any strength. If we are sailing wing and

It takes less than a minute to furl in the poled-out jib

wing with the foresail poled out, I leave the mainsail alone and furl the foresail completely. My method of setting up a pole independently of the sail works perfectly in such situations, as the pole can be left untouched during the squall and, once it has passed, the furled sail, or doused spinnaker, can be returned to its pre-squall status. The technique of setting up a fixed pole is described on page 168 in the chapter on sailing in the tropics.

For most European sailors a transatlantic passage is the first time they experience a tropical squall, and over the years I have witnessed among participants in my rallies countless breakages caused by squalls. Blown sails, damaged autopilots, broken booms, furling gears or spinnaker poles were the most common, and even dismastings on a couple of occasions. In the majority of cases the cause was not reducing sail in time, or simply inattention by not noticing the approaching squall. I am ashamed to admit that it happened on my own boat too.

While crossing the Atlantic with two friends on Aventura III, I was woken up by the noise of the boat accelerating fast. By the time I got to the cockpit the squall and rain were upon us and the boat was flying

A violent squall about to hit us in Patagonia

at over 10 knots. At nightfall I had foolishly left the spinnaker up, as the wind was light at the time and the weather looked settled. Fortunately the speed kept the apparent wind speed down and, equally fortunately, I had set the autopilot to steer to wind, so it kept the boat sailing to a steady wind angle. Even so, our headlong rush into the pitch-black night was quite unnerving. There was little danger of broaching as we had been running with the centreboard fully up. While pondering what to do, I avoided looking at my frightened crew member who had been on watch as my looks, I am sure, could have killed her. When I had passed through the cockpit I had noticed the cushions piled up comfortably in a corner, where she had obviously been fast asleep.

The other crew joined me, and we tried to douse the spinnaker, but to no avail. There was little I could do except try to enjoy the roller-coaster ride while praying between gritted teeth that the spinnaker could take it. I wasn't too worried about it blowing out, as it was my spare asymmetric spinnaker, but I knew that the mess of a shredded sail, some of which might end up under the boat, was the worst scenario. As the squall showed no sign of letting up, I decided not to tempt fate any longer and to take the spinnaker down while the gods were still on our side. Well, they weren't. As I tried to pull down the douser, it jammed, and now we had a full spinnaker to contend with... and another squall on our heels. It was no good pulling and yanking, as the douser just wouldn't budge. Eventually I managed to partly mask the spinnaker behind the mainsail and get it down just as another squall loosened its fury upon us. As I was bagging the sail on the foredeck in a deluge of cold rain, I remembered a quote from a crew member on one of the boats that had blown a total of 28 spinnakers in a Whitbread round-the-world race. 'We put them up and God takes them down!' At the time I found it very funny, but after it almost happened to me, I no longer thought it was quite so amusing. Finally, tropical squalls can be even more dangerous when they strike an anchorage, because often their arrival cannot be predicted as they approach at great speed over the land. The solution is to choose an anchorage carefully and always make sure that you are well anchored and, ideally, not too close to other boats.

White squalls

Sailing in the lee of Tenerife in the Canary Islands

Much more dangerous because they arrive unseen, white squalls can be caused by katabatic winds when sailing in the lee of a high island, or in wind-acceleration zones, a phenomenon encountered among high islands such as the Canaries or Hawaii. The only indication of an approaching strong gust is the sudden darkening of the water to windward, which unfortunately is too late to shorten sail. This is where an electric winch can be such an advantage on short-handed boats as the sail can be furled quickly and efficiently while gradually releasing the foresail sheet. In my case, the furling line is always kept ready on the electric winch, so while I keep a finger on the electric

Caught by a 50-knot williwaw in a narrow channel in southern Chile

winch button to quickly furl in the foresail, I ease the sheet with the other hand.

Williwaws are the worst of this kind of squall as they often strike in restricted waters where there may be no sea room to take evasive action. The Chilean fjordland is notorious for these mini-storms that roll off the High Andes like an unseen avalanche. We experienced several on Aventura III, with the most violent nearly driving us onto a lee shore, as described later in this chapter.

Offshore forecasts

A relatively recent improvement in ocean weather forecasting is GRIB files, which have now become extremely popular with offshore sailors. GRIB (GRIdded Binary) is a World Meteorological Organization code used for exchanging meteorological charts and other data on wind, sea state, temperature, etc. The information is put into a compressed binary

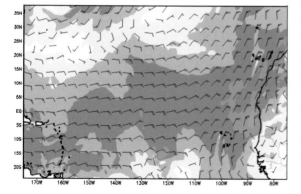

format that enables high-speed transmission. Being able to receive such information over the internet while ashore, or by satellite phone or HF radio while offshore, is a bonus when preparing to leave or already on passage.

I noticed among sailors taking part in the rallies I organise that the majority use almost exclusively GRIB files, and occasionally text forecasts, but surprisingly few use synoptic charts, which are my favourite. I do consult GRIB data occasionally but I don't trust their accuracy and do not let them influence me in my choice of route or course to be sailed. On two passages in the North Atlantic I downloaded GRIB files and saved them so that later I could check their accuracy. On both occasions I found that they were barely correct for the first 24 hours, and that the actual long-term situation did not tally with the one that had been predicted. It reinforced my belief that both before and while on passage you should be able to interpret weather conditions yourself, and for this reason I prefer to consult synoptic charts and draw my own conclusions. At least if my own forecast is wrong, I can only blame myself.

I once expressed my doubts about the reliability of GRIB files at a seminar on long-distance cruising. Two airline pilots, who were in the audience, objected to my comments and said that in fact they used GRIB files all the time when flying and found them quite accurate. I conceded that perhaps at those altitudes weather forecasts might be more accurate because conditions are not as volatile as at sea level. I also pointed out that, in their case, they probably consulted the latest GRIB charts for short-term forecasting while travelling at great speed, in contrast to someone on a slow-moving yacht using the charts for longer-term forecasting. They politely agreed but I could tell that they were not convinced by my arguments.

I do not want to give the impression that I am entirely against GRIBs but I would like to compare them to using satnav in cars and becoming so dependent on them that some people are no longer capable of planning a trip or finding their way with the help of a road map. Just as with GRIBs, I do use a satnav when I'm driving, but when I have doubts about a certain route suggested by the satnav, and decide to take a different one that looks to be more logical, I am often right.

Having airline pilots in my audience or among participants in my rallies seems so common that I asked those two Norwegian pilots what attracted them to offshore sailing. They replied that piloting an aircraft at great speeds may be all right to do as a job but when it came to seeing the world they preferred to move at the more sedate pace that gave them the opportunity to take in and appreciate their surroundings. In fact, both had opted for early retirement and were preparing their boats for a world voyage.

Onboard sources

Weather-wise, our passage-making on the first Aventura could most accurately be described as weather-unwise. All I had were the old pilot charts that were helpful in providing an overall impression of seasonal weather conditions, but otherwise we knew hardly more than our exploring predecessors. In this respect, Aventura II symbolised a true quantum leap in both communications and forecasting capabilities. An SSB radio allowed me to receive synoptic weather charts, while an early version of Inmarsat C provided regional text forecasts. On Aventura III my main source of regional weather information was via the twice-daily transmissions on the much-improved Inmarsat C. On long passages I also had better access to synoptic charts via the SSB radio. These were particularly helpful while in Antarctica, when I regularly downloaded the daily synoptic charts transmitted by the Chilean meteorological office, as they provided a useful indication of impending conditions in the Southern Ocean.

Aventura IV was equipped with an even wider range than its predecessor, as the Iridium Pilot broadband system had put my communications capabilities onto a higher level, which ensured fast transmission of large files, including high-resolution images. Therefore I had access to a much wider range of weather information. In the High Arctic I consulted forecasts from both NOAA and the Canadian Meteorological Office, and found their reliability to be acceptable for short periods but rarely for more than 48 hours. Much more important were the daily ice charts provided by the Canadian Ice Service. Sourced from satellite infrared photography, they provided a fairly accurate image of ice conditions in the Northwest Passage and were invaluable in allowing me to plan our movements accordingly.

On our return from the Northwest Passage, I consulted daily the synoptic charts issued by the British Meteorological Office. They were quite accurate in predicting the unfavourable conditions that we were going to be faced with. Once we were caught in a deepening low and, indeed, by the following day were in the middle of a proper storm. It had been accurately shown on the chart to be exactly on top of our position. However, I believe that being informed about what to expect hadn't helped me all that much because my own prediction might well have been just as accurate, through keeping an eye on the barometer.

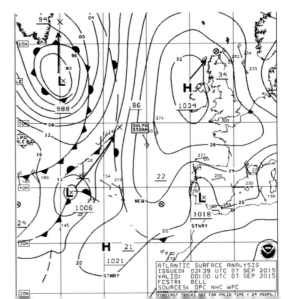

Weather windows

He who will not sail till all dangers are over must never put to sea.

Thomas Fuller

There are two terms, often used by some sailors, that I have taken a deep dislike to: paradise and weather windows. There seem to be so many so-called paradises on earth that there is no space left for hell, which unfortunately is not the case. As to that other term, I once said, and I wasn't trying to be funny, that weather windows can be bad for you. Some examples, picked from my own experience, or that of others, should help bear out that statement.

North Carolina, November 1977

On our first Aventura we had stopped in Beaufort, North Carolina, and were preparing for the passage to the Bahamas and Panama. Most boats around us were bound for the Bahamas or Caribbean, and the main concern was having favourable conditions for crossing the Gulf Stream. Each morning somebody would get the weather forecast and we'd stand around in little groups discussing in great detail every aspect of it. Halloween came and went, we were still there and I was getting worried that we would never leave. After a while it dawned on me that a perfect 'weather window' might never happen, and we may be stuck there for the rest of the coming winter, so I decided that if the weather was at all acceptable, we would leave the following morning, which is what we did.

We had a quite hairy first 24 hours as we crossed the Gulf Stream in a moderate northerly that had kicked up a nasty sea. In the middle of the night we fell off a wave with an almighty crash, but apart from the fright, we came through unscathed. We had a rather uneventful passage to San Salvador in the Outer Bahamas, and eventually made it to Panama. Friends on an American boat, who had been in Beaufort at the same time, caught up with us two years later in New Zealand. They told us that we had been the only ones who had managed to get away and that the weather had deteriorated the day after our departure so that eventually everyone had been forced to make their way south in the Intracoastal Waterway, and that most had spent the rest of the winter in Florida. It sounded as if we had indeed caught the last of that year's 'weather windows'.

That was the last time in my sailing life that I waited for a perfect weather window to set off on a long passage. Normally I set a date of departure, and if we are ready and the weather looks at all acceptable, we go.

Antarctica, March 1999

Having reached the Melchior Islands, our chosen point of departure across the Drake Passage to Cape Horn at the end of the Antarctic cruise, I did not agree with the captains of the other three Millennium Odyssey yachts who were waiting for a favourable weather window for the 600-mile-long passage. As the weather looked settled, and the situation on the synoptic charts did not appear threatening, I decided to leave immediately. This was my fourth crossing of this infamous stretch, and I knew that it was almost impossible to avoid being caught out by a low on this passage. With no imminent depression showing on the daily weatherfax, all of us on Aventura agreed that we'd rather go sooner than later.

For the first two days our gamble paid off and we made excellent progress. The strong northerly winds that had blown in the days before our departure had pushed all icebergs towards the Antarctic Peninsula so, to our great relief, we saw not a single iceberg after we had only sailed 20 miles offshore. A few hours of calm signalled a change in the weather, and when the wind returned it had backed to the northwest; by the afternoon of the third day, it was blowing in the high 30s. As we were now less than 100 miles from Cape Horn and had a good deal of westing in hand, we decided to heave to for the night.

With three reefs in the mainsail, the staysail rolled up to three-quarters of its size and the wheel

lashed to windward, Aventura took the mounting swell quite well, forereaching slightly but making quite a lot of leeway. By morning we had lost all our hard-earned westing and had drifted past the longitude of Cape Horn. A keen debate followed onboard as to whether drifting past Cape Horn counts as having doubled the famous landmark or not.

With the wind later backing to the southwest, our decision to heave to proved to have been wise as it saved us from sailing over the continental shelf extending for some 50 miles south of Cape Horn, the depth of between 50 and 80 metres creating hellish conditions in strong westerly winds. By staying as closehauled as the strong wind would permit, we gradually clawed our way back and reached Cape Horn four days after leaving Antarctica. Those who had decided to wait eventually left a few days after us, giving up on that elusive window. They all ran into bad weather and got quite a pasting in the unforgiving Drake Passage.

Fiji, October 2002

The ancient site of Havaiki on the island of Raiatea, in the Society Islands, is the symbolic centre of the Polynesian triangle whose far-flung corners stretch to Rapa Nui, Hawaii and Aotearoa, or the Land of the Long White Cloud. In 1999 Aventura III had sailed along one side of that triangle, from Easter Island to Raiatea and on to Hawaii. Three years later I was back in the Pacific, this time with Gwenda, and, as the safe season was coming to an end, we were in Fiji preparing to sail to New Zealand. Our route would follow that sailed by the intrepid Maoris whose large double-hulled canoes had plied those waters some thousand years previously.

The ancient Havaiki

One cannot but feel the deepest admiration for those Polynesian navigators who not only managed to sail their fragile craft way beyond the limits of their known world, but also then sailed back and forth between their new home in New Zealand and their ancestral home. What unparalleled feats of navigation those Polynesian sailors had achieved by having colonised the entire Pacific Ocean.

This was the thought that occurred to me as we prepared to leave for New Zealand from Musket Cove, west of Fiji's main island of Viti Levu. Other boats were getting ready too, and the buzzword all along the waterfront was 'weather window'. People pored over weather charts, consulted weather gurus by email or satellite phone, and discussed the best tactics for the 1,100-mile passage. It brought back memories of the similar situation in 1977 in Beaufort, as described above.

So I set a date of departure and we left. The weather was far from ideal and, as is often the case in the vicinity of land, we had a slow first 24 hours, with strong southwesterly winds that forced us to the west of our intended track. This didn't worry me too much as I knew that we would be able to make up the lost ground closer to New Zealand, where the prevailing winds were from the west. This passage is described in detail on page 292.

The above examples should, I hope, make it quite clear that I usually prefer to follow my own nose, which, over the years, I have come to trust more than that of some so-called experts. Perhaps I gave the wrong impression with my earlier statement about weather, when I actually meant that my theoretical knowledge might be limited whereas, thanks to the many years spent at sea, my intuition seems to do a good job at filling that gap.

Las Palmas de Gran Canaria, November 2005

In November 2005, while in Las Palmas for the start of the 20th ARC, I was invited to a farewell party for the 10 Spanish yachts taking part in the event. With the captains fresh from the official skippers' briefing, I was asked to make my own comments on the best tactics in the early stages of their forthcoming Atlantic crossing. I was quite reluctant to disagree with the advice given by the official meteorologist, who had advised the 200 or so ARC captains not to worry too much about a depression that was forming to the west of the Canaries. However, I told the Spanish captains that they should take a prudent course, by sailing close to the Cape Verde Islands, and altering course for the Caribbean only once they had reached the latitude of the Cape Verdes. A few days later I started getting emails from some of the Spanish sailors thanking me for my advice, as they had managed to make their southing without difficulty, whereas many of the other boats, which had left on a more direct course, had run into very strong headwinds. But worse was still to come, even if didn't affect the ARC fleet, as that ordinary-looking depression gradually turned into a tropical storm and by 2 December was upgraded to Hurricane Delta. This was the first-ever tropical storm to hit the Canaries and caused widespread devastation in the archipelago. It was most certainly not any meteorological insight that had helped me make that inspired guess but just a simple hunch that told me that things didn't look right. I suppose that's what makes people bet on an outsider at horse races... So maybe in the future I should put my nose to better use.

ARC start

Mediterranean, April 2006

Shortly after my return to the Mediterranean with Aventura III in spring 2006, we were in Menorca, in the Balearics, getting ready to hop across to Sardinia, a distance of only about 200 miles. For this section of our cruise, Gwenda and I had been joined by Italo Masotti, an Italian friend who has spent all of his sailing life in the Mediterranean and, having followed Aventura's progress around the world, was very keen to sail on her. Italo is a typical Mediterranean sailor who voyages mostly short distances, prefers spending nights in marinas and keeps a wary eye on the weather, which can be quite capricious. So, when on the eve of our departure from Menorca, the forecast was for 25 knots with higher gusts, he looked surprised when I declared that we were going. 'In the Med, as everywhere else, when the wind is from the right direction, you go!' I said, and off we went.

With three reefs in the mainsail and a partly furled staysail, we shot out of Mahon's narrow inlet like a cork from a champagne bottle. Past the last point of land, the sea looked ugly, with a short steep swell and the occasional breaking wave. For a relatively light displacement boat, Aventura was surprisingly well behaved in such conditions, and she more than made up in speed for the discomfort. Gwenda, who is very stoical when faced with rough weather, had settled in her favourite corner of the cockpit, while Italo was trying hard to be useful although there was nothing for him to do. He came below and found me sitting in my armchair reading a newspaper. 'Jimmy, how can you sit there so calmly?' he asked in utter amazement.

'What do you want me to do? We are well reefed down, the boat looks happy and the autopilot is doing an impeccable job. Nothing to worry about.'

With that, I went back to my newspaper. I could tell that Italo was not too happy but, after all, he had insisted that he wanted to sail on Aventura, so at least he could see for himself how I sailed my boat, which may not have been entirely to his taste. The strong winds didn't abate until the mountainous outline of Sardinia

punctuated the eastern horizon the following morning, and we made a perfect landfall. Not long afterwards, when we were tucked up in the marina, the winds turned into the east and would have been blowing hard on our nose had we left later.

French Riviera, May 2006

A few weeks later I was back in France, and while in St Raphael, which had been Aventura's base before her world voyage, I met my friend Patrick Canut, who had sailed with me from Cape Town to the Canaries.

'Nice to see you, but what are you doing here? I thought you were in Corsica,' I greeted him.

'Well, I'm ready to leave, but the forecast is for a strong mistral, and as my crew are quite green, they insisted that we wait.'

'Why wait; the wind is OK now. It may be on the increase, but it is, after all, from the right direction.'

'I know, but I am not too happy about leaving with such a forecast.'

'Good luck then, but I still feel you should be on your way.'

The summer mistral is a regular feature in the south of France, and while the wind can occasionally get up to 40 knots, the forecasts of its strength are quite reliable and local sailors think nothing of playing cat and mouse with Mr Mistral.

Later that year I met Patrick in our village and asked him about his trip to Corsica. He burst out laughing.

'Jimmy, you were absolutely right! We left the following morning, sailed for a few hours, but about halfway to Corsica the wind died and we had to motor. Minutes after I had started the engine, the alarm went off and, when I looked in the engine room, there was oil everywhere and I couldn't find the cause. As I suspected a serious problem, I decided not to restart the engine, but, after we had drifted for about an hour, my crew insisted that we call the Coast Guard in Corsica and arrange a tow. I told them that it was ridiculous as we

were in absolutely no danger but they panicked and, faced with such an impossible situation, I reluctantly caved in and called Corsica. A boat was sent out and towed us into the nearest port.'

'I bet that got your adrenaline going!'

'Yeah, and my wallet too, as I had to pay a couple of thousand euros for the towing operation.'

'Well, at least I hope that's a lesson for you.'

'Of course, from now on I am determined to do just what you would have done.'

'So our South Atlantic trip was not an entire waste then?'

'Waste? It was one of the best things that happened to me and I'll always be grateful that you invited me to come along.'

Heavy weather

I hate storms, but calms undermine my spirit.
Bernard Moitessier

Heavy weather is a very broad term, and I only regard winds over 50 knots to merit that description. Looking back on four decades of sailing, I can only remember perhaps half a dozen times when I experienced truly heavy weather, half of them in the Southern Ocean.

The Southern Ocean showing its might

Bismarck Sea, 1979

The first time I experienced winds over 50 knots was on the first Aventura, while on passage from Rabaul to Madang across the Bismarck Sea north of Papua New Guinea. Initially, as we had sufficient sea room, the situation did not appear to be dangerous. We hove to for the night, but I started getting concerned because I didn't know how much we had drifted and had no idea where we were. In those days I depended on astronavigation, and with an overcast sky it had been impossible to take any sights, whether of the sun or stars. By the second morning the wind had dropped to around 30 knots and the cloud cover started breaking

Peter Haven on Garove Island

up, so I managed to take a quick sight of the sun. To work out a position I needed to have accurate time, which I usually got from the American WWW station broadcasting on shortwave. Unable to pick it up, I tuned into Radio Papua New Guinea and started my stopwatch when they gave the local time as 0800 hours. When I worked out a position line, I was amazed that we seemed to have landed, like Noah's ark, high up on the mainland. Later that day we saw land, so I managed to locate our position and anchor in a beautifully protected bay.

When I eventually got the correct time from the WWW station and compared it with the one broadcast by Radio PNG, there was a discrepancy of about 30 seconds. Several months later I was in the capital Port Moresby and visited the radio station. I asked one of the newsreaders how they got their time so wrong. He broke out in laughter. 'Hey, this is Papua New Guinea. What is 30 seconds between friends?'

Le Maire Strait, January 1999

My worst heavy-weather experience occurred while sailing through Le Maire Strait, which separates mainland Tierra del Fuego from Isla de los Estados, also known as Staten Island – not to be confused with the island of the same name off New York. The sailing masters of yesteryear used to dread this treacherous stretch of water even more than doubling Cape Horn, as mountainous waves can be created by a strong northwest wind blowing against the fierce tides at the meeting point between the Pacific and Atlantic oceans. It is therefore imperative to catch the right tide and sail through the strait on the ebb, which had been our aim ever since leaving the Falklands. As we approached the strait, the northwest wind started increasing in strength, and by the time the tide started ebbing we had 35 knots on the quarter. With wind and tide in our favour, Aventura was flying at 10 knots over the ground. When we had almost reached the southern end of the strait we breathed a happy sigh of relief, but it was too soon. As we approached the southeast extremity of the mainland, the wind backed to the west, then southwest and, funnelled by the Beagle Channel, was gusting at 50 knots. In that strong wind the wind generator was making an awful noise, screeching like a possessed devil, and when caught on its side, making a horrible deep growling sound like a prop plane altering the pitch of its propeller as it comes in to land. Then, with a sudden high-pitched shriek, the generator started shaking so violently that the whole boat was shaking with it. With one final judder, it wrenched itself off its

supports and flew into the sea, one of its blades hitting the cockpit coaming, where it left a deep indentation in the aluminium. Ivan was standing by the wheel and, later, when I saw the deep gash caused by the blade, I realised that if it had hit him it would have killed him.

The wind generator a few minutes before it flew off

Under those conditions we could neither sail nor motor in the desired direction, so we turned tail and ran back through the strait, hoping to find shelter in one of the bays on the north coast of Staten Island. With the tide still flowing in a southerly direction and the wind now blowing from the south, mountainous waves started forming within minutes. From almost a flat sea, the waves had risen to at least 5 metres. It was almost impossible to believe that such changes could be so sudden.

All four of us were huddled in the cockpit, watching in awe as every now and again a massive wall of water would break over the stern and fill the cockpit. As I went below to change into something dry, I saw water sloshing over the floor. When I lifted the nearest floor panel I found the bilge full of water and asked Ivan to give me a hand, as the small bilge pumps couldn't cope. The large emergency Gusher 25 operated by Erick from the cockpit looked as if it was getting the level down. Meanwhile Ivan was doing what is often best: filling bucket after bucket and emptying them in the cockpit. The source of all that water was an absolute mystery so I asked Erick to have a good look when the next wave broke over us. I could already see from down below a massive wall of grey water advancing menacingly towards us. With a growling roar it broke over our stern. Over that terrible noise, I heard Erick shout, 'I've got it. There are two ventilation vents for the engine room on the stern counter and somehow the water manages to find its way into the main bilge.'

That was exactly what was happening, and that one wave must have deposited at least 50 litres of water into the bilge. While Ivan and I were getting rid of it, Erick stuffed some rags into the vents and the problem was, at least temporarily, resolved. It has been said that there is no better bilge pump than a man in a panic with a bucket. I remembered that saying as we were emptying bucketful after bucketful into the cockpit,

but because we had established the source we were no longer in a panic.

At long last we reached the lee of Staten Island and made our way into the perfectly protected Hoppner Bay. At the head of the outer bay, a narrow passage not much wider than Aventura's beam led into a calm pool surrounded by precipitous mountains. By the following morning, their slopes were covered in a dusting of snow, reminding me that, although this was the height of summer, in this part of the world you could indeed have four seasons in one day. It was the perfect place to relax after the beating we had received and put right the damage sustained, which turned out to be more serious as more breakages came to light, the worst being the flooded refrigerator electronics that put the system out of action, but as we were heading for Antarctica it was one piece of equipment we could easily live without.

When I checked the source of that inflow of water into the engine compartment, I was amazed to find that, in order to provide ventilation, the builders had connected the two vents to 100mm-diameter plastic hoses that led into the engine compartment. This may have been an acceptable system for a boat normally used in benign conditions but was an irresponsible solution on an ocean-going yacht like mine. I later changed the vents so they could be closed tightly in case of rough weather. On a few occasions when I

The Beagle Channel

forgot to open them after the weather had passed, the engine never seemed to be starved of air with the vents closed, so it seemed to have been a useless precaution.

A day later, the weather improved and we sailed uneventfully through the strait and reached Puerto Williams, on the southern shore of the Beagle Channel. One lesson I had quickly learned was that in those waters, when the conditions look right you move, but when the prospects look doubtful you let patience prevail and wait for a break. With hindsight, we should not have attempted Le Maire in a rising wind and should have sought shelter sooner. We didn't – and paid the price.

Patagonia, March 1999

Sailing north from the Beagle Channel into the Chilean fjordland, we experienced one of the infamous williwaws. It arrived with a sudden gust of about 30 knots and, having been caught in a relatively narrow channel, we didn't have any sea room to speak of. For a while we managed to sail, and later motorsail, close to the wind to stay clear of the land, but when the wind changed direction we started drifting in the direction of the shore. As the wind was now blowing from abeam, it put us on a deadly lee shore. I knew that we were in a grave situation, as we couldn't clear the land whether we continued ahead or tried to turn around. With the sails trimmed as close as possible to the wind and the help of the engine, we somehow managed to reach a more sheltered area where the wind was lighter. But it had been a very close shave indeed.

North Atlantic, September 2015

While on passage from Greenland to England, we had within three days of each other two force 10 storms. A stationary and very powerful high, west of the British Isles, had been blocking all weather systems in the North Atlantic and preventing any lows from moving from west to east. Caught in a deep low, the wind quickly reached gale force, then moved up the scale with sustained winds of 45 knots, with gusts over 50, and seas to match. Well reefed, Aventura took the strong winds in her stride and, as we had plenty of sea room, there was no reason to be concerned. What surprised me was how quickly the sea mounted, and at the height of the storm, I estimated the swell to be at least 8 metres high.

For a while we continued sailing, but with the wind showing no sign of decreasing and us being well off course, I decided to heave to. This was the first time that Aventura IV had to contend with winds of such strength at sea. With the backed staysail furled to about half its size, and three reefs in the mainsail, it was quite amazing how gentle Aventura's movement became once we were hove to. We were forereaching slightly, making quite a lot of leeway, however even the largest waves were no longer breaking but passing

Chilean williwaw

harmlessly under the hull. We rode out comfortably the worst of the storm and, when the wind went down in strength, we started sailing again. As the storm started abating, a rainbow formed over the towering seas, heralding the end of the show. And a show it had certainly been, providing visceral enjoyment at being witness to the raw force of nature, the raging ocean, the tumultuous swell.

At anchor

Some of the occasions where I experienced strong winds were while at anchor, whether in Bora Bora, Solomon Islands, Suwarrow or Croatia, and I found them to be more worrying than those that occurred at sea. Being anchored close to other boats exacerbated the problem, and while our anchor was holding, some of the others were dragging or swinging wildly, and getting dangerously close to us. At two of those locations I decided that the safest thing to do was to raise the anchor and move out to sea as quickly as possible. Having to manoeuvre under such conditions in a crowded anchorage is not something that I would recommend. On one occasion, when the storm had abated and we returned the following day, we found that some of the boats that had stayed had been blown ashore.

Antarctica, February 1999

The synoptic chart showed a deep low heading straight for the Antarctic Peninsula, and I knew that we were going to be in for a serious blow. So I decided to seek shelter at Port Circumcision, which was a protected spot, and made for it immediately. Having pushed our way through the ice blocking the entrance, we dropped anchor in the most sheltered part of the small bay. To reach it, we had to partly raise the centreboard. The advantage of being able to reduce our draft was that even smaller bits of ice could not make their way into the shallow area and grounded in deeper water. For added safety we took four lines ashore and tethered Aventura firmly in place. Aventura hardly budged even when the wind topped 50 knots.

Port Circumcision

We spent two enjoyable days in this perfectly sheltered spot, much of it ashore in the nearby penguin colony, watching their daily routine and being just happy to be there.

Northwest Passage, August 2014

While waiting in Dundas Harbour for the ice situation to improve in the Northwest Passage, the forecast of an easterly gale turned into a proper storm, with gusts of over 60 knots. Aventura survived it unscathed, owing

Dundas Harbour

to our 33-kg Rocna anchor and 90 metres of 10-mm chain. We had to motor constantly into the wind not so much to ease the strain on the anchor, but primarily to avoid being hit by a boat that had anchored too close to us before the storm. Being anchored with only a short length of chain and the rest line, it was swerving wildly in the strong gusts and coming perilously close. After 27 hours of defensive manoeuvring, our track recorded on the chart plotter had become a solid, almost black shape of intersecting lines, as shown on page 206.

Storm tactics

I do not have any universal rules concerning the actual handling of a boat in heavy weather, nor am I prepared to give any advice, as so much depends on local circumstances, the type of boat and the experience of the captain and crew. Above all else, the two most important factors are an absolute confidence in yourself and in your boat. Any well-built and -equipped boat should withstand conditions generated by winds

of 50 or 60 knots. As with everything else to do with cruising, the secret is good preparation. Just as important is not to panic and to stay calm, because however bad the weather may be, it will eventually come to an end. Whenever I am in a storm, I never fail to remember one of my favourite songs, Dr Hook's Storms Never Last. They never do.

At sea

I need to stress again that in this case, more than with any other subject, I prefer to limit my comments to what I would do in certain situations myself, and shall attempt to summarise my own way of dealing with strong winds.

With a boat like Aventura III or IV, if I had sufficient sea room I would prefer to try and outsail bad weather. I would run or broadreach if existing conditions and my location allowed this to be done safely. I would heave to if there were no sea room, or conditions became too uncomfortable.

Depending on the type of boat, other sailors who find themselves in such situations may consider trying to slow down if the boat became unmanageable, or improve control by streaming a sea anchor. I need to stress that this would not be my way of dealing with such situations, and for this reason I do not carry any type of sea anchor or drogue. But for certain types of boats this approach may work.

At anchor

I would, as always, make sure to be well anchored. If I were in any doubt, I would seek a more sheltered place, and would also make the necessary provisions to buoy and jettison the chain and anchor if forced to leave immediately. Occasionally, being at sea may be the safer option, and to be able to do this at short notice, I would prepare an exit strategy in advance.

If I were on a mooring, I would check that it is a professionally laid heavy-duty mooring capable of handling storm-force winds, and also check the mooring chain or line. But if I had no confidence in the mooring, I would either find a sheltered spot to use my own anchor, or put to sea.

Tips

» Uncluttered decks. The advent of a heavy blow is not the time to start worrying about lashing the dinghy, stowing sailbags, surfboard, jerrycans or any of the clutter that marks long-distance cruising boats. On all my boats, the decks were kept absolutely bare with everything stowed below or in the cockpit lockers, not just on long ocean passages but even when cruising short distances.

» A safe, well-protected cockpit where the crew can sit comfortably and preferably dry.

» Efficient sail handling and reefing systems so that reducing sail can be done quickly and easily, ideally from the cockpit, without putting the crew in potential danger.

» Good-quality sails that can withstand a strong gust or squall for long enough to allow the crew to reduce sail.

» A strong, reliable autopilot. A good pilot is absolutely essential, especially if sailing short-handed. In strong weather, the fact that you can rely on the autopilot to steer the boat allows you to stay alert and deal with other things.

» Carry a few ready meals, such as canned casseroles or stews, in order to have a warm meal when cooking may be difficult.

» Dealing with heavy weather when it arrives is always easier if all necessary preparations have been made in advance: foul-weather gear and harnesses at the ready, a substantial meal prepared, a hot drink in a Thermos flask.

11

Life Afloat

It isn't that life ashore is distasteful to me. But life at sea is better.

Sir Francis Drake

There is nothing more enticing, enchanting, and enslaving than the life at sea.

Joseph Conrad

For me life afloat is just a pleasure.

Silvana Masotti

The attitude to life at sea may not have changed much over the years, as the above comments attest, but the standard of comfort, and our expectations, certainly have.

A comfortable life afloat has been a top priority for me from the beginning, and even if our means were limited at the time, we made a great effort in making our first Aventura as comfortable as possible. Early on we established an offshore routine with regular meals, rest periods and watches, a pattern that I have continued throughout my sailing life even when I was not sailing with my family. The importance of such a routine was inherited from the days when I sailed with Gwenda and our two children, Doina and Ivan, and realised how important it was for them to grow up in an environment similar to the one they had lived on land. Some of my later crew found my insistence on a regular routine, as pedantic and at odds with the tenets of a carefree cruising life.

The rather modest personal comforts that we considered adequate in the 1970s have changed considerably over the years. In 2001, as Gwenda and I passed through Gibraltar on Aventura III, we were greatly surprised to see Aventura I on her way into the Mediterranean. In spite of her age, she looked in tiptop condition and much better than when I had sold her in 1982. Her latest owner, a cabinetmaker by profession, had ripped out the interior, got rid of all my clumsy amateur work and refitted her to the highest

standard. The main thing that shocked us was how we had managed to survive for six long years in such a confined space.

One lesson that I learned from the writings of cruising pioneers was how important it was to lead as normal a life as possible. This meant having proper and regular meals, ideally seated at the table, and that at least the main meal should be taken with all the crew together. I took this so much to heart that on our first ocean passage, while crossing the Bay of Biscay, when the time came for our first lunch I hove-to and asked Gwenda to lay the table.

'You must be crazy. I can hardly hang on in all this rolling and you'll never get the kids out of their bunks.' Gwenda commented, trying to inject some realism into my harebrained idea.

'But Eric Hiscock said that you must try and keep the crew happy by....'

'Why don't you go and sail with Hiscock then,' she cut me short. 'We were sailing along so well, so why do you have to spoil it now?'

The sea was indeed quite agitated so I got the boat sailing again and the movement got better. Gwenda fed the children first, then handed me a bowl of steaming stew.

'That tastes good. When did you manage to cook it?'

'Well, Susan Hiscock suggests that you prepare a nourishing dish before you set off on passage so all you have to do is heat it up.'

'You women always seem to know best.'

'Yes, and also we are usually right.'

That was probably the first time I realised that not only did I have a lot to learn from all those famous predecessors, but also that I had a ready source of common sense much closer to hand and started listening more to my wife. Over the years I have come to appreciate and value Gwenda's judgement. Whereas by nature I am impulsive and quick to take decisions, Gwenda is very English in her manner, never rash, always calm and cool, pragmatic and open-minded. She rarely reacts immediately to whatever I may suggest, but takes her time to consider the issue before expressing her views on the matter, her realism being occasionally irritating, although usually justified.

Both on Aventura II and III life followed a regular pattern and I kept the same routine on Aventura IV. After so many years spent at sea, most things had become second nature. However rough it may be, I try to shave and wash every day because this always makes me feel better. Unfortunately this daily routine was often incompatible with sailing in high latitudes, whether in Antarctica or the Arctic, and, especially when under way, I occasionally let it lapse. Peeling off several layers of clothing just to wash was too much of an effort, and I found an easy excuse by saying to myself that you hardly perspire in the constant cold. However, I remembered a skipper once pointing out that 'ample water keeps you from getting sick; daily showers keep people from fighting because they feel yucky.' So, as we had plenty of warm water when motoring in the Northwest Passage, all the crew had a chance to have regular showers.

Meals

On all my boats, whenever conditions were right we tried to eat at the table, either in the cockpit or below. The food was either dished out onto individual plates in the galley straight from the pot, or brought to the table in a serving dish, never in the cooking pot. Both in Antarctica and the Arctic, we usually had warm meals at both lunch and dinner, and everyone, whether on watch or resting, was expected to join these meals.

Breakfast was usually cereal, porridge, and, on special occasions, pancakes. Toast was also on the menu, grilled at sea on a special toaster placed over a burner, or electric when we were on shore power. Porridge is my favourite, and I have my own recipe, not the bland variety boiled in water, but in milk with a generous helping of raisins or sultanas. The breakfast routine was flexible as it was dependent on the watches.

Lunch with Dunbar and Pablo on passage to Dutch Harbor on Aventura IV.

On every Aventura, lunch was served at noon, shortly after the day's position had been entered in the logbook and the last 24 hours mileage announced to the crew. It usually consisted of soup followed by a substantial salad, made with fresh lettuce or tomatoes, supplemented by canned sweet corn, tuna, heart of palm, olives, and accompanied by bread, cheese, ham, salami or hard boiled eggs with mayonnaise. When salad leaves were not available, they were substituted by potatoes, rice or pasta, cooked in advance. One of my favourite salads on passage is cabbage salad. Cabbage keeps up to two months in a dark and dry place. The white cabbage with a dense interior is the best, as it keeps longest. The implement to grate it is the type of square metal grater with four sides. Occasionally

I also add some grated carrots; I then add capers, mustard, maybe a little bit of salt, although I am not keen on using salt in my salads, as I believe that there is sufficient salt in the ingredients. I also believe that most people use more salt in cooking than necessary, and ready-made and most restaurant meals are often too salty for my taste. The exception is boiling pasta and potatoes, when I always add some salt to the water, usually seawater. The dressing is made up of lemon juice, which I prefer to vinegar, and a substantial amount of olive oil. When I introduced my crew to this East European dish, albeit greatly modified for West European tastes, it was met with much scepticism. But that didn't last long, as eventually all agreed that it was indeed a tasty and wholesome dish. It went very well with frankfurters or hard-boiled eggs with mayonnaise. Ideally, the salad should be made a few hours before lunch because it improves by being left to stand. It tastes even better the following day, so it is always a good idea to make enough for two meals.

The main cooked meal of the day was dinner served shortly after nightfall. While preparing the shopping list for the Northwest Passage with Gwenda's help, I devised, as I had previously done for Antarctica, a rolling menu spread over six days. Two of the dinner meals were fresh meat or sausages, served with potatoes, rice, tinned peas or other vegetables. The potatoes were either freshly mashed or from a packet, or pre-boiled and fried up with onions. To save gas and also time, I often boiled a full pressure cooker of potatoes, and then used them as a side dish or in salads. When the fresh meat ran out, I substituted it with fish. When fish was not available I had a selection of large French tins of gourmet meals, from duck confit to coq-au-vin.

On two evenings we would have stew, also of East European inspiration, prepared to last for two meals. The meat, preferable diced lamb, is fried up with onions in the pressure cooker, with diced potatoes, carrots, cauliflower or other fresh vegetables. Two

large tins of peeled tomatoes are added next, also one cup of seawater, with a large helping of paprika and herbes de Provence, bay leaves and pepper, before the pressure cooker is sealed. When its valve starts hissing, the flame is lowered and the stew is usually left to simmer for eight minutes. When the time is up, the gas is turned off, the pressure cooker is allowed to cool for a few minutes before the pressure valve is slowly and carefully released to let the steam escape. The advantage of using a pressure cooker is that after the first meal is served, the cooker can be sealed again, brought up to the boil and let to cool down with the lid closed. If the stew is too successful and there are too many second helpings the first time, it is very easy to add a tin of peas, white beans or mushrooms to make up the quantity for a second meal. Occasionally, I varied the routine by using pulses, such as red beans or lentils, cooked with smoked ham or sausages, such as chorizo.

The two other meals on the rolling menu were pasta in all its shapes, and with various sauces. The latter is normally one of the prepared ones, but only used as a base, with my own spices and ingredients added to it. For long passages, I buy mincemeat in a larger quantity, divide it up, and vacuum pack it in separate bags for a single use.

Provisions

Just as I chose not to have a separate diesel generator on any of my boats, having witnessed so many problems with gensets on other boats, I also decided against having a freezer, not so much because I suspected its reliability, but because I could not see any good reason for having such a power-hungry piece of equipment. After all these years I still feel the same, mainly because I prefer to eat fresh food whenever possible, but also because I found that a capacious refrigerator is more than adequate for my needs. On Aventura IV, the refrigerator had two large drawers, the lower one being kept for long term storage and vacuum packed food. When provisioning for a long passage I always try to buy meat that had been vacuum packed already, or ask for it to be done for me. Otherwise, I do it myself as I have a 220V vacuum packer, which makes it possible to keep meat stored in the bottom drawer of the refrigerator for at least two weeks.

The vacuum packer also comes in handy to preserve freshly caught fish that cannot be consumed all at once and will keep for several days. Besides the vacuum packer, a liquidiser is very useful both for making soups and fruit juice.

Provisioning for all long passages I use a comprehensive list that covers all planned meals, snacks, special treats, hot drinks, long life milk, wine, as well as the entire range of domestic consumables

from garbage bags to toilet paper, cloth pegs to eco-friendly washing up liquid. I am pleased to say that we missed nothing on my latest voyage and we ended both Arctic seasons with a surplus of provisions. My basic passage shopping list can be consulted on our website cornellsailing.com/Aventura.

Farmers' market in Santa Cruz de Tenerife

For long passages, I always buy large quantities of fresh fruit and vegetables. Potatoes, onions, carrots, white salad cabbage, onions, garlic, as well as apples, oranges, and lemons keep well. Others, such as aubergines, green and red peppers, courgettes, celery, cauliflower, green beans and avocado, have a limited storage time. Tomatoes keep well if bought slightly unripe. Every morning I would go on an inspection tour checking the fruit and vegetables, and picking out the ripest to be consumed first.

All fruit and soft vegetables were stored in large hanging nets, whereas those that are vulnerable to light were kept carefully separated from each other on shelves in the forward cabin. Bananas should never be stored next to other fruit as an enzyme in the bananas accelerates the ripening process in adjacent items. On Aventura IV, potatoes, onions, garlic, cabbage and carrots were kept in bins in the dark and airy space under the deck salon.

Markets

I always enjoy going to local markets as often you find there an aspect of community life that can no longer be found elsewhere. Although buying provisions may be the main reason for my visit, what I really enjoy is watching the ever-changing scenery, and attempting to catch some of its colourful aspects. In all my travels, some of my best photographs are scenes snatched in the market.

On a more practical level, I prefer to buy fruit and vegetables from a farmers' market, where they are fresh and not chilled. I usually go to the market a few days before my planned departure, pick out the best looking stall, explain to the owner that we are on a boat about to leave on a voyage, and ask him or her to bring some fresh supplies on the agreed day. Fresh eggs are also best bought from the market and kept in a dark, well-aired place. For my first attempt at the Northwest Passage I had to buy provisions for a crew of eight, and did all my fresh shopping at Stromness, in the Orkney Islands. I managed to track down a local farmer who kept hens, and bought twenty dozen freshly laid eggs. They were kept in a cockpit locker and lasted all summer, albeit in Arctic and not tropical temperatures. I still had some on the passage south from St John's in Newfoundland when one morning I prepared an omelette for my crew. Both my crew found it very tasty and asked me if they were freshly bought eggs from the last stop. 'No', I replied, 'I bought them earlier... three months ago, in fact,' and burst out laughing. They didn't find it funny and probably didn't believe me either.

This incident reminds me of my friend Antti who sailed with me on several long passages. His favourite breakfast was fried eggs. As he was a cardiologist, I once asked him if he wasn't worried about the cholesterol content.

'Not at all,' he replied, 'just take your statin and stop worrying. And now that you mentioned it, can I have some eggs for breakfast?'

'The usual two?'

'How about three... sunny side up?'

One of the most interesting and memorable times on Aventura I was while sailing from the Solomon Islands to Papua New Guinea and stopping at the islands on the way. In some places we were the first ever yacht to been seen there.

One afternoon we dropped anchor off a small village and, within a few minutes, we were surrounded by a dozen small outrigger canoes paddled by one or two children. We tried to communicate with them but without much success. They looked so friendly and welcoming that we decided to give them some gifts. We were well prepared for this eventuality and carried a good supply of coloured pencils and balloons. So we gave each child a balloon and after a while they paddled happily away. Hardly had one lot departed that another lot arrived, each one clutching an egg, which they offered us as a gift. Guessing what they were after, we handed over more balloons for each egg. That evening Gwenda decided to make an omelette, but when she cracked the first egg open, it had a small half grown chick inside, as did most of the others. We guessed that they had been liberated from under a hatching hen and could only laugh at this clever trick. It was exactly what I would have done myself at their age to get something that I really wanted.

We soon found that provisioning in remote places in the South Pacific was almost impossible. Fresh vegetables have always played an important part in our diet, and we realised that the sooner we learned to appreciate the local produce the better. We greatly missed having fresh salad, and one inspired improvisation was green papaya salad, based on our well-tried cabbage salad. The unripe papaya was peeled, grated and seasoned with a small amount of salt, ground pepper, lemon juice and salad oil. It made a tasty and perfect substitution for my favourite cabbage salad, and in most islands the supply of green papayas was almost unlimited. Gradually we learned to adapt our taste to local produce, such as palisami, a kind of spinach, taro leaves, plantain, breadfruit, as well as banana, mango, papaya, and green coconut. The latter's tasty juice made a perfect sundowner when mixed with a dash of rum.

In places where there was no market, we usually bartered, not always very successfully or with the expected result, as with the eggs. After a memorable 600-mile passage through the uninhabited fjordland of southern Chile we arrived at the settlement of Puerto Eden where we could buy diesel fuel but little else. I asked the man at the ramshackle fuel station where we could get some fresh provisions, and he told me that we may be able to get some scallops at a nearby packing factory. We tied up to the small dock and were met by a young man, whom I greeted in Spanish.

'I have been told that we can buy some fresh scallops here. Is that right?'

'Oh no, señor, absolutely not, that is strictly forbidden.'

'That is a great pity as we need some fresh food.'

I must add here that the area of southern Chile, that we had sailed through, was experiencing a red tide, when neither mussels nor fish were safe to eat.

'Please can you sell us at least enough for one meal?' I pleaded.

'I am sorry señor, we are not allowed to sell anything.' He repeated, then gave me a meaningful look, 'But we can give you some. Wait here.'

A few minutes later he returned carrying two large boxes, which he handed over one by one. Each weighed several kilos, one containing white, the other pink scallops. As obviously money could not change hands, I asked him what we could offer in exchange.

'Do you have any jam or marmalade?'

'I am sure we do.' I replied. Fortunately we had several jars, so the barter was completed to both sides' satisfaction. But the ensuing daily diet of scallops, fried, seared, stewed, baked, boiled or battered has turned me off this delicacy for life.

Our Chilean benefactor

The galley

By the time I came to equip Aventura IV's galley, where I expected to do much of the cooking, I knew the importance of good utensils and useful aids. I will list them here in no particular order, and start with a comprehensive set of non-stick sauce and frying pans of various sizes, each with fitting lids, their overall dimensions to allow two of them to sit on top of the cooker at the same time. A good-sized pressure cooker is essential, and so is a kettle with whistle, plus a range of utensils: sharp knives of various sizes, swivelling potato peeler, tin-opener, garlic-crusher, pasta tongs, salad centrifuge, waffle iron, microwave dishes and assorted silicone baking dishes.

For a large crew an insulated pump-action coffee dispenser was very useful on night watches, as well as insulated Zyliss cafetiere-type mugs. The advantages of a vacuum packer have been described earlier. Finally, an ingenious gadget, which I had on Aventura III, and wished I had on her successor, was a holder made of 3-mm stainless-steel plate, that fitted on top of the cooker and had holes cut out for mugs and cereal bowls. Being gimballed, it was ideal to use while making coffee, preparing breakfast, or putting down a mug in a hurry.

Aventura IV being an eco-friendly ship, we only used eco-friendly washing up liquid, and the special laundry balls for the washing machine, a natural alternative to chemical detergents. Garbage disposal on passage was another important aspect we considered. We disposed of all packaging in a responsible manner before leaving port, and while on passage kept all garbage that could not be disposed of safely at sea in bags stowed in the tender, to be disposed of when we arrived in a port with recycling facilities. Both grey and black waters were treated by an Electroscan purifying system.

The social side

Any damn fool can navigate the world sober. It takes a really good sailor to do it drunk.

Sir Francis Chichester

I have no strict rules about alcohol consumption at sea maybe because all my friends only drink in moderation. A sundowner is normally served just before sunset, usually a glass of wine, but only if the weather looks settled. Drinks are usually served in proper glasses not plastic and I still have my favourite heavy bottomed glasses that we bought in Fiji 40 years ago and have travelled thousands of miles on every Aventura since.

Our daily bread

On the suggestion of some cruising guru, or his wife, Aventura I left London with a large sack of wholemeal flour. For a while Gwenda valiantly baked bread at least once a week but eventually the flour got so infested with weevils that the sack was visibly moving. Eventually we learned not to buy large quantities of flour or rice, as the outcome was always the same. Later Gwenda switched from loaves to rolls, as they were easier to bake. I once looked into buying a dedicated breadmaker, but was put off by the large amount of electricity they use. Once I did opt for the next best thing and took along a baker as crew. Unfortunately Patrick, who sailed with me from Cape Town to the Canaries, refused to even attempt to bake bread away from his state-of-the-art bakery. He only managed to produce once some pitiful-looking rolls that tasted fine, but he never repeated the effort. It certainly made me feel very good as it set my own inadequacy as a baker in a new perspective.

On long passages, a good substitute for bread is crispbread of the Ryvita or Wasa type that keeps very well on long passages. One other good supplement, and one of my favourites, is pancakes. I always carry a good stock of ready-made pancake mix and often treat my crew to a special breakfast.

Freshly baked bread became a special treat while sailing with Doina in the Arctic, and I was impressed how well she rose to the occasion by producing not only tasty loaves, but also buns, cakes, puddings and other treats. Although I do not mind cooking all meals on passage, baking bread is a chore I don't enjoy. Instead, I found sliced bread perfectly adequate and my crew didn't object either. The wholemeal type is best as it is more nourishing and also keeps better. I usually store the bread in the hanging netting, and after a bag is opened, in a breadbin or airtight container. Sliced bread will keep for up to three weeks even if towards the end there may be mould growing on the crust, which I try to get rid of out of sight of my crew. If this makes me feel bad all I have to do is think of what the crew and officers ate on Captain Cook's ships. At least they had some compensation as each seaman was supposed to get two gallons of ale and about a pint of rum per day, so life must have been quite bearable, as most of the time they were half-drunk. I once saw the list of beverages loaded in Madeira for Captain Cook's first voyage. It included 3,000 gallons of wine, a staggering amount that worked out at two litres of wine plus one litre of spirits per day for every officer or gentleman. One must remember that they did not have good drinking water, but I still wouldn't suggest trying out such a regime on your own crew.

Cooking gas

The most common types of cooking gas used on boats is butane, which is used mostly in tropical and temperate climates, and propane in colder countries. As there is no universal standard, and the type of tank and fittings differ widely, deciding on the right type of tank for a boat setting off on a world voyage can be a real challenge. Connectors and regulators differ from country to country, as do regulations concerning filling steel, aluminium or fibreglass tanks. Filling the tanks in countries used to visiting yachts is usually possible, even if it may take time to find the right place to do it. Carrying a universal set of adaptors may solve the problem, but assembling such a set can be a frustrating if not impossible task. The only tanks that can be filled in most places are the blue Camping Gaz tanks. In desperation, as happened to me on a few occasions, I resorted to buying or renting a full local tank, connected it with a hose to my own, hung it upside down above it, and decanted the contents. I usually managed to get half my tank filled, but it is not a solution I would recommend. Eventually the only reasonable solution is to switch over to using local tanks, especially if you are spending longer in that country.

Fishing

One of my greatest pleasures while cruising is catching fish. Fish used to be, and still is, my main source of protein on long passages. There are various ways of getting your fish. On ocean passages trolling a line with a good lure will usually achieve results. As I do not use a fishing rod, and cannot play the fish as professionals do, I use a double hook. It may not be sporty but it seems to ensure better results than a single hook. It's worth mentioning the importance of the type of lure used.

On offshore passages in the tropics I found those looking like a squid yield the best results. In temperate and cold waters successful fishing becomes more of an art than a gamble. When trolling at sea you should reel in the line if there are birds about as they may mistake the lure for a fish and get hooked. The worst are boobies, of which I caught at least two and so realised how they have got their silly name. Albatross can be just as vulnerable and there is an ongoing campaign to protect the albatross population of the Southern Ocean that has been decimated in recent years in this way by longliners.

While we were making our way into the Salomon lagoon in Chagos, a young boy of about ten came over in his dinghy, greeted us and asked permission to come on board. He directed us to the best spot to anchor then briefed us on all essentials. He told us that the lagoon was teeming with fish and that the tastiest were a kind of snapper. He stressed that the best time to get them was at seven o'clock in the evening. After he left I rowed to the beach, picked up a couple of hermit crabs for bait, returned to the boat and by 6.30 had set up a line and sinker with the creature impaled on the hook. I lowered the line until I felt the hook touch the bottom some 20 metres under the boat. Nothing much happened and I felt a bit foolish sitting on the stern platform wiggling a fishing line. My crew saw the hilarity of it and started making fun of me. He had been more impressed on our passage from Cocos Keeling when I managed to land a large fish every time I let out the line. In spite of the ridiculousness of the situation I decided to wait until seven and, lo and behold, on the dot of seven I

felt a strong tug on the line, I pulled it up and when it broke the surface I had the most beautiful snapper hooked on it. It made an excellent supper, perhaps one of the tastiest fish I had ever caught. I took that perfect timing to be just a happy coincidence but decided to have another go and disprove the theory, so around the same time the following evening I repeated the operation and at precisely seven o'clock had another large snapper on the line. QED. But I hope no one asks me for an explanation.

During our first voyage, we tried to live as much as possible off the sea and land, and while in Greece I became very proficient with my speargun. Unfortunately Greek waters had been fished out over the years by the widely used barbaric method of dynamite and in those days one could still see older fishermen with missing limbs. I soon found out that fishing with a torch on a moonless night was much more productive. With a powerful torch I would scan the waters around me, and if lucky would catch a fish in its beam, the mesmerised creature making a perfect target. I would feed it on to a wire ring that I was carrying at my waist and continue my hunt. If I was really lucky I got a conger eel or an octopus, which, after I had learned how to tenderise them, would provide two or three tasty protein-rich meals. I rarely came back before midnight, but in this way I managed to feed my family.

Life became much easier once we reached the Caribbean where fish was plentiful and could be caught easily by day. Octopus was replaced by crayfish or spiny lobster, which were an easy target once I had learned how to locate their hiding places. So lobster became

our staple diet until we reached the Bahamas where we didn't seem to eat anything else and Doina exclaimed one day, 'Oh Daddy, not lobster again!' I got the point and reverted to ordinary fish. However justified that massacre may have been at the time to feed my family, now that I am aware of the depleting stocks and the destruction of the marine environment, I feel really bad about it, so on my latest world voyage I only fished when sailing offshore. Eventually the fish had their revenge as at Tikehau in the Tuamotus, I broke my own rule and speared a grouper that gave both Gwenda and me a serious dose of ciguatera poisoning. This is the most serious risk associated with fishing in tropical waters and is described on page 282.

Diving

As part of the preparations for our first voyage I joined the British Sub-Aqua Club and qualified as a diver. I have carried a full set of diving gear on all my boats, Aventura II even having its own diving compressor. On both Aventura III and IV I had two sets of gear with two tanks, which were always kept full. I had a wetsuit as well as a dry diving suit that allowed me to dive in

cold waters in an emergency. The tanks were rarely used when I was younger and in better shape, and could easily free-dive to 15 metres. The dry suit was used in a real emergency in the Arctic when we caught a rope around the propeller and I was forced to dive in the ice-cold water to attempt to free it. The incident is described on page 227.

Creature comforts

One comment that has stayed with me all my life is some terse advice to moaning cruisers issued by rally founder Jimmy Cornell: 'If you want things to be like home, stay at home.' We elect to go sailing because we want to be in the thick of the elements: wild, free, exciting, unstable, brilliant, sometimes ugly, but more often thrilling and beautiful, an experience that brings life fully to life.

Elaine Bunting

Personal comfort is a relative matter and I must admit that when I was young my tastes and habits were quite Spartan, undoubtedly a result of growing up in a place where shortages and privations were the norm. It may have been a useful attitude in my youth, but not when planning a long voyage with my family. Bearing in mind our limited means, we managed to make the first Aventura reasonably comfortable. Aventura II was a great improvement, but when I started planning a world voyage on Aventura III, I knew that if I wanted to persuade Gwenda to sail with me, I had to raise the standard even higher. Fortunately Gwenda decided to take matters in hand and Aventura III ended up having the most comfortable armchairs on any boat that I have visited before or since. She also conceived her own watch-keeping corner with all instruments at her fingertips, a feature also incorporated in Aventura IV's cockpit.

Gradually I came to realise that creature comforts are essential not just for the general wellbeing of the crew, but also for safety. This is particularly true in high-latitude sailing, and therefore personal comfort was a high priority on Aventura IV. The interior layout was designed with this in mind, and the Spectra

watermaker provided a generous supply of water so that we could have hot showers anytime we wanted, while the diesel heater kept the inside temperature at a comfortable level.

Entertainment

One of the great pleasures of life afloat is reading and whereas ashore I rarely manage to read more than one book per month, when I am sailing I devour them virtually by the day. I always make sure that I take a good supply of books with me, as generally the ones that interest me are much harder to find away from home. Book swapping with other sailors rarely seemed to work as tastes differ so greatly and in all these years I don't think I got more than half a dozen books in this way. As I am not too keen on novels, and prefer non-fiction, I always like to have a good stock of factual books on history and economics, or biographies. The latter are the best reads on long passages, as they are easy to put down and pick up again. Much of my own

onboard library was made up of reference books, such as manuals on maintenance, first-aid and medical emergencies, cruising guides for the various countries we intend to visit, books on seabirds, fish, cooking and a frequently used book on knots. Guides to specific countries are best bought in advance, as often they are unavailable locally.

Music can be just as important as books and on the first Aventura we left with stacks of pre-recorded tapes that we played on one of my tape recorders. Both Aventura III and IV had a proper sound system with stereo speakers in the main cabin and cockpit. Eventually we also progressed to a DVD player and screen.

On our early voyages, the preferred pastime was listening to the BBC World Service but the BBC has now discontinued most of its radio transmissions. Short wave radio is now mostly a thing of the past, but there are various satellite radio and television services that sound attractive but I have not used them myself.

Communications

From nothing to virtually everything is how the change from the first Aventura to the current one can be described. When we first set off we did not even have a VHF radio although towards the end of the

Aventura IV's Arctic communications hub

voyage we did acquire an SSB radio. Aventura II was much better equipped while Aventura III had the whole range of communications, VHF and SSB transceivers, Inmarsat C for text, and later an Iridium satellite phone for voice and email. Aventura IV went one step up being equipped with VHF, SSB and AIS transceivers, as well as Iridium Pilot broadband for both data and voice communications. This was a great boon while in the Arctic as I was able to not only receive daily ice charts for the Northwest Passage but could also send photographs to the websites and magazines to which I was contributing.

As an emergency backup I have owned an Iridium satphone ever since they became available. Over the years I have used my Iridium phone not just on the boat but also when travelling in areas where I expected not to have reliable mobile phone coverage, whether trekking in the Alps, skiing in the Sierra Nevada, or on a foray by Jeep into the Sahara in Tunisia.

Email is my main means of offshore communication and as a service-provider I use Mailasail, a British company specialising in satellite communications, used to dealing primarily with pleasure craft and thus familiar with the requirements of cruising sailors. The system worked very well on the last two Aventuras, although some people find the use of a satellite phone for emails to be expensive. Mainly for this reason some cruising sailors use one of the SSB radio-based systems, such as Sailmail and Winlink, that are more economical, even if slower and not suitable for volume users such as myself.

Mobile phones have become almost indispensible, and in recent years I realised that many marinas no longer use VHF radio, but expect to be contacted by phone. As roaming charges and costs of making calls while abroad can often be very high, it is well worth buying a local SIM card if spending a longer time in a certain country.

For long-range communications SSB radios were very useful in the not-so-distant past when I often used to make calls home via one of the shore relay stations. Most have closed down now, bringing to an end over one century of ship-to-shore communications. As a result, my own use of the SSB radio has gone down considerably. Occasionally I have joined one of the cruisers' radio nets that have proliferated in every corner of the world, and can be a most valuable source of local information, providing a means of reporting one's position, getting updates on weather, and having a place to appeal to in case of trouble.

In the old days postal mail was virtually the only means of communication between sailors and their families as international phone calls were unaffordably expensive. For those who are still dependent on the postal system the most reliable holding addresses continue to be those of yacht clubs or marinas. It is advisable to contact them in advance to ask permission to use them as a holding address, and give them your ETA to hold your mail until your arrival.

Pets

Obviously it is better to have a small pet on a big boat than a large pet on a small boat.

Luc Callebaut

We never had pets on any of our boats, nor at home for that matter. Knowing how strongly some people feel about this subject I am quite reluctant to be too outspoken on the controversial subject of cruising pets. My main objection is of a practical nature. The restrictions applied to pets are similar to those concerning firearms, and there are a number of countries where importing a pet illegally is considered no lesser crime than trying to hide a gun. Regulations concerning cruising pets are extremely stringent in some countries and this is the main reason why the number of cruising boats with pets is still very low, probably less than five per cent. To have or not to have a pet is a difficult question and anyone considering having a pet should think very carefully before setting off on a long voyage. I feel that especially in the case of large dogs, confining them on a boat is both selfish and cruel. Small dogs or cats may be a different matter.

A couple, whom we met in many places, admitted that having a dog during their world voyage had been a major mistake, mainly because their freedom of movement had been severely restricted. Luc Callebaut disagrees. 'Cruising with a pet on board is so nice that I plan to get a couple so we can start breeding Schipperke dogs, those intelligent barge dogs.' He did and called the first-born Jimmy.

Luc and Jackie with my namesake on the left

Pests

Uninvited pets are a very different matter and cockroaches are the worst, especially in the tropics, as once they are in residence they are almost impossible to eradicate. This is why it is so important to avoid being gate-crashed by those nasty squatters by observing some basic rules: thoroughly rinse fresh fruit and vegetables, and especially stems of bananas, before taking them on board (some people suggest adding one or two chlorine water-purifying tablets to the rinsing water), immediately remove from the boat cartons and other packaging after unpacking, never leave food remains in the open, always clean the area around the galley. If laying up the boat in the tropics, sprinkle anti-cockroach powder in all critical areas including the bilges. Once the boat is infested the only way to get rid of the roaches is to have the boat fumigated. Because we didn't know what precautions to take, Aventura I got badly infected with cockroaches, and although we regularly fumigated the interior we barely managed to keep matters under control. We only got rid of that nuisance when we returned to temperate zones. Having learned from that experience, I never had a cockroach on any of my subsequent boats.

Mosquitoes can be an even greater nuisance and in some countries also carry the risk of malaria, dengue fever and other diseases. On our first voyage we took prophylactic antimalarial tablets in critical areas but because of their side effects and also the fact that some malaria strains have become drug resistant, many people have stopped using them. Instead, it is best to avoid being bitten by mosquitoes in the first place. The first rule is to anchor far enough from the shore so as to be out of their range. Mosquito nets or screens should be fitted to all openings, and using burning coils or ultrasound devices is also recommended. When going ashore always use a good repellent spray or cream, and try avoiding the critical times, such as dusk and early evening when mosquitoes are most active.

Flies can be bad too and in Croatia we were invaded by huge swarms of fat black flies. Sprays and sticky hanging tapes seem to work and, if one has the patience, swatters too. In Croatia, for the first time on a boat, we were pestered by some very aggressive wasps. Fortunately some friends presented us with a Zephyr, a battery operated electronic wasp zapper obtainable from local hardware stores.

Photography

Photography has played a major role in my voyaging and, in fact, in all my life. The first job I got after leaving school was as a roaming photographer for a studio whose owner gave me a camera and flashgun

and told me to go to restaurants in the evenings, take pictures of people eating or dancing, give them a card with the address of the studio and tell them to pass by if they wanted to order the finished result. When I handed out the card I charged a small deposit, and this I could keep whereas the studio kept whatever it made out of the order. It was an easy job, I was earning well and I enjoyed it. Soon afterwards my father came home on one of his regular shuttles between prison and freedom, and I proudly took him shopping and bought him a suit. I was sixteen.

When Aventura I arrived in Fiji and I saw the low prices in the duty-free shops I decided to go for the best and invested in two top of the range Nikon cameras and assorted lenses. It was a wise decision because over the years they have paid handsome dividends. Excellent results followed almost immediately, which was not surprising as we were cruising in one of the most photogenic areas in the world. I now have a huge selection of colour slides from our many years of cruising, but eventually I decided to move with the times and switch to digital photography. This means

that the best of my old slides had to be scanned, which was a daunting task, as I must own over ten thousand of them.

On Aventura IV, I found a GoPro camera to be very useful, as it had an underwater housing, and, attached to a long pole, allowed me to inspect the propeller, rudders or engine water intake. Mounted at the top of the mast, I let it film some of our transit of the Panama Canal.

My earlier attempts in the field of movies were quite disappointing, and came to an abrupt, and ultimately fortuitous, end on Easter Island. As the weather was unsettled, we could not leave the boat unattended in the open anchorage off the main settlement of Hangaroa, so first Gwenda and Ivan visited the site of the giant statues, then Doina and I. As the site was several kilometres from the anchorage, we hired two horses from a local man. Lucia and Gloria looked quite a sorry pair, but the owner assured me that they were gentle and obedient animals. We took his word and set off towards the distant quarry where the giant statues had been carved and left abandoned by the mysterious earlier inhabitants of the island. As we got to the bottom of the extinct crater I prodded Lucia to stop, which she did. I dismounted and my feet had hardly touched the ground when Lucia jerked her head violently, the reins slipped off her head as they had not been well tied, and galloped away. Leaping wildly as if possessed by devils trying to get rid of the saddlebag, I watched in horror as the bag emptied its contents, starting with my Super 8 camera that described a high arch before crashing onto the stony ground followed by my other accoutrements. Once the bag had stopped banging against her sides, Lucia calmed down and started grazing. Meanwhile Doina's Gloria looked on placidly with a sympathetic expression in her beautiful large eyes, as if saying, 'Nothing to do with me, Guv.'

We tied Gloria's reins to a large boulder, left Lucia to fend for herself, and climbed to the top of Rano Raraku crater to wander among the huge half-finished statues. That place, and Easter Island generally, is a fascinating place that exudes not just the sense of mystery that one expects on that magical island, but an almost palpable feeling of a further dimension, something indefinable that I felt just as strongly on my return 25 years later with Aventura III.

Sightseeing over, we untied Gloria and walked gently towards her neurotic sister. As we got closer, Lucia stepped back and kept the same distance from us whatever we did. Eventually it became clear that I would never manage to get hold of her, so we set off on the long trek to Hangaroa, Lucia walking at a safe distance behind us. It was well after dark by the time we got to the village, where we found the owner blind drunk on our rental fee and incapable of understanding what had happened.

Thus Lucia put a premature end to my amateur filming career and although I managed to get the camera repaired when we got to Tahiti, I realised that Super 8 was a very expensive hobby and, decided to stick with what I knew best. So I stayed with still photography, and have also tried to keep away from any mode of transport with four legs.

On the practical side, as with everything else on a boat, it is worth getting two cameras: a small compact one that fits easily in a pocket for quick trips ashore, and a professional model for special occasions, with a selection of lenses; a versatile zoom lens for general photography, a telephoto lens for action shots, such as breeching whales, leaping dolphins or wheeling birds, and a wide-angle lens, which is essential for taking photos of what is happening on the boat itself.

Health matters

With good nutrition and such a healthy life as most cruisers lead, it is not surprising that most are in good health. I was never ill during the five years of my voyage on Aventura III and only once had to use my medical chest to treat my crew for an ear infection that he had picked up while diving. The most common complaints that I came across on other boats were ear and eye infections, burns and superficial wounds, scratches or insect bites. Sailors are particularly vulnerable to skin infections caused by grazing or insect stings. The infection is normally caused by the staphylococcus bacteria of which there are various strains. As the infections may take long to heal and cannot be easily kept dry, especially in the tropics, they should not be treated by standard antiseptic or antibiotic creams, but with one of the powders recommended for such conditions.

In over 40 years of sailing there has been only one accident on any of my boats that could be described as potentially serious. While sailing in the Solomon Islands and getting close to the anchorage we were making for, Ivan decided to make himself some custard, his favourite dessert. We were in the cockpit and unaware of what he was doing. Suddenly the boat lurched, the saucepan on the cooker tipped over and most of the hot custard ended up on Ivan's bare chest. After washing off all the custard immediately with cold water, Gwenda assessed it as a third degree burn. After sterilising the area, she applied one of the burn dressings we carried in our medical kit and wrapped a body sock around his chest to keep it in place. Being

Rano Raraku crater on Easter Island

in such a remote area, he was also given a course of antibiotics as well as being forbidden to swim. The skin healed without even a scar.

Ivan showing his train set to local children

Prevention

In the old days, some people setting off on a long voyage would have their appendix removed. Nowadays this may be an exaggeration, as I have not heard of any sailor that had appendicitis while on passage. What is more important is to have a thorough medical check-up before leaving, and get some international health insurance. It is therefore advisable to arrange such health travel insurance before the planned voyage so that it can be renewed more easily once the voyage has started. A comprehensive travel insurance that covers health and emergency evacuation in serious cases, is ideal, although may be quite difficult to get, and premiums can be quite high. Many travel insurances limit the length of an individual trip to 30 days, so may be invalid for those living permanently on the boat. The British insurance company Topsail offers comprehensive travel insurance with no time restrictions for cruising sailors, whose yacht is insured with them (www.topsailinsurance.com). For those who are divers, Divers Alert Network www.dan.org is a global association offering worldwide insurance cover for diving accidents and also normal travel insurance. DAN has local branches in some countries and is also open to cruisers without a home base.

As there is always a much higher risk of catching an infectious disease while ashore than on the boat, it is essential to check what vaccinations are necessary for the countries you plan to visit. Ideally such vaccinations should be done while still at home, but if they need to be done abroad, because of such real risks as HIV and hepatitis, always make sure that disposable syringes are used and, if necessary, provide your own. The same advice applies if having any blood tests done. It is also advisable to keep a vaccination card showing all vaccinations and their expiration dates.

First Aid Kit

» Cotton wool and sterile gauze
» Skin disinfectant such as antiseptic spray
» Bandages of various widths
» Crepe bandage
» Waterproof strapping
» Cleansing wipes
» Waterproof adhesive dressings in various sizes
» Butterfly sutures
» Skin closure strips or plasters that pull the edges of a cut together
» Artificial skin patches
» Special, non-stick sterile dressings for burns
» Sodium alginate dressings for wounds that won't stop bleeding (Kaltostat)
» Eye bath/drops
» Surgical adhesive tape
» Scissors, tweezers, safety pins
» Thermometer
» Disposable needles and syringes (5 ml is the most useful size)
» Sterile needles with sutures for stitching
» Disposable gloves
» First aid manual

Onboard pharmacy

Having a well-equipped medical chest is of utmost importance if cruising in remote places where medical help may be impossible to reach quickly in an emergency. It is worth carrying all items that may be needed, such as sufficient antibiotic and antiseptic creams, bandages, painkillers and some broad-spectrum antibiotics.

Regulations regarding drugs vary enormously from country to country, and some customs officials may confiscate certain strong painkillers such as morphine. In several countries however, the laws are more relaxed, and many drugs that normally are only available on prescription, such as antibiotics, can be bought over the counter. Many sailors use this opportunity to stock up their medicine chest or replace drugs that have passed their expiry date. The effectiveness of antibiotics decreases with age and storage in tropical conditions, but some antibiotics can still be used after the expiry date by increasing the dosage.

All medicines should be labelled and kept in their original containers with their explanatory leaflet. As each preparation has both a trade name and a generic name, and trade names differ from country to country, a foreign doctor may not be able to advise on the use of some medications if the generic name is not known. It is useful to carry a pharmacopoeia or formulary for reference.

Except in an emergency, prescription medicine should only be used on medical advice, which may be obtained over the radio or satellite telephone. Excellent information is also available on the internet. Unfortunately the wide and often irresponsible use of antibiotics has resulted in some bacteria becoming resistant to even the most powerful antibiotics currently available, so antibiotics should only be used if prescribed by a qualified doctor. Families sailing with young children should have specific children's remedies. In an emergency, it may be possible to use adult medication for children if the tablets or capsule are divided carefully with a sharp knife so that the reduced dose, as listed in the formulary, can be administered to a child. It is often possible to improvise. Cotton and linen clothing and sheets can be cut up to make bandages and be sterilized by boiling for five minutes. Sail battens make good splints.

When setting up the medicine chest for a long voyage it is advisable to consult your own family doctor, who is the best person to give advice on what to take. Most doctors will also prescribe certain drugs, which are on the restricted list, once the reason has been explained. It may be worth doing a first aid training course and get advice on how to use scalpels, sutures and syringes, should the need arise. As Gwenda is a trained pharmacist, her skills did come in useful on many occasions.

Fortunately I very rarely had to resort to my comprehensive pharmacy but was often able to help sailors on other yachts or people ashore. While on the island of Tanna in Vanuatu on Aventura III, I met a local man who had an awful open sore on his leg. I took him back to the boat, disinfected and bandaged the wound as well as I could, but realised that the infection was so far advanced that if it weren't properly treated he would probably lose his leg. I told him that he needed to go to the local hospital, but he objected saying that it wasn't really necessary. I would have none of it, called a taxi and we both drove there. On the way he admitted that he had been there already, but that he had been sent away as he couldn't pay the fee. The 'hospital' was a small clinic run by an overworked nurse. I insisted that my charge was properly treated and told the nurse that I wanted his dressing to be changed every day, and that I'd like to pay for the entire treatment in advance. I was amazed when the bill came to the equivalent of only seven dollars for seven days. This poor man could have lost a leg because when he first came to the clinic he couldn't afford to pay one dollar!

Also while in Vanuatu, we anchored in Gaua Bay on the island of Vanua Lava and went ashore to pay our respects to the local chief. We found him in a darkened hut moaning with pain. He pointed to his sore legs, and explained that he had been attacked by wild dogs while he was walking home from the nearest village. He managed to get hold of a low branch and pull himself up a tree, but the dogs had snapped at his legs and bitten him badly. The bites had by now gone septic, so I rowed to Aventura and brought back my first aid kit, disinfected the wounds, applied antibiotic cream, and dressed them. I also gave him a course of antibiotic tablets.

During the time we spent there his wounds started healing and I was greatly relieved that he did not seem to have got rabies as well. One day his wife stopped me to say that she had terrible toothache, so I gave her some Paracetamol tablets, which temporarily relieved the pain. As the nearest clinic was on the other side of the island, and there was no path through the impenetrable jungle they had no choice but fend for themselves as well as they could. Before we left, I gave them all the medicines I could spare. To show their gratitude on the morning of our departure the family put on a show of water music for us. Standing in water up to their waist the 'musicians' slapped the water with the open hands producing a sound not unlike the deep base of an organ.

Basic medical chest

» Local anaesthetic to allow cleaning and stitching of a major wound
» Specific local anaesthetic drops for removing foreign bodies from the eye
» Drops and ointments for eye infections, e.g. chloramphenicol
» Ear drops for bacterial ear infections
» Antibacterial cream e.g. fusidic acid, neomycin sulphate, silver sulphadiazine for infected burns or tropical ulcers
» Antibiotic powder or spray e.g. neomycin sulphate. These are better than creams under moist tropical conditions
» Hydrocortisone cream to relieve reactionary rashes, insect bites or sunburn
» Antiseasickness tablets or patches
» Antihistamine tablets, such as cetirizine, for allergies to food, insect bites, jellyfish or coral stings, etc.
» Antibiotics. Two broad-spectrum antibiotics should be carried in case one is ineffective or there is sensitivity.
   » Penicillin e.g. ampicillin or amoxicillin (available in a syrup for children)
   » Tetracycline (not recommended for under 12 years or pregnant women. Large doses can suppress appendicitis).
   » Ciprofloxacin for stomach bugs
» Analgesic: Paracetamol or Ibuprofen for minor pain and reducing fever. Pentazocine for more severe pain
» Sulphonamide antibacterial for urinary-tract infections
» Laxative
» Antidiarrhoeal tablets (or kaolin mixture for children)
» Sleeping tablets, useful for helping someone in severe pain to go to sleep
» Promethazine elixir, such as phenergan, useful as a sedative for a sick child and also for allergic conditions, nausea, etc.
» Antifungal preparations for athletes foot and other fungal infections
» Insect repellent
» Sun screen lotion
» Antimalarial tablets for prophylactic use

In the above list generic not proprietary names have been given for all medicines.

Medical advice should be sought as to which antibiotics to take as some people are sensitive to penicillin and, like all powerful drugs, antibiotics should not be taken lightly. Taking the wrong antibiotic can hinder the correct diagnosis of an infection and sometimes make the condition worse.

Tips

» Never swim on passage except in emergencies (to clear a fouled propeller).

» If stopping in a place where provisioning is good, stock up on items that may not be available in places you plan to visit later.

» Install a stern light on a separate switch from the bow navigation lights, so it can be used to shed light on the stern platform making it easier to board from the dinghy, handle fish caught in the dark, deal with the hydro-generator, or adjust the self-steering gear if fitted.

» Keep some water from the watermaker separately in a jerrycan by the galley for drinking, making coffee or tea. It tastes better than out of the main tank and saves electricity by not having to operate the fresh water pump every time you need small amounts of water.

» The gas supply to the galley should have a remote automatic cut-off at the tank end, not in the galley.

» Refill your gas tanks at the first opportunity and always carry enough to last for at least three months.

» Carry a good supply of disposable gloves to be used for doing dirty jobs: cleaning the toilet or handling oil and filters when servicing the engine.

» Have a well-planned medicine chest and carry sufficient antibiotic and antiseptic creams, bandages, painkillers and broad-spectrum antibiotics to be able to help people living in isolated places.

» Never eat lagoon fish unless you are told by a local fisherman that there is no risk of ciguatera fish poisoning in those waters.

» Invest in a good quality camera with wide-angle and telephoto lenses.

» Have some gifts for children such as T-shirts, pens, exercise books, coloured pencils, balloons, but no sweets!

» Produce a postcard with a photo of your boat and details of the crew to hand over to new friends ashore and afloat.

12

Sails and sailing routines

Sailing a boat calls for quick action, a blending of feeling with the wind and water, as well as with the very heart and soul of the boat itself.

George Matthew Adams

Having left on my first voyage without any offshore experience I had to find out by myself how to choose the right sails for certain conditions or when to reef. Learning by trial and error is undoubtedly the best way and it doesn't take long before you get in tune with your boat and start understanding what it is trying to tell you. The first Aventura can best be described as a docile sailer, never exciting but very reliable. With her heavy displacement Aventura II was utterly forgiving, as she could continue with full sail when, in the same conditions, another boat would have been sailing on its ear. Everything changed when Aventura III came on the scene and with her relatively light displacement soon showed me how exciting sailing could actually be. What I also soon learned, in contrast to her predecessor, was the importance of reefing the mainsail early when closehauled or beamreaching if I wanted to keep the boat sailing at her best. This method of reducing sail by starting with reefing the mainsail in a strengthening wind continued to be a routine also on Aventura IV.

At this point I need to mention one fundamental factor that set my latest two boats apart: the centreboard. To take full advantage of this special feature you need to sail a centreboard yacht quite differently to a boat with a standard keel. When sailing closehauled or beamreaching, the board is fully down, so there is no real difference to a keeled boat. It is off the wind when having a centreboard becomes a great advantage. When sailing off the wind I start gradually raising the centreboard so that by the time we are broadreaching or running the centreboard is normally fully retracted. As I mentioned elsewhere, this is not only an advantage from the point of view of performance, but in my view even more important is the safety aspect, as the risk of gybing is virtually eliminated.

Reefing

Depending the point of sailing I normally put in the first reef in the mainsail when the true wind speed gets to about 15 knots. As the wind increases I may start also furling in some of the Solent jib. By the time the true wind rises to between 18 and 20 knots I would put in the second reef and furl in some more of the Solent. If the wind continues increasing I would swap the Solent for the staysail and take in the third reef. If we were broadreaching or running, I would continue sailing like that gradually reducing the size of the staysail until the true wind is in the low 30s. At some point I would furl in the staysail completely and continue with the fully reefed mainsail. On both Aventura III and IV there was a provision to put in a fourth reef, but I normally I preferred to continue with three reefs. On a number of occasions, when the wind got up to the high 30s or low 40s, I continued just with the reefed mainsail but at some point I would decide to heave-to.

On Aventura IV the first reef needs to be set up at the foot of the mast, the second reef is one-line that can be controlled from the cockpit, as are the two lines of the third reef.

Heaving to

I would heave-to in very strong winds, when I prefer to wait for a weather system to pass over us, or to slow down so as not to arrive at my destination during darkness. In the above photo we hove-to when winds reached 50 knots during a storm in the North Atlantic. On both Aventura III and IV, I would heave-to with three reefs in the mainsail and the staysail furled to half or one-third of its size.

Downwind sails

The sails used on my various boats were discussed briefly in chapter 6, but downwind sails are so important on a cruising boat that I will deal with them here. Downwind sails was certainly the most discussed subject in my early days of cruising and, like virtually everyone else setting off on a long voyage, I equipped the first Aventura with twin forestays so that I could hoist my hanked-on twin running-jibs independently of each other.

The system worked reasonably well but it induced an awful rolling motion that was very hard to take during the long Atlantic crossing. I tried to dampen the rolling with the trysail sheeted in hard but it didn't make much difference. So on the second Aventura I went straight to a spinnaker and have used spinnakers as my preferred downwind sail ever since.

For some reason, many cruising sailors seem to have a deep aversion to spinnakers and regard them as unmanageable and even dangerous. Some try to solve this by using a cruising chute, and some even twin jibs. In the earlier rallies boats with spinnakers were in the minority, but the situation is changing, as in recent transatlantic rallies more boats were equipped with spinnakers.

By the time Aventura II was ready to leave on her world voyage her sail wardrobe included both a triradial and a reaching spinnaker. Aventura III also started off with a triradial and one asymmetric spinnaker. The triradial was perfectly cut but the asymmetric was a disappointment. In the late 1990s asymmetric spinnakers had just appeared on the market and their cut was inefficient, so I kept it as a spare and ordered a second asymmetric spinnaker. Halfway through the voyage, while in New Zealand, I acquired one of the new Parasailor spinnakers. On her return voyage home, Aventura III covered some 18,000 miles along a route that took us through the Torres Strait, across the South Indian Ocean and Cape of Good Hope to the Mediterranean. Besides the Parasailor, I still had the other spinnakers: the standard triradial and two asymmetric spinnakers. After I acquired the Parasailor the asymmetric spinnaker was used on a couple of occasions, and never the triradial, as I found the Parasailor to be so versatile that it could be used in a much wider range of conditions than the triradial. Looking through my logbook I reckon that the Parasailor was used for well over one third of that distance, which must be at least 7,000 miles.

The main features of a Parasailor spinnaker are the wide slot that runs from side to side about one third down from the top and, on the forward side of the sail, a wing across the slot. Once it is up, the Parasailor acts just like a normal triradial spinnaker but this is an illusion, as the slot and wing help the Parasailor stay full even in light winds. I have used it on a few occasions in as little as 5 knots of true wind, and every time it looked like collapsing, the backpressure exerted by the slot kept it full. It is in strong winds, however, that the Parasailor comes into its own.

Normally I drop the spinnaker when the wind reaches 16 knots true, but soon after I used it for the first time, when I saw a squall approaching, I decided to leave it up and see what happened. From 15 knots the wind went up and up and settled at 27 knots. Aventura III took it all in her stride, accelerated to 9, then 10 knots and once, when it caught the right wave, surged to 14. Meanwhile the Parasailor behaved as normally as before, the wing streaming ahead and the slot wide open almost visibly spilling the wind. Wonderful! Of course, one thing that must be avoided at all cost, as with any spinnaker, is not to broach. In my case this was easy, as the centreboard was fully raised at the time. Usually this makes it very easy to steer the boat even in strong winds, as there is no keel to act as a pivot if a mistake by the helmsman or a large wave forces the boat into a broach.

With her flat bottom and no keel, Aventura III acted just like a large windsurfer, with the rudder having no difficulty keeping the boat on course. With her twin rudders, Aventura IV was tracking even better and was a joy to helm. However, I would suggest to owners of boats with a fixed keel to play it safe and drop the Parasailor if the wind threatens to get close to 20 knots true, and the risk of a broach becomes real. Although I know that the Parasailor can be safely left up in winds of such strength, as I have negotiated several squalls of around 25 knots, I now prefer to douse it, mainly because if the wind continues to go up it may be quite a struggle to get the spinnaker down. I should add here that dousing the Parasailor is very much helped by the generous size of the rigid douser-collar and the equally well-designed dedicated sailbag. It has been suggested that on long runs one should consider using the Parasailor rigged with two poles and drop the mainsail. I am always reluctant to drop the mainsail while on passage, as in strong winds it is so much easier to douse the spinnaker by having it masked by the mainsail. Also, hoisting the mainsail again when sailing downwind can be very difficult. Therefore I prefer to keep up the mainsail even in strong winds, but well reefed. On two occasions, in the South Indian Ocean, when the wind was very light (6 to 8 knots true) and no swell I did put up the Parasailor with two poles, and it worked, but as soon as the wind got up, I dropped one pole and the Parasailor set much better.

I normally keep the Parasailor poled until we are sailing at 120 degrees off the wind, then, if the wind continues moving forward of the beam and the pole is about to touch the forestay, I release the pole and fly the Parasailor from the bows by connecting the

pole downhaul to the tack of the sail. Flown from the bows, the Parasailor acts as an asymmetric spinnaker and could be kept up until the wind got to 70 or even 60 degrees off, but as I also had a Code Zero sail on Aventura IV, I usually preferred to make the switch earlier.

The Parasailor is even easier to deploy on catamarans as this can be done without a pole, as I found out on a delivery trip of an Outremer 49 from St Martin to Florida.

I hope it is very clear from this that I am happy with the Parasailor and would recommend it to anyone who is considering buying a new spinnaker. One further advantage of the Parasailor is that it tends to stay full even if not perfectly set, so you don't need to constantly adjust sheets and guys, a chore that will not be missed by a lazy crew.

Sailing with a fixed pole

My favourite downwind technique is to set up the spinnaker pole independently of the sail I intend to

Going...

going...

going...

gone.

use, so that the pole is held firmly in position by a topping lift, forward and aft guys – all three lines being led to the cockpit. Regardless of whether I decide to pole out a foresail or a spinnaker, the sheet is led through the jaws of the pole, which is then hoisted to the desired position.

Once the pole is in place and is held up firmly by the three lines, the foresail can be unfurled, or the spinnaker hoisted and its douser pulled up. With the pole being independent of the sail, the foresail can be furled partially or fully with the pole being left untouched. This is a great advantage when sail has to be shortened quickly, usually when threatened by a squall.

When the squall has passed the foresail can be easily unfurled, as the pole is still in place. If sailing under spinnaker and threatened by a squall, I would douse the spinnaker and lower it onto the foredeck. Once the danger had passed, with the pole still in position, the spinnaker can be hoisted and its douser pulled up.

I have often raised or doused the Parasailor on my own with this tried and proven fixed-pole system, and would highly recommend it to anyone, not just to those sailing short-handed.

Boom brake

This is an essential feature that I have used on my boats and regard as indispensible. As a swinging boom can cause a serious or even fatal injury, preventing such an accident should be a priority. Temporary preventers help, but it is much better to use a permanent arrangement provided by a boom brake. The reason why I prefer a boom brake over a preventer is that the former is, or should be, permanently set up. This means that in an involuntary gybe, possibly caused by the autopilot, windvane, large wave or human error, the gybe is controlled. Furthermore, as the helmsperson attempts to bring the boat back on course, that first gybe is often followed by a second gybe in the opposite

direction (and I speak from personal experience). Even if the preventer had stopped the boom on the initial gybe, on the second gybe that preventer will be useless, whereas a boom brake would control the boom on either gybe.

On Aventura IV the two ends of boom brake line are led over blocks to the cockpit. As the boom brake works by the friction exerted on its drum by the lines, they need to be taken up on winches on either side of the cockpit, and be kept taught at all times. Spinnaker jamming blocks can be used to free the winches for other uses.

Dousing the Parasailor...   *going...*   *going...*   *gone.*

13

A transpacific marathon

There is no other landmark in maritime lore to equal the awe-inspiring Cape Horn. The southernmost of a group of islands lying off Tierra del Fuego at the tip of the South American continent, the island was named Hoorn in 1616 by the Dutch navigator Willem Schouten after his native town. In fact, there is now evidence that Sir Francis Drake landed there in 1578, but this was suppressed by the English authorities as the discovery of a clear passage between the Atlantic and Pacific oceans was deemed too important to be shared with other nations.

Aventura III off Horn Island

Whoever landed there first might have done so in the same spot where we landed ourselves, a small cove on the northeast side of the island, close to the old lighthouse. Having been forced to abandon a similar landing three years previously, this time I was determined to land come what may, so Ivan and I donned our survival suits and took to our smaller dinghy, which would be easier to handle once we reached shallow water. As the bay was too deep for anchoring, Erick and Muriel stayed on board, hovering at a safe distance offshore. Even in calm weather, the landing was far from easy as the swell broke over the rocky beach and the smooth stones were treacherously slippery.

The former military presence on the windswept island had been replaced by a Chilean family. As the new lighthouse was automatic, the keeper's main job was to check the identity of any passing vessel by VHF. The rare visitors were warmly welcomed in their home, where a modest range of souvenirs were displayed for sale. The most sought after memento was the Cape Horn stamp, which now adorns Aventura's logbook and the passports of her crew. Next to the keeper's house stands a small chapel, built of driftwood and erected in memory of the countless mariners who had lost their lives in these stormy waters over the centuries. On a nearby hill stands an impressive steel sculpture of a wandering albatross, commissioned by the Cape Horners Association.

As the weather was unusually calm, I asked the keeper if we could walk to Cape Horn itself. With an embarrassed smile, he warned us that the path might be all right but as the entire area had been mined by the military during the conflict with Argentina, he wouldn't advise us to do so. Cape Horn mined! It was too much to bear, and so we returned to Aventura, happy to have landed there, but also disappointed to have come across such human stupidity at the very end of the world.

Back in Puerto Williams, we checked in with the Chilean authorities, who regard not only the area south of the Beagle Channel as far as Cape Horn to be part of Chile's territorial land and waters but also the Antarctic Peninsula. We then sailed across the Beagle Channel to Ushuaia, in neighbouring Argentina, a busy cruise-ship base and therefore the best place to stock up for the trip to either Antarctica or through the Chilean fjordland. I had been warned that going north absolutely nothing would be available as far as Puerto Eden, the nearest settlement at a distance of some 600 miles, so we stocked up well on fuel and fresh produce. We set off in March sailing from south to north, which is not the best way to go as the winds were almost invariably from ahead and usually very strong. Anyone planning to visit this beautiful part of the world should attempt to sail from north to south. A network of fjords and narrow channels allows almost the entire distance to be sailed in protected waters.

The south of Chile is in every respect a sailor's paradise; the scenery is ever-changing, with sparkling glaciers, tumbling waterfalls and primeval forests, and there are countless sheltered anchorages, with not another boat in sight for hundreds of miles. It is difficult to comprehend the vastness of this country with a coastline of some 3,000 miles. On a stretch of 600 miles, while we sailed through fjords and narrows, anchored at the foot of mighty glaciers, we met only four cruising boats and about as many local fishing boats. Indeed, from Puerto Williams to Puerto Eden, there is not one single settlement, not a farm, not even a house. Isolation is complete.

There were many more settlements once we reached the large island of Chiloe, and by the time we arrived in Valdivia, we were back in civilisation. This is undoubtedly the best port on the west coast of South America to prepare the boat, either to continue into the South Pacific or for a cruise south through the Chilean fjordland. After weeks of wilderness it was a good feeling to finally arrive in this welcoming town, where we joined up with the other Millennium Odyssey boats. The route to Antarctica, Cape Horn and southern Chile had been a great test of endurance for both the yachts and their crews, so the stop at Alwoplast, a boat-

Anchored off Romance Glacier

building yard and marina operated by our host Alex Wopper, was essential to prepare men and machines for the next stage of their round-the-world adventure.

From Valdivia, we struck out in a northwesterly direction: destination Easter Island. Our friends Erick and Muriel, who had sailed with us to Antarctica, left us in Valdivia. This was the first long passage that Ivan and I were on our own, and I was very happy with how well we got on. We made a good team, as Ivan liked to stay up late and get up late, whereas I always enjoy the dawn watch, which I regard as the most beautiful time of day. We worked out an ideal system: Ivan would take the first watch, immediately after dinner, around 9pm, until 1am or 2am. I would take the rest of the night and let him sleep late. Those night watches, alone in the cockpit, with the boat silently rushing along, were full of magic, especially the last hour of darkness, watching the sky turn slowly from black to dark blue, then start taking on all the colours of the rainbow before the sun rose over the horizon. Exquisite moments!

When Ivan got up I would make breakfast, and on special occasions our favourite pancakes. The rest of the day was routine: we did maintenance work, read, listened to music, but as our tastes didn't mesh, we each had our own Walkman. One thing you soon learn on a small boat is to respect each other's space. We had plenty of time to talk, to comment on what we were reading, on the latest news on the BBC World Service, or Ivan's future plans. The wind vane and autopilot did all the work so we hardly ever had to steer. Also, as the boat was easily handled by one person, I very rarely had to wake up Ivan to help me change sails, or vice versa – except on one dark night when I managed to wrap our tri-radial spinnaker around the forestay. I had noticed what looked like a small squall approaching, but had neglected to move the autopilot from steering to compass to steering to wind, which is what I normally do when overtaken by a squall. I tried everything possible to unwrap the large billowing sail on my own, but without success. Eventually I gave up

and called Ivan. He offered to climb up the mast with his harness clipped to a spare halyard and swing out to the forestay to unwrap the spinnaker, but it sounded too risky in the dark.

'Let's wait till morning,' I said.

'Why not do it now?' Ivan insisted.

'I have three spinnakers but only one son,' I retorted and sent him back to bed.

I did call him when it got light and we did save the spinnaker. It was one of the very rare moments of disagreement between us, perhaps the only time when I acted as father as well as captain, and had the last word. The tension didn't last long because the next day we sighted Easter Island. Although we had made a reasonably fast passage and had covered the 2,000 miles in exactly 15 days, it had been my hope to arrive at Easter Island on Easter Sunday. Light winds and the damaged spinnaker had scuppered my plans, and in spite of our best efforts, we only managed to arrive on Easter Monday. Gwenda had been waiting for us for three days, and we had a wonderful reunion after the long separation of nearly six months.

Light winds on the way to Easter Island propelled by two asymmetric spinnakers

There are few places in the world more enigmatic than Easter Island, and arriving there on your own boat, making landfall at this very special island after 2,000 miles of an empty ocean, must be one of the most powerful experiences for any sailor. This was our second visit, having called at this Polynesian outpost on our first circumnavigation, nearly quarter of a century earlier. Much had changed in the intervening years, yet much had remained the same. The anchorage off the main settlement at Hangaroa was just as precarious, the landing through the breakers just as exhilarating, and the weather just as unpredictable. The island's triangular shape offers little protection from wind or swell, so after several yachts had got into difficulty, and at least two lost when the wind changed direction unexpectedly and drove them ashore, the port captain now insisted that one person must remain on board all the time.

What was immediately noticeable was how much more geared to tourism the island had become. Fortunately, this first impression was confined to the main settlement of Hangaroa itself, because out of town the island looked just the same windswept place that I remembered from before. The giant statues were as awesome as when I first saw them, and so was the air of mystery that surrounded them. The experts still puzzle over how a Stone Age people managed to carve the enormous statues out of rock with rudimentary flint chisels and then transport them for several miles to erect them singly or in groups along the shoreline. In recent years, some of the fallen statues have been re-erected onto their original platforms, albeit by using modern lifting equipment, so now the island is ringed with dozens of statues looking inland with their backs to the sea, just as they had done all those hundreds of years ago.

No less fascinating, although for very different reasons, was our next landfall, Pitcairn. As this section of the Millennium Odyssey, from Valdivia to French Polynesia, was run as a pursuit race, with individual boats stopping the clock when they arrived at one of the islands, and restarting them as they left, both at Easter Island and at Pitcairn there were only three Millennium boats there at the same time. Because of the very special significance of Pitcairn, the leading boats had agreed to coordinate their arrival so as to be there together. Furthermore, as the islanders are Seventh-day Adventists, it was decided to perform the Millennium Flame ceremony on a Sabbath. The arrival of three Millennium yachts at the same time caused such a stir in the tiny community that any other day would have done just as well.

As on Easter Island, we were strongly advised not to leave the boats unattended as, according to our concerned hosts, several boats had been lost in Bounty Bay while the crew were visiting ashore. Unbelievably, two of the incidents involved the same owner, and happened on subsequent visits, several years apart. The joke among the islanders was that the original Bounty was finally burned by the mutineers not in order to destroy any evidence of their presence on the island, but because they could not cope with moving the ship every time the wind shifted, just as visiting yachts have to nowadays. We certainly sympathised with the mutineers!

Their descendants continue to be intrepid sailors, which they showed by the impeccable manner in which they manoeuvred their longboat through the raging surf into the tiny harbour. Four men had come out to bring us ashore at first light, their names sounding like a roll call of the original mutineers: Young, Warren, Brown and, as to be expected, Christian. They were too young to remember us from our previous visit, but once ashore we met several old friends who greeted us warmly. Ivan met some friends of his own age whom he and Doina had joined in the tiny classroom 22 years previously.

Millennium Odyssey yachts at Easter Island

On arrival, we were all loaded onto several quad bikes and whizzed up a rough track into Adamstown, to be greeted at the church by what looked like the entire island's population of 67. I had kept in contact throughout the intervening years with Tom Christian, a direct descendant of Fletcher Christian, the man who started it all.

Tom accepted the Millennium Flame on behalf of the small community, a gesture that I found highly symbolic, listening to his comments as the heir of the best-known mutineer in history. We were treated to some beautiful singing, including two moving goodbye songs that Pitcairners normally sing to departing ships. Each Millennium crew was adopted by a separate family, first for lunch, followed by a tour of the island on one of those four-wheeled monsters.

Just before nightfall, loaded with tropical fruit, we were taken back to the boats. As the anchorage looked as precarious as when we had arrived, rather than spend another rolly, sleepless night, we all decided to leave immediately. The small island stood out clearly in the gathering dusk for a long time as, one by one, we set our spinnakers and headed for Mangareva, 300 miles away.

In the 1970s, while the French nuclear-test programme was still underway at nearby Mururoa atoll, visits by foreign vessels to the Gambier Islands, of which Mangareva is the main island, were not permitted. All that has changed, and the Gambiers, one of French Polynesia's five groups of islands, made a perfect landfall.

Being finally able to drop the anchor in a quiet, protected, tropical lagoon after so many thousand miles was sheer bliss. This was our second visit to Mangareva, having spent one unforgettable month there on Aventura I in 1977, when we had made a long detour from Panama to Peru and then turned west to visit Easter Island and Pitcairn before making landfall there. On that occasion we stayed for one month, Doina and Ivan went to school, and we easily integrated into the lives of the 100-strong community.

The island had changed a lot since our first visit. The population had shrunk and the friendly, laid-back atmosphere seemed to have gone. The arrival of the fortnightly supply ship, and its large supply of beer, was eagerly awaited, and I could no longer detect the strong community feeling that I had noticed during our previous visit. We met our friend Lucas Paeamara, still the mayor, and he sadly agreed that things would never be the same again. In every sense, this was paradise lost.

Never content to sail in a straight line when a detour would do as well, on leaving Mangareva I decided to visit the Australs, a remote group of islands lying some 500 miles south of Tahiti. By the time we left Mangareva it was already late April and thus close to the austral winter. We had strong westerly winds and had to tack most of the way. Gwenda, who had been expecting tropical sailing conditions, was not impressed.

'This is about as nice as sailing in the English Channel in winter. It still beats me why you had to be so stubborn and come here!'

'OK, you are right and I apologise, but as you may remember we were going to come here in 1977 and this time I just could not resist the temptation.'

The history of Rapa is as mysterious as that of its eastern namesake, Rapa Nui (Easter Island). There are several hilltop fortresses, whose origin is still under debate. The long detour was certainly justified as we were warmly welcomed everywhere. Yachts rarely visit the Australs, and we were told that Aventura was the first boat to call in more than a year. We caused quite a stir among the children going home from school, who had great fun piling into our dinghy.

Situated just outside the tropics, the weather in Rapa is so damp and cold that there are no palm trees. These grow in abundance on Raivavae, 300 miles further north, on arrival at which we suddenly we felt we were back in the tropics.

Raivavae is one of the most beautiful islands we have seen anywhere and is certainly on a par with Bora Bora: the mountainous island and its lagoon are similarly ringed by a coral reef. As on Rapa, we went walking into the interior, and in a clearing in the dense forest came across a man building a small yacht. He was a retired Frenchman who had worked in the islands and, as he told me, his greatest pleasure during the long and lonely evenings was to read the stories of adventurers just like us. His dream was to set off one day on his boat and sail the world to the end of his days. How well I understood those feelings.

We had better winds on our way to Tahiti, whose main port of Papeete was overflowing with boats; this is where we joined the rest of the Millennium Odyssey fleet. After sailing separate routes for the previous eight months, the smaller South American fleet merged here with the 32 boats that had taken the Panama Canal route. It was a time of happy reunions, swapping stories and, for Aventura, of preparing for the next instalment of our Pacific Odyssey: Tahiti to Alaska.

The sustained rhythm of our long trek from Antarctica to Tahiti had left its mark on both Ivan and I, and we savoured to the full our leisurely one-month-long interlude in French Polynesia. There are few places in the world to better the cruising attractions of the leeward group of the Society Islands. The four islands of Huahine, Raiatea, Tahaa and Bora Bora are close to each other, making it is easy to visit them all. Each has its own lagoon, except Raiatea and Tahaa, which share one; the winds in winter (May to October) are the fairly reliable southeast trade winds; shore facilities are of a high standard and the cuisine is French. What more can one ask for?

We had agreed on a rendezvous for the entire Millennium Odyssey fleet in Bora Bora, where the Millennium Flame was accepted on behalf of his people by the mayor of the island, Gaston Tong Son, an old personal friend. A lavish farewell dinner was laid on by our host, while the famous Bora Bora Mamas entertained us with their well-honed repertoire of entrancing Polynesian songs.

On the day of the start, the imposing silhouette of Mount Otamanu provided the perfect backdrop as the large fleet tacked around a windward mark at the far end of the lagoon and then, one by one, the boats rushed through the pass into the open sea, bound for Tonga and beyond. Gwenda left us in Bora Bora and we were joined by my niece Marianne, who was going to sail with us all the way to Hawaii.

Having fulfilled our job as committee vessel, immediately after the start we tacked back to Raiatea for a symbolic stop at the ancient site of Havaiki, reputed to be the largest religious site in Polynesia. It was from this very point that the intrepid sailors set off to colonise Aotearoa (New Zealand), the southwest point of the Polynesian triangle.

Our own route took us towards the apex of that magic triangle, as on leaving Raiatea we headed almost due north towards distant Hawaii. We must have pleased the Polynesian gods, and in particular Tangaroa, the god of the sea, because we had excellent winds right from the start. In early June the winds were from northeast, so we were closehauled and, in hindsight, I can say that in all my thousands of miles of offshore sailing I have never had a more perfect week.

With winds at a constant 15 knots, Aventura rarely sailed below 7 knots, so that in one week we clocked 1,100 miles, and that included stops at Flint and Malden islands. Fishing was also excellent; therefore the only word to describe this week was perfection.

Our first stop was at Flint, an uninhabited island, about 330 miles due north of Tahiti. We had a wet and exciting landing through the breaking surf and could well understand why the island is hardly ever visited. To get ashore, we used our smaller inflatable dinghy, which we rowed up to the surf line, then jumped out and waded ashore. We would probably have ruined the outboard engine if we had taken it with us as the following surf capsized the dinghy when we reached shallow water. But the effort was justified by landing on a pristine beach probably untouched by human feet for a long time. The island was covered in coconut trees, and an impenetrable curtain of vegetation that came down to the waterline made it impossible to advance more than a very short distance inland.

Excellent winds gave us a fast passage to our next stop, the also-uninhabited Malden Island, which had been used by the US military during the nuclear-testing programme of the 1950s. The island still bore the scars of that devastation, with rusting military equipment abandoned all over the place. We anchored on the west side out of the swell and rowed ashore. Just as we approached the surf line and were getting ready to jump in, we saw two large blacktip sharks cruising along. As they seemed interested in us, we continued rowing until we touched the bottom, with the result that, as on Flint, the surf overturned the dinghy and threw it on top of us. Fortunately, our cameras had been packed in a sealed container and we escaped with just a few scratches. As with our previous dunking, Marianne found this to be extremely hilarious and kept pointing at the black fins, laughing her head off. Ashore, the landscape was punctuated by mounds of rusty steel drums and abandoned hardware. But life was visibly returning to this devastated island as nature was making a determined effort to reclaim the land, with bushes growing out of decaying trucks and scores of seabirds nesting in the few trees.

The following day, we crossed the equator and made landfall at our next stop, which had its own nuclear past. Christmas Island was used by the British for nuclear tests in the 1950s, and several decades later the islanders were still struggling to wipe out the consequences. Even if radiation was said to have ceased to be a hazard, the amount of military hardware that still littered the island and lagoon was beyond belief. Mountains of rusting metal and huge abandoned fuel tanks lined the beaches and, as the local population was either unable or unwilling to use whatever natural building materials were available, such as palm and pandanus, the main settlement, grandly called London, consisted of sad-looking shacks patched together from bits of corrugated tin. Malden and Christmas are permanent reminders of how 20th-century man raped the environment without any thought for the consequences of his actions. The contrast to what the Polynesians had left behind on Raiatea was not only striking, but also an unforgivable indictment of modern man's attitude to the environment. Perhaps the same rules should be applied in these islands as in Antarctica, where the former polluters are now obliged to return and clean up the mess they had left behind.

After what we saw at Christmas Island, we were quite concerned that the next Line Island, Fanning, would be no different. How pleasantly surprised we were!

As we reached the protection of the large atoll, we came across a dozen outrigger canoes out in the ocean, trolling for fish under sail. The perfectly formed atoll encloses a wide lagoon with a narrow opening to the ocean. The pass can be easily located on the west side of the lagoon, but one can only enter at slack water because at certain times a fierce 6-knot current sweeps through the narrow passage, which locals call 'the river'. We timed our arrival to coincide with the moon meridian passage and must have guessed right because we did arrive at slack water. We made our way in and anchored off the nearest village.

As the island was rarely visited by cruising boats, and even the supply ship from Tarawa only called four times a year, the islanders were extremely welcoming. It was a pleasure to walk through the neat villages and be greeted warmly by everyone. Suddenly we were back in the Pacific as I knew it a quarter of a century previously. The island, whose correct name is Tabuaeran, was neat and tidy, and every house was made of local materials.

One day we borrowed some bikes and cycled along the west side of the atoll, which is made up of several smaller islands linked by bridges or causeways. Every house was built from traditional materials of palm and pandanus and surrounded by a cleanly swept courtyard where hens were pecking in the dust. Pigs were kept in separate enclosures on the shore of the lagoon, well away from the villages. The islanders appeared to be remarkably self-sufficient, this being more than obvious in the one and only store that had just a few basic supplies: flour; rice; corned beef; the perennial Pacific staple of cabin bread, which is a hard baked rusk-type biscuit; and, surprisingly, canned fish. The sea, lagoon and well-tended land supported several villages, and everyone looked well nourished and healthy.

As we cycled quietly along, we heard some beautiful singing that reverberated all around us. We looked around but could see nothing. As we got closer to the source of the sound, it appeared to come from above, and indeed this was the case: on top of a tall coconut palm we saw a man wielding his machete while singing at the top of his voice. We leant the bikes against the trunk and waited for him to climb down. In surprisingly good English, he explained that he was collecting toddy and offered us some to taste. The fresh unfermented variety is sickly sweet, but once fermented the syrup produces a potent drink. He pointed to a number of bottles suspended from the fronds of the surrounding palms, every one of them collecting the thick sap drop by drop.

We cycled as far as we could go, then turned around when the track came to an end. On the way back we stopped in several places to talk to people, but one memory that sticks in the mind more than any other was that of a group of children, sitting in the middle of the dusty track... busy playing cards. We stopped, looked again and could barely believe our eyes. This small incident epitomised better than anything else the carefree and relaxed existence those people were living.

All too soon it was time to go. By then we had made a number of friends, Ivan had repaired the priest's CB radio and I had given a young fisherman enough material to make himself a sail for his canoe. There were a few tears on both sides while our friends waved us off as 'the river' got hold of us and spewed us into the ocean.

Our next stop was Palmyra, the northernmost of the Line Islands. We had heard on the cruising grapevine that a French sailor and former chef, Roger Dextrait, had settled on this island, which in those days was privately owned by a family from Hawaii. The owners employed Roger, who had arrived there on his 40-foot yacht a few years previously, to keep an eye on things and make sure that visiting sailors did not misbehave or overstay their welcome. The entire atoll had been declared a nature reserve and Roger was doing his best to correct some of the abuses of the past.

Roger led a truly Robinson Crusoe life on this large atoll, where nature was gradually returning things to normal after its occupation by the US military during the Second World War. Diving in the lagoon was among the best experiences in the entire Pacific, with a profusion of tropical fish, giant manta rays and turtles, but perhaps too many sharks. On land, the birds reigned supreme and there were tens of thousands of them everywhere, especially on the former airfield, now occupied by thousands of sooty terns, where one could hardly walk without risking stepping on a hatching bird, its eggs or its young.

The future of Palmyra Atoll as a nature reserve is now guaranteed, because shortly after our visit it was purchased jointly by The Nature Conservancy (TNC) and the US Fish and Wildlife Department. All visits to Palmyra must now be prearranged with TNC, there are permanent caretakers based there, and only one-week stops are allowed.

We left Palmyra with a heavy heart, not only because of Roger's unmatched hospitality – his heart-of-palm salad defies description – but also because we knew that the passage to Hawaii was likely to be hard on the wind. The accepted tactic is to make as much easting as possible before reaching the area of prevailing northeast trade winds. Unfortunately, that summer the Inter-Tropical Convergence Zone (ITCZ) was virtually on top of Palmyra and strong northeast winds were expected all the way to Hawaii. After leaving Palmyra, we tried to keep south of the ITCZ and make some easting while still in lower latitudes. Then, to our great fortune, Adrian, the first hurricane of the season forming off the coast of Baja California, came to our help. After blowing from almost dead ahead, the winds started veering east and gave us a better angle to sail on course. By that time we had already managed to make some 200 miles of easting, but still had 1,000 miles to sail on the wind. We managed to stay on the starboard tack all the way to Oahu, and arrived in Honolulu less than nine days after leaving Palmyra. At dawn, as we closed with the shore, scores of surfers were bobbing up and down ahead of us trying to catch the right wave. This was Hawaii as I had always imagined it.

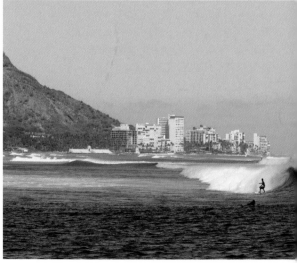

We were welcomed at the Waikiki Yacht Club, and for one indulgent week we enjoyed the unlimited attractions of Honolulu, where everything was available and life was obviously there to be enjoyed.

My old friend Alan Sitt, who had sailed with us from Peru to Easter Island in 1977, was now living on the west coast of Oahu, having built himself a large house right on the beach with reputedly the best surfing conditions in the world. His title of surfing champion had been taken over by his elder son, and Alan was working as a pilot, towing up gliders from a nearby airstrip. We arrived in great style at his spacious house in a hired Jaguar XK8 convertible, a treat to myself but appreciated even more by Marianne, who insisted on jumping in and out without opening the door as she had seen done in Hollywood films. Alan took us up in his plane in turns to see Oahu from above, and also treated each of us to a glider lesson.

Marianne left us in Honolulu and, in preparation for the long trek to Alaska, we sailed to the island of Hanalei, from where in early July we set off on the 2,500-mile passage to Sitka in Alaska. A huge North Pacific high was generating strong northeast winds, so we sailed as close to the wind as possible on a course that pointed dead north along the meridian of Hanalei (159°W), and thus kept to the west of the high-pressure area. While we were sailing north, the high-pressure area started moving west, so by the time we had reached 29°N we were right inside the high and, not surprisingly, the wind fell to almost nothing and soon we were totally becalmed. We had no choice but to motor through this extensive calm patch, and by the time we had reached 33°N we started picking up southwest winds. For a while they were light but good enough for a spinnaker. Most of the time we had only 10 knots of true wind, so we kept changing from the triradial to the asymmetric spinnaker and back again, making consistently good progress. As we moved into colder waters, the fog came down and we had to rely on radar as visibility dropped to a boat's length. We encountered several fishing boats, mostly Japanese, and had to avoid them as they took no notice of us.

For several days the fog was so thick that we could see absolutely nothing, so we set the radar alarm with a guard at 6 miles... and carried on sailing blindly into the milky void. A very eerie feeling! By 53°N, the wind started going to the westnorthwest, and although the fog was still with us, and occasionally also rain, with 15 to 18 knots of wind we were sailing fast. We arrived in Sitka 17 days after leaving Hanalei, managing this time to get there one day before Gwenda joined us from London.

Sitka is probably the best place to make landfall in southeast Alaska because it has excellent facilities. We spent the next five weeks cruising southeast Alaska and British Columbia. The scenery was in many ways a mirror image of the Chilean fjordland, except for, notably, the heavy traffic of cruise ships, fishing and pleasure boats. The highlights were: watching salmon jump an almost vertical waterfall, an unexpected encounter with a grizzly bear and its cub in a shallow bay where we had dried out overnight, the picture-postcard beauty of Glacier Bay, where we were surrounded by a large pod of killer whales and, in British Columbia, the wild grandeur of Princess Louise Inlet.

Having achieved our objective of sailing in one season from Antarctica to Alaska, while covering more than 12,000 miles in only four months, I realised that it would be impossible for me to manage the complex programme of the Millennium Odyssey while sailing. In Vancouver I loaded Aventura onto a transporter ship for the long trip to the Mediterranean. Six weeks later, she was unloaded in the French port of Toulon.

Johns Hopkins Glacier

14

Automatic pilots and wind-operated self-steering gears

The goal is not to sail the boat, but rather to help the boat sail herself.

John Rousmaniere

There is little doubt that the development of wind-operated self-steering gears and automatic pilots for sailing boats has contributed more than anything else to the popularity of offshore cruising, and, for that matter, short-handed racing too. This may sound like a bold statement, but I know that, with the exception of fully crewed boats, few if any sailors would set off on a long voyage if they had to be at the tiller or wheel 24 hours a day.

Dependency on a robotic helmsman can be as bad as a drug addiction, and the withdrawal symptoms just as unpleasant. I know of several examples of crew on an ocean passage, usually a couple, being prepared to abandon their boat because of a broken autopilot, forced to such a decision by the sheer exhaustion of steering by hand, day and night, in boisterous trade-wind conditions. No wonder that few other items on an offshore cruising boat have been debated more fiercely than these two stepbrothers, who seem to attract love and hatred in equal measure. In fact, wind-operated self-steering gears and electronic automatic pilots do not compete but complement each other, and anyone planning to leave on a voyage on a boat that could have both should acquire one of each. For the sake of simplicity, and common usage, occasionally they will be referred to as windvanes and autopilots.

Wind-operated self-steering gears

Oh ye seekers after perpetual motion, how many vain chimeras have you pursued? Go and take your place with the alchemists.

Leonardo da Vinci

When I equipped the first Aventura in the early 1970s, wind-operated self-steering gears had been around only for a decade, pioneered by those legendary early circumnavigators, the main contribution to their development having been made by Sir Francis Chichester. In his epic voyage around the world on the 53-foot Gipsy Moth IV, he used a large contraption that he had designed and built himself. His singlehanded circumnavigation showed that such a device not only worked but that it actually made such a strenuous voyage possible. As a qualified pilot, Francis Chichester was able to deal with the technical problems of this ingenious device, the closest thing to the mythical perpetuum mobile, a perpetual-motion machine. As far as I know it is the only piece of equipment on a cruising boat that can work continuously without any visible energy input from the crew. The energy is derived from the movement of the boat through the water as well as from the wind, but I still prefer to regard it as a perpetual-motion machine.

My windvane doesn't eat, sleep or have an opinion

Thomas Hahn

Aventura's Aries windvane

By the time Aventura I was ready to leave London, I had acquired what in those days was regarded as the best and most reliable self-steering gear. This was the British-built Aries, several of which had been used in the OSTAR, a transatlantic singlehanded race from the UK to the USA. Although it was possible to connect the gear to a steering wheel, I decided to stick to the original concept of such gears and lead the steering lines to a tiller. Installing an auxiliary tiller was not an easy solution as Aventura had an aft cabin, so I had to use a long stainless-steel extension that passed through the cabin from top to bottom and was connected to the rudderstock. Its top end emerged in the middle of the poop deck, where a large wooden tiller fitted neatly onto the square head. Although it restricted space in the aft cabin, it proved to be an ideal arrangement as not only did the windvane manage to steer the boat more efficiently, but I also had a permanently installed secondary steering system.

During the following six years I estimate that the gear steered the boat for about 80 per cent of the time. It didn't always keep the most accurate course, but it saved us from the drudgery of steering by hand, a worthwhile consolation on a short-handed boat that included two young children. When sailing downwind, the gear made Aventura meander about 20 degrees either side of the desired course. It didn't bother me too

much at the time, although later I realised that those extra miles had added at least two days to our slow 26-day crossing of the Atlantic.

Unfortunately, when this perpetual-motion machine reverts to its natural state and is idle, ie, when the wind stops, there is only one solution and that is to steer by hand. On the first Aventura an autopilot would have been a godsend, but there were as yet no suitable autopilots for small boats, and even if there had been, we wouldn't have had the money to buy one. Some simple tiller pilots started to appear on the market around that time, but we only managed to get one in Singapore a few months before the completion of our voyage.

Aventura II's steering position in the centrally located cockpit was far from the stern, making it difficult to connect a windvane directly to the steering wheel. For this reason I chose a Hydrovane gear, which had the advantage of being independent of the main steering system. Its large rudder was quite capable of steering a 40-foot boat on its own, provided the sails were well trimmed and that there was enough wind to move the large windvane, because the wind was its only source of energy. Owing to her heaviness, Aventura II needed a lot of wind to make any progress, and so did the Hydrovane. Aventura II was also equipped with an automatic pilot, so at long last we had the best of both worlds.

The same principle was followed on Aventura III, and I acquired what in the late 1990s was considered the best wind-operated self-steering gear, the German-made Windpilot.

The gear was mounted on a special support on the stern platform, the two control lines being led over blocks to the steering wheel. Because Aventura III's large stern arch interfered with the windvane, I had a custom-made smaller but wider vane that fitted under the arch. I also bought a Brookes & Gatehouse automatic pilot, which was integrated with the rest of the Hydra system. Just before the voyage to Antarctica, it was converted to a hydraulic system, which significantly increased its power. The autopilot was very reliable and worked well for thousands of miles, suffering only a couple of breakages.

A non-standard vane had to be used on Aventura III to fit under the stern arch

To play safe, Peter Förthmann, the maker of Windpilot, also supplied Aventura III with a Navico tiller pilot which could be used as a backup for the main autopilot, or to save electricity when the wind was too light, as the main pilot consumed on average 6Ah while the Navico only 1Ah or 2Ah. With the small autopilot linked to the Windpilot's windvane, the vane mimicked the wind and prompted the self-steering gear to keep the boat on course. The movement of the vane was transmitted to the steering lines via the servorudder, and the additional power derived from the movement of the boat through the water helped the small autopilot operate on very little electricity.

Whenever conditions were right I preferred to use the windvane, and over the years I learned its strengths and weaknesses, and we became good friends. I wish I could say the same about some of my crew, especially Gwenda, who, in spite of her offshore experience, seemed incapable or unwilling to come to terms with what she considered an uncooperative macho monster. Fortunately, as with everything else on Aventura, there

185

was an easy solution to that, so as soon as Gwenda came on watch, on came the automatic pilot and marital harmony prevailed.

As Aventura III's voyage progressed I used the windvane less, especially when I made a sail change, such as hoisting a spinnaker, and preferred to let the boat be steered by the autopilot. Because I often did this work on my own, there was a critical moment after I had hoisted the spinnaker and needed to dash to the cockpit to adjust the sheet and guy. In such situations I needed to be able to rely on the autopilot, which had been set to steer to wind, to keep an accurate course. Once the sail was properly set, and the boat was moving happily along, I would revert to the Windpilot, mainly to save electricity and also because it was silent.

I agree with those who argue that the advantages of a windvane outweigh its disadvantages, but this is only when looking at this subject from the technical point of view. Early in Aventura's III voyage my use of windvane versus autopilot was probably around 70 to 30, but as the voyage progressed, and I was trying to sail faster, usually under spinnaker, the windvane went into semi-retirement. This was not the windvane's fault but my own, as being short-handed and keen on sailing the boat efficiently at all times, I found the autopilot to be more convenient to use. There is no doubt that a good autopilot, especially a top-of-the-range model such as the one I had, keeps a more accurate course than a windvane, which for me was a crucial consideration.

On the wind, the Windpilot steered impeccably as this is a windvane's preferred point of sailing. Its performance when reaching was also good, provided the boat was not overpowered, in which case the mainsail needed to be reefed promptly to avoid too much weather helm. Broadreaching is any windvane's weakest point, and however well the sails are set, a larger wave or stronger gust will push the boat off the desired course. Often in such situations the gear is either incapable of bringing the boat back on course or takes a long time to do it. When running downwind with the sails well adjusted the windvane coped well, although because of the risk of broaching or gybing, when on this point of sailing I never dared leave the cockpit, so as to be able to intervene promptly if necessary. Running downwind either wing and wing or with twin jibs was easiest on the windvane. It also worked well when sailing downwind with a spinnaker, but I always kept a careful eye on it.

A possible disadvantage of a windvane is that it keeps steering the boat to the same wind angle regardless of changes in the wind direction. Admittedly, this is also the case with autopilots if they are set to wind and not to a compass heading. In both cases, this means that the wind direction should be monitored constantly, the sails trimmed if necessary and the course readjusted accordingly. The same practice also applies to changes in wind strength or direction.

This is exactly what happened on an overnight passage on Aventura III between two island groups in the Chagos archipelago. At the end of my watch I adjusted the windvane and set a safe course to pass well clear of any dangers. I asked my crew to keep an eye on the windvane and the course we were sailing, and to call me if there was any change. When he called me at the end of his watch, I checked our position on the GPS and realised that we had gone badly off course and were heading towards the nearest reef. During his watch the wind had changed direction and we were now sailing at about 30 degrees off our intended

A smaller plywood vane was used in the strong wind conditions of the Southern Ocean

course. We were pointing straight for the edge of the Caicos Bank, and had I come up 20 minutes later we would have run onto that reef.

The decision whether to have a windvane or not on Aventura IV was taken out of my hands as the need to carry a RIB tender in the stern davits on my voyage to the Arctic made it impossible to also install a windvane. If I had continued on a world voyage, I would have attempted to find a compromise solution, as I am still convinced of the usefulness of a windvane as a backup. To make up for this, I decided to have two totally independent Brookes & Gatehouse automatic pilots. As an added safety provision, I also considered carrying a spare rudder, which, in an emergency, could have been mounted on the universal stern bracket normally used for the hydro-generator, and fitted with a tiller-type autopilot. But I realised that the twin-rudder configuration of the Exploration 45, and the additional autopilot, provided a perfectly adequate backup.

Automatic pilots

The sails must be properly trimmed and adjusted before handing over the steering to either autopilot or windvane.
Carlton DeHart

Automatic pilots have been around for a long time. The first aircraft autopilot was developed by the Sperry Corporation in 1912, and in the early 1920s the tanker JA Moffett became the first ship to use an autopilot. In 1974 the British inventor Derek Fawcett produced the Autohelm, a tiller-mounted system that steered a yacht to an apparent angle using a hydraulic arm, an external windvane and the boat's 12V supply. Fawcett later developed a more advanced model that included an internal gyrocompass, which made it possible to set a course based on wind angle or compass information.

Current models are based on the same principle, but are much more user-friendly: they will not only steer the vessel on a pre-set compass course, but when connected to a GPS receiver or the boat's instruments, the autopilot can deal with a wide range of other tasks. Operating an autopilot is very simple, but good seamanship requires that the autopilot and course steered be monitored constantly.

'Compass' is the default mode of the autopilot, and once activated, it will steer the course selected. Normally I only use this mode when under power or for short periods when hoisting or reefing the sails. The 'wind' mode allows the autopilot computer to steer the boat according to the wind direction. On most autopilots, either true or apparent wind angle can be selected. Usually true wind angle should be selected when sailing downwind, as it will keep the boat on track avoiding the risk of gybing. The 'apparent wind' mode is more efficient when sailing upwind because it will allow the pilot to keep closest to the preferred wind angle. When sailing to wind, it is advisable to set a windshift alarm if available to alert the crew of any wind changes. In the 'navigation' mode the autopilot will steer to a waypoint or selected route. Such full integration between navigation and autopilot is undoubtedly useful in the case of commercial ships, but is not recommended on sailing boats because an error made in plotting a waypoint could have grave consequences if the course steered is not constantly monitored. It is a function that I never use.

An autopilot would have been a great boon on our first voyage, but leaving just before the launch of that first Autohelm, we had only a windvane to ease the drudgery of hand steering. The Aries windvane coped well when there was enough wind to move the boat, but in light winds or when motoring we had to take over and steer by hand.

The following three Aventura all had Brookes & Gatehouse autopilots. Aventura II and, initially, Aventura III had a linear electro-mechanical steering ram; the latter converted later to a hydraulic ram. On the advice of the boatbuilders, on Aventura IV the two Brooke & Gatehouse autopilots were equipped with Jefa linear drives, which worked very well.

Maintenance

Maintenance of a windvane is simple as most models only need to be rinsed with fresh water occasionally, the lines checked for chafe and the various nuts regularly tightened. I carried several spare vanes and servorudders, and although the latter are of the sacrificial type and would break if they hit something hard, this never happened to me. However, carrying a spare is essential, a bitter lesson learned by a couple

during the maiden voyage of their boat between New Zealand and Fiji. About 200 miles into the passage, the servorudder hit something and sheared off. As they had left without a spare, they switched on the autopilot, but that wasn't working either. Because there was only the two of them, and they were not prepared to hand-steer all the way to Fiji, they had no option but return to New Zealand. By then the season was too far advanced and they had to wait another six months before being able to resume their voyage.

Routine maintenance of an automatic pilot is quite simple. On Aventura III I regularly checked the bolt connecting the hydraulic ram to the rudder quadrant. I had several of those 12mm stainless-steel bolts because they tended to break on average about once a year. I also checked the level of hydraulic fluid daily and always carried at least 10 litres of it. About once a year I checked the brushes on the electric motor, usually when I also inspected the brushes on other electrical appliances. As an emergency spare, I carried an electric motor for the pilot's hydraulic pump. Before the system was converted to hydraulic I also carried a spare ram.

The most serious autopilot breakage on Aventura III happened in Chile, but as there were four of us on board, and we were using the windvane extensively, this was not a major inconvenience. I had a replacement ram couriered to Valdivia, and the system worked well for a while, but that same year, while on passage between Hawaii and Alaska, the autopilot stopped working again. At the time we were motoring across the North Pacific High in thick fog, and there were lots of fishing boats around us. As there was hardly any wind and we were motoring, we could not use the vane, so I set up the small Navico autopilot, which did an excellent job and steered all the way to Sitka. That breakage was one of the reasons I decided to upgrade the autopilot for Aventura III's forthcoming round-the-world voyage.

Autopilot maintenance on Aventura IV consisted of regularly visually checking the drive units and,

Easy access on Aventura III to the autopilot ram and rudder sensor connected to the quadrant

if necessary, tightening the steering cables. Also, as part of my usual routine, I would regularly activate the backup autopilot to ascertain that it was working properly.

Having been, so to speak, at the receiving end of thousands of boats completing an ocean passage, I have witnessed a fair amount of autopilot breakages. Over the years, their reliability has improved considerably, but in the early days the electronics of some of them were simply not up to the job. In fairness to the manufacturers, I must add that the fault, both then and now, may have been that of the user. As I have pointed out already, some autopilots were undersized for the size and displacement of the boat, or exposed to too much strain by the boat being over-canvassed or having badly trimmed sails. It was interesting to notice how the reliability of autopilots increased as their owners acquired more experience.

In a recent survey on the size of crew on boats undertaking a long voyage, I found that the majority of such boats were crewed by a couple. As I mention in chapter 20, being left without a functioning autopilot or windvane on a long ocean passage can be a serious problem, especially when sailing shorthanded.

North Atlantic, January 2015

A couple sailing on their own, from the Canaries to the Caribbean, on a 53-foot yacht in the Atlantic Odyssey reported a serious emergency and asked us to arrange a tow because their autopilot had broken down and they were too exhausted to continue. As it was a US-flagged yacht, we advised them that their request had to be passed on to the US Coastguard. We also warned them that, with their yacht being some 900 miles from the Caribbean, a tow might be impractical, and if the US Coastguard mounted a rescue operation it would seek assistance from a vessel in the vicinity to save them, and they would be forced to abandon their boat.

We managed to persuaded them to attempt to continue their passage by limiting the time spent

steering by hand, reducing sail at night, and letting the boat drift with wind and current in the general direction of the nearest landfall. They took the advice and managed to cover the remaining distance in 10 days and make landfall unassisted.

Barbados 50 yachts in Tenerife... and not a windvane in sight

North Atlantic, November 2016

A similar situation befell another couple taking part in the Barbados 50 transatlantic rally, when a steering cable broke on their 50-foot yacht. With the autopilot also out of action, they had to steer with the emergency tiller and found it extremely hard and exhausting to keep the large yacht on course in the strong winds and large swell. Alerted to the emergency, seven yachts taking part in the same rally changed course, either to catch up from behind or slow down if they were ahead. One of the boats caught up with the disabled yacht and they considered coming alongside to transfer one of their crew, but were dissuaded by the large swell. In the words of the captain of the rescue boat:

'We discussed the option of inflating our dinghy, but as we wanted to complete the transfer before darkness fell, my decision was to run a warp with a fender from our leeward quarter and, as a precaution, asked them to lower their bathing ladder, and also trail a warp from the stern. Our crew used the warp as a safety line and swam downwind from us to the other boat. We then got closer and threw a line across to haul a waterproof bag with his personal effects. It was all quite straightforward.'

The crew who had swum across was an experienced mechanic and managed to repair the steering and also get the autopilot to work. To be on the safe side, he remained on board until they made landfall in Barbados.

South Pacific, March 1999

Ten days after leaving the Galapagos Islands on the 3,000-mile leg to the Marquesas, the autopilot stopped working on Dreamtime of London, which was sailing in the Millennium Odyssey. Initially, Alison and John continued with their windvane. 24 hours later, a huge wave hit the stern and tore the windvane support arm from its mounting. They now had to steer by hand, which was extremely tiring in the 20 to 25-knot wind and large quartering seas. Two days later, Alison described their predicament on the daily SSB radio schedule, and several Millennium yachts responded immediately, with the captain of the Italian Jancris offering to transfer two of his crew. Four other yachts changed course, and they all converged to stand by for the transfer. Dreamtime hove to windward of Jancris, lowered their dinghy on a long line, and safely brought young Franco and Nico on board. For the next 1,400 miles they took their turn at the wheel, and 10 days later Dreamtime arrived in the Marquesas for an emotional reunion with the other yachts. At the welcoming reception in Tahiti, Alison and John were awarded a special prize of two large blow-up dolls, their new crew.

Backups

In spite of their happy endings, these three stories should be an important lesson to any couple or short-handed crew leaving on a long voyage. While windvanes are quite robust and may be mended if they break, autopilots can rarely be repaired at sea, unless you have all necessary spares and the skills to repair the equipment. For ordinary mortals, the only answer is a suitable backup. Ideally, such a backup should be

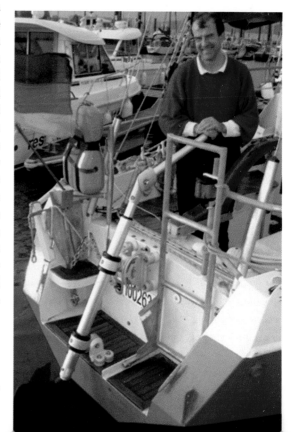

entirely independent of the main unit. This means that it should not be dependent on the main navigation system, and should have its own rudder sensor, compass and GPS input. The speed-over-ground function can be acquired from the latter.

A backup for the steering system itself is an emergency rudder. The Hydrovane self-steering gear incorporates its own rudder, which can be used as a spare rudder in an emergency. The Windpilot Pacific model has an ingenious system to mount an emergency rudder-tiller on the existing unit. Windpilot also produces a stand-alone rudder-tiller combination, which can be installed even on boats that are not equipped with a Windpilot self-steering unit.

Windvanes surveyed

Wind-operated self-steering gears have been examined in a number of surveys, and it would be interesting to look at the results with a historical perspective. In a major equipment survey conducted among participants in the second ARC in 1987, among the 197 yachts surveyed, 43 per cent had a windvane and 67 per cent an autopilot, while 10 per cent had both. Things have changed dramatically over the years: in ARC 2004, among the 197 boats surveyed, only 25 boats (13 per cent) had a windvane, while almost every yacht had an automatic pilot. Ten years later, among the 189 ARC boats surveyed, only 20 boats (11 per cent) had a windvane. Among these, 18 also had an autopilot, as did all other boats surveyed. Not included in the total figure were racing boats with a full-crew complement, most of which had an autopilot that was not used.

These findings were confirmed when I compared them to the situation in the non-competitive rallies that I have been involved with of late. While not as drastic as in the ARC, a similar drop in the number of cruising boats equipped with windvanes points to a general downward trend, with approximately only 20 per cent of cruising boats having a windvane, with a slightly higher percentage among boats undertaking a world voyage.

Autopilots surveyed

The use of, and dependence on, automatic pilots has reached the stage where there are hardly any cruising boats without one. Among the captains interviewed in the Global Cruising Survey who had both, many expressed their concern over the electricity consumption of their autopilots. Although the hourly consumption on all surveyed boats averaged 3.9Ah, in reality the figure was probably higher because several skippers admitted that they had no idea how much power their autopilots consumed. This prompted me to keep a careful record of my own consumption over a period of 24 hours. I ended up on Aventura III with an average of 6Ah, which is probably normal for a boat of that size. In spite of Aventura IV being longer and also heavier than Aventura III, I arrived at a similar average, probably due to her twin-rudder configuration, which made her very easy to steer.

A survey on the reliability of autopilots among participants in three transatlantic rallies showed that approximately 20 per cent of the boats experienced problems with their autopilot during the Atlantic crossing. One of the most frequently cited causes was the fact that many autopilots were considered by their owners as insufficiently powerful to steer a boat under prolonged conditions of strong winds and high swell. For various reasons, whether because of wrong advice by the manufacturers or the need to save money, some owners may have bought an underpowered unit, so it is not fair to put the blame on the autopilot if it was being used under conditions that it was not designed for. The overall conclusion I drew from talking to some of those with autopilot breakages was that often they had neglected to trim and adjust the sails, thus forcing the autopilot to work hard to keep an unbalanced boat on course.

In my view, most autopilots are very efficient and, if the sails are properly trimmed, will steer the boat effortlessly. My advice is to regularly monitor the rudder indicator on the autopilot display, and if it yaws widely it means that the autopilot is struggling to keep the boat on course, therefore the sails need to be reefed or adjusted to the existing conditions.

Autopilot or windvane?

Looking at the general picture, as boats become faster and sailors get a taste for speed and efficient sailing, a boat steered by windvane may look like a thing from the past. Windvanes were perfectly suitable when 6 knots was the top speed of most boats and many sailors were happy to average 120 miles per day. When I discussed this matter with Peter Förthmann of Windpilot, he disagreed and pointed out that the sales of windvanes proved that most cruising sailors, for whom safety and comfort not speed are the first priority, are still happy to use the more environmentally friendly windvane than the power-hungry autopilot.

My answer to the above question is that those who plan a long voyage, and can afford it, should get both a wind self-steering gear and an autopilot. I would also advise not being tempted to buy a cheap autopilot just to save money. A reliable, accurate and powerful autopilot is of such vital importance to the comfort and, above all, safety of an offshore voyage that this is one area where only the best will do. The choice of a windvane is more complex, and the final decision will depend on the size and sailing characteristics of the boat, the configuration of its stern, the location of the steering wheel and the style of your sailing. A good starting point is to read Peter Förthmann's book on this subject, where he describes all windvane models currently available. He also deals with the main aspects of autopilots. The book is available at windpilot.com.

Tips

» Always keep an eye on changes in wind direction when sailing with an autopilot that has been set to steer to wind, or when steering by windvane.

» If planning to leave on a long offshore voyage, consider having both an autopilot and a wind self-steering gear.

» A backup autopilot should be carried on long ocean passages with a short-handed crew. Ideally, it should be entirely independent of the main unit.

» Make sure that you have a powerful enough autopilot to cope with long runs under strenuous conditions.

» The main autopilot should be connected directly to the rudderstock, independent of the steering system, so that in an emergency the boat can be steered with the autopilot.

» Carry spare servorudders and vanes for the self-steering gear.

15

Anchors and anchoring, tenders and outboards

Anchors are right at the heart of cruising. Ensuring you have the best anchor possible is one way to stack the safety odds in your favour.

Peter Smith

In more than 40 years of cruising I have used all types of anchor: CQR, Bruce, Danforth, Océane, French FOB and, occasionally, a Fisherman. I feel that, having acted as a guinea pig in the evolution of anchors, I must point out that each one had its limitations and none could be entirely trusted. It was only when I got a Rocna for my latest Aventura that I finally found what could be the perfect anchor. The 33kg model was tested in a variety of conditions on Aventura IV's 25,000-mile voyage and performed well throughout.

Ideally an anchor should do all of the following:

» Dig in fast and bury itself deep
» Continue to provide good holding power even if it drags
» Hold and not roll out despite wind, tide or current shifts
» Resist both lateral and vertical movements even if submitted to extreme loads
» Hold well in any kind of seabed, whether mud, sand, grass or kelp

Anchor design has greatly evolved over the years, and there are now types of anchor, such as the Rocna, whose holding power is much better than any of the above. But, as with everything else in cruising, no anchor should be regarded as being 100 per cent reliable under any conditions. One lesson that I have learned in many years of sailing is that there is no such thing as a perfect solution for any given situation: this certainly includes anchoring gear and anchoring techniques.

This is obviously quite a tall order, but having seen and heard of so many boats lost as a result of being badly anchored, I cannot stress enough how seriously this matter should be taken. Acquiring the best possible anchor should be one of the main priorities when equipping a boat.

Anchor rode: chain, rope or a mixture?

Personally I prefer all-chain to a chain-and-rope combination, but your choice should be dictated by the area where you plan to cruise and the type of ground you may encounter, as well as the kind of anchorages you are most likely to be using. If you plan to go to the tropics and spend time in areas of coral, all-chain should be your preferred choice. One disadvantage of using rope, besides the risk of it being damaged by coral or rocks, is that you have to let out more scope and thus need to have a much wider swinging space than with all-chain. Because many anchorages in the Mediterranean and Caribbean are often crowded, you must take such limited space into account.

I have always had all-chain for the main anchor, and usually about 6 to 10 metres of chain plus rope for a second anchor. Aventura IV had 100 metres of 10mm chain with a 33kg Rocna anchor, a combination I consider as being adequate for her displacement. To keep the weight centred, the chain locker and anchor winch were sited at the foot of the mast. I also had a permanently installed anchor reel at the stern with 50 metres of leaded anchoring line. The secondary anchor was a 14kg aluminium Fortress anchor, which I deployed with 10 metres of chain plus the leaded line.

While in the Northwest Passage, we experienced a storm with gusts of over 60 knots. It lasted 22 hours and the anchor held, but as there was another boat that had anchored too close to Aventura, we had to motor into the wind throughout the storm, not so much to help the anchor, but to keep out of the way of the neighbouring boat, which was anchored with rope only and was swinging widely, often getting dangerously close to us. We survived that long storm unscathed, as did our friends on Suilven, an Oyster 47, who also used all-chain with an identical Rocna anchor to mine (more details later on in this chapter).

Anchor types

My preferred anchor? One that doesn't drag.

Don Babson

I agree with Don Babson's remark, and fortunately there is now a new generation of anchors to choose from. Peter Smith, the designer of the successful Rocna anchor, made this comment: 'There are still many sailors who carry the older generation anchors such as CQR, Delta, Bruce and Danforth types. They may not be fully aware of the benefits of the newer generation anchors now widely available, which have raised the bar significantly in anchoring performance.'

Alain Poiraud, the designer of the Spade and Océane anchors, made a similar observation when he said: 'Out of all the equipment on today's boats the anchor is the one that attracts the least interest from sailors. In the age of satellite navigation many boats are still equipped with anchors that look as if they had been invented by the Ancient Greeks. Like all other techniques in recent times, anchors have evolved, old wisdoms have been replaced by new theories, anchors no longer have to be heavy, and new designs are proven to be more efficient. There is no doubt that current-design anchors improve security for those who are wise enough to try them.'

Two of the most successful new-generation anchors are the German Bügel or Wasi anchor, and the French Spade. The main novelty of the former is its rollbar; of the latter, its concave fluke shape. The New Zealand designer, Peter Smith, incorporated these two features in the design of the Rocna anchor that I had on Aventura IV.

All this was far in the future when I was preparing for my first voyage in the early 1970s, and practically every cruising boat was using the British-designed and -built CQR. As a result, I automatically opted for a 15kg CQR, which worked reasonably well in the Mediterranean but was not so good when we reached the tropics. No type of anchor is suited for anchoring among coral heads, and while any anchor may hold once itself or the chain, or both, have fouled on a coral head, a plough-type anchor is more vulnerable to fouling in such situations than most other types.

Before Aventura I left the London docks, a friend presented me with a mighty 60kg Admiralty-type anchor that he insisted I should take along as a

CQR

Océane

Spade

Wasi

Rocna

hurricane anchor. It was never used but it certainly made me feel good just knowing that I had it. For lack of inspiration, Aventura II also ended up with a CQR as her main anchor, this time upgraded to 20kg. In the case of Aventura III, the decision was taken out of my hands as she came supplied with a 15kg FOB anchor, which I was assured was quite adequate for her relatively light displacement.

Eventually I replaced the FOB with a Bruce anchor, but it turned out to be just as disappointing. While in New Zealand, I was contacted by the manufacturer of Spade anchors who asked me to test their new Océane model. The Océane was of a similar design to the Spade but was supposed to incorporate some improvements on its successful predecessor. To test it, I started making a note of the type of bottom, depth and how much chain had been let out, and this made me pay more attention to my anchoring technique than in the past. It came as a surprise to find, when I double-checked, usually with a mask, that often I was not as well anchored as I had presumed. We never dragged badly enough to put the boat in danger, although there were a couple of close calls. A few times we dragged not because I had done anything wrong, but because, while we were away, some other boat had dragged over our chain and had displaced our anchor, or someone had picked up our anchor with theirs and then dropped it without any thought of what might happen to our boat. One such incident happened in Greece, and could have had serious consequences had it not been for an alert taverna owner who told us to return quickly to our boat. This probably saved the boat, but ruined my traditional Greek Easter lunch. After that, I was very reluctant to leave the boat unattended while paying long visits ashore.

Before sailing on Aventura III to Antarctica, I acquired a 5kg Fisherman that I used in a tandem arrangement with the main anchor. The Fisherman was shackled to a length of 6 metres of 10mm chain, which was connected to the main anchor. The small anchor was let go first, and being held down by its short length of chain, would usually settle in firmly and help the main anchor dig in well.

Anchored with the tandem arrangement in a shallow Antarctic cove

We never dragged when anchored in this way, and even later, whenever I was in a dubious place or planned to stay longer, I used this reliable system. Retrieving the anchors was easy because the main anchor was hauled in normally with the electric winch, and when the smaller anchor's chain broke the water it could be either handled or grabbed with a boathook, and lifted onto the foredeck. If I planned to anchor again soon, I would leave the whole caboodle shackled up on the foredeck ready to go.

Anchoring techniques

I have often been amazed at just how lazy people are about re-anchoring, even if their anchor is obviously not holding well, or they have dropped it in the wrong place.

Klaus Girzig

Nothing shows up better someone's inexperience than their anchoring technique.

Some sailors seem to have an entirely wrong attitude. One of the best examples in this respect is that of a singlehander who stopped at Pitcairn Island, dropped his hook in Bounty Bay and went ashore to enjoy the hospitality of his hosts. Later that day the wind came up and the Pitcairners warned him that winds blowing from that direction eventually back and end up blowing straight into the bay, thus putting his boat on a dangerous lee shore. They strongly advised him to return to his boat immediately and re-anchor in a better place. Being happy ashore, he ignored them... and lost his boat. He managed to get a lift on a passing ship and, a couple of years later, was back in Pitcairn with a new boat. Incredibly, the situation repeated itself and, once again while ashore, the wind came up, he was warned to return to his boat, but laughed it off, saying that such things never happen twice. Well, they do... and did, and he lost his second boat in exactly the same spot as the first one!

Boats can get into trouble even if anchored well under prevailing wind conditions, if put on a lee shore by a wind change. This is what happened to a yacht anchored in Port Resolution on the island of Tanna in Vanuatu. When the wind changed direction during the night and started blowing strongly into the anchorage, putting the yacht on a dangerous lee shore, the crew tried to leave in the dark. As they were making their way out of the bay with the help of the radar and GPS, the yacht clipped the corner of the fringing reef and was quickly pushed onto the rocks by the large swell. The crew managed to save themselves but the boat was a total loss.

This is the kind of nightmare scenario that I fear more than anything else, so whenever I am anchored in a doubtful place I make sure I have an exit strategy. Usually, on arrival I make a note of the GPS coordinates of the entrance and mark down an exit track with suitable waypoints. After we have anchored, I write down the coordinates of the spot. These coordinates can be a useful indication of the boat dragging, especially at night when it is reassuring to see that the boat is still holding its position. As a precaution, the bitter end of the anchor chain should be secured to the boat with a line that can be cut in an emergency, so that the chain and anchor are buoyed and can be retrieved later. However, as a rule, if the weather looks at all like changing, I prefer to play safe and leave the anchorage before I have to put my exit strategy into practice.

Sailing past Pitcairn's unprotected Bounty Bay

Wrecked yacht in Chagos

While in Chagos on Aventura III, I went for a dive on the wreck of a cruising boat that had been lost on the fringing reef off Fouquet Island shortly before our arrival. A violent squall had caught the crew unaware, as the strong wind quickly turned and blew from the opposite direction to the prevailing southeast wind. The wreck of the ferrocement hull lay in about 4 metres of water, a gaping hole on its port side teeming with fish of all colours, shapes and sizes. It was a sorry sight and made me think how such a tragedy could have been prevented. Every year boats are lost under similar conditions while anchored in a place that is protected from the prevailing winds by an island or a reef. A passing front can suddenly generate violent gusts from the opposite direction to the prevailing wind. As the boat swings on its anchor, it can be pushed by wind and swell onto the shore or reef. If this happens suddenly, getting up the anchor and leaving is rarely possible, and all one can do is pray that the anchor will hold until the front has passed or the squall has blown itself out. There is a way to pre-empt such a situation, which I have tried out on Aventura III.

This prudent system of anchoring is basically a modified Bahamian moor and consists of using two anchors, both streamed from the bows. It can be very useful when anchoring in areas where changes of wind direction are expected, which is a known phenomenon in the tropics. As this system of anchoring takes some time to set up, it will appeal primarily to those planning a longer stay, although if in doubt it should be done even for short stays.

With the wind blowing from the prevailing direction, the main anchor is let go at a reasonable distance from the beach or fringing reef. The chosen spot should be far enough from the beach or reef to allow the boat to swing around safely should the wind change direction.

A second anchor is then taken by dinghy and dropped in at a safe distance from the beach or reef. Ideally, this inshore anchor should be checked with a mask and, if necessary, set by hand. The anchor should be buoyed in case it has to be retrieved in an emergency. The rode is then taken to the boat and made fast at the bows. This is now the holding anchor. The inboard end

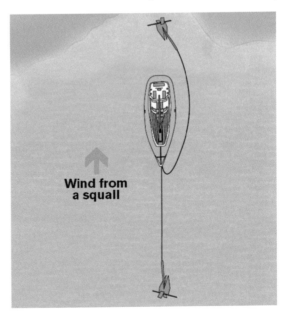

Prevailing wind

Wind from a squall

of the rode should be buoyed also in case it has to be dropped in a hurry. When setting the inshore anchor, the rode on the main anchor may have to be let out to its full length so as to be able to pick up the end of the second rode. Both rodes should then be adjusted so that the boat is held firmly by the inshore (windward) anchor. Ideally, the two anchors should be roughly in line, both with each other and the direction of the wind.

The spot at which to drop the main anchor can be estimated as approximately two-thirds of the total length of the two anchor rodes. During my test, the main anchor was dropped in a depth of 12 metres at approximately 100 metres from the beach, while the inshore anchor was dropped in 4 metres at about 25 metres from the beach. In order to pick up the end of the second rode (50 metres of 25mm nylon line plus three metres of chain), I had to let out almost all my 100 metres of chain holding the main anchor. Once both anchors had been set, I hauled in some of the main chain, and Aventura was now lying to the secondary anchor at approximately 50 metres off the reef.

Anchored in this way, if the wind swings around, the boat would swing with it and would be held by the main anchor. This should hold the boat off the reef or beach, and ride out the squall. However, should the situation deteriorate, it may be prudent to leave. This set-up makes it possible to jettison the second rode and anchor (both of which had been buoyed), ride up to the main anchor, retrieve it and move into deeper water or to a sheltered spot. In extremis, the main anchor and chain may also have to be abandoned, so a line and a buoy or fender should be prepared for such an eventuality.

The basic idea of this technique is to be prepared for the worst, so if a strong wind starts blowing from the opposite direction to the prevailing wind, and puts the boat on a lee shore, you are in a position to do something about it, and do not risk being stranded on a reef or beach.

Safely moored with two anchors in tandem and secured with lines ashore in preparation for an impending storm

Anchoring routine

Over the years I have honed my anchoring technique to a simple routine and a few rules that I observe whenever possible. For a start, I always try to anchor in a depth where, in an emergency, I could dive to dislodge a fouled anchor or untangle the chain. If the water was too deep, I had diving tanks on board for just this kind of eventuality. The mask and snorkel were always kept by the companionway, and it is surprising how often I have had to dive quickly to sort out a fouled anchor, or check if it had set properly. Not being able to dive can be a serious handicap. The very first money I earned as a sailor happened a few days after we had arrived in Greece. The captain of a charter boat, who had lost their anchor in deep water, asked me if I had diving tanks to find and retrieve it. He offered me the equivalent of 50 dollars if I would do it. I wasted no time, donned my equipment, found the anchor, secured it with a line, and not five minutes later was back on the surface, all smiles. I was paid the promised fee, which in those days was as much as I was paid by the BBC for my weekly programme.

The usual anchoring routine whenever I sailed with Gwenda was for me to be at the bow looking for a suitable spot while she motored slowly, keeping an eye on the depth sounder and, after we had acquired it, on the forward-looking sonar. When we reached a suitable depth, I dropped the anchor and let out chain to between four and five times the depth. I then asked

Gwenda to go slowly astern with the engine, and the stretching chain would indicate that the anchor had set. Normally I would then dive to check the anchor. Occasionally I had to re-set it by hand, but if I was not happy with what I found, I would return on board, haul in the anchor and look for a better spot. Even with all these precautions, we often ended up having to repeat the procedure two or three times until I was perfectly satisfied that the job was as well done as it could possibly be. This was particularly important if we planned to be away from the boat and leave it unattended for any length of time. Being lazy about anchoring is simply not an option.

To stop the boat swinging in a crowded anchorage, especially in tidal areas or when the wind is light, I usually set a stern anchor or took a line ashore. To make life easier, on Aventura IV's stern I had two drums, one with a leaded line for the anchor and a floating mooring line on the other.

Getting your anchor fouled is an unavoidable hazard, especially in tropical waters, and if you are not able to dive, sooner or later you may lose your ground tackle. The way to avoid this is to try to find a sandy spot in which to anchor. To be able to do this, it is essential to arrive at a chosen anchorage in good light, when sandy patches are clearly seen. If possible, you should always avoid anchoring near coral heads, and it is a good idea to first have a look around with a mask to identify a suitable spot.

While in the Pacific, where the chain often got entangled with coral heads, I learned a simple but efficient trick when anchoring in such an area. After I dropped the anchor and started releasing more chain, I would insert, at intervals of about 5 to 8 metres, plastic floats attached to the chain with a one-metre-long line. By holding up the chain, the floats stopped it from getting entangled. I found several fishing floats of about 40cm in diameter among the debris stranded on a windward beach, and provided each with a line and carbine hook so they could be quickly attached to the chain. After I started using this system I never had a fouled chain again.

Anchor winch

The first Aventura had a manual anchor winch that was not only poorly manufactured but was also not powerful enough, so often I ended up hauling in the 6mm chain by hand. On all my later boats I used 8mm galvanised chain. The electric winch installed on Aventura II was a well-known British brand, but it proved to be just as bad as its predecessor, and winching in the heavier chain manually was frustratingly slow and tedious, especially when I had to do it repeatedly. So I made sure that Aventura III had the best, and indeed the Lofrans vertical anchor winch worked impeccably for the 13 years I owned her.

On Aventura IV the powerful Quick Aleph 1500W winch was installed at the foot of the mast, as was the chain locker. Thus the considerable weight of the chain was transferred to the middle of the boat, with the added advantage that the chain locker was easily accessible from the forward bathroom. I also had an electric capstan installed on the foredeck to make it easier to handle docking lines if necessary; this would have acted as a backup in an emergency.

How much importance long-distance sailors attribute to the anchor winch was demonstrated by the fact that in a survey of cruising sailors, nearly one-third listed a powerful and reliable electric anchor winch among the five essential items on their ideal cruising boat. It is a view I entirely agree with, as I know from personal experience just how much easier life can be with a good-quality anchor winch. And not just easier, but also much safer because re-anchoring several times if necessary is no longer an effort, as the operation can be easily repeated.

Never anchor too close to the shore and always allow sufficient swinging space

Moorings

We lost our boat when her mooring broke loose during tropical storm Felix in Saba, when she drifted ashore. The mooring was supposed to be hurricane-proof and we checked the line the week before. Never trust a mooring, especially if you leave your boat unattended for any time.

Luc Callebaut

This is what happened in almost exactly the same spot in Saba in an incident described on page 319. We almost had a similar experience in Croatia when we tied Aventura to a harbour mooring in the port of Porec. Having been assured that it was a professionally laid and checked mooring, we went ashore to visit this picturesque medieval town. Virtually out of a blue sky, a violent wind swept over the anchorage, instantly churning up the sea into an infernal maelstrom.

This was a bora, a katabatic wind and dreaded local phenomenon that can reach hurricane-force within seconds. We were watching helplessly from the quay, hoping that the mooring would hold. It did, but I still blamed myself for not having dived and checked with my own eyes that it was indeed reliable.

The conclusion is quite obvious: never use a mooring unless you are absolutely sure that it is reliable. I should also add that moorings are normally owned by somebody, so obtain permission first too.

Tenders

Tender jam at Great Exuma in the Bahamas

Choosing the right tender for a long voyage can be just as difficult as selecting a suitable anchor, and as there is such a wide choice, it is very easy to make the wrong decision. On the first Aventura, we set off with a small Avon inflatable, but by the time we got to Gibraltar I realised that we needed a bigger backup for longer expeditions, so we bought a larger inflatable. As it was almost impossible to row, I also bought a 2HP Seagull outboard engine – a noisy, smoky and smelly yet reliable workhorse. In New Zealand we acquired a fibreglass dinghy, which I fitted out from a bare hull. It had a centreboard and mast and could double up as a sailing dinghy, to the delight of our junior crew.

This two-dinghy configuration was repeated on all my subsequent boats. Both Aventura II and III had two inflatables, a smaller and a larger one that were stowed deflated in a locker when on passage. Aventura III had two Honda outboards: a smaller 2HP motor that could be used on both dinghies, and a 5HP that was used on the larger inflatable on longer outings. If I needed to land quickly, maybe to complete formalities in a new place, I could get the smaller dinghy ready in 10 minutes. On longer expeditions I always clamped the 2HP as a backup next to the 5HP motor. As an added precaution, I always carried a pair of spare wooden oars. To avoid losing them, I had drilled holes through the handles and tied each with a long lanyard to the dinghy, so they were not lost when making a wet landing. Both inflatables could be easily rowed, even the larger one, which was also fitted with retractable wheels to make it easier to pull up on a beach.

Aventura III's larger tender

The choice of tender is a matter of personal preference. As on passage I prefer to stow all gear in lockers and have no loose gear on deck, the tenders had to be inflatable. This may not be to everyone's liking, and if an RIB can be safely and adequately stowed, it is probably a better choice. RIBs have a number

201

of advantages over ordinary inflatables. They take the ground better, which is very important on rough beaches, where I had to be very careful not to puncture my inflatable dinghies. Also they are easily driven and steered, and use less fuel. The main disadvantage of a RIB on a smaller yacht is that of stowage, and the only solution is to have them held in davits. On larger yachts they can be stowed on the foredeck, either upside down or the right way up with a well-fitting cover to keep the water out.

Aventura IV's stern arrangement

On Aventura IV an aluminium-hulled RIB was the obvious choice for the Arctic voyage, where we would have to land on rocky or ice-covered beaches. As a backup I also carried a four-man inflatable dinghy, stowed in the forward sail locker. Having a large RIB hanging in davits was not to my liking, but in spite of my concerns it was never a problem when we encountered rough seas.

A great advantage of the Highfield aluminium hull, which we used in the Arctic is the weight factor, as in spite of its size, two of us could easily lift and carry it when we made a wet landing on a rough beach. The red colour is an option recommended when sailing in remote areas.

Choice of tender

I have often been surprised at some people's choice of tender, and perhaps more than anything else, it indicates the owner's lack of cruising experience. A recent observation is that some sailors, especially those used to docking in marinas, cannot resist the temptation of getting a large, comfortable RIB equipped with a powerful outboard. It is only when they start cruising that they realise that most of the time they need to land on a beach, often reached

Wet landing on Flint, in the Line Islands

through shallow water, and some times breaking surf as well. I asked such an owner what had made him buy a heavy RIB with a steering console and a huge outboard. He admitted that he had been only thinking of longer expeditions and never of the problems of landing on a beach through the surf. That same evening I saw him and his crew swim ashore to have dinner at a beachside restaurant, carrying their dry clothing in waterproof bags.

Photo shoot in Davis Strait

Outboard motors

There is indeed a certain technique in landing from a tender if there is surf breaking on the beach where you intend to land. As you reach shallow water, the crew should be ready to jump out, take hold of the tender on both sides and walk it ashore. As the tender might be swamped in such situations, all vulnerable possessions should be kept in a watertight container. It is certainly easier to land on such beaches with a light rowing dinghy, but if it has an outboard, it should be stopped and lifted before reaching shallow water. In case the tender capsizes and the outboard is swamped, the motor should be rinsed in fresh water immediately, the spark plug removed and a little oil poured into the cylinder when it has dried. For larger or heavy tenders, the alternative is to anchor them off the beach and for the crew to wade ashore.

If landing on a coral reef, it is advisable to wear plastic sandals or diving booties to protect the feet from the sharp coral. An inflatable dinghy must never be dragged on such beaches. When landing in extreme conditions – such as those Ivan and I encountered at Horn Island – wearing a survival suit, as we did, might be the answer.

My obsession with having a backup for everything, including a second tender, proved useful in Antarctica, when the captain of one of the Millennium yachts had the uninspired urge to tease, with an oar, a leopard seal that was swimming close to the boat. These creatures have no enemies, and obviously no sense of humour either. Unable to retaliate against its tormentor high up above him, the enraged animal vented its fury on the nearest thing it could find, and attacked the yacht's RIB with amazing ferocity, reducing its Hypalon tubes to shreds. With a large charter party now stuck on board, and knowing that I had two dinghies, he begged me to lend him one of mine until we returned to the mainland. This is but one example, albeit not a very commonly occurring one, of why it pays to have a spare tender.

If you plan to go any distance in your dinghy be sure you have enough fuel as well as a way of communicating with others.

Bob Hall

The choice of outboard motors is so vast that I wouldn't know where to begin. With two-stroke engines having been gradually phased out in favour of less polluting four-stroke models, I would start by looking first at an outboard motor's impact on the environment. For this reason, Aventura IV carried two Minn Kota electric outboard motors. The arrangement worked very well, especially as the actual time spent propelling the tender was usually of short duration and the battery could be charged between uses. I opted for automotive batteries, and on longer trips always carried a spare fully charged battery.

Most tenders continue to be equipped with gasoline outboards, although there are some models that run on LPG or diesel fuel. The advantage of the latter is that they use the same fuel as the yacht, and there is no need to carry gasoline, which can be a hazard. The one drawback of diesel outboards is that they are heavier than gasoline models of similar power, but as in the case of cars, the future is undoubtedly electric.

Outboard power

The question of adequate power is, once again, a matter of personal preference. For a smaller tender, a 2HP or 2.5HP model is usually sufficient, and has the great advantage of being light and using less fuel. An observation that I have made over the years is that the majority of outboard motors are far too powerful for the job they are supposed to do. Consequently, they are too heavy to handle safely (some boats need a special derrick on the stern to lift or lower them), they use a lot more fuel and are also more expensive. What I cannot understand is this: if most sailors are quite happy to sail at 6 or 7 knots, why do they need an outboard that pushes their dinghy at twice that speed, so that they reach the nearest beach in one and not two minutes? This is a question that puzzles and infuriates me in equal measure, watching inconsiderate sailors, especially children, zooming noisily and at great speed around a beautiful tranquil anchorage.

My advice is to resist temptation and get for your main tender the outboard you really need and not the maximum power that the tender can handle. An advantage of less powerful outboard motors is that they have an integral fuel tank. An even greater advantage is that they are lighter, because sooner or later you'll have to carry the tender and its outboard through the surf onto a beach. Could you do it? Finally, consider the fact that there is absolutely no need for the outboard to be powerful enough to get the tender to surf, when a steady slower speed will get you where you want to go just as well. Whatever kind of outboard you have, it is important to always carry the essential spares. On all my boats I had a waterproof plastic box with spare spark plugs, replacement shear pins and the necessary tools. The list of spares was reduced to zero when I went electric.

While anchored in a bay in Vanuatu, we lingered too long on a beach, and when we left for Aventura, anchored about half a mile away, the light was fading. In the failing light, I hit an isolated coral head and broke the sacrificial pin on the propeller. I tried to row but we made little progress, so I headed for the nearest beach, where, by the light of a torch, I managed to replace the

pin and make it back to the boat. This is the kind of incident that can have serious consequences, and I have come across several such cases. I will mention only one that happened while we were anchored in Abemama lagoon in Kiribati.

Having spent the day and part of the evening ashore, digging into the freshly arrived supply of beer with their local friends, a couple from a yacht anchored in the lagoon left the beach and headed for their boat. In the pitch-black night, they missed their yacht, and as they lost the lee of the low island, the small outboard could no longer cope with the strong wind. They realised that they were being driven towards the wide pass and thus into the ocean, so the man made an abrupt turn for what he hoped was the nearest beach, but in doing so the outboard got swamped and it stopped. Their flimsy plastic oars were even less help against the strong wind, but with a desperate effort they managed to land on the shallow reef on one side of the pass. They dragged the dinghy over the reef, badly cutting their feet and, exhausted, spent the night on the beach. In the morning, the wind having died, they managed to row to their boat. None of the surrounding yachts had noticed their absence and, with absolutely no land for 1,000 miles, they would have certainly lost their lives. They were still in shock when I met them later that day and they told me of their narrow escape.

One other problem that I want to highlight is that of serious accidents caused by outboards, two of which happened to participants in the Millennium Odyssey. In both cases the dinghy operator was on his own and fell overboard not wearing the outboard cut-off cable on his wrist. While attempting to hold onto the dinghy, both were badly cut by the racing propeller, and both had to be hospitalised because they suffered extensive lacerations. Unfortunately one of them was a boy of 10, who had been driving his over-powered tender in ever decreasing circles, enjoying the mini tsunamis he was creating and rocking the nearby boats while his overindulgent parents were watching his antics from the cockpit.

Abemama lagoon

Similar accidents were caused by colliding either with other high-speed tenders or with a yacht being driven around blindly while the crew were looking for a suitable place to drop the anchor. Collisions at speed with another dinghy occur regularly in crowded anchorages such as in the Bahamas. Worse still is being run down by a local fishing boat or one of those fast fantail boats used all over southeast Asia. Just as bad are jet-skiers, water-skiers, windsurfers, water-scooters or fast, powerful RIBs towing a parachute. The latter can be a menace as, by necessity, the operators of such boats have to look backwards at their tow, with only the occasional quick glimpse to see what is ahead of them. Tenders commuting between shore and their boats are not the only potential victims: swimmers are at even greater risk. I have been forced to take avoiding action on several occasions while swimming off my boat when suddenly I saw a fast tender heading for me.

Memorable anchorages

My memorable anchorages are a diverse lot, some remembered for their sheer beauty, others for what happened there. From among the later, I have chosen two examples relevant to one of the subjects of this chapter.

Port Circumcision, Antarctica, February 1999

Picking a safe anchorage in Antarctica is of vital importance as the weather can change for the worse without warning, when a sudden onshore wind drives the ice. One of the best anchorages off the Antarctic Peninsula is Port Circumcision. The small cove is almost landlocked, with just a narrow entrance. As it was too shallow for our draft, we had to raise the centreboard to be able to anchor in its most protected part.

The weather looked settled, but black clouds started gathering on the horizon and a falling barometer foretold of worse things to come. We had a late dinner and slept a quiet night, totally unconcerned by the whistling of the rising wind in the rigging. When we got up in the morning, the small bay and all the sea outside were blocked with solid ice; the only tiny patch of clear water was the pool where we were anchored. I landed on the nearby beach in the midst of a penguin colony, overwhelmed by the beauty of the wild scenery.

We stayed until the ice cleared because we were neither able nor in any hurry to leave such a beautiful spot, and would have been quite happy to spend all our Antarctic time there.

Dundas Harbour, Northwest Passage, July 2014

While waiting for the ice to retreat in the central area of the Northwest Passage, we spent some time in Dundas Harbour, a perfectly protected bay on the south coast of Devon Island in Lancaster Sound. We had an enjoyable time, dealing with routine maintenance jobs, reading, watching DVDs, listening to music, receiving visitors from other boats that were waiting, like us, for an improvement in the ice situation, and returning those visits. We also went on long walks ashore, watching the wildlife around us, mostly seabirds, and the odd walrus from a nearby resident colony. For the first time on this trip I was successful in my fishing, and caught three odd-looking fish with wide mouths and large spinal fins looking like wings. Unable to feed our crew of eight on that meagre fare, we ended up using the fish as a base for a tasty bouillabaisse soup.

There was much excitement when one of our neighbours came on the VHF radio to inform everyone that a polar bear was seen walking on the nearby shore. With everyone's cameras and binoculars trained on the majestic beast, one boat launched its dinghy with three

the neighbouring Gjoa started unfurling. With the crew fighting to tame the billowing sail and the boat yawing dangerously closer and closer to us, I somehow managed to power Aventura out of their way.

As our friends on the yacht Suilven appeared to be dangerously close to the shore, we called them on the radio, but they assured us that their anchor was holding well. They even found the time to take photos of us, so we reciprocated and photographed Suilven being hammered by repeated gusts.

Aventura survived the storm unscathed lying to the 33kg Rocna anchor and about 70 metres of chain, although we had to motor constantly into the wind not only to ease the strain on the anchor but to keep out of the way of our wayward neighbour. The storm lasted 22 hours, and our defensive manoeuvring track, recorded on the chart plotter, shows a solid, almost black shape of intersecting lines.

crew on board and went as close to the bear as they dared. The bear gave them a bored look, turned around and walked nonchalantly away. Obviously sailors were not on his menu that day.

Our peaceful sojourn was interrupted when a forecasted easterly gale turned into a proper storm with gusts of over 60 knots. As the wind increased, my main concern were the two boats that had arrived later and had anchored quite close to us. In the middle of a particularly violent gust, the foresail on

Tips

» Take your time to find the right spot and anchor properly, even if it takes several attempts.
» Be considerate of others when choosing an anchoring spot.
» Always check that the anchor has set well, ideally with a mask.
» Ensure that the bitter end of the anchor chain is attached to a fixed point with a line that can be cut in an emergency.
» Write down the coordinates of the spot where you are anchored, and if you have any concerns, prepare an exit strategy by plotting a safe track to follow if you are forced to leave in the dark.
» If in any doubt, leave an anchorage before it is too late.

» Never anchor too close to a reef or beach, and allow sufficient space to swing safely should the wind turn.
» Consider using the CAM technique if spending longer in a tropical anchorage.
» Avoid returning to the boat by dinghy in the dark.
» Leave a light on the boat and take a torch with you in case you are delayed ashore.
» Have proper oars that can be used for rowing, and secure them to the tender.
» Prepare a waterproof box with essential spares and tools for the outboard motor.
» Make sure the outboard motor is fitted with a safety cut-off lanyard, worn by the operator on their wrist.
» Never tow a dinghy at sea.

Spot the dinghy

16

Return to the South Seas

An Atlantic crossing followed by a leisurely Caribbean cruise marked the start of Aventura III's long-delayed world voyage. Having transited the Panama Canal, she was based at a marina in Ecuador in preparation for the passage to French Polynesia.

I was looking forward to my return to the South Pacific, and the relatively short hop to Ecuador's offshore island group was a perfect way to slide back into my offshore routine. As Gwenda had made it clear that long ocean passages were no longer to her liking, I was joined for this section by my Finnish friend Antti.

This area of Ecuador has one of the most benign climates in the world. I was told that winds over 20 knots had never been recorded and they have never had storms of any kind. We soon picked up a light southwest wind, and with a freshly painted bottom Aventura romped ahead, happily doing 6 knots in the flat seas. We were enjoying ourselves so much just being at sea that Antti agreed to my suggestion to bypass the usual ports in Galapagos, and go straight to Puerto Villamil on the island of Isabela, still an oasis of peace and tranquillity in a sea of change. Strictly from the legal point of view, unless one has an official permit, cruising boats are not allowed to stop at the Galapagos Islands except in an emergency. Those who have obtained the compulsory permit with the assistance of a local agent are allowed to stop for a maximum of 21 days. Normally visiting boats are only allowed to clear in at one of the two main ports of entry, Baquerizo Moreno or Puerto Ayora, but as we were coming from mainland Ecuador I was sure that I could manage to persuade the port captain in Villamil to let us stop there for a few days.

Our second day at sea was followed by a splendid night, with a starry sky and virtually flat seas. The southwest wind continued blowing at 7 to 8 knots and Aventura managed to make 4 to 5 knots closehauled. As the wind slowly drew more into the south, up went the asymmetric spinnaker, which was now in its element.

Day three followed the same pattern, and as the wind drew more into the east on day four we swapped the asymmetric for the larger triradial spinnaker. During the night we passed the island of Española. I remembered my visit there a few years previously, when we had chartered a 10-cabin excursion boat with a number of participants in the second round-the-world rally. On that occasion we cruised around the Galapagos archipelago for one week, visiting the various islands and enjoying their unique wild life. Española has the largest colony of blue-footed boobies, and I will never forget watching the gentle dance performed by courting couples.

Española is also an important breeding ground for sea turtles, which come to lay and bury their eggs on its sandy beaches. On that week-long cruise among the islands we were fascinated not just by the abundance of wildlife – ashore, in the air and in the sea – but also its variety. Every island seemed to have its own resident species: penguins on San Salvador, sea iguanas on Santa Fé, land iguanas on Fernandina, frigate birds on

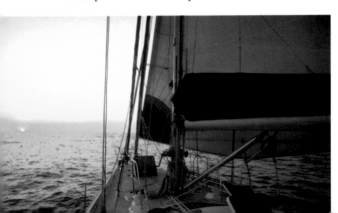

Seymour, sea lions on San Cristobal, giant tortoises on Isabela and white-tipped sharks at Bartolomé.

The following day we were visited by a school of very large dolphins, the largest I had ever seen in the Pacific. A pod of humpback whales swam close by, snorting noisily but ignoring us. We passed south of Floreana, one of the four islands that have settlements on them. Floreana's past is probably the most colourful of all the Galapagos Islands as it was a pirates' lair. Later it was a convenient resting place for the crews of whalers who visited these islands to load hundreds of the giant turtles. The poor creatures were laid on their backs in the ship's hold waiting to be slaughtered for food, their main attraction being the fact that they could survive without water or food for many months. Some of those sailors started the fashion of leaving letters for home in a barrel hoping that some kind soul would pick them up and post them, a practice that has continued to the present day.

There was also a bloody side to Floreana's past, involving murders and suicides among its early German settlers. But nothing has contributed more to the fame of these islands than the visit by Charles Darwin. His long stay here in 1831 resulted in the theory of evolution that profoundly changed scientific thought.

Unfortunately this unique world is in grave danger, mainly as a result of its own success. Although the Ecuadorean authorities have made great efforts to control the number of visitors that are allowed to land at any one time on one of the nature-reserve islands, they have been far too lax in terms of their own population. In recent years thousands have come over from the mainland, attracted by job opportunities that were absent back home. While one can accept the motivations for this, the consequences are now badly threatening the delicate nature of the islands and their habitat. The main settlements at Puerto Ayora and Baquerizo Moreno are growing at an exponential rate, causing not just overcrowding but also serious pollution. On my last visit to Puerto Ayora, I was dismayed by the changes that had occurred in the 10 years since I started visiting the islands regularly. This is the reason why I decided to stop only at Isabela, as I preferred to preserve the beautiful memories of my earlier visits.

Early on the fifth day after our departure from the mainland, we made our way into the sheltered anchorage in front of the small settlement at Puerto Villamil, where the port captain agreed to a 48-hour emergency stop, which he later extended just as readily. Although the largest island of the archipelago, Isabela is off the beaten track with only a handful of visitors and there was only one other boat there when we arrived.

One day Antti and I walked to a former US airbase, which, after the Second World War, had been transformed into a penal colony. For a dozen years, until 1958, the worst criminals from a number of South American countries were kept in this high-security prison under extremely tough conditions. To keep them occupied, they were forced to build a high stone wall, which was dismantled every time it was completed so that work on it could start again, an unending punishment worthy of the labours of the mythical Sisyphus.

Close to the main settlement was a tortoise regeneration and breeding centre. Giant tortoises were brought here from other islands to regenerate before they were returned to their place of origin. Tortoises were also bred here, and kept until they were two years old, so as to be large enough to resist attacks by rats and cats, which are the biggest danger for young tortoises. It was a splendid effort to put right the wrongs of the past.

Twelve different species of tortoise survive on Isabela, their large number being due to the fact that Isabela was rarely visited by pirates or whalers and was colonised very late. The largest colony is in the north of the island, comprising an estimated 10,000 giant tortoises, many over 100 years old.

Our forays ashore whetted our appetite to see some of the interior of this largely untouched island. We agreed with a local guide to join a small group to trek on horseback to the Sierra Negra volcano, which has the second largest crater in the world. My rather small horse looked strong enough to carry me, but what worried me was the look of the rudimentary wooden saddle. With stirrups of the old-fashioned Spanish style, it felt like being back in the age of the conquistadors. It took us nearly three hours of rough going to reach the rim of the giant crater.

The long walk down to the bottom of the crater ended at an area of fumaroles belching steam in large clouds, the pestilential smell of sulphur pervading everything. The surrounding rocks were covered in thick layers of sickly-yellow sulphur. It was almost impossible to breathe, and I nearly choked trying to hold my breath to take a photograph of a particularly active fumarole. The atmosphere and setting looked straight out of hell, and we wasted no time in returning to our horses, which had been left on the rim of the crater. The return trip was even more painful because, going downhill, the wooden saddle dug deep into my posterior, and it took a week before I could sit down without wincing. After my Easter Island experience I thought I had finished with horses, so following the Isabella trek I renewed my vow to never attempt to be a cowboy.

For the long passage to the Marquesas I managed to get a local farmer to supply us with some of his produce: bananas, avocados, watermelons, grapefruit, oranges and eggs. The day before departure I cooked a large stew to last us for at least three dinners. We bade goodbye to the port captain and headed out into the ocean. Ahead of us lay the longest continuous stretch of any of the world cruising routes, with nothing but water for 3,000 miles.

For the first time in my sailing life, on the eve of departure I decided to get some outside advice and contacted Bob McDermott of the New Zealand Meteorological Service to suggest the best course to sail to reach the area of steady trade winds. After a slow start, the winds became more consistent; up went the asymmetric spinnaker, to be replaced by the triradial when the wind settled in the southeast. With over one knot of favourable current and the wind rarely blowing at more than 14 knots, those were truly perfect conditions. We ate every meal at the cockpit table and, as the sails needed little adjusting, split the night into two watches, so that each of us could have a nice long sleep. It was almost too good to be true... until one afternoon Aventura was surrounded by a large pod of several dozen pilot whales.

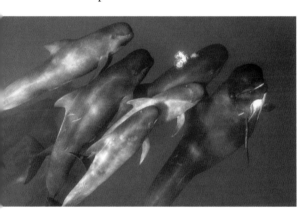

Their blunt heads gave them a menacing look, especially when I remembered that this was the area where several boats had been rammed and sunk by this kind of whale. With these thoughts at the back of my mind, I wasn't too thrilled by our uninvited companions. Antti, who had lost his own boat on a reef in the Red Sea a couple of years earlier, and until then had greeted any sea life with great interest, looked even less excited by our escort. Fortunately the whales soon lost interest and left us alone. With a sigh of relief, I told Antti, 'Obviously aluminium wasn't on their menu!'

The following day the weather changed dramatically, the blue skies turned to a dull slate colour, and we had several squalls with little wind in between them and a large confused swell. Even the temperature dropped, and it felt so chilly that we could easily have believed that we were sailing in the North Sea and not some 200 miles south of the equator. These were typical doldrums conditions and apparently a known phenomenon on this route. Right on cue, an email from Bob McDermitt advised me to alter course for 5°S, 105°W, where we should find good winds. The promised winds arrived soon and were blowing steadily from southeast. With all sails up and also a favourable current, Aventura picked up her skirts and was happily galloping on her way west. The sky took on the typical trade-winds look with fluffy clouds dotted about the horizon. Looking at my logbook, I see that it was at that point (4°40'S, 104°W) that we picked up the proper South Pacific trade winds, and our tactic appeared to have paid off.

Under those benign conditions we enjoyed a stable routine, with lunch served immediately after plotting our noon position. Around sunset we would have a sundowner, then I would cook dinner, which was served at 1900 while listening to the news on the BBC World Service, a habit that I have followed during all my cruising years. After dinner Antti would wash up while I did a tour of the boat, checking all systems, and also deciding if we should continue with the same sails during the night.

Another pleasant night lit by a splendid full moon, while doing over 7 knots in 14 knots of wind, brought us to our halfway point. In spite of the variable conditions at the start we had managed to keep up a good average speed. I called Gwenda on the satellite phone and Antti called his wife Nina, who was just as averse to long passages and happily agreed to stay on her own while us boys were playing sailors. In fact I suspected that Nina, who is a well-known writer in her native Finland, was probably quite happy to have Antti out of the way so she could work on her latest novel. I wondered if Gwenda felt the same.

A special occasion calls for a special dinner, so I retrieved from the bottom of the fridge the last vacuum-packed steaks I had bought in Ecuador. They were accompanied by the last bottle of vintage Rioja wine, while for dessert I used up the last of our bananas, which I flambéed with a generous lashing of brandy.

As we were sailing through such an effortless area, more for my own sake, I decided to relax one of my strict night rules of not reading on watch because having a light on affects your night vision. In this fashion, the nights passed by pleasantly, the bright starry sky reflected in our sparkling wake being of a beauty that only those fortunate enough to experience such exquisite moments can comprehend.

That night I finished reading an excellent biography of Che Guevara. Like most people of my generation, I had been intrigued by this man whose anger at the inequalities that affected the world I could readily identify with, but whose political views I could not share, primarily because of my experience of having lived under a communist regime. My visit to Cuba had not changed my opinion, rather it had confirmed my view that while Fidel Castro may have started off as an idealistic revolutionary, once the struggle had succeeded, his utopian intentions were abandoned in favour of the temptation of absolute power. Having died before those changes, Che has ensured that his image will forever be that of a true revolutionary and an inspiration for young people everywhere. We will never know how he would have turned out in old age.

My log entry for the following day notes that sailing wing and wing with the yankee poled out and full mainsail we were going 'like a train' in the now stronger trade winds. The seas around us were full of life, with lots of sooty terns darting about. Shortly after noon we saw a sail far in the distance. After we had made contact on VHF, we agreed to switch over to a better frequency on SSB radio. The elderly New Zealand couple told me that they had left Galapagos one week before us, and as their autopilot could only cope with reduced sail, they had to keep their speed down or steer by hand. I asked if they needed any help with food, water or fuel, but they assured me they were all right and expected to take another 10 days to reach the Marquesas. We altered course to pass closer and lost sight of their masthead light around midnight.

The last week passed very quickly. I lost my best lure to a monster marlin, who struck with such force that I am sure it would have towed us backwards had the smoking line not parted with an almighty twang. For a long time the large fish kept somersaulting furiously in our wake, and I felt really bad about the agony he was going through.

On day 19, with only minutes to spare before dark, we dropped anchor in the small harbour below the village of Atuona on the island of Hiva Oa. In every respect, it had been an extremely pleasant passage and one of my most enjoyable ocean crossings. Having made such good time, Antti and I had several days to kill before Gwenda's arrival. After resting for a couple of days, we got some fresh supplies and early one morning left for Fatu Hiva. Luck was on our side as there was no sign of the expected strong southeast trades, and we had to motor all the way in virtually calm seas. Shortly before arrival I landed a small tuna and by early afternoon dropped anchor at Hanavave, 11 years after my visit on Aventura II. Considered to be one of the most beautiful anchorages in the world, the surroundings are truly spectacular, with huge rock formations overlooking the tranquil bay. As we had arrived in the Marquesas well ahead of the annual migration, Aventura had the beautiful bay all to herself.

The small village at the head of the well-protected bay now had a breakwater and short quay, which made landing from the dinghy much easier than in the past. Walking through the small village, we were warmly welcomed by everyone, and, as we were the first yacht to arrive that season, I was told several times how everyone was looking forward to the annual arrival of the cruising yachts. This was because visiting sailors had helped the villagers in various ways, repairing outboards, fixing television sets or playing soccer with the youngsters.

Being in such a calm spot, I decided to do some maintenance work, and as I always like to start with the most difficult job first, I took Antti by surprise when he found me giving the forward toilet a long-delayed service.

'Jimmy, what you are doing is almost blasphemous. Have you got nothing better to do than work on your toilet here, in the most beautiful spot on earth?'

'I agree, but one thing I always make sure is that everything works on this boat when Gwenda arrives, and that means a spotless galley and a functioning toilet. So, now that I've mentioned it, you'd better tackle the galley while I finish here.'

A captain must always have the last word.

17

Engines, maintenance and spares

Diesel engines are extremely reliable but are often mistreated by sailors, who do not run them under load, do not let them reach their working temperature and generally treat them as a convenience and not as a friend.

Chester Norman

Diesel engines are indeed reliable and if they are looked after well can give years of trouble-free service. In more than four decades of sailing I have had few engine failures on any of my yachts, but those that did occur each taught me a lesson. So, rather than start with a general discussion of engines and how to look after them, I prefer to relate those incidents.

Corsica, September 1975

There have been many memorable moments in my sailing life, but none has remained as fresh in my mind as one that happened more than 40 years ago on our passage through the Strait of Bonifacio between Sardinia and Corsica. We were at the beginning of our world voyage and, after having spent the summer cruising in the Aegean, had reached Sardinia. Our Perkins engine broke down in Porto Cervo, even then the most expensive marina not just in the Mediterranean but probably in the whole world. As we couldn't possibly afford to have the engine repaired there, the helpful mechanic suggested that we sailed to Bonifacio in neighbouring Corsica where there was a Perkins agent. He then offered to tow Aventura out of the marina... and we were on our own.

Between us and our destination lay the Strait of Bonifacio, a treacherous stretch of water where a maze of rocks is swept by strong currents, and which has been the graveyard of countless ships. Light winds helped us reach the strait, and just as we set a course for a distant mid-channel buoy, a school of dolphins positioned itself at the bows, delighting Doina and Ivan with their gambolling. As we tacked back and forth in the narrow fairway, the dolphins kept changing direction as well, always staying in front of us, until I realised that this perfect display of synchronised swimming could not possibly be pure chance.

'Let me try something,' I told Gwenda, 'and don't worry whatever happens.' When the time came for the next tack, rather than tack back into the fairway, I continued steering for the nearby rocks. All of a sudden the dolphins became extremely agitated: they jumped out of the water, and swam backwards and forwards as if trying to point in the safe direction we should take.

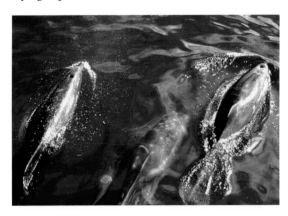

Close to the rocks, we tacked into deeper water, and just as suddenly the dolphins calmed down and took up their previous position at the bows. We did the same test at the end of that tack, and their behaviour repeated itself. We finally reached the end of the strait, and as soon as we got into clear water our escort left us. Mission accomplished. It was hard to believe, but the dolphins had been clearly trying to protect us.

We made it safely into Bonifacio late that night, slowly tacking into the narrow canyon-like inlet. We anchored in a small bay, and in the morning I went by dinghy into the port. The local boatyard towed Aventura in and, having inspected the engine, the yard manager informed me that the engine had to be completely rebuilt. As the season was far advanced, that meant we would have to spend the winter there and postpone our cruising plans by one year. The yard did a good job and not only repaired the engine, but the manager wrote a report to Perkins, pleading our case and explaining that, although the engine was out of warranty by a few months, the breakage had been caused by a manufacturing fault. Eventually Perkins agreed to supply all parts for free and we only had to pay labour costs.

New Zealand, January 1978

That same engine was put to the test two years later in New Zealand, where, quite foolishly, I had agreed with a teacher from Whangarei, who had befriended us, to swap Aventura for his car for one month. The idea seemed very attractive because both Gwenda and I had our mothers visiting, and this would give us the opportunity to see more of this interesting country. Without a further thought, I agreed to the suggestion, explained to the car owner everything about Aventura that I could think of, loaded the family into the car and set off on a complete tour of New Zealand's two main islands. The old Wolseley showed its age right at the start, when it could barely splutter its way to the top of the hill overlooking Opua harbour, where Aventura lay at anchor. By the time we had reached the main road, there was a thick ill-smelling oily cloud pouring from the exhaust. As all the cars we had had in London had not been much better than this old lady, I wasn't too concerned, so at the first station bought a supply of engine oil, and ended up topping her up with oil in almost the same proportion as her fuel consumption.

Miraculously, we made it all the way to the tip of South Island and back again, although we seemed to spend as much time waiting by the side of the road for the engine to cool down as actually driving. While we were virtually on the home stretch, Lady Wolseley decided to give us a final adrenaline kick when we heard the two grannies scream that the back of the car was on fire. With smoke pouring out of the boot, I wrenched it open and managed to put out the flames before they devoured our luggage. It was an electric fire that was put right, at some painful cost, by a local garage. Greatly relieved, we made it back to Opua and handed our friend the car keys.

'I hope it went all right,' he said, and I was convinced he must be pulling my leg.

'Well,' I said, 'it all depends how you look at it. Let's say it could have been worse, much worse.'

'That's all right then,' he said, visibly relieved.

'And what about Aventura?'

He looked away rather shiftily and I expected the worst. The first thought to cross my mind was that he had wrecked my boat.

'We had... a small problem but I am sure it can be easily sorted out.'

'What's that?' I asked.

'The engine wouldn't turn. I think the starter motor is ruined.'

'Well you could at least have had it fixed before our return.'

'Oh, I thought you'd like to deal with it yourself.'

'Thanks very much, mate, I see I have no choice!'

Back on board, I checked the batteries, but when I turned the key nothing happened. Unless the engine had seized up just as it had in the Mediterranean, it could only be the starter motor.

And when do such things happen? Late on a Friday afternoon, of course. With the two grannies due to fly home two days later, we didn't have much choice: 'We have to get to Whangarei,' I said.

'Hire a car?' Gwenda asked, hopefully.

'No, we'll sail there.'

'You must be joking! Not through this busy bay at a weekend, then up that winding Whangarei River.'

'Now listen, I am really surprised that after Bonifacio you don't trust my judgement.'

'That was totally different, we had no choice.'

'Well, as far as I can see, we don't have a choice now either. And, by the way, I heard that Kiwi dolphins can be very friendly.'

'Fantastic, now that certainly gives me some hope.'

As it was getting late, I suggested we sailed a few miles to a bay where we had stopped before, and anchor there for the night. We left immediately, reached the bay before dark and anchored in a place where we could sail out the following morning.

As soon as we were anchored, Gwenda's English mother piped up: 'I'd love a cup of tea. I haven't had one all day.'

'And nothing to eat either,' added my mother, just to rub it in.

While I was preparing to hang out a gill net for the night, Gwenda went to heat up some water. I heard her yell.

'There is no gas. Those friends of yours have used up the whole tank.'

'No problem, said I calmly, settling into my Tarzan role, 'we will make a fire on the beach.'

'And heat up the kettle?'

'No, we'll grill something.'

'Like what?'

'Like the fish that has just committed suicide in my net this very instant.'

Indeed the net was shaking as if some monster was trying to tow us away. I pulled it in and there was a beautiful red snapper. To Ivan and Doina's delight, a fire was duly lit and we had a most enjoyable picnic on the moonlit beach.

'There are compensations for everything in life,' I said as we were rowing back to the boat.

The Bay of Islands

The sail down the coast took all day, and we did have a school of dolphins accompany us for a while. Although one of them would occasionally lift his head and look back at Aventura, as if to make sure she was following, they didn't seem to be the navigator type. We reached the entrance to the Whangarei River just as night was falling, but fortunately it was a well-lit channel with lots of flashing buoys, there was a little wind to help and the tide was slack. We short-tacked from side to side, making slow progress, and by midnight had reached a spot where we could anchor out of the way and were close enough to row to the town dock. In the morning, this being helpful New Zealand, the very first boat to pass by responded to my call, and although he was on his way out for a day's fishing, the helpful man brought his boat alongside and skilfully manoeuvred Aventura into a free slip.

'Miracles do happen,' I couldn't resist saying smugly to Gwenda.

'Well, this was a lot easier than Bonifacio.'

'It was... and next time it will be easier still.' And so it was to be, even if it happened a quarter of a century later and half a world away.

Those early incidents had given me confidence both in Aventura's sailing capabilities, and even more in my own ability to handle the boat under sail alone. From then on, the prospect of not being able to use the engine never worried me. We had two more incidents in the South Pacific, when dirty fuel had put the engine out of action, and each time we managed to sail to the nearest harbour and have the problem fixed.

Malta, May 1992

Aventura II had fewer engine troubles, maybe because it had two and so there was a permanent working backup. The only trouble I ever had was in Malta, close to the end of her circumnavigation in the first round-the-world rally, when one of the transmission gears seized up, so it wasn't really an engine failure. Repair facilities in Malta are very good, and there was no problem getting the failure fixed. The mistake I made was that, being there in an official capacity as organiser of that rally, I expected to get special treatment. I could not have been more wrong because when I got the bill I nearly fainted. It came to a staggering £1,000 – I could have easily bought a brand-new transmission with that amount.

That experience taught me that you must always ask for a written estimate before you commission a job, and whenever possible attempt to be present when it is carried out. Unfortunately there are too many repair shops and boatyards that regard visiting sailors as easy prey and will charge whatever they can get away with. Even worse are the yards that take an imprint of your credit card as a guarantee, which means that, if they wish, they can charge you above the original estimate. It happened to me when I left Aventura IV in a well-known US boatyard in the Newport area, to put right the damage sustained by catching a rope around the propeller while in the Arctic. In the event, they charged me over 2,000 dollars more than the estimate. In spite of my complaints, they debited my card and I never got a refund.

South Africa, October 2004

Aventura III's most memorable breakdown happened in the worst possible place, while on the daunting passage from Richards Bay to Cape Town around the bottom of South Africa. The area is notorious for the hellish conditions that are caused when strong contrary winds blow against the fast south-setting Agulhas Current. An unexpected spell of good weather had persuaded me not to waste such an opportunity, and to make a dash along the aptly named Wild Coast. The start could not have been more enjoyable. With the spinnaker up and the help of the current, we were doing 10 knots over the ground. When the wind dropped, and I guessed that the weather would probably change, I decided to make for the commercial port of East London, about 70 miles away. I started the engine to motor out of the current. It ran for a while then slowed down and stopped. I tried to restart it but, from the sound it made, I guessed that it had drawn air. I primed the engine, tried to start it but it refused to turn, so I presumed that it was due to a faulty solenoid on the starter motor. As I had a spare and it was calm, I decided to replace it. Meanwhile, we were drifting with the strong current, doing 4 knots

Rally boats leaving Malta   217

over the ground but without enough wind to even fill the sails. With the new solenoid installed, I turned the key, but the starter still refused to budge. So what was the one essential spare I did not have on board? Of course, a starter motor.

Fortunately, the wind came up later in the day, so up went the spinnaker again and we sailed well for a few hours, doing 6 knots of boat speed plus a bonus of 4 knots from the current. The wind fell at night when we still had about 20 miles to go, and it took us several hours to edge out of the current so as to avoid being swept past East London. Eventually we made it, but by then it was midnight and I decided not to push my luck and enter an unknown harbour at night without an engine, so we tacked up and down, off the harbour entrance, for the rest of the night, then entered at first light. I had already installed on the stern the emergency outboard bracket, but as we had enough wind to sail we tacked into the outer harbour, then tacked... and tacked again, trying to pass through the narrow gap that led into the inner harbour.

The outflowing current from the Buffalo River, on whose banks the town stands, was strongest at that point, and it took us ages and all my sailing skills to ease Aventura past it. More tacks took us up the narrow river until eventually we managed to drop the anchor near a spot where some yachts were docked. I mounted the outboard motor on its emergency bracket. It started first time, but the current was too strong and we could not even turn the boat. Meanwhile, the anchor dragged in the soft river mud, we drifted slowly and hit, ever so lightly, the local police launch docked alongside the quay! We proceeded to tie up to the launch, trying to give the impression that this had been our intention all along. Two officers came to see what was happening and, when I explained our predicament, they were very nice and told us not to worry and to stay there.

The captain of a nearby tug, who had been following our earlier manoeuvres, came over and recommended a local electrical-repair shop. The starter

motor was taken off, and when it was dismantled at the workshop its plastic planetary gear was found to be badly worn; it had to be replaced. Unfortunately neither this part nor a complete starter motor could be found locally, so it looked as if we were going to be stuck in East London for a long time. After I got my contacts in Durban and Cape Town, as well as Ivan in London, lined up to help locate a replacement starter motor, I decided to have one more go, got into a taxi and started scouring the town's electrical workshops and breakers' yards. The owner of a small shop looked at my defunct starter motor and said, 'Wait a minute. I had one of those for years and don't know why I kept it. Now I know!' His was a left-hand-side mount, mine a right-hand-side, but the parts could be transferred, and that same afternoon I had a reconditioned starter motor.

With the engine repaired, there was nothing to keep us in East London, so as soon as the weather looked right we left and made a beeline for the axis of the Agulhas Current. We eventually made it to Cape Town, where the first thing I did was to order a new starter motor.

Gwenda at Krka Falls with Dan, Nera and Doina

Croatia, August 2006

Another breakdown on Aventura III that deserves to be mentioned happened in Croatia as we were motoring down the Krka River after having visited the spectacular Krka waterfalls. The engine temperature alarm sounded suddenly, so I switched off the engine and found that it had overheated. Being in a river, I naturally suspected that we had picked up some weed or debris, but when I checked the seawater trap I noticed a lot of water in the engine bilge, so I realised that we might have a more serious problem. I dropped the anchor where we were, which unfortunately was right in the middle of the river, and in the way of the numerous excursion boats. When I lifted the floorboards in the aft cabin to look at the back of the engine, I was met by a strong smell of exhaust fumes. The plastic exhaust mixing pot had a large hole in its side through which both exhaust and cooling water had been able to escape. While Gwenda was trying to make clear to passing excursion boats that we had not anchored there for afternoon tea, but because we had a problem, I got a tube of underwater epoxy, rolled and mixed the two components and managed to cover the hole. We waited one hour for it to set, turned the key

and the engine started up and ran happily. It was quite a minor problem that could be dealt with easily, but it could have had very serious consequences. We had with us Doina and our grandchildren Nera and Dan, who slept in the aft cabin. If this problem had happened at night, when they were asleep, they could have been overcome by the highly poisonous carbon monoxide in the exhaust fumes, as these would have leaked out of the mixing pot long before the engine would have overheated, triggering off the alarm. Just the thought of what could have happened got me worried then, and makes me shudder still.

North Atlantic, September 2016

Having completed the transit of the Northwest Passage without any problems, on the passage south from Greenland the engine kept overheating. I suspected a blocked seawater inlet, checked it with the submersible GoPro camera, but could not see any obstruction. I then checked the seawater pump impeller, but it looked undamaged. I tested the engine again, but after a few minutes the temperature started rising, so I stopped it to avoid damaging the impeller. I was now convinced that there was an airlock somewhere in the cooling system, and although I checked every possibility, I could not locate it.

Concerned about setting off on such a long passage without a working engine, I had a chat with my crew Dunbar about whether we should detour to the nearest port in Greenland, about 150 miles away. I realised that I was in a similar situation to the previous year, when passing with Doina through the same area. Dunbar's reaction was the same as Doina's: if I decided to carry on, he would have no objection. So carry on we did, and from that point we just sailed. Without the engine, we had to rely on charging the batteries with our solar panel, wind and water generator, which they did perfectly and covered all our energy needs. Sailing the remaining 2,000 miles proved to be no real handicap because we had more than enough wind, even if not always on our desired course. We also had two fully-fledged storms thrown in for good measure. Looking back now, I found the experience of crossing the North Atlantic without an engine satisfying and even enjoyable.

Maintenance

Regular maintenance of the engine is essential, and is something that I have always done conscientiously – not just to the engine but all my equipment. One of the general observations I made, among participants in the various rallies, is that the newer someone was to cruising, the less inclined they were to carry out regular maintenance work, and they usually waited until something broke before tackling it. This kind of attitude may be acceptable on land, where people are used to being able to call on outside help, whether to fix something in the house or get the car going if it breaks down. At sea the situation is very different, and you have to be self-sufficient and tackle the jobs as they occur. Initially I behaved in the same way, until damage from chafe or small breakages that could have been easily prevented finally made the penny drop. Once

maintenance turned into a routine, I became almost obsessed by my daily inspection tour. All of a sudden, many of those niggling problems disappeared and life became much more enjoyable. It is indeed surprising what can be discovered by having a good look around the boat at least once a day. Most things are simple matters: a suspect split pin, an unsecured shackle, a chafed sheet running over a block that is out of line, or a sail rubbing against a spreader.

Potentially more serious problems, such as a loose strand of rigging, a cracked turnbuckle or a loose rudderstock, could result in a lost mast or steering. My luckiest discovery was to find, one morning, Aventura IV's spinnaker pole loose on the foredeck. During the night we had experienced strong winds and rough seas, and the probable explanation was that, while tacking, the flogging jib sheet had knocked open the jaws of the pole so that it became dislodged from its parking position on the side deck.

Bearing in mind its vital importance, the engine deserves special attention and that means a visual check every time it is started, having a look to see that the exhaust is discharging water, and making sure that the engine is fed clean fuel. One of the most important things I have learned is the value of preventative maintenance. I look after my gear and the gear looks after me. Over the years, I developed an affectionate relationship with my engines, and was always guided by the wise advice given by my friend Chester, quoted at the beginning of this chapter. Engines, after all, are similar to the human body: they need to be fed and watered well. That means ensuring that they are supplied with clean, properly filtered fuel. Regular maintenance such as oil and filter changes, and checking the cooling fluid, transmission and engine oil and transmission levels, as well as alternator belt tension, must become routine.

Having talked to rally captains who had reported engine-overheating situations on an offshore passage, some admitted that they had used the engine in a seaway, whether for propulsion or charging. By running the engine when the sea is rough, the rolling or excessive heeling may result in air being drawn into the cooling system, stopping the flow of seawater and causing the impeller to burn out. One point that many sailors do not seem to understand is that the neoprene impeller on the seawater pump is ultimately sacrificial. Otherwise I suppose that it would be made of metal, in which case much more damage would ensue if the pump no longer drew water and the metal impeller continued turning. It is worth pointing out that engine overheating will also occur if old bits of previously damaged impellers have lodged in the cooling system, causing an obstruction.

On all my voyages, every year I tried to find a convenient place to give the engine a thorough overhaul, when injectors, compression and all other essential aspects were checked and, if necessary, put right. In spite of all the care and regular maintenance, almost every time the engine was dismantled the mechanic found something wrong in its guts, which could have ended in disaster if not detected in time.

While in New Zealand, I had Aventura III's engine submitted to a thorough overhaul and the Volvo mechanic discovered that the aluminium exhaust manifold was badly corroded. Initially it looked so bad that a complete replacement seemed unavoidable, but, with typical Kiwi ingenuity, a local metal shop managed to build up the missing aluminium and make it as good as new.

At the end of Aventura IV's 24,000-mile Arctic voyage, I sailed her back to the Garcia boatyard in Cherbourg, where she had all systems checked. Because of the need to motor through the ice or during calm or light-wind spells in the Northwest Passage, the engine had clocked up a high number of hours, but it was still working well. The colour of the exhaust fumes alerted the Volvo mechanic to a possible problem with the injection pump, which had to be dismantled and reconditioned. He suspected that somewhere along the way we must have filled up with polluted fuel. He was probably right, as in Cambridge Bay all we could get was Jet-A aviation-type fuel, to which we were advised to add outboard engine oil as a lubricant. As we had no choice, I reluctantly took the risk and the engine got us safely through the Northwest Passage, but it may have been the cause of the damage.

Soon after I started running the ARC, I decided to compile at the end of each rally a list of all reported breakages. Later, I went further and handed out questionnaires to all captains, both in transatlantic and round-the-world rallies. In the case of engine failures, most were caused by the fuel supply, whether it had been polluted by dirt, water or bacteria. I came to the conclusion that on many production boats the fuel supply and filtering systems were often inadequate.

Aventura IV's day tank with filter and glass water separator

On each Aventura such problems were avoided by having a day tank. Like my previous boats, Aventura IV also had a 40-litre tank mounted higher than the engine so that the fuel was gravity-fed to the engine. The tank was topped up every four or five hours by manually activating a fuel-transfer pump. I had deliberately avoided having an automatic filling system so that the person who filled the tank could see what was happening. The pump switch was placed in a position that allowed the operator to monitor the glass water separator on the filter to make sure that the fuel that entered the day tank was clean. Apart from this pre-filter, there were two more filters before the fuel reached the injection pump.

Another advantage of a day tank is that when the amount of fuel in the main tank is getting close to being used up, all remaining fuel can be transferred into the day tank, so you know how much fuel is left and can monitor its consumption. As a backup on Aventura IV, in case there was a problem with the supply of fuel from the day tank, the activation of a two-way valve would switch the fuel supply directly from the main tank to the engine.

Anodes

Regardless of the hull material, zinc anodes are essential in protecting seacocks, propellers and their shafts. Some engines may also have sacrificial anodes in the heat exchanger, in the seawater cooling system, and possibly in the cooling loop of the transmission. Normally there is also an anode in the cooling system of the refrigerator. All these anodes should be inspected regularly and replaced at least once a year. Bronze propellers are protected from electrolysis by anodes mounted either on the shaft or propeller hub. These are easy to inspect regularly with a mask. On boats with bolt-on keels, the bolts may be vulnerable to electrolysis, and even if the keel itself looks fine on the outside, the bolts should be inspected regularly. Steel and aluminium hulls have both advantages and disadvantages, their intrinsic strength being their main advantage. As for the disadvantages, in the case of steel it is the need for the best possible preparation of the hull and decks when they are first painted, with careful maintenance to follow in later years. In the case of aluminium, the almost irrational fear of electrolytic reaction, which so many people continue to associate with these hulls, is quite unjustified. Modern alloys have taken care of that, as have the sacrificial anodes. As an added precaution, aluminium yachts should be provided with a stray-current meter that shows instantly if there is a negative or positive current leak detected in the hull. Provided the boat has the correct electrical installation, any possible damage caused by electrolytic action can be avoided if such simple precautions are taken.

There are a few situations that must be avoided, and among the worst are poor electrical installations on marina docks or pontoons, where the wrong polarity is used in the shore supply or there is an accidental current leak. Just as bad is being moored next to a metal boat that is running its generator and/or air-conditioning unit most of the time. Any stray current from either can seriously affect your own boat or, hopefully, only your anodes.

This is what happened when I had left Aventura III for three months in the care of a Tunisian marina. While I was away, the marina moved a large steel boat next to mine. It must have been running its generator for much of the time because when I had Aventura hauled out on my return to be antifouled, I was shocked to find all the anodes, which had been renewed recently, to have been eaten away down to their bases. The propeller anode was also gone, and the prop itself had taken on a sickly colour. Fortunately I discovered this in time and the damage was only superficial, but the situation could have been much worse if I had come back a couple of months later. It was my fault because usually when I left the boat unattended for a longer period, I would hang two large sacrificial anodes from the bows and stern, each connected to the hull, but I had failed to do it on that occasion.

Talking about anodes, I would like to mention what happened to an old friend whom I visited with Aventura III in southern Spain. When we arrived, his yacht was being hauled out and he explained that a toilet bronze seacock had almost disintegrated. When he checked the others, he found them also to be a suspicious colour. All the seacocks had to be replaced, but as I was looking at the gleaming hull just about to be launched, I was struck by the complete absence of any anodes. Not even the propeller and shaft had been provided with zinc anodes, so I asked my friend the reason for it.

'I contacted the builder and he assured me that anodes were a complete waste of time on a fibreglass hull.'

'And you believed him?'

'Of course.'

'But what about the prop and shaft?'

'Same thing, not really necessary.'

'What happened to your seacocks then, or was it divine intervention?'

'Yes, the guys at the yard were puzzled, so I called the builder again, and he assured me that it had nothing to do with the absence of anodes, but were most likely faulty seacocks, which he offered to replace.'

I expressed my serious doubts on this matter, but in spite of what had just happened, my friend preferred to listen to this well-known Scandinavian builder rather than to common sense. In his place I would have installed a few anodes, just in case.

Tools

The first Aventura was, at least in the beginning, a floating workshop and, if I remember well, there were a few jobs that I never managed to finish before our return six years later. Therefore, on the second Aventura I had sacrificed the entire forepeak and turned it into a workshop/storage area. On the portside there was a full-length workbench and a vice, with a wide selection of tools stored in the lockers above. On the starboard side were a diving compressor, three tanks and enough space to stow an inflatable dinghy. While the compressor proved to be useful in those days when I was still a keen diver, the workbench was very rarely used. As the boat had been fitted out professionally, nothing had been left 'to be done later', as had been the case with its predecessor.

Because of my endeavour to learn from my own mistakes, I had incorporated a lot of 'useful' features in Aventura II that I had missed on the first. Many of them turned out in the end not to be really that useful. Fortunately I drew the right conclusions the next time, and on Aventura III the nearest thing that came to a workshop was a portable vice that fitted into the top of a cockpit winch.

On both Aventura III and IV I carried such essential tools as a complete set of spanners, socket sets and Allen keys (both metric and imperial), riveting gun, hacksaw, bolt cropper, woodworking tools and screwdrivers of all types and sizes. I had, too, a selection of 220/240V electrical tools: a drill, angle grinder, jigsaw, rope cutter (hot knife) and soldering gun, as well as a battery charger and 12V dinghy pump. There were also a whole lot of bits and pieces that I felt may come in useful (and often did): stainless steel plate, threaded studs, various lengths of wood, plywood, etc. All small items such as nuts and bolts, screws, solder, electric bulbs, fuses, blocks, tapes, toilet spares, etc, were kept in separate plastic boxes, with the function of the contents marked on the cover. Two very useful items were a small magnifying mirror with a long flexible arm, and a litter-picker to retrieve items that had fallen into the bilge.

Spares

On Aventura III I carried a comprehensive range of spares, which were kept in various lockers, their contents and location being listed in alphabetical order in an address book. Each locker was identified by a code, and the layout plan was drawn on the first page of the spares book. This is a useful idea in an emergency situation when you may need to find something in a hurry. Similarly, all instruction manuals and equipment booklets were stored in alphabetical order in a concertina-type folder.

When I started compiling a list of spares for Aventura IV, I realised that some of the systems were so complex that, even if I had spares, I wouldn't be able to make a repair. I still had all essential spares for the engine, including a starter motor, fuel and oil filters, impellers and belts, and replacements for the various pumps, as well as individual Brookes & Gatehouse items that could be easily replaced. In the case of some of the electronics that could not be replaced, I had a complete backup system, such as an entirely autonomous autopilot.

List of spares

Engine
» Starter motor with solenoid
» Complete seawater pump
» Seawater pump impellers (at least four)
» 20 litres of engine oil
» 10 litres of engine coolant
» Oil filters
» Fuel filters
» Alternator belts
» Fuel-transfer pump
» Anodes
» Propeller-shaft anodes
» Three-bladed fixed propeller
» Liquid gasket

Electronics and electrics
» Paddle-wheel unit for B&G speedometer
» B&G masthead unit
» Complete B&G Triton unit
» Forward-looking sonar transducer
» Wind-generator blades, and assorted parts
» Battery-operated emergency navigation lights
» Bulbs, fuses, connectors, terminals, including spare deck light
» Hand-held VHF radio
» Emergency SSB radio whip aerial
» Satellite-phone antenna
» Satellite-phone battery (always kept charged in the emergency grab bag)
» Alkaline batteries for all equipment
» 1500W inverter
» Electric outboard motor

General
» Two diving tanks with regulator
» Two masks, snorkels and fins
» One mast step
» Dinghy pump
» Repair kit for the inflatable dinghy
» Two-part underwater epoxy-repair kits
» Assorted sealants, water-repellent sprays, WD40, Loctite
» Two sets of oars (for RIB and inflatable tender)
» At least 2 metres of each size of plastic hose used on the boat
» 20 metres of webbing tape
» Assorted blocks (two large snap blocks)

Sails
» Adhesive repair material for white sails and various colours for spinnakers
» Complete sewing kit, palm, twine and needles
» Grub screws for the furling-gear profile
» Lazy-bag battens

Tips

» Carry out a visual inspection of the engine every day, or every time it is started after an idle period longer than 24 hours.

» Check that cooling water is discharged from the exhaust each time you start the engine.

» Regularly check the engine oil, transmission and coolant levels and seawater trap. Look for possible leaks around injectors, filters and the seawater pump.

» Check the seawater impeller every 200 hours, and replace it if it shows any sign of damage.

» Check the tightness of the alternator belt; fine black deposits are a first indication of wear.

» When motorsailing and heeling, regularly right up the boat so the oil gets circulated around the engine.

» Do not run the engine for propulsion or battery charging when in a seaway because the rolling may cause air to be drawn into the cooling system, which will result in overheating.

» Some engine makes do not have a temperature gauge installed on their control panel. Make sure you have one installed with an analogue display and a loud alarm, both in the cockpit and, ideally, below.

» Stop the engine after having motored for a few hours, carry out a visual inspection and check the oil level.

» Regularly check for leaks from the stern gland, and always inspect it when the boat is launched after a haul-out. Some stern glands need to be squeezed to fill them with water after a haul-out.

» Carry all essential spares and consumables, especially if leaving on a voyage to remote places.

» Make a detailed list of all engine and parts numbers, and leave a copy at home or with a reliable friend in case parts need to be ordered and shipped to the boat.

» Add the recommended amount of biocide to the fuel at every fill-up.

» Treat any fuel bought in less-frequented places as suspicious and filter it with a Baja-type filter.

» Avoid completely emptying the fuel or water tanks.

» Keep the tanks separate by closing them off so they cannot be completely emptied inadvertently.

Motoring in the Northwest Passage on an unusually calm and sunny day

18

Dealing with emergencies

The art of the sailor is to leave nothing to chance.

Annie van de Wiele

I have been in a number of emergency situations and have been able to deal with all of them successfully. Fitting out the first Aventura myself taught me to be self-sufficient, and ever since then I have attempted to do all that is necessary to be prepared for the worst. One golden rule that I have learned is not to panic. It is indeed crucial in an emergency situation to keep calm, take time to properly assess the situation, draw up a plan of action and then act.

Some of the incidents mentioned in previous chapters highlighted two other essential points: the ability to deal with an emergency when it happens, and to put anything right that has broken, or at least find a temporary solution. Once again, I am going to start by describing some of my own emergencies.

South Indian Ocean, September 2003

While on passage from Reunion to South Africa, sailing on Aventura III with my friend Antti, we encountered bad weather off the southern tip of Madagascar, where sudden changes in weather can cause very rough seas. During my night watch, with the wind steady at 35 knots and our speed never going below 9 knots, with occasional higher bursts as the boat surfed down the high following seas, the pattern of the waves changed and the swell started to look menacing. I had seen higher waves in the Southern Ocean while returning from Antarctica to Cape Horn, but was not expecting to see anything as bad in what I believed should be more benign waters. Earlier that evening there had been a warning on Inmarsat C that a ship had seen one or several large logs afloat in that area.

The threat of colliding with one of those logs was at the back of my mind as I was savouring the thrill of seeing 12.5 knots on the speedometer while surfing down a big wave when, above the hiss and rumble, I heard a louder noise. The boat pulled out

of its slide and settled on its haunches, and I heard a louder noise coming from the direction of the steering. Almost instantly, the movement of the boat changed, and I suspected that the autopilot had gone off. I grabbed the wheel and it felt heavy and unresponsive. I lifted the cockpit grating and shone the flashlight onto the steering mechanism and saw that the 12mm bolt joining the hydraulic autopilot ram to the rudder quadrant had sheared. As the steering also appeared to be faulty, I decided to heave to and called Antti. I lowered the centreboard, as it had been raised while we were broadreaching. As we were sailing under reefed mainsail and staysail, I hauled in both sheets and turned into the wind, the steering feeling unusually heavy. Hove to with the wheel lashed to windward, Aventura was closereaching slowly into the large swell.

I found a replacement bolt and replaced the broken one, brought the boat back on course, still wondering why it was so hard to steer, and re-engaged the pilot. Only then did it occur to me to check the rudder hydraulics. I tried to pump down the rudder but it felt dead, thus confirming my suspicion that this was probably the cause of our troubles. If the valve controlling the rudder or centreboard was not left in the open position, and one or the other hit something, the resulting pressure blows a sacrificial copper disk that opens the hydraulic circuit. As I had spare disks taped to the hydraulic pump in a plastic bag for this eventuality,

it only took me a couple of minutes to replace the copper disk. Only then did it occur to me that we may have hit one of those logs that were reported to have been washed off Madagascar. Whatever it was, the boat had ridden over it and, as there was nothing under the boat to stop it, it ended up hitting the rudder.

Thanks to its design, the rudder had absorbed the shock without suffering any apparent damage, but nearly one year later, when the boat was hauled out, I noticed a suspicious crack in the main rudder body. The rudder had to be taken off and welded, and it could have only been a consequence of that collision, which must have been very violent to crack the massive aluminium plate.

Dealing with the emergency had taken less than half an hour, not much more time than it took me to describe it now. Later, I heard that the upturned keel-less hull of the South African yacht Moquini had been discovered soon afterwards south of that same area. Of its crew of six there was no sign. The 42-foot yacht had been taking part in the Mauritius to Durban race when it disappeared. I am sure that they must have hit something similar, as violent thunderstorms that had devastated parts of Madagascar around that time had washed a lot of debris out into the ocean.

North Atlantic, September 2015

A mysterious leak was also the cause of another emergency on Aventura III, which occurred on our way to Antarctica, as described on page 140. I was reminded of that incident when we were caught in a storm while sailing on Aventura IV from Greenland to the UK. Reefed down well, we were broadreaching fast, with the boat taking the high seas in her stride. While enjoying the exhilarating ride, I went below to check that everything was in order. I lifted the engine cover to check the main bilge, and found it full of water. The bilge pump was running, but the water was coming in faster than the pump could deal with. I asked Dunbar to use the manual bilge pump located in the cockpit,

and the water level went down, but suddenly it rose again. While Dunbar continued pumping, I lifted each floor panel to find the source, and deduced that the water was coming in from somewhere at the front, but I was unable to establish the actual source. By then, the wind had increased to 40 knots and to continue sailing seemed reckless, so I decided to heave to. The water ingress stopped immediately, and it was later that I realised that the water could only have found its way via the anchor chain tunnel into the anchor locker, and then overflowed into the bilge. On Aventura IV the anchor winch is located at the foot of the mast, with the chain running from the bows to the winch via an aluminium duct. Bashing into the heavy seas at high speed, enough water was forced through to fill the bilges. Having been flooded once from the stern on Aventura III, I now had the experience of being flooded from the bows. From then on, I made sure to plug the tunnel with a rag on passage, and informed the builders to advise other Exploration 45 owners of this risk.

Northwest Passage, August 2014

After the decision was taken to abandon the attempt of a transit of the Northwest Passage because of the unfavourable ice conditions, we turned around to sail back to Greenland. With gale-force winds forecast for the following day, and being in the typical calm before a storm, we were motoring fast towards the open sea. During Doina's watch I was woken by a loud noise from the engine. I rushed into the cockpit and stopped the engine as it was making a rattling metallic sound. It sounded like we had picked up something on the propeller. I restarted the engine briefly but the noise persisted.

With the engine out of action and an imminent gale upon us, I needed to find out if we had indeed caught something in the propeller. I mounted the GoPro camera with an underwater housing onto the end of an ice pole, lowered it over the side and managed to get a good view of the propeller.

quite comfortable and easily rode out the gale. After a dozen hours, the wind started going down and I could work on the engine. Although I had no spare bolts on board, I found some longer bolts and cut them down to size with the electric angle grinder. I retrieved from the bilge the sheared-off bolts, and recuperated their nuts. Hanging upside down over the back of the engine, I managed to pull back the propeller shaft sufficiently to reconnect it to the transmission.

A thick black rope was wound around the propeller shaft, with its end trailing behind. I realised that something more serious might have happened, so went to look at the engine and found that the bolts between the propeller shaft and transmission had sheared. To have picked up a rope in those pristine waters, where we had not seen a single fishing boat, was almost impossible to believe. But we had, and it had been strong enough to immobilise the propeller shaft and rip it off its mounts. With much drifting ice as well as large icebergs still about, and the nights getting longer as we moved south, not being able to use the engine for the remaining 1,000 miles to Nuuk would have been a serious handicap.

My mind was soon focused on the imminent gale, so we reefed down and continued sailing until we had consistent winds of over 35 knots. We hove to with three reefs in the mainsail and most of the staysail rolled up. In spite of the large seas, we were

It was now time to deal with the remains of the rope. Although I was able to turn the propeller shaft by hand and it felt as it were free, I dared not start the engine and put it in gear. I donned my dry diving suit and kitted myself out with all the gear needed for a dive in ice-cold water, but decided not to use a tank for a job that may only take a few minutes. Attached to the boat with a safety line, I came close to the trailing rope and managed to cut off some of it, but the violent rolling of the boat, with my head banging against the hull, forced me to give up. But at least I had been able to ascertain that the propeller was indeed free.

Getting out of the water weighed down by 12kg of lead weights, with the boat bouncing violently in the rough swell, required a superhuman effort. Although

I was wearing a dry suit, the hood was not dry and I could feel the cold getting to my head. I knew that I was in a critical situation and, as an experienced diver, was aware that I had to get out of the water quickly because I had only about one minute before serious hypothermia would set in and I may no longer be able to act rationally. It was the sight of Doina standing helplessly above me that gave me the strength to lie on my back and lift my feet one by one out of the water so that she could reach down and pull off my large fins. I then managed to put my foot on the lowest rung of the ladder and was helped up the rest of the way. I dropped exhausted into the cockpit, and Doina later told me that I could hardly speak and sounded incoherent.

When I had recovered, I started the engine and engaged the forward gear, but kept it at slow revs. I checked the propeller with the underwater camera and could see it turning freely, the end of the rope trailing harmlessly behind. After half an hour of motoring, I checked the bolts and they were all tight.

Eight days later we were in Nuuk, where once again I donned my dry suit, but this time also a diving tank. In the calm clear water I reached the propeller, where the black line was still trailing idly in the current. I cut it off with a serrated knife, but could not manage to cut the rest, which was coiled so tightly that it had fused to the propeller-shaft housing. That was a job that had to wait until Aventura could be hauled out at a US boatyard, 3,500 miles from where the incident had happened.

Emergency management

There is no harm in hoping for the best as long as you're prepared for the worst.

Stephen King

Over the years I have witnessed many emergencies at sea, and I am pleased to say that in the vast majority of cases they were resolved without tragic consequences, either by the crew being able to deal with it themselves or with outside assistance, whether from other yachts or, in extremis, the international rescue authorities. The main factors that contributed to a solution were being part of a rally, availability of satellite communications and, above all, self-sufficiency.

Mike Johnson, a former jet pilot and mountaineer, who took part in one of my surveys, said: 'How you deal with an emergency depends on knowledge, preparation and constant review. We use a simple acronym for most of our decision-making, DODAR: diagnose the problem, options available, decide on the most appropriate, act upon it, review how it is working. If necessary, return to step one. This may sound simplistic, but we have seen so many minor situations develop into disasters because people didn't begin at the first step.'

Emergencies experienced on transatlantic passages, whether by sailors in a rally or on their own, are a good indication of this safety aspect of offshore voyaging. I estimate that between 20 and 25 per cent of boats experience some kind of breakage, among which perhaps five per cent could be described as serious emergencies, such as dismasting; rigging, structural, engine or steering failure; and medical emergencies. Among all these, only an estimated one per cent could be described as truly serious emergencies. Even in such cases, the majority managed to find a solution and make a safe landfall, with very few needing outside assistance. This shows the absolute importance of self-sufficiency, and why this factor should be at the core of preparations for an offshore voyage. It is a subject that will be discussed in detail in the chapter dealing with safety.

Man overboard

The danger of losing a crew overboard is something that I dread more than anything else and, I must admit, that should something like this ever happen, I'd much prefer for me to be the one lost, because I simply could never live with the thought that I had been responsible for somebody's death. Strict rules on all of my boats have thankfully avoided any such situation, but the loss of one young man in the first round-the-world rally shook me to the core. That was the only life lost by someone who had fallen overboard in any of the rallies I had organised, although there have been a few man-overboard situations, all of the others with a happy ending.

This young Norwegian had the luckiest escape when he fell overboard from his 33-foot boat. Fortunately he was wearing a life jacket that kept him afloat. Several ARC boats responded to the crew's Mayday and spent the next 24 hours doing a wide search. Eventually the man was found by a young couple on another Norwegian boat. What is even more incredible is that they had already saved a man shortly before the start of the ARC. While sailing close to the Canary Islands to join the ARC, they saw something afloat that made them suspicious; they got closer and found an exhausted African man who was close to drowning. They pulled him on board and took him to Gran Canaria, where he told the authorities that he had stowed away on a Ukrainian ship with a large group of other potential asylum seekers. As the ship was passing Gran Canaria, the captain ordered his crew to push all the men overboard, forcing them to swim to the island. The young man rescued by the Norwegian yacht was the only survivor.

Abandoning ship

To my great relief, my knowledge of this matter is based only on second-hand experience, but as I regard the possibility of having to abandon ship as something that could happen to anyone, I have given the matter serious thought and have made the necessary preparations. I always discuss such an eventuality with my crew, preferably before leaving on a passage, as I find the subject rather upsetting if broached when we are already at sea. Here are the six separate steps that I decided should be dealt with promptly and in the right order if the decision to abandon Aventura were ever taken:

I have timed the above tasks and, with help from the crew, they can be done in about two minutes. The EPIRB, which is registered with Aventura's details, is close to the companionway so that it can be quickly activated and put in the liferaft. The raft itself can be easily launched from its recessed bin on the aft platform.

One often overlooked point is to ensure that the liferaft painter or tether is secured to the yacht. This is one of the items that is checked during the safety inspection conducted on all yachts taking part in a rally, and it is surprising to find that on as many as one-third of the boats, the owners had failed to actually secure the liferaft to a strong point. On pleasure craft the liferaft is inflated by the pull of the painter, which activates its CO_2 bottle. Some liferafts, especially on commercial vessels, are fitted with a hydrostatic release, which is activated by increased water pressure as the vessel and its liferaft sink.

The liferaft should only be launched as a matter of last resort, as a yacht still floating is always safer than a liferaft. This is why anyone at the point of abandoning their sinking yacht should step up into the liferaft. The liferaft should always be launched to leeward, and care should be taken that it cannot be damaged.

I regard a satellite phone, preferably the Iridium 9575 with its in-built GPS, as providing the best chance of prompt assistance. Therefore a fully charged spare battery for the sat phone should always be kept in one of the survival containers. The phone numbers of the US and UK Coast Guards and SAR authorities closest to the route should be written in indelible pen on the lid of one of the survival containers, and also on a piece of paper kept inside one of the containers. In all emergency situations involving rally participants, their ability to communicate directly with the SAR authorities, and later with the rescue vessel, has resulted in the victims being rescued in a matter of hours. In more remote areas, the rescue operation may take longer, hence the need to carry a more comprehensively provisioned survival container.

From the suggestions made by sailors who described the contents of their survival containers – some containing the bare minimum, others being able to support the crew for several days – I compiled a list of the best and most popular ideas:

Safety
EPIRB, battery-operated GPS, satellite telephone with spare battery, portable VHF radio with spare batteries, flares (in separate waterproof container) or flare pistol, dye marker, torch and batteries, signalling mirror, sea anchor, survival handbook.

Food
A mixture of dry and concentrated food, not all of which has to be reconstituted with water, food in selfheating tins, chocolate, glucose.

Medicine
First-aid kit, vitamins, laxatives, sunblock cream, painkillers, anti-seasickness medication, personal medication.

Miscellaneous
Hand-operated watermaker, knife (pocket knife with various blades), drinking cup, spoon, plastic plate, fishing gear, can opener, sponge, liferaft repair kit, assorted plastic bags.

Personal
Passports, money, credit cards, pen and paper.

Comfort
Survival suits or aluminium blankets, spare clothing, sun hats, sunglasses, folding umbrella (can be used to shelter from rain or sun, to catch rainwater and even as a sail, if strong enough).

The above list is so comprehensive that one would almost need a second yacht to carry all that stuff, so in my case I tried to reduce it to more reasonable proportions and ended up with what I regard as the most essential items necessary for survival. My two survival containers were of waterproof plastic, with a wide mouth and screw top of the type normally used for flares. Both had lanyards to make fast to the liferaft and were kept close to the companionway. As liferaft emergency packs contain very little water, I always kept in the cockpit a jerrycan of water that was not completely full, so it floated if thrown overboard. A hand-operated watermaker may not be needed, but even if one is available, some additional water should be carried as well.

The contents of Aventura III's two survival containers were as follows:

» Selection of flares (one orange smoke, two parachute, two red flares)
» Hand-held VHF radio, torch, 48 AA alkaline batteries
» Satellite phone
» Portable GPS, as the older Iridium 9555 did not have a built-in GPS
» Charged spare battery for the satellite phone; emergency telephone numbers (all these were kept in a separate waterproof box)
» Fishing gear, hooks, monofilament line
» Two knives, one with cork handle
» Leatherman compact tool kit
» Liferaft repair kit
» Personal medication, antibiotic tablets, antibiotic cream
» Sunblock cream, first-aid kit, anti-seasickness pills
» Notebook and pen

On long passages, passports and money were always kept in one of the containers. Ideally, all battery-operated items should use the same alkaline AA type batteries, rotated regularly so that those in the container are always the latest batch.

Tips

» Prepare an abandon-ship procedure, discuss it with crew and assign individual tasks

» Prepare a survival container

» Check and rotate its contents regularly

» Keep an emergency jerrycan of water in the cockpit

Young rally participants checking out a liferaft during a safety demonstration

19

A Polynesian interlude

In a place like Atuona nothing much seems to happen, and the time spent there by the painter Paul Gauguin is still mentioned as if it were yesterday. So it is not surprising that every living soul on the island seemed to have descended onto Hiva Oa's small airport to welcome the flight from Tahiti. Gwenda stepped off the small plane looking diminutive among the burly Marquesans returning home. After a separation of two months, I was very happy to be with her again, and was looking forward to the prospect of a long cruise on Aventura III with just the two of us all the way to New Zealand.

We had called at the Marquesas on Aventura II in 1991, and had enjoyed that cruise so much that we were hoping to repeat the experience a dozen years later. We also planned to spend some time on Hiva Oa, an island that we had not had time to explore at leisure.

One of the first things we did was to walk the steep road that leads to the small cemetery where Gauguin was laid to rest in 1903. The tomb is overshadowed by a gnarled Tiaré tree, whose fragrant flowers fluttered down gently onto the simple grave. Nearby is the grave of Jacques Brel, a Belgian singer who had also chosen to end his days on this remote island.

Our visit coincided with the 100th anniversary of Gauguin's death, an event that had galvanised Hiva Oa's small community into a burst of civic activity. The painter's Maison de Jouir (house of pleasure), which was burnt down by the villagers on his death, had been faithfully restored and now contained reproductions of the famous canvases he had painted during his troubled sojourn on the island. Shunned by the locals while he lived in their midst, he was now commemorated as a local celebrity.

Those Gauguin reproductions that adorned the walls of his restored studio had a story behind them worthy of the peripatetic painter himself. On my previous visit to Atuona I had met a French singlehander who had just arrived in his yacht from France. Alain had set up an easel under a large tree that overshadowed Gauguin's former abode, and was busy painting. He told me that he was planning to reproduce all Gauguin's paintings in time for the centenary of his death.

The canvas he was working on looked almost identical to the reproduction he was copying from a large art catalogue, and when I commented how good it looked, he said if I was interested he would paint one for me as well. We agreed on one of my favourite Gauguins, and Alain's painting is now in our London apartment.

This is by no means the end of the story, as in the meantime I had found out that Alain was one of the most famous art fakers in France, who ended up in prison after one of his many scams. When he had finished his sentence, he vowed never to get into trouble again and to use his undoubted talents to produce original work. Unfortunately the ever-alert French Inland Revenue had other ideas. One day a taxman paid Alain a visit and presented him with an enormous bill for unpaid taxes on all the money he had made from the fake paintings he had sold to various dealers over the years. Alain promised to find the money, but asked to be given some time to do so. Instead, he wasted no time in buying a sailing yacht and set off for the South Seas. After he finished his work in Atuona, he disappeared without trace, and the unforgiving French taxman is probably still looking for him.

A bumpy four-wheel drive took us to the opposite side of the island to the archaeological site at Puamau, whose centrepiece is an ancient stone tiki about 3 metres high, the largest of its kind in the Marquesas. Due to their isolation, the Marquesas – named locally Te Henua Enata, meaning Land of Men – had developed a thriving civilisation, whose death knell was sounded by the arrival of the first Europeans. The first to call was the Spanish navigator Alvaro de Mendaña in 1595, who called the islands Las Islas de la Marquesa, after the Marchioness of Mendoza. Extensive ruins on every island are a sad reminder of the thriving community of at least 100,000 people that once lived there. Their massive fortification complexes proved to be of no avail against an invisible enemy: the various diseases brought by those early visitors. Their tragic fate was later compounded by the forced abduction of men to work on plantations, the infamously called blackbirding, which completed the decimation of the native population, so that by the middle of the 19th century their number had been reduced to only 6,000. The Marquesans never managed to recover from those traumatic years, and even today the total population of the islands is less than 9,000.

After having spent several days in Atuona's rolly harbour, we sailed across to the nearby island of Tauhata and anchored in Noe Noe Bay. The nearby golden beach looked very tempting, but having made the mistake of visiting it 10 years previously, when the infamous Marquesan sandflies had almost eaten me alive, we preferred to enjoy the scenery from the safety of our cockpit. The last time I had been anchored there was with Aventura II, in the company of several yachts taking part in the first round-the-world rally. A local Marquesan and his son had come from the nearest village, unable to understand what had brought about such an invasion. After I explained to him what was going on, he kindly offered to go into the nearby hills to, as he put it in his simple English, 'kill some piggies with my doggies'. He did just that, and the two of them returned with a piggy each on the shoulder, made a huge fire on the beach and treated us to the most delicious barbecue that I can remember; nor will I ever forget those nasty sandflies either, whose only role in life, I am told, is to take revenge on any outsider for the sufferings visited on the natives of these islands, who seem impervious to their attacks.

The spectacular scenery of the Marquesas, their jagged soaring peaks and lush vegetation, make them among the most beautiful islands in the world. As we sailed out of Noe Noe Bay, the sharp peaks of Ua Pou pierced the sky to the south, while Nuku Hiva's majestic silhouette beckoned from the north. While Hiva Oa thrives on its

association with Paul Gauguin, the claim to fame of the main island, Nuku Hiva, is that it's the setting for Herman Melville's Typee. Although most of the story is fictional, Melville did call at the Marquesas on the whaler Acushnet in 1843, where he jumped ship with a friend. They spent some time among the people of Nuku Hiva, so his description of locals and places rings true. We decided to corroborate this at the village of Taipivai, which inspired the title of the book. Hidden in the dense forest above the village is one of the best-preserved maraes (sacred sites) on the island. In the profound silence, large stone tikis stand guard over ancient graves, the oppressive atmosphere and sultry heat almost bringing to life Melville's gruesome story.

We drove across the island to its northern shore, and halfway there stopped at two other ancient sites, at Kamuihei and Hikohua. Just as on Easter Island, ceremonial demands and rivalry amongst chiefs had led to the construction of massive stone terraces, large temples and impressive statues. Close to a group of tikis, a huge mango tree had shed its golden fruit, which was covering the ground in a thick fragrant layer. I could not resist the temptation to pick up a few, as fruit that I gather myself always tastes better.

As I had not been able to treat Gwenda to her favourite lobster meal for a long time, at Hatiheu we stopped for lunch at a small restaurant that we remembered from our previous visit. In spite of her French-sounding name, the owner, Yvonne, was a larger than life Marquesan lady who insisted that she remembered us from before, and she produced a most delicious meal. Having enjoyed an excellent lunch in the open-sided restaurant, set on a beach against a backdrop of craggy mountains, we both agreed that the Marquesas had once again lived up to our highest expectations.

Our last stop in the Marquesas was Haka Hatau, a small village on the west coast of Ua Pou. Before leaving for the Tuamotus, I went ashore to buy bread and some fruit. A large swell was breaking in a shower of spray on the small quay, and the continuous surge made it difficult to land from the dinghy. Ashore, a burly Marquesan was watching my pitiful attempts to control the wild buckings of my inflatable. As I was trying to time myself to leap onto the slippery concrete steps, I felt myself grabbed under the arms and lifted onto the quay like a sack of potatoes. With a friendly smile, the man greeted me in broken English, and I replied in French.

'No French,' he said. 'You must speak English to me'. He then explained that he had been sent by his teacher, who had seen our red ensign and wanted to invite me to their class. Nearby, in an open-sided building, sat a dozen men, all local fishermen who were learning English to be able to deal with the tourists who were arriving on their island in increasing numbers. The teacher prompted each pupil to introduce himself in English, and I was then asked to describe my voyage, family and occupation. I tried to summarise the latter part of my life in a few simple words, but I doubt that they understood much of it. After I had got my bread and fruit and was getting ready to board the dinghy, they all came down to the quay to wave me goodbye. As I rowed back to the boat, it occurred to me that what really sets the Marquesas apart is not just the natural beauty of the islands, but the unique beauty of their inhabitants, so magnificently portrayed in Gauguin's work.

Squally unsettled weather caused by a stationary front over the Tuamotus stayed with us for the four days that it took to get there. After the near-perfect voyage from Ecuador, I felt really sorry for Gwenda, who always seemed to get the worst deal. On the last night, we deliberately slowed down to avoid arriving too early at the island of Raroia. On my watch, I kept thinking back to the anxious moments I had passed in this same area 25 years earlier, when we had sailed nonstop from the Gambiers to Tahiti. Our route took us right across the Tuamotus, and it still filled me with satisfaction to think of having overcome that challenge without any problems. With only my sextant for navigation, and even that being restricted to day sights, as cloudy skies made it impossible to take any star sights, we had to sail blindly throughout the hours of darkness. How different things were now: I had GPS and radar, and could pinpoint my position any time I felt like it.

Raroia's serrated outline of coconut trees was spiking the horizon as we closed with the island's northern shore at dawn. This was a highly symbolic landfall for me, as it was on this atoll that the Kon-Tiki raft finished its epic 101-day voyage from Peru in 1947. The Norwegian explorer Thor Heyerdahl had tried to show not only that such a voyage was possible in a balsa raft, but also that people from South America had sailed a similar route to Polynesia in days gone by. Even if the expedition didn't prove that Easter Island and other Pacific islands had been colonised by people from South America, rather than Polynesians arriving from the west, Kon-Tiki still stands out as one of the greatest adventure stories of all time.

Thor Heyerdahl's international bestseller, which described that great adventure, was also published in my native Romania, the book having somehow slipped past the Communist censors. I was around 12 and can still remember the excitement I felt reading that thrilling adventure, and my amazement that free people could do what they liked and travel where they wanted. I have no doubt that it was that very book that sowed in me the wanderlust that has never left me.

In his tumultuous life, Heyerdahl had been involved in many similarly controversial projects, and he has attracted much criticism, such as this rather ungenerous quote from the author Paul Theroux: 'Heyerdahl's single success was his proof, in Kon-Tiki, that six middle-class Scandinavians could successfully crash-land their craft on a coral atoll in the middle of nowhere.'

Timing our arrival to coincide with good light was not enough in the Tuamotus, as I soon found out when we came to the pass leading into Raroia lagoon and were confronted by a strong contrary current. We eventually managed to get through, but I knew I had to do better next time and pay closer attention to tides. Hardly had our anchor gone down in front of the one and only village, than a small canoe left the broken-down quay and headed for us. A young girl asked permission to come aboard, and then spread out a dozen black pearls on a towel, eyeing Gwenda as a potential customer. The production of cultured black pearls is now a major industry in the Tuamotus, with pearl farms in almost every lagoon. The prices must have gone up because we found them much too expensive, and declined to buy any. Later that day, while walking ashore, we met the girl again, and when we still refused to make a deal, she picked one of the pearls and gave it to me, probably thinking we were too poor to buy one.

An overnight passage took us to Makemo, our next destination. As we sailed along its northern shore, I was puzzled that, according to our GPS position, we should have been level with the Tapuhiria Pass, on the atoll's west side. For a while I thought we had missed it, and was even considering turning around, but when I checked with the radar I realised that something was not right. What I saw on the screen did not in any way match my chart, which, for a change, was not my usual recycled lot but a brand-new recent acquisition. At last the narrow break in the reef came into view and, because this time I had made sure that the tide was not against us, we got through without difficulty and anchored close to an abandoned copra shed. As we entered the pass, I took down its GPS position to compare it with the chart. While the pass was located at 16°26.83'S, 143°57.99'W, on the British Admiralty chart 83023, the coordinates of the pass were 16°21.75'S, 143°58.60'W, a difference in latitude of close to five miles! Maybe changing the name from the Dangerous Archipelago to plain Tuamotus had been rather premature.

Our most memorable stay in the Tuamotus was at the uninhabited Tahanea atoll, now a nature reserve. One morning we saw a yellow catamaran approach our anchorage, and I immediately recognised the bearded man at the helm, whom I had last met in Paris. In the 1960s Antoine was a major star on the French pop scene, and he still has lots of fans. He gives the occasional performance, but is now better known for the books and videos he produces while roaming the seas on his Banana Split. He persuaded us to up anchor and follow him to his favourite spot in the southeast corner of the lagoon, which he had been visiting regularly since 1986. We spent a highly enjoyable time with Francette and Antoine, who regaled us with stories from their peripatetic life.

Also memorable, although for different reasons, are two other incidents that occurred at Tahanea. It was there that both Gwenda and I fell ill with ciguatera fish poisoning, and, to cap it all, we had a most hairy exit as we were leaving the lagoon through the narrow pass. Both incidents are described elsewhere in this book.

Our next destination was Fakarava, some 40 miles from Tahanea. As by now I knew that passes into most lagoons can have very strong currents, it was essential to time both departures and arrivals carefully, because the best – and often only – time to leave or enter a pass safely was just after slack low tide. With an optimum arrival time at Fakarava of 6am, I decided to sail there overnight. Some Tuamotu bad spirit must have taken a dislike to me because we had such strong winds for the 80-mile passage that I had great trouble slowing

Aventura down, and instead of arriving there at dawn we had to heave to off the island at 2am. As soon as it got light, we went through the pass and dropped the anchor close to a trimaran. Sloepmouche, a 46-foot Cross, has been home for Jackie Lee and Luc Callebaut since 1995, when they left the Caribbean and headed west. As I am writing these lines 22 years later, they have reached the Philippines. Luc has pointed out that their voyage around the world may never end, but if it eventually did it will surely qualify for the slowest ever circumnavigation.

As both Luc and Jackie were keen divers, later that morning I joined them for a drift dive through the pass we had just negotiated. By now the tide was sweeping through at a good rate, so it took me no time at all to virtually fly over the amazing coral formations, a sensation that felt like watching an underwater film in fast motion. We then sailed in company across the well-beaconed lagoon, past several pearl farms, to anchor close to an islet on the windward side of the lagoon. This proved to have been a very inspired move because during the night that same bad spirit brought very strong winds with several violent squalls, and we would have been in real trouble if we hadn't left our previous exposed anchorage. I was starting to see why the Tuamotus might never become a cruising destination to most people's liking.

Under normal conditions, the 250 miles to Tahiti should have taken us just under two days, but by the time we reached the open sea, the trade winds had piped up to their usual level, and were blowing a steady 25 knots. With Aventura reefed right down, we were still doing over 6 knots, and once again it looked increasingly like, rather than arriving at our destination at first light, we would probably get there in the middle of the night. As we got as close to Tahiti's north coast as I dared go, we hove to until it got light. Then we passed through Matavai Pass, with the lighthouse on Point Venus to our portside. Its name was given by Captain James Cook during his stay with a team of scientists in 1769, to observe the rare phenomenon of the transit of the planet Venus across the face of the sun.

As we made our way into the small Tahiti Yacht Club marina, my friend Michel Alcon, the manager of the club, was waiting to take our lines. I have the good fortune of having friends all over the world, many of them made during our first voyage, and I have kept in regular contact with most of them. Often on my travels I feel like I am walking down the main street of that mythical global village, stopping here and there to chat with an old friend. Having a drink with Michel on the airy yacht-club terrace felt just like that.

Papeete's waterfront had changed greatly since my last visit, and docking facilities for visiting yachts had been much improved. Papeete has one major advantage for yachts engaged in a long voyage: due to an active local yachting community, its repair facilities are the best this side of New Zealand. Provisioning is just as good, even if the prices are less so, but that didn't deter us from stocking up with French delicacies, including a good supply of wine that we knew would not be available in the places we were heading for.

Spending even a short time in Papeete was a shock after weeks of peaceful cruising in the Marquesas and Tuamotus. The capital of French Polynesia is now a busy, noisy, polluted town, with fast traffic and impatient drivers. Gone forever is much of that unique charm that had seduced so many travellers in the past, and had made countless dreamers abandon their home and family to run away to the South Seas. The natural beauty of the Society Islands, and that includes Tahiti's interior, still makes them one of the most attractive places in the world, but whenever I return to Papeete I have a feeling that something has been irretrievably lost.

After the hubbub of Papeete, neighbouring Moorea, only nine miles away, was a world apart. Its natural beauty has been preserved almost intact, and tourist development has not been allowed to go unchecked. As a result, the picturesque anchorages on its north coast are still among the most beautiful on the world cruising circuit. With Aventura safely anchored in Cook's Bay, overlooked by the needle-sharp profile of Mount Mou'a Roa, one afternoon we climbed to the Belvedere, a high point that overlooks Moorea's spectacular north coast. We waited until the setting sun cast a veil of pinks and reds over the surrounding mountains, and then started on the long walk down. As is usual in the tropics, there was hardly any dusk, and we had to make our return trip in almost complete darkness.

Once again, because of the distance involved, I decided on an overnight hop to Huahine, the smallest of the Society Islands. Huahine was exactly as we remembered it from our first visit; tourism has not been allowed to destroy the island's fragile fabric, and life continued at a tranquil pace. Huahine has some of the best-preserved remains in the Society Islands, although the most important marae in all of Polynesia was on neighbouring Raiatea, our next stop.

Raiatea shares a lagoon with her smaller island sister Taha'a, and as there is deep water all around the islands, we made a complete circuit of Taha'a, just as we had done on our first Aventura. Because of its ideal setting, Raiatea has become one of the major charter destinations in the Pacific, its main attractions being the sheltered waters of its lagoon and its central location at the heart of the Society Islands, with Bora Bora only a short sail away.

We stopped at a tiny island where I had once taken some photographs of Gwenda walking on the pristine beach, in order to show the beauty of Pacific cruising. As we got closer in the dinghy, I saw a large notice in French and English nailed to a palm tree: Private Island Keep Out. A Polynesian family were having a picnic by the beach, so I walked up to them and asked in French if they would allow us to walk around their little island. 'Of course, just go ahead. And would you like to join us for a drink?'

So things may not have all changed for the worst, and from this brief encounter, and other similar incidents involving local people, such as the girl with the black pearl on Raroia or the fishermen on Ua Pou, I felt that in French Polynesia, as everywhere else, what meets the eye may not necessarily be a reflection of the true situation.

I wish I could have felt the same at Bora Bora, our last stop in French Polynesia. James Michener once described it as the most beautiful island in the world, and for many years I agreed with his comment and considered Bora Bora one of my favourite cruising destinations. Tied to one of the moorings of the

Bora Bora Yacht Club, we were watching the ever-changing scene around us. There was certainly a lot more movement than we ever remembered, with fast launches coming and going from the airport located on one of the outer islands, excursion boats taking tourists on sightseeing tours of the lagoon, and dive boats heading for a session of shark feeding or swimming with giant manta rays. We decided that it was time to move on and explore some of the South Pacific's less frequented areas. As we headed out through the pass and felt the gentle embrace of the ocean, I realised that for the first time I could ever remember I was leaving a place without hoping to return. An inveterate traveller once said that you should never return to a place you had enjoyed, because your first impressions can never be matched by what you may find on subsequent visits. In the case of Bora Bora, that comment could not have been truer.

20

Crew and watches

The ideal crew would be a fairly laid-back character, who can keep it together under pressure, can fix most things and, of course, be a good cook.

Steve Spink

That sounds like quite a tall order, although Steve, who sailed as captain on one of the Millennium Odyssey yachts, and as crew in two previous round-the-world rallies, has all those rare qualities.

The crew of Taratoo

Fabio Colapinto, who sailed his own yacht in the same event, and who has had more than his fair share of crew problems in his long sailing life, was of the firm opinion that 'nothing can spoil the pleasure of a voyage more than problems with your crew'. Fabio echoed my own feelings, as I believe that more voyages have been abandoned because of crew problems than by the wrong choice of boat, gear failure or financial difficulties. This conclusion is based in part on my personal experience, but mostly drawn from countless examples that I have come across as the organiser of cruising rallies. Even allowing for the fact that I was dealing with very large numbers of people, the proportion of boats that experienced crew problems was much higher than I would have expected.

The scenario is simple: you invest all your energy and probably much of your savings in the boat of your dreams, and finally set off on your planned voyage. Unless you are sailing with your family, you are likely to be accompanied both by people you know well and others that you know less well. But however well acquainted you may be with your crew, you know them from another dimension: a comfortable life ashore. The sea is different, an alien and occasionally dangerous medium where a person's true character may quickly reveal itself as selfish, anxious, stubborn, lazy, mean, greedy, inconsiderate or humourless, not to speak of the physical or psychological problems that might manifest themselves. On top of that, they may have irritating habits: being noisy or untidy; eating messily; not washing; not sharing cooking, washing up and other tasks; smoking; drinking too much or, worse, being addicted to drugs. There may also be problems with discipline, sleeping on watch and being generally unreliable. However skilful and tolerant the captain may be in trying to make allowances for a difficult crew member, the situation is often impossible. If all this sounds like a description of the crew from hell, I should point out that there are also many crews who exhibit none of these faults and are a pleasure to have on board.

Types of crew

I will look at crew first from a general point of view, and then examine the same subject from both my own experience and that acquired as an event organiser. Getting crew for a long voyage is certainly not a simple matter, as I know too well from the various rallies. Basically, there are five types of crew:

Sharing crew: these are often friends who join a boat for a shorter or longer period. Normally they are expected to contribute towards their living expenses and do a fair share of the work.

Casual crew: people who may not be well-qualified but are willing to work for their trip. Such people need not be paid, and normally the owner covers their onboard living expenses. This category also includes so-called hitchhikers, often young people who hang out in ports frequented by cruising boats, who are keen to do some sailing, even if they may not have much experience.

Paid crew: sailors who are experienced, whom it should be possible to trust, to tell them what to do, and who are not joining a yacht just to have a good time. These sailors expect to be paid a wage and have all their onboard expenses taken care of.

Paying crew: people who want to join an adventure or log offshore miles for their qualification, are prepared to play an active role on board, and also make a contribution to the overall costs, or even pay a reasonable fee per day.

Charter guests: normally these are not expected to do much, although they may take watches and help where necessary. They expect to be fed and looked after well, so boats who charter need to have a full crew to do that, including a cook. As such people are often paying substantial charter fees, their expectations are high, and therefore such operations must be approached as a purely business undertaking.

Briefing of charter guests in a round-the-world rally

The level of sailing experience will vary greatly in all the above categories, and so will attitude and behaviour. The best crew are usually sailors whom you know reasonably well, who have their own boats, some offshore experience, and are interested in the opportunity to sail with you because they may not be able to do it on their own boat, or to gain the experience to do it themselves later. Even among such people, there may be some who will not live up to your expectations. The worst are those who believe they know everything, insist on doing things their way, dispute your decisions and are incapable of accepting the fact that, even on a small boat, the captain has the last word.

Financial arrangements

Regardless of the type of crew, owners have to be very careful about whom they take on board, what arrangements are made, financial and otherwise, and what their responsibilities are in regard to accidents, injury, illness, repatriation, etc. There are many hidden problems, some serious, that can show up, so this matter should not be taken lightly.

Those who decide to go down the paid charter-guest route, must approach that option in a proper, businesslike manner. One should not mix the owner's personal friends with paying guests. Many sailors hope to supplement their cruising kitty in this way, and although taking on paying guests may look like an attractive solution to finance or at least underwrite some of the cruising costs, there are many pitfalls. People who pay have high expectations. They want service, and are not prepared to compromise and make allowances. If you are determined to still go ahead, adequate preparations should be made.

A few cruising couples have made this a successful business, and in most cases they were competent sailors who ran a well-organised ship. A good example is John and Amanda Neal, who have been running their Mahina Tiare III for many years as a navigation and sail-training ship. Fee-paying crews join up for offshore training stages in ocean voyaging, seamanship, and safety and navigation, the operation being backed up by regular cruising seminars held in various locations, usually at boat shows.

Some owners, who may be put off by the complications of running a properly set up charter operation, may consider going for a mixed solution. If the owner is not going to be on the yacht for much of the time, it is better to take a chance, go only for proper charter guests, and run the boat with a permanent crew of three persons (captain, cook and deckhand), provided the yacht is large enough for this kind of operation. Whatever decision is made by the owner must be agreed with the captain, as he will have to deal with any problems, and should always have the last word when crew is chosen. Professional captains are renowned for being extremely touchy, so owners often have to treat them with kid gloves, which many find difficult. This may be the reason why professional captains seem to change jobs so frequently. In fact, although I mentioned earlier that crew can cause the biggest problems on a voyage, equally serious problems can be caused by these professionals, who are often arrogant and difficult to get on with.

I am giving these warnings because I have seen too many bad situations caused by friction between owner and captain, owner and crew, captain and crew, owner/captain and paying guests, etc. So anyone planning to dive into this potential quagmire must be prepared to do their best to tread carefully. You will not be able to avoid every problem, but at least you should attempt to minimise the chance of a major falling out.

One other matter to be borne in mind if running a charter operation is that in some countries this is liable to various legal restrictions, and chartering may be limited to locally flagged boats. Occasionally, to avoid such problems, you can say that the crew are personal friends, but this should not be overdone because the authorities soon get suspicious if there are too many crew changes. The captain's qualifications, specific insurance requirements and the owner's legal liability are other matters that must be taken into account.

Taking on crew

Only go on trips with people you love.

Ernest Hemingway

This is certainly my preferred solution and undoubtedly the ideal setup for anyone. But even if sailing with old friends, it is good to have agreed on all essential aspects in advance, from onboard responsibilities to financial arrangements. If you have no alternative but to sail with people you don't know well, or possibly not at all, to avoid possible legal problems it is advisable to make sure that everything that is agreed is set out in a written document, even if this is only a simple letter signed by both parties. A friend of mine, who usually sailed alone, occasionally took on crew. Every time, he made sure that a proper contract was drawn up and signed by both parties, detailing everything from the captain and crew's obligations to sharing costs and other financial matters. At the time I found this rather extreme, but over the years I realised that it is the wise thing to do.

A similar precaution is to ask that the crew deposit with the captain a sum of money equivalent to their return fare home. This can be used in cases where the crew has to be repatriated quickly, whether in an emergency or if they demand this. Crew repatriation is the responsibility of the captain. This precaution applies to both professional and casual crew. It is exactly what happened to the owner of a boat in one of the round-the-world rallies. While in Ecuador he had taken on a young man not so much because he needed an extra hand but because he felt sorry for him. In Tahiti the crew got involved with a girl on another rally boat; both decided to leave the rally and fly to her native New Zealand. They went to immigration and demanded to be repatriated by their respective captains. Legally, this was their captains' obligation, and although the captains asked me to help, there was little that I could do. The captain who had taken on the young man was very annoyed because he felt he was being blackmailed, so I agreed to accompany him to the immigration office. The head of immigration explained that there was nothing he could do, and asked the captains to produce the crews' tickets before he would clear their yachts. I pointed out that, whereas the New Zealand girl should return home, the man, who was British, should be repatriated to London, not New Zealand. The officer agreed, and the crews' scheme collapsed because that was not what they had in mind.

Round-the-world-rally fleet in Tahiti

One of the most frequent problems is that of owners taking on crew they don't know, as in the above case. I have been amazed, both in the ARC and the Odysseys, how some owners agreed to take on crew on the eve of the start, being prepared to set off on a long ocean passage with people they knew nothing about. Sometimes it worked out, but there have been just as many unpleasant outcomes.

When a captain is faced with a difficult crew member at the very beginning of a voyage, a quiet talk with them, but never in front of the others, often

works. Ideally it should be done on their night watch, when one can talk without being overheard. It normally calms down the situation, but if it doesn't, one may be forced to seek a drastic solution by making for the nearest port and disembarking the crew. This is what happens every year in transatlantic rallies as, soon after having left the Canaries, a few boats make a detour to the Cape Verdes to land their troublesome crew.

Mindelo marina

Before moving on from this complex subject, I ought to mention that occasionally the main source of friction in such unhappy situations was neither the crew nor the captain, but the boat itself. Often this was the case on boats whose owners were taking on paying crew and were attracted to what they believed was an easy source of earning money. What they failed to realise was just how important it was for their yacht to be adequate for that passage: spacious enough to accommodate extra crew, well equipped, comfortable and safe. Starting off with an unsuitable boat and the attitude that 'we'll manage somehow' is a recipe for disaster.

Some of the above comments were drawn from a detailed report I compiled for the owner of a 53-foot yacht, who was planning to set off on a world voyage and was hoping to finance it by taking on paying guests. At the time I was doing consultancy work, so I had to put some serious thought into it and give clear advice. I expressed grave doubts about the viability of the project, but it was to no avail. Unfortunately all the pitfalls that I had warned my client about eventually came true. He had a serious falling out with his professional captain before they had even left the Mediterranean, and the mixing of paying crew with the owner's friends proved to be a toxic cocktail. After a disastrous season in the Caribbean, the owner decided to abandon the whole project, sell the yacht and give up. What made him especially bitter was that originally he had bought the yacht for a round-the-world voyage on which occasionally he would sail with his wife or grown-up sons. By tackling the project from the wrong angle, he ended up with nothing but bad feelings. Owing to his determination to find a way for the voyage to pay for itself, while being just as keen for it to be enjoyable, my client fell right between those two incompatible positions. As the saying goes, you cannot have your cake and eat it.

Crew competence

The best arrangement is to have crew who you know personally. You know both their experience and their personality.

Barry Esrig

One important point to bear in mind when choosing crew for an ocean passage is that at least one of the crew members should be competent enough to stand in for the captain in an emergency. Among many examples that have come to my attention of what can go wrong when the captain is the only person capable of handling the boat, I shall mention only the most significant.

The captain of a yacht sailing in the ARC was taken ill and virtually incapacitated when a pre-existing mental condition reoccurred halfway across the Atlantic. After five sleepless nights, the crew felt that they could not continue because they did not have the confidence to sail the yacht on their own. They alerted the organisers, who made arrangements for all crew, including the captain, to be evacuated onto a superyacht that had come to their assistance, and the yacht was abandoned. This incident shows the importance of having at least one experienced person besides the captain on board.

Ivan, the best crew any captain could wish for

Captain competence

I believe firmly in democracy. On my yacht all decisions are taken by unanimity... as long as I agree with them.

Fabio Colapinto

Trying to blame problems on the crew is not always fair, because there is just as good a chance that the fault may lie with the captain. Some of the bad traits I outlined earlier can apply as much to the captain as to the crew. An observation that I made in the rallies was that yachts having crew or captain problems were in fact a small minority, and there were many more happy boats and happy crews. It was also interesting to notice that some captains never seemed to have crew problems whoever sailed with them, while others seemed to have them regardless of who they sailed with. The greatest handicap for a captain is lack of experience, both in sailing and dealing with people. I saw this on my very first sail, and have never forgotten the valuable lessons I learned on that short weekend cruise in coastal waters. I hate to think how a long passage with that captain would have turned out.

As far as the crew is concerned, there is little that can be done to improve a bad captain, as the mutiny on the Bounty had clearly shown. Leaving a boat helmed by such a captain at the first opportunity is certainly recommended. As even the smallest yacht is, after all, a ship, the crew must accept the fact that some basic rules must be respected, and that discipline is not only essential but vital. Just as in the Navy, the surest way to achieve discipline is through routine; this should be imposed, and insisted upon, from the very beginning. This means having regular meals, regular watches, a fair distribution of tasks, tidiness and respect for the captain and other crew members.

Onboard compatibility

I had over 300 people sail with me over the last 40 years and only had three bad experiences – and all were with couples.

Roger Swanson

Peter Noble, whose book The Mind of the Sailor deals with the psychological aspects of sailing and the effects on captain and crews, comments, 'The importance of the human factor to the success of a sailing crew has been increasingly recognised. Small crews, particularly husband-and-wife teams, get on best. Compatibility is everything; be reluctant to sail with strangers. A small boat at sea, except possibly for the singlehander, is not an emotional escape. People take their problems with them. The successful and happy sailor was usually successful and happy before putting to sea.'

Some cases of tension between owner and crew are caused by the fact that the crew are more experienced than the owner of the boat. Although there are captains who are wise enough to accept their shortcomings, problems can occur with vain owners who always insist that they are right. Even worse is the situation where a crew believes that he knows more than the owner, even if this is not the case. This can certainly end up in an explosive situation, as I have witnessed on two recent rallies. In both cases the crew were a couple, who had been taken along to help on a long passage by the less experienced owner and his wife. In my view, two couples on the same boat on a long passage can be an unfortunate mix, and there is rarely a happy ending. In one case it got so bad that the couples stopped talking to each other, each spending their off-watch time in their own hull (it was a catamaran), and communicating by email. In the other case the clash was even worse, as before the voyage the two couples had been friends of long standing and the separation was painful and unpleasant. The crewing couple had spent time and some of their retirement funds contributing to the preparation of the boat, and were cruelly dismissed halfway through the voyage.

I have no doubt that the ideal crew on a long voyage is a romantic partner, and/or other family members, a subject that will be discussed in the following chapter. In the case of couples, leaving on a long voyage is often the man's dream, some wives going along just for his sake. This may not turn out to be a major problem if the pair have a healthy relationship and each is prepared to compromise. After sailing many years and tens of thousands of miles with me, when Aventura III arrived in New Zealand, Gwenda told me that she was no longer keen on long ocean passages, and made it very clear why. 'I think it is important to know your interests and limitations, and in my case I have reached the point where I no longer enjoy it. Of course I can do it if necessary because I've done it before, but if you don't enjoy something you are just a dead weight on the others.'

From New Zealand onwards, Gwenda only joined me for the cruising stages, so I had to complete the voyage with various crew, usually one or two. My first crew on leaving New Zealand were two experienced Kiwi sailors, one of whom I had known for many years, and we had a great sail together to New Caledonia. By the time I completed the voyage about two years later, a total of 12 different crews had sailed with me. I am happy to say that with one exception it all worked out well, and Aventura III successfully completed her circumnavigation. The main reasons were threefold: I chose my crew carefully, briefed them extensively beforehand on what to expect, and – probably most important – I had the experience not just to deal with my crew, but to show them by example that I knew all there was to know about my boat and sailing it.

Unfortunately I had a very different experience on Aventura IV's voyage, possibly explained by the tensions caused by an Arctic expedition. As half the crew were family members in the first attempt at the Northwest Passage – my daughter Doina, granddaughter Nera and niece Marianne – I attempted to maintain a relaxed and happy atmosphere on board, being more tolerant of mistakes than I should have been. This was interpreted by some of the other crew as a sign of weakness, and their condescending and disrespectful manner became hard to bear. Eventually the situation became so bad that I had no alternative but to ask them to leave the boat. In hindsight, that unhappy situation certainly had some bearing on the decision to abandon that first attempt.

On my second attempt I was determined to avoid making the same mistake, and was quite firm in my dealings with the crew. I tried to set the scene from the very beginning by stressing the fact that we were setting off on an expedition, and that in order to bring the voyage to a successful end, we needed to be disciplined and committed. We did complete the transit of the Northwest Passage, but the atmosphere on board was often tense. Regardless of my own feelings at the time, I am happy to have done it and grateful to my crew for their role in making it happen.

Dealing with crew

Do your best to find the right crew but expect relationships to change during the voyage.

Paul Donnerup

All owners have their own manner of dealing with other people, and also different ways of doing things on their boat. Therefore, there must be some compatibility between owner and crew, and the willingness on both sides to compromise. Such situations occur in everyday life, certainly in an office where the hierarchy is well established and needs to be accepted, however reluctantly. The difference with a boat on passage is that you are exposed to it 24 hours a day. Some crew have no problem accepting this situation, and get on well with the owner and vice versa, while others find it impossible – the outcome is not difficult to predict.

I need to point out that some of these comments are made from my own perspective. By nature I am a rather forceful character and, certainly in my younger days, also rather impulsive. But, by being aware of it, over the years I have made an effort to control myself, and be more tolerant and patient in dealing with my family, friends or crew. Unfortunately what I found on a few occasions, both in my professional and sailing life, was that my willingness to be flexible or accommodating, and my attempts to do things by consensus, have been interpreted as a sign of weakness, as happened on Aventura IV. As the person in charge, unless you are dealing with people who are close to you, occasionally you cannot expect to be both loved and respected.

What I found when sailing on longer passages with crew who were not family or close friends was that the critical parts of a passage were the very beginning, the middle and the end. Of those three stages, the start is the most important because it sets the tone for the rest of the passage. As so much seems to depend on the initial contact, when the crew and captain try to figure each other out, and when even a small thing can be blown out of proportion, I decided to introduce a three-day rule. When they join, I explain to my crew that during this initial period whatever I say is not meant as criticism, but an attempt to make them understand how my boat functions. They must take no offence at anything I say, or how I say it, because I do not mean to tell them off. I also assure them that if they can bear this for three days, the rest should be easy.

Marc and Patrick

The three-day rule came in extremely useful when Patrick and Marc joined me in Cape Town on Aventura III. Both had their own boats and sailing experience in the Mediterranean, but not offshore. Right from the start, Patrick started questioning my orders, so I reminded him of the three-day rule, and although he didn't seem to like it, from then on he tried to be more cooperative. As both of them were planning to set off on a long voyage, even before the three days were over they had realised that I knew what I was doing, and that it was in their own best interest to go along with what I kept reminding them: 'You are here to learn, so just do as I tell you and you won't regret it.'

Generally, by the time a long passage has reached its mid-point, it is not uncommon to notice among the crew a sense of boredom and perhaps irritation with others after a long period of close proximity. This was most certainly not the case with Patrick and Marc, who by that time had settled in perfectly and were clearly enjoying the passage and life at sea. One way to deal with boredom on long ocean passages is to prepare something that the crew can look forward to. On the first Aventura we had presents for everyone, to be opened as we crossed another 10° of longitude. The children loved it, and we kept it up throughout our six-year-long voyage. It was such a simple idea that I continued doing it later with adult crew, and it is surprising how much pleasure even a simple treat or gift can give when there is little else to look forward to.

A special treat for crossing the Arctic Circle

More accidents have happened at sea because the captain needed to be in a certain place by a specific date than any other reason.

Joseph Conrad

As a passage gets close to its end, the prevailing feeling is often one of impatience to arrive. If there have been previous clashes among the crew, the atmosphere can become explosive. Even simple matters like concern over a flight to catch, or missing home and the family, can create a tense atmosphere. This can be the most difficult stage, and there is little one can do to improve it. One thing that a captain should do is to not allow the crew to cut it too fine when they are booking their flights home. This time pressure can have a serious effect on both captain and crew, and can often spoil an otherwise successful ocean passage. On my boat, I normally insist that I am consulted on the date of a crew's return flight, and if I am in any doubt about how long it will take to reach our intended destination, I strongly advise the crew to book a flexible ticket. In these days of budget airlines, crews are often tempted to buy the cheapest fare possible, and by the time the captain finds this out it is often too late, and the choice is either for the crew to miss their flights or for the captain to do everything possible to make landfall before the flight.

Firmly booked flights are one of the most common causes of friction among crew and captain in the ARC, and, as I watched boats arrive in St Lucia at the end of the event, it never failed to amaze me how many crew had their bags packed and were ready to step off the boat even before it was properly docked. It was easy to guess what must have been going on during the crossing, and what an unpleasant time they must have had.

Assigning tasks

It's much easier to be crew than captain.

Charlie Doane

Assigning tasks is the most common source of friction, for the simple reason that most people do not like being told what to do. Often this puts the captain in an impossible situation, as I know only too well because, when faced with a touchy crew, I often end up doing a job myself rather than trying to delegate it.

Just as the crew have to obey certain rules, so does the captain. Paramount among these is not telling off a crew in front of others or shouting at the crew unless the captain makes it clear that if he raised his voice it was not in anger, but because he wanted to make sure that he had been heard. I am very much aware of this problem because several of my crew have had hearing problems. One of the most popular T-shirts for sea wives is one that simply says in large letters on the front: DON'T SHOUT!

I am ashamed to admit that in my early sailing days I did shout at my crew, and usually that meant Gwenda. My lack of experience meant that I was unsure of myself, made lots of mistakes and often ended up shouting. I know that lack of experience is hardly an excuse, but I am still annoyed with myself for my attitude in those days. Not to shout at the crew is another valuable lesson that I have learned and followed, without fail, to this day.

The problem with crew that are hard of hearing is that, by necessity, the captain is forced to raise his voice to make himself heard, but this can be easily misinterpreted, and unfortunately some people with hearing problems are even more touchy when yelled at than people whose hearing is normal. This is why I insist that such crew wear their hearing aid at all times, and I also make it very clear, as I do to any crew, that if I need to raise my voice, this is only because I want to make sure that I am heard.

While in Vanuatu I was joined by Dieter, an experienced sailor and good friend, who had sailed with me before. As we made our way into a lagoon and were looking for a place to anchor, I shouted to Dieter, who was on the foredeck: 'Prepare the anchor.'

The rumble of the chain running out fast made me realise what he had done, so I shouted even louder, 'Stop, stop.'

At least 30 metres of chain had already gone down, and although I immediately tried to stop the boat, we had run over the chain and the anchor was now lying on the bottom somewhere behind us. We managed to retrieve it, make for a better spot and re-anchor.

'What did you do that for?'

'You shouted: drop the anchor, and I did just that!'

'No, I shouted prepare the anchor. And anyway we were still moving, so how could I have asked you to drop it? Aren't you wearing your hearing aid?'

'Sorry, no.'

'OK, from now on please wear it all the time and, to be safe, we'll start doing things the Navy way. You repeat whatever I tell you to do, so I know that you heard.'

'Yes, sir. Understood, sir!'

Next time we anchored and everything had been tidied away, I saw Dieter walk to the stern and dive in. He suddenly resurfaced screaming as if possessed, and trying to swim as fast as he could back to the boat. As he grabbed hold of the boarding ladder, I asked, 'What on earth happened?'

'I left my expensive hearing aids in. I hope they are not ruined.'

'I'm sorry, I know I asked you to wear them all the time, but I didn't mean in the water.'

Fortunately, after being rinsed in fresh water and dried in the sun they were saved. Both incidents joined the list of things that we often had a good laugh about, which wasn't all that difficult because Dieter has a really good sense of humour. That may be about the most important quality in any crew.

One other important lesson I have learned is not only to make sure that crew have understood an order, but also to check that they have actually carried it out, especially when the crew are new. I always try to do this as discreetly as possible. Most crew, especially if they are experienced, dislike people looking over the shoulder, so the captain has to be very careful not to upset them unnecessarily. On the other hand, not checking what a crew is doing or whether an order had been carried out can be just as bad, as I found out when sailing with a friend on Aventura III in Sweden. With an imminent gale approaching, we ran for shelter in a small port. I spotted a space alongside what looked like a home-built steel boat. As I eased Aventura alongside, a grinding noise made me fear the worst. My friend had failed to put out any fenders! Fortunately, Aventura's unpainted aluminium hull only suffered a few superficial scratches, but more damage was done to my friend's ego as he was an experienced sailor. The mistake I had made was to trust my crew to use his own initiative, rather than tell him specifically what to do.

Crew briefing

Crew briefing on the eve of the ARC start

Whenever new crew join me, they get a detailed briefing on all aspects of the boat and its running routine. However, my first priority on the crew's arrival is to take everyone out to dinner as this eases the atmosphere, no doubt helped by a glass or two of good wine. I feel that it is essential that this introductory meeting takes place on neutral ground, away from the distractions of the boat, because in such informal circumstances people seem to be more relaxed about discussing matters and they ask questions without inhibitions.

The following morning, I take the crew around the boat and explain everything in detail. Although both Aventura III and IV were very easy to handle once the sails were up, their deck layout was quite intricate, with dedicated lines and blocks all over the place, which for a newcomer could be quite bewildering. After dealing with the sailing side of things, we then discuss the engine, self-steering gear and autopilot. Safety comes next, followed by what to do or not to do if it comes to the worst and we have to abandon ship, so that everyone knows what role they have been assigned. Some hypothetical emergencies are also discussed, such as losing a crew overboard, the steering or the mast.

Perhaps the most important part of the briefing is left to the end, as it involves onboard routines. I regard enjoying a normal civilised life on passage as paramount, and always make sure that the crew know this by sending them in advance details of the meals and food generally. I also ask them to let me know their likes and dislikes, as well as possible allergies or special dietary requirements. Before doing the provisioning, I describe the kind of meals I intend to provide, and we then troop to the chosen supermarket. Once everything on the list has been chosen, I ask everyone to pick any special treats they might like. This approach hasn't always worked, and on three occasions, although the crew assured me before joining the boat that they were happy to eat whatever was available, I only found out when we went shopping together that they were much fussier than they had led me to believe. Two were quite choosy about what they ate, which I managed to make allowances for. The third was following a strict diet and also had an allergy to gluten, none of which he told me beforehand. Diet was only part of the problem, as his behaviour was quite unusual. We parted company at the first opportunity because I realised that his lifestyle would be incompatible with the rest of us on a long passage. Just as bad were two crew who had lied when I had asked them about smoking (which I don't approve

of on my boat), and only when I discovered cigarette-filter stubs on the aft deck did I realise that they must have been smoking on their night watch.

Initially, supermarket and other bills involving provisions were split equally between all of us, myself included. I soon realised that money matters could cause problems and decided to cover all the boat costs myself. I therefore pay for provisions, fuel, docking, any port fees and the cost of any spares or repairs. After all, I regard my crew as my personal guests, so why apply different rules at sea to those of guests to my house.

A happy crew makes a happy ship

Crew incidents

The most important attribute of a crew is congeniality.
Doug Decker

For many years I was convinced that bad experiences with crew only happened on other boats, but I was proven wrong soon after I stopped sailing with family members or old friends, and had to take on crew on certain voyages. Initially the incidents were not too serious and could easily be ignored, but when it came to unpleasant personality clashes, I realised that I was now as vulnerable to such situations as participants I had witnessed in the various rallies.

My very first lesson in the delicate field of human relationships happened right at the beginning of my sailing life. when I decided to take Aventura I across the English Channel on a shakedown cruise to Brittany. I had a crew of four, a friend who brought along two of his colleagues from the same London hospital, and Dominic, a neighbour whom I had met on a navigation course. As he was a carpenter, Dominic kindly offered to spend every free weekend doing the more difficult woodwork on Aventura that I was totally incapable of. His help was one of the reasons I managed to get that boat completed in such record time.

We had hardly made it into Brest's well-sheltered inner harbour when a violent storm broke over the area. The storm continued for several days with no sign of abating. Stuck in port in the confined space of a small boat and with no prospect of sailing soon, the situation became terribly testing. As the days passed, the three doctors drank and played cards all day long. The situation came to a head after another bout of cards and booze, when one of the doctors started blaming me for having ruined his long-awaited holiday. He was quite drunk and also so insulting that I couldn't take it any more.

'If that's how you feel, you should leave my boat immediately.'

As they had come together, they decided to leave together. My friend, who had brought his two colleagues along, apologised profusely, but I assured him that I understood, and that it would be better for him to go as well. After they had left, Dominic, who had witnessed all this in complete silence, turned to me and said, 'And they call themselves educated people?'

Watch systems

Over the years I have worked out a watch system that I consider particularly suited to boats with a crew of two or three. Throughout our first voyage Gwenda and I were very disciplined in keeping night watches, although it wasn't always easy. We were often tired, but as the children grew up they would take an afternoon watch together so we could catch up on sleep. They could be trusted and always called one of us if they thought it necessary. In those days we only had the Aries windvane, so whenever the winds were too light or we were motoring we had to steer by hand. As I had other jobs to do, and often did a longer night watch, Gwenda generously took the larger share during the day, and I hate to think of the many hours she spent perched on her seat trying to keep the boat on course while fighting hard not to fall asleep. An autopilot of any kind would have turned our life from beautiful into perfect.

Night watches started after the evening meal at 8pm local time. As I can easily go to sleep at any time, and usually do so the moment my head hits the pillow, I went to sleep first. If Gwenda could stay awake until midnight, she would let me sleep until then, those blissful four hours being so restful that I rarely had to call her again. I had another sleep in the day, usually while Gwenda switched from mate to teacher, and supervised the children's daily schoolwork.

The prospect of the person on watch falling asleep is a serious concern for me when sailing with friends, but not with Gwenda as I can never remember her doing this. She has an incredible ability to stay awake however tired she may be. During the long years while we were waiting for permission to get married, Gwenda regularly commuted by car between England and Romania. We once worked out that over a period of five years she had done that trip across Europe in each direction on 17 occasions. To complete the 3,000km journey in the shortest time possible, she would drive for 14 hours a day, only allowing herself two overnight stops. One of her worst trips was in the spring of 1968, when she had nine-month-old Doina with her, who slept while she drove but woke up and became active and demanding once they stopped, just when Gwenda was yearning for some rest.

I continued the same routine when sailing with other crew, by starting night watches usually at 8pm and ending them at 8am, with day watches being more flexible.

Whenever possible, I try to get the last dawn watch as I never tire of sunrises at sea. This way I can let the off-watch crew sleep in the morning until they wake up on their own. If there are only two of us sailing, the night is divided into four three-hour periods, so that we each have two night watches. Whenever I am joined by new crew, I explain the system, and ask if they find it acceptable. Occasionally, less experienced crew ask to have the watch reduced to two hours, as they find three hours on their own too long on an unknown boat, but we usually revert to three-hour watches when they realise that a two-hour sleep is rarely sufficient.

On a few occasions, I had an inexperienced crew who became frightened when they realised where they were, on a dark night on a nutshell in the middle of a vast ocean, which they would be unable to leave for many more days. If I noticed this kind of anxiety or the crew mentioned it, and if there were three of us, I doubled the watch so that the two crews would stand watches together for three hours, while I covered the rest.

My worst experience of such a situation happened while I was sailing with a friend from Saint Lucia to the Dominican Republic. One morning he confessed that, when he realised we were passing Puerto Rico by only some 15 miles, he was caught by a sudden attack of panic, shivering uncontrollably and being terrified that he might die. He was so desperate that he was about to call Puerto Rico Coast Guard on the VHF radio and ask to be evacuated. Fortunately he got himself under control, calmed down and finished his watch. He said nothing at the change of watch, but told me everything over breakfast and apologised profusely. We are still good friends, and that night off Puerto Rico was never mentioned again. He was just the kind of person to be able to bring himself under control, because he is normally calm and composed. He also has a great sense of humour and was helplessly laughing at his bout of irrationality.

My friend's experience taught me to be more careful with fresh crew, especially when left to do a night watch on their own. My niece Marianne, who sailed with me from Tahiti to Hawaii, expressed the same kind of feeling, and admitted that she was sick with fear when sitting alone in the cockpit at night, being overcome by the vastness of the surrounding ocean and the immensity of the starry sky above. Gwenda shares this general anxiety when she is sailing offshore, and it is this feeling of uneasiness that probably explains her dislike of long passages, rather than her complaint about the boredom of spending a long time at sea. I find it quite strange to be anxious when, for me, this is the most exhilarating part of offshore sailing: the feeling of being on your own small boat, far away from everything, and in total control of your fate.

Night watches

The off-watch crew sleeps in his bunk; the on-watch crew sleeps in the cockpit.

Thomas Hahn

Falling asleep on night watch is a common occurrence, but few people are prepared to admit it. With the boat gliding along effortlessly, the gentle movement can be a powerful soporific. Occasionally I have dozed off myself, but fortunately I always wake up, with a start, after a few minutes. Whenever it happens, I make myself a coffee, walk around, check the sails and do my best to keep awake. While singlehanding from Panama to Ecuador with Aventura III, I set the radar alarm at 6 miles and the alarm clock to ring every 20 minutes, but usually I managed to wake up before the clock sounded. I had at least two incidents that I know of when my crew had fallen asleep. The first occasion occurred during an Atlantic crossing on Aventura III, when we were caught by a squall with the spinnaker up, as described on page 131.

On the other occasion, I was off-watch and fast asleep below, and probably quite relaxed as it was a quiet night, when I woke up suddenly with a distinct feeling that something was wrong. I rushed into the cockpit, where my crew was happily snoring in a corner. Abeam of us, a large yellow ship with lights blazing was ploughing through the swell at over 20 knots, going in the same direction as us. My heart almost stopped as I estimated that a mere 30 metres separated us from disaster. Everything happened so quickly that by the time my crew was fully awake the ship was already well ahead of us. I realised that with our masthead light showing and Aventura's aluminium hull giving a good radar signal, the officer on watch had obviously seen us, altered course slightly and passed at a safe distance. I was furious but managed not to say anything, and the matter was not mentioned again. My friend was such an experienced sailor that there was no need to dwell on such a fundamental error.

What woke me up? I have no idea, but Gwenda is convinced that I have a sixth sense. Occasionally I get a sudden feeling that something is wrong, and I can usually sense from the movement of the boat that the sails need to be trimmed or reefed. I sometimes wake up seemingly for no reason, and almost every time the reason soon becomes apparent. Twice I woke up suddenly on Aventura IV when I sensed that something was not right. The first time, as I walked towards the cockpit I smelt diesel fuel, and realised that the crew on watch had left on the pump filling the day tank, and had failed to turn it off when the tank was full. The fibreglass tank had cracked, and all the fuel had poured into the bilge. I found my crew in the cockpit watching a film on his tablet. At the next stop, the tank was replaced with an aluminium one, but this incident should not have happened.

On the other occasion, I was woken by a change in the sound of the engine. As I rushed to the cockpit, I heard the temperature alarm sound, but it was too late. As there was no wind, we had been motoring and rolling badly in the lumpy sea. At some point, we must have rolled over so much that the seawater intake had drawn in air. As a result, the engine overheated, and the seawater pump impeller was damaged and had to be replaced.

Gwenda once remarked jokingly how some of her subliminal messages miraculously seemed to get through to me while she was on watch. Just as she was thinking that she needed to call me, I would pop up in the cockpit. But I put this down simply to my being so much in tune with my boat that I detect even the smallest changes in its behaviour.

Off watch

Being able to have a proper rest between watches is of utmost importance, especially on a long passage. When drawing up a watch system, it is crucial to ensure that everyone has a period of uninterrupted deep sleep. It has been established that deep sleep is a state of nearly complete disengagement from the environment, and its main function is to restore us physically and mentally. Many important physiological processes occur during deep sleep, and there are various psychological benefits. It is believed that deep sleep is the most refreshing part of the sleep cycle, and it is very difficult to awaken a person from it. Those who are woken out of it abruptly may feel sluggish and confused, and I remember it happening to some crew who took minutes to wake up properly. Without a period of deep sleep, a person may feel physically rested, but not mentally. This is when wrong decisions may be taken in emergency situations, and for this reason it is essential to ensure that no one is deprived of adequate deep sleep.

After I read about this phenomenon, I amended my watch routine on long passages to allow everyone an undisturbed sleep of at least four hours in each 24-hour period. When sailing with two experienced crew, we each take a three-hour watch, and thus get a six-hour rest period. I have also found that rotating watches is not advisable, and a fixed night-watch rota helps sustain a regular sleep pattern.

Dunbar enjoying the view after the storm

Night rules

There were some firm rules on all my boats, and first among them was for the crew not to leave the cockpit for any reason whatsoever without calling me. If the weather was settled I would not insist on wearing harnesses and let this to be a personal choice, as I considered the cockpit to be very well protected. Urinating over the side was completely forbidden, even in daytime, and I insisted not only that men use the toilet at all times, but also that they sit down. Both Aventura III and IV had a second toilet right next to the companionway, which was easy to reach in the dark without disturbing the rest of the crew.

Two other night rules I started imposing only of late: no reading and no listening to music. To be able to read you need a light, and that impairs your night vision. Crew reading on watch would occasionally put down the book or, more often, the tablet to have a look around, but I suspected this break to be too short for their night vision to be restored. Being able to see well at night was so important, not just for spotting other ships, but also to check the sails, sheets and that the hydro-generator had not been fouled with seaweed, etc, that I believed this admittedly unpopular rule to be justified.

I felt just as strongly that not being able to hear was similarly unacceptable. Being shut off from any outside sound can be dangerous, and having radar or AIS is not enough. There are many sounds on a boat that can foretell an impending problem, such as a flapping sail, a loose sheet, a strange sound from the autopilot or the engine if motoring, whales blowing nearby, and many others. Also, the faint sound of an engine, which can travel a long way through the water, can indicate a ship somewhere in the vicinity.

Cooking and washing up

Delegating cooking on Aventura was never a problem because I enjoy cooking at sea and I am happy to prepare all meals, as that also puts me in better control of the provisions. Also, I am quite fussy and would get annoyed by the mess that some crew created in the galley when they volunteered to cook, so that by the time a meal was ready to be served, empty dishes, various utensils and ingredients were spread all over the place. This is because people who are used to large kitchens with generous surfaces seem unable to adapt to a compact galley. When I cook, I normally put ingredients or utensils back in their place after using, and wash some of the dishes that have been used, so that by the time I am ready to serve the meal the galley looks orderly.

I have candidly described in this chapter, and also elsewhere in this book, some of my personal experiences with crew, not only because I believed them to be significant or relevant, but also because I don't want to give the impression that I never had crew problems. The few that I had, I regard as exceptions. As with everything else in my life, I have been lucky in this respect.

Tips

» Do not take on crew that you do not know well.
» On long passages there should be at least one competent crew who can stand in for the captain in an emergency.

Tips

» It is always advisable to part company with a difficult crew early, rather than hope that matters might improve.
» Never trust a new crew until they have proven themselves.
» New crew should be briefed on all onboard routines as well as on emergency procedures. This should be done before setting off on an offshore passage.
» All financial arrangements should be agreed in advance and, if necessary, set down in writing.
» The captain should send crew joining during the voyage a covering letter, stating that they are joining the boat and giving their personal details. Such a letter, or a return ticket, may be requested when checking in at the airport of departure, or by immigration on arrival.
» Make sure that the crew have booked flexible airline tickets for their return voyage so they can be changed if a passage takes longer than expected.
» Instruct joining crew to bring their belongings in soft bags, as hard luggage may be difficult to stow.
» Caution should be exercised if taking on paying guests because such operations may infringe local laws, and may also invalidate your insurance.

21

Sailing as a family

A cruising family is like a pioneer or explorer family; they must be self-sufficient, independent and creative.

Saundra Gray

Having enjoyed six wonderful years in the closest companionship with Gwenda and our two children, Doina and Ivan, on our first voyage, we continue this happy relationship to this day, so no wonder that I consider the family unit as the ideal set-up on a long voyage. Indeed there are plenty of similar examples, but among those that stand out among my sailing friends are Erick and Muriel Bouteleux, who sailed with their children on Calao; the three generations on Duen, on which Albert and Dottie Fletcher, their children and grandchildren spent 14 incredible years travelling around the world; and Arthur and Germaine Beiser, who continued to sail into their eighties, as they have done for the previous 60 years.

Although most of my comments on this aspect of cruising come from my personal experience, I have learned countless valuable lessons from participants in my various rallies, which always attracted couples sailing either on their own or with their children. In recent years this has become a much more common phenomenon, as young families decide to give their children the chance to see this world before it is too late. It was a father in his early thirties who told me recently why he had decided to put his successful professional life on hold, buy a state-of-the art yacht and leave on an indefinite voyage with his wife and two young daughters. He reminded me of my own decision all those years ago, and he was not the only one.

I always prefer to let figures tell their own story, so, looking at the total of 70 boats that took part in the three transatlantic rallies that I organised in 2016, 61 boats were sailed by couples with or without crew. Among the 61 boats, 20 couples sailed on their own and 20 with their children. Among the latter, eight sailed just with their children while 12 also had additional crew. There were a total of 43 children under 18, with several older

children sailing with their parents, including a couple sailing with their three daughters, all in their twenties. There were also three grandfathers sailing with their sons or daughters and grandchildren to lend a hand for the Atlantic crossing, including an 81-year-old man accompanying his son and daughter-in-law. Cruising is undoubtedly a family affair.

Decision to go

Twenty years from now, you will be more disappointed by the things that you didn't do than by the ones you did do. So throw off the bowlines. Sail away from the safe harbour. Catch the trade winds in your sails. Explore. Dream. Discover.

Mark Twain

The decision to go can have such an important bearing on one's life that I decided not to limit its discussion just to my personal experience, but to bring in the comments and advice of other sailors faced with the same dilemma. Indeed, the decision to turn one's back on shore life in favour of a life at sea can put an enormous strain on a marriage, and even some of the most harmonious relationships may end up being seriously affected. I have come across such examples among participants in my various rallies, and occasionally have been asked to advise on how to reach a mutually acceptable solution. All too often the initial idea to go sailing comes from the man, and there is no doubt that the urge to explore, the love of adventure and the desire to pit oneself against the forces of nature are very much male characteristics. In my own case, it was my desire to see the world in my own boat that made me take my family along. I was very fortunate that Gwenda had a keen spirit of adventure and had always liked travelling, so my task of persuading her to throw in everything and set off into the blue was not too difficult.

From what I observed in later years, Gwenda was quite exceptional, and many women whom I met sailing with their partners were doing it more or less reluctantly. Some were bold enough to admit that it was the price they paid to save their marriage. There were also husbands who, while not being prepared to abandon their dream, were equally determined to preserve their marriage, so they managed to work out a solution that satisfied both parties. In most cases it meant sailing the long passages with friends or hired crew, to be joined by their wife for the more relaxed cruising stages. Almost invariably, this proved to be a workable solution, and I met several cruising couples happily sailing around the world in this way. In each of the round-the-world rallies there were some wives who preferred to follow their husband by flying from place to place, so avoiding the longer passages. Occasionally, even the best will in the world cannot overcome a partner's unwillingness to compromise, and I cannot think of a better example than that of an Australian participant in the Millennium Odyssey who, on reading about that round-the-world rally, told his wife that he would very much like to do it. The wife objected vehemently, but he refused to be swayed.

'I have spent my entire life being a responsible family man, but now the children have grown up, we are well off and so I feel it is time that I do something for myself.' To which the wife retorted, 'It's either the boat or me.'

'In that case, I am sorry, but it's the boat!' And off he went.

There are some exceptional stories that I have come across, the most remarkable being that of a woman whom I met in Tahiti. All his life her husband had dreamed of going cruising, and as he was nearing retirement he started building his dream boat. Unfortunately his untimely death brought that dream to a cruel end, but determined not to abandon her husband's long nurtured dream, his wife decided to complete the building of the boat. When I met her, she and her teenage son were in the second year of their voyage, her husband's dream having become her own.

Never have I come across a better example of sheer determination to go against the odds than that of an ARC participant in his seventies who had been warned by his doctor not to risk an Atlantic crossing because of his heart condition. Undeterred by this, he continued with his preparations, but then had a skiing accident and this time his doctor insisted that he call off his voyage. 'If you are so concerned about the state of my health,' he told his family doctor, 'then you, the cardiologist and the orthopaedic surgeon must come along, because I am definitely going!' And so he did, being accompanied on his large yacht by several children and grandchildren as well as three doctors.

Facing reality

The most important and difficult action is putting your dream into practice. The highlights arrive by themselves.

Klaus Girzig

A better title for the previous subject might have been 'the decision to go and continue going', as unfortunately some voyages come to a premature end when one or the other partner decides that this is not the kind of life he or she is prepared to live. The importance of having a good relationship is a major factor, and one should never start off on a voyage if one has any doubts about the strength of one's relationship. For many people the cruising life can be a cruel eye-opener, making them realise that they hardly knew their partner. This particularly applies when the couple have both had demanding careers ashore, and have only spent a few hours a day together. Living 24/7 in close proximity can have an effect on any relationship, and one woman observed cynically that life afloat was very good at pulling people apart. The most telling example was a couple sailing in one of my round-the-world rallies. Both had had successful professional careers, and once their children had grown up they decided to leave on a long voyage, just the two of them. But after only two months their relationship reached crisis point, and both agreed to bring the voyage to an end. They were very distressed by this outcome and spoke to me separately of their painful decision. Each stressed that while still in love and with no intention of separating, they simply could not stand being together 24 hours a day. Therefore they decided to return home and resume their previous life.

I had come across similar examples in the past, and in most cases a mutual agreement was reached for the husband to continue the voyage and for the wife to return home, rejoining him occasionally as the voyage progressed. It may not have been the case in the example I described, but often the passive role played by some women in the initial decision lead to problems later on, endangering not just the continuation of the voyage but the relationship itself.

I have been fortunate in being able to count on Gwenda's support throughout my life but, of late, even her boundless tolerance seems to have been exhausted. The decision to build Aventura II caused no problems between us because I was not planning to set off on a long voyage. However I did end up doing a circumnavigation as part of the first round-the-world rally, dictated primarily by the convenience (or excuse) of providing a floating base for our staff. When Aventura III came along, and from the way she was equipped, Gwenda realised that I had some serious voyaging in mind. She was very clear in letting me know not to count on her full participation, which I understood and accepted. As a result, she did not accompany me on the trip to Antarctica, but when Ivan and I continued the transpacific voyage to Alaska, Gwenda joined us in Easter Island and sailed all the way to Tahiti, and later cruised with us in Alaska and British Columbia. We had the same arrangement during Aventura III's subsequent round-the-world voyage, when Gwenda missed most ocean passages but joined me on all cruising stages. It was a win-win situation and the ultimate credit for its success goes to Gwenda, who accepted that I was a lost cause and, as I would never get the sailing bug out of my system, she might as well live with it. The main reason why Gwenda did not join me for the trip to Antarctica was that she does not like the cold. Aventura IV's Arctic challenge attracted her even less, although she agreed to join me in the Bahamas and Florida. But when my Arctic voyage had come to a successful end, I finally had to accept that the game was up and pay Gwenda the due she overwhelmingly deserved, and in March 2017 Aventura was sold.

Christmas lunch in the Bahamas

Some of the sailors I interviewed tried to bring a dose of realism into the argument, such as Glynn Beauchamp, who pointed out that passage making can be exhausting and even boring at times. In some cases, couples decided to take on crew to help handle the boat on long passages. This worked for some, but not for others. As Anne Harsh commented, 'Our first thought was that an extra crew was a desirable safety factor on long passages in case of bad weather, illness, etc. Having made many long passages with just the two of us, we decided that it was not really necessary and we now agree that sailing alone as a couple is preferable because we found that the crew can often be lonely and ends up feeling the odd person out.'

Ideal age

There is no ideal age but I know that if at all possible the best time is now as tomorrow may be too late.

Jimmy Cornell

Although I made that statement many years ago, I still stand by it, because I know of several recent examples that have only reinforced its validity. Many of the round-the-world rallies attract retired sailors in their sixties who finally seize the opportunity to do something that they had not been able to do during their busy lives. In the Millennium Odyssey we had three owners who were diagnosed with prostate cancer within months of each other. They all had to return home for treatment while their crews, with help from sailors on other rally boats, continued the voyage. Two of them rejoined the rally later, while the third could only attend the final ceremony in Rome. They all admitted how happy they were to have been able to do it, but also how much they regretted not having done it earlier. 'Whatever you do, and whenever you decide to go, don't leave it too late' – more words of wisdom, from Carlton DeHart.

Although there may not be an ideal age, in hindsight, our own decision to leave on our world

voyage at 35 was probably right, as both Gwenda and I were in good physical shape, and the age of our children also fitted in well into our six-year-long voyage.

I continued sailing into my seventies, and intend to be active as long as possible. As I have gotten older, I have noticed that some of my friends and acquaintances have started behaving like older people, as if this were expected of them. I remember reading a remark on the subject of aging made by a psychologist, who wondered whether people are getting slower because they are getting older, or are they getting older because they are getting slower? In my case, I prefer to believe the latter.

Cruising couples

A boat is not the place to fix anything wrong with a relationship, whether it is with a partner, a child or a friend. If someone irritates you ashore, they will irritate you more on a boat. Some people are not emotionally geared for life aboard. They are not wrong or misfits, they are just not boat people.

Saundra Gray

Saundra has sailed for many years with her husband Charlie; they have cruised with their children, and took part in both America 500 and the Millennium Odyssey.

Saundra and Charlie Grey

Saundra and Charlie are one of the most exceptional cruising couples that I have met, and their comments and advice to other sailors stand out for their realism and common sense. Although earlier I highlighted some of the problems that may beset cruising couples, I must stress that there are many more happy stories. Among the most remarkable couples that I have met are Bob and Judy Hall, Betty and Duke Marx, and Lois and Don Babson, who all, just like Saundra and Charlie, sailed in both America 500 and the Millennium Odyssey. Therefore our friendship stretches to more than 25 years, during which time we have shared many enjoyable moments. They are examples of perfect sailing couples. In Judy's words, 'We love sailing together and have a wonderful, close, loving relationship.' Lois and Don Babson, who also sailed in the Millennium Odyssey, commented, 'We sail as a couple and are happy with our closeness while cruising.'

Another good example of an enduring relationship is that of John and Amanda Neal, who sailed many thousands of miles teaching seamanship and navigation to their students. Erick and Muriel Bouteleux also have outstanding longevity, as do Arthur and Germaine Beiser, who have kept sailing well into their eighties.

Asked to advise other couples planning to embark on a similar life, Germaine sounded a note of realism. 'One should never start off on such a voyage unless you already get on well with each other ashore.'

Arthur and Germaine Beiser

Marcia Davock stressed that in certain situations women have a greater capacity for endurance than men, while Saundra Gray admitted that there were occasions when she didn't find it easy to cope when there were just the two of them. 'We enjoy being alone on the boat but on long passages, especially during rough weather, it is nice to have extra experienced hands. However, there can be problems with additional crew as the relationship between people changes when others are introduced into the equation.'

Lack of sailing experience combined with the anxiety associated with a long passage can have serious consequences, as in the case of two fathers who admitted being extremely worried about their responsibilities towards their families. One of them arrived in the Caribbean mentally and physically exhausted, having stayed awake for the last few nights due to his apprehension about the impending landfall. The other sailor also expressed his disillusionment as he had been looking for peace at sea, but the only thing he had found was anxiety. He was therefore determined to give up the voyage at the earliest opportunity. This was a painful realisation for someone who had dreamt for 30 years about such a voyage but had never considered the practicalities of this dream. It was ironic that his wife, who admitted having been reluctantly dragged along on the voyage because of his dream, had come to love the cruising life and was very reluctant to give it up. This was the kind of outcome suggested by Paulette Vannette in the advice given to husbands: 'Make sure she loves the sea and not only you.'

A former racing enthusiast, who joined one of our round-the-world rallies with his wife upon his retirement, informed me two months after the start that he was not able to continue because he was exhausted both physically and mentally. He admitted that while off watch on long passages he could not sleep, as he did not trust his wife to be able to even deal with the simplest task on her own. This feeling of anxiety was even more pronounced in her case, as she was very concerned that if something happened to him she would be unable to handle the boat by herself, to navigate or deal with any breakages. They eventually agreed that the only solution was to abandon the voyage and have their boat shipped home.

I have had to deal with this kind of painful situation on several occasions, so have realised that often women are reluctant to admit their doubts or shortcomings so as not to spoil or even jeopardise their partner's long-nurtured dream.

At a seminar on voyage preparation held in France, I was taken to task by an older man in the audience for the fact that in my comments I appeared to regard wives differently from ordinary crew. 'I cannot see any difference; on my boat I regard my wife as crew.'
'I disagree, and I have the feeling that your wife may

disagree too,' I replied. 'In my experience, husbands ought to have a different kind of relationship with their spouse than with their crew, be it their friends or just acquaintances.'

His wife, who was sitting by his side, looked embarrassed during this exchange, and came to see me on her own during the next interval.
'I'd like to apologise for what happened, but he has always raced just with friends. We haven't been married for long and he seems incapable of accepting that cruising with me is not the same thing. He will soon retire and is keen to leave on a big voyage, but I have absolutely no desire to go.'

A few days later I was at a boat show, where I met another couple that had been at the same seminar. Later that day the wife came to see me on her own and asked me to visit the boat they had ordered because it was exhibited at the show.
'Please come, as you may be able to persuade my husband to order a backup autopilot. As we shall be sailing our own, I am very worried that if the autopilot breaks we'll have to steer by hand. For some reason he won't do it, but I know that he respects you and I am sure you could persuade him.'

I did; and both these examples only reinforced a view I have held for most of my life: that men are often their own worst enemies.

When I started running a new series of more family-orientated rallies, one of the first features I introduced at the preparatory seminars was a women-only session. Such closed meetings gave the women the opportunity to express freely their own views, doubts and concerns. It was an instant success, and such sessions are now being held regularly. From what I have been told, a wide range of concerns are being raised: being able to handle the transition from a comfortable life ashore to an uncertain one afloat; being alone on night watch, or in heavy weather, and concerns with safety generally; worries about not getting on when they are living together for 24 hours a day; concerns about ageing parents or being away from the family, children and especially grandchildren. Another major concern was the risk of selling up, spending everything to go cruising, and not having a secure base to return to, or of being forced to return home sooner than planned.

Labour division

Some of our roles are shared and some are not, each of us doing what we like best or do best.

Judy Hall

The sharing of responsibilities is a crucial ingredient in a harmonious relationship, and a fair division of labour is as important on land as it is at sea. During the first summer on Aventura I, we agreed that it made more sense for Gwenda to steer the boat, while I, being stronger, would handle the lines, docking and anchoring. Gradually Gwenda became very efficient at handling the boat, and we kept this system throughout that voyage, although we rarely saw it on other boats. While in Fiji we met Susan and Eric Hiscock, and among many other things discussed over dinner on our boat, Susan made some sharp comments on this very subject. 'Men are simply just macho. They want to be seen to be in control.' Indeed, I have witnessed many situations where a burly male shouted instructions from the wheel while his tiny wife struggled with a huge anchor or tried to fend the boat off the dock. This reminded me of an older sailor's advice to fellow captains: 'Don't be too hard on her. You wouldn't be the first man who finished the voyage as a singlehander!' The subject of labour division interested me so much that I returned to it in a later survey. Whereas the earlier surveys showed that women were usually cast in a secondary, passive role, according to this later survey tasks were designated more according to ability than to the traditional roles that still seem to dominate shore life.

'As the female, I handle provisioning, communications, navigation, stand watches and steer the boat during emergencies when male strength is needed on deck,' commented Judy Hall.

Sailing children

A sailor's joys are as simple as a child's.

Bernard Moitessier

Indeed, many cruising children seem to enjoy their peripatetic life more than some adults. At the start of our first voyage, Doina was seven and Ivan five, so they could take an active part in sailing and also be old enough to appreciate the places we visited. On our return, Ivan was 11 and Doina nearly 14, which, in her case, was probably one or two years beyond the best age for this kind of life. I once asked Doina to comment on this subject, and she pointed out that reintegration can be the most difficult problem faced by a child who has been away from shore life for a long time. 'The problem wasn't so much me having difficulty in adapting to life ashore, but other children not being able to accept me because I was so very different to them. It was just as hard for Ivan. Some children can be very cruel.'

As children are by nature very adaptable, even the very young seem to have no difficulty in coping with life on a moving boat. Over the years I have met a number of children who were born during their parents' voyage and who grew up successfully in this environment. As we found out ourselves, the difficulties only started when Doina reached puberty, and showed that teenagers can be as much of a problem afloat as ashore.

Although our experience of bringing up children on a boat was quite successful, I have come across several examples that would not fit that description. In every case the fault lay squarely with the parents, who were either too lax or who never thought seriously about what was best for their child. One such example was a young child of between one and two who sailed with his parents in one of the round-the-world rallies. The parents were of the 'let the child grow up without any constraints or inhibitions' persuasion, and as a result the little boy had not been potty trained, so he was always walking around with a bare bottom, or completely naked, which caused raised eyebrows in several of the places the rally visited.

A few of the children I met were spoilt and ill-behaved, and usually as inconsiderate as their parents. By far the worst were boys in their mid or late teens, who were obviously frustrated by not having the company of their peers, which is so important at that age. Usually these were also the children whose education had been neglected by their parents, either because they could not be bothered, or because not having had an education themselves, they found dealing with it beyond their capability. The main disadvantage for such children is that they don't learn to socialise with groups of other children as they would in school.

The above examples were clearly the exception, and we have met many more families who had brought up their children successfully. One of those parents believed that, 'The pros outweigh the cons by such a large measure that the cons don't really count. Children on a boat learn how to entertain themselves with reading, crafts and schoolwork in a way that kids in school with a TV at home could never equal. They learn how to find information in books, which benefits them for the rest of their lives, how to make friends quickly, and how to interact with adults when other children are not around. They get to see their parents making difficult decisions.'

This ability that cruising children have to entertain and look after themselves was brought home to me when I came out of a seminar at the Tenerife yacht club and found all the rally children quietly absorbed in various activities while their parents were attending the seminars in the next room.

Saundra Gray, who had cruised with her own children, had seen 'Some very successful parenting aboard boats and some that didn't seem to be working out so well, not far different from land-based parents. Much maturity on the part of both partners must be exercised to make a cruising lifestyle workable with children.'

Children growing up on a cruising boat are normally self-confident and, if guided in the right direction, will grow up successfully. At our dinner table the main topic of conversation was usually politics, which is not

Swimming

surprising with a journalist father fed on daily doses of BBC news, to which we all listened regularly. One other major topic was the culture and the people of the country we happened to be visiting. From those often-heated discussions, Doina and Ivan learned to express their own opinions, and even now, some 40 years later, a family dinner at the Cornells is never a quiet affair.

Children from visiting boats playing happily with pupils from an orphanage in the Cape Verde Islands

Our rallies attract many more parents with young children than in the recent past. What is remarkable is how much the children enjoy meeting other children in the countries visited. Because of this, we have made a point of arranging meetings between youngsters in our rallies and local children. The visits are always extremely successful, and it is quite remarkable how quickly children can make friends even if they don't speak the same language.

While spending the cyclone season in Papua New Guinea, we witnessed a terrible tragedy on a neighbouring boat, where an unattended toddler had fallen in the water and drowned. Ever since Doina and Ivan were small, we had made an effort to teach them to swim, and once we started sailing it became much easier. Finally, by the time we got to Bequia in the Caribbean, Ivan managed to swim around the boat

unaided, and got a big prize for his achievement. I used the same incentive for our granddaughter Nera, who impressed us all when she managed to swim the entire length of the boat, although the water was quite cold and, from her expression, it was clear that she was scared. But she persevered and made it as far as the anchor chain. I was quite impressed by such determination and willpower in a six-year old. No doubt she takes after her mother, as Doina was always a good swimmer. Diving for shells was Doina and Ivan's favourite activity while we were in the tropics, and while in New Zealand Doina won the school swimming championship. On her return to England, Doina decided to join a diving club, which in those days was a very male-dominated activity. The instructor told her that she would only be accepted if she could show that she could swim underwater. Doina dived into the pool, swam its entire length under water, and when she surfaced at the far end, shouted across, 'Will that do?' It was just the kind of lesson the instructor and his macho mates deserved.

Rally children visiting a school on arrival in Barbados

Education afloat

As part of Doina and Ivan's education, whenever we arrived in a new place, Gwenda would not only read to them about its history, but would also make a quick research trip to a nearby site or museum. She would then compile two worksheets, which the children had to complete as part of their schoolwork. We spent that first summer in Greece, when Doina was eight and Ivan six, and our frequent visits to historic sites nurtured in them an interest in Greek mythology and ancient history, which Doina has kept to this day. Shortly after our arrival in Iraklion, the capital of Crete, we had visited the Minoan remains at Knossos. In the ancient labyrinth beneath the Royal Palace, Gwenda read out the legend of the Minotaur, the unique setting so impressing Doina and Ivan that they never forgot that special day. In Iraklion Gwenda had set her sights on the museum of antiquities, which houses the best frescos retrieved from Knossos, skilfully displayed to great effect on the museum walls. One day, about two hours before closing time, she took the children to the museum, where they started completing their worksheets. The questions were not difficult, but were meant to make them look properly at the items on display.

'Where was the fresco with dolphins located?' Ivan: in the Queen's bathroom.
'Why were the ancient Cretans so scared of the Minotaur and what did they associate it with?' Doina: earthquakes.

The children were busy copying some of the frescos when one of the museum attendants told them that it was closing time, and they had to leave the museum. At this, both of them started crying and saying they didn't want to go. Not knowing what to do, the attendant called her boss.
'What wonderful children you have,' he told Gwenda. 'We've had plenty of children crying in the museum, but never when being asked to leave.'

Gwenda took her job very seriously, and unless the weather was really bad, school was never missed. I only contributed one subject and that was navigation. If they worked hard while at sea, Doina and Ivan were given time off while in port, which they highly appreciated. Gwenda's work paid dividends as both children fitted easily back into the British system upon our return, and finished their schooling with good exam results. Our six-year-long voyage does not seem to have greatly affected their education because both children went on to university in London, Doina to study international history at the London School of Economics, and Ivan computer science at University College London.

As part of the preparation for our voyage, Gwenda had qualified as a teacher and taught in a London school for two years in order to be able to deal with our children's education, which she did very successfully. For parents who are planning to leave on a longer voyage with school-age children, there are various options, depending on the country of origin. Australia, Canada, New Zealand, Great Britain and the USA are among the countries that have programmes developed initially for children in isolated rural locations. France has CNED (Centre national d'enseignement à distance), the National Centre for Distance Education. Among the many curricula for home education on offer, it is wise to choose one that is similar to those used in local schools, so as to make reintegration into the standard school system easier when the time comes.

Forty years later and nothing has changed

22

Chasing a dream

Every voyage starts as a dream, and dreams are often inspired by a book. When I first read An Island to Oneself by Tom Neale I could only fantasise that one day I would step ashore at Suwarrow, an uninhabited atoll halfway between Tahiti and Samoa. As it lies off the traditional route, a visit to Suwarrow entails a long detour, and so on both my previous trips through the area I missed the chance to stop there. This time, however, I was determined to follow up a 40-year-old dream, and so on leaving Bora Bora I laid a course for distant Suwarrow, 680 miles away in the Northern Cooks.

After several weeks of easy sailing among the Society Islands, I was looking forward to a longer offshore passage and had promised Gwenda some nice trade winds... but, once again, I was wrong. Two days out of Bora Bora, the western horizon turned into a menacing dark mass and I knew that we were in for a hiding. The area between French Polynesia and Tonga is known for its unsettled weather, and in my previous passages through this area I had experienced some of the worst conditions I had met anywhere in the Pacific. The culprit is the South Pacific Convergence Zone, a meteorological phenomenon that affects weather conditions in a swathe that stretches all the way from the Solomons to Tahiti. Its position and movement are updated by the Fiji meteorological office in its daily broadcasts.

As the system got closer, we were swept by a series of violent squalls, accompanied by black clouds shaped like gigantic anvils, which were rent apart by forked tongues of lightning straight out of the Apocalypse. Reefed right down, we managed to avoid the worst by slaloming between those monsters, then the wind dropped and there was an eerie lull before the heavens opened with a deluge of solid water that could hardly be described as rain. By the following morning it was all over, the sun came out, the sea turned blue, flying fish were once again streaking over the wave tops, and Aventura was sauntering merrily towards our destination with a light wind humming sweetly in the rigging.

A week in Suwarrow

On the morning of day five, a smudge on the horizon slowly transformed into a bristling line of palm trees, then into a small island, then into a whole string of them: Suwarrow!

We sailed through the pass into the sparkling lagoon, passed Anchorage Island and dropped anchor among nine other boats sheltering in this idyllic spot. Suwarrow is a typical Pacific atoll and was named after the Russian military hero General Alexander Suvorov by the Russian explorer who first set eyes on it. The spelling has undergone several versions and seems to have settled on the present Suwarrow.

The eight-mile-wide lagoon is surrounded by a reef, studded with a dozen small islands. Tom Neale had made his home on Anchorage Island, where he lived a truly Robinson Crusoe existence, fishing in the abundant lagoon, growing vegetables and breeding chickens, some of whose descendants still roam his island. After Tom's death in 1977, Suwarrow returned to its previous solitude. It was occasionally visited by itinerant fishermen or a fisheries patrol boat, but the only people who spent any time there were cruising sailors. Eventually, the Cook Islands government declared Suwarrow Atoll a nature reserve, and had a caretaker posted there during the cruising season from May until October. However, cruising boats continue to be welcomed without any restrictions. The special affection in which Suwarrow is held by sailors is shown by the various plaques and mementos that have been left there over the years. Some thoughtful soul had nailed a sign to a coconut tree: 'Take but nothing leave but footprints', while one of the most famous of all Pacific wanderers, Frenchman Bernard Moitessier, who was a frequent visitor, left his own memento made from a slab of coral that reads: 'Tom Neale lived his dream on this island 1952-1977.'

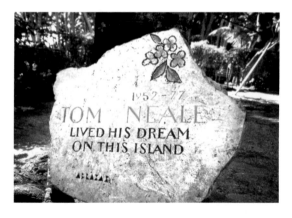

Next to Tom's original wooden house, the Cook Islands government has erected a solid hurricane shelter, known as the yacht club and decorated with flags from visiting yachts. It was also the home of the current caretakers, Ioane Kaitara, or Papa John as he was affectionately called by everyone, and his assistant Mareko Leikal, nicknamed Baker. They made us feel really welcome and asked us to sign the visitors' book, in which I counted an average 50 boats per year. I then paid the mandatory 50 dollars that covered our entire

stay – however long we wanted it to be. Never have formalities been simpler! Both caretakers were in their seventies and quite obviously enjoyed the presence of all those sailors, some of whom lingered on for several weeks.

Anchored further out was a steel catamaran that looked like a small cargo vessel and flew the flag of the Cook Islands. The captain told me that it had been chartered by the Cook Islands Environmental Association, some of whose members had come to Suwarrow to lay poison for the rats that were decimating the bird colonies. To my great surprise, I found out that one of the passengers was Tom Neale's daughter Stella. She hadn't been back to Suwarrow since her childhood, and revisiting her father's atoll was a very moving experience. We talked much about her father, whom Stella described as a complex person who relished solitude to the point of neglecting his family, his absence clearly having affected her as a young girl.

Meanwhile, we enjoyed this truly relaxing spot to the full. The presence of the caretakers did not seem to deter sailors from treating Anchorage Island as their own, and much had been done by previous visitors to provide some simple comforts. Hammocks were slung between trees, lounge chairs had been knocked together from driftwood for comfortable reading, a barbecue had been made from an old 55-gallon drum, and a pit dug for burning garbage, while a large tank next to Tom's old house held enough rainwater for everyone to do their laundry. Every second night, Papa John and Baker invited everyone in the anchorage to a potluck dinner. One or two large fish caught in the pass by Papa John with a traditional mother-of-pearl lure were cooked in an earth oven. Beautifully displayed on a tray plaited from coconut fronds, the fish was accompanied by breadfruit fritters or tasty pancakes made from germinating coconut. The sailors' contributions were salads and highly appreciated cold beers. While Papa John strummed on his ukulele under the flickering light provided by a small generator, the party stretched far into the balmy night.

One day the indefatigable Papa John invited all sailors to join him on a day's outing. Two yachts, one of them Aventura, took the party across the lagoon for a first stop at an island used for breeding by a large colony of sooty terns. As we stepped ashore, thousands of birds took to the sky with a lot of noise, abandoning their nests and eggs, visibly disturbed by the unexpected invasion. We repaired to a nearby island whose main attraction was hidden under our feet rather than dive-bombing us from above. Papa John had tempted us with the foremost culinary delicacy of the Pacific: coconut crab, of which he assured us there were thousands on this island. Followed silently by a rather sceptical group of sailors, he kept poking under trees and looking into cracks in the ground, but without any success. Having built up the suspense to the highest degree of anticipation, and probably realising that we might soon lose interest, he suddenly poked his pointed stick between the roots of a tree and told us that he could feel a large crab hiding in its burrow. He started digging with both hands, throwing loose earth in all directions, then, with a deft movement, pulled up a wriggling shape from the hole and held up a large crab for all to see.

Papa John handed me the wriggling creature, before producing another victim. When it looked like there were enough to feed us all, we returned to the spot where we had left Baker. While we had been away, he had built a large fire from old coconut husks, and had also opened several green coconuts, some to drink their refreshing juice, while others had been split open for their tasty flesh.

While the crabs were being roasted on the open fire and Baker was opening more nuts, Papa John plaited trays from palm fronds, on which the cooked crabs were served. I don't think that I have ever tasted anything more delicious or enjoyed a meal more than this kingly feast. As we sat on the ground, eating with our fingers and quenching our thirst with green nuts, I willed myself to grasp that moment and freeze it in my memory. It was, in every respect, a dream that had come true.

The pass into Suwarrow lagoon is reputed to be one of the best diving spots in the South Pacific, so one day I went to check it out for myself. The underwater scenery was indeed magnificent and teeming with fish, some quite large, but there were also many sharks. They did not take much notice of me so I spent a long time watching the activity below me through the crystal-clear water. In spite of the horror stories one hears from time to time, shark attacks are quite rare, and I do not know of any fatal incident involving a cruising sailor. Nevertheless, basic precautions are imperative, and while in Suwarrow we heard on the radio that a person had been attacked by a shark in Moorea. Apparently he was spearfishing on the reef, and this is indeed one of the situations when attacks are most likely as sharks are attracted by blood from an injured fish. The best tactic is to avoid spearfishing in areas where there are sharks, or to land the fish in the dinghy as soon as it has been speared, which is what I normally do. Sharks very rarely attack directly, and this is why the best protection is always to swim with a mask to be able to see what is happening around you. If a shark shows any interest and continues to stay close, it is time to beat a retreat while watching the shark all the time. Over the years I have swum and dived close to sharks on innumerable occasions, and I regard them as one of the most beautiful creatures of the seas, so perfectly adapted to their environment that they have remained unchanged for millions of years.

Having seen the large numbers of tasty fish swimming idly in the pass, on the morning we left Suwarrow I made sure that the fishing line was run out as we sailed through it. Within minutes, the telltale shriek of the line running out fast heralded a strike. As I was reeling it in, I could see a lot of commotion behind us, and I guessed that our hoped-for dinner might be feeding other hungry mouths. By the time I had reeled in the line, all there was left on the hook was the sorry head of the fish, the rest having been surgically removed by those beautiful creatures of the deep.
Sharks 1 – Aventura 0.

There are only about 500 miles between Suwarrow and Niue, our next destination, so we expected to take three days to get there. 'Only 500 miles' is the kind of distance one has to sail from one island to the next in the Pacific, and is something that those used to cruising in the Caribbean or Mediterranean find difficult to imagine. At least the weather on this leg was reasonably good, and for the first two days we had light but steady winds. The large triradial spinnaker stayed up while the autopilot did all the work, Gwenda baked bread and I managed to catch a large mahi-mahi, that tastiest of pelagic tropical fish, confusingly known as a dolphinfish although it has nothing to do with dolphins. The beautiful creatures of the deep kept their distance from our dinner this time, but then that party pooper, the South Pacific Convergence Zone, had another go at our marital harmony. A front detached itself from the SPCZ and made the wind back from northeast to northwest. As the front passed, we were hit by several squalls in which the wind changed direction rapidly. Such wind shifts are hardly a problem at sea, but can have serious consequences at anchor. Friends who were still at Suwarrow told us on the radio that, as that same front passed over them, the boats had to quickly leave the anchorage to find shelter elsewhere in the lagoon, while in the Ha'apai group of Tonga, a New Zealand boat was lost when caught on a lee shore by an unexpected wind shift. By the following morning the winds had gone back into the southeast, and we could see our destination in the distance.

Niue

Niue is a very strange island indeed, a massive slab of coral that was pushed up by tectonic activity. Surrounded by 20-metre-high cliffs, it has no natural harbour, and the only shelter from the prevailing winds is an indentation on the west coast, where a number of moorings had been laid for the use of visiting yachts. In settled conditions this is a safe spot to leave the boat while visiting the island, although the ocean swell is forever present, and the constant surge makes landing a very exciting affair. Thoughtfully, the Niueans had provided a crane for hoisting tenders onto the quay, but perfect coordination is needed to hook up the tender to the waiting strop while trying to keep your balance on the slippery steps. Knowing what to expect, I had inflated the smaller Avon so Gwenda and I would have no problem dragging it behind us onto the dock. Having been contacted by radio, the various officials were waiting when we landed ashore, and entry formalities took only minutes to complete.

As a dependency of New Zealand, Niue has a special status. Its citizens have the right to work and settle in New Zealand, and as a result there has been a steady drain, with more Niueans now living abroad than on the island. Although some 1,500 people still lived on Niue, the island had a deserted look about it, and when we rented a car and left the main settlement of Alofi, we felt that we had the place almost to ourselves.

Because of its unusual geological formation, Niue is riddled with underground tunnels and caves, while on the east coast, which is constantly battered by huge Pacific rollers, a number of deep chasms have been carved out of the massive coral cliffs. When we reached the bottom of one such chasm, we were surprised to find a cool oasis of tall palms growing by the side of a limpid stream.

We stopped for lunch at the Washaway café, whose young owner Willie explained that he had given it this name after he had been repeatedly told that he had chosen the wrong spot, and his café would end up being washed away by the waves, which obviously had not yet happened. As we were the only customers, Willie was happy to talk. He had worked for several years in New Zealand, but had returned home as he felt that Niue was still the best place to live. This may indeed be the case because while we were there, Niue became the first country in the world to offer all its inhabitants free wireless internet access, and shortly afterwards every school child was given their own laptop computer.

The Niueans who chose to stay knew what was best for them, and this was what I was told when we stopped in a small village on the north coast. What had caught my eye were several dugout canoes that were being built by the side of the road. We were shown around by Taumafai Fuhiniu, who told us that he had been concerned about the old skills being lost as everyone was using aluminium runabouts powered by large outboards, so he decided to teach young men how to build their own paddling outriggers or sailing canoes. Taumafai's workshop was very successful, and several canoes that had been adzed out of tree trunks were nearing completion.

As the supermarket in Alofi only stocked chilled and frozen produce flown in from New Zealand, we tried our luck at the nearby market, but the selection of fresh vegetables was disappointing. A friend on another boat told me that we might have better luck at the prison, which apparently had its own vegetable garden. It sounded a bit far-fetched to me, but as we still had the hire car, I drove up to the prison. A man in blue overalls was working in a well-tended garden with rows of tasty-looking vegetables. He told me that his name was Cosini, and as he seemed eager to talk, I asked him how he had ended up there. Apparently there had been a family argument during which he had threatened his mother-in-law with a gun, without realising it was loaded. The gun went off and she got killed. As even in Niue killing your mother-in-law is a crime, regardless of whether it happened by accident, he was sentenced to eight years in prison, of which he had already served three. Because he had a wife and five children to support, he tried to earn some money growing vegetables. At weekends his family, whom he kept referring to as his 'juveniles', came to help. There was only another inmate in this open prison, but, as Cosini pointed out, he was a real murderer and was not at all interested in gardening, which, from Cosini's disapproving tone, he seemed to consider as the greater crime.

Driving around the island, one got the impression that Niueans liked keeping everything in the open, and even family graves were erected in front of their homes rather than hidden away in a cemetery. Elaborate structures adorned with framed photographs of the dead stood by the side of the road, but it was a taller memorial that made us stop and have a closer look. The modest white obelisk commemorated the surprisingly high number of men from one of the smallest nations on Earth who had fallen in the first and second world wars while fighting with the New Zealand forces. A line that had been added at the bottom of the memorial mentioned five Niueans who had died in the Vietnam war. It seemed so incongruous on this small peaceful island. May all of them rest in peace.

Swimming with whales in Vava'u

Tonga's northern group of islands has been one of the most popular cruising destinations in the South Pacific for a very long time. The perfectly sheltered anchorage off the small town of Neiafu looked very different to how I remembered it from our first visit in 1978, when

we had chosen it as a rendezvous with our friends Erick and Muriel on Calao. As they were in Peru and we were in New Zealand, we each drew a line on a chart of the South Pacific, and those lines crossed in Vava'u. We had agreed by mail to meet there the first weekend in May and, in spite of the vast distance, both our yachts arrived on the same morning.

The strategic location of Vava'u at the crossroads of several sailing routes, along with the reputation of the main anchorage, Port Refuge, as a safe hurricane

hole had, unsurprisingly, turned it into a busy yachting centre. Several charter companies are based there and, as a result, there is a good range of repair facilities. Although the improvement in facilities is also of benefit to cruising sailors, there is no doubt that it is the needs and requirements of charter clients that really count. However convenient it may be to find a small restaurant in every bay, as we first noticed in Raiatea and rediscovered in Vava'u, there comes a point when I'd rather have a place to ourselves, even if we have to cook our own dinner.

In spite of all that, Vava'u continues to be a most beautiful place, its tranquil waters being the favourite destination of some travellers of a very different kind:

scores of humpback whales that gather here to breed. We met them frolicking with their young throughout the islands, and heard their chatter reverberate through Aventura's aluminium hull. There were several boats specialising in whale watching, taking clients to within feet of those benign giants, snorkelling with them being the latest thrill. The morning we were leaving for Fiji, a large female and her newly born calf were ambling slowly next to us, only metres from the shore, so I asked Gwenda to stay as close to them as possible while I donned my mask and fins. It was only when I tried to catch up with them that I realised that their idle pace was a lot faster than I could swim. Just as I managed to get reasonably close, they both sounded, the sight of their disappearing tails sending me a clear message that the interest was definitely one-sided.

23

Sailing in the tropics

Sailing in the tropics is like married life. When things go well life is perfect but when things go wrong it can turn to sheer hell.

Tom Williams

During the safe season, sailing in the tropics can be highly enjoyable because the weather conditions are generally benign and, especially on long passages, you can have days on end of trouble-free sailing. This is what trade-wind sailing is all about, so not surprisingly the main route passing through the South Pacific is called the milk run, or, more poetically in German, the barefoot route. However, for sailors arriving from a temperate area the tropics demand a different approach to sailing, as they may encounter many unfamiliar situations in this new environment.

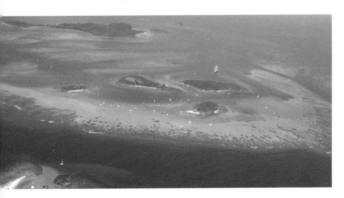

Tropical weather

After God had created the tropics, he was sitting in heaven on his throne with a smile on his face when St Peter stopped by.

'You look very happy with yourself, my Lord,' St Peter said.

'Yes, just look at what I have created. Sheer perfection.' St Peter looked down at the Blue Planet and replied. 'It's not right. Only you can be perfect, nothing else should be. You can't launch a perfect product, and then sit back and relax. You need to build in some small imperfection

or people will simply take it for granted.'

So God looked at the tropics again and, to balance things out, endowed them with two seasons: one of hurricanes, cyclones and typhoons, and left the other unchanged, so that for half the year the tropics could still be regarded as a perfect creation. And so it has remained, with the worst of the tropical-storm seasons coinciding in each hemisphere with the summer and early-autumn months, while the tropical winter months are normally as pleasant as God had always intended.

Photo from space of a tropical storm over Mexico

In spite of current anomalies in world weather, this ideal set-up has remained generally unchanged, so that a voyage can still be planned to take advantage of the best and safest possible conditions. I have enjoyed close-to-perfect conditions on most of my long ocean

Storm damage

A squall about to break over a tropical anchorage

passages, notably our crossing of the North Indian Ocean in February-March 1980 on Aventura I, a highly enjoyable Atlantic crossing in 1989 on Aventura II, and fast passages through the South Indian and Atlantic Oceans on Aventura III in 2004 and 2005. The most enjoyable passage from Galapagos to Marquesas was, at nearly 3,000 miles, also the longest. Aventura IV was definitely short-changed as her only tropical sailing was from the Bahamas to Costa Rica, just about enough for a boat built for high latitudes.

Tropical squalls

Unfortunately I am now going to throw a fly in the ointment by outlining some aspects that can spoil that attractive picture. The main culprits are undoubtedly those irritating tropical squalls, which often catch newcomers by surprise and can cause damage to gear. While squalls at sea can usually be easily dealt with by a vigilant crew, abrupt changes in weather caused by the passing of a depression can cause havoc among boats at anchor. With the strengthening wind often changing by as much as 180° in direction, boats anchored in places that were deemed to be safe and well-protected suddenly find themselves on a dangerous lee shore. When this is combined with a violent short swell produced by several miles of fetch across a wide lagoon, a boat can easily be driven ashore. Severe damage can also be caused by the chain being caught under coral heads.

The first time I got a taste of such a frightening experience was in 1978 in Bora Bora, where we were anchored in the sheltered lagoon with about a dozen other cruising yachts. Around midnight I was woken up by the screaming wind and the slap of waves in what until then had been a calm and quiet anchorage. From the cockpit, I looked out at a situation that was straight out of hell. The sudden wind, which I estimated at between 40 and 50 knots, had turned all the boats around, and we were all now hobbyhorsing violently

with our sterns towards the beach. As the anchorage was over 15 metres deep, the stretched chains already had some boats dangerously close to the fringing reef. While Gwenda powered ahead with the engine at full revs, I tried to get up the anchor and chain, but the anchor was well dug in and we ended up riding over the entire length of chain, narrowly missing a small Swedish yacht whose petrified crew must have thought we were going to run them down. As we reached deeper water, the anchor was finally dislodged, but as I was unable to raise the accumulated weight of the chain hanging vertically in the water with the manual anchor winch, we could only crawl into the wind at a snail's pace. Slowly, dragging the anchor and chain with us, we manoeuvred around the corner into a more protected bay and tied to a small dock. Looking back, I was surprised to see that we were the only boat to have moved, and by the time a few others decided to follow our example a couple of boats had already been driven onto the reef, sadly among them the well-travelled yacht of Alex du Prel. This colourful character had arrived there with his family in the early 1970s, and founded the Bora Bora Yacht Club, which for many years was one of the favourite watering holes along the world-cruising circuit.

Our prompt action probably saved us from more serious trouble, and I was to apply the same tactic throughout my sailing life. A Canadian sailing friend reminded me of how we had left the crowded anchorage at Honiara in the Solomon Islands as soon

277

Seasons

as a sudden thunderstorm started venting its fury on the anchored boats. He was surprised to see us pick up the anchor and spend the night hove-to off the island, but he understood why after passing an anxious, nail-biting night in the cockpit. Such local wind changes are usually unpredictable, although warnings of unsettled weather accompanied by thunderstorms or squalls should not be ignored. If anchored in a lagoon that does not offer all-round protection, the best solution is to use what I call the CAM system as described on page 197. I conceived this safer way of tropical anchoring while in Chagos, where a 50-foot yacht had been driven onto a reef by just such a sudden change in weather a short time before our visit.

Also worth mentioning are the so-called reinforced trade winds that are more common in the South Pacific than in other tropical areas. It is a phenomenon that occurs throughout the winter months, and is particularly frequent in French Polynesia, where it is called maramu. It also occurs on passages between New Zealand and the tropics. One other phenomenon is the South Pacific Tropical Convergence Zone, which stretches in an arc all the way from Tahiti to the Solomon Islands, and which can affect weather conditions throughout the area.

When the end of the safe season approaches, my firm opinion is that it is imperative to leave the tropics and head for an area unaffected by tropical storms. In my early days of cruising this was accepted as the thing to do by practically all sailors, but over the years attitudes have changed, and by the time I reached the South Pacific on Aventura III I reckoned that about one third of the cruising boats remained in the tropics during the cyclone season. Most managed to find a place in a marina or boatyard and were usually left unattended. A few continued to cruise, their crews keeping a wary eye on the weather. Those who decide to take this line of action should make sure that they know of, or preferably are close to, some hurricane-proof shelter. The situation is similar in the Eastern Caribbean, where many boats spend the hurricane season in a marina or boatyard, provided they are located south of 12°40'N as stipulated by the insurance companies, or have obtained a special dispensation if north of that line.

Undoubtedly a sign of changing climatic conditions, in recent years there have been some notable exceptions to those well-defined tropical-storm seasons, with a number of storms occurring during the accepted safe season, or in areas that had never experienced such storms before, such as Brazil, the Canaries and Azores: Hurricane Catarina formed off Brazil in Match 2004, Hurricane Delta hit the Canaries in early December 2005, and Hurricane Alex the Azores in January 2016. As I am writing this in May 2017, Cyclone Donna, which developed in the Coral Sea, has just passed over New Zealand, two weeks into the hypothetical safe season. The worst situation is in the northwest Pacific, where typhoons have now been recorded in every month of the year, so a safe season can no longer be counted on. Meteorologists warn that because of climate change, extra-seasonal cyclones may now occur in any month, especially during an El Niño episode.

Tropical tactics

Lagoon in French Polynesia with the reef marked by beacons

The tropics demand a different approach not just to offshore sailing, but to navigation as well. By their very nature, many tropical destinations are remote, and as some areas may still not be accurately charted they should be approached with the utmost caution. In French Polynesia most passes into lagoons are marked by beacons, and although other Pacific island nations have improved their aids to navigation, they should not be relied on because lights and beacons are often reported to be missing.

As many tropical islands and atolls are protected to windward by massive reefs, few of which are lit, making landfall in such places can be a risky undertaking, and the situation is often compounded by the presence of strong currents. Thus it is always wise to set a landfall waypoint at a safe distance from the intended destination, and only make landfall in daylight and good visibility.

The problems are far from over once landfall is made, as entering a lagoon is rarely a simple matter of just pointing the bows for the middle of the pass. Because most lagoon passes are swept by strong currents, you should attempt to time your arrival at the beginning of the incoming tide, just after slack water, when there may still be a slightly contrary outflowing current. This is the time when passes are normally at their calmest. What makes the situation difficult is not just the force of the tidal streams, but also the fact that lagoons are constantly filled by the seas pouring over the windward reef, as a result of which the water level in some lagoons can be considerably higher than that of the surrounding ocean. It is not uncommon for an outflowing current to reach 6 knots or more, and in some places even double digits. All these facts must be borne in mind, and it is therefore essential to have access to a worldwide tide table.

Eyeball navigation

Coral patches can be clearly seen when the visibility is good

Most lagoons can be crossed relatively easily in good light, but while passes and some lagoons may be beaconed, in most places you have to find your own way. You must quickly learn the tricks of the trade, better known as eyeball navigation. Many tropical lagoons or anchorages are strewn with isolated coral heads, some of which reach up almost to the surface. In more frequented lagoons these may be marked by perches, but often they are not. Depth sounders are of no help because the depths are usually quite constant and there is no early warning of the presence of such coral heads. However, in good light, they can be easily seen in the clear water. Good light means having the sun behind the observer so the timing must coincide with favourable conditions. In other words, you should plan on going west through a lagoon between early and mid-morning, when the sun should be behind you, and, conversely, move in an easterly direction in mid-afternoon.

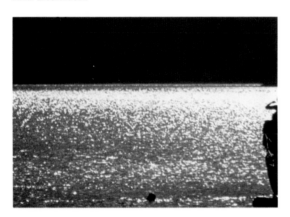

With the sun ahead of the observer, the surface of the lagoon turns into an impenetrable opaque mass, where not even obstructions that are close to the surface are visible to the naked eye. Polaroid glasses can help if the sun is not too low ahead. Being able to climb the mast, ideally provided with steps, can be a great advantage, as the visibility from a higher point is much better than from deck level. An absolute godsend for this kind of lagoon navigation is a forward-looking sonar (FLS), which shows the profile of the bottom and any dangers that may lie ahead. Depending on the model and strength of the signal, a FLS can see as far forward as 40 or 50 metres, and more recent models even further still. Having had a FLS on both Aventura III and IV, I can vouch for its usefulness; it got us out of tricky situations on several occasions.

The Tuamotus

The Tuamotus were until fairly recently little visited by cruising yachts, and for a very good reason: navigation among the reefs and atolls is, even in these days of GPS, a daunting task and calls for a high degree of alertness and vigilance. It is a price worth paying because some of these remote atolls fit perfectly the ideal image of a tropical destination: turquoise blue lagoons, deserted islets shaded by swaying coconut palms, and magnificent underwater scenery with a profusion of fish and colourful corals. There are some basic rules to be followed, such as choosing an anchorage carefully and avoiding a long fetch if strong winds are expected or a front is predicted to pass. Most sailors used to cruising in the Eastern Caribbean are surprised by the drastic wind changes that commonly occur in this area of the Pacific.

Aware of what to expect, I had worked out the optimum time for entering Raroia lagoon, Aventura III's first landfall in the Tuamotus. From the way the water was gushing out through the pass, it looked obvious that our timing was wrong, but as I didn't want to spend several hours waiting outside, I decided to go for it and, with the engine at full blast, pointed for the middle of the half-mile-wide pass. Half an hour later, we were little more than 50 metres from where we had started. Fortunately a local fisherman must have guessed our predicament, as he motored over with his boat powered by a large outboard and beckoned us to follow him. He headed straight for the edge of the pass, where obviously he knew that there was a slight countercurrent, and within minutes we were inside. The friendly Raroian slowed down so we could catch up with him and led us to a spot close to the village, where he told me to anchor, and then left with a wave.

Special considerations

These balmy sun-kissed tropical islands are not the healthiest places on Earth either, as the early sailors soon found out. Now that we know so much more about UV light and other associated risks to our skins, the main concern is overexposure to the sun. A hat and long-sleeved shirt should be worn, the boat should be provided with a bimini or awning, and those who have a particularly delicate skin should use strong sunblock cream.

The skin should also be protected from bites by mosquitoes or the irritating sandflies common to some of the beaches in the Marquesas. Repellent sprays are quite useful, but better still is to avoid being ashore at the critical times, around dusk and early evening, when mosquitoes are most active. Of the mosquito-born diseases, dengue fever is present throughout the Pacific, while malaria is the main hazard in islands west of Fiji (Vanuatu, Solomons and Papua New Guinea). In these areas it may be worth considering taking antimalarial tablets, but as several strains of malaria are now resistant to prophylactic medication, the best protection is still to avoid being bitten. Not going ashore at dusk, using a strong repellent while ashore in doubtful areas, using smoking coils and screening all openings are simple precautions that often work.

Swimming has its own risks, and although sharks are often present in lagoons, they are rarely dangerous if some simple precautions are observed. As in the case of mosquitoes, the time to avoid is around dusk, which is shark feeding time. If fishing with a speargun, the speared fish should be taken out of the water immediately and put in a dinghy because the blood and vibrations emitted by a wounded fish will attract any sharks that happen to be in the vicinity. One serious hazard in all tropical waters is ciguatera food poisoning. The culprit is a toxic microscopic algae that is ingested and concentrated in the flesh of reef-feeding fish.

As in much of the Caribbean there are either few fish left or spearfishing is prohibited, it was with great anticipation that I looked forward to the Tuamotus, where fish are still abundant and the underwater scenery is almost without equal. En route from the Marquesas to Tahiti we stopped at various atolls, most attractive among them the uninhabited atoll of Tahanea. The pass into the large lagoon had beautiful coral formations and was teeming with fish. Aware of the risk of ciguatera poisoning, I only speared a couple of smaller fish, which I considered to be safe. Gwenda marinated one of them in lime juice, which we ate raw in Polynesian style, and pan-fried the fillets of the other. Halfway through the afternoon, while beachcombing on a nearby islet, we were both overcome by terrible stomach cramps. By the time we got back to the boat, other symptoms were telling me clearly that after 30 years of catching and eating tropical fish, I was now on the receiving end. The first 24 hours were the worst, but not severe enough to risk sailing the 300 miles to Tahiti to seek medical assistance. We chose to deal with the matter ourselves and, although we felt very bad for a couple of days, very slowly we recovered, but it took one month before all symptoms disappeared. The last to go was the tingling and a queer reversal of sensations whereby a hot drink felt cold, and ice cream burnt my mouth.

In most instances the symptoms subside after a few days, although the itching and alteration of sensations can last for several weeks. Ciguatera has been treated successfully with IV mannitol. The usual dose is one gram of mannitol per kilogram of body weight. The medication is infused intravenously as a 20 per cent mannitol solution. It is believed that mannitol acts at the cellular level by rendering the toxin inert. Antihistamines, calcium gluconate, atropine and vitamin B have also been used to ameliorate the symptoms.

The risks can be minimised by gutting fish as soon as it is caught and by not eating the head, liver, roe and viscera, as the toxin is concentrated in these organs. All large fish caught inside a lagoon, or close to a reef, should be treated with suspicion, especially snappers, groupers, barracuda, jacks and moray eels. It pays to take local advice, as most islanders know only too well which fish and which areas of their lagoon have to be avoided. Freezing, drying, cooking or marinating the fish does not destroy the poison, and affected fish look, smell and taste normal. Various traditional tests have been recommended but none is truly effective.

One message is abundantly clear: every outbreak of ciguatera indicates that something is wrong with the reef. Nature exacts a high price for interfering with the fragile ecosystem of living coral.

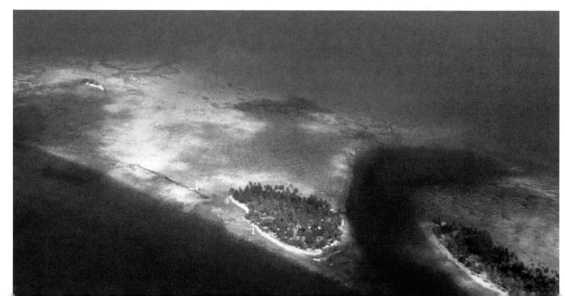

Tackling atoll passes

Having missed the best time to leave our anchorage at Tahanea, by the time we were ready to go the sun had moved into the west, turning the surface of the lagoon into a shimmering silvery mirror. Crossing the three-mile-wide lagoon with the sun in our eyes proved to be a nightmare. We had crossed it in the opposite direction in good light, but now had to dodge the numerous coral heads that littered the lagoon under the worst possible conditions. I climbed to the first set of spreaders for better visibility, but even with my Polaroid glasses could only see a short distance ahead. With her eyes glued to the FLS mounted next to the wheel, Gwenda was moving cautiously ahead, frequently changing course abruptly before I could even see the reason why. After a while I realised the futility of my presence up the mast and climbed down. Gwenda and the FLS were doing an excellent job, managing to weave a circuitous path around the coral heads, and we made it to the main pass safely.

I had timed leaving the lagoon to just before slack low water, when the incoming tide hadn't had time to get established. We lined up with the middle of the pass and, with all sails set and full power, forged ahead. Outside the pass, the incoming tide had already created a massive wall, with 2-metre-steep waves breaking all over the entrance, the change from the outgoing to the incoming tide being almost instantaneous. Soon we were caught in this violent maelstrom and, as we crashed down from the breaking crest of a large wave, the engine alarm sounded. Gwenda immediately turned off the engine and, with difficulty, we managed to sail through the breaking waves into deeper, calmer water. When I opened the engine compartment I was confronted by black oil sprayed onto everything and presumed that, under the tremendous pressure caused by Aventura crashing from the top of that steep wave, the oil had been ejected through the air breather. We stayed in the lee of the large atoll while I cleaned up the horrible mess with oil-absorbing pads and old rags. I poured fresh oil into the engine, started it, and it fired up as if nothing had happened. We headed offshore and set course for the next atoll, ready to face new challenges.

Some of the above comments and observations may seem quite daunting, but you should never forget that the tropics include some of the most attractive anchorages in the world. As we all know, there is always a price to be paid and, however difficult it may appear to be, the islands of the South Seas are certainly worth the sacrifice.

Tips

» Entering a lagoon should be timed for just after slack high water, and departure immediately before slack low water.

» Perfect your eyeballing techniques at the first opportunity and always attempt to cross a lagoon in good light by having the sun behind the observer.

» While on passage the watch-keeper should keep a good lookout to windward for any approaching squalls. Sail should be shortened promptly, and if the autopilot is engaged it should set to steer to wind.

» Many charts in remote places are still inaccurate and do not agree with GPS, therefore islands, especially those protected by reefs to windward, should not be approached at night but given a wide berth.

» Always have an exit strategy if anchored in a large lagoon, because if there is a change of wind direction the boat may be put on a dangerous lee shore. Leave a doubtful anchorage for the open sea if a change in weather looks likely, while there is still time and good light.

» Attempt to anchor in an area that is free of coral heads. Check that the anchor is well set and, if possible, inspect it with a mask.

» Only eat lagoon fish if you know that no cases of ciguatera have been reported in that area.

Aventura III anchored with a fleet of traditional sailing canoes on their way to the South Pacific Festival of Arts in Port Moresby, Papua New Guinea

24

Offshore utilities

Electricity is the heart of your boat; it keeps everything ticking.

Bill Butler

Over the years I have come to the conclusion that, with the exception of the choice of the boat itself, no other element of offshore cruising has improved the quality of life on board, and ultimately the success of a voyage, more than the easy availability of an adequate supply of water and electricity. This viewpoint has been confirmed by reports on the problems experienced in this respect by participants in three recent transatlantic rallies. In most cases, the existing arrangement for electricity generation could not cover the demands of the array of power-hungry equipment carried on present-day cruising boats. Those who are not prepared, or able, to forego or limit the use of equipment that may not be absolutely necessary have no alternative but to ensure that their generating capacity is up to their requirements. Until not so long ago, the solution would have been a separate diesel generator, but the surge in the use of renewable sources has made it possible to satisfy your needs in a more eco-friendly manner. For larger consumers of energy, with larger boats to match, a genset may still be the answer. A global survey conducted in 2016 on the profile of cruising boats undertaking a world voyage showed that the average length was 45 feet. I would expect that in most cases a well-thought out charging system based on renewable energy sources should be able to take care of the needs of a boat of that size, without the need for an additional diesel generator.

Generating electricity

When I had to decide on the charging system for Aventura IV, a far more complex boat than any of her predecessors, I was much influenced by the findings of both my surveys and observations made on other boats. The final decision was the same: no diesel generator.

In certain situations the engine would still be the main source of charging the batteries, but would be backed up by alternative sources: a D400 wind generator, a 140W solar panel and a Sail-Gen hydro-generator. The system worked better than expected, and this was proven on the passage from Greenland to England in September 2015 when the engine was out of order and could not be used to charge the batteries. For two weeks all our energy needs were fully covered by renewable sources.

The concept was not new as I had a similar system on Aventura III, although in that case the engine was fitted with two alternators, the standard 55A alternator and a more powerful 120A model with a double pulley and two belts. The latter charged the house batteries, whereas the former charged the engine-starting and anchor-winch batteries. As a backup, either alternator could charge both banks on its own and, in an emergency, a switch allowed the house batteries to be used to start the engine. However, I made sure that the banks were always kept separate. The system was supplemented by two 40-watt solar panels mounted on the coachroof, a Rutland 913 wind generator and an Aquair 100 towing generator. On passage, the latter provided enough power to run the autopilot and fridge.

The system worked satisfactorily throughout a long voyage, and coped well with all energy requirements. The addition of the high-capacity alternator was a useful improvement, and made it possible to bring the batteries to a full charge in a shorter time than before. The solar panel and towing generator provided a useful boost on long passages, although the wind generator was quite inefficient when sailing downwind. In 13 years, I had to replace the batteries four times, which was far from perfect but was probably caused by the boat being left unattended for several long periods, when the batteries could not be charged under optimum conditions and suffered as a result. I still find the idea of a second alternator very attractive, not just for charging but also as a useful backup, the latter being a feature that I regard as essential on a long-distance cruising boat.

On Aventura IV, the charging system was based on a Sterling Power alternator-to-battery charger complemented by a Victron Quattro 12V/3000VA/120V charger/converter. The system worked well, but I also had a portable 12V/1500W inverter as a backup in case I had to use my power tools in an emergency.

The surveys

Energy consumption on cruising boats has been a subject that has interested me since my earliest surveys, and I have interviewed hundreds of sailors on both consumption and generation. One of the main conclusions was that perhaps as many as 90 per cent of owners, myself included, underestimate their consumption, or overestimate their charging capability, which is saying the same thing.

Another observation highlighted by the surveys was that many owners were seriously concerned about the higher-than-expected consumption of electricity, and often the only solution they could think of was to turn off the power-hungry item. Automatic pilots are one of the pieces of equipment that can raise the consumption of electricity considerably, and several owners were annoyed to find out that their autopilots consumed more than they had been led to believe. This may be explained by the fact that compared with coastal cruising, autopilots have to work much harder to keep a yacht on course in the vigorous downwind conditions of an ocean passage. In a recent survey conducted among sailors who reported autopilot failures in three transatlantic rallies, several admitted that they did not, as a rule, trim the sails for minor changes in wind strength or direction. As a result, the autopilot had to work harder and thus used more electricity. This confirmed the reason not just for the higher consumption but possibly also for the failure of their autopilot.

Another observation from my latest survey was the steep increase in energy consumption compared to the past. The increasing need for additional sources of electricity generation is virtually unavoidable, bearing in mind the many accessories that most sailors now regard as essential: autopilots, watermakers and freezers, as well as certain items that normally run off mains power such as washing machines, microwave ovens, breadmakers, etc. As a result, a higher proportion of even smaller cruising boats than in the past are now equipped with diesel generators.

As electricity consumption is a cause of so much concern among those planning an ocean voyage, I asked each skipper for suggestions based on their personal experience. While the majority seemed resigned to the fact that their personal comfort could only be maintained at the price of high energy consumption, and therefore adequate preparations needed to be made to meet this task, a few owners stressed that rather than be obsessed with the need to produce more electricity, you should rather try to consume less. It was one of the latter who pointed out that it was a mistake to rely solely on an automatic pilot, and stressed the advantage on long passages of a wind-operated self-steering gear. Needless to say, the former group often included larger boats equipped with diesel generators, whereas the latter group were owners of smaller boats, most of which sported wind generators, solar panels and windvanes.

The owners were also asked to comment on the generating system they would have on their ideal yacht. Without exception, all agreed that some kind of additional means of electricity generation was essential, preferably from renewable sources. A useful tip given to would-be voyagers was to make a realistic assessment of their estimated daily needs, and then double that figure for good measure. The battery capacity should be at least twice the latter amount, and this should then dictate the size of the alternator, as the standard alternator provided with the engine may not be powerful enough. But things appear to be changing, and the latest survey highlighted a gradual move away from diesel generators and a definite increase in the use of renewable sources.

Average electricity consumption

The average consumption on Aventura III while on passage was 346Ah, which was reduced by the input of my renewable sources to about 202Ah. That meant that I usually had to run the engine once every 24 hours to make up the difference. Aventura IV's consumption on passage was considerably higher at 465Ah, and I estimated that the input from renewable sources would reduce it by half. I was proven quite wrong in my calculation when it was put to the test on a passage from Greenland: to my surprise, those renewable sources kept the batteries topped up, although we were continuously using the autopilot, chart plotter, instruments, Iridium broadband, VHF radio, refrigerator and, occasionally, also the radar, electric winches and electric toilets. I must admit that I found it hard to believe then, and even now still regard it as almost a miracle. The strong winds that we encountered did have something to do with it, but it

was still satisfying to know that I had run my ship for two weeks without using one drop of fossil fuel.

The highly efficient Sail-Gen covered all our electricity needs when we were sailing at over eight knots

Energy consumption was addressed in my two latest surveys, but there were such large differences between the various boats that I concluded that working out an average consumption would be irrelevant. What I found to be perhaps more helpful was battery capacity, which came to an average of 550Ah per boat. Although most users described their capacity as adequate, I regarded it as possibly insufficient. On Aventura IV, the total capacity of the six domestic batteries was 720Ah, and even in my own case I believe that it should have been higher. The state of the batteries was permanently shown by a Philippi monitor that, among other things, also showed the amperage being consumed at the moment, as well as the total amount left in the batteries. For good practice, I never allowed the batteries to be discharged below 70 per cent of their capacity.

Alternative energy sources

Solar panels

Having used this wonderful means to supplement my energy needs on both Aventura III and IV, I am convinced that this is the future of sailing, not just for the provision of energy for general consumption but eventually also for propulsion.

Solar panels on Aventura III

Photovoltaic cells have been with us for a long time, and their discovery is attributed to a 19-year old French physicist, Alexandre-Edmond Becquerel. In 1839, while experimenting with metal electrodes and electrolyte, he observed the phenomenon of light-to-electricity conversion. In 1888, the American Edward Weston received the first US patent for a solar cell, and this was followed in 1901 by Nikola Tesla taking out a patent on this method for utilising solar energy. Photovoltaic cells came into commercial production in 1954, and were first used on the US satellite Vanguard. What is less known is that the one and only Nobel Prize awarded to Albert Einstein was for a paper he had written on the photoelectric effect in 1904, which was only recognised in 1922.

In May 2012 the catamaran Tûranor PlanetSolar completed a 19-month-long circumnavigation of the globe, the first by a solar-powered vessel. Conceived by the Swiss electrical engineer Raphael Domjan to promote renewable energy, the 31-metre vessel carried 537 square metres of black solar panels. In July 2016, the aeroplane Solar Impulse 2 completed the first round-the-world flight by a solar-powered aircraft. The plane spent more than 23 days in the air and was powered by 17,000 solar cells.

The advantage of catamarans is that they can accommodate large solar panels at the stern

Solar panels started being used on cruising boats in the 1990s, but their use continues to be limited by the available surface, although the development of sail and other materials incorporating photovoltaic cells will expand that potential. I saw on a 50-foot yacht an ingenious solution to increase the available surface: several hinged solar panels were installed along the sides of the boat. Because of their considerable windage when displayed, at sea they were usually kept in the parked position, but they were raised to horizontal, or to the best angle to the sun, when at anchor.

Wind and water generators

Wind and water mills have been around for millennia, but the concept of wind- or water-driven turbines on boats is a relatively recent phenomenon. Wind generators appeared on boats first, but water generators are catching up fast as the older, towing-type generators are replaced by more user-friendly and efficient models, such as Sail-Gen, Watt & Sea, or Aquair-UW. Having used an Aquair 100 towing generator extensively on Aventura III, I upgraded it to a Sail-Gen on Aventura IV, and found it to be a great improvement.

Wind generators will continue whirring away more or less silently as long as there is any wind. In stronger winds, depending on the make, some can become quite noisy and may need to be stopped. As this is not always easy, it should be done before the wind starts picking up. There is no consensus whether they should be stopped in high winds, and having experienced two incidents in winds over 50 knots, I now believe that they should.

While sailing on Aventura III through Le Maire Strait, which separates Patagonia from Staten Island (Isla de los Estados), we were caught by a storm with winds gusting at 50 knots. As described on page 140, the wind generator started shaking the boat violently, and eventually wrenched itself off its support and flew into the sea. I discussed this incident with the manufacturer and they were of the opinion that one of the blades might have been damaged, causing the unit to become unbalanced.

I had the same experience on Aventura IV during a storm while at anchor in Dundas Harbour, in the Northwest Passage, where we had sustained winds with gusts over 50 knots. During a particularly violent gust, recorded at 64 knots, one blade of the wind generator became dislodged and flew off. Knowing what might happen next, I managed to throw a line around the other blades and stop them turning. The generator was saved and the blade replaced when we got to Newfoundland.

Fuel cells

This is another alternative source of energy that has been used on cruising boats, but for the time being fuel cells seem to be more suitable for coastal or weekend sailing. More advanced models are being developed that may appeal to those on a longer voyage.

A fuel cell is a compact unit that generates direct current through a chemical reaction. The byproducts of the process are water, some heat and carbon dioxide, if the unit uses methanol fuel. Fuel cells were used by NASA on the Apollo missions, space shuttles and other space projects. They can be connected to 12 V lead-acid, gel, AGM and lithium batteries. The common models provide between 3A and 14A of charge for up to 30 hours of continuous use.

Portable generators

These are usually of the gasoline type as they are lighter than the diesel units. I had a Honda generator on Aventura III, and although I never used it for charging the batteries, it provided current to power my tools when I had to do some repair work ashore where there was no power available. It was a useful backup and used the same fuel as the outboard motor.

Water and watermakers

My water consumption dropped to less than half once I turned off the electric pump and the crew had to use the foot pump instead.

Volker Reinke

Watermakers are a major advance that has greatly enhanced the quality of cruising life. Gone are the days when I used to row ashore with empty jerrycans, beg someone to let me take some water from their tap, then lug it to the dinghy and get it back to the boat. When spending time in remote anchorages we could never have a freshwater shower, as water was only for drinking and cooking. On Aventura III's voyage, I don't remember filling my tanks with shore water on more than three or four occasions, and then only when we were leaving a marina and I knew that my crew were using water faster than the watermaker could produce it.

Not only did I enjoy this great luxury, but I could also let others share it. The first time it happened was in the San Blas Islands off Panama, where we met a Kuna family living on a tiny island. The man had to paddle or sail his canoe some 20 miles to the mainland to get water. I made enough water to fill several jerrycans, and when I took them ashore they were so impressed that the women started crying, led by the young mother of a few-weeks-old baby who obviously found it very hard to cope with the shortage of water.

The Kuna family of Moro Du

Later, in the Pacific, I did the same on a couple of occasions, regretting that I didn't have a watermaker with a larger output. My wish came true on Aventura IV, whose Spectra watermaker worked surprisingly well even when the seawater temperature was close to freezing, continuing to produce copious amounts to the delight of my shower-addicted crew.

Watermaker maintenance

Routine maintenance of watermakers is quite simple. Most important is to make sure that the watermaker is drawing clean, unpolluted seawater. This means that water should not be made while in marinas, ports, crowded anchorages, or anywhere the water does not look clean. On Aventura III, my most time-consuming job was to properly prepare the HRO watermaker when the boat was left unattended for longer periods. To protect the membrane, the unit needed to be thoroughly rinsed with previously made water, and then preserved with a special chemical product. The fact that the HRO watermaker and its membrane lasted for 13 years speaks for itself, but this was at the cost of countless hours of effort on my part.

In total contrast, the Spectra watermaker on Aventura IV was provided with an ingenious Z-Ion protection system. This runs automatically during the final freshwater flush cycle, by flooding antibacterial silver and copper ions through the entire system. Each freshwater flush kept the system disinfected for up to 30 days, and the watermaker only needed to be preserved when the boat was left for longer periods. Even that could be avoided by leaving the system pre-programmed to carry out regular freshwater flushes, provided the onboard freshwater pump as well as the power were left on, and there was sufficient clean water in the tanks.

Because the water available in marinas is often chlorinated, it should always be filtered with a charcoal-type filter, not only because of its taste but, in the case of aluminium tanks, also the risk of the chlorine reacting with the aluminium. However careful you may be, though, sooner or later the taste of the water drawn from those tanks may no longer be perfect for drinking. On both Aventura III and IV, the watermaker had a secondary hose to the galley, where bottles or jerrycans could be filled with freshly made water to be used for drinking, making tea, coffee or soft drinks.

Tips

» Make a realistic assessment of the estimated daily needs of electricity and then double that figure. The latter figure should dictate both the choice of an adequate charging system and battery capacity.

» Have an alternative means of charging the batteries should the main system fail.

» Always monitor the energy consumption carefully, and have a charging routine on long passages.

» Resist the temptation to use the engine-starting battery if your domestic batteries are discharged or you may end up not being able to start the engine when needed.

» Water tanks should be separated by a valve so they cannot be emptied at the same time.

» Even if you have a watermaker, always leave on long ocean passages with full tanks and take some additional water in jerrycans.

Moro Du in San Blas

25

To the land of the long white cloud

Musket Cove Resort

There are some unique places along the world-cruising circuit that have earned the affection of sailors, and Musket Cove on the Fijian island of Malolo Lailai is one such place. Musket Cove resort is the creation of Dick Smith, who arrived in the South Pacific on his own boat in the 1960s and after working for a while in the hotel business bought Malolo Lailai. He set up a resort and marina that eventually mushroomed into the Musket Cove complex. Every one of our round-the-world rallies stopped at Musket Cove, and on her arrival Aventura III was given a royal welcome by Dick and his staff.

After a very pleasant stay at Musket Cove, Gwenda and I were ready for the long passage to New Zealand. Surrounded by many cruising sailors, it was not the best place to leave from, as my unorthodox approach to weather often generates a debate as to the rights or wrongs of the decision to go. What I usually do, I set a date for departure, and if the weather looks at all acceptable I normally leave, an attitude many find impossible to understand. This is exactly what I did in Musket Cove. The weather was not ideal, but waiting for a change did not seem like a better prospect, so we left. We had an unpleasant 24 hours, with strong winds that forced us to the west of our intended track. This didn't worry me too much as I knew that we would be able to make up the lost ground closer to New Zealand, where the prevailing winds are from the west.

The winds continued to have too much south in them, so we were pushed more and more to the west. By the third day we had to go on the starboard tack, as I didn't want to stray too far from the direct course. Then luck was on my side, as conditions started to improve. A low that was heading our way across the Tasman Sea began generating northwest winds, and soon we were broadreaching. Gradually the wind crept up to 30 knots, and frequent squalls kept me on my toes.

This new wind direction resulted in an uncomfortable swell, so Gwenda spent much of the time in her bunk. I was certainly glad that Aventura was so easy to handle on my own. Earlier in the trip, when the winds were lighter, I had left the steering to the windvane, but when the winds got stronger and there was a risk of gybing, I preferred to put my trust in the autopilot. After I while, I took the wheel and was surprised how hard it was to keep the boat on course, as with just the reefed mainsail she was rather unbalanced. Probably the worst drawback of a fully battened mainsail is the difficulty of dropping it even in moderate following winds, as the sail is plastered against the spreaders and the battens get caught in the rigging. On long passages I avoid dropping the mainsail and keep it up well reefed as long as possible. The result is that when the wind gets to over 30 knots, and I need to reduce sail further, all I do is furl up the foresail and thus end up sailing with only a deeply reefed mainsail. I know that this is a rather unusual way of sailing, and may not suit other boats, but Aventura seemed to cope well with this arrangement, and I got used to it.

By the seventh day the wind had levelled off at 35 knots, with occasional stronger gusts. Every now and again I would disengage the autopilot and steer for a few minutes, enjoying the boat surfing down the waves, the speedometer rarely going below 10 knots. Admittedly, the movement was quite lively, but at that speed keeping the boat on course with the wind on the starboard quarter wasn't too difficult. Occasionally a large following sea would catch us up and lift the stern, and I could feel the acceleration as Aventura shuddered slightly under my feet. The speedometer needle kept going up and peaked once at well over 14 knots. It stayed there for a few exhilarating moments, then the wave pulled ahead and Aventura settled back in her groove, still doing 10 knots. This went on for at least one hour, in the middle of which Gwenda put her head through the hatch and, as she later told me, saw me standing at the wheel with a huge grin on my face. 'You are absolutely crazy,' was all she said before going back to her bunk, and she repeated those words more colourfully later, when the weather had calmed down.

The day before our expected landfall, I called Taupo Radio to inform New Zealand Customs of our arrival, which all incoming vessels are required to do. I told the officer on duty that it looked as if we might arrive in the Bay of Islands after dark, and I requested permission to anchor for the night and proceed to Opua for clearance the following morning. Permission to do this was firmly denied as all boats arriving from abroad had to proceed directly to an officially designated clearance dock.

Fortunately I knew the large bay from previous visits, but even so it was not easy to follow the buoys across the bay, then make our way up a narrow channel in pitch darkness. It was near midnight when we finally tied to the quarantine dock at the new Opua marina. The trip from Fiji had taken just over eight days, and with all the tacking we had sailed close to 1,200 miles. Once again, I had been right to leave when we did, as a delay of one or two days in our departure would have put us right into the path of that same depression, and we would have ended up with strong southwest winds rather than the exhilarating broadreaching conditions that we actually had.

Opua

In the previous six months Aventura had sailed from Ecuador to New Zealand, covering more than 8,000 miles, so both Aventura and her crew were ready for a long period of R&R. Having totted up almost 50,000 miles since her launch in 1998, Aventura needed a lot more than just a well-deserved rest, and I was planning to give her a thorough overhaul. New Zealand was the perfect place to do this as it has some of the best yachting facilities in the South Pacific. This is one of the main reasons why hundreds of cruising sailors leave the tropics every year to spend the cyclone season in New Zealand. This is also what brought the first Aventura south in 1978, and why I had returned a quarter of a century later. What I found this time around was very different to the quiet backwater of my previous visit, when we had arrived on a weekend and found that the whole country had virtually shut down, meaning we could not even buy a pint of fresh milk. New Zealand was now a vibrant modern country that during our absence seemed to have leapt from the 19th century straight into the 21st. What had not changed, however, were the Kiwis, whom I rate among the most welcoming and helpful people in the world.

New Zealand is, by any standard, an outstanding country, and so are its people. For a nation of barely four million, the Kiwis have totted up some truly remarkable achievements: the first man to climb Mount Everest, the best rugby team in the world, not to speak of winning the America's Cup as well as several victories in the Whitbread (now Volvo) round-the-world race. Those sailing achievements should not be too much of a surprise, as this is a nation of sailors, and the Maoris, who are the original New Zealanders, made one of the most remarkable ocean voyages in the history of seafaring when they sailed their double-hulled canoes in search of a new home from Havaiki (present-day Raiatea) to what they called The Land of the Long White Cloud (Aotearoa).

Aventura spent several months at Half Moon Bay marina, near Auckland, and I took full advantage of its range of repair and service facilities. First on my long list of jobs was a complete engine service. This started off as a fairly routine operation but became more complicated, and more costly, as a host of hidden problems were uncovered. At the same time, all sails were checked, repaired and restitched. Although the mainsail was still in reasonably good condition, I decided to order a new sail as the prices were relatively low. The old one I gave to a Kiwi sailor building his own boat, who could not believe that someone would throw away a sail before it actually fell apart. The standing rigging was checked and tested, and I had the forestay replaced as well as the lifelines, while the yankee and staysail furling gears were taken apart and serviced too. The electrical system was completely revised and the charging system, which had given me some trouble in the past, was upgraded with a new 120A alternator, a new solar panel and new gel batteries. The least work required was on my Brookes & Gatehouse instrumentation and autopilot, with only new brushes needed for the latter. Among the safety equipment, the liferaft had its usual service, while the 406MHz EPIRB, which needed new batteries, ended up being replaced with a new unit that cost less than the set of special batteries.

Considerably poorer than when I had arrived, but with a boat in tiptop condition, by the end of the southern summer I was ready to resume my voyage. As Gwenda had decided that long passages were no longer her cup of tea, I had two Kiwi friends as crew on the first leg to Noumea in New Caledonia. I had first met Paul Ewing in Greece, when we arrived with Aventura I on completion of her long voyage and he was about to hand over the boat that he had built and sailed from New Zealand to her new French owner. Roy was a friend of Paul's, and as they were both keen sailors they sounded like the perfect crew to join me for the passage north.

Leaving Auckland

Back to the tropics

The time to leave New Zealand for the tropics is after the end of the cyclone season, which, at least on paper, is 30 April. Paul and Roy were quite amazed when I told them that we'd leave Auckland, as I had always said, on 31 March. From what I was told by the customs officer when I cleared out of Auckland, we were the first boat to leave for the tropics that season. I was aware that we were departing earlier than we should, but there was a good reason for this. I was very keen to be in Vanuatu by the end of April when there would be a land-diving ceremony on the island of Pentecost. This rare occurrence was something I had missed on all of my previous visits and was determined to see this time. Leaving early was a calculated risk, and in hindsight the land divers were really not a good enough reason to leave for the tropics before the cyclone season had come to an end.

We had light winds for the first three days, but by the fourth day we had moved sufficiently north to pick up the southeast trade winds. After one day of perfect sailing with the asymmetric spinnaker, we had to endure 24 hours of miserable conditions, with violent squalls and torrential rain, while the wind was getting stronger and stronger. I had no doubt that we were in for a bout of reinforced trade winds, which is a frequent feature in this area, but at least the wind continued to blow from the right direction, even if it did creep up towards the 30-knot mark. The strong winds and large southerly swell put paid to my long-nurtured plan of stopping at Norfolk Island, which lies almost halfway between New Zealand and New Caledonia. Once used by the British as a penal colony, in the 19th century the island was turned over to settlers from Pitcairn. That tiny island, where the Bounty mutineers and their Tahitian wives managed to hide for many years from the long arm of the Royal Navy, could no longer support its expanded population, so the offer of Norfolk was gratefully accepted. The majority of those transferred to Norfolk settled there happily, and their descendants continue to live there, but a number of Pitcairners were consumed by nostalgia and returned to their abandoned island. Having twice visited Pitcairn, I was very keen to call at Norfolk as well. The island's only harbour is on the south side, which was untenable in winds from that direction. As we came within sight of Norfolk and its verdant cliffs, the course was regretfully altered because I considered it too risky to enter the exposed harbour. We sailed on all day before we lost sight of this tempting landfall. What a disappointment!

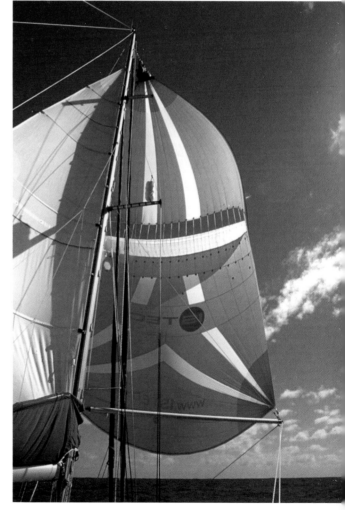

At least we had some compensation because the winds gradually eased, the sun came out, and we could hoist the brand-new Parasailor spinnaker, which I had received the day before our departure from Auckland. This novel type of spinnaker, which I described in more detail on page 166, had been advertised as the best invention since sliced bread. Both this kind of statement and the comments made by those who had used such a sail in the past sounded too good to be true, so I had some serious reservations, as did my crew. Hoisting the Parasailor was no different to a standard triradial spinnaker and, once it was up, it didn't behave all that differently either – or so we thought. After a while I noticed that, in spite of the confused swell that had been left over from the previous squally night, the spinnaker remained full and stable. Roy, who was a professional racer and former sailing champion of New Zealand, soon realised that his tweaking and playing with the lines didn't seem to make any difference as the Parasailor was quite happy to be left alone. After two days of perfect sailing, with the Parasailor doing all the work, we crossed the Tropic of Capricorn and, almost on cue, saw the first flying fish.

There was a full moon on the last night, as we sailed slowly along the southwest coast of New Caledonia. At first light we went through Amadé Pass and followed the long beaconed channel into Port Moselle, where we tied up to the visitors' dock. The marina was full of French liveaboards, most of whom had found jobs locally and seemed happy to take a break from sailing to fill up their cruising kitty. In spite of my disapproval of France hanging onto its former colonies, I must admit that the French certainly know how to enjoy life to the full, especially in their overseas territories. Among the main beneficiaries of this global network are French sailors, who can count on a 'home from home' every few thousand miles. Nowhere is this more obvious than in Noumea, which is a thriving city with well-stocked supermarkets, restaurants for all tastes and a distinct feeling of being somewhere in mainland France, not on the opposite side of the world.

Having taken a two-week holiday to sail with me, Paul and Roy had to return home to go back to work. Their place was taken by Juan Francisco Martin, a Canarian friend who had sailed with me on various occasions, and Dieter Walz, a Swiss friend who had last sailed with me in the Bahamas.

NB On this very day (12 May 2017), I read the news that Cyclone Donna has just passed over New Zealand after having caused havoc in Vanuatu and parts of Fiji. It has been described as the strongest off-season South Pacific tropical cyclone on record during the month of May.

Sunset over Havannah Pass near Noumea

26.

Practical aspects of cruising

The real voyage of discovery consists not in seeking new lands but seeing with new eyes.

Marcel Proust

Dealing with formalities is an unavoidable aspect of cruising and, especially for newcomers, it can be both daunting and irritating. Whereas in most countries that are used to cruising yachts, formalities are simpler than in the past, there are still many more restrictions imposed on cruising sailors than on ordinary tourists arriving by air. Formalities were not any simpler in the days of Columbus, and he was arrested when he reached Lisbon on his first return from the New World. Admittedly, he wasn't flying a yellow Q flag, so no wonder he was treated with suspicion.

Formalities and documents

There is a certain routine, almost an etiquette, which must be observed whenever clearing into a new country. The first rule is to make for an official port of entry or a listed clearance facility for visiting yachts, and show your intentions by flying the yellow Q flag as well as the courtesy flag of that country as soon as you enter its territorial waters. Never stop and go ashore anywhere before having cleared in first. It is important to remember that it is the intention that counts. Sometimes it is sufficient to make a call to customs whether on VHF or, as in the USA, from one of the special telephones installed on arrival docks. If you clearly state your intention, no one can later claim that you tried to sneak in. Some countries insist that they are notified 24 hours in advance of one's arrival, while Australia has the most stringent rules, requiring at least 96 hours' advance notification. On arrival, follow VHF instructions and only dock where advised. Normally one can ascertain by VHF whether officials will visit the boat or the captain is required to attend offices ashore.

Clearing immigration on arrival in Barbados

Arriving boats are usually visited by officials from customs and immigration, but in some countries yachts are also visited by plant and animal quarantine (biosecurity) officers, port officials, security and even secret police. In some countries, marinas are authorised to handle clearance formalities, or at least to act as a first point of contact. This must be ascertained before arrival. Increasingly, marinas do not respond to VHF radio and prefer to be called by phone. To complete the clearance procedure some, and occasionally all, of the following documents may be needed:

» Ship's registration certificate
» Passports of all crew
» Clearance papers from last port
» Captain's licence, or certificate of competence for the captain
» Crew lists
» Vaccination certificates
» Licences for equipment that may need it: radio, amateur radio, even diving gear in some countries
» Gun permit
» Fishing licence
» Cruising permit
» Insurance policy

Some countries are very strict about boats stopping anywhere before clearing in, so this matter should not be taken lightly, as sailors have got themselves into serious trouble for ignoring this rule. A few years ago, a British yacht stopped briefly at St Thomas in the US Virgins to drop off a crew who had to catch a flight. When the crew got to the airport with minutes to spare, the immigration officer asked about his entry stamp and soon realised that he had come off a boat that had not cleared in. The crew was immediately arrested but by then the offending captain had already left. It took several months of legal wrangling and a fine of $5,000 before the crew was released from prison.

Royal Canadian Mounted Police officers visiting Aventura IV on arrival at Tuktoyaktuk

In a few countries, such as Chile, Greenland and Arctic Canada, visiting yachts must report their position at regular intervals, but may cruise unimpeded until they reach the first port with clearance facilities.

A number of countries insist that arriving yachts advise the relevant authorities of their impending arrival well in advance of their ETA. Several foreign captains have been fined heavily in Australia for failing to give at least 96 hours' notice of their arrival.

The European Union is a special case, and EU-flagged boats and nationals can move freely within the area without the need to complete any formalities. If non-EU citizens are on board, the captain is required to inform immigration officials. Non-EU-flagged boats need to clear in at the first EU country whose waters they enter, and nationals who need visas for the EU must have acquired these in advance. Non-EU nationals may spend a maximum of 90 days in the EU in any 180-day period.

Regulations do vary from country to country within the EU, so while in some countries non-EU boats have freedom of movement once cleared in, in a few countries such as Greece, all boats, both EU and non-EU, have to clear in and get a cruising permit as well as contacting port authorities in every major port or marina.

Special requirements

Some countries require that passports must be valid for at least six months beyond the date of arrival. Passports should have sufficient blank pages because many visas use up an entire page. When applying for a new passport, it is advisable to try and get one with more than the usual number of pages.

Visas must be obtained in advance for some countries where the crew of yachts cannot get a visa on arrival. Although the USA has a visa waiver scheme (ESTA) with some countries for air travel, a visa must be obtained in advance if arriving by yacht, and that includes not just mainland USA but also Puerto Rico, the US Virgin Islands and Hawaii. This ruling does not apply to Canadians.

Crew or family members joining a boat should have a letter signed by the captain so that it can be shown at check-in at the airport of departure, or to immigration on arrival. The letter should state the name of the boat, give details of the crew and mention that they are joining the boat and will leave the country on a given date. Occasionally such a letter may be sufficient to allow the crew to arrive on a one-way ticket, as airlines are responsible for the repatriation of passengers if they are denied entry at the airport of arrival. Most airlines will not accept a passenger with a one-way ticket to fly to a country where, on arrival, immigration demands to see a return ticket. In cases where the crew arrives with what is known in the airline business as an open-jaw ticket (for example: flying from Los Angeles to Tahiti and returning from Auckland to Los Angeles), immigration at the airport of arrival may insist that the crew buy a ticket for the missing section. If this cannot be avoided, the best solution is to buy a fully refundable ticket so the fare can be redeemed later if the ticket had not been used.

Having two passports can be very useful if visiting such countries as Israel, because arriving in some Muslim countries with an Israeli stamp is prohibited or can lead to complications. Having a second passport is also good if one needs to be sent away to get a visa. A cruising permit is required in a number of countries, and in some cases it must be obtained in advance.

Guns and ammunition must be declared on arrival and, unless they are allowed to be kept on board in a sealed locker, they will be impounded and kept at the port of arrival for the duration of one's stay in a country. This can become quite complicated if the boat will leave the country from another port. In such a case a customs officer will have to take the gun to the port of departure, which can be quite an expensive operation. It must be stressed that attempting to avoid such a situation by hiding the gun would be extremely unwise, as penalties for this can be very severe.

Fishing licences are compulsory in a number of countries (Bahamas, Canada) and can be purchased on arrival.

Diving tanks need to have a certificate showing when they were last tested or they may not be refilled.

A clearance certificate (zarpe) from the last foreign port is required on arrival in some countries and should be requested when clearing out if it is known that it will be needed in the destination country.

If planning to work when underway it is essential to be able to show to a potential employer any professional qualifications, diplomas or degrees. It also helps to have an attractively produced CV and recommendations from your last employer(s). In most countries, working without a work permit is illegal and may lead to deportation. In the USA even expressing an intention to work, unless you have a green card, may lead to penalties. Similarly, if you try to sell a yacht in the USA and customs finds out, they may impose import duties based on that intention alone.

If a crew intends to fly out of the country, their ticket may have to be shown to the port immigration office. The captain must make sure to sign off the crew before their departure.

In some countries yachts in transit are allowed to keep a certain amount of duty-free drinks on board, although they may have to be sealed in a special locker. Regulations and requirements differ from country to country and this must be born in mind, as ignorance

Carrying a rifle while ashore is compulsory in
Spitsbergen to protect against attacks by polar bears   299

is no excuse. In some countries different restrictions apply to the yacht than the crew. In certain places leaving a boat unattended between seasons must be cleared with local customs, because the yacht may have to be sealed and put in bond.

In French Polynesia, EU nationals are granted a three-month visa-free stay on arrival, which can be extended to a maximum 18 months. Non-EU nationals are allowed to stay for an initial three months, and this can be extended to six months. Yachts are allowed a stay of 18 months.

In some countries (South Africa, New Zealand) visiting yachts may buy equipment tax-free, or the tax paid will be returned on one's departure. Similarly, in the European Union VAT (value added tax) may be redeemed if locally bought equipment is exported. If having a major overhaul done, it is worth asking the yard to get permission from customs not to charge local taxes on any of the equipment that will leave the country with the yacht. Consumables such as antifouling paint are usually excluded, and so are labour charges.

Quarantine regulations are very strict in some countries, Australia and New Caledonia being the strictest as most food will be confiscated and destroyed.

It is therefore advisable to arrive in such countries with no fresh produce and no prohibited items (honey, tinned pork, souvenirs containing feathers or bones, etc). Arriving in Australia should be avoided at weekends and on public holidays, when the already high quarantine charges are doubled.

Transit formalities for the Panama and Suez canals are time-consuming and best done with the help of a local agent. Although an agent is not absolutely necessary in Panama, they will not only handle all formalities but, if booked in advance, will considerably shorten the time one needs to wait for a transit. The use of a local agent in the Galapagos is compulsory, and the agent will deal both with obtaining the compulsory cruising permit in advance and with formalities on arrival.

In some countries it is much easier to arrive as part of a rally whose organisers take care of all these necessary formalities, including cruising permits. My book World Cruising Destinations has details of formalities and practical information on all maritime nations of the world, and was written to assist cruising sailors planning to sail in foreign waters.

Insurance

Some people say they cannot afford insurance, I say we cannot afford losing our boat without insurance.
Luc Callebaut

Although the yacht insurance policy is rarely requested when clearing in, most marinas will not accommodate a boat whose owner cannot show that they have at least adequate liability cover. Those who are planning to set off on a longer voyage should contact their marine insurance company at an early stage to be sure that it would be prepared to insure the yacht for the forthcoming voyage. Some companies are reluctant to insure yachts for longer voyages, and some have various stipulations such as a minimum number of adult crew, and a specified level of experience for the captain and at least one other crew member. Insurance companies may also insist on having the boat hauled before an ocean crossing and possibly being inspected by a marine surveyor. The British marine insurance company Topsail, which insured Aventura IV for the transit of the Northwest Passage, is used to dealing with yachts on longer voyages. The cost was very reasonable bearing in mind the risks associated with a transit of the Northwest Passage. What I also found attractive was the option of an additional payment to protect the no-claims bonus. In the event I did have two claims, both of which were settled in full, and without my no-claims bonus being affected.

Email and internet

There is now an internet café on every rock.
Michelle LaMontagne

Most cruising boats have some email facility on board, and although there are cyber cafés in the most unlikely places, you should not count on finding internet access everywhere. Marinas and yacht clubs may allow visiting sailors to use their wifi, but some cruisers abuse this hospitality and this makes life difficult for anyone following in their wake.

The internet is the best source of information, both at home and once underway, and should be consulted regularly on countries to be visited, their visa and entry requirements, marina and repair facilities, and also to check the latest security situation. A good source of information is noonsite.com, which I originally set up for just this purpose. Accessing the internet from your boat while on passage or cruising in remote areas is slowly becoming possible. Currently this is primarily a matter of cost, but it can only be a matter of time before access to the internet will become an affordable global feature.

Travel

Many cruising sailors travel widely away from their boats and there are few who do not take this opportunity to see more of the world. Some specific points concerning travel while leaving the boat unattended are discussed on page 332. There are also a number of aspects that must be borne in mind when booking flights.

When booking flights online, some airlines may only accept payment by credit card if the account is registered in the country where the flight originates. One way to overcome this problem is to use a local travel agent. When travelling overseas, it is strongly recommended to book your flights directly with the airline you will be flying with. The temptation to save money on flights by buying a cheaper ticket from an online booking agency should be resisted because, in the case of any problem, or even such matters as changing the date of your flight, you will not be able to deal with the airline itself but will have to do it via the booking agency. However tempting it may be to buy the cheapest tickets, this should be avoided, as they usually are unchangeable in case your plans may change. It is more prudent to either buy a flexible ticket or to ensure that the airline in question will allow changes to be made on payment of a penalty fee.

An easy matter to overlook, which can have annoying or even serious consequences, can occur in some countries, such as South Africa, where the crew of an arriving yacht gets a different visa from that of a normal tourist. This is a seaman's landing permit, which in principle restricts movement to the port of arrival. Those who leave by air must first clear out with the port immigration office and have their passport stamped accordingly. These formalities are essential or the crew may risk being stopped at the airport and missing their flight.

Finally, if travelling extensively away from the boat, it is important to have a comprehensive travel insurance that covers not only flight cancellations, but also personal health. Obtaining this type of policy may be difficult for those who are already underway, so it is advisable to attempt to arrange such insurance before the planned voyage in the hope that it can be renewed more easily once underway.

The UK based marine insurer Topsail Insurance, offers a very flexible travel insurance policy to sailors insured with them, which provides cover for emergency medical expenses, repatriation and other travel benefits. This type of year-round travel insurance allowing for longer periods of time spent abroad is aimed at cruising sailors and is quite exceptional.

Yacht transport

In today's world there seems to be a solution to everything, as I found out when Aventura III reached Vancouver in British Columbia after the transpacific marathon that had taken us from Antarctica to Alaska in only four months. Rather than continue west and thus around the world, as I had planned, I decided to return to Europe, but the eastern route would have taken just as long. My doubts came to an end when I heard about the company Dockwise Yacht Transport, which had regular runs between Vancouver and the Mediterranean. Six weeks after we had loaded Aventura

in Vancouver, she floated off in Toulon, France, and I had my boat where I wanted her to be.

I was in a similar predicament in April 2015, after Aventura IV had reached the Pacific Ocean via the Panama Canal and I realised that I did not have sufficient time to sail to Dutch Harbor if I wanted to attempt a transit of the Northwest Passage that same summer. The logical solution was to load Aventura on a Sevenstar yacht-transport ship that was due to sail from Golfito, in Costa Rica, to Victoria, in British Columbia. This allowed me to start the transit of the Northwest Passage at the most favourable time.

Several participants in the Blue Planet Odyssey round-the-world rally, who were concerned about the safety situation in the North Indian Ocean and were not prepared to sail around the Cape of Good Hope, chose the same solution to reach the Mediterranean from Southeast Asia.

Sevenstar has now joined forces with Dockwise Yacht Transport and expanded its operations to reach the most popular cruising destinations. It is being used regularly by owners who cannot fit a long passage into their busy schedule, or sailors who prefer to reach their favourite destination in the shortest time and with the least effort possible.

Languages

Although English is now almost universal, speaking another language, or trying to learn at least a few useful words of the local language (which is not difficult), can be a great advantage. One should at least learn two expressions: hello and thank you, so you can greet a local with as-salaam-alaikum in Arabic-speaking countries, bula (pronounced mbula) in Fiji, hola in Spanish-speaking countries or iaorana in Tahiti (apparently a derivation of 'your honour', which the Tahitians heard their early English visitors use frequently).

I never have great difficulty picking up the basics of another language having grown up with Romanian (father), Hungarian (mother), German (school) and Russian (compulsory in communist Romania), and later learning English (university), French (a place in Provence) and Spanish (working in the Canaries with various rallies). The Romance languages that I am familiar with help me get by in Italian and Portuguese. I was less successful in Vanuatu and Papua New Guinea, where there is a local language (Tok Pisin), basically pidgin English, developed by the early traders and plantation owners. It is called Bislama in Vanuatu, a derivation of the French bêche-de-mer, from the times when sea slugs were a main export item of the area. Despite my lack of fluency, because most words have some semblance to English I found it possible to get the gist of it – essentially the language is simple and quite logical. A sign outside an electricity substation read: 'Yu go in yu ded!'

One of the best reads is the Bislama New Testament, in which Jesus chides the devil, 'Yu no bagar ap mi church'. Bugger up, a favourite expression of those colourful Australian planters, means to spoil in Bislama. There are many other such gems, such as titibasket for a lady's bra, meri (Mary) for woman, and numbawan (number one), meaning the best or very important; while mifela means I, yumi means we (you and me), weit smol is a short delay, dipsea is the ocean, hamas means how much, yu save is do you know, mi no save is I don't know, mi glad tumas means I am happy, and ale mi go is I am leaving (from the French aller). Sori tumas mifela ask, how can anyone not be interested in languages?

New Guinea man smoking a cigarette rolled up from the Tok Pisin Niugini Nius, which used to pride itself on being the 'most smoked newspaper in the world'

In Egypt I only got as far as learning to read the numbers, but it helped. I even tried to get by in Japanese and was puzzled that every time I asked a taxi to take me to the railway station the driver always dropped me at the back of the station. After three such incidents, I realised that I was saying something wrong so asked a Japanese friend for his advice. When I told him that I was telling the taxi driver 'iki mae' he burst out laughing, because they were doing exactly what I had asked them to: go behind (iki) the railway station (mae).

At the insistence of my parents, and especially my father, who was fluent in several languages and believed that being able to communicate with other people in their own language was the best way to achieve harmony in the world, at the age of nine I was enrolled in a German school, where I arrived speaking not one word of that difficult language. I somehow muddled through the first year, at the end of which we had to pass some exams. In preparation for my German exam, I had learned by rote a few details about the lives of Karl Marx and Friedrich Engels. My German master received me with a smile and told me to pick from the desk one of several folded papers. I picked one, and all I could understand was that it had something to do with Goethe. I read out the question as well as I could, then quickly added, 'Goethe lived in the century before Karl Marx, who was born in Trier in 1818. His father was...' and trotted out some other trivial details.

'Very good, very good, Cismasiu. So what else do you know?'

'Friedrich Engels lived around the same time. He was born in 1820 in Barmen...'

'That is even better,' he said, and passed me with a sour grin. The poor guy had no choice. How could he not reward a pupil who had learned so diligently the biographies of the sacred founders of communist dogma?

Official incidents

For as long as I can remember, I have had a deep aversion to uniforms of any kind. In my early days of cruising, this aversion probably showed, but I gradually learned to control it, especially as most officials I met were decent people. Over the years, I usually had only good experiences with the officials that I had to deal with in the nearly 100 countries that I visited by boat. Unfortunately there were a few bad apples among them, and it annoys me that it is those that I remember more easily than the much more numerous nice officials.

The port of Pythagorion on the island of Samos

There have been times when I have attracted an official's suspicion, one of the most serious occasions being on the Greek island of Samos. In common with other cruising boats, we were regularly commuting between the Greek islands and the Turkish mainland coast only a few miles away. When we returned to Samos from yet another brief foray into Turkey, I was hauled in to see an officer. It soon became clear that he was no ordinary police or immigration officer but something more sinister. He looked, behaved and sounded just like a Romanian secret-service clone, of whom I had seen plenty.

He addressed me abruptly in English. 'What business do you have in Turkey?'

'None, just sightseeing.'

'That's a lie. Out with the truth! This month you have been across three times. You call that sightseeing?'

'What else can I call it? Is it illegal?'

'Don't be cheeky or I'll soon put you in your place. What's your job anyway?'

'I am a sailor.'

'Yes, yes, but what do you do to earn a living?'

'I am a journalist.'

'Oh, a journalist, that's interesting. And who do you work for?'

'Freelance really, but mostly for the BBC.'

'Did you say BBC? Now that's really interesting.'

He proceeded to grill me more and more, and I realised that he was not going to give up until he found something to nail me with.

'Look, officer, I understand your concern. I know enough about Greek history to understand your suspicions. Furthermore, as we Romanians have suffered just as

much from the Turks in the past as you Greeks, I have only the deepest sympathy for the sufferings of your people. But a spy I am not and I swear it.'

'Why did you not tell me you were Romanian from the beginning?'

'You didn't give me a chance.'

'OK, let's leave it at that, but no more trips to Turkey or I'll be forced to act.'

The worst incident happened in Peru on Aventura I. We were warmly welcomed at the Callao Yacht Club near the capital Lima, where we met Alan Sitt, a young American whose father had a small factory in Peru. Alan agreed to look after Aventura and assured us that she would be safe while we toured the interior of Peru and neighbouring countries.

After Christmas, we embarked on a two-day bone-rattling trip on a rickety bus that took us over the High Andes to Cuzco and the ancient Inca remains at Machu Picchu. Our trip continued by train to Lake Titicaca, from where we crossed on foot into Bolivia. The border guard took a look at our passports and shook his head.

'You should not be here at all. You have a seaman's shore pass, not a visa. You must go back to Callao and sort it out.'

I thought we had completed all the necessary formalities when we had arrived from Panama, and it never occurred to me that we needed to obtain special permission to leave the port area. I begged and argued, but he was adamant: we had to go back.

'Señor, I see what we have done was wrong, and as such we should be punished. Why don't you fine us, say 20 dollars, so we learn the lesson and never do it again.' While saying this, I slipped a 20-dollar note between the pages of my passport.

His eyes lit up. 'That sounds better. Let me have those passports and see what I can do. In fact, to help you, I will alter the date and place of entry and give you the proper entry stamp as well.'

'That is ever so helpful, señor, thank you.'

This was the first and only time I have bribed an official, as it is something that I am very much against. He put all the necessary stamps in our passports and waved us on our way. Over the next six weeks, we visited by train, bus and taxi some of the highlights of South America: Bolivia's stunning interior, carnival in Rio de Janeiro, the Iguazu Falls in northern Argentina. From Paraguay we flew back to Lima and started preparing Aventura for the passage to Easter Island, on which we were to be joined by Alan.

The morning of our planned departure, I went to do the usual clearing out formalities. As I stepped into the immigration office, the official who had cleared us in on arrival looked at me and said, 'Aren't you from that English boat?'

'Yes, Aventura.'

'And where have you been all this time? Didn't I tell you to come and see me to get your proper visas?'

'I am sorry, I must have misunderstood, but anyway, we are now ready to leave.'

'OK, let me have those passports.'

He suddenly looked up and said, 'What on earth have you done? You have not only left the port without express permission, but have also faked your visas. This is a serious offence.'

I tried to explain what had happened, but he was adamant.

'This is no joke. This is very serious. I must take it up with my superiors.'

I knew that he meant it and I also knew that I was in very serious trouble.

'Can I please make a phone call?'

'You can call God if you want but it won't help you!'

Alan's father, who everyone referred to as Colonel Sitt, had been an officer in the US Army and had retired to Peru. I somehow felt that there was more to it than that, so I called Alan and briefly described my problem. 'Alan, please talk to your father. Maybe he can help.'

'OK, I will. What is your number there?'

The officer told me to wait outside. Even compared to some of my troubles in Romania, I felt that this time my luck had run out. Worse still, on our return we had been told that the crews of two yachts that had arrived during our absence had all been thrown in jail after cocaine had been found on one of them. I was sure that I would probably share their fate. After a while, the officer called me in.

'Mr Cornell,' he addressed me in a surprisingly friendly manner, 'why did you have to involve other people in this simple matter that could have been easily resolved by the two of us? I agree that you have made a mistake but, after all, we are human, aren't we?'

I could not believe my ears.

'Yes, and believe me I am very sorry for being so stupid, but I only made that call because my friend is going to sail with us to Easter Island.'

'I am glad to hear that you have such an important friend in our country. You must have got him worried, so why don't you call him to say that it was, as it were, only a storm in a teacup. Please use the phone.'

I called Alan to say that it all seemed to have been sorted out.

'I am glad to hear that, even if my dad had to revert to some really heavy guns, but he is very good at that.'

'Here are your passports,' the official said as he handed them to me. 'You will see that I have retroactively granted you the necessary visas, so now you are in perfect order.'

'Thank you so much.'

'That's OK, but don't do it again as in other countries you could get into some serious trouble. Fortunately, here in Peru we are much more tolerant.'

The following morning Alan joined us on Aventura and brusquely waived off my embarrassed but sincere thanks. I have remained in contact with Alan ever since, and visited him in Hawaii when I stopped there with Aventura III on the way to Alaska. He lives on Oahu with his Peruvian wife and works as a commercial pilot. I never asked, and he never told me, what Colonel Sitt's real role was, but it didn't really matter. What mattered was that he managed to save my skin.

There are two other, rather more trivial, incidents that I'd like to mention. When we arrived in Fort Lauderdale with the first Aventura, one of the many officials who inspected the boat rummaged through all our lockers and came up with a bunch of garlic.

'What is this?' he asked.

'Garlic. Do you want some?'

He looked at me as if I were mad.

'This is a prohibited import and you should have declared it, not hid it out of sight.'

'It was not out of sight, but out of light.'

'You boat people have an excuse for everything. I'll confiscate it and I could fine you as well, but I'll let you off... this time.'

Many years later I arrived in New Caledonia with a lot of fresh food from New Zealand, not realising that this was not allowed. The plant quarantine officer went through every locker, emptied the fridge and vegetable basket, and started putting everything in a large plastic bag. I saw her pick up a box of eggs.

'Do you have to take those as well?'

'They are fresh so they must go.'

'What if they are broken? Are you worried about their contents or the shells?'

'The shells really.'

'Then let me deal with them myself,' so I broke the whole dozen into a bowl and handed her the shells. For lunch we had the largest omelette south of the equator.

These examples are some rare exceptions, as there were many more situations where officials had been more than friendly and helpful. When we arrived in Cocos Keeling from Bali with Aventura III loaded with fresh provisions, to last us the month it would take us to sail via Chagos to Mauritius, the Australian officer understood our situation and allowed us to keep all fresh produce, provided none of it was taken ashore. Just as helpful was the US immigration officer in Honolulu, where Ivan arrived on Aventura III without a passport, which he had somehow lost while in Bora Bora. American officials are known to be absolute sticklers for rules, but this one was a gentle older person who made no fuss at all. He fined Ivan 170 dollars and granted him a one-month waiver that allowed him to get to Alaska and wait there for a new passport.

While I may recall some of the more troublesome officials, my lasting memory is not of them but of the warmth and friendliness we encountered everywhere we stopped. My firm conviction after all this voyaging is that most people are kind and generous, and that bad ones are a tiny minority. So nothing will ever make me change my opinion that the world is full of wonderful people, and it has been my great fortune to meet so many of them.

Tips

» Fly the yellow Q flag as soon as you enter a country's territorial waters, and head directly for the nearest official port of entry. Never stop anywhere before properly clearing in.

» Contact the relevant authorities by radio, phone or email in countries where advance notice of arrival is compulsory.

» Respect the dress code of the country you are visiting and never go to an office unsuitably dressed. Treat officials with respect and courtesy, and whatever happens never allow yourself to lose your temper.

» Try having two passports if planning to visit sensitive countries, or to have one as a backup if a passport needs to be surrendered or sent off to get a visa.

» Check the validity of your vaccinations and get any vaccinations that are needed for the countries that you plan to visit before leaving, as it is both easier and safer to get them done in your home country.

» Produce and print or photocopy several crew lists with all personal details, so they can be handed out when clearing in.

» Crew joining the boat should have an official letter from the captain/owner of the boat to be shown at check-in at departure, or to immigration on arrival.

» Have a boat stamp, which, for some strange reason, is appreciated in some of the more bureaucratic countries.

English Harbour in Antigua

27

Safety afloat and ashore

He who will not sail till all dangers are over must never put to sea.

Thomas Fuller

Safety has been a major concern for seafarers from the earliest days of sailing, and whereas in the old days mariners were willing to put their fate in the lap of the gods, today's prudent sailors prefer to play safe by reducing the risks as much as possible. It is quite uncanny that almost every time I start working on a new chapter of this book, I read about some incident or disaster that is relevant to it. This time it was the gruesome news of a German sailor who had been murdered by pirates in the Philippines after the ransom they had demanded had not been paid.

Jürgen Kantner and his partner Sabine Merz had been sailing for many years aboard their 53-foot yacht Rockall. In 2008, while sailing off the coast of Yemen, they were abducted by Somali pirates and held for 52 days. They were freed after a high ransom was paid for their release. In 2009, they retrieved their yacht from Somalia and continued sailing. Seven years later, in November 2016, their yacht was attacked while sailing in an area of the southern Philippines under the control of the terrorist group Abu Sayyaf. During the attack, Sabine Merz was killed and Jürgen Kantner was abducted. In recent years Abu Sayyaf has abducted several foreign tourists as well as sailors, and if the demanded ransom was not paid on time, the victims were killed. This is what happened to Jürgen Kantner, whose body was found on Jolo island in the Sulu Sea, in early March 2017.

In 2015, the same group had abducted from a marina near Davao, in the central Philippines, Canadian John Ridsdel of the catamaran Aziza, Canadian Robert Hall and his Filipino partner Marites Flor of the yacht Renova, and Norwegian Kjartan Sekkingstad of the yacht Wiskun. The two Canadians were murdered in April 2016 when the Canadian government refused to pay the ransom. Marites Flor was released shortly afterwards, and Kjartan Sekkingstad was released in September 2016.

Thinking of this and similar incidents with fatal consequences, I am tempted to believe that some people must have a death wish. What other explanation could there be for the disastrous decision by the crew of Rockall to sail into an area known for repeated abductions for ransom and murders of foreign captives?

Reeling back the memories of other real or potential tragedies, I can only conclude that in some situations sailors had brought such disasters upon themselves. Indeed, when I consider the total losses mentioned in these pages, it is remarkable that virtually every one of them could have been avoided. Several boats were lost for being anchored in an unsafe place, their captains not being prepared to leave when the weather deteriorated. The above tragedy was just as avoidable, as no sane sailor should sail anywhere near a notorious area such as the southern Philippines.

Having written these lines, I decided to contact some search and rescue (SAR) authorities to find out if they kept records of incidents involving sailing boats. The Australian Coast Guard responded immediately with details of two recent cases. In March 2017, an Irish yacht that was caught in a storm while sailing from New Zealand to Sydney capsized and broke its rudder. The two sailors were rescued, but the boat had to be abandoned. The same month, a South African yacht on passage to New Zealand was dismasted in the Southern Ocean. The Australian Navy sent a ship to the location, and the three crew members were winched to safety by

Davao marina

helicopter, but the yacht was abandoned. The Falmouth Coast Guard reported an incident involving the 60-foot Clyde Challenger. While on passage to the UK, the yacht lost both its mast and rudder when it was hit by a rogue wave 400 miles west of Portugal. The 14 sailors were rescued by the Royal Navy, but the yacht had to be scuttled as it posed a hazard to navigation.

The Falmouth Coast Guard keeps a record of all rescue operations, and what is remarkable is that in 2016, among the approximately 2,300 reported incidents, only 44 involved sailing yachts. In almost all cases the latter were close collision situations in the English Channel, with no serious consequences being reported. This point was emphasised by Colin Struman, a former Coast Guard official: 'The real problem are the inexperienced people who set off in unsuitable boats and get into trouble while coastal cruising. Offshore, many more racing boats get into serious trouble than cruising boats, probably because cruising sailors going offshore are usually well prepared and know what they are doing. Bearing in mind the number of boats sailing the world's oceans, very few boats are lost offshore.'

The US Coastguard does not keep records that refer specifically to sailing vessels. The most recent annual report lists a total of 2,211 incidents involving recreational craft, with 174 fatalities among them. Virtually all incidents happened in coastal or inland waters, the findings of the US Coastguard confirming those of its British counterpart. The encouraging conclusion is that offshore sailing can be quite safe.

Personal safety

In recent years personal safety has become a major concern among cruising sailors. This is in total contrast to the situation during my early days of cruising. In all my years of sailing, neither my family nor myself have ever felt seriously threatened, and the few thefts that we suffered were quite insignificant. In spite of this, in later years I started observing some basic rules such as always locking the boat when going ashore and usually, but not always, when going to visit another boat. My outboard engines were always kept padlocked on the aft rail. Some people go as far as locking the boat at night when they are on board, while others have installed alarm systems. A simple precaution is to remove everything on deck that can be easily picked up, and to make sure that there are no tempting loose items in the cockpit when visited by locals.

Dinghy theft seems to be more prevalent than theft from inside yachts. It is advisable to secure the outboard motor and its tank with a combination padlock on a steel cable, both when going ashore but also at night when the tender is tied to the boat. The most vulnerable items are inflatable dinghies and outboards. In suspicious areas, the tender and outboard should always be brought up on deck at night.

Safety rules

Over the years I have compiled a number of safety rules that became routine on all my boats. At night or in rough weather no one is allowed to leave the cockpit, unless I am present. Similarly, if anyone is taking a shower on the stern platform, there should be another person on standby in the cockpit. Urinating over the side is strictly forbidden. The boom must be prevented at all times, and especially when broadreaching or running. This is easily done on Aventura IV with the help of the Walder boom brake.

When climbing the mast to do a job, whether with the help of steps or being hoisted in the bosun's chair, a harness should always be worn and clipped to a secure point while working. While in the tropics, a mask should always be worn when swimming from the boat to be able see if there are any sharks about. Sharks very rarely attack without warning, so if one is seen to be lurking about you should get back on board immediately. Swimming in the open ocean while on passage is not permitted, unless it has to be done in an emergency such as when a line or net needs to be cut from the propeller.

Travel

In my early surveys personal safety was rarely mentioned, whereas now the subject is often raised when I give lectures or take part in cruising seminars. In fact, in spite of the concern over acts of piracy or violent robberies, sailors are much more vulnerable when sightseeing ashore, or travelling as ordinary tourists, than when on their own boats. In such situations the precautions to be taken are the same as if arriving in another country by aeroplane or car. Most cruising sailors travel widely away from their boats and there are very few who do not take this excellent opportunity to see more of the world. The subject of cruising in stages and leaving the boat unattended while travelling inland is discussed on page 330.

Avoiding troublesome areas

If safety becomes a serious concern then I would rather not be in such a place at all, as the boat becomes like an albatross around your neck.

Skip Novak

The best precaution is to avoid doubtful areas altogether. This means not only places where attacks on cruising boats have been reported recently, but also regions undergoing a period of political uncertainty, such as the Red Sea, North and East Africa, Venezuela, Honduras, Belize and some areas of Nicaragua, Panama and Brazil. This was the case in 2017, but the latest information should always be checked because things are continuously changing. While there is no doubt that avoiding countries or areas with a known record of violence is highly recommended, cruising sailors are usually in little danger in places where such acts of violence have an underlying political cause. In such cases, sailors should try to keep abreast of developments by monitoring the news before arrival, staying in contact with their embassies and, if already in the country concerned, keeping a low profile. Avoiding doubtful areas is a good policy whether travelling by boat or on land.

Piracy and violent robberies

Besides personal safety when cruising, a more serious concern is the possibility of a piracy attack. The term piracy describes attacks against a vessel by another vessel on the high seas, so strictly speaking many recent incidents involving yachts should not be described as piracy but robbery. Cases of both violent robbery and actual piracy involving cruising sailors are relatively rare. The situation in the previously infamous Gulf of Aden seems to have improved, with no attacks on cruising yachts as the result of naval vessels of various nations patrolling that area in recent years. The International Maritime Bureau runs a Piracy Reporting Centre that covers incidents involving both commercial vessels and pleasure craft. The website icc-ccs.org covers maritime crime issues, and publishes news and warnings on dangerous areas, reports on incidents and has a 24-hour maritime-security hotline.

The Caribbean safety and security website safetyandsecuritynet.com publishes reports on any reported incidents, whether theft, assault, armed burglary or piracy attacks, in a wide area covering the entire Caribbean Sea basin, from Barbados in the east to Panama in the west. Details of a total of 81 incidents were listed in 2016, the most serious being six reported armed burglaries and six piracy attacks. Among the latter, one each occurred in St Croix (US Virgin Islands) and Belize, and two each in Nicaragua and the area between Grenada and Trinidad, the latter perpetrators suspected of being from Venezuela.

The website noonsite.com keeps a record of piracy attacks going back to 1999 and is a useful site to monitor updates on the latest security situation, as well as on formalities and related issues for all cruising destinations.

Guns

I doubt I would knowingly go to a region where a couple of Uzis and a rocket launcher would be needed.

Arthur Beiser

Whether to carry arms or not is a difficult decision, and the proportion of cruising boats that do is very small. Regulations concerning firearms vary enormously from country to country, and their presence on board a cruising boat can cause certain difficulties because of the formalities involved. In some countries firearms are bonded on board, but more often they are removed for the duration of the boat's sojourn in a particular port or country.

A much-publicised incident involved the yachts Mahdi and Gandalf, which were attacked by armed pirates off the coast of Yemen in March 2005. The pirates started firing as they approached the two boats. The captain of Mahdi, a retired US Navy officer, started shooting back and hit at least one of the attackers, after which the two boats retreated. The incident caused much debate in cruising circles and re-ignited the controversy over the issue of carrying guns or not. Jay Barry of Gandalf said. 'As much trouble as they are, in some circumstances, they can help. That's why we're alive.'

Among 100 captains questioned on this subject in a survey conducted in the Caribbean and South Pacific, the majority were firmly against the idea, including both those who had a gun and also some of those who did not. Only 11 captains considered firearms to be essential for their protection. Six captains, who were reluctant to carry arms, stressed nevertheless that their possession might be justified in certain parts of the world. Several owners described their guns as a deterrent and not an offensive weapon. For some sailors who did not wish to carry guns, the solution to this problem was to avoid areas with a bad reputation. Because of the disadvantages of having firearms on board, several people had acquired mace or pepper-spray containers, regarding them as an acceptable alternative for self-defence against burglars and casual intruders, which are more common than pirates. As one captain pointed out, 'It's far better to have a potential robber crying his eyes out than to discover you have shot dead the cousin of the local police chief.'

Luc Callebaut summed up the dilemma faced by those who might consider having firearms: 'If you produce them when threatened, you may scare the aggressors away or, more likely, you may encourage them to fire at you. If taken by surprise, you may not have time to get your gun, and you cannot have it at the ready every time you meet someone you don't know.'

This is exactly what went through my mind when I was sailing on my own from Panama to Ecuador on Aventura III. Having just left Colombian waters, I was still apprehensive because that was known as a dangerous area. Early that morning I was approached by a large whaler-type boat with three men on board. They looked quite menacing as they came at great speed towards Aventura. They slowed down a few metres away and shouted instructions about how to avoid their fishing long-lines deployed nearby. If I had been armed, I should have had my gun ready to fire before they got too close. Fortunately I was not armed, otherwise what turned out to be an entirely innocent incident could have had tragic consequences. I am sure that, like me, most sailors have given the subject of firearms a great deal of thought, and probably decided that arms and yachts are not a good combination. This was confirmed recently at a skippers' briefing for participants in a transatlantic rally when not one of the captains present had a gun on board.

There are a few places where having a gun is justified, such as when cruising in Spitsbergen or Arctic Canada, where it is in fact compulsory to always carry a gun as there have been several attacks by polar bears, and a number of people have been killed.

The threat of an attack on the high seas is one of the reasons why some sailors prefer to join a rally, as there is an element of safety in numbers. This is what happened towards the end of the Millennium Odyssey while the yachts were crossing the Gulf of Aden and the British yacht Nori was intercepted by a boat coming from the direction of northern Somalia. Three other Millennium yachts sailing in the vicinity were alerted and closed in with the threatened yacht. The French military authorities in Djibouti, who, at our request, had been monitoring the progress of the Millennium

fleet, were alerted by us and immediately dispatched a helicopter to the scene. By the time it got there, the offending boat had disappeared over the horizon. The helicopter gave chase and intercepted the boat as it was making full speed towards the Somali coast.

I must stress once again that areas prone to piracy attacks should be avoided at all costs. The fact that there have been so few victims of piracy among cruising sailors in recent years is due to their alertness and prudence. The tragic incident mentioned at the beginning of this chapter is a sad exception. For those who, for some reason, need to sail through, or close to, a suspicious area, the following list includes some practical suggestions.

Tips for piracy waters

Attempt to form a convoy of between three and six boats of similar speed whose crew are prepared to remain in close contact and, if necessary, slow down to allow slower boats to catch up.

Maintain visual contact with all boats in daytime and find a way to keep in contact at night (ideally by radar) without showing masthead lights or any other lights that can be seen from beyond the range of the convoy.

Maintain radio silence on the standard VHF channels and turn off the AIS, as both can be easily monitored by other parties. Ideally, keep permanently open a SSB channel on a frequency agreed and available to all other boats in the convoy. The alternative is to keep in contact with the others by satellite phone.

Have a crew member on permanent listening watch on the agreed SSB frequency and have the SSB radio connected to a speaker in the cockpit.

Monitor the immediate area on radar, and if anything suspicious approaches alert the others immediately. Even if the suspected vessel is still out of visual range but appears to be on an intercepting course, the convoy should close ranks.

All boats in the convoy should be equipped with satellite telephones and have the numbers of maritime or naval authorities in neighbouring countries, as well as those of the international SAR authorities, so that they can be contacted promptly in an emergency.

Make sure that a responsible person ashore receives regular position reports from the convoy and can contact the relevant authorities promptly in an emergency.

If the worst comes to the worst, do not resist the attackers, keep calm, hand over all valuables and follow their instructions. In most known recent cases, when the crew being attacked offered no resistance, the pirates appeared satisfied with just robbing the boat and refrained from killing or being violent to anyone.

In case of an attack
» Do not resist
» Avoid making eye contact
» Avoid any action that may be deemed to be aggressive
» Hand over valuables and have some cash prepared for such an eventuality

Collisions

We always have someone on watch 24 hours a day. We have had to make rapid course changes when we have overtaken or been overtaken by a vessel with no one on watch. A potential collision was avoided only because we were watchful.

Bob Hall

Collisions with ships, containers, whales or unidentified objects are probably the main cause of boat losses on the high seas. Among all those hazards, I consider ships to be the greatest risk to sailing boats, and although I have only had a couple of potentially dangerous encounters, there is always somebody on watch on my boat, and whenever I feel that a ship is too close for comfort, I prefer to be the first to take avoiding action. AIS has greatly improved the situation but, just like GPS, it can result in a false sense of security. For some reason, some ships do not have AIS, or have turned it off. While sailing off the west coast of Greenland, a large fishing boat passed us at great speed. Because the visibility was good, our radar was not turned on, but we had seen the boat approaching, although it did not show up in AIS. Later, while motoring through a large fjord near Bergen, in Norway, we also encountered a large fishing vessel that did not show up on AIS. It made me wonder whether in both cases it had been done on purpose, as it is known that some fishing vessels do occasionally operate illegally in areas where they are not supposed to.

Possibly the worst incident in the pre-AIS days happened in the Bay of Biscay, while I was sailing with a friend on Aventura III from the Isle of Wight to Porto. During his night watch, my friend called me to come up quickly and, as I stepped into the cockpit, I saw a large ship some 50 metres away bearing down on us. As we were broadreaching, there was no time to gybe in a controlled manner, so I started the engine, turned the wheel, the mainsail gybed, and the ship missed us by not more than 10 metres. As it sped by with all lights blazing, we could see the crew working on deck, but they didn't seem to have noticed us although we had our masthead navigation light on. After we had sorted out the sails and gone back onto our original course, my friend explained that the ship was overtaking us on a parallel course when it suddenly changed course, made a sharp turn and headed straight for us. The only explanation that I could think of was that it may have been on automatic pilot and, having reached its waypoint, it had automatically altered course for the next waypoint. This seemed a most plausible explanation as we were close to Cape Finisterre, where ships do alter course having passed that important landmark. Whatever the reason, it was a frighteningly close call and we could easily have been run down.

While on passage from Cape Town to St Helena with my friends Patrick and Marc, we were sitting in the cockpit one evening when a large tanker appeared out of the darkness and passed close to our portside, without showing any lights or signs of life. We were so taken by surprise that we didn't have time to react. As it disappeared like an evil phantom into the night, I called on VHF channel 16, but my call was not answered.

As to actual collisions at sea, I have experienced two, fortunately not with another vessel. One happened on passage from La Reunion to South Africa after we had received a warning by Inmarsat C that some large logs had been seen in the area south of Madagascar. We were sailing fast in a strong wind when there was an almighty bang. The shock of the collision brought Aventura III to a dead stop, and I realised that we must have hit one of those logs. Fortunately, the aluminium hull sustained no damage and we managed to continue. The incident is described in more detail on page 226.

The Indian Ocean seems to have it in for me because my very first collision happened while en route to the Red Sea on Aventura I, and it also involved a floating log. Before I took over the night watch, Gwenda had asked me if it was prudent to continue blindly under full sail.

'Oh, there is really nothing to worry about in this area,' I assured her.

She reminded me of my overconfident statement when she was abruptly woken up by a loud bang. In the light of the torch I saw a large tree with thick branches appear astern from under our keel.

'What was that?' Gwenda asked as she rushed into the cockpit.

'It looks to me that we have landed in a forest.'

Aventura had been stopped in her tracks by the collision, but she slowly extricated herself and left the tree behind. A quick inspection of the bilges showed there was no water coming in and it looked as if we had not suffered any serious damage.

'Nothing to worry about?' Gwenda asked.

What could I say? I let Gwenda go back to sleep and continued my watch. As it started getting light, I was looking ahead into the half-darkness when suddenly I saw not three boat lengths ahead of us a dark shape undulating in the swell. I disengaged the self-steering gear and managed to avoid it by a few metres. It was a large whale fast asleep on the surface. Nothing to worry about indeed!

Collisions with whales are not that uncommon, and most of the time seem to occur when the whale is asleep on the surface. This is what happened to the French 52-foot catamaran Lama Lo, which was seriously damaged in a collision with a whale off the South African coast in October 2015. One hull was badly holed, so the crew of two activated their EPIRB, and launched the liferaft and their two inflatable dinghies. Before the boat capsized, they took to one of the dinghies, as they considered this to give them a better chance of surviving and reaching the shore. They attempted to row in the direction of the shore but the dinghy capsized in the rough seas, and they also lost the liferaft and the other dinghy. They managed to get back into the dinghy, and were eventually located by a SAR vessel and taken ashore.

My relationship with whales before my move to metal boats was rather ambivalent as I was quite concerned about bumping into one while at sea but at the same time could not resist the temptation to get as close as possible when the risk looked small.

Being in the company of whales was one of the greatest thrills in Antarctica, where there are always large numbers of humpback whales that migrate south for the summer to gorge on the abundant krill. I might have met some of the same whales when I dived with them later in Vava'u, where humpback whales come regularly to breed.

Whenever we encountered whales with the first Aventura, I always tried to put some distance between us. Once, while cruising among the outer islands of Papua New Guinea, we were surrounded by a pod of killer whales. They didn't show any aggressive intentions but just their menacing presence was worrying enough, so I decided to try a small trick. I poured a small amount of diesel into the water, which quickly spread on the surface. As the smelly stuff reached their blowholes, the whales instantly departed. It was a harmless and highly effective solution. Nowadays when I am in an area where whales are present and I am concerned about colliding with them while they may be asleep, I prefer to switch on my forward-looking sonar. The ultrasound signal emitted by the transducer would probably irritate or warn a whale of our presence, without doing them any damage. I have certainly noticed that we never had dolphins accompany us when the sonar was on, although this could be coincidence.

While sailing their 40-foot aluminium Igloo from France to the Canaries, my friends Erick and Muriel Bouteleux collided in broad daylight with a Spanish fishing trawler. They were sailing on a parallel course to the trawler when it suddenly made a 90-degree turn and rammed Igloo in the bows. After the collision, the trawler backed off and sped away. Erick took its name and called on the VHF radio, but there was no response. The violent impact had seriously damaged Igloo's forward area, jamming the foresail furling gear. Erick got out his 220V angle grinder, cut away part of the pulpit and freed the furling gear. As they were in no immediate danger, they decided to continue to the Canaries, where the damage was put right. This is a good example of the importance of having a good selection of tools on board, especially mains power tools.

Groundings

This yacht had spent over 24 hours bouncing on a reef in Tonga but its strong aluminium hull survived the ordeal with relatively minor damage

Collision damage on Igloo

In spite of the much-improved precision of navigation, the major cause of boat losses continues to be that of grounding. A survey, which I conducted on the reported losses of cruising boats, and updated by recent observations, showed that more than half of the total reported were caused by running aground. The main reasons for groundings are: navigational mistake, human error and being driven onto a lee shore.

Several of the reported losses gave the reason as navigational error. Two boats were lost on a reef on the north coast of Tahiti within one week of each other, in both cases owing to their navigators relying on outdated charts. Similar cases were reported from the Caribbean and South Indian Ocean. Human error was mentioned in a number of cases, either the crew on watch failing to steer the assigned course, or taking the wrong decision in a critical situation usually by leaving it too late to call the captain. Finally, being caught on a lee shore has always been a seaman's nightmare and unfortunately it still happens. Boats are lost or damaged every year in tropical anchorages when a sudden squall or passing depression puts them on a lee shore.

There have been three instances where my own boat has run aground. They all happened during our first round-the-world voyage, and I am sure that they served as serious warnings because I managed to avoid repeating the experience. The first and potentially most serious grounding happened in the Turks and Caicos Islands (see page 62). The second incident happened later that year in the Chesapeake Bay, when I tried to enter Annapolis in the dark and we ran aground on a mudbank (see page 105). The third happened in the Solomons, where we went too far into a shallow bay and ran hard aground. With the tide running out, I managed to stop the boat from tipping over by propping it up with the spinnaker poles. At the next high tide we were unable to come off, so I had to swallow my pride and row to a tugboat that happened to be in that remote place, waiting to tow a large raft

Sailing with an A-frame made up of two spinnaker poles

of felled trees. The helpful captain took our line and pulled us into deeper water. It is in such situations that I always remember an old Romanian saying: 'It doesn't matter how stupid you are, as long as you are lucky.'

Structural damage

Several of the reported losses were as a result of structural damage, often caused by rudder or keel failure. On some occasions this may have been caused by a collision, and in this respect unsupported spade rudders seem to be particularly vulnerable. In the last 30 years, several boats taking part in the ARC were abandoned after losing their rudders. In most cases this seems to have been a result of a design fault or inherent weakness. Although some of the crews believed that the rudder might have been lost as a result of a collision, the very fact that they could not be sure that they had actually hit something probably meant that those rudders were not up to the job.

A recent example of a boat that was abandoned after losing its rudder is that of the British 52-foot yacht Dove II. While on passage from Portugal to the Caribbean in December 2016, the couple and two young children on board encountered strong winds. The rough seas caused the rudder to break away from its stock, making the boat unmanageable. Incapable of rigging a jury rudder, they decided to abandon the boat and were rescued by a large yacht.

Around the same time, two catamarans arrived in Barbados at the end of the Atlantic Odyssey, the owners only noticing while tying up to the dock that they had each lost one of their rudders. In both cases the failure was due to delamination. Having two rudders was certainly an advantage.

Losing the mast is possibly the most traumatic experience on a sailing boat, although its consequences are not necessarily as grave as that of losing the rudder. This is shown by the much larger proportion of boats being abandoned after having lost their rudder than their mast. A rudderless boat is unmanageable, and improvising a means of steering the boat is often impossible. In contrast to that, the crew of many dismasted boats have managed to improvise some kind of jury rig and reach safety unaided. A good example is that of a boat in the ARC, shown above, which lost its mast halfway across the Atlantic, but the crew managed to hoist a sail on an improvised A-frame and continue sailing. They even kept pace with some of the boats that still had their masts up.

Bolted-on keels can be another potential weakness, demonstrated by the case of the British yacht Cheeki Rafiki, lost on a passage from the Caribbean to the UK in May 2014. The upturned hull was discovered without its keel, and with no sign of the four crew members. The crew had reported water ingress from an unidentified source, and when the US Coastguard discovered the upturned hull, it sent down a diver who confirmed that the keel was missing and that the liferaft had not been launched.

There have been many such incidents caused by a yacht losing its keel, and in most reported cases the keel had fallen off, causing the boat to capsize. This is instantaneous and the crew have no chance to launch the liferaft and save their lives. Yachting World magazine has published a report showing that since 1984 there have been 72 cases of keel failure, with 24 lives lost.

Anyone faced with water ingress from an unknown source should check the following:

» Seacocks
» Overflowing toilet
» Depth sounder or other through-hull transducers
» Engine seawater pump
» Propeller shaft stern gland or saildrive seal
» Rudder stock
» Keel bolts if the boat has a bolted-on keel
» A cracked freshwater tank

If the source cannot be established, the first test to do is to taste the water in the bilge to find out whether it is salty or fresh. If the source cannot be identified and the water ingress is difficult to keep under control, the procedure is to prepare the liferaft, secure it to the boat and launch it. Prior to launching the liferaft, the boat should heave to so as to stop or slow it down. The liferaft will be held behind the boat by its lanyard.

A common but less reported breakage, which usually occurs as a result of an involuntary gybe, is that of the gooseneck fitting connecting the boom to the mast. I had this experience on two occasions myself, and managed to continue sailing by securing the boom to the mast, and reefing the mainsail so as to reduce the strain. In both cases, I had the cast-aluminium fitting replaced with a part machined from solid aluminium.

The keel bolts should be checked regularly, as on this boat sailing in a round-the-world rally

Weather

Reports of sailing yachts being lost at sea due to bad weather are relatively rare, and when it happens it is often the case of being in the wrong place at the wrong time. On 18 January 2015 a 44-foot catamaran with a crew of three was lost in the South Indian Ocean while on a delivery voyage from South Africa to Thailand. It was the tropical cyclone season and the boat's last reported position was close to Cyclone Bansi, with reported gusts of 85 knots and a 12-metre swell. The upturned hull was spotted a few months later east of Mauritius.

The best documented weather damage suffered by cruising boats while on passage occurred in June 1994, during the so-called Queen's Birthday storm when a group of boats sailing from New Zealand to Tonga were caught by a violent storm. In spite of the severity of the storm, only nine of the 35 boats closest to the centre of it suffered serious damage. One boat and its crew of three were lost, and eight other boats had their crews rescued but the boats were abandoned. The high seas caused some boats to pitch-pole or roll over repeatedly, and seven boats lost their rig. With the help of a Royal New Zealand Navy ship and helicopter, 17 sailors were rescued. What was quite remarkable, and this is why this example is worth mentioning, is that in spite of the damage suffered, all the boats whose crews were rescued were from boats that were still afloat. It appears that some of the boats that had been abandoned would have survived the storm, if left to their own devices. Never was the old wisdom truer that you should only abandon your boat when you have to step up into the liferaft!

The above boats were sailing in company with other boats as part of an organised rally, so it was tempting to find out if this shows that there might be safety in numbers. Looking at the records of the approximately 200 boats that took part in the five round-the-world rallies that I organised between 1991 and 2016, there was only one total loss, the Hungarian Jolly Joker, which ran aground on a reef in the Torres Strait. Besides that incident, the round-the-world rallies produced little drama, with only two dismastings and a few groundings, none with serious consequences. What is quite remarkable about those round-the-world rallies is how very few serious breakages the boats experienced, which shows, as in my own case, just how trouble-free a circumnavigation can actually be – if one is well prepared.

Compared to offshore losses, many more boats are lost while caught on a lee shore or while anchored in an unsafe place. I came across two such cases during my voyage on Aventura III. One was a boat that dragged its anchor and broke up on a reef in Chagos during a sudden squall. The other boat had been anchored in Vanuatu and tried to leave at night, when the wind changed direction. As they were leaving the bay in the dark, navigating by GPS and radar, they clipped the corner of a fringing reef and the boat ended up being smashed to pieces. The crew walked ashore.

As I was working on this chapter, I got news that a yacht had run aground on the Caribbean island of Saba. The crew had picked up a mooring laid down for visitors by the local marine park, and had gone ashore. A change in wind direction and the large swell caused the mooring line to get caught between the keel and rudder, and chafe through. The yacht drifted onto the rocky shore and was eventually towed off by a rescue tug, but it had sustained serious damage and may not be able to be salvaged.

An interesting story is that of a boat that was stranded on a reef in the Chagos archipelago in 2016 after its anchor line chafed through on coral. The crews of other boats in the anchorage helped to get the boat refloated. The same team also removed the damaged rudder and managed to repair it. The boat was saved and was able to sail away. In the words of the person who reported the incident: 'Not often do you find a naval architect, a professional sailmaker and a boatbuilder on nearby boats, ready to help.'

When looking closely at a number of recent boat losses, what is striking is that in many of the cases in which boats were lost as a result of grounding, this appears to have been caused, just as in the old days, by a navigational or human error. Contemplating a number of incidents of near or total losses, I was tempted to draw the conclusion that whereas in pre-GPS days boats were often lost because sailors didn't know where they were, nowadays boats are lost because captains know where they are. Or so they think!

One of the reasons is that in some remote areas the charts have not been updated, and often coordinates of locations on the chart do not correspond to their actual GPS location. I know this too well from my personal experience in the Tuamotus, and more recently from the Northwest Passage. Occasionally GPS can be a false friend indeed!

Dealing with heavy weather

More than any other aspect of sailing, how to handle heavy weather depends primarily on the sailing experience of the person in charge, as well as their attitude in an emergency situation. Other important factors:

» The quality and experience of the crew
» Type and characteristics of boat
» Nature of weather: predicted storm, heavy seas, unexpected violent squall, approaching tropical revolving storm
» Location
  › At sea with sufficient sea room
  › At sea in restricted area
  › Moored in a sheltered place
  › Moored in a doubtful anchorage
» Availability or absence of heavy-weather gear
» Degree of preparation

This is such a complex subject that it would be irresponsible of me to even attempt to give some simple answers. In my own case, I have always done everything possible to avoid being in a tropical storm area during the dangerous season. As result, the instances of heavy weather that I have encountered were never life-threatening. Nevertheless, I was always prepared for the worst, and had I been caught in an extreme situation, I hope that I would have managed. At sea, if I had sufficient sea room and conditions allowed it, I would attempt to outrun the storm. If there was no sea room, I would heave to, and hope for the best. If I were at anchor I would make absolutely sure that I was well anchored. But if I were in any doubt, I would leave the anchorage and have an exit strategy prepared in advance.

Lightning

It is said that lightning never strikes twice in the same place. How come my boat was struck in the same marina berth on two separate occasions?

Italo Masotti

Although I am rarely worried and certainly never frightened while at sea, there are two situations that give me a distinct sensation of unease: being close to large ships whose intentions are not clear, and being in the middle of a thunderstorm with lightning. One of the most violent thunderstorms that I ever experienced happened on Aventura I between Tonga and Samoa. A menacing storm lingered for a long time right over us, and I expected to be struck at any moment as massive forked bolts hit the sea all around us.

An even worse storm greeted us as we crossed the doldrums on our way from Ascension to the Cape Verdes on Aventura III. On that occasion I was less concerned, as I knew that if we were struck the damage sustained by a metal hull would be less serious than in the case of a fibreglass boat. However, I did make sure that all essential equipment was unplugged and also that none of us touched any part of the hull or rigging while the storm was raging.

Mother Nature had another go at me while I was off the coast of Montenegro at the very end of Aventura III's round-the-world voyage. This time I was absolutely convinced that we would not escape unscathed and that somebody up there was trying to show me that no voyage is over until it is truly over. I did my best to avoid the worst of the storm by slaloming from the edge of one menacing black cloud to another. Fortunately, luck was once again on my side, but it's not an experience that I'd like to repeat. I did, however, witness a lightning strike first hand in Singapore. The violence of the so-called Sumatras is well known, and when one of these electric storms that breeds over the neighbouring island broke over Raffles Marina, where the yachts taking part in a round-the-world rally were gathered, their crews were advised to leave their boats. From the control tower I had a panoramic view of the marina and, from the frequency and proximity of the lightning bolts, I felt that it would not be long before a boat was struck. It happened right in front of my eyes as a massive bolt of lightning smashed into the top of the mast of a boat berthed right by the control tower. Although the electronics had been disconnected, the damage was extensive and all electrical and electronic equipment had to be replaced. The only positive side to this disaster was that we were in a place where such equipment was widely available so the boat could be quickly re-equipped and did not miss the start of the next leg of the rally. Fortunately, the boat was insured for such an occurrence, which is something that should be checked, as damage from lightning is sometimes excluded.

While sailing from Vava'u to Fiji, a boat was struck by lightning and lost its computer and the electronic charts that were stored on it. They managed to get their radio to work, and other sailors cruising in the area gave them a series of waypoints to follow on a handheld GPS. Although I have never tried it, it has been suggested that putting electronic instruments inside the ordinary or microwave oven might protect them in case of a strike.

Main areas of concern

The changes in the global climate and its effects have become a major safety concern among sailors preparing to leave on a voyage. From the questions asked at seminars and discussions with rally participants, these were the main worries:

> » Climate change and its effects on global weather
> » Tropical-storm seasons and the possibility of extra-seasonal storms
> » Dealing with heavy weather
> » Personal safety
> » Piracy

All these are justified concerns, but I do not regard them as being serious enough to stop anyone from leaving on a voyage. With good forward planning every one of them can be avoided. So, if that is the case, how does the current situation affect long-term cruising plans?

> » Long-term planning is now even more important than in the past
> » Tropical-storm seasons can be avoided by good planning
> » Leave the tropics during the tropical-storm season
> » Avoid cruising during critical periods or, if you do, keep an eye on the weather and stay close to shelter. Always have a well-thought-out Plan B

Tips

> » Do not spend more than one night in a doubtful anchorage.
> » In doubtful areas consider cruising or anchoring in company with another boat.
> » Bring the tender and outboard on deck for the night.
> » On arrival in an anchorage, prepare an exit strategy by noting down essential waypoints and making a sketch of the anchorage so as to be able to leave at short notice, whether because of a change in weather or a perceived danger.
> » If leaving the boat for travelling ashore, make a mutual arrangement with the crew of another boat to look after your boat during your absence.
> » Take normal precautions when going ashore, never carry too much cash and keep valuables and passport in a pouch close to the body (in some countries it is compulsory to carry ID at all times).
> » Be careful when touring in a rental car, and never leave anything visible inside.
> » If you have a forward-looking sonar, leave it on in areas where you are concerned about the presence of whales (the depth sounder might work too).
> » Besides the masthead tri-colour light, have secondary navigation lights at deck level. Also carry a battery-operated emergency bi-colour set, to be used if one of the two main systems fails (deck level or masthead navigation lights).
> » When at anchor always leave a light on at night. The advantage of solar-powered lights is that they come on automatically at dusk and most batteries will last all night.
> » Have a diving mask and sharp serrated knife in an easily accessible place, in order to be able to cut free a fouled propeller.
> » The boarding ladder should be kept lowered whenever someone is in the water.
> » Have a trailing lanyard permanently attached to the boarding ladder so that in an emergency someone in the water can easily pull it down.
> » If the boat is provided with mast steps always wear a harness and clip it onto a strong point while working. For longer or more difficult jobs use a bosun's chair.
> » Avoid being discourteous or even aggressive to local people who offer things for sale or to do work on your boat. They need to make a living, and never forget that you are a guest in their country.

28

Farewell to the Pacific

Sailors are probably more prone than ordinary people to looking back nostalgically to a golden past when there were still countless unspoilt places to explore and you could sail around the world on a shoestring. It is probably true that cruising in the 1970s was generally more rewarding, but there are still a few places where things have changed very little. Such a place is Vanuatu, formerly known as the New Hebrides Condominium and once administered jointly by Britain and France. When we arrived there shortly before independence in 1979, we came across some of the most isolated and undeveloped communities that we had seen anywhere. A quarter of a century later, life in the outer islands has changed very little, and cruising sailors can still experience a way of life that has disappeared elsewhere.

Stretching in a long chain from south to north, the 80-odd islands have everything one could wish for: scenic anchorages, welcoming villagers and some of the most interesting sights in the Pacific. There are two highlights that stand out above all others: the Yasur volcano on Tanna, and the land divers of Pentecost. Having bypassed both islands on my previous visit, a pleasant overnight sail took us from Maré, in New Caledonia, to Tanna. We anchored in Port Resolution, named after the ship of Captain Cook, who was probably the first European to set sight on these remote islands, which he called the New Hebrides.

As we stepped ashore, a young Ni-Vanuatu man greeted us warmly. Pointing to a couple of thatched huts on the headland behind him, he exclaimed, 'Welcome to the Port Resolution Yacht Club. I'm Wherry.' To make sailors more comfortable and encourage them to stay longer, Wherry's uncle, Chief Ronnie of the neighbouring village, had built a large hut, now adorned with flags and club burgees, to be used as a shore base by the crews of visiting yachts. Unfortunately Cyclone Ivy had hit Tanna recently with 120-knot winds, damaging crops, flattening banana plantations and denuding coconut trees. With no help coming from the central government, the villagers were eagerly awaiting the arrival of the cruising boats that provided their main source of income and barter. As we were the first to arrive that season, our reserves of rice, flour, cooking oil, corned beef and fish hooks were soon exhausted. Entry formalities had to be completed at Tanna's main settlement of Lenakel, on the opposite side of the island, and entailed a bone-shaking trip in a local truck.

Several villages were strung along the rough track and, as we drove through one of them, I saw a scene that encompassed in one image the uniqueness of this amazing country: fixed to the trunk of a large tree was a wooden box with a public telephone, on which a man was making a call, while not 20 paces away another man had just shot a large bird with a bow and arrow.

323

A public telephone was also the central feature on the village green at Port Resolution, where it stood proudly in its own thatched hut next to a solar panel and a large antenna. Two objects lying incongruously in the middle of the village green caught my attention: a large boom and a spinnaker pole. Wherry explained later that these were among the few things left from a 53-foot yacht that had been lost there the previous year.

Tanna's Yasur volcano has been active for many years, and on dark nights its reddish glow can be seen for a long way, a welcome landmark in a country where lighthouses are mostly absent. Wherry offered to arrange a visit to the volcano, but explained that it had been reclaimed by the villagers who lived on its slopes and they were the only ones allowed to guide visitors to the rim of the mighty crater. Looking shyly at the ground and speaking in a whisper, Wherry also told me, sounding apologetic, that the villagers made a charge for this. I told him that there was nothing wrong with that, and that I was happy to pay. But I still felt that something was not right, so I asked him, 'Wherry, what do other visitors do?'

'Some people are not happy to have to pay, but there is nothing I can do because a custom village has the right to charge.'

'In that case, there is no need to worry because, as I said, I'll pay. But can we also visit the village itself?'

'Oh no, the village is taboo, and outsiders must not see the women, but occasionally the men will put on a performance for visitors.'

By now I had realised that everything had to be extracted out of Wherry with a lot of patience.

'Very good, so why don't you tell the village chief that we are very interested in seeing both the volcano and the performance.'

The following day Wherry told me that the chief had agreed and was expecting us. Wherry also arranged for us to be collected by the one and only local taxi, the battered pickup truck that I knew too well from my bone-crushing trip to Lenakel.

Although I had been to Vanuatu on several occasions, I had never had a chance to visit a custom village. In the narrow sense of the word, this usually meant a traditional village where people had returned to the ways of their ancestors, both in their day-to-day life and in their animistic beliefs. The chance of visiting a custom village on Tanna was made even more attractive by the fact that it was on this island that the John Frum cargo cult originated before the Second World War. John Frum was a mythical character who promised his followers that all their needs would be satisfied if they returned to the beliefs and lifestyle of their ancestors. One explanation is that this conviction may have been inspired by the aeroplanes that they saw flying overhead and the western goods that appeared in abundance when US troops were billeted on the islands during World War II. Even if those expectations came to nothing, the movement has survived in some villages, whose people had turned their backs on the doubtful benefits of the modern world.

A cult of the ancestors

A short walk along a narrow muddy path took us to a clearing that was hemmed in on all sides by an impenetrable jungle curtain. Through a small opening at the foot of a gigantic banyan tree, a row of chanting men emerged slowly. They were of all ages, from very young boys to gnarled old men. All were naked except for a tiny skirt at the front, their private parts enclosed in a penis wrapper called a namba sheath, once common throughout Melanesia. Chanting and stamping the packed ground with mighty thuds, they danced around in a circle, never raising their eyes. It looked straight out of the Stone Age.

At the end of the performance the men disappeared through the banyan curtain, and we made our way slowly to the rim of the volcano. This was about as close as one wanted to get to a live volcano, as even at the safe distance of about 100 metres the spewing volcano was a sight to behold. Every now and again, a deep rumble foretold of a more forceful eruption, when large boulders were thrown sky-high. The sight was awesome and so was the pestilential smell, and it was easy to imagine where the vision of hell may have originated.

While Captain Cook may have enjoyed a warm welcome on Tanna, at our next stop, the island of Erromango, we were told that early visitors had met with a less friendly reception. When the first two missionaries, John Williams and James Harris, stepped ashore, like us, at the village of Unpongkor, the locals took them to a sacred place, drew their outline on a large flat rock on which they were laid spread-eagled, then cut them up, cooked and ate them. We had the privilege of being taken to that gruesome place by Joe Mete, the son of the current chief, who admitted that his own ancestors had quite probably feasted on the two unfortunate missionaries.

The following day, Joe came on board Aventura and we sailed along the coast to Suvu, a small bay fronted by a sandy beach overshadowed by tall coconut trees. He explained that the beach was taboo and no one was allowed to land there because in a nearby cave were the remains of his family members going back several generations. We landed on the beach and made our way up a steep path, slipping on the moist soil. We stopped in front of a wide crack in the cliff face that led into the sacred cave. Before going in, Joe called into the cave, warning his ancestors that he had come to visit them with some friends, and asking their permission to enter.

Down in the damp and gloomy cave were piles of bones and about two dozen skulls. As we were leaving, Joe explained that until not so long ago, when an older person felt that the end was near, they would ask to be taken to that place and left to die alone. The family would visit regularly with food and water until their relative had passed away. They would then be placed in the cave.

The land divers of Pentecost

The best-known custom village on the island of Pentecost is Bunlap, home of the famous land divers of Vanuatu. This special ceremony is normally held at the end of the yam season, a root vegetable that is their staple diet. Young men perform this unique feat of daring to appease the gods and ensure another good harvest. An overnight sail from the capital Port Vila brought us early one morning to Waliap, on the southwest coast of Pentecost. For the last few weeks I had been communicating with a friend in Port Vila to help me attend such a unique performance. I had first met Ian Irving when we arrived with Aventura I in what was then the New Hebrides. He had been seconded by the BBC to set up the local radio station, and he helped me in my freelance work with his local contacts. He never left Vanuatu, and we have remained in intermittent contact during all these years.

Ian had contacted Chief Willie on the island of Pentecost, who reigned over that area and was the only person who could arrange for us to see a land-diving performance. When we arrived at the island we were met by Chief Willie at the head of a large reception committee made up mostly of children. The chief welcomed us warmly and told us that, although we had arrived one day early, the men were ready to do the land dive that same day.

We were accompanied by several members of Chief Willie's large family to a nearby forest, where a tall tower stood in a clearing. Chief Willie explained

that diving towers are normally only used once, and take about one week to build, but he had managed to persuade the divers to use their tower for an extra performance for our benefit. What's more, the divers were from Bunlap, the famous land-diving village. It was almost too good to be true.

The tower was much higher than I had expected, and must have been about 25 metres high. Pairs of lianas were hanging down from platforms inserted at various heights. There were seven divers as well as two young boys, one of whom cannot have been more than seven and who looked quite terrified as he prepared to jump from one of the lower platforms.

Before jumping, the diver stood on the edge of the platform, calling out in defiance to the other villagers, and, by tradition, was free to shout out any indiscretion he liked. He then threw himself forward, as if into a swimming pool, the fall being surprisingly swift as the diver fell rapidly towards the ground. The impact was lessened by the lianas tied to his ankles, the green vines having enough stretch in them to act as shock absorbers and slow down the fall. Even so, what I had not realised was that the diver actually hit the ground, and, as part of the ceremony, was supposed to touch the loosened soil with his forehead. How hard they hit was difficult to tell as on landing they all curled up in a foetal position.

A chief quickly came to help the stunned-looking diver to his feet and cut with a machete the vines that had been tightly bound to his ankles with strands of pandanus fibre. The diver then retook his place among the dancers at the base of the tower. Throughout the performance, several dozen men, women and young boys danced, stomped and chanted while the divers made their preparations for the jump.

Neither words nor photographs can describe the sheer excitement that I felt as diver after diver hurtled towards the ground, the adrenaline coursing in my veins as if it was me and not them who had taken that awesome death-defying leap.

The Louisiades

Aventura lay at anchor in a most delightful bay on Panasia, an uninhabited island in the Calvados group of the Louisiades archipelago, a cluster of small islands in the far southeast corner of Papua New Guinea. On the chart of this part of the world the tiny specks of islands look as if some flies had had a busy time. The Louisiades are remote even by New Guinea standards, and the small villages we visited would not have looked any different if we had landed there 200 years earlier. The few people we met were all very friendly and welcoming, and a great bonus was that almost everyone spoke English, some of them surprisingly well, thanks to their missionary-school education. This made it possible to have a proper conversation, to find out how they lived and what they did. Unlike in some other parts of the world, the people were shy and unobtrusive, and when they paddled out to our boat they hung about quietly, waiting to be noticed, and invariably brought a small gift. The islands themselves are a cruising paradise, probably what the Virgin Islands looked like 50 or more years ago. There are scores of tiny islands, mostly hilly but also a few low-lying ones, with beautiful sandy beaches and lots of anchorages sheltered from the prevailing trade winds.

Some of the small communities were completely cut off from the outside world. They were very much on their own, without any help or interference from the local government. Soon after we had dropped the anchor behind Bobo Eina island, an outrigger canoe with two women and three children paddled out to greet us, and gave us a bag of small tomatoes and a bunch of greens. Both women spoke English and enquired if we had any items to trade, so I asked them what they needed. From the items they mentioned – paint, sealant, a diving mask, as well as the more usual requests such as fish hooks and rice – I realised that they were used to visiting yachts. They told us that they lived with their family close by, and invited us to visit.

We took up the invitation and landed on their beach later that day. Drawn up on the beach were several canoes of various sizes, the largest having a sail and being used for longer inter-island trips, the others having smaller sails or just paddles. Under a large tree a young man was hewing a small canoe out of a tree trunk, his only tool a simple adze. This versatile tool, a few pots and pans and some plastic containers were the only items that were not made of natural materials. I was told that their extended family had moved over from one of the neighbouring villages and had made their base there: grandfather, father and mother, son,

daughter-in-law and three children. Granddad was quite old and was sitting on a shady open platform playing with the baby. The houses were all made of woven pandanus and coconut thatch. A well-tended garden had been cleared out of the bush to grow papaya, yam, taro, sweet potato, beans, pumpkins and tomatoes.

What we found both there and in the more remote islands of Vanuatu was self-sufficiency in its purest form, as people lived from the land and sea, grew and caught what they needed, and did not seem to require all that much from the outside world. Soon after the first traders arrived, the local people were persuaded to gather or grow a cash crop: sandalwood, sea cucumbers, mother-of-pearl shells, copra or timber. Later, planters arrived and set up large coconut plantations providing employment for local men. So money began circulating, allowing people to buy their basic supplies. This encouraged them to live in villages, each with a store, school and church. In recent years, as a result of a drop in the demand for and price of copra, most plantations have been abandoned, so a reverse phenomenon was now in evidence. As there was no market for cash crops, nor any demand for work on plantations, there was no source of income, so people had no choice but to become self-sufficient again. Rather than live in a village, some families set up on their own. Usually they resettled on ancestral land and lived in harmony with nature, just as their forebears had done. If the children needed to go to school, they were usually sent to stay with relatives. For some of those isolated families, trading with visiting sailors had become a way of life, and wherever I came across such examples I felt that the human contact with passing cruisers was probably more important than what the locals actually got out of the visitors.

Back at Panasia, once again we had the small island to ourselves. The evening of our arrival, two men had come over in a sailing canoe from the neighbouring island to offer us two large lobsters, which we traded for some T-shirts. The following day, we were visited by a large canoe with eight men, who brought carvings, shells, eggs and some vegetables to trade. Having recently heard of cases of robberies in other parts of Papua New Guinea, I was rather concerned to be faced with a bunch of rough-looking men with only two of us on board. However, it soon became clear that they meant no harm and were in fact enjoying having someone different to talk to. Owing to my shame at having automatically suspected these innocent people, and being so relieved, I only bargained with them to keep up appearances, and was actually quite happy to give away all my trading goods. Their young chief, John Mwasi, told me that his Meisoga clan had recently won a court case confirming their ownership of the island and surrounding reef. He was hoping to attract more visiting boats to the area, so Panasia's deserted days might be over soon.

They left us as the sun was going down and, as I sat on the deck, it occurred to me that this was my last stop in the Pacific, and I wished I could turn such splendour into a lasting memory: the craggy cliffs overlooking the bay, the ring of islands on the horizon, the psychedelic colours of a tropical sunset. In the last quarter of a century I had left the South Pacific by boat three times, but this was the first time that I was leaving without the certainty that I would return.

29

Cruising in stages

Cheaper travel and more places to leave your boat safely for the season have made cruising more enjoyable, as it is now possible to return home more frequently when leaving on a voyage of several years.

Amanda Neal

Breaking up a long voyage into shorter stages is an increasingly common phenomenon, as by dividing the voyage into convenient sections it is possible to take advantage of favourable seasons and weather conditions, which can be a major safety factor in the current climate. A more relaxed schedule of this sort is very attractive to people whose professional or personal interests require their presence back home on a regular basis, and also allows family or friends to join the boat at some of the more attractive destinations. It also seems to suit some wives who are not keen on long passages, like Gwenda, but who are quite happy to join the boat to cruise in certain areas. Some men, keen to realise their dream voyage and not wishing to risk the harmony of their marriage, have found this a truly win-win situation.

During our first circumnavigation between 1975 and 1981, Aventura covered 68,000 miles and we spent the entire six years away from home. Flights in those days were very expensive and there was no real reason to return home because we were sailing as a family. During Aventura II's voyage, as part of the first round-the-world rally, I commuted regularly between boat and home, with the crew sailing the boat on their own during my absence. It worked but was not an ideal solution, so on Aventura III's world voyage between 2001 and 2006, I sailed the entire distance and left the boat at convenient stopover places along the way. The 38,000-mile route was divided into 12 stages, allowing me to fly back home on average twice a year. Now that so much more is known about carbon emissions and global warming, I am quite embarrassed by this.

Some of my absences from the boat were as short as two months, while the longest was nine months

Puerto Lucia in Ecuador

when, for family reasons, I could not rejoin the boat at the appointed time, thus missing an entire favourable season in the South Pacific. Whenever I left Aventura, I made sure that she was safely laid up, usually ashore, in a secure place and always outside the tropical-storm areas. The wide availability of such safe places is another feature that was almost absent in the past, and is one of the reasons why this phenomenon has become so widespread.

A suitable place to leave the boat

There is a wide choice of safe places strategically located along the main world cruising routes. Whether planning to leave the boat in a marina or boatyard, such a place must meet a number of criteria: good security, a properly prepared area for storing boats ashore, a good range of repair facilities, availability of spares and equipment, reasonable shore facilities and closeness to an international airport. Finding a place that incorporates all these features may not prove to be easy, and this is why I stress that careful forward planning is much more important when cruising in stages than on a continuous voyage, when one can improvise and change plans at short notice.

In order to help would-be voyagers plan the individual stages of a proposed route, I wrote

World Voyage Planner, while for selecting potential destinations its companion volume, World Cruising Destinations, has all the necessary information on specific places, to help both in the planning stages and later, when a new stopover place needs to be found.

The internet is a helpful source to find out what is available, but as with almost everything in life, the best advice is usually by word of mouth. As you sail closer to an intended destination, you start meeting sailors who may have first-hand experience of such a place or be a resident of that country. The research should start well in advance, and once you have drawn up a shortlist of potential destinations you should start contacting marinas or boatyards by email. Some of this research can be quite frustrating, as some marinas or boatyards reply promptly with plenty of detail, while others do not answer at all. Facilities available and costs should be discussed at this stage, but a firm booking based on cost alone should not be made, however tempting this may be, because a lower-than-average price might mean that the facilities of the marina or boatyard are not of a good enough quality or range.

Power Boats yard in Trinidad where boats are stored on the hard during the hurricane season

Cruising in stages is dictated primarily by seasons, and this is reflected in the way I planned my own voyages. From my very first foray into the tropics, I always planned my route carefully so as to avoid being in a critical area during the established tropical-storm season. While the majority of prudent sailors continue to do this, those who decide to remain in the tropics during the storm season are taking a calculated risk, even if they are insured. This is why it is essential to inform your insurance company about your intentions well in advance, so as to avoid finding out too late that they may not be prepared to provide cover unless you cruise or leave the boat in an area that is considered low risk.

Those who decide to continue cruising during the cyclone season should take certain precautions. You should identify any cyclone-proof sheltered areas in the vicinity and attempt to get there in case a cyclone comes your way. In some places such sheltered spots may only be known to the locals, and may be full by the time you get there. A crowded anchorage can be particularly dangerous in such situations as even if your anchor holds, your boat may be seriously damaged by another boat dragging and colliding with yours. Damage from other boats can also be sustained when stowed ashore in a boatyard, and for this reason several yards now stow the boats with their keels dropped into a trench, and tethered to strong points in the ground, so that they cannot fall over and get damaged themselves as well as damaging nearby boats.

The greatest danger of an open anchorage in an approaching storm is that of fetch and surge. As

Tradewinds anchorage in Fiji is reputed to afford good shelter in case of a cyclone

a tropical storm approaches, the wind direction may change drastically, putting the boat on a lee shore. For this reason, mangrove areas, such as the Tradewinds anchorage in Suva, Fiji, are considered the safest shelters. On the first Aventura, I carried a very heavy oversized Admiralty-type anchor as a safety precaution, but it was never used.

If you are sailing in low latitudes and there is no safe hurricane hole anywhere near, the best tactic is to proceed as fast as possible towards the equator because, until now, cyclones have never reached below 6° regardless of hemisphere. In the worst case you should cross the Intertropical Convergence Zone and the equator and switch hemispheres, thus leaving the critical tropical-storm area altogether. However, leaving the tropics themselves is, in my opinion, still the wisest tactic, especially as the cyclone seasons seem to be getting longer as a consequence of climate change.

There are a number of hurricane holes spread out across the South Pacific, but because of the large distances that separate the various island groups, running for shelter if a cyclone is predicted may be a hazardous affair. The best tactic is either to stay close to a chosen shelter, or cruise on the edges of the cyclone belt, so as to be able to possibly sail out of danger. In the eastern South Pacific, the area immediately south of the equator is considered safe, which, for example, can be reached by sailing north from the Marquesas. This is not the case in the central South Pacific, where Tuvalu, north of Fiji, has been affected by several cyclones in recent years. It is only in Papua New Guinea, in the western South Pacific, that low latitudes can be considered safe. A similar tactic may work in the eastern North Pacific, where a hurricane that threatens Mexico may be avoided by sailing as quickly as possible south to get outside the tropical-storm area. The same is also possible in the Caribbean, but it needs to be stressed once again that you have to get quite far south to reach a safe area.

Wherever you may be, once you have done everything possible to secure your boat, take yourself ashore because saving your own life is the only thing that really matters. In most cases it is foolish to stay on the boat as nothing much can be done in hurricane-force winds, and sailors have died trying to save their boat rather than their own life.

Flights

Before leaving the boat, make sure that all necessary arrangements have been agreed with the marina or boatyard, as well as undertaking any necessary formalities with customs and immigration. An easy matter to overlook, but one that can have serious consequences, is the fact that in some countries leaving a boat unattended for a longer period must be cleared with customs, as the boat may have to be put in bond. In places such as South Africa, yacht crews get a different visa from that of normal tourists. Anyone departing a yacht must clear out first with the port immigration office and get the passport stamped accordingly, or the crew will have difficulties at the airport. Also, in Cape Town the captain needs to obtain a release paper from the Port Authority stating that all marina and boatyard fees have been paid, because obtaining an exit visa from immigration depends on this. None of these things should be left to the last day, especially if planning to leave on a weekend. As to visas, do make sure to obtain one in advance if you plan to interrupt your voyage, and lay up the boat, in a country where a visa is necessary.

Also in the way of formalities, some marinas insist on being left a copy of the boat insurance certificate. Do make sure that your insurance company is kept informed of your intentions, as some do not allow boats to be left unattended in certain countries. This needs to be cleared in advance to avoid the risk of having the insurance policy voided.

Aventura III laid up in Greece between seasons

Tips

» Choose the marina or boatyard carefully especially if it is located in a tropical storm area. Have the boat well supported with strong props. Ask to have it laid up away from other sailing boats whose masts can cause serious damage if they fall over.

» Prepare the boat properly for a long period of being unattended as suggested in the laying up tips at the end of this chapter.

» Even if the marina or boatyard promise to look after the boat as part of the contract, it pays to make a private arrangement with a reliable local person to keep an eye on the boat and occasionally give it a wash. Inform the marina of such arrangements.

» Ask the marina or boatyard to draw up a proper contract and take a copy to have in case the authorities ask to see at the airport.

» Leave a set of boat keys with the marina or yard and have another set for yourself. The set for the marina should only give access to main accommodation, not to cockpit lockers, etc., all of which should be secured with strong padlocks.

» Always pay for longer than intended, as delays do happen and most marinas offer a better deal if fees are paid in advance.

» Complete necessary formalities with customs if the boat needs to be left in bond.

» If sending or taking parts overseas to be repaired and returned, clear this with customs so as to avoid paying import duty when they are returned. Bring back on your return essential spares that are not available locally.

Laying up the boat ashore or afloat

The state that some owners leave their boats in when unattended for a long time never fails to amaze me. I am exactly the opposite and have almost an obsession about leaving the boat as tidy and well prepared as possible. Usually my boats were left entirely bare, with all sails, tenders, outboards and running rigging neatly stowed away. This was not just a safety measure, but also a good opportunity to check everything so any broken equipment could be repaired or replaced before my return and the start of another cruising period.

To make sure I did not forget anything important, I drew up a list of jobs, which was thoroughly honed over the 13 years I owned Aventura III, during which time I must have laid her up on at least 15 occasions. In Aventura IV's case, she was only laid up twice during the two and half years that I owned her.

The laying up procedure was generally the same whether the boat was left afloat or ashore, but if possible I preferred to leave the boat laid up ashore. I realised the benefits of doing this, even for relatively short periods, with Aventura II, which was made of steel and needed special care when left afloat unattended. Having a boat hauled out ashore was very useful as I was able to inspect all systems, check and service the propeller, and clean and antifoul the hull before she was put back in the water. Although an aluminium hull needs less attention than steel, I continued this practice with Aventura III. Having sailed 70,000 miles since she was launched in 1998, Aventura III looked half her age when I sold her in 2010.

This routine can be adapted to a boat made of any material. As normally the boat will have to be hauled out on your return to apply a new coat of antifouling paint, it makes sense to have the boat stored ashore. Furthermore, the cost is often similar, and in some busy places leaving the boat in a wet berth is, in fact, more expensive than leaving it on land. For all the above reasons, when I started looking for a place to leave Aventura III unattended for a longer period, the first priority was somewhere where she could be hauled out and left ashore safely.

Watermaker

Normally I prefer to tackle the most difficult job first, so once it is out of the way I can continue with easier or more pleasant tasks. The most time-consuming job on my list of things to do when I laid up Aventura III was to 'pickle' the watermaker. If the watermaker was not going to be run for a period longer than two weeks, it had to be properly flushed through and preserved so as to protect the membrane. As this job could be done in advance of actually laying up the boat, I always tried to find a nice anchorage where I could relax and do a number of jobs that need not wait until I arrived at the chosen marina or boatyard for the haul-out.

Being in an anchorage had the added advantage of being able to make water (I only made water offshore or

in clean uninhabited bays), as I needed about 80 litres for this procedure. The watermaker was first flushed out with half of this made water. The next step was to add the chemical preservative to the final rinsing water. If freezing temperatures are expected, glycol or food-quality antifreeze needs to be added at this stage. Once the final rinse is completed the watermaker can be shut down, its seawater-intake seacock turned off and the electricity supply switched off. In places where winter temperatures could drop below freezing, it may be advisable to also lag the unit.

That time-consuming procedure was the main reason why I decided to have a Spectra watermaker on Aventura IV. These are provided with an ingenious Z-Ion long-term protection system, as described on page 290.

Sails, sheets and halyards

Once we were berthed in the marina or boatyard where Aventura would be hauled out, the laying up procedure could start in earnest. The jib and staysail were always the first to come down, be rinsed, dried and folded neatly. I frequently handed them over to a local sailmaker to do a thorough inspection and any necessary repairs. Often I was surprised at what a sailmaker's trained eye discovered on a sail that I would have sworn was in perfect order. On a couple of occasions I had the anti-UV strips replaced on the two foresails when they started showing signs of wear. I am very pleased that after all the miles she sailed, I still had the original jib and staysail when I sold the boat, and they looked almost like new. I am just as pleased that I had never blown out a white sail on any of my boats, and even the damage to spinnakers has been relatively minor.

Initially, when laying up the boat I usually took off the mainsail as well, a lengthy and difficult procedure that also entailed taking out the battens, reefing lines and blocks. For a while I only did it for longer stays,

but then realised the futility of the operation as the mainsail was perfectly protected by the lazybag. On later occasions, I normally left the mainsail on the boom as it saved about half a day's work when the boat was recommissioned. Even so, at least once a year I made sure the mainsail and its cover were checked and serviced by a professional sailmaker.

All sheets, guys, jackstays and the boom brake were taken off, rinsed in fresh water, dried, coiled and stowed. I always stowed the various lines in such an order that the first things to be needed on my return were stored on top. With the exception of the boom topping lift, all halyards were taken off, rinsed and stowed. Every halyard was replaced by a messenger, a strong thin multi-ply line marked with a tape showing the name of the halyard it was replacing. The two ends of the messenger lines were tied to one of the granny bars, well away from the mast, to stop them banging or chafing against the standing rigging.

Deck gear

All loose deck gear was taken off and stowed: danbuoy, horseshoe buoys and their lights (all batteries are taken out so they don't get discharged if the light falls over and is activated), fishing reel, steering wheel. Initially I used to stow the liferaft, but this seemed an unnecessary precaution, and later I left it in its recess by the stern platform. As regular inspections are always best dealt with during long absences, I normally arranged for the liferaft to be collected by an approved agent, and only had it returned serviced when I came back, so I knew that it had been stored in a dry place.

Spars

As the main boom was open-ended, I blocked it with rags so as to stop birds getting in and making a nest, as happened to me twice, the second time with serious consequences. On my return to the boatyard near Athens where I had left Aventura during the winter, I found a nest halfway inside the boom, but managed to get it out and clean up the mess. In Cape Town it was only when a local rigger was trying to sort out my jammed reefing that he realised that something was amiss. A bird had built itself a nest far inside the boom that completely blocked all lines and blocks, and could not be cleared. The rigger had to take the boom to his workshop to sort out its insides, so after that I made sure the end of the boom was always sealed with rags.

In places where I had doubts about security, I used to stow away the two spinnaker poles, as well as the aluminium passerelle. They were among the last things to be put inside the boat, so as to leave the decks entirely clear.

Masthead unit

While in Ecuador, I noticed a large black bird perched on the top of the mast of an unattended boat. It suddenly took off, making the whole mast and rigging shake. It was an adult frigate bird, which can easily weigh more than 5 kilos. It flew a few circles then landed clumsily on the same masthead unit, which I expected to snap under its weight. I had seen enough, so I put on a harness, climbed to the top of the mast and removed my masthead unit. This was also a good opportunity to have a visual check of the rigging as

I passed close to it. I have continued removing the unit ever since. It might have started as an anti-bird measure, but it also meant that on my return I needed to go aloft to replace the unit, when I would also check the masthead lights, antennas, rigging terminals, spinnaker blocks, and the top of the jib and staysail furling gears. Having maststeps made it all easier, and also I could deal with such jobs on my own.

Anchor and chain

After the boat had been hauled out, I dropped the main anchor and all chain onto the ground, rinsed it and left it spread out neatly under the boat. Worn chain with some of its galvanising missing can easily start rusting during a wet winter if left in the chain locker, and may end up in a solid heap that can only be loosened with a hammer. Having to reach into the chain locker, which on some boats is difficult to access, is another good reason for this precaution. Not only does this prevention help protect the chain, but it also meant that on my return I could replace any of the missing length markers. For markers I used coloured cable ties inserted at five-metre intervals.

Electronics

This equipment is the most vulnerable if not used while the boat is left unattended. A humid tropical environment is the worst and, unless someone will turn on the equipment regularly and air the boat, the best way to protect it is to leave a dehumidifier on board. Such a unit may only run on mains power, and provision must also be made for the condensed water to be discharged safely overboard.

At the other extreme, on boats exposed to freezing temperatures, a heater could be left on inside the boat, but it should be checked regularly.

Bilges

If there is any water in the bilges, they should be emptied, dried and thoroughly cleaned. Once they are clean and dry, on boats that are left in a tropical country anti-cockroach powder should be sprinkled in the bilges, and also in the galley area.

Seacocks

Whether the boat was left ashore or afloat, I normally turned off all seacocks. Because Aventura III's seacocks were made of plastic, they didn't need to be greased, but this must be done on boats with bronze seacocks, which should be inspected regularly. This was easier on Aventura IV, whose seacocks were above the waterline on top of standpipes welded to the hull.

If work needed to be done on the boat during my absence, or the engine had to be run if the boat was left in the water, I clearly marked the location of the seawater intake. In case the engine seacock was not left open, I also left a sheet of paper on the steps by the companionway so that it could not be missed: Engine water intake seacock CLOSED. The location of the main electrical switches was also clearly indicated.

Batteries

What to do with the batteries during a longer absence is a difficult decision: whether to leave them as they are and not charge them, disconnect and separate them, or leave them on a trickle charge. It all depends on the type of battery. Lead-acid batteries are the worst in this respect as they cannot be left uncharged for long periods or they will be ruined. Gel batteries are easier to manage because they can be left charged and, if they are in a good state, will keep their charge almost indefinitely. Initially I left my gel batteries not on charge, and also disconnected the cables linking the separate batteries. On my return I measured their respective voltages and was often surprised to see how much better some were than others after an absence of several months. This was a first indication that some of the batteries were no longer in their best state. By the time they were three years old, and gave signs of nearing the end of their lives, I decided to leave them connected to the solar panel. They were thus on a permanent charge, which should have done them no harm, as they were charged via a regulator. Mainly for this reason, I believe that gel, or similar maintenance-free batteries, are better suited for cruising in stages. In my own case the choice was easy because one should not have lead-acid batteries on an aluminium boat in case of a capsize and the risk of spilling sulphuric acid into the bilges, which can have grave consequences. Even without capsizing, I feel that however well the batteries may be secured, the danger of an acid spill remains. So my advice is to avoid lead-acid batteries if planning a long voyage, not just on an aluminium boat, but with any hull material.

Whatever kind of batteries one has, they should be checked and cleaned before leaving, and if they are of the lead-acid type should be topped up. Gel batteries must not be opened or they will be ruined, as happened to two of my new batteries when the New Zealand electrician who had installed them unscrewed their tops while looking for the source of some spilt liquid. They had to be replaced. What was amazing was that the electrician had never heard that this type of battery must remain permanently sealed or it will lose the pressurised hydrogen inside it.

Boat cleaning

This routine was added to my list by Gwenda and can be easily done while lockers and other things are being sorted out prior to packing up the boat. Gwenda also discovered that wiping the insides of drawers and hanging lockers with vinegar will inhibit the growth of mould or mildew, and prevent the development of that typical stale boat smell.

This is a good time not only to give the heads a good clean, but also to check the state of their discharge hose to see if it empties satisfactorily. If it does not, it probably means that the hose is partly blocked with limescale deposit and during the long period of inactivity may seize up completely. This may mean having to replace the entire hose, which, as a precaution, should be done every five years or so anyway. Once when I arrived in the Canaries I found that the discharge hose on the forward toilet was completely blocked. As it would have been very difficult to replace it, I bought a bottle of hydrochloric acid from a shop supplying professional plumbers. Handling it is very dangerous because it is extremely corrosive, and it should be treated with the utmost caution. The acid does not react with plastic hoses, or with the toilet material or usual components, but I was warned that the reaction would be spectacular, and so it was. I disconnected the hose, put one end in an empty bucket, and as soon as I poured some acid into the toilet bowl there was an immediate reaction with rumbling, hissing and choking plumes of gas pouring out. The hose got increasingly hotter as the acid made its way slowly through it. A few minutes later, the acid had reached the end of the hose, and pieces of solid grey limescale started falling out. Some pieces fitted neatly together, having the shape of the pipe with a small hole in the centre, which explained the restriction I had been experiencing. When I reconnected the hose, I was amazed how easy it was to pump, just as it was when the boat was new.

The tidying up period was also the best time to get rid of any useless stuff: books that were no longer wanted, etc. The galley and provisions were gone through too, and any opened bottles or containers, or those whose expiry date was due soon, were thrown out. Finally, I tided up my navigation desk and chart locker, went through the cruising guides and took home those that I would no longer need. I made a list of all guides and charts that were left behind. I also went through the chart catalogue and wrote down the names and numbers of charts I might need to order for my return, all the way to the next destination. Normally I bought or ordered before leaving anything that I would need on my return, such as charts, antifouling paint, spares or consumables.

I usually took the boat laptop with me, and also the logbook, because I often needed to refer to them. All easily removable items that were of value were hidden in a suitable place. Having had Aventura II broken into once, when all such items were stolen, I regarded this as a simple precaution.

Timing

Dealing with all the above jobs may sound time-consuming, but some of them need not be left until the last moment. And as the laying up operation was repeated and became routine, it ended up taking less time to complete. Initially I allowed two or three days for the entire operation, but it often took less because some jobs had been done in advance.

The last things to be taken off were the ensign and courtesy flag. I used to leave the latter up as a courtesy to the host nation, but it rarely outlasted my absence so it came down too. A final check, a last look and a farewell caress of my faithful companion and I was off, invariably with a heavy heart, as I would feel when parting from a good friend for a long time.

I had two sets of keys, one for every lock, which I took with me, and one that had the main companionway key. The latter was left with the marina or boatyard office if they were going to do any work in my absence. I usually tried to avoid this because I had had a few bad experiences and preferred to be around when any work was done, but occasionally I had to compromise if some essential job couldn't wait.

The job list

The following list is a personal aide-memoire that includes all essential laying up jobs on Aventura III, but it could be easily adapted to any boat.

» Flush, preserve and winterise the watermaker.
» Lag watermaker and hot water tank; add food-grade glycol, if freezing temperatures are expected.
» Service the engine, change oil and filter, replace main fuel filter, check and empty water trap on fuel filter, clean seawater trap, check engine coolant, winterize engine.
» Defrost and clean refrigerator/freezer.
» Check refrigerator anode.
» Empty and clean bilges.
» Test automatic bilge pump(s) if left afloat.
» Service, winterize and stow outboard(s).
» Check batteries, clean terminals, top up lead-acid batteries. Arrange for lead-acid batteries to be checked and charged regularly. Disconnect and separate batteries if they are not being charged while away.
» If the boat is left afloat sink additional anodes if in a doubtful situation.
» Take down sails and sail covers, rinse, dry and fold; have sails serviced if necessary.
» If the mainsail is left on the boom, cover and secure it, stow reefing lines inside the sail cover.
» Secure the boom and if open-ended block its end as an anti-bird measure.
» Take down wind masthead unit.
» Take in all sheets, guys, jackstays, rinse, dry and stow.
» Power rinse furling gear(s), foresail(s) and mainsail travellers.
» Take down all halyards, replace with messengers, rinse, dry and stow.

» Secure messenger lines well away from the mast to stop them banging in strong winds.

» Take in mainsheet, replace with messenger, rinse, dry and stow.

» Take down running backstays and stow.

» Take off selfsteering lines, windvane and servorudder.

» Take down cockpit dodger and bimini, check for tears, rinse, dry and stow.

» Stow danbuoy, horseshoe buoys, fishing reel, and all loose deck gear.

» Take in boom break, rinse and dry lines, stow.

» Take off steering wheel, cover instruments and steering console.

» Release the backstay tensioner.

» The wind generator should be immobilised in case of strong winds.

» Disconnect solar panel (take out fuse) if not in use during absence.

» Empty and rinse all water tanks.

» Flush out, rinse and clean toilet(s), use strong disinfectant for final flush.

» Empty and rinse grey and black water tanks.

» Drop main anchor and chain to the ground, rinse, lay out neatly under the boat.

» Turn off and disconnect LPG tank.

» Wipe the insides of lockers with vinegar. Leave all lockers and drawers open for air circulation.

» If leaving the boat in warm countries set cockroach poison in critical spots and sprinkle some in the bilges.

» Install dehumidifier or heater.

» Take in the solar cockpit light.

» Pump up centreboard and rudder (if applicable).

» Close all seacocks except the seawater intake if the boat is afloat and the engine will be run while away.

» Mark visibly the locations of the engine seawater intake seacock and main electrical switches.

» Hide in a secure place small items, portable GPS, VHF radio, laptop, binoculars.

» Take home logbook, used guides and charts.

» Take in flags.

» Turn off power.

» Lock up boat and all lockers. Leave a set of keys with the marina or boatyard.

For those who plan to lay up a boat in a cold climate with freezing temperatures, it needs to be thoroughly prepared for the harsh winter conditions in order to protect both the boat and its equipment from serious damage. The best solution is to have the boat hauled out, and stripped of all loose equipment and gear. It is a major procedure that could take at least a week of work to recommission the boat in spring. These are some specific tips in addition to those already listed.

Tips

» Haul out boat, pressure wash hull, but leave applying antifouling paint until return.

» Service the folding propeller and lubricate its gears with approved grease.

» Service winches and lubricate with approved grease.

» The engine and diesel generator should have a full service and be winterised by a professional mechanic.

» All batteries should to be left on a trickle charge

» Outboard engines need to be winterized also if stowed in a place with freezing temperatures.

» Ideally, if the boat is left under supervision, there should be a heater left on permanently inside the boat in order to protect electronics and also to avoid mold forming on surfaces, upholstery and mattresses.

» Make sure that your insurance company agrees for the boat to be left afloat in a marina that may freeze.

Port of Refuge in Tonga's Vava'u group of islands

The main factors that may affect the success of a voyage

Success is not final, failure is not fatal: it is the courage to continue that counts.

Winston Churchill

From the cases of unhappy or abandoned voyages that have come to my knowledge over the years, and from conversations with owners and crews, I have tried to narrow down the most common factors that can contribute to the success or failure of a long voyage. These are the boat itself, the crew, inadequate funds, inability to be self-sufficient and, finally, the wrong attitude to cruising and life at sea generally. As these are such important matters for anyone planning a long voyage, I conducted a wide-ranging survey among a large sample of long-distance sailors. The results of the voyage-planning survey were first published in my book World Voyage Planner, and its findings have been updated from observations made in the intervening years by participants in the transatlantic rallies.

The boat

I start from the premise that no object created by man is as satisfying to his body and soul as a proper sailing yacht.

Arthur Beiser

What kind of boat to acquire for a long voyage is often a more difficult decision than deciding to do the voyage itself, especially when there is such a bewildering range available. There is no doubt that the choice of boat can seriously affect the quality and enjoyment of a voyage, and a wrong choice may even lead to the voyage being abandoned. There are many factors that can make a boat unsuitable for a long voyage, and the most common is it being the wrong size – either too large to be handled easily by a short-handed crew, or too small to be comfortable, having limited storage capacity or not being fast enough on long passages. Comfort is indeed a major consideration and has a bearing not only on the well-being of the crew, but also on safety. Important as size and comfort may be, the most essential consideration when choosing a boat for a long voyage is safety. There are many boats on the market that are perfectly suitable for weekend sailing or short cruises but which may not be up to the demands of a voyage in tough offshore conditions.

A common reason for some people setting off with what turns out to be an unsuitable boat is that it was the boat they happened to own at the time. Whether for financial reasons or owing to a lack of offshore experience, they decided that it would do. By the time their mistake becomes obvious, it is too late to put it right and they either choose to carry on regardless; cut short; or, in some cases, abandon the voyage.

As the choice of the right boat is such an important factor, participants in the voyage-planning survey were asked to point out the design features that would make a considerable contribution to the quality and enjoyment of a voyage. A few owners complained about their boats being too small, and stressed that for a long voyage a boat under 40 feet might not be suitable. Other owners found that a more serious handicap on long voyages than actual size was the lack of storage space, which they blamed on the fact that many boats were designed for weekend sailing or charter, with storage capacity not a priority.

Crew

Regardless of size, the most desired features mentioned were a comfortable, sheltered watch-keeping position and an ergonomically designed cockpit, if possible with a hard dodger, which would make passages more comfortable in both hot and cold climates. Another desirable feature was shallow draft, because it would extend the cruising range, such as on catamarans or centreboard boats. Other features mentioned were good access to the engine room for maintenance, a compact and user-friendly galley, comfortable sea berths and a proper double berth for when in port. In terms of sail handling, a well-thought-out reefing system was considered essential, with the lines being led to the cockpit, ideally to an electric winch. Also important was easy access to the chain locker, with a vertical drop to avoid the chain getting snagged and serviced by a powerful and reliable windlass.

As most of those interviewed had spent long periods sailing in trade-wind conditions, several mentioned having easily handled downwind sails, such as a cruising chute or Parasailor spinnaker. The four most commonly mentioned pieces of essential equipment were a strong autopilot, preferably backed up by a wind-operated self-steering gear, a reliable watermaker, AIS and bow-thruster. For communications, satellite phones were regarded as an essential safety feature, but also mentioned as very useful on long voyages were SSB radios for voice communications with other boats, as well as email.

When it came to giving practical advice to would-be voyagers, it was pointed out that many of those with limited experience seem to be unaware of the high electricity demands of a boat equipped for a longer voyage, so they should ensure that those demands are satisfied by a diversified portfolio of options.

Several sailors stressed the need to keep things simple – a strongly built boat, good quality winches, anchoring gear and a reliable engine being paramount. It was stressed that the safety aspect should be the overriding factor when choosing a boat for a long voyage.

Trust no crew, no matter how fabulous his sailing career and credentials, until he is fully proven aboard.

Bill Butler

Many a voyage has failed because of crew problems, and this may explain why the majority of boats on a long voyage are sailed by couples. While many voyages have been completed successfully by couples, the same cannot always be said of boats crewed by friends, acquaintances or occasional crew taken to supplement the permanent crew. Anyone choosing crew for a long voyage, or just one ocean passage, should take into account not just their experience, but also their physical condition and reliability, as well as their compatibility with other crew members. Concerning boats crewed by just a couple, an important point raised was to ensure that in an emergency the other person would be able to deal with any essential tasks.

Practical demonstration at a medical seminar for Atlantic Odyssey participants

Health and general fitness should be given a high priority as part of the preparation for a voyage, whatever the age of the crew – and many long-distance sailors are no longer in their prime. This is especially true for long voyages where medical assistance will not be easily available. After a long period of an urban, sedentary existence, it is essential to get into good physical shape for the impending voyage, and Erick Bouteleux, of the yacht Igloo, stressed the fact that many people do not realise how important physical fitness can be on a boat. 'You must prepare yourself physically but also mentally for what can be a demanding way of life.'

Over half the boats in the survey were crewed by couples, who only occasionally took on additional crew, and several stressed that they preferred this arrangement. Among the later was Nancy Zapf of the yacht Halekai, who wrote: 'The advantages of doing long passages as a couple are huge, provided both are fully competent. You only need one decent sea berth, watch-keeping routines are easy and you haven't got the responsibility towards other crew. Less is more. The more people in a small space, the more potential for problems. Modern technologies such as autopilot, windvane, radar and AIS have made it much easier to sail short-handed. Although for watch-standing we would prefer to have at least one extra crew member aboard, the logistics of doing so, and the limited space available, mean that just the two of us is a better choice.'

Finances

Make a detailed estimate of anticipated expenses, double it, and then decide if you can stretch your resources to afford it.

Roger Swanson

No voyage should be embarked on without having adequate funds, not just for day-to-day expenses, but also a reserve for possible emergencies. The situation is now very different from the days when it was still possible to sail the world on a limited budget.

Financial matters and the cost of cruising were an important part of the voyage-planning survey, and its findings have been updated recently. The average annual expenses quoted by couples sailing on boats between 40 and 45 feet varied between $18,000 and $24,000, to a maximum of $36,000. For couples on boats between 50 and 55 feet, the annual costs generally spanned $30,000 to $36,000, the maximum being $48,000, spent by a couple on a recently completed 10-year world voyage. These figures included all living expenses, marina, maintenance and repair costs, while the higher figures covered also the costs of going out, car rental and occasional flights home.

A pelican couple waiting for the bank to open so they can retrieve their savings

My own advice on cruising budgets generally is to allow more than planned and have recourse to funds in a serious emergency. But I also urge everyone to think carefully before making a clean break with shore life during the current economic uncertainty and creeping inflation. If possible, you should keep a shore base so if you are forced to change plans, whether for health or financial reasons, you have somewhere to return to.

Self-sufficiency

Necessity is the mother of invention. When you're in the middle of nowhere and something breaks, you've got to be resourceful and imaginative enough to make things work.

Dave Lynn

In today's world, when help is usually just a phone call away, the ability to be self-sufficient has been lost by many people – not just the skills required, but also the attitude to try to deal with a problem before calling on outside assistance. Many of those interviewed stressed that this kind of approach is no good on a boat in the middle of the ocean, where you must be able to deal with any emergency yourself. Many are the skills required of the crew of an offshore boat, such as the ability to repair and improvise, navigate without electronic aids, dive, give first aid in an emergency and most certainly sail the boat if the engine is out of order. To be able to deal with emergencies, the boat should carry a comprehensive set of tools, essential spares and backups for the most important pieces of equipment. There should also be a well-stocked medical chest and at least a rudimentary knowledge of how to deal with a medical emergency.

The right attitude

If you want to build a ship, don't drum up people to collect wood and don't assign them tasks and work, but rather teach them to long for the endless immensity of the sea.

Antoine de Saint-Exupéry

A boat that incorporates your main priorities is absolutely crucial for the successful outcome of a voyage, but there are other factors that can have a serious effect on its success, and they are, as mentioned before, crew, finances and self-sufficiency. There is, however, an even more important factor that can have a bearing on the success of a voyage, and that is your attitude to the sea and sailing, and to cruising life in general. Setting off on a life on the ocean is a major decision that entails a complete change of both lifestyle and mentality, something that some people may not have considered carefully. Leaving on a voyage in a sailing yacht just because it is a convenient way to see the world is not a good enough reason. I have come across this attitude among sailors I have met, some of whom were unwilling, or more often unable, to make the transition from shore-based person to full-time sailor. This may not be a great problem on a relatively short voyage, such as going to the Caribbean or Hawaii and back, but it can have serious consequences for those who leave on a longer journey of several years. In the final analysis, the ultimate success of a voyage does not depend on the boat, but on you and your attitude.

In over 40 years of sailing I have met many outstanding people, and invariably what made them stand out was their attitude. What I most admired in them was their profound respect for the sea, and how being on the ocean came to them naturally, undoubtedly because they loved what they were doing. Some I met while cruising, others as participants in the various sailing events that I organised, and over the years several have become close friends. What they all had in common was that special mindset to embark on a long voyage, which required such qualities as courage, perseverance, determination and self-confidence. The

The height of improvisation: defrosting lines with a hairdryer

fact that we live in an age when it is so much easier and safer to sail to the remotest parts of the world has not changed those requirements in any way.

The safety situation in certain parts of the world may be causing concern, as do the effects of climate change. But there are still plenty of peaceful places to explore and exotic destinations to enjoy. All that is needed is a positive attitude. In the final analysis, how satisfying and enjoyable your life on the ocean will be is not determined by how big or small, how comfortable or well-equipped your boat may be, nor on how much money you have, but primarily by your own attitude.

Alone on a small boat in the middle of an ocean, far from land and outside help, a captain has his destiny, and that of his crew, in his own hands. Nothing can describe this situation better than the words of the poet WE Henley.

It matters not how strait the gate,
How charged with punishments the scroll,
I am the master of my fate:
I am the captain of my soul.

Roman mosaic of Odysseus tied to the mast by his crew to resist the bewitching calls of the sirens

31

South Indian Ocean hideaways

I had a nice surprise when I pulled out my old chart covering the approaches to the Torres Strait and saw on it the cats-cradle of position lines I had drawn on my first passage through those waters almost exactly one quarter of a century ago. That was in the good/bad old days of astronavigation and I can still remember vividly the feeling of anxiety as we approached these treacherous waters with nothing but a sextant and depth sounder to tell me where we were. As soon as the sun was up I took the first of several sights hoping to pinpoint the gap in the reef that led into the buoyed shipping channel. A small islet, Bramble Cay, marks the northern edge of Bligh Entrance and would have been concrete proof that we had arrived in the right place. By mid-morning I gave a great sigh of relief as we found the first buoy and thus the main shipping channel, but I never saw Bramble Cay.

And now? My GPS told me exactly where we were, so making landfall was child's play...well, almost, as I still had a knot in my stomach while setting a zigzag course among all those reefs. History repeated itself, as I did find the first buoy, turned the corner and, just as that first time, Bramble Cay refused to show its face. But once we had found the well-buoyed main channel, all we had to do it was keep to it and it took us all day and the following night to reach Thursday Island, on the edge of the Arafura Sea.

Having completed entry formalities into Australia, as well as the stringent quarantine requirements at Thursday Island, we caught a four-knot current that sent us flying into the dull green waters of the Arafura Sea. The change from the dark blue waters of the Pacific was so abrupt that it was hard to believe. Even the winds felt like having a different texture after the boisterous trade winds that we had enjoyed since we had left the Louisiades. We were quite clearly entering not just a different ocean, but also a different world.

Balmy southeasterly winds settled at around 15 knots, which were ideal spinnaker conditions, the Parasailor keeping the boat at a steady speed of between six and seven knots. Our target was Darwin about 800 miles almost due west of Thursday Island. There are two ways to reach the port, the easier but longer route that passes west of Bathurst Island, or a shorter route through the Dundas and Clarence Straits. The latter route is usually avoided by cruising yachts, as the straits are swept by strong tides and the intricate route through a maze of reefs and small islands makes for challenging navigation. In spite of, or to be honest, because of this, I was tempted to try that route. In order to be able to do that we had to catch the right tide by arriving at the northern entrance of Dundas Strait at exactly the right time.

Where is the wind? We have an appointment!

Nothing helps focus the mind better than having a rendezvous with Lady Tide at 2100 hours on a Friday night at Cape Don some 580 miles distant. We had to keep up an average speed of six knots, which with the help of the spinnaker we managed to do, although the wind had dropped to 10 knots. We even managed to catch a large kingfish, one of the tastiest pelagic fish.

We arrived off Cape Don at precisely the agreed time and Lady Tide was there waiting. With a smile on her face she waved at us to follow her, so we turned

Aventura's bows south and, once we were pointing in the right direction, Lady Tide gave another wave, and was gone. But she kindly left us with a strong favourable current that helped us make fast progress. The wind had by now increased to 20 knots so we were flying, which would have been a thrilling experience in the open sea, but not when I had to plot an absolutely accurate course to pass the Abbot Shoals at a safe distance, which we zipped past in the dark night doing 8 knots. The next gap to find was the entrance into Howard Channel, where we arrived just as it was getting light. As we still had the tide with us, the current in the narrow channel was 3.2 knots, and our speed over the ground 9 knots. Fortunately the entrance of the channel was marked by several lit buoys, but I would have preferred to have had them earlier, while it was still dark. As we shot past the last pair of buoys, having managed to do the entire 75-mile-long shortcut on one tide, I could see far ahead the outline of Darwin's tall buildings.

The capital of Australia's Northern Territory is a pleasant modern city, which has had to be re-built from scratch twice, once after it was almost pulverised in the second world war, and then in 1974 when cyclone Tracy tried to complete the unfinished job of the Japanese bombers. As the base of a large shrimping fleet, Darwin has excellent repair facilities and Cullen Bay marina has turned it into a favourite place among long-distance cruising sailors. Darwin is also a good starting point for inland trips whether to the nearby Kakadu nature reserve, the spectacular Kimberleys, or the Red Centre and its famous Ayres Rock, now known by its original Aboriginal name as Uluru. Although the Territorians, as the locals are referred to, are keen to project Darwin's reputation as a frontier town, it is in fact a pleasant, modern place, with pastel-coloured buildings, wide tree-lined avenues, and a slow measured pace perfectly adapted to the usual 40°C temperatures.

We made landfall at Darwin on 29 May, almost exactly two months and 4,000 miles since leaving Auckland. It had been a busy, but highly enjoyable, three months, and the stops in Vanuatu and the Louisiades were already etched in my mind as the undisputed highlights of this voyage.

Into the Indian Ocean

As the closest Australian port to Indonesia, Darwin is also the ideal starting point for a cruise to that archipelago of 10,000 islands, amongst which Bali continues to be the preferred destination for most sailors. Benign weather conditions for the 1,000-mile passage across the Arafura and Timor Seas gave us one week of glorious sailing, all of it under spinnaker. In Darwin I had a change of crew as Dieter had to return to his architectural practice, and I was joined by an acquaintance who had recently bought a boat and was keen to do some offshore sailing.

The only hiccup on an otherwise perfect passage occurred right at the end when a strong contrary current slowed us down so that it was already dark by the time we arrived off the entrance channel into Bali's Benoa harbour, but I managed to find my bearings and tie to a pontoon in Bali marina.

Over the years I had visited Bali on several occasions, and was pleased to see that in spite of the massive impact of tourism, traditions are still very much alive and the Hindu religion, to which most Balinese belong, plays an active part in their day-to-day lives. Each home has a shrine dedicated to its patron god, and, to appease the gods, small square baskets are put out every day in front of shops and offices, usually right on the pavement. Every taxi that I took had a similar offering on its dashboard.

While having breakfast at the marina restaurant one morning I saw one of the waiters set a small offering in front of the statue of a deity overlooking the marina. I later noticed that the offering was renewed throughout the day, the small basket containing rice and food as well as flowers. Statues of various deities, usually shaded by a dainty umbrella, could be seen everywhere, their lower half prudishly obscured by a black and white checkered sarong. Even a sacred banyan tree, which I saw while driving across the island, had its lower part covered by such a sarong.

With one week to kill on my own as my crew had to return home for family reasons, I spent the time visiting the interior of the island. What I found amazing was that, in spite of the large number of tourists that had made Bali one of the most popular holiday destinations in the world, all those crowds were confined to the beach resorts. In the interior life continued at a pace that had hardly changed for centuries, with people tending their fields with buffalo-drawn ploughs scouring the deep mud of terraced rice paddies. On narrow lanes I came across women walking to the nearest temple with a layered pile of offerings precariously balanced on their heads. On our first visit on Aventura I we had spent some time in Bali's interior visiting various temples and the sacred Gunung Batur Mountain, and I was happy to see that virtually everything was just as I remembered it. As we were preparing to leave Bali and head west, I set my own little basket of offerings in front of the god overlooking the marina, and asked him to bless Aventura and those who sail in her.

A favourite hangout

That Balinese deity must have taken notice of my prayer because we had the most perfect sail to Cocos Keeling, with only two noticeable occurrences during the week-long passage. One night I saw what I first thought to be a bright white flare to the east but as it kept growing larger and plummeting fast towards the sea I realised that it could only be some space debris burning up as it entered the atmosphere.

That same night we were bombarded by aliens of a more friendly kind as an entire school of flying fish landed on Aventura's deck. Some managed to wriggle their way to freedom, but in the morning I still found a total of 22 large flying fish in the scuppers. Before turning them into a delicious breakfast, I lined them up on deck for a photo, which I emailed to Gwenda, Doina and Ivan.

Because of Cocos Keeling's remoteness, this Australian outpost has gained the affection of all long-distance cruisers who call there. The authorities have made a visible effort to welcome sailors, having cleaned up Direction Island, installed a barbecue pit, toilets, and built an open-sided covered terrace with tables and benches. There was even a phone for free local calls, and two large water tanks to use for a shower or your laundry, and so I did.

Paradise lost?

The so-called clubhouse was adorned with hundreds of mementoes of boats that have passed through. Faced with the opportunity to leave behind something for posterity sailors had given free rein to their artistic talent whether in the form of carved name boards, inscribed fishing floats, decorated pieces of driftwood, a stuffed puffer fish, even a couple of quite beautiful paintings that reminded me of the wall paintings of Horta in the Azores.

There were nine other yachts there when we arrived and tied Aventura to the yellow quarantine buoy. An Australian police officer came over in a boat from the main settlement on West Island, and quickly dealt with all formalities. Kindly ignoring the strict quarantine rules, he allowed us to keep all our fresh provisions provided they were consumed on board, and made us promise that any garbage that was taken ashore would be burnt. Later that afternoon we joined the other sailors for the daily happy hour, everyone bringing their own drinks and snacks. A hurricane lamp was lit when it got dark and the party continued late into the night. My crew, who had only sailed in the Mediterranean before, was absolutely delighted. 'This is what I always dreamed of as being the true cruising life,' he exclaimed as we made our way back to the boat.

Jetsam art

Refreshed and refuelled, we tore ourselves away, and set course for Chagos. The southeast trade winds that I described as balmy on the leg to Bali increased steadily the further west we moved into the south Indian Ocean and never dropped below 20 knots on this leg. We also had frequent squalls, usually at night, so the spinnaker was given a rest, and most of the time we sailed with two reefs in the mainsail and a poled out yankee rolled up to half or even one third of its surface. Even so we moved at a fair clip and covered 1,500 miles in a little over nine days.

As so often at the end of a long ocean passage, at the rate we were going we would have arrived at our destination in the middle of the night, so after midnight I slowed down. With none of the hazards being lit and a strong current pushing us westwards, I was anxiously monitoring the radar, but the low islands refused to show up. They only appeared at a distance of four miles, by which time dawn was breaking and the low islands on the windward side of Salomon Atoll were already visible with the naked eye in the half-light. We entered the large lagoon through Centre Pass and dropped the anchor in 21 metres off Fouquet Island in the southeast corner of the large lagoon.

A small dinghy with a young boy at the helm made his way towards us and asked permission to come on board. He told us his name was Janni, that he was Austrian, sailing with his parents, and that they were now on their fourth circumnavigation. He proceeded to give us the local lowdown as well as some fishing tips and suggested that if we wanted to have more privacy we should anchor off Takamaka Island near their yacht Mapopo, that stood conspicuously apart from the others. There were altogether nine yachts anchored in the lagoon but as it was still early in the morning there was no sign of life on any of them.

It didn't take long to realise that the atmosphere among the sailors anchored around us was very different from our experience at Cocos. Whereas those who called there could best be described as birds of passage, those whom we saw at Chagos seemed to have grown roots there. In recent years these uninhabited islands, which are part of the British Indian Ocean Territory, had become a semi-permanent base for some cruisers who spent months there. A British patrol vessel made the rounds of the islands on a regular basis, charged an anchoring fee, but generally left people alone provided they observed some basic rules: no spear fishing, no collecting of shells, coral or coconut crabs, no living ashore. Diego Garcia, the largest island of the archipelago, had been leased by the UK to the US as a military base, and was strictly out of bounds.

Among the three atolls: Salomon, Peros Banhos and Egmont, the former has the best anchorages. It was also here that the original Ilois inhabitants had some of their settlements. In 1971, all Ilois settlements on Salomon and Diego Garcia had to be vacated to clear the entire area for the US military base. The entire population of approximately 1,500 people was forcibly removed by the British authorities to Mauritius and the Seychelles. Over the years the Ilois have won several court cases against the British government for the right to return to their ancestral lands, but I suspect that as Diego Garcia is such a strategically important base, their hope to resettle the islands may never happen.

During the week we spent at Salomon we moved between Fouquet, Takamaka and Boddam Islands, all of which used to be inhabited. The largest Ilois settlement used to be on Boddam, now reduced to a roofless church, a few ruined houses, and a cemetery. The latter looked as if it had been cleaned up recently, as occasionally Ilois are allowed to visit the graves of their families, but the rest of the island was an almost impenetrable jungle. In one of the deserted houses someone had spray-painted a graffiti, which summed up Chagos better than I could ever do: 'Welcome to the yachtie hangout par excellence'.

With little else to do on the island, we took the dinghy to a tiny islet on the windward reef and snorkelled on a nearby coral patch. It had some of the most beautiful underwater scenery I had seen in years with lots of fish and brightly coloured coral.

On our return we anchored off Takamaka, close to Mapopo, whose crew Hans and Karin invited us to join them ashore. They had been there six months and it was their fourth visit on as many circumnavigations in the previous 20 years. Their friendly attitude was quite a contrast to that of the others we had met. Some of the long-stayers were quite strange, they rarely went ashore, and a few never left their boats during the week we spent there. I could not make up my mind what made these people tick. All I could say is that they ticked very slowly.

An overnight sail done mostly in the lee of the extensive Chagos Bank took us to Egmont, one of the least frequented spots in the Chagos archipelago. We found the entrance, but navigation through the Egmont lagoon was not easy as it was peppered with isolated coral heads, but with the help of the forward-looking sonar we managed to make our way slowly into the far southeast corner, where we anchored off a beautiful golden beach. In my long cruising life I had anchored in many attractive spots but none came close to Egmont. Knowing that this was going to be my last anchorage in the tropics, I was hoping to stay for a few days, but an unexpected spell of easterly winds cut short our highly enjoyable stop. However tempted I might have been to stay longer in that lovely place, the prospect of a fast passage to Mauritius quickly wiped out the temptation. Both in Bali and Cocos whenever I mentioned the fact that I planned to sail to Chagos and from there to Mauritius, the reaction had been the same. 'You'll have a hell of a hard time beating all the way to Mauritius,' I was invariably told. I had heard this so many times that I had almost started to believe it myself, but I still decided to visit Chagos come what may.

Indeed, the 1,200-mile passage from Chagos to Mauritius can be quite tough, especially later in the season when there is more south in the strong trade winds. But in sailing, as in everything else in life, you need good luck on your side. Once again fortune was with me, as a depression that had formed to the east of us brought favourable winds, and we had a perfect eight-day passage to Mauritius, mostly closehauled but comfortable nonetheless. Meanwhile the news on the daily radio net that acted as a forum for boats heading west was going from bad to worse. While we enjoyed almost perfect conditions, further east the weather produced by that same depression sounded atrocious, with gale force winds and a nasty cross swell that caused a lot of damage.

Caudan Marina

Old and new in Port Louis

After the tranquillity and slow pace of Chagos, the noise and constant traffic of Port Louis, the busy capital of Mauritius, was almost too much to bear. A major development programme had given the once rundown waterfront a welcome facelift with a neat little marina huddled among the tall new buildings. Not far behind this picture postcard image, the bustling street markets of the old town retained the true character of this ethnic melting pot, where Asia, Africa and Europe had come so harmoniously together. When the writer Somerset Maugham described Mauritius as the 'sugary pearl of the Indian Ocean,' he undoubtedly meant the crop that has shaped the island's history and contributed to its prosperity. While sugar continues to play an essential part in the local economy, its importance has been supplanted by tourism. Mauritius is now a trendy holiday destination with new resorts mushrooming among the old plantations, but has little to offer as a cruising destination.

My crew, who had sailed with me from Darwin, left in Mauritius and I was joined by Gwenda. As she was going to sail only as far as La Réunion, I had already arranged to be met there by my friend Antti, who had agreed to join me for the long trek to Cape Town.

A French enclave

In spite of their shared history, as both islands were originally colonised by French settlers who started the sugarcane industry, neighbouring La Réunion could not be more different from Mauritius. For some strange reason, La Réunion was declared a department of metropolitan France, an administrative legerdemain that ensured that this island in the midst of the South Indian Ocean remains a remote corner of France. Rather than opt for the new marina at Les Galets, near the capital St Denis, where most visiting boats go, I decided to head for St Pierre, a small town on the south coast.

The entrance into St Pierre marina is quite tricky as it is constantly silted up by a river that empties into the ocean. When we arrived after an overnight passage from Mauritius, a high swell was breaking outside the harbour to the obvious enjoyment of local surfers. Having been assured that the swell in the harbour entrance looked worse than it was, somewhat reluctantly, I decided to have a go. The channel was buoyed and we made it through safely at the cost of nothing more than a few more white hairs. The small marina was located right in the middle of the lively town, with dozens of restaurants and bars within walking distance. As I have said before, and will gladly repeat, the French do know how to enjoy life, and eating well is not just part of this joie de vivre, but absolutely central to it. St Pierre is a case in point.

The mountainous interior of La Réunion is dominated by the remains of three huge craters called 'cirques' whose sheer walls rise to well over 2,000 metres. The volcanic scenery is quite breath-taking and the best way to appreciate it is to go on one of many walks, the island being crisscrossed by several paths.

With the season by now being well advanced, a planned detour to Madagascar was no longer feasible. However, being so close, it would have been a shame not to see this fascinating island, so Gwenda and I left the boat in St Pierre, and flew to Madagascar. We hired a 4WD car with a local driver, and explored the island from north to south stopping at several of the nature reserves for which Madagascar is famous. Having been isolated from neighbouring Africa for millions of years, its flora and fauna are unlike anywhere else on earth. Hundreds of species of plants and animals are unique to the island, perhaps none more distinctive than the lemur, a primate of which several species survive.

African landfall

Oh, the joys of cruising! We were motoring in a flat calm south of Madagascar on passage to South Africa when just 24 hours previously it felt as if we were in a boiling cauldron with waves crashing, thunder cracking and lightning exploding as if Armageddon had descended upon our poor heads. It is almost impossible to say what was the worst: the wild breaking waves, the wind gusting at 40 knots, or the awesome thunderstorm that even the forecast had described as severe. The same forecast had warned that large logs had been seen in the area we were passing through, and were posing a serious hazard to shipping. With night approaching there was little we could do, except keep our fingers crossed. Before we were hit by the front that brought with it all the above ingredients, we had been sailing along nicely in 25 knots. As the sky darkened and the wind kept rising, I rolled up the yankee and continued with two reefs in the main. I had often sailed in winds over 30 knots broadreaching like this, so there wasn't much to worry about... or so I thought.

During my night watch, with the wind steady at 35 knots, sometimes gusting more, and our speed never going below 9 knots, the pattern of the waves changed and the swell started to look menacing. Suddenly we hit something hard, quite likely one of those logs that had floated off Madagascar. Whatever it was, the boat had ridden over it and, as the centreboard was up, there was nothing under the boat to stop it, so it ended up hitting the rudder. Thanks to its design, by swinging upwards the rudder had absorbed the shock without suffering any obvious damage. The incident was described in more detail on page 226.

The rest of the passage was uneventful and we made landfall at Richards Bay nine days after leaving St Pierre. While the port and nearby town had few attractions, the proximity of one of the largest game parks in South Africa was a great temptation. After the clearance formalities had been completed, we were going to spend a couple of days touring the large park, but Aeolus, divine keeper of all winds, had other plans for us. The prospect of two days of favourable weather sent us racing out of Richards Bay and, as the weather looked like holding, I also decided to bypass Durban, and try to make it as far as East London. I knew that in this notorious part of the world if conditions look right, you go, so that's what we did, even if there were a few raised eyebrows among our neighbours seeing us leave in such a hurry when we had hardly arrived.

The promised northeast wind held the whole of the second day and we made excellent progress with a welcome boost from the current. By midnight the wind had dropped to almost nothing, so with only 70 miles left, on came the engine and we continued, hoping to arrive in East London by early afternoon. Suddenly the engine slowed down and stopped. I suspected fuel starvation, purged the engine, but when I tried to restart it, it would not turn. It could only be a faulty starter motor, the only engine spare I did not have on board.

We had no option but sail and eventually made it into East London. With my usual luck, I tracked down a reconditioned starter motor and, with the engine working again, we left as soon as the weather looked all right and made a beeline for the axis of the Agulhas current. Its strongest rate is along the 200 metre line, which we found about 15 miles offshore. Soon we had the thrill of having three knots in our favour, but the

excitement was short lived as during the night the wind started to shift into the southwest foretelling a blow from that direction. The first thing to do in such a situation is to move as quickly as possible inshore, into shallow water, so as to be out of the current before the wind gets too strong. Even winds of 25 knots against that mighty current can create hellish conditions with huge breaking waves. We made it into shallow water before the wind got too strong, and spent the rest of the night taking short tacks along the coast and making painfully slow progress.

By the morning the wind had gone into the southeast, so up went the Parasailor and I plotted a course that wasn't too far offshore, but would still benefit from a favourable current. Listening to the next forecast, the weather appeared relatively settled for the following three days so I decided to push on rather than stop at one of the tempting places along the way: Port Elizabeth, Knysna or Mossel Bay.

At dawn on the third day after our departure from East London we could make out in the distance the low outline of Cape Agulhas, the southernmost point of Africa. Agulhas means needle in Portuguese and the early navigators had given it this name because the compass needle showed true north when their ships were level with the Cape as, in those days, there was no significant magnetic variation in this area. In the intervening years the magnetic north pole had shifted a long way and the current charts show a hefty 25°W variation.

The featureless headland is a highly significant landmark as it is the point where the waters of the Indian Ocean meet those of the Atlantic, and it was a great thrill to sail past it. The low cape may not have looked very dramatic, but the sea life around it was quite prolific. Earlier we had seen dolphins and whales, but it was the countless seabirds that held centre stage here: white and painted petrels, gannets, and several kinds of albatross, the majestic wandering albatross among them. The last time I had seen so many birds had been off Cape Horn. I wondered what made them congregate at such significant locations.

It took us all day to reach the more famous Cape of Good Hope. Initially called Cape of Storms, it was on Prince Henry the Navigator's suggestion that it was changed to the current more positive sounding name. True to form, by nightfall the wind came up stronger and stronger from the southeast, and was soon blowing at over 30 knots. It was also bitterly cold with a true whiff of the Antarctic in it. Even with three reefs in the mainsail Aventura was romping along at over eight knots and my planned dawn arrival at Cape Town now looked more like an ETA of two am, yet another night arrival in an unfamiliar port. For all of two seconds I thought of heaving to and wait for dawn, but the temptation proved irresistible, and I called Port Control. Permission to enter the harbour was granted, and we crossed the huge port past several sleeping ships all the way into the far corner where the Royal Cape Yacht Club has its base. Having phoned the club the previous day we slowly crept in and tied up to our assigned berth. I had a feeling of deep satisfaction, but also of great relief to be there having covered close to 12,000 miles in the six months since I had left New Zealand. A bottle of champagne, which I had bought in La Réunion with this very celebration in mind, was duly popped and Antti and I drank a toast to our safe arrival. Happiness is made up of small moments like this. Small maybe, but unforgettable.

32

Choosing and equipping a boat for offshore cruising

Accept nothing as nearly good enough.

Sir Henry Royce

Forty years after preparing the first Aventura for a world voyage I had a unique opportunity to conceive a boat that would fulfil my long pursuit of the ideal cruising boat. In the process I learned much about design and boat building, and had the opportunity to work closely with the builders in deciding on the essential elements concerning safety, comfort, performance or functionality.

As I mentioned in the previous chapter, the choice of the right boat and its main features lies at the very core of a successful voyage, and my own voyage on Aventura IV has comprehensively proven that point. In previous chapters I have dealt with some of the other factors that might affect the success of an offshore voyage, such as crew, health, security concerns, weather and practical considerations. In this chapter the boat itself takes centre stage and the most important features on a boat suitable for an offshore voyage will be examined. Some of the points discussed in the following pages may have been mentioned earlier, but I decided to bring together here all the relevant features that ought to be borne in mind by anyone planning a long voyage.

In search of that elusive ideal cruising boat, I have conducted various surveys over the years, from the wide-ranging Global Cruising Survey to the Voyage Planning Survey. The views of the sailors interviewed differed widely but there was one point on which they all agreed: the choice of a suitable boat for an offshore voyage is of such paramount importance that the final decision should not be taken lightly. This is echoed in the advice quoted above of Sir Henry Royce of Rolls Royce fame, who should know that only the best is good enough.

With the wisdom of hindsight, I can say that I am happy with the choice of every one of my boats, each being right for my circumstances, experience and plans at the time of choosing. In contrast, among the more than 3,000 yachts that have sailed in the transatlantic or round-the-world rallies that I have been involved with, I noticed many obviously unsuitable choices. A few were so bad that their owners were eventually forced to abandon their voyage. Although I could fill a book with examples of the bad choices that I have come across, I will limit myself to the most recent. It involved a couple sailing on their new 50-foot boat in a transatlantic rally. They had a series of frustrating problems on their way to the Canaries, but the worst occurred halfway during their passage to the Caribbean when the steering cable broke followed by the autopilot. They were helped by other participants in the rally and managed to make it safely to Barbados, but were totally exhausted by the effort, and decided to get rid of the boat come what may. A dream shattered.

Length overall

Too many of my friends follow the erroneous belief that a yacht should be as long in feet as the years of your age.

Bill Butler

Bill Butler

Sailing with Erick Bouteleux who has played a major role in my choice of boats

Deciding on the size of a boat is not only the most important but also the most difficult of the entire decision making process and it is here that most serious mistakes are made. More often than not people choose a boat that is too large for their requirements, difficult to handle shorthanded and more expensive to run and maintain. The temptation is hard to resist, as the same money nowadays will buy a much larger boat than it did ten years ago. Also equipment such as electric winches, powered furling gears and bow-thrusters have made even large boats much easier to handle. The used boat market is awash with excellent offers and, as more and more used boats become available, prices become proportionally even more attractive. If there is one single aspect to be borne in mind and stuck to firmly before any decision is taken, is to ask, 'Can I sail this boat with just my partner or, in an emergency, on my own?'

I will quote here my good friend Arthur Beiser, author of the classic book The Proper Yacht, who points out: 'There are four essentials for a proper yacht. These are, not in order because all four are needed, that the boat be (1) beautiful; (2) fast under sail and under power; (3) able, well-designed and engineered, strongly built and well-equipped and (4) comfortable at sea and in port, on deck and below.'

In a survey on the global movement of sailing yachts in 2015, I obtained data from 50 locations around the world and was able to calculate the average length of the boats that had passed through some of the most frequented cruising destinations. To arrive at a realistic figure, only boats under 60 feet were taken into account as very few of the larger boats would fit the description of a standard cruising boat. Among the 775 boats that arrived in Horta, in the Azores, on completion of their passage from the Caribbean, the average length was 43.8 feet. The average among the 556 arrivals in Tahiti was higher, at 45.2 feet. The Bermuda average for the 560 boats was 46.9 feet, while 45.9 feet was the average for the 617 boats that had transited the Panama Canal.

The overall average length for the 2,508 boats under 60 feet that called at the above locations was 45.3 feet. The above results included both monohulls and multihulls. More efficient and better-equipped boats, with reliable automatic pilots, electric winches, furling gears and countless other accessories, have resulted in an overall reduction in the size of crew. This was evident from the figures obtained from St Helena, where visiting yachts had an average crew of 3.3, whereas in Vava'u, Tonga, it was 3.5, in Cocos Keeling 2.6, and 2.7 in the Marquesas. It is indeed worth adding that at both Cocos Keeling and the Marquesas, over half the boats were sailed by just a couple. An even higher proportion of boats were sailed by couples in the three transatlantic rallies that I organised in 2016. Among the total of 70 boats, 61 were sailed by couples, 40 of them alone, 13 with their children, and 8 also with additional crew. In this case, the average number of crew per boat, including children, was 4.4, or 3.8 if taking into account only crews over 18.

Skip Novak

Skip Novak, who had sailed in several round-the-world races and now runs a successful charter operation in the Antarctic with his 55-foot steel Pelagic and the 80-foot aluminium Pelagic Australis, gave the following advice, 'The length depends entirely on the purpose of the boat and how many will sail on her. For a couple or up to four people, and your goal is to explore remote areas rather than make long ocean passages, the boat should not be longer than 50 to 55.'

Aventura IV's clean decks

That size might be too large for most short-handed crews, especially if they are not experienced. Both in the rallies and during my voyages I came across several couples sailing on 50 to 55-foot yachts, who found them difficult to handle on their own and ended up being forced to take on extra crew, a solution that they didn't like at all. As one of them advised, 'Don't go for a bigger boat than you need just because you can afford it.'

While all my previous surveys had shown that most owners were happy with their choice, whether large or small, in every survey there were also a few disgruntled owners. Whereas a few complained that their boat was too large to handle, more owners complained about their boat being too small. It is a well-known fact that lack of space or privacy can have a negative effect on morale and lead to friction among crew on a long passage.

Another cause of complaint was not having enough space to store all the gear necessary for a long voyage. Often this meant that surplus gear was stowed on deck, which can lead to a potentially hazardous or unseaworthy situation. Having been on the dockside watching the arrival of boats at the end of their Atlantic crossing, I was often amazed at the clutter on the stern of some boats, as the person throwing the line struggled to clear a forest of obstructions from wind generator mast to danbuoy, fishing rod, flag pole, spare anchor, whip aerial, outboard motor, barbeque and even a bicycle, not to speak of surfboards or paddling canoes on the side decks. I wondered how in a real emergency the crew would be able to throw a line to a man overboard or launch the liferaft past all such obstructions.

Monohull versus multihull

I was very happy with the performance of our catamaran during our circumnavigation. I believe that it was the ideal boat for that voyage, for that route and also for our budget. In spite of which, I feel that if you want to sail in the Southern Ocean, a monohull would be better but not just any monohull.

Javier Visiers

Javier Visiers

357

To go for one or more hulls is perhaps an even more difficult decision than that of size. Although there are a few cruising trimarans on the market, I still need to be persuaded that trimarans are suitable to be sailed on offshore passages by a small family crew. However things may be changing as a new generation of cruising trimarans may show that their designers have learned from past mistakes and have managed to improve their safety credentials. In the early days there were similar doubts about the suitability of catamarans for offshore sailing, but their design has greatly improved, architects have put a lot of thought into their safety, while builders have done their best to produce strong seaworthy craft. Their ever-increasing popularity among long-distance cruisers is the best proof of that. As they have many advantages over a monohull of the same length, I have an open mind on this subject.

Those who plan to set off in a catamaran on a long voyage must choose their route carefully to minimise the risk of encountering dangerous weather, observe the safe seasons, and always be aware of a catamaran's weak points. Catamarans are much less forgiving than monohulls when weather conditions deteriorate, and whereas a catamaran needs to be helped to overcome extreme conditions, a well-found monohull can be battened down and left to its own devices. It may capsize and lose its mast but it will probably survive upright.

Javier Visiers, who is quoted above, is a well-known Spanish naval architect, and took many by surprise when he chose a catamaran for the Millennium Odyssey round-the-world rally. Javier did in fact what many other sailors do, and chose what he thought was the most suitable boat for a particular voyage, a pragmatic attitude that I fully share. Other sailors may consider a catamaran, even if with some provisos, as in the case of David Beauchamp. 'I am considering a catamaran for cruising, as a catamaran over 12 metres can be handled by a couple on most occasions with more ease than a monohull. I have spoken to owners of large cats. They are best kept between 30 degrees north and 30 degrees south for safety's sake.'

The number of catamarans on long voyages has been steadily increasing and my global survey was a good opportunity to find out their actual proportion among cruising yachts. Once again, I referred to the detailed statistics obtained from the Azores and found that among the 775 boats that had arrived in Horta, 103 (13%) were catamarans. That percentage had risen to 17% (185 of 1058) among the Panama transits, with the highest percentage (19%) recorded in Noumea (New Caledonia), with 61 catamarans among a total of 328 boats. The situation in some rallies confirmed this trend, with 17% in the Blue Planet Odyssey, 19% in the World ARC, 14% in the ARC (35 of 259), and 17% among the 209 boats in the Pacific Puddle Jump. The Atlantic Odyssey achieved the highest percentage, with 18 catamarans among the 70 boats (26%) in the 2016 event.

Rudders

Based on the reported rudder failures in the ARC and other offshore rallies, as well as similar emergency situations handled by the search and rescue authorities, more cruising boats have been abandoned in the last

30 years because of rudder failure than for any other reason. The most recent example is that of the yacht Dove II that lost its rudder 400 miles east of Barbados while on passage to the Caribbean. The crew were unable to improvise an emergency steering system and had to abandon the boat. The crew, a couple with their children and another crew member, were rescued in a coordinated salvage operation.

Rudder losses also occurred on two catamarans in the Atlantic Odyssey, their crew only noticing their absence when they arrived in Barbados. Having two rudders was a definite advantage in such a situation as their owners only noticed their absence on arrival.

One of the most common failures experienced by boats taking part in the ARC is to their steering systems. Over the years several ARC boats had lost their rudder during the Atlantic crossing and some were abandoned. The organisers' comments on this frequently occurring problem are very clear. 'Those yachts were not the only ones with rudder problems; there were many reports of steering cables and systems breaking due to the pressure on them and the amount of rudder movement needed to keep the yacht on course. Another contributing factor is overloading; this is an easy mistake to make as piles of stores, water, fuel, crew gear and cruising equipment are added before departure. All this extra weight adds to the strain on the steering systems, especially in heavy seas, and doubly so if the sails are incorrectly trimmed and the yacht is unbalanced. Bad trim can often go unnoticed when the autopilot is used for long periods and the crew do not hand-steer.'

The potentially serious consequences of rudder failure highlight their importance as one of the essential design features that should dictate the choice of boat. Chief among them are those to do with safety, such as suspended rudders. Unprotected by at least a partial skeg such rudders are extremely vulnerable and have gradually migrated from racing to cruising boats. If you cannot avoid a boat with this kind of

rudder, at least insist that the lower half of the rudder is sacrificial, as this is where it is most likely to be hit by debris or damaged if making an accidental hard landing. Regardless of the type of rudder, an adequate emergency system should be prepared in the event of the loss of the rudder and steering. Such an emergency backup should be easy to set up and known to all members of the crew. This subject was discussed in more detail on page 190.

On Aventura IV, the two aluminium rudders are supported by skegs and, as an added protection, the upper section of the rudder blades incorporates a crumple area. This sacrificial area is made of light composite material that will crumple and compress without causing any damage to the hull itself in case of a collision. This is exactly what happened in a collision with large lump of ice in the Arctic, with only the sacrificial part being affected and the main rudder continuing to function normally for several thousands of miles until repairs could be made.

The aluminium hull and rudders had two coats of International Trilux 33 antifouling paint, which stood up extremely well during a long voyage in both Arctic and tropical waters. Quite remarkable was its good adherence to the hull in spite of some brutal scrapes with ice floes.

Keels and draft

Keel configuration and ideal draft on a cruising boat were also examined in my surveys when many owners expressed their concern about the vulnerability of a fin keel. Some owners qualified both their choice of keel and maximum draft by pointing out that their final decision would depend on the particular cruising area they were spending most time in.

In all the surveys dealing with the subject of ideal draft there was a consensus that a fixed keel may be better suited for ocean passages, whereas shallow draft, whether with a shorter keel and bulb or a centreboard arrangement, was preferable when cruising. Skip Novak spoke for many when he commented, 'if your priority is to explore, rather than see from a distance, then some lifting appendage is necessary. A centreboard allows you to get into shallower places.'

My two last boats had a centreboard and I can state unequivocally that both from the safety and convenience point of view, a centreboard is a great advantage on a cruising boat, both when exploring inshore areas and on passage.

As to actual hull shape the only general comment I am prepared to make is that a fine V entry makes for a more comfortable ride when going to windward. I know this only too well because the pounding of Aventura III's flat bottom when going hard to windward could be quite tiring. Aventura IV's hull had a better configuration and as a result was both more efficient and comfortable when sailing close to the wind. Sailing to windward is the main weakness of cruising catamarans although significant design improvements have been made in this respect, usually by the use of daggerboards. It is an essential feature to consider by anyone looking for a performing cruising catamaran.

Displacement

What fun can anyone get from sailing in a floating safe?
Erick Bouteleux

Erick's barbed comment was addressed at sailors who built themselves massive steel boats, which used to be regarded not only the safest option but also best suited for cruising. Fashions do change and nowadays it is rare to see heavy displacement boats while homebuilt boats are even less common.

Displacement should be a serious consideration for those interested in sailing performance, as I know too well from personal experience. At 9 tons for her 36 feet, the first Aventura was on the heavy side and, having a rather short main mast, was an indifferent sailer in light winds. After my first voyage, when I had come across a number of boat losses, I was also attracted to the idea of a strong steel boat and ended up with Aventura II. My intention was to have a boat of reasonable displacement, but while the designer followed my suggestion, the builder had other ideas and Aventura II ended up with a displacement of 17 tonnes rather than the 12.5 tonnes envisaged by the architect Bill Dixon. While Aventura II sailed well in moderate winds, in light winds she was a source of continuous frustration. So I was determined to get a boat with a lighter displacement for my third Aventura.

An Outremer 4X performance cruising catamaran on passage to the Caribbean

Indeed Aventura III's designed displacement of 9.5 tons for a beamy 43-footer was as close to perfect as possible and I always made sure to keep her weight down to a reasonable level. Aventura IV's designed displacement was 14 tonnes and even when fully loaded with provisions behaved very well on every point of sailing.

Hull material

There is no good or bad construction material, but unfortunately there are good and bad boat builders!

Javier Visiers

As in the case of displacement, this is another decision that may very well be taken out of your hands, unless hull material is put at the top of the list of priorities or you order a one-off. In most cases boat are built in the most suitable material the architect and builder have agreed upon. For a long voyage the builder might be persuaded to put some additional strength in critical areas (bows, along the waterline, rudder area) so it is worth discussing this early with the builder so that such modifications can be done during the initial building stages and not as an afterthought.

Aventura III's spotless unpainted aluminium hull at age 13

Metal hulls, whether steel or aluminium, have both advantages and disadvantages, their main attraction being their intrinsic strength. As for the disadvantages, in the case of steel it is the need for the best possible initial preparation of the hull and decks for painting, which must be followed by careful maintenance throughout the boat's lifetime. In the case of aluminium hulls some people are concerned about the risk of electrolytic reaction but this is quite unjustified. Modern alloys as well as building methods have taken care of that. Having had two aluminium boats and never experienced the slightest problem of electrolysis, that myth should be laid to rest, just like that of the Bermuda Triangle.

Rig

A cutter rig is ideal because when the going gets rough our little staysail gets tough.

Don Babson

Don's view was shared by Dave Beauchamp. 'A cutter rig with furling jib and staysail is best when shorthanded.' Arthur Beiser has no doubts that a cutter rig is best for long-distance cruising. 'No other rig makes sense these days except for very small boats when a simple sloop might be OK.' Initially I was determined to have a cutter rig on Aventura IV, but was eventually persuaded that a fractional rig with backswept spreaders would be more efficient than a standard cutter rig. Indeed, the Solent jib performed very well when close-hauled and the mast was also much better stayed than on the previous Aventura. But I still insisted on a split rig, with a staysail set on an inner forestay to be used in stronger winds. It was a good solution and reinforced my conviction that the flexibility provided by a two-foresail configuration is a major advantage on any boat over 40 feet.

Running rigging

As synthetic ropes have got stronger, I don't like the current trend of using thin lines for sheets, as I prefer them of adequate diameter to be comfortable to the hands. While setting up the running rigging it is a good idea to have a good look at the existing deck layout and the run of the various sheets and lines, which should have a clear unobstructed run back to the cockpit helped by turning blocks at critical points.

As to halyards, the mast should have enough dedicated channels for spinnaker and foresail halyards, and their backups. On Aventura IV, the mainsail halyard was of Dyneema non-stretch material and I decided to have the boom topping lift from the same material so as to have a permanent backup for the mainsail halyard. I always prefer to have two spinnaker halyards so they can be used on the lee side when the sail is hoisted. The same halyards were used for the code zero sail.

Deck layout

A well-thought out deck layout makes it possible to sail the yacht singlehanded and preferably without leaving the cockpit.

John Ellis

Clear unobstructed decks are of paramount importance on an ocean going yacht and due thought should be given to an efficient deck layout and to the run of the various lines. An efficient and functional deck layout has been one of my main priorities as I regard this matter as an essential safety feature that allows me, and my crew, to do most of the sail handling jobs from the cockpit.

It is essential that lines, which come to the cockpit, are colour coded and brought to individual clutches. The same goes for the control lines from the furling gears. Some production boats fail badly in this respect, and this should be put right by making sure that the system is adapted to your own needs and preferences.

I shall point out some other essential features that I have used on my boats and which I regard as indispensible, such as a boom-brake. The reason why I prefer a boom-brake to a preventer is that the former is, or should be, permanently set up. This means that in an involuntary gybe, possibly caused by the autopilot or windvane, the gybe is controlled. A first gybe is often followed by a second gybe in the opposite direction. Even if a preventer had slowed down the boom on the initial gybe, on the second gybe that preventer will be useless, whereas a boom brake would control the boom on either gybe.

Another point to consider is that if a spinnaker will be used frequently it is advisable to have sheets, guys and blocks permanently set up, certainly when on passage. I once went on an afternoon sail on a large yacht used for crew training. Out of the marina, the captain decided to put up the spinnaker but as the decks were absolutely bare, all blocks and sheets had to be retrieved from lockers. As we were sailing in the Mediterranean, by the time everything was ready, the wind had died so all those lines and blocks were neatly gathered and stowed safely away, the whole procedure being probably repeated next time the captain deemed conditions to be right to hoist a spinnaker. I couldn't help wondering what those paying crew were going to learn from such a traditionally-minded captain.

In my view, the best improvement in your sailing technique, especially if planning a voyage in trade wind conditions, is to make the necessary arrangements to use a fixed pole when running or broadreaching. It is a simple and efficient system that I have been using on all my boats, and I highly recommend it.

For efficient sail handling, especially when shorthanded, I regard having two electric winches almost indispensible. A good example of one of the situations when this extra help can be very handy is when a foresail needs to be furled in quickly, such as when threatened by a squall. The furling line is always kept wound around one of the electric winches, and while pressing its button with one finger, with the other hand I ease the sheet gradually as the sail is being furled. This effortless operation rarely takes more than one minute. It worked equally well on Aventura IV when reefing the mainsail from the cockpit, with the reefing line being hauled in by the electric winch while the halyard was paid out.

Interior comforts

Comfortable sea berths on any tack or angle of heel are an absolute must.

John Wicks

As comfort is so important on a cruising boat, everything should be done to make the boat as homely as possible. Comfortable sea berths are essential on an offshore passage and there should be at least one all-weather bunk for the person off watch. As one normally spends most of the day sitting, serious thought should also be given to comfortable seating both in the main cabin and cockpit. One aspect that is easily neglected if planning to sail with crew is to have two toilet compartments.

Good insulation as well as adequate ventilation with sufficient hatches and dorade boxes for rough weather are features often missing on production boats built for temperate climates. They are vital for cruising in the tropics. Good ventilation and sound insulation are essential for the engine room.

A well thought-out galley should be a priority. Compact, U or L-shaped galleys are to be preferred over open-plan ones, which are unsuitable on an offshore cruising boat. There should be sufficient storage space in the immediate area of the galley so that all essential items are within easy reach. On many production boats, which are most likely to be used for charter in sheltered waters, the galley is quite inadequate when used on passage or in rough seas.

The importance of ample storage space was often mentioned in the surveys probably because it is an aspect neglected on some production boats. This was a high priority when I planned the Aventura IV, as I knew that there would be occasions when I would sail with a full complement of crew. That was also the reason why I wanted to have as many comfortable sea-berths as possible. At one of the boat shows where Aventura was exhibited, a visitor asked me.

'Why do you have so many berths and not enough cupboards?'

'For the simple reason that you can stow things in a berth, but you cannot sleep in a cupboard.'

He gave me a strange look, and thought that I was joking. I wasn't.

Cockpit protection

The ideal yacht should provide total shelter to the cockpit.
Antti Louhija

Good cockpit protection was one the main items mentioned by the surveyed captains when questioned about essential features on an offshore cruising boat. Some designers have managed to provide this useful feature by incorporating a hard dodger without spoiling the overall looks of the boat, but the majority continue to be limited to soft dodgers.

A compromise solution was found on Aventura IV by extending the coachroof so as to create a protected corner for the watch-keeper in the forward part of the cockpit. Aventura IV also had an inside nav station with good visibility, so the person on watch had this more comfortable option to retreat to in inclement weather.

Sails

I do like a fully-battened mainsail but if I were a little older I would consider in-boom furling.

Don Babson

Books have been written on the subject of sails so I will focus only on the essentials. For a long voyage one should make sure that the mainsail is made as strong as possible, with double, ideally triple UV resistant zigzag stitching and protection patches in the areas where the sail may touch the spreaders when fully let out. The furling foresail(s) should be provided with anti-UV strips.

I have discussed the subject of the type of mainsail on a cruising boat elsewhere, and I stand by the fact that a fully battened mainsail, with slab reefing, is still the answer for those who are interested in performance. There are three ways of reefing the mainsail: doing all the work at the foot of the mast, taking all lines to the cockpit and dealing with the halyard also from there, or taking only the reefing lines to the cockpit and handling the halyard and reef cringles at the foot of the mast. On Aventura IV, I had the second and third reefs being handled from the cockpit, and the first reef at the mast. In this way I did not need to leave the cockpit in stronger winds.

Mainsail furling systems have evolved, and some of the boom furling arrangements combine the best of two worlds, by offering a quick and easy way to reduce sail surface, and, as the furling mainsail is provided with battens, the loss of performance is quite minimal. Spinnakers should be provided with adequate dousers or it will be difficult to douse them in strong winds when this needs to be done quickly. While there isn't much to choose between well-cut spinnakers, some dousers are better than others. Ideally, as on the Parasailor, the collar should be rigid and not made of soft material. The douser collar should also have a wide enough mouth to snuffle the spinnaker easily. As an added protection, the sailmaker should be asked to strengthen the corners and top panel of the spinnaker.

Various light weather sails, such as asymmetric spinnaker, code zero, cruising chute, gennaker, etc., come with their own furling gear, and can be a useful addition to the sailing wardrobe as they are relatively easy to set up and take down on a shorthanded boat.

Aventura IV's code zero

Engine

As I get older the ability to hang upside down into a dark cavity to reach an oil filter is both more difficult and less fun.

Alastair Duncan

The engine location and general accessibility are features that can easily be overlooked although they should be a high priority. All points that need regular inspection or maintenance should be easily accessible so there will be no reason to neglect the latter. Equally important is easy access to the main components: alternator(s), belts, starter motor, seawater pump and impeller, injectors, oil changing, oil and fuel filters, engine intake seacock, seawater trap, transmission and stern gland. This is a very tall order and few, if any, production monohulls under 40 feet would meet half of those requirements. This is one aspect where catamarans win hands down as their engines are normally located in the stern, and in most cases there is enough space around the engine to make them accessible from all sides.

The first Aventura's Perkins 4108 had been thoughtfully provided with a dedicated sump pump that made oil changes easy and clean. Aventura III's Volvo MD22 engine had no oil changing provision. To empty the oil you had to do it via the dipstick tube by feeding a thin plastic hose through it. The oil was then emptied with the help of a manual or electric pump. It was a messy job and I hated it. Other regular maintenance jobs on Aventura III were not necessarily easier because Volvo, like most other engine manufacturers, try to compress the engine into the most compact shape. This is made worse by some boat builders, who try to fit the engine into the tiniest space possible so that those essential parts become virtually inaccessible. On Aventura IV, the builder had provided removable access panels opposite such parts so that the engine could be reached from any side. I also insisted on having a hand-operated pump installed on the side of the engine to make oil changes easier.

Therefore my advice is to look not just at easy accessibility for regular maintenance jobs on the engine, but whether it will be possible to dismantle and remount an alternator or starter motor on a dark and windy night at sea.

Optimum power

Engine power is never enough.

Skip Novak

For various reasons, most cruising sailors, and that includes me, never seem to be satisfied with the power provided by the designer and, if given the choice, would choose a more powerful engine. Aventura III's engine was a standard Volvo of 50 hp. Initially I asked for a more powerful engine of 62 hp, but the engine compartment was too small for it, and reluctantly I gave up. I was glad that I hadn't insisted as I could not think of many occasions when I would have needed that additional power and, in exchange, I would have paid with proportionally higher fuel consumption. Aventura IV's engine was upgraded from 55 to 75 hp and, bearing in mind its displacement, the decision was justified.

This subject was examined in several of my surveys and the conclusions were always the same: while some owners agreed that there was nothing to beat the old yardstick of one horse power per foot of length, others would have preferred a slightly higher ratio of 1.2 hp per foot of length. Other captains suggested a different yardstick by aiming for 5 hp per ton of displacement. I broadly agree with the latter.

Optimum fuel capacity

Ideally the boat should have sufficient fuel capacity to be able to motor for at least one third of a given passage.

Antti Louhija

Fuel capacity and range under power were also examined in various surveys. Among the boats surveyed, the average fuel capacity was 400 litres, although several owners pointed out that additional fuel was taken for longer passages or when cruising in areas where diesel fuel was difficult or impossible to obtain. The average range under power, when motoring at relatively low revs in calm conditions, was 750 miles per boat. Motoring or motorsailing under such conditions, the reported average consumption was 2 litres per hour. Asked about the ideal amount of fuel to be carried, some owners suggested that when setting off on a long passage, one ought to have enough fuel to be able to motor between one quarter and one third of the entire distance should there be a serious emergency.

Aventura III's fuel capacity was almost exactly the average mentioned above (380 litres) which provided an autonomy of about 800 miles under power. On a few occasions, such as when cruising in Antarctica or Chile, an additional 120 litres of fuel was carried in jerrycans. Aventura IV had a fuel capacity of 740 litres, augmented by 200 litres in jerrycans for the Northwest Passage to ensure an autonomy of 1500 miles under power.

Martin and Dunbar topping up the tanks in the Northwest Passage

Propellers

A fixed propeller on a modern sailing yacht is like a Model T Ford, reliable but boring.

Tom Williams

Although most production yachts continue to be fitted with fixed blade propellers, there is now a wide range of folding or feathering propellers for those who are interested in better efficiency and also wish to reduce drag. There are so many different types and models available that I prefer to limit my comment to the make I know best. Having had a Max-Prop on both Aventura II and III, I can vouch for the quality of this well-engineered product. Aventura IV had a 3-bladed feathering J-Prop, which worked perfectly. To avoid it being damaged by ice I replaced it with the standard 3-bladed fixed propeller for the Northwest Passage.

Equipment

We had access to too much money, too much equipment, and little by little, we went insane.

Francis Ford Coppola

As part of my preparations for my first world voyage I joined a weekend course in seamanship and navigation. I still remember the person holding the course, a former Royal Navy officer, trying to put our mind at rest by assuring us that marine navigation was quite simple, and was not rocket science. It wasn't then, but most certainly is today. There is a truly bewildering range of electronic equipment and for anyone without extensive offshore experience it must be very difficult if not impossible to make the right choice. There are almost too many options, too many clever gadgets. In the same survey among participants in the transatlantic rallies run by Cornell Sailing Events, several owners expressed their disappointment in having bought some equipment that proved to be unnecessary, at the price of not buying something that could have been more useful.

In the case of Aventura IV, I seem to have made the right choices regarding electronic equipment and would make the same choice if I were to equip another boat now. I must admit that at the beginning I was rather overawed by it all, and it may have driven me insane, but I managed to keep my sanity with Ivan's help. No wonder he is doing so well working in the film business.

The Brookes & Gatehouse Zeus MFD (Multi-Function Display) combined inputs from charts, instruments, weather, radar, autopilot, GPS, AIS, depth sounder, with two 12-inch displays, one at the nav station, and one in the cockpit. The latter was backed up by a smaller 8-inch display at the portside wheel. In spite of its complexity, the system was simple to use, very reliable, and an absolute delight to work with, as every conceivable item of information was at my fingertips, not just current inputs but also historic graphs showing wind speed and direction, barometric pressure, sea and water temperature over a certain period of time, as well as global tidal data, phases of the moon, sunrise and sunsets. The two autopilots were entirely independent of each other, each with its own compass, rudder indicator, and GPS input. For communications I used the Iridium Pilot broadband, and also an ICOM M802 SSB radio. As on Aventura III, I also had an Echopilot forward-looking sonar, but I should have gone for a B & G unit, as it would then have been integrated with the rest of the onboard instrumentation.

Useful features

The beautiful thing about the ocean is that the only thing out there is what you bring with you.

Paul Dunn

I entirely agree with this statement, and this is why it is so important when you equip your boat, that things that are really useful are not forgotten. This subject was examined in detail in two surveys by asking the captains to name the most important features they would have on their ideal cruising boat. The five most quoted items were a powerful electric anchor winch, watermaker, dependable reefing system, a powerful and reliable autopilot and an electric cockpit winch. To narrow down their priorities the captains were asked to limit their choice to three items they considered as absolutely essential. Perhaps not surprisingly by forcing them to focus on the essential aspects of their ideal boat, the priorities changed, with safety and seaworthiness now becoming the number one priority. This aspect was summarised by Antti Louhija whose ideal would be 'a solid, sturdy and comfortable boat even if it means sacrificing some speed. If you are comfortable you gladly spend more time on passage.' Steve Dashew considered as essential features 'water tight bulkheads, the ability to hit the ground at slow speed without having to go into a boatyard, and a good turn of speed when one needs it.'

Several captains highlighted the importance of good sailing capability such as for the boat being able to point high. Beside their concern for safety and performance, several owners stressed the importance of comfort. Among them, as many as one third specified a permanent structure that provided shelter to the cockpit, as an essential feature. These results were confirmed by the findings of the voyage planning survey, and have greatly influenced the concept and equipment of Aventura IV. Although they may have been mentioned elsewhere, here is my list of the items and features that I find to be very useful on a cruising boat.

- » Day fuel tank
- » Boom-brake
- » Fixed pole set-up
- » Mast steps
- » Universal stern bracket for:
  - » Water generator
  - » Outboard motor
  - » Emergency rudder and tiller
- » GoPro camera with underwater housing
- » Wifi booster
- » Capstan if anchor winch is centrally located
- » 12V socket in cockpit for:
  - » Emergency bilge pump
  - » Emergency autopilot
  - » Dinghy pump
  - » Spot or other light

Safety

Safety and seaworthiness are the most important features followed by comfort and easy sail handling.

Bob Hall

Whenever I visit a yacht and am asked by the owner to express an opinion, I always start by looking at the boat primarily from the safety point of view. How well protected is the cockpit? How exposed is the person at the helm? How safe is it to work at the foot of the mast or on the foredeck? Are there sufficient handrails provided? Do stanchions and lifelines look strong and reliable? How dangerously low does the boom pass across the cockpit? How easily accessible is the main bilge and is it provided with a pump of adequate capacity, as well as an emergency backup? How accessible is the steering mechanism and what provision has been made for an emergency? Is the liferaft stowed in an easily accessible place from where it can be launched by the weakest member of the crew? How can the dinghy be stowed safely while on passage? How easily accessible is the anchor chain? How easy it is to board the boat from the water or retrieve an overboard person?

This may sound like the Ten Commandments and I must admit that very few boats that I have visited passed all those tests. If this was the case I felt that it was my duty to point out to the owner some of the most serious shortcomings. My remarks were not always accepted graciously and this put me in an awkward situation but I still preferred to be honest, even if my frankness was not necessarily appreciated. A lesson that I learned in my youth, and I have observed throughout my life, is that you should never ask a question if you don't want to know the answer.

Final decision

Anyone who has never made a mistake has never tried anything new.

Albert Einstein

Mast steps on Aventura IV

This is why it is so important to learn from your own mistakes, but also from those made by others, something that I have been doing throughout my life. An observation that I made among participants in recent rallies was how well equipped most of their boats were; yet at the same time how unprepared they were themselves. Too much seemed to have been neglected or left until the last minute, from onboard email capability to essential spares, not to speak of a backup for the autopilot. Could this be a generational phenomenon?

Because my old friend Erick Bouteleux had played such an important part in the choice and the fitting out of Aventura III, and also in some of the special features on Aventura IV, I asked him if he had any advice to give to anyone faced with the decision to choose and equip a boat for a long voyage. He replied that he was reluctant to be too specific as nowadays there was such a choice of boats and equipment that finding a suitable boat should not be difficult provided you knew your priorities. Knowing just how opinionated he can be on any subject that is of interest to him, I was taken aback by his reluctance, and said so. Erick had an answer to this.

'We have the great advantage of having started off by sailing on simple boats with no sophisticated equipment. Once you have sailed on such a boat you can easily adjust to a more sophisticated boat, but not the other way around. Current sailors planning to set off on a long voyage have a much tougher job, mainly because there is so much to choose from. This is why it is so important to decide first on your main priorities. For us it was dead easy as the choices were so limited that most people like us left in whatever they could afford, and, with very few exceptions, we all managed to complete our voyages.'

So the choice of a boat that satisfies your main priorities is crucial but, as I pointed out earlier, crew, finances and self-sufficiency are equally important factors that may affect the success of a voyage. As I stressed when discussing this aspect of voyage planning, an even more important factor is your attitude to sailing and cruising life in general. I say this because I know just how I feel about the sea and sailing, and I have absolutely no doubt that it is because of this attitude that Mother Nature has treated me so kindly.

Tips

» Resist the temptation to buy a larger boat just because you can afford it. The deciding factor should be ease of handling by the proposed crew.

» Avoid a boat with a vulnerable unprotected rudder that is unsuitable for offshore cruising.

» The engine and essential components must be easily accessible for routine maintenance and emergency repairs.

» A functional deck layout is essential to be able to sail efficiently shorthanded.

» The boat must have a well-thought-out mainsail reefing system that ideally can be handled from the cockpit.

» The boat must have adequate engine power and sufficient fuel capacity for the planned voyage.

» There should be a backup for the autopilot, either a wind-operated self-steering gear, or a second autopilot entirely autonomous of the main unit.

» There should be backups for all halyards.

» The cockpit must have good protection for both safety and comfort.

» A well-planned compact galley that is safe to use in rough weather.

» There must be at least one comfortable all-weather berth for the off-watch crew.

» The boat must have sufficient storage space for a long voyage.

» The liferaft should be easily launched.

» There should be strong attachment points for safety harnesses in the cockpit.

» There must be adequate man overboard provisions: such as stern platform with boarding ladder.

Aventura IV in Disco Bay, Greenland

33

Closing the loop

The tough leg around the bottom of Africa made me appreciate even more the warm welcome we received on arrival at the Royal Cape Yacht Club. Throughout the dark days of apartheid this well-endowed club tucked away in a corner of Cape Town's huge harbour had hosted cruising and racing sailors from all over the world. The open-mindedness and hospitality of its members had ensured that the club never lost its royal warrant. The club's active racing community is supported by a wide range of repair facilities of which Aventura took full advantage. In the six months since leaving New Zealand we had clocked up a lot of miles of often hard sailing, so I wanted to make sure that everything was properly checked and serviced before taking on the Atlantic Ocean. By the time we were ready to leave, Aventura was in tiptop condition and that included a replacement of all standing rigging.

Two French friends, Marc Martinez and Patrick Canut, joined me for the 5,000-mile leg to the Canaries. As we sailed out into Table Bay on a sunny Saturday morning, scores of racing yachts were piling on the canvas in the unusually light breeze, while several large catamarans full of sightseers were chasing whales. We joined in the fun, slaloming among the countless dolphins, seals and pods of whales, which congregate in this sheltered area to breed and nurse their young. One large humpback gave us a fright when it surfaced a few feet from Aventura and for a few seconds it looked as if we were going to collide.

As the distinctive shape of Table Mountain faded into the far distance, we were finally on our own, surrounded by the vastness of the South Atlantic. The solitude embraced us like a velvet cloak as day after day and night after night we ploughed the waves on our way north, often the only sign of life a lonely albatross. Three days after leaving Cape Town, the southeast trade winds set in, so up went the spinnaker and it stayed there all the way to St Helena. The weather on this stretch of ocean is among the most benign and reliable in the whole world. The trade winds blow

throughout the year and although Catarina, the first recorded South Atlantic hurricane tried to spoil this picture of perfection when it formed off the coast of Brazil in March 2004, hopefully it was an exception that will not occur again.

The weather was so settled and the sea so calm that we had every meal at the cockpit table. One evening, in the middle of dinner, this dream-like routine was shattered when a tanker passed us at what seemed like hailing distance. Our own tricolour masthead light was on, but the large ship had no running lights and it glided past like a ghost ship. All three of us were so shocked we could hardly speak, and after that we made sure that whoever was on watch scanned the horizon every few minutes, but no other ship was sighted until we reached St Helena.

Napoleon's exile island

St Helena is a truly fascinating island, not least because its most famous visitor arrived by force, spent nearly six years of exile there, and ended his life on this remote speck of land. Her very isolation is probably St Helena's main attraction and, until recently, the lack of an airport meant that only determined travellers actually set foot on this remote island lost in the vastness of the South Atlantic. Its most regular visitors are cruising sailors, most of whom stop here on their way from South Africa to Brazil or the Caribbean.

St Helena's checkered history is reflected in the island's 3,000 thousand inhabitants called Saints, a rainbow mix of colours and races: African, English, Irish, Portuguese, Indian, and probably a lot more. In this small place, everyone greeted us warmly in the street, so it was not just the language that made me feel immediately at home. Quaint is the term that springs to mind whenever I think of St Helena, from the name of her inhabitants to those of some landmarks, such as Longwood, Levelwood, Deadwood or Alarm Hill, where a canon was placed in wartime to sound the alarm if an enemy vessel was sighted.

One day we hired a taxi to take us on a tour of the island, which measures some six by ten miles, with steep roads and a hilly interior that rises to 800 metres. Some of the interior was surprisingly lush, with grassy meadows sprinkled with all kinds of wild flowers, whereas the western, lee side was parched brown. A winding road led to Longwood, Napoleon's residence, now a museum, set in a landscaped garden, and declared sovereign French territory. Ever since Napoleon's death, the British have tried to make amends for the rather awful way they had treated their recalcitrant prisoner. The house where he spent his exile, and where he died of stomach cancer at the age of 51, is now in much better shape than it was when the former emperor and his entourage lived there. Then it was a draughty, damp, rat-infested place with sagging floorboards, dripping walls and smoking fireplaces. As we walked around on the squeaky floors, Napoleon's presence was almost palpable, a feeling that was helped by the fact that some of the original furniture had been preserved: his desk and chair, an ornate mirror, the large zinc bath in which he spent endless hours feeling sorry for himself.

The subsequent 700-mile run from St Helena to Ascension was one of the most enjoyable passages of this entire voyage, a pleasant spinnaker run in dream-like trade wind conditions. The night before our landfall, we were overtaken by RMS St Helena, one of only two vessels to carry the title of RMS, Royal Mail Ship, and which makes regular runs between the UK and South Africa. Besides mail and supplies, it also carries passengers to the few remaining outposts of the former British Empire: Ascension, St Helena and Tristan da Cunha. The ship overtook us on my watch, so I had the opportunity to have a long chat on the radio with the officer on duty. He told me that they had first picked us up on radar at 11 miles and saw our masthead light at nine miles, both of which I found quite reassuring. He also said that earlier in the evening they had passed another sailboat that showed no lights and there was no sign of anyone on watch. They passed so close that they shone a searchlight on the yacht expecting to get a response on the radio, but to no avail. I knew immediately whom he meant: a South African yacht had left St Helena at the same time as us with three young men and one woman on board who, I believe, were delivering the boat to Brazil. The officer sounded quite irritated by such irresponsibility and echoed the remarks made to me earlier by the port captain in St Helena, who had received complaints from several ships' captains that sailing boats often failed to keep a watch at night, and many didn't show lights either. This reminded me of a survey I once did among ARC participants, when they were asked what watches they kept, if they showed lights at night, and how many boats they had seen during the Atlantic crossing. When the results were processed it became clear that boats with large crews, especially those in the racing division, where watches were kept on a regular basis, reported seeing several boats, whereas boats with smaller crews rarely saw any boats at all. As one of the interviewed skippers remarked, 'It's only those who don't keep watches who never see other boats. We see them all the time.'

Miracle on a space-age island

Compared to sleepy St Helena, where people lead a normal life, running shops, tending small farms or fishing for a living, Ascension is firmly set in the space age. The island bristles with antennae of all shapes and sizes, gigantic dish aerials, satellite tracking gizmos, and communications towers. The US Air Force has a sizeable presence here as does the British Royal Air Force, the European space program has a tracking station, and the BBC maintains several antennae to relay its international broadcasts. There is a military airport used also by the twice-weekly flight between England and the Falkland Islands. Cruising boats are welcome to make a short stop provided their crew keep out of restricted areas and do not spend the night ashore. Getting ashore was a serious test of stamina as landing from the dinghy on the slippery quay steps, with a violent surge breaking against the high wharf was a major feat. Entry formalities were quickly completed at the police station, and we were free to do what we liked, which wasn't very much until we found a small hotel that also rented cars, so we hired one for the day.

The interior was rather barren and less attractive than St Helena, but there was a surprising amount of wildlife, mostly formerly domesticated animals that had been let loose. A couple of wild donkeys ran over when we stopped the car expecting to be fed and looking very disappointed when it didn't happen. Shaggy sheep walked around in a daze obviously very uncomfortable in the 36°C heat as no one bothered to shear them. No Aussie yachties around here, I thought. Back in Suwarrow I had met an Australian couple who had a farm in South Australia with several thousand sheep. Every year they had to return home in October to round up and shear the sheep, then back they went to their small boat to continue their voyage. When we met them they had been doing this for some ten years and were close to completing their circumnavigation.

One of the great pleasures of cruising, especially after a long passage, is treating yourself to a nice meal ashore. The hotel where we had hired the car also served lunch so, full of anticipation, I asked for the menu.

'What can we have?' asked my crew, who, being French were probably expecting a three course gourmet meal of local specialities.

'Hamburger and fries,' I said meekly.

'What, no other choice?' Patrick asked visibly shocked.

'Oh yes. Cheeseburger.'

Marc was the owner and chef of one of the best restaurants in our village and Patrick ran the local patisserie and bakery so both of them knew a thing or two about food.

By the time we got back to the dock after that unmemorable lunch, the swell was even worse than when we had arrived, but we managed to launch the dinghy and cast off without being swamped. Having cleared the long mooring lines holding various launches, I pulled the cord of the outboard motor and it failed to start. Pushed by the strong wind we started drifting quickly in the direction of Brazil, and rowing the inflatable under those conditions proved futile. Marc managed to grab a mooring as we drifted past it and while he held onto it, I tried desperately to get the outboard started. Somebody ashore must have observed our antics because a big launch detached itself from the quay and zoomed in our direction, on board two St Helenians wearing overalls with badges of the US Air Force. They took one pitiful look at us, threw us a line and towed us to Aventura.

'Hang-on guys,' I said as I dove below to put some cold beers in a plastic bag. Long after they'd left I was still trying to take it in. Saved by two Saints... on Ascension Island! Would it rate as a miracle?

In Neptune's role

For many years the accepted tactic for anyone planning to sail from South Africa to either northern Europe or the Mediterranean was to stay with favourable winds as long as possible by making a long detour via the Lesser Antilles and continue from there to Europe. An alternative route via the Azores is considerably shorter, but entails being hard on the wind for some 1,500 miles north of the equator. I decided that there was little to lose by trying out a third alternative and sail the shortest route from the south Atlantic to the Med. Two groups of islands, the Cape Verdes and Canaries, sit temptingly astride such a route and would allow the long passage to be broken into shorter sections.

The start from Ascension was very encouraging as we held the steady southeast winds all the way to the equator. Up to that point, ideal trade wind conditions had given us several days of perfect sailing, with gentle seas, the most wonderful skies at night, and excellent fishing. As we were busy preparing for the traditional celebration of crossing the Line, and not paying much attention to the weather, we were hit by a most violent squall. Too late to take down the spinnaker all I could do is pray that, as on one memorable previous occasion, the Parasailor would hold. I disengaged the autopilot, and although the centreboard was up, as it normally is when downwind sailing, I found that steering was quite a struggle. With the wind gusting at 27 knots I tried to point dead downwind thus keeping the apparent wind

to a reasonable level, which was helped by us surfing at over ten knots. My two friends were watching wide-eyed from the corner of the cockpit, their eyes darting between the spinnaker and the instruments. Both were visibly awed... or more likely just worried. Maybe this is what is meant by the term shock and awe.

As the wind started abating, the heavens opened and the most awesome deluge broke over us. Solid water came down in cataclysmic quantities while the skies were rent asunder by blinding rods of lightning accompanied by ear-shattering thunder. Streaking flashes were bombarding the sea all around and I expected to be struck at any moment. I told my crew to go below and keep away from any metal, while waiting for final confirmation that an aluminium hull was indeed safer when hit by lightning. Fortunately it did not come to pass, the rain stopped and when the GPS finally displayed all those zeroes, we opened a bottle of champagne to celebrate not just my crew's first crossing of the Line but also surviving that mother of all squalls unscathed – an unforgettable farewell from the South Atlantic. A dram of 12-year old whisky was poured into the ocean to thank the gods, both Neptune and Aeolus, for the perfect winds they had given us for the 3,000 miles from Cape Town.

Patrick's baptism

As this was my eighth crossing of the Line, I had dressed up as Neptune, sporting a cardboard trident attached to a deck brush, and a crown made from an empty box of cornflakes, which fitted snugly over my head. Around my neck I wore a Swedish Cruising Association tie, which I felt to be suitable for the occasion as it was adorned with tridents. To complete the picture, I draped myself in some netting because I had always wondered why mermaids wore it. Seated on my throne, I had my crew prostrate themselves at my feet and performed their baptism by smearing their faces with shaving cream and dollops of ketchup.

I have often wondered why crossing the equator used to have such a mystical significance for sailors and now I felt that I had the answer. For sailors from northern countries crossing the equator on their way south meant that they were well and truly on their way to whatever destination they were going to. Coming north, as in our own case, they knew they were getting closer to home and the safe completion of their voyage. Besides that, the equator is a permanent marker where weather systems change and you feel you are entering a different world, and this is exactly what happened. While we were still celebrating, the wind died completely, the skies turned into a menacing slate grey, punctuated by massive electrical discharges, like silent lightning. The sea was dull, ugly and black; no wonder the French refer to the doldrums as 'pot au noir' – a black pot.

Cape Verde landfall

We motored out of this nightmare scenario and around 5°N started having some northeast wind, but it was too light and also from the wrong direction, so our progress became frustratingly slow. We tacked and tacked again, and on some days only managed to cover 60 miles in a straight line. But even the slowest passage eventually comes to an end and we finally crept into Praia, the capital of the Cape Verde Islands. The port

captain directed us to tie up alongside a tug, a rust-covered monstrosity that looked as if it had not seen a paintbrush for half a century.

Even by African standards this former Portuguese colony is a poor country, but the Cape Verdians more than make up for it by their sunny attitude. Provisioning the boat for the next leg was a delight as the market was overflowing with a most amazing range of fresh fruit and vegetables. But it was the fish market that left us with our mouths gaping: never in my life have I seen such a profusion of fish of all species and sizes, proof that this area is one of the richest fishing grounds in the world. Poor the Cape Verdians may be, but I am sure that nobody goes hungry.

Closing the circle

After the short stop in Praia, the rest of the passage to the Canaries was more or less the same, as we kept taking short tacks trying to stay close to the rhumb line in the hope that a change of wind would give us a better sailing angle. It was a tactic that seemed to work and in some 24-hour periods we managed to make as much as 120 miles in the right direction. On the eighth day after leaving Praia, Aventura crossed her outward track when she had set off from the Canaries for the Caribbean at the start of this voyage almost five years previously. For the third time in so many decades, I had safely closed the circle.

Shortly after midnight we crept into San Sebastian de la Gomera and tied up to a pontoon. It had taken us eight and a half days to cover the 880 miles from Praia, although I reckoned that with all the tacking we must have covered close to 1,100 miles. I was greatly relieved that my gamble had paid off, but even happier to be back in a familiar place.

Marc and Patrick left here, but rather than continue immediately to the Mediterranean, I had asked Gwenda to join me for a leisurely cruise among these islands that I knew well, but where I had done little actual cruising. I was as guilty as most sailors who pass through the Canaries every year and regard the Canaries just as a convenient stepping stone on the way to somewhere else.

One morning we left San Sebastian to sail to the two westernmost islands: La Palma and El Hierro. The wind was unusually light, but I knew that it wouldn't last. The Canaries may boast having one of the best climates in the world with benign winters and pleasant summers, but local sailing conditions are not to everyone's liking. The high islands generate their own weather similar to that encountered in Hawaiian waters with wind acceleration zones in the channels separating the islands. We had a taste of this at the start of our 40-mile trip to La Palma, when the wind went from 10 to 30 knots in a matter of seconds, and I understood why local sailors call these sudden gusts 'mosquitoes', as you only hear them when they bite.

The capital Santa Cruz de la Palma is one of the most attractive towns in the Canaries and its main cobbled street, named Calle O'Daly after a local dignitary of Irish origin, has preserved many of its ancient buildings. Many houses have the charming enclosed balconies that are a special feature of this island. Most buildings date from the 16th century when

Santa Cruz was a prosperous town, as all Spanish ships heading out to the Americas were obliged to stop there to report before crossing the Atlantic.

The interior of La Palma is dominated by Caldera de Taburiente, a huge extinct crater, the largest of its kind in the world. The enormous circular bowl is surrounded by sheer rock walls that soar to over 2,000 metres. La Palma's prime attraction are the various volcano walks, and the island is crisscrossed by many tracks. One morning Gwenda and I took a taxi to the starting point of the Ruta de los Volcanes, a long trail that runs along the spine of the island past a string of extinct volcanoes before it ends at the southern tip of the island where the very last volcano Teneguia is only dormant. The last time it erupted, in 1971, it entirely changed the shape of the southern end of La Palma and left behind a large area of devastation that looks as fresh as if it only happened recently.

Our next stop, the island of El Hierro, was considered until 1492 and the discovery of land to the west, the end of the world. Even today El Hierro feels more remote than any of the other Canary Islands, its unique landscape, vegetation and climate making it a UNESCO biosphere reserve. The south of the island is a barren area covered in volcanic badlands, deeply eroded lava fields that are pierced by tunnels and caves produced by volcanic bubbles. Even the vegetation has a tortured look about it, the gnarled trees having been twisted by the wind into odd shapes. An old lighthouse stands on the wind-swept headland of La Orchilla at El Hierro's westernmost point. As I looked out over the grey Atlantic waters, my thoughts went to that great sailor whose deeds had done so much to bring the world closer to how we know it today.

In the wake of Columbus

Carved into a black marble slab overlooking Las Palmas marina on the island of Gran Canaria are the names of the 146 yachts that sailed in the America 500 transatlantic rally commemorating Columbus's original voyage to the New World. Where else in the world would local authorities take cruising boats so seriously as to erect a monument in their honour? In fact, this is not at all surprising as throughout the history of these islands, ships and sailors have been the lifeblood of their existence. A small settlement surrounded by a palisade of palm trees (hence Las Palmas) stood on the shores of this bay when Columbus called here in August 1492. Some medieval buildings still survive in the oldest part of town, called La Vegueta, where narrow cobbled streets are flanked by beautiful homes built around cool central patios. To the north, the modern town prosaically called El Puerto has developed around what is now one of the busiest ports in Spain thanks to its strategic location astride the shipping lanes between Europe, Africa and South America. Las Palmas is also a great favourite among yachts on their way from Europe to the Caribbean with over 1,000 yachts calling here every year attracted by the wide range of repair facilities and excellent provisioning.

Bucking the westward trend, one fine morning Aventura set off in the opposite direction on the first stage of a long delayed return to the Mediterranean. As we rounded the massive breakwater that protects the large port of Las Palmas, I set a course for Lanzarote about 100 miles away. On cue, having blown from an easterly direction for a couple of days, the wind turned to the northeast and was now blowing smack on our nose.

'Here we go again,' Gwenda exclaimed bitterly, 'as soon as I get on board, the winds start blowing from the worst possible direction.'

'Don't take it so personally. After all, this is their prevailing direction,' I commented rather meekly.

'OK, if it's not the wind then it can only be Aventura who doesn't seem to like me.'

'It's neither one nor the other... just bad luck. There is no need to exaggerate.'

'I still find it strange that as soon as I join you, all your talk about balmy winds and perfect passages turn to nothing. So who is exaggerating? Let me just mention recent longer passages that we did together: Bora Bora to Suwarrow, lousy weather almost all the way; winds of over 30 knots for most of the passage from Fiji to New Zealand; strong headwinds even on that shortest of trips between Mauritius and La Réunion. So am I really exaggerating?'

Gwenda was absolutely right and as we were in no great hurry, I eased the sheets and altered course for the southern end of the nearer island of Fuerteventura. Just before nightfall we crept into the port of Morro Jable, where the local council had provided a number of floating pontoons for the use of visiting yachts.

Next morning we left at crack of dawn for the 60-odd miles to Lanzarote. The strong winds that are a local feature, and have given Fuerteventura its name, making it a windsurfers' paradise, never rose above a gentle breeze so it took us all day to motorsail along the island's eastern shore. While the western Canaries are mostly lush and green, their eastern sisters are barren and sun-scorched, a constant reminder that Africa is only 50 miles away. As we got closer to our destination, the scenery in neighbouring Lanzarote looked even starker, its skyline punctuated by a panorama of brooding extinct volcanoes.

A local artist, whose work was greatly influenced by these surroundings and whose mark is evident everywhere on the island, is Cesar Manrique. Having achieved international fame as a painter and sculptor he returned home and set about applying his vision to his native land. By the late 1960s the island's tourist potential had started a development boom that threatened to scar forever the island's unique environment. Manrique skilfully managed to persuade the local authorities to draw up a set of wide-ranging standards, such as a strict control on the height and style of buildings, a ban on roadside hoardings, and the highly effective edict that hotels can be of any colour as long as it's white. The eye-catching white houses, dotted about the black landscape, have a definite charm, and as a result Lanzarote is architecturally the most attractive island of the entire archipelago.

Cesar Manrique, who died in 1992, did a lot more for his island than just trying to preserve its uniqueness. By applying his fertile imagination to some special features of his island he created a number of highly original projects, such as an auditorium with excellent acoustics in an underground cave, an exquisite cactus garden with scores of species unique to these islands, a modern art gallery inside a medieval fort, to name just a few. Nowhere, however, is Manrique's bold style and exquisite taste more noticeable than in his own home and studio, built in a series of volcanic bubbles in the middle of one of Lanzarote's volcanic badlands, and now open to the public.

A windy passage

As it was still March and northeast winds prevail north of the Canaries, I expected to have strong headwinds on the passage to Gibraltar, so rather than risk exposing Gwenda to more misery, I had asked Ivan to sail with me from Gran Canaria to southern Spain. Two days before our planned departure, a depression forming in the north Atlantic started tracking east towards the Iberian Peninsula with a forecast of southwest winds in the area we were going to sail through. My Canarian friend Juan Francisco could not restrain his amazement at my never-ending good luck.

'Jimmy, you picked this day of departure one month ago, and now just as you are getting ready to leave, the winds turn in your favour. I don't think there is a more fortunate sailor than you in the world.'

Instead of headwinds, Ivan and I left Las Palmas in strong southwest winds gusting in the low 30s, but it was far better than having to beat into the usual northeasterlies. Broadreaching with the staysail and three reefs in the main we rarely sailed below eight knots. It was in every respect an exhilarating sail, and only four days after leaving the Canaries we picked up the light on Cape Espartel, at the northwest point of Africa. By dawn we were greeted by the unmistakable shape of the Rock of Gibraltar bathed in blushing pink by the rising sun, and yet another passage safely completed.

34

Cruising rallies

The most significant decision for us was to join a rally. Had we not joined America 500, there would have been no Atlantic crossing for us in 1992. Without that experience, and without the Millennium Odyssey, there would have been no round-the-world voyage for us either. Without those rallies the friendships amongst the whole fleet, which will last for many years, would have never developed. The shared accomplishments will live in each of us forever.

Don Babson

The launch of the first transatlantic rally in 1986 is one of the main achievements of my life. The immediate success of the annual ARC inspired similar rallies all over the world and I am credited with having conceived the format of such offshore cruising rallies. One of the main advantages of cruising rallies, whether across an ocean or around the world, is that the organisers take care of formalities, docking, weather and routing information, also transits of the Panama and Suez Canals. There is also the safety in numbers factor, and being able to get help or advice in an emergency from fellow participants. Another advantage is that there is a fixed schedule, which imposes a certain discipline. As some of the participants are business people, retired or close to retirement, they appreciate this aspect and also the fact that they can delegate responsibility, what they normally did in their professional lives.

The Atlantic Rally for Cruisers (ARC)

From the very beginning, one of the primary aims of the ARC was to provide a framework of safety and support to sailors who lacked offshore experience, and this continues to be one of its main attractions. There have been many changes in the 30 years since I stopped my involvement with the ARC, and not all for the better. What I find most objectionable is that what started as an event for cruising sailors has been allowed to become a convenient backdrop for racing boats, their owners boasting to have been successful in the largest transocean event in the world.

Round-the-world rallies

Symbolic historic events or anniversaries have a special fascination for me, so when I started organising international sailing events I had a readymade vehicle to promote and celebrate some of the most significant

dates of our times. The success of the ARC served as an inspiration for the first round-the-world rally, something that had never been done before. Having briefly mentioned the idea to a number of ARC participants, by the late 1980s I knew that such a rally was feasible. This was instantly confirmed when the project was launched and the maximum number of participants (40 yachts over 40 feet) was quickly reached and a waiting list started. Being a

Start of the first ARC November 1986

great believer in the European concept. I had decided to call the first round-the-world rally Europa 92. I contacted the sports and special events department at the European Community headquarters in Brussels for their support, but unfortunately my enthusiasm left the narrow-minded bureaucrats visibly cool and I left empty-handed.

Europa 92 started from Gibraltar at the beginning of January 1991, Gibraltar's far-seeing government doing everything possible to support this international event, whose aims coincided so closely with Gibraltar's own endeavours and hopes. A Gibraltar start was both logical and convenient. The weather was acceptable for a winter start, it was perfectly located for both the start and finish, and was easy for the participants to get to. The route and timing of the rally had been chosen carefully to take advantage of favourable seasons and weather conditions along the projected route. Also, knowing that most participants wanted to accomplish a round-the-world voyage in the shortest time possible, and were not interested in dallying too long en route, the rally was to last only seventeen months. This was rather a tall order but in the end proved to be the ideal solution and it was not altered for the following rally.

Choosing the route was almost as simple as the timing. After stopping in the Canaries, the rally crossed the Atlantic to the Caribbean, passed through the Panama Canal in February and, via the Galapagos Islands, headed for the South Pacific, which was reached at the start of the safe tropical winter season. Stopping at a number of island nations on the way, the rally reached the Torres Strait and entered the Indian Ocean. From Bali the route turned north to Singapore, before crossing the north Indian Ocean during the favourable northeast monsoon that blows constantly in the early months of the year. A final stage through the Red Sea brought the fleet into the Mediterranean and eventually to the finish in Gibraltar.

The fleet that left from Gibraltar was joined in the eastern Caribbean or Panama by a number of US boats. Being the first of its kind the rally was received with great enthusiasm everywhere it stopped, local people and officials welcoming the participants with open arms. Cruising stages had been carefully planned in between the offshore legs, giving participants, their crews, and family members, who were joining the boats underway, a perfect opportunity to visit some of the most attractive cruising grounds in the world.

Europa 92 yachts transiting the Panama Canal

Rally fleet in Papeete, the capital of Tahiti

One of the main attractions of such a rally was the safety it offered to participants, especially those who were rather inexperienced and drew comfort from being able to draw support from other more experienced sailors. The overall safety record of the six round-the-world events that I organised is quite outstanding; unfortunately it was in that first world rally that there was one fatality, and one boat was lost. A young Finnish sailor was lost overboard on the long leg from the Galapagos to the Marquesas, when the 53-foot boat he was sailing on, went into an uncontrolled gybe while flying a spinnaker at night. In spite of frantic efforts by the crew, who were joined by eleven other rally yachts, he was never found. The only loss involved the Hungarian 43-foot Jolly Joker, whose captain had handed over the control of the boat to his young crew, having to return home for urgent family reasons. Jolly Joker ran aground and eventually broke up after it had strayed from the main navigation channel in the notorious Torres Strait. The crew were saved almost immediately by another rally yacht.

Rally participants received by the King of Tonga, H.M. Taufa'ahauTupou IV

As in all other rallies of this kind, competition played a certain part, which was taken to heart in a greater or lesser degree by the participants. There were two divisions, racing, in which the use of engines was prohibited, and cruising, in which the hours of motoring had to be declared so that a penalty could be applied when the results were calculated. Competition was keen in both divisions and added a special zest on long ocean passages. The boats were in constant contact both with each other and the organisers, initially by SSB radio and in later rallies by Inmarsat C, satphone or email.

Traditional welcoming ceremony on arrival in Fiji

Europa 94

The success of the first round-the-world rally proved the validity of its basic concept and was followed three years later by a similar event along the same route. Having been unable to elicit any response from Brussels even after its successful completion, I gave up on the suits in Brussels, but not on Europe, and as I could not think of a better name, the second rally also ran under the generic name Europa.

The various difficulties encountered in the first round-the-world rally were mostly ironed out in the second, chief among them an improvement in communications between the shore-based rally staff and participants, and also among the participants themselves.

The rally attracted a number of boats crewed by fee paying guests, a new phenomenon which was to become wide-spread in the ARC too and was not entirely to my liking. Overall, though, Europe 94 was as successful as Europa 92 and, apart from one dismasting on the leg from Madeira to Gran Canaria, and one boat running aground off the coast of Brazil, also fraught with less problems.

America 500 participants in Palos de la Frontera

Compared to the first rally, participants in Europa 94 were more competitive. Such interest in competition, which was also becoming evident in the ARC, showed the need for a round-the-world race for amateur sailors that eventually led to the Hong Kong Challenge.

America 500

Long before the first round-the-world rally took off, I became intrigued by the imminent approach of one of the most important nautical anniversaries of the 20th century, the quincentenary of Christopher Columbus's voyage to the New World in 1492. There were to be several major sailing events following the historic route from Spain to the Bahamas, and I could not resist the temptation of making my own contribution. The idea of America 500 was soon born, a rally for cruising yachts that would follow Columbus's original route. The initial enthusiasm with which America 500 was greeted by the international sailing community, was somewhat affected by the negative comments in the US media highlighting all the bad things that followed Columbus's arrival in the New World. This may have dissuaded some potential US participants from joining, but even so half of the 146 yachts that took part came over from the New World, with the largest national contingents from the USA, followed by Canada, Mexico and Argentina.

Columbus and his three ships left from the small Andalucian port of Palos at dawn on August 3, 1492. Following in Columbus's footsteps, I managed to obtain permission to bring our own captains to the same room in the ancient La Rabida monastery, where Columbus had briefed his captains on the eve of their departure 500 years earlier. Thus the America 500 captains had their briefing in the very same room as their illustrious predecessors. The highlight of the festivities was an unforgettable flamenco opera based on the Columbus story that was performed in an amphitheatre below the walls of the monastery, and attended by thousands of people and all our participants.

At dawn on 3 August 1992, the America 500 skippers and their crews attended a special mass and blessing in the small St George Church where Columbus and his crews had worshipped on the morning of their departure. They also left by the same rarely-used side door to make their way to the boats floating on the river Odiel nearby.

America 500 was hailed as the only international sailing event of the quincentenial celebrations to accurately reflect the historic significance of the Columbus anniversary. King Juan Carlos and Queen Sophia flew over from the Olympic Games in Barcelona to give the start of America 500, as it set off on its long way to the New World.

While Columbus had unknowingly crossed the Atlantic at the height of the hurricane season (September), it would have been irresponsible for us to do the same. For this reason I decided that the Atlantic crossing should be done later in the season to avoid the risk of encountering a tropical storm.

On the eve of the start from Las Palmas de Gran Canaria on 15 November 1992, every boat was presented with a two-foot high sapling of a Canarian palm tree to be planted on arrival in San Salvador. Before embarking on the 3,000-mile passage, a two-hour symbolic stop was made at the island of La Gomera where Columbus himself had left from on 6 September 1492. After the crews had had their special souvenir logbooks signed by the president of the island council and the mayor of San Sebastian, they walked to the nearby Church of the Assumption where Columbus and his sailors had prayed all those years ago.

By late November the hurricane season had come to an end, and the fleet made a fast and generally uneventful passage to the small island of San Salvador in the Bahamas. On arrival, the crews planted their trees next to the Columbus monument, and then sailed over to George Town in Great Exuma. Its large protected harbour was the only place capable of sheltering such a large fleet, which was the reason why it had been chosen in preference to San Salvador. It was there that the final America 500 celebrations took place, an unforgettable finale to a unique event.

Hong Kong Challenge

Never at a loss for inspiration, the rapidly approaching date of the return of Hong Kong to China in 1997 provided the theme of yet another special event. Because of the location of Hong Kong, as well as other practical considerations, I soon realised that this was not to be another cruising rally. The route and weather conditions were much tougher and could only suit larger yachts sailed by experienced crews. For all these reasons the Hong Kong Challenge was a proper round-the-world race for ocean-going yachts. Once again the idea was greeted with enthusiasm, and eventually a dozen yachts sailed in the event.

From the start in London, where the famous Tower Bridge was specially opened for the fleet to commence its passage down the River Thames, the yachts sailed via the Canaries to Panama, transited the Canal, proceeded to Hawaii and Japan before arriving in Hong Kong. The return voyage took the yachts via the south Indian Ocean around the Cape of Good Hope to Brazil, and finally back to England.

The race marked several significant firsts and will be remembered as such: the first round-the-world ocean race to transit the Panama Canal, and the first world event to visit Hawaii, Japan, Hong Kong and Singapore. In spite of its toughness and length, the Hong Kong Challenge was completed without serious mishaps by all yachts, sailed mostly by amateurs.

Expo 98 round-the world rally

Soon after the end of the second round-the-world rally, I started planning a third one and, having drawn a blank with getting any support from the European Union, was now actively looking for a suitable theme that might attract a sponsor. One day I read a long report in a London newspaper describing the ambitious plans that the Portuguese government was drawing up for the anniversary of Vasco da Gama's voyage around Africa in 1498. The planned celebrations were to be incorporated in a big world exhibition to be held in Lisbon. The theme of Expo 98 was 'The Ocean, our heritage for the future', and I knew instantly that there couldn't be a more suitable theme for my rally, so I started making overtures to my Portuguese contacts. I flew to Madeira where my generous supporter João Carlos Abreu, Director of Tourism, had worked wonders in 1992 when America 500 had passed through his island. He welcomed me warmly, listened carefully to what I had in mind, picked up the phone, called Lisbon and spoke to the Minister of Commerce, who was responsible for Expo 98. After a short conversation, he turned to me, 'OK, all done, but you must go immediately to Lisbon as the minister is very busy and he can only see you tomorrow at 6 am. He is an old friend and he is coming to the ministry early just to see you.'

I arrived punctually at the Ministry the following morning, but the guard refused to believe what I told him, and asked me to wait outside. A few minutes before six an official car pulled up and a smartly dressed man of my age stepped out. He realised who I was, shook my hand with a strong manly grip, and invited me into this office. I briefed him on America 500, of which he knew more than I expected, and also the success of the previous two round-the-world rallies. I then told him that the theme of the forthcoming world exhibition was so attractive that I was very keen to be associated with it.

'OK, that's no problem at all. What can you do for us?' Not knowing what to expect I had come without my usual wish list, so I decided to play for time.

'For Expo 98 to be the title sponsor of the rally we would expect your full support throughout the event.'

'No problem,' he replied.

'Bearing in mind the dates of the proposed exhibition we could easily plan to start and finish the rally in Lisbon. In fact we could adjust the timing in such a way that we could be back in Lisbon for the grand opening of the world exhibition in May 1998.'

'That sounds interesting, but could you include some current or former Portuguese territories on your route?'

I thought for a moment and then said, 'Stopping in Madeira at the start is no problem. After we have sailed through the South Indian Ocean we could pick up the traditional Portuguese route at the Cape of Good Hope.'

'Excellent.'

'From South Africa we could make a detour to Brazil, then sail to the Azores before the final leg to Lisbon.'

He was now all smiles.

'It sounds fantastic! Anything else?'

I hesitated for a diplomatic moment.

'Well, yes, and I hope won't you mind a final request, but with an event of this scale and nature, which is going around the world on a totally new route, the entry fees will not be able to support the budget on their own.'

'How much?'

'150,000 pounds sterling.'

He thought for a moment, then said simply, 'done. And thank you for thinking of us. I like the idea very much and can guarantee that you have made the best decision.'

'I know and I am very grateful.'

We shook hands and when I walked out of the ministry I realised that it wasn't even 6.30 am. I had secured my first commercial sponsorship in record time. I was on cloud nine.

Christmas 1996 found our 32 yachts tethered to a couple of pontoons in a commercial dock on the River Tagus close to the imposing statue dedicated to Prince Henry the Navigator and the explorers and sailors who had pioneered the modern era of maritime exploration.

The following day all yachts headed for the start line in front of Henry the Navigator's monument.

Four of the yachts were flying the Portuguese flag and not surprisingly we were welcomed warmly in all the Portuguese territories. The first stop in Madeira was an excellent foretaste of things to come. An Expo 98 official, João Gonçalves, who had been seconded to the rally, joined us in a number of significant stopovers, such as Cape Town and Salvador da Bahia, where he put on large receptions for local dignitaries and rally participants. On our arrival in South Africa at Richards Bay, the rally was welcomed by the King and Queen of the Zulus, who presented all participants with exquisite carvings of wild animals.

The stop in Salvador da Bahia was timed to coincide with the colourful carnival and the famous samba groups were joined by our participants with great enthusiasm even if less dancing skills. The long leg from Brazil to the Azores finished in the picturesque marina at Horta. From there we sailed to the Azorean capital Ponta Delgada and on to Lisbon. With perfect timing, the fleet sailed up the River Tagus on the day of the opening of Expo 98, and the yachts were docked in a special pool inside the large exhibition. Our crews, including the scores of friends and families who had joined them, had the run of the place as they could roam freely around the exhibition, day and night. It was a wonderful atmosphere that kept some of them there for weeks. The end was not too painful, as I knew that we would be back with the Millennium Odyssey before Expo 98 closed. And so we were.

Millennium Odyssey

The impending new millennium and its huge potential had my mind already spinning in the early 1990s, long before even the idea of the Hong Kong Challenge had been born. Not only was I keen to organise something unique and original for this very special occasion, but the year 2000 coincided also with my own 60th birthday when I was determined to retire and therefore had one more reason to try and leave the rally scene with a big splash. A round-the-world rally was quite obviously the logical answer but, for a while, I could not think of a suitable theme. I mulled over the millennium's historic significance, international implications, and its Christian dimension, but still could see no light at the end of the tunnel. Slowly those very elements started to coalesce, come into focus and an idea started to take shape. This would be an opportunity not only to celebrate the arrival of a new millennium, but much more important, to mark a milestone in the history of humankind that, after the fall of communism, promised to usher in an age of peace, international harmony and understanding. Looking back into the early history of man I saw that the gift of fire to another clan or tribe must have been the original symbol of peace, an early instance of man stretching out his hand in friendship to a fellow human being. My idea therefore was for a symbolic Millennium Flame to circle the globe and bring everywhere a message of hope, understanding and, above all, peace.

The true meaning of the millennium celebrations imposed its own parameters and, in spite of a certain reluctance, I realised that the Christian dimension could not be ignored. The rally, therefore, had to have a symbolic start in Jerusalem and an equally symbolic finish in Rome - with the wide world in between.

A small fleet of Millennium Odyssey yachts gathered in the Israeli port of Ashkelon early in August 1998 for the start of the most ambitious project I had ever undertaken. One morning we all drove the Church of the Holy Sepulchre in Jerusalem, where the Greek Orthodox Church, which has administered this holy place throughout its turbulent history, had agreed to put on a special ceremony for the lighting of the Millennium lamps. These had been specially designed and each participating yacht was to carry a flame in its lamp and around the world. At every stop the flame was to be handed over to local dignitaries in a special ceremony.

Gathered in the smoky gloom in front of the tomb of the Saviour, a venerable Greek Orthodox monk emerged from the narrow tunnel leading to the Holy Sepulchre and, from a blazing torch that he had lit from a candle on the tomb, transferred the flame to the expectant sailors. The moving ceremony completed, we proceeded to a neighbouring side chapel, where the Papal Nuncio, Monsignor Pietro Sambi, blessed us, prayed for the safe completion of our endeavour, and then ended with a statement that brought tears to my eyes.

'My heart is filled with joy that your very special event has already borne fruit because, as far as I know, this is the very first time in the 2,000-year old history of this sacred place that our two religions, Catholic and Orthodox, had actually agreed to give their support and cooperation to one project. Thank you all, but above all, thank you Jimmy Cornell.'

While the Jerusalem fleet made its way across the Mediterranean, a similar fleet had left London, with Aventura III among them, for a rendezvous in Lisbon. Having opened Expo 98 in May, the organisers of the international exhibition had enthusiastically agreed to host the Millennium Odyssey fleet inside the exhibition.

The merging of the two fleets in Lisbon was a joyful occasion made even more enjoyable by the many families joining the crews during the exciting last days of the highly successful show. With perfect timing, we left Lisbon just as the curtain fell on Expo 98. Sailing down the River Tagus on the last day of the world exhibition, the rally made its way towards Madeira and Gran Canaria.

In Las Palmas the fleet split in two, as in order to cover as much as possible of the world, I had devised two very different routes: a warm-water route that went through the Panama Canal and the tropics, which attracted the bulk of the fleet, and a cold-water alternative via Cape Horn and the Cape of Good Hope.

A unique feature of the rally were the special souvenir logbooks that had been produced for each yacht. Each log had the usual pages for daily entries and notes to refresh the memory. Specially designed pages were inserted in the logbook for the relevant stopovers to be signed by a high official at each of the flame handing-over ceremonies. Among those who signed were the Papal Nuncio in Jerusalem, the President of Panama, the Mayor of Rio de Janeiro, the Governor of the Falkland Islands, The President of the Suez Canal Authority, HRH Princess Pilolevu of Tonga, and many others. The pages that I treasure most in Aventura's logbook are those signed by all the scientists at the Ukrainian Vernadsky station in Antarctica, the distinctive stamp added by the keeper of the lighthouse at Cape Horn, and the signatures of my Pitcairn friends.

While the warm-water fleet was to head west via the Panama Canal, seven of the more daring yachts set sail south from the Canaries towards Brazil, Argentina, the Falklands and Southern Chile. Nowhere was the symbolic gesture of the handing over of the Millennium Flame appreciated more than in Mar del Plata, where the Bishop gave us a message of peace and friendship from the people of Argentina to take to the Falkland Islands. The Millennium Odyssey was the first international event to link the two previously warring communities since the tragic conflict that had marred lives on both sides.

Equally impressive had been the flame ceremony at the Cathedral of Rio de Janeiro, where a famous Brazilian sculptor had created a huge frame to hold the tiny Millennium Lamp, which was guarded by a Republican Guard in full ceremonial uniform.

At Puerto Williams on the Beagle Channel the small fleet split into two: three left on a leisurely cruise

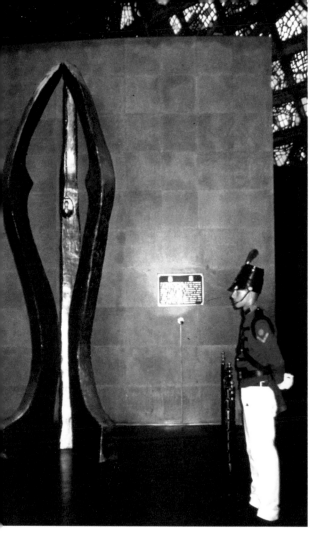

After a moving welcoming ceremony in the Cathedral in Papeete, the combined fleet proceeded westward to Tonga, where the skippers were received at the Royal Palace by HRH Princess Pilolevu, who gave participants a warm welcome, something that our royal hosts had done for every previous rally. Princess Pilolevu's interest in our events went back to the very first round-the-world rally, when she had graciously agreed to come to Gibraltar to give the start of Europa 92.

Special ceremonies, combined with cruising interludes, marked the rally's passage through the rest of the South Pacific with the highlight of an unforgettable traditional Fijian welcome ceremony at the resort of Musket Cove. In Bali it was time for the two fleets to go their separate ways again. A smaller fleet headed along the more difficult route across the South Indian Ocean and the Cape of Good Hope, while a larger group pointed their bows for the Red Sea and Mediterranean.

through the Chilean fjordland, while the other four yachts crossed the Drake Passage to Antarctica. We met again in the Chilean port of Valdivia from where we proceeded via Easter, Pitcairn and the Gambier Islands to Tahiti. There, the cold-water fleet was reunited with those that had transited the Panama Canal and who had been joined by a number of American yachts that had started from Florida.

What stood out in this part of the world was the enthusiastic welcome the flame ceremony received everywhere, from Buddhists, Hindus and Muslims, just as in previous countries we had been warmly welcomed by various Christian denominations. In Mauritius the ceremony was attended by each of the island's three main religions, a unique occasion that marked yet another first for the Millennium Odyssey.

A warm welcome in Papeete   389

While the main fleet spent some time in Southeast Asia, the smaller fleet sailed across the south Atlantic to Salvador da Bahia in Brazil, where, once again, the arrival coincided with that city's unique carnival. From Brazil, the fleet continued to the eastern Caribbean and, on reaching Antigua, it was time to bid farewell to the American participants, who were sailing home from there. The other yachts, which were going to sail either to the Mediterranean or to northern Europe, set sail from Antigua bound for the Azores.

Meanwhile, after stops in Singapore, Malaysia and Thailand, early in 2000 the larger Millennium fleet sailed across the Indian Ocean to Djibouti, and thence via Eritrea and Sudan to Egypt. Being docked in a marina south of the Suez Canal gave participants the opportunity to visit the ancient sites of Luxor and the Valley of the Kings before finally reaching the Mediterranean. After a last stop in Crete, the fleet arrived in Rome's ancient port of Civitavecchia where the yachts were joined by scores of families and friends who had flown in from all over the world.

Millennium Odyssey participants in Rome

Millennium Easter Monday had been set aside for a large outdoor ceremony in St Peter's Square where the Millennium Odyssey contingent had been reserved places in a special enclosure among the 100,000 pilgrims from around the world.

I had the honour to hand over the Millennium Flame to Pope John Paul II, an occasion which filled me with immense satisfaction. I was very moved to hand over the Millennium Lamp to this frail, but remarkable man, who had done so much to shape the closing years of the 20th century. With a warm smile on his face he asked about our rally and I described briefly how the flame had reached him, and how our message of peace had travelled around the world.

But that was not the end, as with the help of a Roman friend I also managed to secure an appointment with the Mayor of Rome. Our reception at the Campidoglio Palace with the President of the Rome Municipal Council took place in the ancient Roman Senate overshadowed by a statue of Julius Caesar who had once presided over proceedings in that very spot. We were then taken on a private tour of this famous building that overlooks the ancient Roman Forum, and is not open to the general public. The participants were quite blown over by the setting, and I am sure that all that happened that day would be remembered by them to the end of their lives.

A final ceremony awaited the few yachts that had decided to end the rally where they had started – on the Greenwich Meridian in London. Once again, I was fortunate to find just the right place, the 15th century chapel set in the grounds of the Tower of London, where the Millennium Lamp now rests not far from the remains of the martyred Sir Thomas More.

The Blue Planet Odyssey

From among the many comments made by the Millennium Odyssey participants, I wish to conclude with the words of Saundra and Charles Gray, as they so well crystallised my own hopes for this truly unique event. 'The idealism of the journey takes visible form in the people we encounter. Only through meeting people one to one can we hope to find peace. A big dream of Jimmy Cornell's, an adventure for all of us, and the hope that understanding can grow between people through encounters like these.'

Lois and Don Babson of the yacht Que Sera Sera receiving the 'Spirit of the Millennium Odyssey' award

The Grand Finale

The successful finish of the Millennium Odyssey was also meant to mark the end of my career as a rally organiser. Shortly before the Rome ceremony we sold World Cruising Club, which Gwenda and I had founded in 1986. Eventually I came to regret not so much the actual sale of World Cruising Club, as it gave me the long delayed opportunity to do what I like best and go sailing, but the direction the ARC took after my departure.

The Millennium Odyssey brought to an end my involvement with sailing rallies, and indeed the freedom thus gained allowed me to enjoy my subsequent round-the-world voyage on Aventura III. With no more major sailing voyages planned, in 2010 I decided to sell Aventura III and spend more time smelling the roses at our place in Provence. However it soon became clear that an idle retirement didn't suit my style, and I started thinking of some new challenging project. During my second voyage to Antarctica, as part of the Millennium Odyssey, I had noticed some changes that were probably related to the phenomenon of global warming. The visible deterioration of the environment was a subject that started to cause increasing concern in the early days of the new millennium, as was the realisation that the root cause may be man's impact on global climate. This impression was reinforced during my third world voyage when I revisited some of the places I had visited on previous voyages, and was disturbed by the changes that had occurred in the intervening years. Some of the damage was man-made, but other signs indicated a change in the global climate. Scientists had predicted this for some time, and it reminded me of the message that Expo 98 had carried around the world, 'The Ocean, our heritage for the future'. Quarter of a century later that message seemed to be even more relevant, and I felt that there ought to be a global sailing event to raise awareness of climate

Blue Planet Odyssey fan club

change, and its impact on the oceans.

Unfortunately the rally could not have been timed at a worse moment, as the deterioration of the safety situation in the Indian Ocean meant that from the 25 boats that had signed up, only ten took the start from Key West in Florida in early January 2015, with a few more boats joining them in Panama and Galapagos. As the route passed through some of the less-travelled areas of the oceans, arrangements were made with oceanographic institutes and research centres to use this unique opportunity to receive environmental data

Terry Singh of the yacht Libby launching an Argo float en route to the Marquesas

gathered by participants.

As part of a unique partnership with UNESCO's Intergovernmental Oceanographic Commission and the World Meteorological Organisation, drifter buoys supplied by NOAA and Argo floats from the Scripps Institution of Oceanography in San Diego, were deployed by several BPO yachts between Panama, the Galapagos and Marquesan Islands. Some rally participants were also in contact with school children in their country of origin, as well as in some of countries along the route by way of a comprehensive

educational programme.

By the time the fleet had reached Tahiti, the worsening situation in the Gulf of Aden and Red Sea, and the possibility that the route of the rally may need to be altered to continue around the Cape of Good Hope, persuaded some participants to remain in the South Pacific. With the safety situation in the north Indian Ocean showing no improvement, at the end of a highly successful cruise through Indonesia, the decision was made to reach the Atlantic Ocean via South Africa. As a result, some participants decided to have their boats shipped from Southeast Asia to the Mediterranean. Those who persevered, sailed to western Sumatra, Cocos Keeling, Rodrigues, Mauritius and La Réunion, and reached the south Atlantic in late 2016. After stops at St Helena and Brazil, the Blue Planet Odyssey came

The crews of No Regrets, Tahawus and Maggie happily celebrating the safe completion of their arduous voyage

to a successful end in Barbados in late January 2017.

The Odysseys

The Blue Planet Odyssey inspired me to launch in 2013 a series of noncompetitive transatlantic rallies with the aim of bringing back the original non-commercial

Barbados 50

favourable weather conditions.

This special transatlantic event to commemorate the 50th anniversary of Barbados independence had a start in London on 31 July 2016. Several more boats joined as the fleet made its way to the Canary Islands with stops in various ports along the coasts of Spain and Portugal. During their five-week Canarian sojourn, the participants visited all islands of the archipelago. While in the Cape Verdes, they took part in a cruise to some of the most attractive islands. From there, a fleet of 33 yachts crossed the Atlantic to Barbados arriving in capital Bridgetown in time for the anniversary celebrations.

The Future

I am very happy that my rallies have provided the framework that has allowed so many sailors to cross the oceans in safety and an atmosphere of friendship, to travel the world in a spirit of goodwill, and to bring them in closer contact with the people of the countries visited.

As to the future, only time will tell.

spirit of my earlier rallies, with the emphasis on safety and the enjoyment of taking part in a purely amateur event. The Atlantic, Caribbean and Islands Odyssey, have been a great success, with most boats in these transatlantic rallies being sailed by family crews with over 46 children under 16 sailing in the 2016 events.

The hub of these events is Marina Santa Cruz, located in the centre of the capital of Tenerife. The Caribbean host is Barbados, the logical landfall at the end of an Atlantic crossing. Participants have a choice of sailing to the Caribbean on a direct passage with the Atlantic Odyssey in November, the Caribbean Odyssey in January, or join the Islands Odyssey that sails first from Tenerife to São Vicente in the Cape Verdes. During their stopover, participants have the opportunity to visit various islands in this remote archipelago of attractive anchorages and spectacular scenery. As the Cape Verdes are located in the subtropical area of prevailing northeast trade winds, the subsequent passage to Barbados has a good chance of encountering

Barbados 50 yachts in Mindelo, Cape Verdes

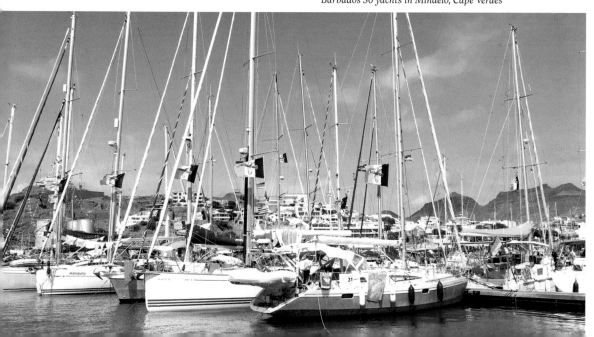

35

Where do all the boats go?

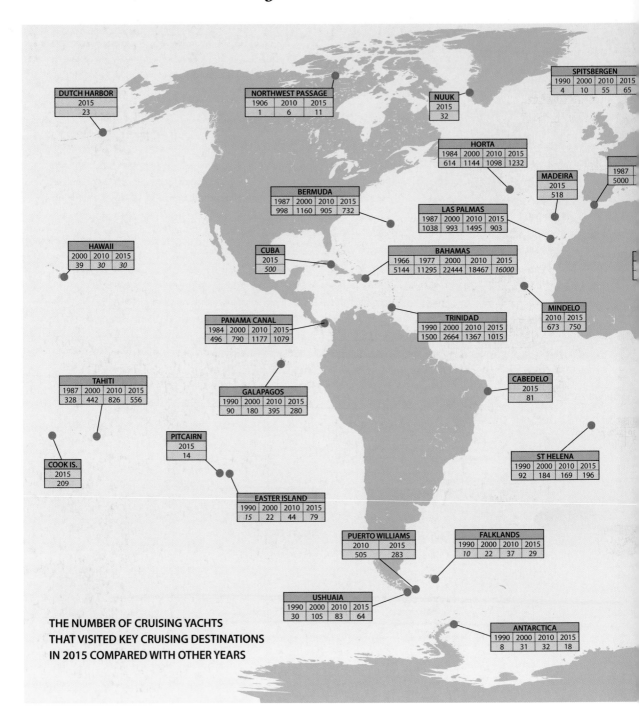

SPITSBERGEN

1990	2000	2010	2015
4	10	55	65

DUTCH HARBOR

2015
23

NORTHWEST PASSAGE

1906	2010	2015
1	6	11

NUUK

2015
32

HORTA

1984	2000	2010	2015
614	1144	1098	1232

MADEIRA

2015
518

1987
5000

BERMUDA

1987	2000	2010	2015
998	1160	905	732

LAS PALMAS

1987	2000	2010	2015
1038	993	1495	903

HAWAII

2000	2010	2015
39	*30*	*30*

CUBA

2015
500

BAHAMAS

1966	1977	2000	2010	2015
5144	11295	22444	18467	*16000*

MINDELO

2010	2015
673	750

PANAMA CANAL

1984	2000	2010	2015
496	790	1177	1079

TRINIDAD

1990	2000	2010	2015
1500	2664	1367	1015

TAHITI

1987	2000	2010	2015
328	442	826	556

GALAPAGOS

1990	2000	2010	2015
90	180	395	280

CABEDELO

2015
81

PITCAIRN

2015
14

ST HELENA

1990	2000	2010	2015
92	184	169	196

COOK IS.

2015
209

EASTER ISLAND

1990	2000	2010	2015
15	22	44	79

PUERTO WILLIAMS

2010	2015
505	283

FALKLANDS

1990	2000	2010	2015
10	22	37	29

USHUAIA

1990	2000	2010	2015
30	105	83	64

ANTARCTICA

1990	2000	2010	2015
8	31	32	18

**THE NUMBER OF CRUISING YACHTS
THAT VISITED KEY CRUISING DESTINATIONS
IN 2015 COMPARED WITH OTHER YEARS**

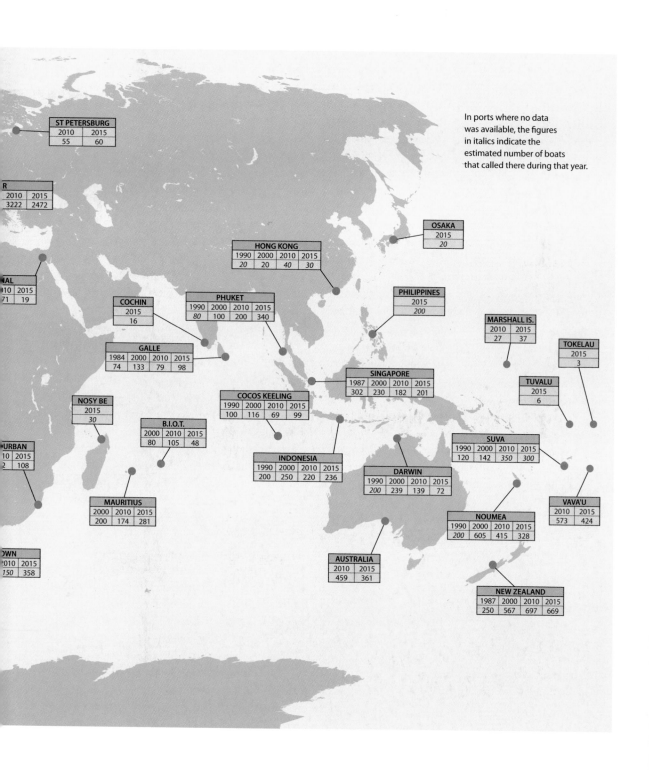

In ports where no data was available, the figures in italics indicate the estimated number of boats that called there during that year.

ST PETERSBURG

2010	2015
55	60

R

2010	2015
3222	2472

OSAKA

2015
20

HONG KONG

1990	2000	2010	2015
20	20	40	*30*

AL

010	2015
71	19

COCHIN

2015
16

PHUKET

1990	2000	2010	2015
80	100	200	340

PHILIPPINES

2015
200

MARSHALL IS.

2010	2015
27	37

TOKELAU

2015
3

GALLE

1984	2000	2010	2015
74	133	79	98

SINGAPORE

1987	2000	2010	2015
302	230	182	201

TUVALU

2015
6

NOSY BE

2015
30

COCOS KEELING

1990	2000	2010	2015
100	116	69	99

B.I.O.T.

2000	2010	2015
80	105	48

URBAN

10	2015
2	108

INDONESIA

1990	2000	2010	2015
200	250	220	236

DARWIN

1990	2000	2010	2015
200	239	139	72

SUVA

1990	2000	2010	2015
120	142	*350*	*300*

VAVA'U

2010	2015
573	424

MAURITIUS

2000	2010	2015
200	174	281

NOUMEA

1990	2000	2010	2015
200	605	415	328

OWN

010	2015
150	358

AUSTRALIA

2010	2015
459	361

NEW ZEALAND

1987	2000	2010	2015
250	567	697	669

Atlantic Ocean

My interest in the global movement of cruising boats goes back to 1987, when I published the results of my first survey on this subject. In the intervening three decades I have conducted every five years a follow-up survey; the latest was done in 2016 and examined the global situation during the previous year. Since the publication of my previous survey on movement and distribution of sailing boats in 2010, the world has been confronted by two major phenomena that have affected offshore cruising both in the short and long term. The political upheavals in the Middle East and North Africa have greatly affected cruising in the Mediterranean as well as passages through the North Indian Ocean and Red Sea, but while those effects can be regarded as regional, the consequences of climate change are now affecting the entire world. Global weather conditions in 2015 were also affected by a prolonged El Niño episode that exacerbated the ongoing effects of climate change, most notably in the north west Pacific where at least one typhoon occurred in every month of the year, with a safe sailing season now sadly a thing of the past.

As on previous occasions, in order to construct a realistic image of the global movement of sailing yachts, I contacted officials in the most important hubs in every ocean requesting statistical data on the number of foreign flagged yachts that had passed through those ports in 2015. The resulting global canvas was filled in with figures obtained from the most popular destinations on the world cruising circuit as well as some of the least visited places in the world.

The port of Las Palmas in the Canary Islands boasts a larger concentration of boats preparing for an ocean passage than any other place in the world, with the majority setting off across the Atlantic to the Caribbean from there.

The port authority recorded a total of 903 visiting boats in 2015, a significant drop from the 1,495 that had called there five years previously. The lower number may be explained by some boats leaving from other Canary Islands, but, according to Juan Francisco Martin, commercial director of the port of Las Palmas, 'A gradual downward trend has become noticeable in recent years and could point to a general reduction in the number of boats crossing to the Caribbean.'

Approximately 75 per cent of the boats that called at Las Palmas continued across the Atlantic to which should be added an estimated 200 boats that left from other Canarian islands, some that left from Madeira or directly from Gibraltar. An increasingly popular departure point on a transatlantic passage are the Cape Verde Islands, where Mindelo Marina, on São Vicente Island, recorded a total of 750 visiting yachts. Lutz Meyer-Scheel, the founder and manager of the marina, reckons that: 'Most took from here the route to the Caribbean, while some continued south to Brazil or Cape Town. Located in the trade wind belt, the Cape Verdes are increasingly regarded as a better launch pad for an Atlantic passage, which is also much shorter from here.'

Extrapolating from the figures obtained from the Cape Verdes, Canaries and Madeira, it can be assumed that every year approximately 1,200 boats cross the Atlantic along the northeast trade wind route. This indicates a significant reduction of 20 per cent from the estimated 1,500 boats based on the figures provided by the same sources in 2010.

Even if the numbers in Las Palmas were smaller, the nationalities of sailors have remained generally unchanged compared to the recent past, with French yachts in the lead (199), followed by Britain (163),

The port of Las Palmas de Gran Canaria

Germany (98), USA (62), Netherlands (57), Sweden (49), Belgium (39), Norway (31), and others. The flags seen in Mindelo paint a similar picture.

Most of the European boats that sail to the Caribbean usually complete an Atlantic circuit by sailing from the Canaries to the Caribbean after the middle of November, and returning home the following year in May or June by sailing to the Azores, either direct or via Bermuda.

As the westernmost of the Azores, the port of Lajes on the island of Flores makes a welcome landfall at the end of a long passage. The small marina recorded 184 transatlantic arrivals in 2015, of which 83 originated in the Eastern Caribbean, 68 in Bermuda, and 31 in USA or Canada. However, many more boats bypassed Lajes and made straight for Horta, on the island of Faial, which continues to be the preferred landfall at the end of an eastbound transatlantic passage. The port authority has been keeping detailed records of visiting boats since 1985 and this treasure-trove of data made it possible to extract a raft of interesting facts about the boats, their crews and routes sailed. The data also confirmed the downward trend highlighted by the figures from Las Palmas.

Horta marina in the Azores

Horta's tradition of hospitality is legendary as every sailor who sets foot ashore there at the end of a long passage will testify. The very first was Joshua Slocum, who was welcomed here in 1895 on completion of his transatlantic passage at the start of his single-handed voyage around the world. In the intervening years Horta has become the most important sailing hub in the world, both by the number of visiting yachts and the multitude of their ports of origin or destination, from Panama to Iceland, Cape Town to Greenland.

While the total of boats (1,232) that cleared into Horta during 2015 was in fact 12 per cent higher than in 2010 (1,098), on closer inspection it became clear that just over half of them were undertaking a longer voyage. Combined with the figures from Lajes, the data confirmed that the majority of boats on passage from the Caribbean to Europe sailed directly to the Azores, with far fewer making the detour to Bermuda than in the past.

The data obtained from Horta reconfirmed the predominance of French yachts. Among the total of 1,232 visitors, 358 were flying the French tricolour, 143 were from the UK, Germany (94), Netherlands (77), USA (59), followed by the surprisingly high number of boats from Belgium (35) and others.

While Horta has overtaken Bermuda in sheer numbers of visiting yachts, Bermuda continues to be just as important in its role as a point of transit by North American boats sailing between the mainland and the Caribbean or Europe, as well as by boats returning from the Caribbean either to the US east coast or Europe. The total of boats that called at Bermuda in 2015 was 732 and confirmed a 37 per cent decline that has been noticeable since 2000. This is mainly due to the large number of American boats that nowadays bypass Bermuda and sail directly to the Eastern Caribbean. The situation is reversed in May and June, when many more boats returning to the US mainland call at Bermuda. Another reason for the overall reduction of visitors to Bermuda is that many more European boats now sail directly from the Caribbean to the Azores.

Over half the boats that arrive in the Caribbean from either Europe or America used to spend at least one full season there, but in recent years concerns over the effects of climate change have resulted in a significant increase in the number of sailors who prefer to limit themselves to a one year circuit, be it from Europe or North America. Those who decide to stay longer in the Caribbean usually have their boats stored on land in a secure place during the hurricane season. The island of Trinidad has set up several boatyards for this purpose with 1,015 boats spending the summer there in 2015, which shows a significant reduction from the 2,664 in 2000 and 1,367 in 2010. According to Donald Stollmeyer, president of the Yacht Services Association of Trinidad and Tobago, 'The explanation is the gradual decline in the number of sailors who are prepared to keep their boats in the tropics during the hurricane season, but also local issues such as increased crime, piracy incidents between Grenada and Trinidad, archaic immigration and customs formalities, and many others.'

The total number of boats that spend the winter season cruising in the Caribbean has remained relatively stable in recent years but one country that has seen a significant increase is Cuba. Its major ports and marinas recorded in 2015 a total of 1,256 foreign flagged yachts, both sail and power. As several of them had cleared into more than one port, the actual number of individual boats was probably closer to 500. Even so, this is a marked increase as it is double the figures for 2010 and points to a trend that is going to accelerate now that relations with the USA are being normalised. According to Commodore José Miguel Escrich of the Hemingway International Yacht Club of Cuba, 'By the summer of 2016 the figures for 2015 had doubled again as we witnessed a steady influx of visitors from the United States. We are so happy to be able to welcome and offer our friendship to all those who love the sea'.

While warm-water cruising has remained generally stable on a global level, cold-water sailing may become more popular as sailors strike out for more challenging destinations. Two high-latitude destinations in the North Atlantic that are now regularly visited by cruising yachts are Spitsbergen and Greenland. The former showed a small increase over 2010, but Greenland is poised to become more frequented both as an attractive cruising destination in its own right and as a base for preparing for a transit of the Northwest Passage, which has become more accessible as a result of climate change. An estimated 32 boats called at Nuuk, the capital of Greenland, in 2015 with most limiting their cruising to the spectacular west coast. The more intrepid struck out west to brave the challenges of the Northwest Passage with eight succeeding to complete a transit of that elusive shortcut to the Pacific. Three boats completed an eastbound transit, among them my own Aventura, the 87th sailing vessel to achieve that feat unassisted.

At the other extreme of the Atlantic Ocean, voyages to Antarctica showed a remarkable decline from 32 boats in 2010 to only 18 in 2015, among them eight sailing boats, three motoryachts, with the remaining seven engaged in charter work. The busy Argentinian port of Ushuaia, at the tip of South America, is where boats planning to sail south to Antarctica or north to the Chilean fjordland prepare and provision for their voyage. The 64 arrivals in 2015 were down from the 83 in 2010 or a peak figure of 105 in 2000.

The spectacular Chilean fjordland

Across the Beagle Channel from Ushuaia is Puerto Williams, a Chilean military outpost and the southernmost settlement in the world. The small port is only a short distance from Cape Horn and as the Chilean authorities have jurisdiction over an area that includes the Antarctic Peninsula as well as parts of Tierra del Fuego, any boat planning to sail that way must complete formalities here. The movements of all vessels are monitored by the Chilean Navy and show that 2015 was a busy year with a total of 283 yacht movements, but well below the 505 of five years previously. As the former figure includes several repeat visits, the actual total of new visitors was 140. Skip Novak, who has been operating in those waters since the early 1990s, does not sound optimistic about the future: 'The Chilean government has banned all foreign charter yachts from Cape Horn and the Beagle Channel circuits. We are trying to find a solution for the future, but it won't be easy.'

From Puerto Williams and Ushuaia most cruising boats turn north for the spectacular fjordland of Southern Chile and continue their voyage westward into the South Pacific and the rarely missed stop at Easter Island. On the opposite side of South America, most yachts heading for the South Atlantic from Tierra del Fuego and the Beagle Channel call at Port Stanley in the Falklands, which saw 29 yachts in 2015. From there, the routes diverge and either follow the contour of the South American mainland, or continue nonstop to St Helena or Cape Town. Both of these have seen a steady increase in the number of visiting yachts, initially as a result of the risk of piracy in the North Indian Ocean that had been replaced more recently by the safety concerns caused by the volatile situation in the Middle East, from Yemen through the Red Sea to the Suez Canal. Compared to 2010, when 171 yachts transited the canal, their number had shrunk in 2015 to 19, with only 14 of them northbound. According to Ashraf Sukar of the Prince of the Red Sea Yacht Agency: 'Nine were from overseas and on a world voyage, two from the Persian Gulf area and five were returning to the Mediterranean from Red Sea ports.'

As a result of the dangers involved with sailing the North Indian Ocean route, any sailor on a westbound world voyage was confronted with four options: brave the risks of a passage through the Red Sea, have the boat shipped from Southeast Asia to the Mediterranean, continue the voyage around South Africa, or abandon a passage through the Indian Ocean altogether. The few who took the first option in 2015 were indeed very daring and as the situation in that part of the world continues to be extremely volatile, it should not be attempted while there are no signs of a real improvement. The Sevenstar transport company shipped 25 boats from Southeast Asia to Turkey in 2015, and continues to offer this service to those who are not deterred by the high cost of the operation. With good planning, the route around the Cape of Good Hope should present no great problem, and has the added attraction of several interesting places along the way, the best being undoubtedly South Africa itself.

All boats that clear out of South Africa must now be docked at the Royal Cape Yacht Club before leaving, which made it fairly easy to obtain their details. Compared to 2010, the increase was indeed remarkable

Pacific Ocean

with a total of 358 long-distance sailing boats calling here, 236 bound for the Atlantic, the rest for the Indian Ocean. The northbound figures were borne out by the statistics from St Helena, the 196 arrivals also showing a net albeit more modest increase. St Helena is such an important port of call in the South Atlantic that, with the exception of a handful of boats that sail directly from Cape Town to Argentina or Brazil, virtually no boat on a world voyage sails by without stopping. Therefore it was interesting to notice that British boats were the largest contingent (30), followed by South Africa (29), USA (26), France (24), Germany (16), Australia (11), Canada (9), Netherlands (6) and others. From St Helena, the most common destination was the South American mainland (38 per cent), followed by Ascension Island (31 per cent), Caribbean (17 per cent) and the Cape Verdes (6 per cent).

Brazilian ports, such as the ancient capital Salvador da Bahia, used to be the favourite mainland destination, but the deteriorating safety situation in Brazil coupled with an unwelcome attitude by the authorities has resulted in a drastic reduction in the number of cruising boats. Sandoval Matos, the manager of Marina Pier Salvador, described the main reasons: 'The Brazilian Federal Police no longer renew visas for European nationals, claiming to be applying the law of reciprocity. Violent incidents involving foreign visitors have exacerbated this situation by giving Brazil a bad reputation, the number of visiting boats having dropped to 20 per cent of what it used to be.'

Against this background, Marina Jacaré, near the town of Cabedelo, and run by two French expat sailors, has somehow managed to remain an oasis of tranquility with 81 visitors in 2015. Not surprisingly, the French contingent was the largest (38), followed by UK (8), Germany (6), Belgium (5), USA (4), and a few other nations. Most European boats appeared to be on an a one-year sabbatical tour with virtually all planning to sail north to the Caribbean before returning home, with only four intending to sail south.

The Panama Canal is the most valuable indicator of yacht movement both between the Atlantic and Pacific and on a global level, and the latest figures show that the steady increase in the number of transits by pleasure craft may have peaked in 2010 when 1,177 yachts transited the Panama Canal compared to 1,079 in 2015 (725 Pacific bound and 354 Atlantic bound). What has remained mostly unchanged are the Pacific destinations after the transit, with two thirds of the boats turning north, towards the west coast of Central and North America, and the rest heading for the South Pacific.

The restrictions applied to visiting yachts in Galapagos are still in force, but since the use of a local agent in dealing with formalities has become compulsory, entry formalities have been streamlined, albeit at a very high cost. Visiting yachts are now granted stays of up to 20 days by the port captains in the two official ports of entry: Baquerizo Moreno and Puerto Ayora. Just as in Panama, the record high of 395 arrivals in 2010 had dropped in 2015 to 280 boats, some sailors being obviously deterred by the complex formalities and the expenses associated with them. This is undoubtedly the reason why many sailors no longer plan on stopping in the Galapagos Islands and prefer to sail a different route to French Polynesia.

For those who are determined to bypass Galapagos, the logical option is to sail directly from Panama to the Marquesas. A somewhat longer but potentially more attractive alternative is to make a detour to Easter Island and continue from there via Pitcairn Island to French Polynesia.

The fact that the number of yachts calling at the Polynesian outpost of Easter Island has almost doubled in the last five years probably proves the above point. According to Ricardo Astudillo Duran, the port captain of Hanga Roa, 'Compared to the 44 yachts that called here in 2010, we welcomed a record of 79 yachts here in 2015.'

The increasing attraction of this southern route is also shown by the fact that 70 boats made landfall at Mangareva, the southeastern point of entry into French Polynesia. Among those, 14 stopped at Pitcairn, the legendary island that served as the secret retreat for the Bounty mutineers, whose descendants continue to live on this remote speck of land.

Landfall in the spectacular Marquesas at the end of a 3,000-mile-passage is an uplifting experience that no sailor can ever forget, nor should any miss. In 2015, 397 boats arrived there, the majority at Atuona on the island of Hiva Oa. The total of arrivals for the entire French Polynesia was 556, which included 11 that made landfall in the southern Austral Islands at the end of a passage from New Zealand. The number of arrivals in 2010 showed a drastic decline from the record 826 reported in 2010.

The largest contingent was from USA (143), followed by France (90), UK (66), Australia (43), New Zealand (39), Germany (6), Canada (23), Netherlands (22), Switzerland (15), Belgium (12), Norway (6), Italy (5), and a host of other nations.

The boats which transit the Panama Canal and head for the South Pacific are joined in the Marquesas and Tahiti by boats that have sailed from Mexico, the west coast of USA or Canada, and Hawaii. In 2015, 166 American and Canadian boats arrived in French Polynesia, but compared to the past, when many continued on a circumnavigation, or at least sailed as far as New Zealand before turning around, about half of the North American boats now turn north from Tahiti and head for home.

Sailing west from Tahiti there are several detours that can be made from the main trunk route, such as to the once rarely visited Palmerston atoll, which was visited by 71 boats. Another highly popular place, also in the Cook Islands, is Suwarrow, an uninhabited atoll where a caretaker is based during the peak arrivals time and welcomed a total of 69 boats. The total

Fatu Hiva in the Marquesas

of arrivals for the entire island group was 209. In neighbouring Tonga, the main island of Tongatapu was once again eclipsed by the northern island group of Vava'u. This long time favourite among sailors roaming the South Seas welcomed 424 arrivals.

All the above places are close enough to the main transpacific route not to entail much of a detour, and this may explain the fact that only 3 boats called at Tokelau, and 6 at Tuvalu, two small and isolated Polynesian communities that would have justified the effort to drop by and say hello, especially as both are likely to be the first victims of the rising sea levels caused by climate change.

By the time they have reached Tonga or Fiji, most cruising boats leave the tropics before the cyclone season and sail to New Zealand or Australia. Although ports in South Queensland and New South Wales have been attracting an increasing number of boats, New Zealand continues to be the favourite destination. This was borne out by the 669 arrivals in New Zealand, the majority making landfall at Opua in the Bay of Islands, with late October and November being the bumper time. Of the total, 491 were foreign flagged: USA (102), UK (70), Australia (65), Germany (32), France (30), Canada (22), Netherlands (15), Italy, Switzerland and Belgium with 7 each, followed by 37 other nationalities.

While in New Zealand the numbers have remained stable, in Australia the number of foreign vessels has dropped by 21 percent from 459 in 2010 to 361 in 2015. The situation was similar in neighbouring New Caledonia which saw 328 arrivals compared to 415 five years previously.

The figures recorded along the South Pacific trunk route show a certain decline in the total number of cruising boats and this trend is now reflected on a global level.

While the South Pacific continues to attract most of the yachts undertaking a world voyage, the situation in the North Pacific has remained almost unchanged compared to 2010, although there was a considerable decline in the number of foreign visiting boats in the Western North Pacific. This is the first area in the world to suffer the consequences of climate change on a large scale, with weather conditions being noticeably affected by the warming of the oceans. The worst affected were the Philippines, with a tropical cyclone striking the country in every month of the year. A defined safe sailing season can no longer be counted on. A similar trend now appears to affect all of Micronesia, which was visited by 27 tropical cyclones in 2015.

Although rarely affected by tropical storms, and enjoying benign conditions throughout the year, foreign flagged yachts are still a rare sight in Hawaii. Probably for that reason, the authorities do not keep a record and the best guess is that only an estimated 30 foreign yachts called at the islands in 2015. In fact, Hawaii does attract many American boats and is visited every year by between 200 and 250 boats, both cruising and racing. Some sail from there to French Polynesia and a few continue west towards Micronesia and the Asian mainland. Some of them were among the 37 arrivals in the Marshall Islands, which is probably a fair estimate of the approximate number of boats calling at the Micronesian islands generally.

In spite of the uncertain weather conditions mentioned above, the Philippines continue to attract visiting boats, but most of them limit themselves to the southern part, which is rarely affected by tropical storms. On the Asian mainland, the expected boom in cruising boats has so far failed to materialise and the estimates from Hong Kong show in fact a decline compared to the previous survey. This comment of a long-standing member of the Royal Hong Kong Yacht Club points to the reason: 'Hong Kong's new "mainland" style bureaucracy has pretty much stifled visiting yachts as they are not allowed to operate in Hong Kong waters without a Hong Kong captain's license.' There was not much more movement in China either where formalities for visiting yachts continue to be both complicated and expensive.

A small number of cruising boats make it as far as Japan every year with an estimated 20 foreign yachts passing through Osaka in 2015. Ten of them could be traced, as they made their way east, with some stopping at Dutch Harbor on their way to Canada or the US west coast.

Dutch Harbor

This busy fishing port at the western edge of the Aleutian Islands saw a record 23 visiting yachts in 2015. Both its provisioning and repair facilities are excellent and this is a good base to prepare the boat for those planning an eastbound transit of the Northwest Passage.

Indian Ocean

Because of the serious threat of piracy in the North Indian Ocean, 2010 was the first year when more boats on a world voyage sailed the Cape of Good Hope route than crossed the North Indian Ocean to the Red Sea and Suez Canal. This trend continued in the intervening five years with very few sailors taking the risk to reach the Mediterranean that way. However, due to the presence of an international naval force in the North Indian Ocean, the threat posed by the Somali pirates has been virtually eliminated. As a result, 2015 saw the first cruising boats braving that northern route, with a total of 14 boats arriving in Suez from the North Indian Ocean. In spite of the fact that these boats had passed safely through the critical area of the Gulf of Aden and Red Sea, it must be stressed that sailing in that area is still potentially dangerous.

As a result, there has been a noticeable reduction in Southeast Asia in the number cruising boats on a world voyage as many avoid the North Indian Ocean altogether. By contrast, there continues to be a fair amount of coastal traffic with more local and regional boats, both racing and cruising, joining the rallies and regattas held during the winter season in Western Malaysia and Thailand. The Singapore port authority recorded just over 200 foreign flagged boats calling in 2015, with the figures obtained from Phuket confirming an increase in visitors from neighbouring countries.

With very few sailors daring to risk a passage to the Mediterranean via the North Indian Ocean and Red Sea, on reaching Southeast Asia their only reasonable option is to switch hemispheres and head south. A convenient port en route is Galle, on the south coast of Sri Lanka, where 98 arrivals were recorded in 2015. Some made a further detour to Cochin in South India, but few boats persevered on a westbound course, with the notable exception of the 14 boats that reached Suez. Among them, 12 were on a world voyage that had originated in Australia or New Zealand, and the remaining two had started from ports in the Persian Gulf area.

Rather than face the challenge of a passage to and around South Africa, many Australian and some New Zealand sailors are now buying a boat in Europe, mostly catamarans, and sail home via the Panama Canal avoiding the Indian Ocean and thus completing a safe and convenient semi-circumnavigation. In contrast to that, some French sailors do it the other way round: they leave home, stop at various French territories in the Caribbean and South Pacific before finishing in New Caledonia where they sell their boats and return home having completed a similar semi-circumnavigation.

It is estimated that approximately 200 yachts transit the Torres Strait every year. Some of those that are heading directly for the South Indian Ocean usually stop at Darwin in Northern Australia, which saw 72 arrivals in 2015. The alternative is a cruise through the Indonesian archipelago and 236 foreign vessels obtained the required cruising permit issued by the Indonesian Ministry of Foreign Affairs. That requirement has been discontinued in 2016, in an attempt to attract more visitors to what continues to be one of the most interesting and diverse cruising grounds in the world.

Heading west from either Darwin or Indonesia, the Australian outpost of Cocos Keeling continues to be a popular stop with 99 visitors in 2015. Among them, 29 were from the UK, USA (17), France (14), Germany (9), Australia (8), Netherlands (5), Sweden (3), and a few others.

From Cocos Keeling the westbound route splits into a southern branch to Rodrigues and Mauritius and a northern branch bound for Chagos (British Indian Ocean Territory). The latter recorded 48 arrivals, a significant reduction of 54 per cent from the 105 boats five years previously, as the British authorities, who administer this territory, now limit the issuing of the compulsory permit to those who can justify the need for a stop in those islands, and seem determined to discourage those who regard them as an interesting cruising interlude.

The most popular stop along the more frequented southern route is Port Louis in Mauritius, with 281 boats being recorded, a major increase over 2010 and a definite proof of the predominance of the Cape of Good Hope route among boats on a world voyage. The largest contingent (67) flew the South African flag, thus pointing to a steady two-way traffic. The rest of the boats all seemed to be on a world voyage with UK (34), France (29), USA (25), Germany (12), Netherlands (7), Belgium (4), Italy (3) and others.

When first discovered as an as yet unexplored cruising destination, Madagascar was expected to become the major attraction in the South Indian Ocean, but the lack of facilities, cumbersome bureaucracy and the ever lingering threat of piracy has put paid to those hopes. The activities of the Al-Shabaab terrorist group in East Africa and its attacks on tourist resorts have engendered a profound sense of uncertainty in this part of the world that has cast its shadow over neighbouring cruising destinations such as Northern Madagascar, the Seychelles and even Mozambique.

Nosy Be, on Madagascar's northwest coast has established itself as a modest base but few world

Cocos Keeling

voyagers bother to make the lengthy detour from Mauritius or La Reunion over the top of Madagascar. An estimated 30 boats visited the Nosy Be area in 2015, half made up of South African boats undertaking a one-season round trip. On the eve of a new cyclone season, all boats make their way south. Richards Bay and Durban are the usual South African landfall ports, with arrivals evenly split between them. A total of 110 boats arrived in Durban from the north in 2015.

The Mediterranean

Some of the most important changes on the world sailing circuit in the last five years have occurred in the Mediterranean. The political turmoil in the Middle East and North Africa, the war in Syria and surrounding area, the refugee crisis, have disrupted or entirely closed some of the most popular cruising grounds of what used to be once described as Mare Nostrum.

Perennially popular places such as the Balearics, Croatia and Greece continue to be uncomfortably crowded during the summer and even outside the high season visiting yachts have difficulties finding places in marinas thus deterring visitors from coming. The stricter application of the Schengen regulations has also led to a reduction in the number of non-EU sailors, especially from the USA.

As the gateway into the Mediterranean, Gibraltar recorded a total of 2,472 transits in 2015, a substantial decline compared to 2010 and a possible sign that the number of visiting yachts is on the way down in the Mediterranean, just as in most places covered by this survey.

Sailing hubs

This latest survey has highlighted three interesting factors: the small size of crew on long voyages, with many couples sailing on their own, the number of couples with young children setting off on a shorter or longer sabbatical leave, and the steadily increasing proportion of catamarans among cruising yachts. These factors are possibly interrelated and the data gathered from some of the most important hubs along the world sailing routes may show that. I therefore decided to widen the scope of this global survey to find out more about the boats than just their numbers or flags, but also average length, size of crew, and whether they were monohulls or catamarans.

Early in 2016, the tourism office of French Polynesia conducted a wide-ranging survey to assess the impact of pleasure craft on the communities in the various island groups they visited during 2015. The survey drew on three sources: entry and exit data compiled by immigration, customs declarations submitted by each vessel, and a questionnaire completed by each captain. 234 captains responded positively and the results are highly informative as they provide a unique insight into such a significant sample of long distance boats and voyagers.

Among those questioned, 43 per cent described themselves as being on a world voyage, 46 per cent on a round Pacific voyage and 11 per cent on an open-ended cruise. As for crew, 51 per cent of the boats were sailed by just a couple, 13 per cent had a crew of 3, 20 per cent a crew of 4 and 13 per cent had larger crews, while as many as 10 per cent were singlehanders.

Conclusions

Since my first global survey in 1987, the cruising scene has seen important changes and while this survey has found that in a few places there has been an increase in the number of visiting yachts, the figures from Las Palmas, Bermuda, Panama, Galapagos, Tahiti, Tonga and Australia seem to indicate that the popularity of long-distance voyages may have peaked in 2010. Those numbers may also point to a global trend among potential world voyagers.

There are various reasons for this, but they all seem related to safety concerns. Although climate change has only started to visibly affect offshore weather, most sailors are worried about conditions becoming less predictable, with safe seasons no longer being taken for granted. The world is also regarded as less safe on a personal level, not only in such high risk areas as the North Indian Ocean and Red Sea, Venezuela, Brazil, Honduras, North, East and West Africa, but also in parts of the Eastern Mediterranean and Caribbean. The prevailing economic uncertainty may also deter some sailors from setting off on a world voyage not knowing what to expect on their return.

To assess the approximate number of boats that are undertaking a long voyage, I estimate that worldwide there are approximately 8,000 either cruising in a certain area or actually voyaging. About half are in the Atlantic, 1,500 to 2,000 in the Pacific, 1,000 in the Indian Ocean, and 1,000 in the Mediterranean. This estimate is about twenty percent lower than the conclusion I drew in 2000 and 2010, when I reckoned that there were between 10,000 and 12,000 boats roaming the oceans of the world.

Finally, those who are planning a world voyage should take heart from the fact that, in spite of some concerns, such attractive destinations as the Azores, French Polynesia, New Zealand, Tonga, Vanuatu and Indonesia, not to speak of more remote or high-latitude destinations, have not been overrun by visitors and show no signs of that happening soon. A definite result, caused mainly by the above concerns, is a move towards regional cruising with many sailors now preferring to limit their voyages to one area or just one ocean. In line with this trend, for many sailors the aim of completing a circumnavigation seems to have lost its aura and whereas in the past most of those who set off on a world voyage were hoping to eventually sail round the globe, nowadays it is only the most determined who find the motivation to go all the way.

Epilogue

As the above title suggests, this book marks a turning point in my life. Having achieved my aim of a transit of the Northwest Passage and, with no plans for another voyage, I decided to sell Aventura, as I had promised Gwenda when she had agreed for me to have a boat built for this project. It was a sad and painful decision, but by way of compensation, her new owner is going to sail in the Arctic, so she will be in her element and doing what she had been conceived and built for.

The coral waxes, the palm grows, but man departs.
Tahitian saying

Acknowledgements

This book was inspired by the voyage of Aventura IV and therefore my grateful thanks are due first of all to those who created her: Stéphan Constance and the entire team at Garcia Yachting – Benoit Lebizay, Marc d'Arbigny, Antonio Costa, François Tréguet, Philippe Hasne, and their skilled workforce at both Condé-sur-Noireau and Cherbourg. I am also greatly indebted to naval architect Olivier Racoupeau, who turned my concept into reality.

I wish to thank all those who supported my voyage in various ways – Rob Stevens and Chris McGowen of Topsail Insurance; Julien Carussi and Yves Brintet of Highfield Boats; Günther Wörl, Alexander Knuth and Volker Lamp of Parasailor; Pete Anderson of Eclectic Energy; Steven Bowden and Pamela House of Sea Tech Systems; Mark Pocock of Rocna Anchors; Philippe Gie, Mike Sudgen, Brian Gifford and Rufus van Gruisen of Brookes & Gatehouse; Ed and Sue Wildgoose, Danny Saify and Helle Kristjansen of Mailasail; Francesco Altamura, Chiara Tognoni and Laura Fanti of Jeppesen (C-Map); Odile Bernhard of International Paints; Philippe Wyatt of Walder; Mike and Susan Philips of Echopilot. Thanks also to Pradip Patel for the advice on essential onboard medication.

I am very grateful to Victor Weir, Peter Semiotuk and Eric Brossier for sharing with me their considerable local knowledge, both in the planning of my voyage and during the transit of the Northwest Passage.

I wish to thank all those who have taken part in my various surveys and have contributed valuable comments, which were quoted in this book; in particular Erick Bouteleux, Skip Novak, Elaine Bunting, Arthur Beiser, Luc Callebaut, Don Babson, Saundra Grey, Bill Butler, Italo and Silvana Masotti.

My thanks are also due to all those who have crewed on Aventura IV and have thus contributed to the success of her voyage: Dunbar Lewis, Chris Eakin, Martin Frey, Charlie Doane, Lou Morgan, Ryan Helling, Pablo Aguilera, Dave Skolnik and Matthias Osthoff.

Jörg Baginski has made an invaluable contribution to the attractive design of this book. I am equally grateful to my daughter-in-law Vicky McGinlay for her efforts in dealing with a host of grammatical and spelling inconsistencies. My most heartfelt thanks are to Gwenda, not just for her generous help with editing, checking and proofreading this book, but also for having agreed to my Arctic voyage.

Photo credits

Although the bulk of the photos in this book are my own, I am very grateful to my following sailing friends for allowing me to use theirs when I did not have anything suitable myself: Linda Andrews (pages 15, 144, 206, 272, 27), Jon Antrup (2), Lucas Bernardin (319, 360), Erick Bouteleux (316), Luc Callebaut (158), Vincent Depoortere (266), Chris Eakin (202, 207), Pascale Guiraudou (265, 393), Dunbar Lewis (20, 21, 29, 39), Skip Novak (356), Dena Singh (392), Donald Stollmeyer (331), Jacques Huguet (406) and José Ramón Martín (396).

My thanks are also due to my daughter Doina for the photos taken during our Arctic voyage (pages 12, 13, 14, 205, 228, 342), as was the one taken by Ivan (page 41), and my niece Marianne Aschenbrenner on page 89 and the back cover. Many thanks also to Li Erben for the photo on page 52.

I am also indebted to various organisations or companies for providing the following photographs: Calero Marinas (99), Garcia Yachts (81, 84, 193, 364), Musket Cove Resort (292), NASA Earth Observatory (100), Sevenstar Yacht Transport (399), Windpilot (190), and to the UK Met Office for the synoptic charts featured on pages 38 and 134.

The photographs on the following pages were all supplied by Shutterstock on behalf of the named artists: Aivita Arika (42), Gabriel Petrescu (45), Tatiana Volgutova (48), aaltair (50), Andrew Sutton (211), Chameleons Eye (216), Toscanini (218), Jackie Z (239), Molly Brown (272), Michael Smith (275), Serge Bertasius (276), Seaphotoart (278), Guaxinim (293), Aduro (294), PawelKazmierczak (304), Minerva Studio (321), Stanislaw Beloglazov (325), Tatiana Popova (329), Niloo (339), andrmoel (352), Lisa Strachan (373), lustra (397), Bilderagentur Zoonar (404) and an unidentified artist for the photo on page 108.

Index